Children's
Literature
Review

Guide to Gale Literary Criticism Series

For criticism on	Consult these Gale series
Authors now living or who died after December 31, 1999	*CONTEMPORARY LITERARY CRITICISM (CLC)*
Authors who died between 1900 and 1999	*TWENTIETH-CENTURY LITERARY CRITICISM (TCLC)*
Authors who died between 1800 and 1899	*NINETEENTH-CENTURY LITERATURE CRITICISM (NCLC)*
Authors who died between 1400 and 1799	*LITERATURE CRITICISM FROM 1400 TO 1800 (LC)* *SHAKESPEAREAN CRITICISM (SC)*
Authors who died before 1400	*CLASSICAL AND MEDIEVAL LITERATURE CRITICISM (CMLC)*
Authors of books for children and young adults	*CHILDREN'S LITERATURE REVIEW (CLR)*
Dramatists	*DRAMA CRITICISM (DC)*
Poets	*POETRY CRITICISM (PC)*
Short story writers	*SHORT STORY CRITICISM (SSC)*
Black writers of the past two hundred years	*BLACK LITERATURE CRITICISM (BLC)* *BLACK LITERATURE CRITICISM SUPPLEMENT (BLCS)*
Hispanic writers of the late nineteenth and twentieth centuries	*HISPANIC LITERATURE CRITICISM (HLC)* *HISPANIC LITERATURE CRITICISM SUPPLEMENT (HLCS)*
Native North American writers and orators of the eighteenth, nineteenth, and twentieth centuries	*NATIVE NORTH AMERICAN LITERATURE (NNAL)*
Major authors from the Renaissance to the present	*WORLD LITERATURE CRITICISM, 1500 TO THE PRESENT (WLC)* *WORLD LITERATURE CRITICISM SUPPLEMENT (WLCS)*

ISSN 0362-4145

volume 70

Children's Literature Review

Excerpts from Reviews,
Criticism, and Commentary
on Books for Children
and Young People

Jennifer Baise
Editor

Rebecca J. Blanchard, Thomas Ligotti
Associate Editors

GALE GROUP

THOMSON LEARNING

Detroit • New York • San Diego • San Francisco
Boston • New Haven, Conn. • Waterville, Maine
London • Munich

STAFF

Lynn M. Spampinato, Janet Witalec, *Managing Editors, Literature Product*
Kathy D. Darrow, Ellen McGeagh, *Product Liaisons*
Jennifer Baise, *Editor*
Mark W. Scott, *Publisher, Literature Product*

Rebecca J. Blanchard, Motoko F. Huthwaite, Thomas Ligotti, *Associate Editors*
Jenny Cromie, Mary Ruby, *Technical Training Specialists*
Deborah J. Morad, Joyce Nakamura, Kathleen Lopez Nolan, *Managing Editors*
Susan M. Trosky, *Director, Literature Content*

Maria L. Franklin, *Permissions Manager*
Julie Juengling, *Permissions Associate*

Victoria B. Cariappa, *Research Manager*
Sarah Genik, *Project Coordinator*
Ron Morelli, Tamara C. Nott, Tracie A. Richardson, *Research Associates*
Nicodemus Ford, *Research Assistant*

Dorothy Maki, *Manufacturing Manager*
Stacy L. Melson, *Buyer*

Mary Beth Trimper, *Manager, Composition and Electronic Prepress*
Carolyn Roney, *Composition Specialist*

Michael Logusz, *Graphic Artist*
Randy Bassett, *Imaging Supervisor*
Robert Duncan, Dan Newell, Luke Rademacher, *Imaging Specialists*
Pamela A. Reed, *Imaging Coordinator*
Kelly A. Quin, *Editor, Image and Multimedia Content*

Library of Congress Catalog Card Number 76-643301
ISBN 0-7876-4576-1
ISSN 0362-4145
Printed in the United States of America

10 9 8 7 6 5 4 3 2 1

Contents

Preface vii

Acknowledgments xi

Preface

L iterature for children and young adults has evolved into both a respected branch of creative writing and a successful industry. Currently, books for young readers are considered among the most popular segments of publishing. Criticism of juvenile literature is instrumental in recording the literary or artistic development of the creators of children's books as well as the trends and controversies that result from changing values or attitudes about young people and their literature. Designed to provide a permanent, accessible record of this ongoing scholarship, *Children's Literature Review* (*CLR*) presents parents, teachers, and librarians—those responsible for bringing children and books together—with the opportunity to make informed choices when selecting reading materials for the young. In addition, *CLR* provides researchers of children's literature with easy access to a wide variety of critical information from English-language sources in the field. Users will find balanced overviews of the careers of the authors and illustrators of the books that children and young adults are reading; these entries, which contain excerpts from published criticism in books and periodicals, assist users by sparking ideas for papers and assignments and suggesting supplementary and classroom reading. Ann L. Kalkhoff, president and editor of *Children's Book Review Service Inc.,* writes that "*CLR* has filled a gap in the field of children's books, and it is one series that will never lose its validity or importance."

Scope of the Series

Each volume of *CLR* profiles the careers of a selection of authors and illustrators of books for children and young adults from preschool through high school. Author lists in each volume reflect:

- an international scope

- representation of authors of all eras

- the variety of genres covered by children's and/or YA literature: picture books, fiction, nonfiction, poetry, folklore, and drama

Although the focus of the series is on authors new to *CLR,* entries will be updated as the need arises.

Organization of the Book

A *CLR* entry consists of the following elements:

- The **Author Heading** consists of the author's name followed by birth and death dates. The portion of the name outside the parentheses denotes the form under which the author is most frequently published. If the author wrote consistently under a pseudonym, the pseudonym will be listed in the author heading and the author's actual name given in parentheses on the first line of the biographical and critical information. Also located here are any name variations under which an author wrote, including transliterated forms for authors whose native languages use non-roman alphabets. Uncertain birth or death dates are indicated by question marks.

- A **Portrait of the Author** is included when available.

- The **Author Introduction** contains information designed to introduce an author to *CLR* users by presenting an overview of the author's themes and styles, biographical facts that relate to the author's literary career or critical responses to the author's works, and information about major awards and prizes the author has received. The introduction begins by identifying the nationality of the author and by listing genres in which s/he has written for children and young adults. Introductions also list a group of representative titles for which the author or illustrator being profiled is best known; this section, which begins with the words "major works include," follows the genre line of the introduction. For seminal figures, a listing of major works about the author follows when appropriate, high-lighting important biographies about the author or illustrator that are not excerpted in the entry. The centered heading "Introduction" announces the body of the text.

- **Criticism** is located in three sections: **Author Commentary** (when available) **General Commentary** (when available), and **Title Commentary** (commentary on specific titles).

  The **Author Commentary** presents background material written by the author or by an interviewer. This commentary may cover a specific work or several works. Author commentary on more than one work appears after the author introduction, while commentary on an individual book follows the title entry heading.

  The **General Commentary** consists of critical excerpts that consider more than one work by the author or illustrator being profiled. General commentary is preceded by the critic's name in boldface type or, in the case of unsigned criticism, by the title of the journal. *CLR* also features entries that emphasize general criticism on the oeuvre of an author or illustrator. When appropriate, a selection of reviews is included to supplement the general commentary.

  The **Title Commentary** begins with the title entry headings, which precede the criticism on a title and cite publication information on the work being reviewed. Title headings list the title of the work as it appeared in its first English-language edition. The first English-language publication date of each work (unless otherwise noted) is listed in parentheses following the title. Differing U.S. and British titles follow the publication date within parentheses. When a work is written by an individual other than the one being profiled, as is the case when illustrators are featured, the parenthetical material following the title cites the author of the work before listing its publication date.

Entries in each title commentary section consist of critical excerpts on the author's individual works, arranged chronologically by publication date. The entries generally contain two to seven reviews per title, depending on the stature of the book and the amount of criticism it has generated. The editors select titles that reflect the entire scope of the author's literary contribution, covering each genre and subject. An effort is made to reprint criticism that represents the full range of each title's reception, from the year of its initial publication to current assessments. Thus, the reader is provided with a record of the author's critical history. Publication information (such as publisher names and book prices) and parenthetical numerical references (such as footnotes or page and line references to specific editions of works) have been deleted at the discretion of the editors to provide smoother reading of the text.

- A complete **Bibliographical Citation** of the original essay or book precedes each piece of criticism.

- Selected excerpts are preceded by brief **Annotations,** which provide information on the critic or work of criticism to enhance the reader's understanding of the excerpt.

- Numerous **Illustrations** are featured in *CLR*. For entries on illustrators, an effort has been made to include illustrations that reflect the characteristics discussed in the criticism. Entries on authors who do not illustrate their own works my include photographs and other illustrative material pertinent to their careers.

Special Features: Entries on Illustrators

Entries on authors who are also illustrators will occasionally feature commentary on selected works illustrated but not written by the author being profiled. These works are strongly associated with the illustrator and have received critical acclaim for their art. By including critical comment on works of this type, the editors wish to provide a more complete representation of the artist's career. Criticism on these works has been chosen to stress artistic, rather than literary, contributions. Title entry headings for works illustrated by the author being profiled are arranged chronologically within the entry by date of publication and include notes identifying the author of the illustrated work. In order to provide easier access for users, all titles illustrated by the subject of the entry are boldfaced.

CLR also includes entries on prominent illustrators who have contributed to the field of children's literature. These entries are designed to represent the development of the illustrator as an artist rather than as a literary stylist. The illustrator's section is organized like that of an author, with two exceptions: the introduction presents an overview of the illustrator's styles and techniques rather than outlining his or her literary background, and the commentary written by the illustrator on his or her works is called "Illustrator's Commentary" rather than "Author's Commentary." All titles of books containing illustrations by the artist being profiled are highlighted in boldface type.

Indexes

A **Cumulative Author Index** lists all of the authors who have appeared in *CLR* with cross-references to the biographical, autobiographical, and literary criticism series published by the Gale Group. A complete list of these sources is found facing the first page of the Author Index. The index also includes birth and death dates and cross-references between pseudonyms and actual names.

A **Cumulative Nationality Index** lists all authors featured in *CLR* by nationality, followed by the number of the *CLR* volume in which their entry appears.

A **Cumulative Title Index** lists all author titles covered in *CLR*. Each title is followed by the author's name and corresponding volume and page numbers where commentary on the work is located.

Citing *Children's Literature Review*

When writing papers, students who quote directly from any volume in the Literary Criticism Series may use the following general format to footnote reprinted criticism. The first example pertains to material drawn from periodicals, the second to material reprinted from books.

Cynthia Zarin, "It's Easy Being Green," *The New York Times Book Review* (November 14, 1993): 48; excerpted and reprinted in *Children's Literature Review,* vol. 58, ed. Deborah J. Morad (Farmington Hills, Mich: The Gale Group, 2000), 57.

Paul Walker, *Speaking of Science Fiction: The Paul Walker Interviews,* (Luna Publications, 1978), 108-20; excerpted and reprinted in *Children's Literature Review,* vol. 58, ed. Deborah J. Morad (Farmington Hills, Mich: The Gale Group, 2000), 3-8.

Suggestions are Welcome

In response to various suggestions, several features have been added to *CLR* since the beginning of the series, including author entries on retellers of traditional literature as well as those who have been the first to record oral tales and other folklore; entries on prominent illustrators featuring commentary on their styles and techniques; entries on authors whose works are considered controversial; occasional entries devoted to criticism on a single work or a series of works; sections in author introductions that list major works by and about the author or illustrator being profiled; explanatory notes that provide information on the critic or work of criticism to enhance the usefulness of the excerpt; more extensive illustrative material, such as holographs of manuscript pages and photographs of people and places pertinent to the careers of the authors and artists; a cumulative nationality index for easy access to authors by nationality; and occasional guest essays written specifically for *CLR* by prominent critics on subjects of their choice.

Readers who wish to suggest new features, topics, or authors to appear in future volumes, or who have other suggestions or comments are cordially invited to call, write, or fax the Managing Editor:

Managing Editor, Literary Criticism Series
The Gale Group
27500 Drake Road
Farmington Hills, MI 48331-3535
1-800-347-4253 (GALE)
Fax: 248-699-8054

Acknowledgments

The editors wish to thank the copyright holders of the excerpted criticism included in this volume and the permissions managers of many book and magazine publishing companies for assisting us in securing reproduction rights. We are also grateful to the staffs of the Detroit Public Library, the Library of Congress, the University of Detroit Mercy Library, Wayne State University Purdy/Kresge Library Complex, and the University of Michigan Libraries for making their resources available to us. Following is a list of the copyright holders who have granted us permission to reproduce material in this volume of *CLR*. Every effort has been made to trace copyright, but if omissions have been made, please let us know.

COPYRIGHTED EXCERPTS IN *CLR*, VOLUME 70, WERE REPRODUCED FROM THE FOLLOWING PERIODICALS:

Ariel: A Review of International English Literature, v. 29, April, 1998. Copyright © 1998 by The Board of Governors, The University of Calgary. Reproduced by permission of the publisher.—*Booklist,* v. 85, March 15, 1989; v. 89, June 1 & 15, 1993; v. 90, July, 1994. Copyright © 1985, 1993, 1994 by the American Library Association. All reproduced by permission.—*Books for Keeps,* n. 60, January, 1990; n. 62, May, 1990; n. 119, November, 1999. Copyright © 1990, 1999 by the School Bookshop Association. All reproduced by permission.—*Canadian Children's Literature,* v. 25, Spring, 1999. Copyright © 1999 by Canadian Children's Press. Reproduced by permission.—*Children's Literature,* v. 25, 1997. Copyright © 1997 by Hollins College. Reproduced by permission of Yale University Press.—*Children's Literature: Annual of the Modern Language Association Seminar on Children's Literature and the Children's Literature Association,* v. 3, 1974; v. 5, 1976. Copyright © 1974, 1976 by Francelia Butler. All rights reserved. Both reproduced by permission of the Literary Estate of Francelia Butler.—*Children's Literature Association Quarterly,* v. 14, Winter, 1989; v. 16, Spring, 1991; v. 20, Spring, 1995. Copyright © 1989, 1991, 1995. All reproduced by permission.—*Elementary English,* v. XLV, May, 1968. Copyright © 1968 by the National Council of Teachers of English. Reproduced by permission of the publisher.—*The Horn Book Magazine,* v. LIV, June, 1978; v. LXV, May-June, 1989; v. LXVIII, October-November, 1992; v. XXXIX, July-August, 1993. Copyright, 1978, 1989, 1992, 1993 by The Horn Book, Inc., 11 Beacon St., Suite 1000, Boston, MA 02108. All rights reserved. All reproduced by permission./v. XX, July, 1944; v. XXXIV, October, 1958; v. XXXVI, December, 1960. Copyright © 1944, renewed 1972; copyright © 1958, renewed 1986; copyright © 1960, renewed 1988 by The Horn Book, Inc., 11 Beacon St., Suite 1000, Boston, MA 02108. All rights reserved. All reproduced by permission.—*Journal of Popular Culture,* v. 10, Spring, 1997. Copyright © 1997 by The Bowling Green State University Popular Press. Reproduced by permission.—*The Junior Bookshelf,* v. 27, December, 1963; v. 34, August, 1970. Reproduced by permission.—*Kirkus Reviews,* v. 56, October 15, 1988, p. 1532. Copyright © 1988 The Kirkus Service, Inc. All rights reserved. Reproduced by permission of the publisher, *Kirkus Reviews* and Kirkus Associates, L.P.—*The Lion and the Unicorn,* v. 20, December, 1996. Copyright © 1996 by The Johns Hopkins University Press. Reproduced by permission.—*Mosaic,* v. 10, Winter, 1977. Copyright © 1977 by Mosaic. Acknowledgment of previous publication is herewith made. Reproduced by permission.—*PMLA,* v. 111, May, 1996. Copyright © 1996 by the Modern Language Association of America. Reproduced by permission of the Modern Language Association of America.—*Publisher's Weekly,* v. 241, June 20, 1994. Copyright © 1994 by Reed Publishing USA. Reproduced from *Publishers Weekly,* published by the Bowker Magazine Group of Cahners Publishing Co., a division of Reed Publishing USA. Reproduced by permission.—*School Library Journal,* v. 35, April, 1989; v. 39, August, 1993. Copyright © 1989, 1993. Reproduced from *School Library Journal,* a Cahners/R. R. Bowker Publication, by permission.—*The Times Educational Supplement,* n. 4111, April 14, 1995. Copyright © 1995 by The Times Supplements Limited 1995 Reproduced from The *Times Educational Supplement* by permission.—*Tulsa Studies in Women's Literature,* v. 6, Fall, 1987. Copyright © 1987 by the University of Tulsa. Reproduced by permission.

COPYRIGHTED EXCERPTS IN *CLR*, VOLUME 70, WERE REPRODUCED FROM THE FOLLOWING BOOKS:

Estes, Eleanor. From an extract from a speech delivered at a meeting of the International Reading Association in New York, in *A Sense of Story: Essays on Contemporary Writers for Children.* By John Rowe Townsend. Longman, 1971. Copyright © 1971 by John Rowe Townsend. All rights reserved. Reproduced by permission.—Kingston, Carolyn T. From "The Tragic Moment: The Hundred Dresses," in *Tragic Mode in Children's Literature.* Teachers College Press, 1974. Copyright © 1974 by Teachers College, Columbia University. Reproduced by permission.—Lurie, Alison. From "E. Nesbit," in *Writers for Children: Critical Studies of Major Authors Since the Seventeenth Century.* Edited by Jane M. Bingham. Charles Scribner's Sons, 1988. Copyright © 1988 Charles Scribner's Sons. All rights reserved. Reproduced by permission.—MacAndrew, Donald. From "The Man Who Invented 'Struwwelpeter,'" in *The Saturday Book,* Vol. 23, Edited by John Hadfield. Hutchinson, 1963. Copyright © Hutchinson & Company Ltd, 1963. Reproduced by permission.—Martin, Abigail Ann. From "Bess Streeter Aldrich," in *Bess Streeter Aldrich.* Boise State University, 1992. Copyright © 1992 by the Boise State University Western Writers Series. All rights reserved. Reproduced by permission.—Moss, Anita. From "E. Nesbit's Romantic Child in Modern Dress," in *Romanticism and Children's Literature in Nineteenth-Century England.* Edited by James Holt McGavran, Jr. The University of Georgia Press, 1991. Copyright © 1991 by the University of Georgia Press. All rights reserved. Reproduced by permission.—Moss, Anita. From "The Story of the Treasury Seekers: The Idiom of Childhood," in *Touchstones: Reflections on the Best in Children's Literature.* Edited by Perry Nodelman. Children's Literature Association, 1985. Copyright © 1985 ChLA Publishers. Reproduced by permission.—Petersen, Carol Miles. From an introduction to *The Collected Short Works, 1907-1919: Bess Streeter Aldrich.* Edited by Carol Miles Petersen. University of Nebraska Press, 1995. Copyright © 1995 by the University of Nebraska Press. All rights reserved. Reproduced by permission.—Prickett, Stephen. From "Worlds Within Words: Kipling and Nesbit," in *Victorian Fantasy.* Indiana University Press, 1979. Copyright © 1979 by Stephen Prickett. All rights reserved. Reproduced by permission.—Rutledge, Amelia A. From "E. Nesbit and the Women Question," in *Victorian Woman Writers and the Women Question.* Edited by Nicola Diane Thompson. Cambridge University Press, 1999. Copyright © Cambridge University Press 1999. Reproduced by permission.—Smith, Louisa. From "Eleanor Estes' 'The Moffats': Through Colored Glass," in *Touchstones: Reflections on the Best in Children's Literature.* Edited by Perry Nodelman. Children's Literature Association, 1985. Copyright © 1985 ChLA Publishers. Reproduced by permission.—Streatfield, Noel. From "Oswald Bastable," in *Magic and the Magician.* Ernest Benn, Ltd., 1958. Reproduced by permission of the author.—Townsend, John Rowe. From "Eleanor Estes," in *A Sense of Story: Essays on Contemporary Writers for Children.* Longman, 1971. Copyright © 1971 by John Rowe Townsend. All rights reserved. Reproduced by permission.

PHOTOGRAPHS APPEARING IN *CLR*, VOLUME 70, WERE RECEIVED FROM THE FOLLOWING SOURCES:

Estes, Eleanor, photograph by Jim Theologos. Reproduced by permission.

Bess Streeter Aldrich
1881-1954

(Also wrote under the pseudonym Margaret Dean Stevens) American novelist and short story writer for adults and young adults.

Major works include *Mother Mason* (1924), *A Lantern in Her Hand* (1928), *A White Bird Flying* (1931), *Miss Bishop* (1933), and *The Lieutenant's Lady* (1942).

INTRODUCTION

Best known for her novels set in the early settlement days of the American Midwest, Bess Streeter Aldrich has been honored for her realistic portrayals of the American pioneering experience. Used often as supplemental reading in American history classes, Aldrich's novels and short stories are driven by their characters, many of them strong, fearless, and hard-working women. Her stories of pioneers were inspired by the experiences of both her mother's and her father's pioneer families and are set in the prairies of the Midwest. She took special care to acknowledge the strength, hardiness, and loving sacrifices of pioneer women, and her protagonists are usually female paragons for whom family is of the highest importance.

Aldrich's novels and short stories were extremely popular during the 1940s and 1950s, and her work was much in demand by such periodicals as *Women's Home Companion, McCall's, Cosmopolitan, Good Housekeeping, Saturday Evening Post, Collier's,* and *Harper's Weekly.* Although her writing was not critically acclaimed for its artistry, she enjoyed a wide readership who loved her simple, sentimental stories about hope and struggle, hardship and romance. She sold every story she wrote, although some of them were rejected many times before their sale. Her work was considered wholesome, uplifting, and cheerful, reflecting her personal attitude about life, but while she wrote of love and personal sacrifice, she avoided the subjects of sexual passion and the sordid and seamy aspects of humanity. Her work has been faulted for this, and for her insistence that marriage, family, and the rearing of children is woman's highest and most satisfying calling. These ideals were, however, those that she believed in firmly and exhibited in her own life.

BIOGRAPHICAL INFORMATION

Born in Cedar Falls, Iowa, in 1881, Aldrich came from a family with a history of pioneering. Her grandparents, whose stories appear in her books, traveled with their families from Illinois to settle in Iowa when it was still a wilderness. Aldrich began to write at an early age, and at 14 won a camera in a short story contest. She earned her first writer's fee at the age of 17 when the *Baltimore News* bought one of her short stories for five dollars. She spent her earnings on a black, ruffled parasol. After training as a teacher at Iowa State Teachers College, she taught in high school and college for several years before her marriage, writing articles for teachers' magazines and short stories under the name of Margaret Dean Stevens.

In 1907 she married Charles Aldrich and moved with him to Nebraska. Her husband encouraged her to write under her married name, and she did so, publishing her first book, *Mother Mason,* in 1924 and her first novel, *The Rim of the Prairie,* in 1925. Her husband died suddenly of a heart attack in 1925 when the youngest of their four children was four years old, and she subsequently supported her family with her writing, publishing a book every two years and writing a total of 168 short stories. From 1930 she also served as book editor for the *Christian Herald.* She died of cancer in 1954 at the age of 74. After her death, the street in Lincoln, Nebraska, where she had lived was renamed Aldrich Road in her honor. A greater posthumous honor came to her in 1973 when she became the seventh person inducted into the Nebraska Hall of Fame.

MAJOR WORKS

Aldrich's most famous book, *A Lantern in Her Hand,* became a worldwide best seller. It was written to honor her mother, embodied in the central character, and is based on stories Aldrich heard as a child from her parents, grandparents, aunts, and uncles, and stories sent to her by others who had experienced the pioneer life. Its sequel, *A White Bird Flying*, was one of the three top-selling books of the year, along with Willa Cather's *Shadows of the Rocks* and Pearl Buck's *The Good Earth. Miss Bishop*, about a spinster teacher who devotes her life to her family and her students, was made into a film, *Cheers for Miss Bishop*, in 1941. Her last novel, *The Lieutenant's Lady*, was based on the diaries of an army officer and his wife and also became a best seller.

Many of Aldrich's books are collections of her short stories. *Mother Mason* and *The Cutters* (1926) contain series of stories about those families. Others, such as *The Man Who Caught the Weather* (1936) and *Journey into Christmas* (1949), are collections of stories first published in various periodicals.

AWARDS

In 1911, Aldrich received the *Ladies Home Journal* prize. She received an Honorary Doctor of Literature degree from the University of Nebraska in 1930. In 1931 her short story "The Man Who Caught the Weather" won the O. Henry Award, and in 1949 *Journey into Christmas*, illustrated by her son James, was selected for the Christian Herald Family Bookshelf. In 1973, 19 years after her death, she was elected to the Nebraska Hall of Fame.

AUTHOR COMMENTARY

Bess Streeter Aldrich

SOURCE: "The Story Germ," in *The Writer*, Vol. 54, No. 12, December, 1941, pp. 355-57.

Several times in the past years your editor has asked me to contribute an article and each time I have been too busy, or thought I was, which is nearly the same thing. This morning another pleasant request has arrived and in the same mail a letter from a young woman with that old query: "Can you help a beginning writer? Where do you get your ideas? How can . . . ?" etc., etc. I wouldn't go so far as to say it is the hand of Fate, but the simultaneous arrival of the two causes me to put aside the desk work of the moment and do that article for *the writer*.

Now I have written and sold about one hundred and sixty short stories and have had ten books published with their by-products of serialization, syndication, English sales, foreign translations, plays, and a movie or two. But I still do not know just how to go about helping a young person in his own story writing. It is the greatest lone-wolf profession in the whole category.

One of my sons, home from the University for vacation, is at this moment across the hall in his room engaged in the throes of evolving a story. Brought up in the writing atmosphere of our home, he expects no help but maternal encouragement. If he has not gained anything from his mother about actual construction, he has learned how to do his work diligently, to rely upon himself, and to take those frequent and sickening doses of rejection slips with something approaching equanimity.

"Where do you get your ideas?" the correspondent queries.

Another young person interviewing me once, asked: "When you are writing one story and another just clamors to be told at the same time, what do you do?" With compassion I eyed her and with patience I answered: "Oh, but they never clamor. If I had two ideas at the same time or ever a few weeks apart, I would think it too good to be true."

Fresh ideas do not flock to a writer's head (not to *this* head) like birds to a martin house. One has to labor very hard to catch them. No doubt there are writers who see themes and plots so clearly that they do not have to put the strain on themselves which some of us do. A few times, but so few that they are almost negligible, I have visioned the skeleton of a story in its entirety or have been haunted by some theme which would not down. For those few times I have thanked the gods and hastily sketched the outlines of the stories. But for the most part I have worked hard, walking the floor at times as one would in physical pain, trying to get hold of an idea which would only elude me. Because I know so well in what labor most stories are written, I discount the sincerity of nine out of ten people who say they want to become a writer more than anything in the world. What they want is the satisfaction of seeing their stuff in print, the checks, and that bit of prestige which curiously attaches itself to anyone associated with the business. But they would not want to pay the price,—to spend hours of writing only to tear the story to pieces, or to bear all the early disappointments so familiar to those of us who have come up the hard and slippery way.

Back to the question,—how may we get story ideas when they refuse to present themselves to us as well-defined plots? *By putting intensive thought upon a small idea which, in its tiny form and limited feeling, has not enough substance for a story.*

Personally, I have found that whenever I am emotionally disturbed, there is the germ of a story in that disturbance,—but *only a germ.* Which means, given the cause of that disturbance for a beginning idea, I must work on it, change it, add to it, until the final story may be very far removed from the original nucleus.

If I am moved to laughter over the naive actions of an adolescent, a funny experience of a friend, an item in the newspaper, there is reason to believe that I can draw a smile from my readers with any of those episodes from which to plan. If I feel a suspicious moisture in my left eye over some small happening, there is reason to think I may be able to draw a surreptitious tear from some reader's eye with that bit of an anecdote upon which to work. And *work* is the word, not just a passive attitude, hoping that the story will inspirationally write itself.

Now, a concrete example: I open a newspaper from my old home town and see the headlines: OLD BUILDING TO BE RAZED. WORK BEGINS JUNE FIRST. And, because the editor is an alumnus of the school in question, there is a sentimental third line: GOOD-BYE TO OLD CENTRAL.

I am emotionally disturbed. It brings back a flood of youthful memories and a certain tender regret that the old building is to stand there among the trees no more. After June, the only thing remaining of the rambling brick building will be the memory of it in the minds and hearts of hundreds of men and women. And then, with an eye to business, I begin to wonder how I can work out a story from that uncomplicated emotion of regret at knowing the old building is to be torn down. For the tearing down of a condemned building is not a story nor the son of a story. It is only an incident. And a story must be more than an incident. It must have people in it, real people with hopes and fears. It must have life and color and movement. It must give forth odors and sounds. And something must happen, something to hold the interest or stir the blood, to bring that laughter or that tear.

So I begin the process of fumbling in the dark, putting out tentacles, as it were, from that center of my emotion.

I reason: If I am disturbed, countless other old students will be moved, too. Old teachers, also. I begin to recall some of those instructors, especially those who gave so much of themselves to their students. I'll do the story of a teacher—one who saw the opening of the college and lived through its growth—who will be there at the end of the old building as she was at the beginning. And now I have left the world of reality and slipped into the world of fancy, for my teacher is not to be any particular one but a fictitious person whose characteristics shall embody something from them all. Soon I have named her so that she may seem more real to me. I decide on "Miss Bishop," and some old-fashioned first name,—Ella. That suits her, for living in the seventies,—"Ella Bishop."

This Ella Bishop is becoming very real, so that I understand how lonely and sad she is in her old age without much to show in a material way for all her good works. A new president of the college will ask her to resign. If she is to be pictured as sad and lonely and hurt over the loss of her position, she ought at some time in the story to be quite the opposite, for the greatest characteristic of drama is contrast. And all contrast has a touch of the dramatic in it. The contrasting activities of "Dr. Jekyll" and "Mr. Hyde"—of "Faust" and "Mephistopheles"—of "Jesus" and "Judas"—these are the things of which drama is made. I ponder over the question of what can be done for contrast. The old students must rally to her. They must give her one exalted hour, one evening of adulation. It shall be in the old building itself, the night before it is to be torn down. A satisfactory climax: The alumni coming back to pay her homage—the old building's last appearance—and Ella Bishop's supreme moment after despair.

Perhaps I have not yet written a word, only visualized a woman and a situation. But the climax is there, a point toward which I can now work. I go back to pick up the threads of her life. Why did she never marry? Was her life always as barren as it must appear to the modern student? All this to be worked out, and research to be done for the accuracy of a midwestern college background in its evolution. (This latter, a very exacting phase of story writing, but not under discussion here.)

By this time I am writing,—much of the climax first so that later I may work toward it. Ella Bishop has grown as familiar to me as my next door neighbor.

To live the lives of his characters, crawling into their very skins, is the writer's prerogative, almost his duty. He must be an actor,—an actor who plays all the parts.

Enough of detailed description. *Miss Bishop* went on the best seller list several years ago and on the screen this year through a fine interpretation of the actress, Martha Scott,—a story and a photoplay which had their beginnings in a very small germ, the momentary emotion caused by reading a headline: OLD BUILDING TO BE RAZED.

I hope this has not sounded pedantic. There are other ways to develop a story. This one is mine. And while there is very little which an older writer can do to help a beginner (for each one must "gae his ain gait," as my Scotch mother used to say) there is always the chance that the telling of a personal experience or the explaining of an individual method will find its interested young reader.

Bess Streeter Aldrich

SOURCE: "Working Backward," in *The Writer,* Vol. 63, No. 11, November, 1950, pp. 350-53.

A number of years ago I wrote an article for *The Writer* titled **"The Story Germ."** Several young writers were kind enough to tell me it was helpful to them. In that article I stressed the point that plots for stories seldom come to one in their entirety, but that, given some small situation or dramatic moment or distinctive human trait, one can work out a story based on that little happening or emotional period or outstanding characteristic.

With the editor asking for another article I can think of nothing more practical than to follow that lead with a detailed account of how one can work backward in developing a short story. Any similiarity between this article and the former will harm no one, for those who read the other, written so long ago, no doubt have become sure-fire authors by this time or have given up the literary ghost.

People who have had no experience in writing often hold the idea that turning out a story must be the easiest thing in the world. A story reads smoothly. The people in it seem natural. Events move forward in regular and interesting sequence. It comes to a surprising or satisfactory climax. And there you are. Nothing could be easier. Or so they think. But they do not know with what knitting of brows, chewing of

pencils and discarding of wordage that easily read story is constructed. For more often than not, it is the outgrowth of some little happening, too small in itself to constitute a whole story, which has become one after intensive work.

Over many years of writing I have evolved two methods for the development of short stories. For a character story—one which stresses the person rather than the plot—I begin by getting mentally acquainted with that fictitious character, dwelling on his appearance, traits, mental processes and emotional reactions, until he takes upon himself the semblance of such reality that automatically he moves into action. In this way **"The Man Who Caught the Weather"** was constructed; a story which was rejected by twenty-eight magazines before it was purchased by the old *Century Magazine*. It was chosen for the O. Henry Award volume of that year, has been used in several anthologies, syndicated, resold to a British magazine and read on various radio story hours. I insert that item for the benefit of young writers who lose their courage over a second or third rejection and who, like the shipwrecked brother, "hearing, may take heart again."

The second method—which is the line this little article is taking—is the constructing of a story from some dramatic incident or interesting contrast between two settings or ideas, and working backward from that point. With fine disregard for the law of gravity, I start with the capstone of the structure, slip another stone under it, and another one under that, until solid ground is reached.

Naturally the story which I shall use as an illustration should be read in its entirety if a detailed analysis is to be understood. It was in the 1948 Christmas number of *The Saturday Evening Post* and titled **"Star Across the Tracks."** Also it is to be found in my book *Journey Into Christmas,* a compilation of short stories. Bearing down heavily on the Christmas atmosphere, it has the simplest of plots, but even so, it entailed a great deal of planning, for the little plot grew out of a mere setting upon which this backward method was used.

Very briefly, the story is this: An old day laborer is the yard man for three families who live in a fine residential district of a midwestern city in which there is a city-wide contest for the best outdoor Christmas decorations. The old man assists his three families in putting up their elaborate decorations, but wins the first prize himself with a simple nativity scene at his own little home across the tracks.

The origin of the story was this: On a Christmas night we were taking one of my sons to his train after his holiday visit with us. Our city had gone in extensively for outdoor decorations and as we drove from our suburban section we passed any number of elaborately decorated yards. There were lights in brilliant landscaping effects, picturesque Santa Clauses, and life-sized reindeer, expansive and expensive. At the station we found the train had changed time, and there would be quite a wait, but not long enough to drive back home. It was a mild evening, in contrast to some of our midwestern holiday weather, and we drove leisurely through a section of town beyond the station where the Christmas touch was evident, if on a less extravagant scale. Then we came to it: a hayfilled manger, evidently made from packingboxes, by the side of a small cottage, a whiterobed figure bending over it and lighted with a single faint glow.

The son, who was a young newspaperman, said: "There's a story for you, Mother. That's right up your alley . . . elaborate decorations up town and this little manager scene here across the tracks."

Now any incident which brings laughter or tears, or which calls forth one's sympathy, anger, admiration, in fact, anything which touches the emotions has the germ of a story in it. The sight of the crude manger and the white pasteboard figure here by the little house, far away from those brilliantly lighted ones, touched us all. And I knew, as my son had suggested, there *was* a story in it waiting to be developed if it could be worked out.

But a story is more than a scene and more than the contrast between two settings. There is nothing static about it. Something must happen. Characters must come to life. People must live and move across the pages of the magazine so that the reader lives and moves with them. A few days later I was starting the mental machinery by which a story could be evolved from the small germ of that little manger across the tracks. *And working backward.*

In other words, the climax was to be that the simple scene by the cottage would win a citywide first prize away from all that uptown splurge. But as almost all stories change from fact into fancy, even though based on reality, instead of the mere manger of boxes, I find myself visualizing a shed with open front to the street, a cow and team of horses munching on the hay, pigeons fluttering on the roof, a star overhead, and the Babe and Mother in that stable setting.

(Immediately I am thinking this is a bit incongruous in a city which prohibits stock in its limits, so make a note to state casually, early in the story, that this is the only section where stock can be kept.)

Now, the people who live there—in the story, of course—who are they? What do they do? Some old man and his wife, hard working and obviously with a religious trend. Almost at once I have named them: *Mr. Harm Kurtz* and his wife. Pa Kurtz and Mamma. For fictitious characters immediately named come more readily to life. The rest of the family, if any, stays vague, for I may want to create characters to fit the story needs.

Mr. Kurtz will be a day laborer. Why not connect him in some way with one of those big highly decorated homes? At once he becomes the yard man for three of the well-to-do families, and they are named, too, so they will begin to seem real: the Scotts, the Dillinghams and the Porters. I see them in their homes with Pa Kurtz helping to put up all those brilliant lights, then see Pa going home to his small house across the tracks on an unpaved street, telling the day's happenings to Mamma and fixing up his own shed, with its cow and horses, for the nativity scene. But something there doesn't ring true,—the incongruity of Pa Kurtz, tired to death of the whole thing, coming home and entering into the decorative contest. No, it will be Mamma with the religious bent who arranges the stable scene.

And here is a knotty problem: our midwestern climate so cold at times, and a shed for stock standing open toward the street? One can't state an incongruity and let it go at that, if one's stories are to ring true. Each step must be the natural outgrowth of that which has gone before. So for some reason the one side of the shed has to come off temporarily. Why not have Pa Kurtz yank off the boards in anger? Mamma has chided him for the old shed looking so decrepit. She is expecting Christmas company and her pride will be hurt. Immediately, I am creating a daughter coming home with her little boys, and Mamma is saying: "Just as plain as I'm standing here I can remember your telling Carrie you'd have the new lumber on that old shed by next time she comes." At that, Pa flares up with: "I'll have that new lumber on by the time Carrie comes if it's the last thing I do." And he begins yanking off the siding, exposing the manager, the cow, the horses, the hay. That problem over, I'm trying to think what can be used for the Mother Mary. A mannikin from a store would be just right, but one doesn't simply go into a house and bring out a mannikin.

I digress here to say that nothing is so irritating in a story as the parenthetical statement. As a judge for one of the monthly reading club's books, I recently read a submitted manuscript which was rather good, had it not been for that amateurish dragging in by the hair of the head, so to speak, of properties and people which never had been presented to the reader until the moment they became useful. So, to have a mannikin handily in the house, I create another daughter, Lillie, who works in a department store, and immediately the store belongs to one of those well-to-do families, thus making the little plot more compact.

In order that it will not escape me, I write that part at once, even though the story is not under construction. "Lillie was a whiz with the needle. She made her own dresses at home and tried them on Maisie the mannikin. That was one of the store's moronic-looking models which had lost an arm and sundry other features and Lillie had asked for it when she found they were going to discard it. Now she hung her own skirts on Maisie to get their length. That was about all the good the mannikin did her, for Lillie's circumference was fully three times that of the model."

So, early in the story I plant the mannikin and when the time comes for Mamma to want something for the figure of the Madonna, there is no incongruous break.

There must be a star above the shed, and because Pa is only a grouchy onlooker, not entering into the decorative scheme at all, I create a son, Ernie, who is a mechanic. Lillie says to him: "Mamma wants you to fix a star up over the stable. Mrs. Dillingham gave an old one to Pa." I am writing this also before starting the real construction of the story: "Ernie had been a fixer ever since he was a little boy. Not for his looks had the River City Body and Fender Wreck Company hired Ernie Kurtz. So, after his warmed over supper, he got his tools and a coil of wire and fixed the yellow bauble high over the stable, the wire and the slim rod almost invisible, so that it seemed a star hung there by itself."

And now I have the causes and effects of several movements in the story to come: Pa home from helping with all those elaborate decorations . . . Mamma chiding him about the dilapidated shed . . . his yanking off the boards in anger . . . Mamma seeing how like the Bethlehem scene the old stable looks . . . going into the house to get Lillie's mannikin, draping it with sheets into the form of the Mother

Mary, saying: "I ain't doin' this for show like Pa's families he's been helpin'. I'm doin' it for Carrie's little boys. Something they can see when they drive in . . . something they'll never forget, like's not, as long as they live."

This much will suffice to show the working backward method sometimes used by writers. By working that way I have created a substantial reason for every stone which is going into the structure. Now I can begin to work from the first, putting in the atmospheric descriptive matter, conversation, all the human touches a story needs: the arrival of the children for Christmas . . . the drive up through the fine residential sections of town . . . the family's utter enjoyment of the elaborate lighting effects there, with no thought that their own scene is more effective . . . their wagering among themselves as to which of the big houses will get the prize . . . hearing over the radio the next day that their own has won it . . . the hundreds of cars driving down the little unpaved street on Christmas night . . . the open shed . . . the horses pulling at the hay . . . the cow gazing moodily into space . . . the pigeons on the ridgepole in a long feathery group . . . white Mary bending over the manger . . . and overhead the star.

And then to end on some substantial Christmas thought. With Mamma asking Pa why he can't get to sleep and his saying: "Keep thinkin' of everything. All that prize money comin' to us. Attention from so many folks. Children all home. Folks I work for all here and not a bit mad. You'd think I'd feel good. But I don't. Somethin' hangs over me. Like they'd been somebody real out there in the shed all this time. Like we'd been leavin' 'em stay out there when we ought to had 'em come in. Fool notion . . . but keeps botherin' me."

And then Mamma gave her answer. Comforting, too, just as he knew it would be. "I got the same feelin'. I guess people's been like that ever since it happened. Their consciences always hurtin' 'em a little because there wasn't no room for Him in the inn."

This resumé of the constructing of a story plot has been written for beginning writers, as experienced ones will have worked out their own methods. There is little enough one can do to assist another in the writing line, for it is a lone wolf business if ever there was one. But sometimes a frank personal experience from one who has been at work in it for a long time will strike a helpful note. I know, for thirty-five years ago I was a beginner, avidly searching for all the helps in constructing, and advice for short cuts I could read. Occasionally I ran across some of the helps. But never a short cut could I find.

GENERAL COMMENTARY

Abigail Ann Martin

SOURCE: "Bess Streeter Aldrich," in *Bess Streeter Aldrich,* Boise State University, 1992, pp. 5-41.

"Nebraska," wrote Bess Streeter Aldrich, "is only the state of my adoption, but I am sure that I feel all the loyalty for it which the native-born bears . . . while I am not a native Nebraskan, the blood of the midwestern pioneer runs in my veins and I come rightly by my love for the Nebraska pioneer and admiration for the courage and fortitude which he displayed in the early days of the state's history . . ." (Introduction to *The Rim of the Prairie*).

Certainly both love and admiration are apparent in Aldrich's finest work, *A Lantern in Her Hand* (1928). This novel alone is enough to give her a place among distinguished writers of the American West. Her feeling for—and appreciation of—the Midwest shine out in much of her other fiction, but primarily it is for *Lantern* that she is to be honored. Few other writers have presented so detailed and vivid a picture of pioneer life.

Born on 17 February 1881, in Cedar Falls, Iowa, she was the daughter of James Wareham and Mary Anderson Streeter. Her childhood as the youngest of a large and lively family was a happy one, and during her impressionable years she was imbued with the values and mores of small-town life, values and mores which greatly influenced her writing. From her numerous aunts and uncles she often heard tales of life in pioneering days, for both her parents had, in their youth, come to Iowa from "the East." Her parental grandfather, Zimri Streeter, had been a member of the Iowa Territorial Legislature, his salty character making him a prominent figure among his colleagues.

Educated in the public schools of Cedar Falls, she went on to Iowa State Teachers College in the same town, graduating in 1901. For five years she taught primary grades in Boone and Marshalltown, Iowa, and in Salt Lake City, Utah, and for a short time she was assistant supervisor of the primary training school at Iowa State Teachers College.

In September 1907 she married Charles S. Aldrich, banker and attorney of Tipton, Iowa, where the couple lived until after the birth of their first child, Mary Eleanor, in 1909, when the family moved to Elmwood, Nebraska. Here Aldrich's husband became cashier of the American Exchange Bank, and here the three Aldrich sons were born: James, Charles, and Robert. Here too Charles Aldrich, husband and father, died suddenly on 5 May 1925. And here Aldrich's literary career began in earnest.

She had been writing from an early age. At fourteen she sold a children's story to the Chicago *Record* and received a five-dollar camera as a prize. At seventeen, hearing that the Baltimore *News* was paying five dollars for stories, she wrote a love story, received the five dollars, and promptly spent it for a black chiffon parasol!

For some years she had been producing articles for teachers' magazines, stories for young children, and a goodly number of short stories for the *American Magazine* and *The Ladies Home Journal*. Her story **"The Little House Next Door"** won a prize of $175 offered in 1911 by the latter magazine. Two collections of magazine stories had been published as well as a novel, *The Rim of the Prairie* (1925).

All this success had been pleasant, of course, but not economically necessary. Her husband's death gave her the impetus to make money, and producing fiction thus became her life work.

This work flourished in the midst of her growing children and their activities, interrupted often by household tasks and emergencies. She is quoted as answering a query about housekeeping: "Three huge meals three times a day for a girl and three boys with the largest appetites in the world. I could take a prize for patching at the county fair."

Again, she remarks, "I have written with three babies tumbling over my feet, with a house of paperdolls under my desk and their five-year-old owner demonstrating a cyclone with them, with one eye on a cooking meal and the other on the story in hand, with grammar grade boys making kites and bows and arrows around me".

Beginning under such conditions—and persisting— Aldrich in the end produced 160 short stories and seven novels. Some of this fiction has been serialized, syndicated, sold in England, and translated into Dutch, Danish, Hungarian, Swedish, Spanish, and French. All of her books have been published in Braille.

Aldrich's novels and stories obviously grew out of her background, her environment, her circumstances. And because they all bear the decided impress of her Midwestern life they are worth examining and evaluating. Both the strengths and the weaknesses of her fiction have regional overtones.

Near the end of her first novel, *The Rim of the Prairie,* she describes the way one of the characters writes of the Midwest. Here she seems to be expressing her own credo: "Warner Field writes of the mid-west. He does not credit it with having in its air either the crispness of the mountains or the salt tang of the sea . . . nor will he discredit the sorcery of the odors of loam and sod and subsoil, of dewy clover, and ripening corn and the honey-sweetness of lavendar alfalfa. He does not pretend that it is idyllic . . . nor will he speak of it as bleak and uninteresting. He does not assert that it has attained to great heights of culture and art . . . nor will he sell it for thirty pieces of silver. But in some way Warner Field catches in his writings the gleam of the soul of the wide prairie, dim and deep and mysterious. For here, as everywhere, drama ebbs and flows like the billowing of the seas of yellow wheat".

In the wider perspective of history, Bess Streeter Aldrich will be remembered for her pioneer fiction—four novels and several short stories that tell of the settling of the Midwest. Actually, her first real prominence as a writer came with the publication of *A Lantern in Her Hand* (1928). Those critics are unperceptive who say it was something of an anomaly, this novel about struggling "dirt farmers" that was published in the roaring twenties when flaming youth, bootlegging, and a kind of shrill prosperity dominated the scene. They overlook society's always undiminished interest in its beginnings, in its own local (or national) development.

This interest Aldrich exploited in ways both innocent and clever. It was innocent because, as she said somewhere, she simply wanted to honor the pioneer women who, as her own mother had, had come to a raw country, lived through appalling hardships and poverty, and had never lost their buoyancy of spirit or their sense of values.

On the other hand she was clever. She was careful to research her material meticulously, making use of bona fide records, papers, anecdotes. As a result the novel is richly detailed and true.

On the very first page of *Lantern* the reader is caught up in the story and senses its authenticity. More, the book is infused with Aldrich's warm admiration for the pioneers who, because of almost unbelievable labor, and in the face of devastating frustrations, disappointments, and suffering, settled one of the richest and most productive states of the union.

Her admiration is not only, or even principally, for their strength and perseverance; it is for their unfaltering courage. The note is struck in Joyce Kilmer's verse from which the novel's title is taken:

> Because the road was steep and long,
> And through a dark and lonely land,
> God set upon my lips a song
> And put a lantern in my hand.

The central figure in the book is Abbie Deal, born Mackenzie, whom the reader meets at the age of eight, just coming to Iowa from the East with her widowed mother and her brothers and sisters. The story takes Abbie swiftly through her growing-up years, her emergence as an exquisite young woman with a delightful voice and a dreamy imagination, to her courtship by sturdy Will Deal, and their marriage.

Sometime after the birth of their first child, a son, when she is pregnant with her second child, Abbie learns that Will is eager to go west to the new territory, Nebraska. By "homesteading" he can acquire a fine profitable farm. All it will require is work, and he is suited to that. For Abbie it requires more than work: it requires courage. The land they are going to is new—and lonely. There will be just a handful of people making a settlement. And these people, destined to be her only neighbors and friends, are as yet strangers. She must leave all that she cares for and venture into who knows what perils. (Childbirth will be completely without medical assistance, or even the aid of her own mother and sister.) There will be no school, no church, no stores, no newspaper.

There is as yet no house for them, of course, nor for their few animals. Shelters will have to be hastily constructed of sod, for the country has no stones for building, and for wood only such trees as grow along the small stream near which they will live.

Very little is there to protect them when the bitter winter comes, when raging winds sweep unimpeded over the prairies, and fierce snows make the country blinding and treacherous. In the summers there will be brutal heat, the sun pouring its terrible radiance down through air as clear and dry as glass. There will be crops destroyed in an hour by drought or by insects; there will be, at times, the debilitating lack of ordinary decencies: even sufficient soap, even the most rudimentary things beloved by women—fabrics for sewing, little toys for their children.

There will be moments when life will cease to be worth living, when the fatigue of each day seems to yield nothing in the way of progress or prosperity. And for a long, long time there will be overwhelming nostalgia, the craving of a tender, affectionate heart for her own people, for her familiar surroundings.

All this is shown in Aldrich's lengthy novel. As the narrative of one woman and her family in pioneer conditions, *Lantern* is complete.

Thus it is much more than the story of one woman. It is a piece of social history, showing how Nebraska, and in particular one town, grew through the years. Interesting statistics help give the aura of authenticity referred to above. For instance, Will Deal buys "railroad land" at $2.00 an acre in 1868, when Nebraska had been a state just under a year. The town which he and Abbie and a few other families found is located "35 miles from Nebraska City, and ten miles from Weeping Water." At this time Omaha has a population of 15,000, and contains eleven churchs, five schools, five banks, five breweries, sixty saloons, and a hoop factory. Lincoln had just been designated the state capital, a place, Abbie says, which is "away out on the prairie with just two or three log houses."

Abbie and Will endure a great many crises and hard times. They know what it is to have crop failures: the land is rich and good, but often rain is scanty. In an effort to increase moisture-retention, they drive to Nebraska City to get cottonwood seedlings to plant. Will never loses his faith in the land, and Abbie, worn with work and childbearing and discouragement, stands by him.

Eventually, of course, times improve, and those settlers who have "stuck it out" live to see their state flourish, with fine modern cities and universities and many cultural amenities. Abbie and Will rear children who are a credit to them: a prosperous banker, a successful lawyer, a prominent singer, a university professor. Their oldest daughter marries a physician who becomes one of Lincoln's most distinguished doctors. Through everything the two keep their love for each other and for the land.

In a way—and surely intentionally—Aldrich makes the Deals to stand as symbols of the pioneer spirit that has made her adoptive state great. Abbie is "Everywoman"—that is, the archetype of the pioneer mother whose tired and ravaged body contains the living spirit of enterprising courage and will.

Spring Came on Forever (1935), though not as sweeping in scope as *Lantern,* is also a graphic presentation of frontier life. Here the pioneers are German, leaving Illinois for Nebraska, enduring all the hardships of settling on a raw, untamed land. And, of course, becoming prosperous. There is the blizzard of 1888, the devastating flood of the early 1930s. There are setbacks and grim, unrelenting labor. But there is an undisturbed, a profound, feeling for the land.

The story itself is uncomplicated. Matthias Meier, a hearty young blacksmith, goes into the new land, makes his way brilliantly, and ends up wealthy and respected. As a young man he falls in love with Amalia Stolz, whose overbearing father forbids their marriage. She must become the wife of a coarse, hardworking man, and she ends up a tiny, shrivelled-up woman with very little to show for a life of pitiless toil and privation. Somehow Neal and Hazel, descendants of Matthias and Amalia, meet and fall in love. When they marry they elect to stay on the land, because the love of it is part of their lives.

The title is taken from Vachel Lindsay's poem "The Chinese Nightingale."

> Who shall end my dream's confusion?
> Life is a loom, weaving illusion . . .
> One thing I remember:
> Spring came on forever . . .

Song of Years (1938-39) also tells of pioneer days. This long and lively tale concerns the ebullient Martin family: the father, Jeremiah; the mother, Sarah; their two sons and seven daughters; and their friends. They are early settlers in Iowa, and the story presents an excellent picture of life in the young country beginning in June 1854 and ending just after the Civil War.

The colorful detailed narrative describes the girls' love affairs (especially that of Suzanne). These are full of incident, for the Martin daughters are given to coquetry. More important, the book gives a clear picture of the impact of the Civil War on the everyday life of the little settlement. Because coffee is a dollar a pound, women try many substitutes: these range from rye, wheat, and bran mixed with molasses to sweet potatoes chipped and browned in sugar. Gold and silver suddenly disappear; "money" becomes printed paper, little slips worth ten, fifteen, twenty-five, or fifty cents. The whole is a vivid picture of the settling of the Midwest, obviously modelled on the reminiscences of Aldrich's grandparents.

Then in 1942 when the country was at war, Aldrich published a "pioneer" novel quite different from the three previously described. *The Lieutenant's Lady* tells of the life (full of hardships, danger—and a bit of glamour) lived by the wife of an Army officer. This is, Aldrich explains on the first page, a "fictionalized version of a real diary," and the reader is led to see that the diary tells a complete story.

Linnie Campbell journeys from New York to Omaha in the 1860s, and Omaha, at the time the territorial capital of Nebraska, was, to put it simply, a very primitive place: "Already the young town had begun to put on airs by denying the privilege of stacking hay in the streets and passing an ordinance that any hogs found running loose were to be impounded and sold." The fight to change Nebraska's status from territory to state is told in detail, followed by a description of the dissension over the location of the state capital. Those who wanted it out on the prairie and those who wanted it named Lincoln were finally victorious, but the struggle was long and bitter.

Linnie and Lieutenant Norman Stafford are married after some rather interesting complications, and they go to live at Fort Berthold, in Dakota Territory, and later at Camp Cook in Montana Territory. Conditions of army post living are described vividly: the loneliness, the ever-present fear of Indian uprisings, and the lack of cultural amenities. (Linnie sets up a little school for the children of personnel.)

Hardships abound (as in any pioneer living), but Linnie and Norman never lose spirit and courage and pride of country. Norman remains a career Army man all his life, and Linnie goes with him faithfully as he is moved about. In very trying circumstances they bring up four children.

The book seems to be a tribute to Army wives, as well as to the Army. Significantly, as it was brought out in 1942, Aldrich carefully confirms its timeliness: "The lieutenant's lady lived to be very old, so old that she had seen her son and two of her grandsons in the United States Army and a toddling great-grandson marching and counter-marching with a wooden gun."

Secondary in importance among Aldrich's works are three novels that may be described as "romances," though each is more than that. Their central figures are women who suffer—and find joy—in love. *The Rim of the Prairie* (1925) was the first of all the Aldrich novels; *A White Bird Flying* (1931) takes up the story of Abbie Deal's granddaughter; and *Miss Bishop* (1940), the most nearly comprehensive character portrait of all, details the long life of a college teacher. This latter book proved so popular that it was made into a movie equally appealing, *Cheers for Miss Bishop* (1941) starring Martha Scott and Paul Muni.

Though each of these novels derives its interest from its heroine, they differ as to setting and era. In *The Rim of the Prairie* the reader becomes intimately acquainted with a small Midwestern town, a town full of "characters." Many of the older people have been pioneers, have seen the town grow, and have retained memories of older, harsher times. There is a mystery to be brought to light near the end; there are emotional moments a-plenty; and, of course, there is the triumph of love over what had seemed insurmountable difficulties. The plot is rather more complicated than in any of the following Aldrich novels, and the main character, Nancy Moore, is a vivid young woman surrounded by a number of colorful people— rich and poor, old and young.

A White Bird Flying is much simpler in concept. Readers familiar with *A Lantern in Her Hand* find it interesting because so many of the characters are known in the earlier book. This one tells of Laura Deal, lovely, talented granddaughter of Abbie and Will. From a very early age she is close to her grandmother, and after Abbie's death she finds inspiration in her memory. Her ambition is to become a great writer, to carry out one of Abbie's cherished dreams.

The story takes her through adolescence and university years to her love for Allen Rinemiller, whose grandparents had come to the prairie country with the Deals. A great opportunity for advancement along her chosen career is offered Laura, and she is forced to choose between a glamorous future and marriage. Here, as has been noted before in Aldrich's tales, a flavor of the "early days" can be sensed; here are people linked with the past, "modern" though they may be.

The third of these romances, *Miss Bishop,* is notable for its strong central character. Ella Bishop is one of the most forceful women Aldrich ever created. Her story may be told in a short paragraph.

One of the thirty-two students who attend the first year of what will later be a great university, Ella dominates the situation wherever she is. Graduating, she is taken on as a member of the faculty and spends the rest of her life giving herself to others: to her students, to her friends, to her family. An ecstatic love affair is brutally ended, and Ella later resists the temptation to enter into another with a married man. All her life she keeps steadily at work, depriving herself of one pleasure after another to help various members of her family and to inspire her students. In the end she is accorded enthusiastic appreciation by the university and has acquired a wide circle of friends. There are some dramatic moments in *Miss Bishop*, well calculated to please the Hollywood of the early 1940s, but the main concern of the reader is the character and personality of Ella herself, as well as her impact on those about her.

A great share of Aldrich's writings may be subsumed under the heading "Small-Town Fiction." Such periodicals as *Ladies Home Journal, American Magazine, Good Housekeeping, Women's Home Companion, Delineator,* and *Saturday Evening Post* welcomed these bright tales of "ordinary" people. Because of their popularity many were gathered into collections—six in number.

The first of these is *Mother Mason* (1924). All the stories here are concerned with the doings of the Mason family, including not only Tillie, the hired "help," but also the daughter-in-law. A great many things go on in the lively Mason household. Mother feels so beset that she takes a few days off to go to the city all by herself. Her pretext is exceedingly flimsy, but it satisfies her family, and she has a wonderful (if solitary) time. Each of the three daughters encounters love and reacts characteristically. Junior, the troublesome pre-teenager, gets into an amusing scrape. Tillie decides to embark on a life of her own, only to return crestfallen a short time later. Whatever happens, the Masons never know a dull moment.

The Cutters (1926) is another collection of stories about a single family, with the focal point Nell, the young mother. Nell's marriage is happy, and her energetic children are bouncingly healthy, but she nevertheless has problems to solve and obstacles to overcome. Many of these problems and obstacles are internal: they show her seeking to come to terms with herself, to adjust her values. She is envious of an old school friend's great success in the business world; she is overawed by an older matron's complacent efficiency; she is pricked by an insistent ambition to write; she feels the strain of entertaining an enviably rich businessman and his wife. Some of Nell's experiences are sheer comedy: her entering a "contest" involving a word puzzle; her working on a gala dinner to honor a "home grown" celebrity; her decision about disciplining her two maddening small sons.

Through both these collections breathes the atmosphere of smalltown middle America. In them the life of these towns during the 1920s comes vividly to life.

Throughout the 1930s and into the 1940s, Aldrich produced a large number of stories having to do with a variety of characters. Her locale never changes. No matter what name she gives, it is the small town she has known (and loved) all her life. Many of these stories were published in *The Man Who Caught the Weather* (1936), *The Drum Goes Dead* (1941), *Journey into Christmas and Other Stories* (1949), and *A Bess Streeter Aldrich Reader* (1950). *A Bess Streeter Aldrich Treasury* (1959), *The Home-Coming and Other Stories* (1984), and *Across the Smiling Meadow and Other Stories* (1984) have been brought out posthumously.

All the plots are uncomplicated. An old man keeps tabs on the weather and goes to his wife's grave to comfort her during an electrical storm. A youngish businessman has his hope for the future renewed at a Christmas celebration. All the citizens of a town join in welcoming a returning "boy who made good"—and he finds his childhood sweetheart waiting for him. Near death, a mother comes to a realization of the value of life. A middle-aged couple celebrates a wedding anniversary. Always in the end there is an upward swing: the men and women, the boys and girls, come to a greater appreciation of life—and of each other. Aldrich's endings may not be exactly "happily ever after," but they are definitely upbeat. Her reader leaves her people contentedly, seeing them wrapped in serenity and satisfaction, or at least knowing they will somehow work things out. In these stories Aldrich has definitely caught and reproduced the American longing for security and for fun.

She has done more. As Victor P. Hass, *World Herald* Book Editor, says, "The core of her writings is family. She has few superiors in American writing in showing, through action, the meaning of family in human life. Her families—the Masons, the Cutters, the Moores, the Deals—were complete. They, and thousands like them, were intensely important because they were the foundation on which the American Dream was built".

Children play important parts in Aldrich's family stories, and it is obvious that she is fond of them. We have seen that she worked with her very lively sons and daughter around her. (When he was small, her youngest, Robert, thought that all mothers wrote.)

They and their activities formed a very important part of her everyday life. So it is not surprising that some of her best and most amusing remarks concern boys and girls.

Consider, for instance, small Jakie Cohen in *Rim of the Prairie:* "Because of his great curiosity over a firecracker," he is "the possessor of a glass eye which he would remove for the edification and entertainment of anyone who paid him a cent." Or observe Nell Cutter's skirmish with her obstreperous sons as they put off feeding their rabbits.

As all popular authors are, she was frequently asked to write articles or give statements concerning her philosophy of creative writing, her methods, etc. Her answers were never ambiguous: the reader is left in no doubt as to what she was trying to accomplish and why.

Discussing *A Lantern in Her Hand* she observes that though it was written in the "roaring 20's" it was far from "sophisticated," seemingly apart from the flamboyant life of the times. And she adds, "That it has made new friends each year since that day might be a bit of a lesson for young writers: *Regardless of the popular literary trend of the times, write the thing which lies close to your heart".*

When it comes to writing of life in a modern setting, she has very clear convictions, convictions which any of her readers may see are amply illustrated by her work: "In regard to the modern novel being a true mirror of the American home, the trend, of course, has been to write of the fast, high-strung, disintegrating home. That type of home is as American as the type I write about, but no more so. It no more represents all of America than does my type. But it is heard from far more than the type that I represent. After all, there are not very many of us who are writing of the small-town, financially-comfortable, one-man-for-one-woman, clean, decent and law-abiding families. As stories call for something dramatic, I suppose the idea is that there isn't much drama in that sort of family. But there is birth there, and love and marriage and death and all the ups-and-downs which come to every family in every town, large or small".

She goes on to say, "If you have lived life deeply, touched bottom, as it were, it takes away any inclination to sit and wade through pages of sex stuff, or even wearily to follow somebody's ponderous mental reactions. They call it real life; at least, if it's decent, it's bunk. Are indecency and slime all that constitute real life?".

One notes here what is obviously one of Aldrich's most deeply rooted convictions: "clean and decent" are divorced from "sex stuff"; furthermore, anything not "law-abiding" or "one-man-for-one-woman" must perforce be "sordid." And the work of the artist may be geared to the "clean and decent" and "law-abiding" as justifiably as to the "sordid."

Besides her uncomplicated credo that "clean" and "everyday life" have their drama—and are preferable to the "sordid"—she has a very firm conviction that character portrayal is the foundation of fiction. One must understand and sympathize with people, she says. A writer must empathize completely with his people; only then can he write truly of experiences as they live them. "When I have mentally constructed a personality about whom I wish to write, I find myself somewhat lost in that personality, crawling back into the character's skin, so to speak, and viewing life from his standpoint".

Aside from her deeply felt convictions as to kinds of life to present and characters to create, she holds one about writing as *work.* That is what it is for her and, she implies, for any serious writer. At times she actually walked the floor as if in physical pain, "trying to get hold of an idea which would only elude me".

Interestingly, she illustrates how the "germ" of a story came to her in a news item about an old college building that was to be razed. Working from the simple fact of the demolishment of a landmark, she gradually evolved the novel *Miss Bishop,* one of her greatest successes.

Her finest work, *A Lantern in Her Hand,* had an unusual beginning. It is rooted in the history of her mother's and father's families. Her mother's tart answer to commiseration about the hardships of pioneer life was, "Oh, save your pity. We had the best time in the world." Aldrich never forgot those words, thinking of them as she read—too often—how writers depicted the frontier women as "gaunt, browbeaten creatures, despairing women whom life seemed to defeat".

And so she determined to write a novel that would amount to a tribute to her mother and others like her, women of intrepid spirit, courage, humor, and strength who had helped settle a wide and fertile land. It was to be more than a tribute: it was to be an authentic account of life on the plains during the early years.

Her research was enterprising. In 1927, at the request of the editor of the *Nebraska State Journal,* she spoke over the radio on the subject **"The Pioneer in**

Fiction." At the end of her speech she requested listeners to send her any anecdotes or facts about frontier living they might have. In reply she was flooded with material: newspaper clippings, diaries, letters, scrapbooks. In addition she interviewed many elderly people who could remember their pioneering days.

As a result *A Lantern in Her Hand* is a book rich in vivid—and homely—detail, a book so informative that it has frequently been used as supplementary reading in schools. From it the student gains not only knowledge, but a kind of awed admiration and respect for people like the Deals and their friends. For these people worked with what seems almost superhuman strength. They founded towns and built roads, established schools, staked out cemeteries. And they defied a grim and relentless Nature that time and again burned their crops with scorching sun or lashed at their poor homes with brutal blizzards.

As noted above, Aldrich lets her own attitudes toward life guide her writing. One easily sees, in novel after novel, short story after short story, exactly what values she holds. And these values are clearly recognizable as those of Midwestern rural and small-town society during the first half of the century.

The stories are free from profanity and any other sort of coarse language. As Robert Louis Stevenson was able to write a pirate tale without a single "cussword," so Aldrich manages to give a sense of reality to life on the prairie without one. More, she can write of "modern" young people, university students, who speak clear unadorned English. Their slang is another matter, as will be noted later.

A few people in the Aldrich world smoke (males only), but no one ever drinks anything headier than coffee. As far as sex goes, it is as well hidden as in any Victorian novel. People fall in love; Aldrich tells us they do—indeed, she insists on it. But it is mostly a friendly "let's be partners" type of love. Once in a while a mild hint of something a bit earthier is evident, but this is not protracted. One senses, for instance, pure lust as Ed crushes young Abbie to him and begs her to marry him.

One senses it also in *Miss Bishop* when Delbert is courting Ella. His ardor vaguely worries her. When he yearns, "You're a cool little piece, aren't you, Ella? You *do* love me, don't you?" she assures him she does. She just wants to be "so sure." Love is such a big thing; she wants to understand it. Delbert embraces her passionately, saying, "It's this!"

Aldrich goes on, "But Ella knew better—Ella Bishop knew her love was something more than that—something more deeply beautiful—something infinitely more delicate".

Here the reader sees clearly that for Ella Bishop sex per se is unclean. True, the treachery of Delbert and Amy is a hideous thing. But the actual sex act would today be viewed as incidental. The 1870s (when Ella is young) of course saw this in a different light, and Aldrich is probably correct in her depiction of Ella's attitude, when she has her say witheringly to the little flirt who has seduced her fiancé: "You little *animal*." But the reader understands clearly that Aldrich is in agreement.

In *A White Bird Flying* when Laura thinks of Allen Rinemiller, there seems to be physical desire. She loves him. She loves being with him, for he is the one person she can talk to. But because of her ambition she at first refuses his offer of marriage. She is going to New York, to a writing career! Neither he nor she gives a thought to extramarital sex.

When Kathy's and Jimmy's marriage is imperiled, no indication is given as to what effect on their sex life their disagreements have. Physical passion simply has no place in Aldrich's concept of "family fiction."

There are no divorces in Aldrich's world, either, though there may occasionally—very occasionally—be a reference to an unhappy marriage. A case in point is that of Uncle Harry and Aunt Carolyn in *A White Bird*.

One of the most strongly held convictions of Aldrich's life is her theory of the place of women in society. The subject is one of crucial interest in our day; when Aldrich was writing it was coming disturbingly to the forefront. She has drawn some engaging women: Mother Mason, Nell Cutter, Abbie Deal, Linnie Stafford, and many, many more. Of her whole feminine galaxy only one career woman stands out: Ella Bishop, the teacher.

Ella is shown to be self-sufficient, courageous, energetic—in the end completely fulfilled. But she is alone. Though Grace Deal of *A White Bird* is also a self-sufficient and energetic single woman, she reveals in an uncharacteristic speech that her life has not been all she wished.

Nowhere has Aldrich put her case for "woman's place" so clearly as in *The Cutters*. Entertaining a former classmate who has become a successful businesswoman, Nell voices her envy. Her friend speaks: "Nellie," she says gravely, "for everything in this world we pay the price. You bought your lovely family with your freedom; and the price I pay for freedom is—heartache. I have an infinite capacity for love—and no husband. I have the heart of a mother—and no child. We say the world progresses, and it does. Women have come up out of slavery and serfdom; they can stand shoulder to shoulder now with the men of the business, scholastic, and political world. But there are some fundamentals to which normal women will always look with longing eyes. In the last analysis, nothing can take the place of them. Love, home, children. I've put my heart and soul into the business, and results show it. I'm rather justly proud of what I've accomplished. And yet—all I really want is a corner of my own, green and shady and restful, where I may sit and . . . rock the baby I never had".

There is an echo of these sentiments, couched in much crisper language, in the advice Grace Deal, a successful university professor, gives her niece Laura. Don't do as I did, she says in effect: don't turn down love and home and family for a career!

Thus Aldrich vividly illustrates what Betty Friedan, decades later, was to call "the feminine mystique." And Aldrich's attitude is neatly summarized in what Friedan says of Helene Deutsche: "This brilliant feminine follower of Freud states categorically that the women who by 1944 in America had achieved eminence by activity of their own in various fields had done so at the expense of their feminine fulfillment".

But Carol Fairbanks remarks that, cheerful and optimistic as Aldrich's *Lantern* is, her Abbie Deal is barred from developing her artistic and musical talents; she must see them flower in her children and grandchildren. Thus Abbie "is the archetypal nineteenth-century woman who sets aside her personal needs and arranges finances so that her daughters realize their dreams".

Fairbanks further points out that Aldrich has underscored the position of women in pioneering days. In *Spring Came on Forever* the German immigrant expects to get ahead because he has land, a good team of horses, and a woman. Said woman must work hard and be as unobtrusive as possible in order to escape his wrath.

Contrast the personality of Nell's friend with Willa Cather's Alexandra Bergson, a woman who is stronger than her brothers and who, with superb ability

and great labor, carves a fine farm from the rich Nebraska country. Her life, at the end of the story, is to be completed by her marriage with Carl.

Or turn to Ruth Suckow and see how she handles a similar theme in her novel *Cora*. Cora has done well in the business world, has become one of the successful women of the city: "She could hold her own among them. She was almost 'at the top.' She had wanted to attain this—life would have been a failure if she hadn't done so. Now she struggled fiercely to enjoy what she had won."

"But there was something wrong . . . There had to be something else . . . something *inside* of things . . . she did not know how to put it."

In spite of obvious similarities, Aldrich differs—I believe fundamentally—from other women who have written of the Midwest, precisely in this question of feminine values. Certainly, as has been noted, she shows strong women, women of courage and perseverance, with a decided bent toward independence. But unlike Cather's Alexandra and ántonia and Thea, and Suckow's Cora, their strength and fulfillment come from *womanliness.*

They come, not from meeting the world in the manner of a man, not from managing farms and ranches, or climbing the corporate ladder, or buying and selling. Mother Mason, Nell Cutter, Abbie Deal, and other Aldrich women characters do not lead easy lives, are certainly not immune to physical and emotional suffering. But theirs is not the suffering of marketplace competition nor the frustration of political losses. It is not even the turmoil of the artistic life, the grueling labor and almost intolerable pressures of careers on the stage, the painstaking work of the writer or the painter.

No, Aldrich's women find their greatest satisfaction in being sturdy daughters, devoted wives, strict and compassionate mothers. For instance, we see Laura Deal giving up her writing plans to be happy as wife and mother. We see Abbie sorrowful when her daughter Isabelle tells her she and her husband plan not to have children so they can both pursue their musical careers. And how much more sorrowful Abbie is when daughter Grace announces that she will remain single!

A much more important difference between Aldrich and other Midwest writers is that she never questions the basic assumptions of "moral" middle-class life. She sees heroism in this life, and she sees humor, but she never really probes beneath its surface.

Ruth Suckow, on the other hand, has an uneasy awareness that something is amiss in the structure of middle-class society. She has a sense of unsatisfactory aspects in the relations of the sexes, for example. Willa Cather, with all the poetry of her narratives, feels keenly—and transmits to her readers—some of the profound problems of "normal" people: jealousy, hatred, revenge, ambition. Mari Sandoz, aware as she is of the beauty and promise of the Great Plains, is devastatingly truthful about showing the ugliness that can flourish in the midst of it all. Helen Hoover Santmyer, demure as she seems in her sweeping novel *And Ladies of the Club,* shows what meanness can lie beneath the surface of a quiet Ohio town. Examples can go on and on. Something in the very makeup of society is askew, as American writers have insisted from James Fenimore Cooper on through Mark Twain to our own time.

Since about the beginning of the present century, which signaled the start of the "revolt from the village" movement, small-town life has been a popular theme. From E. W. Howe's *Story of a Country Town* to Sinclair Lewis's *Main Street* down to *And Ladies of the Club* and Garrison Keillor's *Lake Wobegone Days,* writers of fiction have delighted in exposing the faults, the meannesses, the unlovely provincialism, of many Winesburgs and Gopher Prairies. Such fiction has often been scathing, often cynical, occasionally satirical. Aldrich, on the contrary, looks at little towns with loving eyes and warm sympathy. And she is adept at finding amusing incidents in the lives of her characters.

True, she does admit that "culture" is regarded suspiciously. And in one story, **"Welcome Home, Hal,"** she departs from her usual attitude to remark, "A small Midwestern town through alien eyes is sometimes not a lovely thing."

Her basic feeling, however, is illustrated by Nell Cutter's outburst: "All our modern authors have just two types of people in their small town writings: the discontented kind, or the dull, stolid kind who are too dumb to know enough to *be* discontented. I'm not either one—and there are a lot of us—and I'd like to have Miss Duffield know it. We're not all dowdy and we're not all crude."

After all, Aldrich says, "What were the fundamentally big things of life, the things that were eternal? Knowledge . . . appearances . . . sophistication? Or truth . . . friendship . . . love?".

Though she wrote during and after the World War I years, Bess Streeter Aldrich has nothing to say about war hysteria, "the red menace," labor troubles, bread-

lines, voices both loud and quiet who insist that something is amiss, that some sectors of the population are wronged, are restless, are demanding redress.

Her Cutters and Masons, her modern Deals—her businessmen and bankers and university instructors—live their emotional and financial lives apparently untouched by the world around them. Nowhere is there evidence that this author had read and enjoyed Jane Austen, but a reader can conclude that she would have sympathized with her as she kept her characters out of the turbulence of their era.

A rather curious attitude occasionally surfaces in Aldrich's fiction; one feels almost discourteous in mentioning it, for it is so obviously unconscious. This is her feeling against the American East. It stands to reason, of course, that she would be enthusiastic about the Midwest. Never has anyone loved a place more, nor felt so joyous in the love of it. That love breathes through every line of **Lantern,** for instance, the novel written as a tribute to pioneer women. It is everywhere in **Rim of the Prairie,** in **Miss Bishop,** in **A White Bird Flying.** But often it is accompanied by something almost like veiled hostility toward the East.

This hostility is mainly implied. Young Abbie Deal's flashy suitor, Dr. Ed, begs her to come with him to New York. There he can give her cultural advantages, have her lovely voice trained. Her granddaughter Laura has a chance to go to New York to be a companion to her wealthy uncle and aunt (and eventually to inherit their fortune) while taking advantage of the cultural atmosphere to develop her writing talent. Both girls refuse because they love their honest farmer sweethearts more than they crave the "opportunities" of the East.

A White Bird Flying contains one scene that is rather explicit about the East-Midwest problem. Several college girls are discussing the attitude of Easteners toward Nebraska, their ignorance of the state, and their condescension. One tells of the Eastener who, when a story in the *Saturday Evening Post* is mentioned, says, "Oh, do they have the *Saturday Evening Post* in Nebraska?" And, "I would expect the trees here look odd to you?" one visiting Nebraskan is asked.

Another tells of a newspaper woman who, visiting in New York, counters the obvious condescension of her hosts by pointing out that the author Willa Cather, the comedian Harold Lloyd, and the sculptor Gutzum

Borglum are all Nebraskans. She finishes by saying she'll be delighted to visit Coney Island—it was designed by a "Nebraska boy."

Laura and Allen (in **White Bird**) argue about the Midwest versus the East. She tells him there's no "atmosphere" in the Midwest; as one of her professors has said, "no spiritual uplift." Allen asks where she could find "more substantial people," and she counters with the remark that "substantial people" are poor literary material.

According to her professor, there is no "great beauty" in the Midwest—no sea, no mountains, etc. The landscape is "monotonous." Allen answers with the Bad Lands of Dakota, the blue sky over the Nebraska sand hills, the Minnesota lakes and birches.

Thus, here and there in her fiction, Aldrich seems to be on the defensive as far as the Midwest is concerned, repelling possible attacks, as it were. And, as has been noted, her love of her native region is so deep that it permeates her work.

It certainly is apparent in her descriptions of nature. Probably no American writer has been more delightfully graphic when it comes to settings. In her pictures of the country, Aldrich rivals Willa Cather, Mari Sandoz, Ruth Suckow. One *feels* the country as she spreads it before one. Observe her description of spring: "Spring came over the prairie—not softly, shyly, but in great magic strides. It was in the flush of grass on the alders and willows of Stove Creek. It was in the wind,—in the smell of loam and grasses, in the tantalizing odor of wild plums budding and wild violets flowering . . . ".

Compare that passage with Willa Cather's spring day: "It was a beautiful blue morning. The buffalo peas were blooming in pink and purple masses along the roadside, and the larks, perched on last year's dried sunflower stalks, were singing straight at the sun, their heads thrown back and their yellow breasts aquiver. The wind blew about us in warm, sweet gusts" (*My ántonia*).

Aldrich's feeling for the plains, for Nebraska, is more than simple love; it is a vital empathy. Because of this she is as forceful in her descriptions of the frightening aspects of the land as in its more gracious moods. For her, as for Cather and Sandoz, it is a living, breathing presence.

When it comes to making the reader experience the white terror of plains blizzard, she is a powerful artist. Her storm scenes have all the dreadful actual-

ity of Sandoz's. And probably no one has described a tornado more impressively than she has in **Rim of the Prairie.** Her words are worthy of being quoted at length:

"Above the trees an immense yellow-black smoke whirled up into the sky, spiraling, rotating, in great volume . . . it was no fire but a more cruel thing. Greenish clouds had whipped themselves into the bowl of a huge wine-glass. . . . There was no sound anywhere. No wind in the trees. No bird sang. No cock crew. There was silence everywhere save in the frenzied heart of the Thing that moved swiftly across the prairie. It boiled and crackled and roared. It was heavy. But it was not clumsy. Gracefully it moved. Almost daintily it picked its way in and out of the farmlands. It bent and swayed and sung. The stem stretched and pulled away from the bowl. But it did not break. It sucked at the ground and whatever it touched, living or inanimate thing, answered its wild call and was pulled up into the cloud glass to make wine for the fallen gods".

One may note an egregious mixing of metaphors here, and one may object to the prolixity. But no reader can escape a feeling of breathless immediacy. One is *there* living the terror, overwhelmed with the realization of the sheer strength of elemental powers.

Aldrich's easy, almost conversational style lends itself to humor, and here she is distinctive. Her reader is always conscious of a sunny temperament, one that takes pleasure in the small amusements of life, that finds laughter in day-to-day happenings. Life, whether on the grim frontier or in a small Midwestern town, is filled with little chuckles, brief moments of laughter.

Some of the humor seems off-hand. For instance, in **The Cutters** one finds a bit of totally unconscious irony in Grandma's description of the successful careers of her six sons. She ends her statement with the remark that Robbie, the "rascallyest" one of all, is the new governor of the state.

But unfortunately, in Aldrich's amusement she is inclined to go too far. She not only laughs; all too often she points up her laughter with references that make her remarks seem dangerously close to wisecracks.

As an example, see how she describes a committee planning a function: "Over the dinner itself there was enough discussion to have filled a book the size of the classic which Mr. Webster wrote". And the reader winces as an old Civil War veteran remembers Christmas in Atlanta, when they burned the city "before startin' out with Sherman on that little hoofin' jaunt we took to the sea."

Miss Bishop yields several noteworthy examples. Here she remarks that "hundreds of little towns grew to their full size of two or five or ten thousand, paused in their growth, and admitted that none of them by taking Chamber-of-Commerce thought could add one cubit to its stature". When Midwestern College holds its opening ceremony, "There was [sic] prayers, in which the president informed the Lord of the current events of the morning".

Further, "Professor Carter made an heroic attempt to initiate the novices into the mysteries of Chaucer". And, "A Professor O'Neill, representing Messrs Caesar, Ovid, and Livy, taught for a single year, as his radical views on the origin of the human race, which he so often found occasion to wedge in between the Aquitannians and the Belgae, proved his undoing, and he was summarily dismissed".

Often, too, Aldrich is guilty of an embarrassing affectation: she is fond of parodying famous lines of poetry. *The Rim of the Prairie* contains a statement about a young teacher: "By the next night Nancy's head, pedagogically speaking, was bloody but unbowed". And in *The Cutters* another teacher, near the end of summer, remarks that "in one week I go like the quarry slave at night, scourged to the dungeon of his schoolroom". A very little of this kind of thing goes a long way, and regrettably Aldrich overdoes it.

Some readers might find the conversations of her young girls excessively irritating. Many of these girls seem interchangeable, from Nancy Moore of *Rim,* through Katherine Deal of *White Bird* to Gretchen of *Miss Bishop.* All of them exhibit an airy flippancy supposed to be funny, but which all too often ends in making one flinch.

Nancy says to Aunt Biny, "Real love, Aunt Biny, belongs to another generation. It went out with rubber-tired buggies and castors for centerpieces". And she assures the worried little woman about her engagement: "I'll try to idolize Mr. Farnsworth. He's getting a bit bald on the north mansard roof slope of his head and he's a little too short and a little too fat and a lot older than the hero ought to be. But I'll do my best to moon over him". Abbie Deal's granddaughter Kathy flaunts a like breezy cynicism, though she does marry for love.

In *White Bird* Laura's college friends, discussing campus affairs, show a studied cleverness. Jealousy is "acid raisins"; an assignment in a literature course is "a date with the Russian writer Tchekov"; Shakespeare is always "Billy."

The most egregious case of strained flippancy can be found in the character of Gretchen, Ella Bishop's foster grandniece. This young woman is hardly bearable. Utterly uninhibited, she seems never to express a worthwhile idea. Not only are all male professors "papa" to her, she can apparently take nothing—and no one—seriously. Rummaging in an old trunk, she finds poor Ella's unfinished wedding gown, and without permission tries it on. "Am I not *perfect?*" she says, coming before her aunt. "Isn't it the answer to a maiden's prayer? May I wear it? What does the sweet old auntie say? . . . You're stunned speechless at my gorgeousness, aren't you? . . . What's the answer, sweet pumpkin?".

When Ella supplies the money so Gretchen can live in the sorority house, the girl expresses her appreciation with, "I think you're a luscious old peach. I suppose I ought to be noble and say I couldn't think of accepting the offer, but I'm crazy to do it, and will take you at your word that you really want me to". Later on she tells Ella, "You're an old smoothy,—in fact you're probably the noblest soul that ever trod over campus dandelions".

If humor lightens Aldrich's narratives, an irritating tendency toward didacticism gives occasional heavy moments. This writer simply cannot keep from pointing a moral—and too often it is a moral that readers are quite capable of finding for themselves. Further, most of her "moral" passages are interwoven with a sugary sentimentalism quite unworthy of so gifted a teller of tales.

An excellent example may be quoted from a Christmas story, **"The Drum Goes Dead"**: "And so suddenly that it seemed a new thought—though it was as old as the silent stars—a bright-colored strand wove itself across the gray warp of his mind. *The world was not in chaos to these children.* Through their eyes it was still the same world of limited dimensions he and these other burdened people had know as children, and because this was so, it was still a good world.

"Humanity must hang fast to its faith and its hope. It must never let them go as long as there remained in the world a child and a song,—a gift and a star" (65 . . .).

This didacticism sometimes extends to descriptions of characters. Aldrich presents many interesting people; even her minor actors are colorful. However, she feels obliged to discuss them with the reader; they would do very well if she just left them alone. An especially vivid example is that of Nancy Moore, of **Rim.** She is charming, but her author is not content to show us that she is; she must tell us: "She could no more have abandoned that gay little way of hers than she could have changed the color of her eyes".

Despite flaws such as these, Aldrich's style is smooth and lucid, shot through with the good-natured humor of a pleasant, good-natured personality. Her readers are both soothed and gently amused.

As I have attempted to show, Bess Streeter Aldrich gives faithful pictures of frontier life. The bulk of her work, however, concerns small-town families living according to the tenets of what George Bernard Shaw once called "middle class morality." Clearly she has presented what she sees as truth about life. Indeed, one interviewer has observed that "perhaps her strength has been in the fact that she has not lost contact at any time with the *real people* in this land". If her vision has been affected by her own sunny disposition and the values she learned as a child, she is no different from many other earnest writers of fiction. She has a right to be called a realist according to her own lights.

But the term is not technically applicable to her work. Her predilection is for a pleasant romanticism, a deft veiling of the darker aspects of life. She certainly knew they existed; every now and then a reference is made (in some cases almost reluctantly) to lust, to greed, to sorrow, to frustration. But the overall picture is one of satisfaction in being alive, in doing one's work well, and, above all, in loving one's family and friends.

A critic is wrong to fault a writer for not doing what he or she did not intend to do, and Aldrich has said plainly that she did not intend to write of sophisticated people, of perverts, of "sin." "Life has been wholesome, sane and happy for me," she writes, " . . . I have set down life as I have found it, knowing that many, many people in the world have known it as I have—a thing of mingled happiness and sorrow, little pleasures and little disappointments, deep courage, high faith, grief, laughter, and love".

In a very revealing article, **"Why I Live in a Small Town,"** she is almost militant: "Why quarrel with a writer over realism and idealism? After all, an author is glass through which a picture of life is projected. The picture falls upon the pages of the writer's manuscript according to the mental and emotional contours of that writer. It is useless to try to change those patterns. If one writer does not see life in terms of grime and dirt, adulteries and debaucheries, it does not follow that those sordid things do not exist. If another does not see life in terms of faith and love, sympathy and good deeds, it does not follow that those characteristics do not exist. I grow weary of hearing the sordid spoken of as real life, the wholesome as Pollyanna stuff. I contend that a writer may portray some of the decent things of life around him and reserve the privilege to call that real life too. And if this be literary treason, make the most of it".

A publisher's note confirms her words; speaking of how she "sought to convey the sturdy cheerful realism of her mother," it points to her "intelligent optimism that has illumined all of her . . . work, setting her apart from the mass of current writers, who tend too often to view the American scene darkly and despondently".

And a bit of grudging—almost reluctant—praise occurs in the entry devoted to her in *Twentieth Century Authors* (1942): "Her typical book covers the entire life, from youth to age, of a Middle Western woman, and her thesis is that love, marriage, and children are the most important things in life. Her intense feeling for nature, a natural gift for characterization, and her humor place her work in a rather higher category than its philosophy might indicate".

A less gracious reviewer acknowledging the virtues of **Lantern,** observes that "Mrs. Aldrich does make the settlement of the West seem an epic accomplishment . . . She does make bearing children and loving them, and teaching them, and cheerfully giving up all the world that they might have it instead, seem worth doing." This is obviously written tongue in cheek, for the writer adds sneeringly, "Novels will go on telling about these things forever, and people will read them, and laugh over them, and cry over them. And it will do people no harm" (*Saturday Review of Literature* 17 Nov. 1928: 371).

One excellent proof of her views concerning writing is the fact that for a while she read book manuscripts for a monthly book club called "The Family Bookshelf." The object was to eliminate literature not suitable for children. (Other members of the reading committee were Drew Pearson, Dr. Daniel Poling, and Edwin Balmer, editor of *Redbook*.)

Certainly many readers found her outlook on life and literature congenial. When the Lincoln Kiwanis Club honored her, one tribute began, "Books that sneer at the frailties of mankind, or books that discourage human aspiration, will always impress me as nothing better than bad books. It is the glory of Nebraska, I think, that we have a writer who has never been touched by the frost of what is cynical or bitter. She walks bravely with a lantern in her hand, always a mellow light shines from her fiction. Sanity and a gracious spirit are the soul of her work."

However, even those who agree with Aldrich's convictions might feel a little restless when reading some of her fiction. *Miss Bishop,* for example. This is a charming novel in many ways, and colorful in its delineation of the start and growth of a great university. Ella Bishop is a likeable heroine—except for the fact that she has no flaws. Time after time she gives up her desires for other people, mainly her family. One of her more painful decisions is consenting to rear the child of her faithless lover and the woman with whom he has betrayed her.

Yearning to go to Europe, she twice relinquishes her plans for a trip abroad. On the first occasion her aged mother is ailing, and on the second her supremely selfish foster niece needs money in order to live in a sorority house. Later Ella sends the girl on a trip to Europe to escape a disastrous love affair. In all the crises of her life, Ella Bishop's first thought is for someone else.

But how one would have liked to see her, if only a few times, succumb to selfishness, to irresponsibility, yes, to passion! If only just once she had told her selfish family that she was going to do as *she* wished! (As a matter of fact, many of her sacrifices are made over the protests of her family and friends.)

One wishes she had had at least one glorious, ecstatic night with John Stevens, instead of refusing him because he is married (even though she knows his wife gives him nothing), and because she must stay "pure" so she can, in her own eyes, be a proper role model for her students. One would have liked her to be a little indiscreet, occasionally, and perhaps been rapped over the knuckles for it. One wishes, in sum, that she hadn't constantly been loving and giving and idealistic—and always with a merry quip at her own expense!

Miss Bishop may be an extreme example, but the romanticism that suffuses it may be seen here and there in all Aldrich's work. Nor is she above a bit of gentle

mysticism. A good instance of this can be found in *Lantern.* It occurs at the end of the chapter telling of the ingenious ways Abbie and Will, in spite of crushing poverty, made Christmas for their little children.

The youngsters, before going to bed, look out at the silent, snowy night and see a star which, they say gleefully, is stopping right over their house. Aldrich meditates:

"Historians say, "The winter of 'seventy-four to seventy-five was a time of deep depression. . . . ' Deep depression? To three children on the prairie it was a time of glamour. There was not much to eat in the cupboard. There was little or no money in the father's flat old pocketbook. The presents were pitifully homely and meager. And all in a tiny house,—a mere shell of a house, on a new raw acreage of the wild, bleak prairie. How could a little rude cabin hold so much white magic? How could a little sod house know such enchantment? And how could a little hut like that eventually give to the midwest so many influential men and women? How, indeed? Unless . . . unless, perchance, the star *did* stop over the house?".

Twin to romanticism is a certain innocence that crops up now and then in her work. One is amused to read of college-educated Nell Cutter's failed attempt at short-story writing. Her first effort is rejected by an editor who tells her to "go into the technical construction of story work." Nell's reaction is amazement: "Technical!" she says. "Whoever dreamed that there was any technical construction to a story? I thought when popular writers wrote they just sat down and *wrote.* It looks so easy, as though it just rolled off their pens".

And Laura Deal, just out of the University, thinks there's not enough "scope" for the creative writer in the Midwest. The people are "ordinary," the scenery "uninspiring." It is as if she'd never heard of Madame Bovary, or the one passion and four walls of Dumas, as if she were ignorant of the dramatic possibilities inner conflicts can present.

However, for all the flaws in style—the excesses of over-done humor, of didacticism, of sentimentality— Bess Streeter Aldrich remains a notable figure, fully worthy to be ranked as one of the gifted writers of Midwestern fiction—a group including Willa Cather, Mari Sandoz, Ruth Suckow, Martha Ostenso, to name a few of the women. Fairbanks links her with Cather and Laura Ingalls Wilder as one of "three prairie women writers".

In Abbie Deal, Aldrich has created a woman to compare favorably with Cather's Alexandra Bergson and ántonia Shimerda. With her courage and spirit Abbie is very like Sandoz's Dr. Morissa Kirk in her resourcefulness, in the practical way she makes use of the materials about her. She never flinches at hardship or pain, though she has moments, as is natural, of feminine longing and resentment, moments when life seems too hard to bear. But she always straightens her shoulders and goes on. She is, when all is said, the epitome of the courage, the endurance, and the ethical constancy which Americans like to think make up the spirit of the pioneer. *A Lantern in Her Hand* accomplishes what Aldrich planned it should: it pays tribute to the intrepidity and fearlessness of the women who left their homes to accompany their men to an unsettled land fraught with unknown dangers.

Perhaps Aldrich knew the writings of contemporary Midwestern authors such as Cather, Sandoz, Suckow, and Ostenso, but no indication of such knowledge exists. Perhaps she would have felt a distance between her and these women, all of whom refuse to ignore the sordid aspects of rural life. None of them has the determined cheerfulness that wins out in Aldrich's fiction.

But it may be that very element of cheer that made her appreciated by so many readers—surprisingly different readers. For instance, Admiral Chester Nimitz wrote her that he and his officers gained courage reading *A Lantern in Her Hand* during the worst days of World War II in the Pacific. And his is only one of many letters expressing like sentiments.

One is struck by the tone of some of these letters. They seem to attest to the charm of Aldrich's personality, the pleasant graciousness that one senses between the lines of her stories. Acknowledging biographical materials Aldrich has sent her, one woman says, "It means a great deal to my friends and myself to discover that a person who knows fame and success, could be interested in just ordinary folks."

Again, a fifteen-year-old girl writes with adolescent emotion, "It seems funny—we have never seen each other, you didn't even know I existed and yet you are one of my best friends—one to whom I tell my secrets to [sic]—one who I feel will understand me . . . I love you, Mrs. Aldrich, because you know and can put into beautiful words all that I feel within me."

Near the end of his detailed critique of one of Sarah Orne Jewett's short stories, Louis A. Renza inserts a significant quotation. Jewett, in one of her letters, says, "I often think that the literary work which takes the least prominent place, nowadays, is that belonging to the middle ground. Scholars and so-called intellectual persons have a wealth of literature in the splendid accumulation of books that belong to all times, and now and then a new volume is added to the great list. Then there is the lowest level of literature, the trashy newspaper and sensational novels, but how seldom a book comes that stirs the minds and hearts of the good men and women of such a village as this".

These words seem peculiarly apropos to Aldrich's work if we read "village" to mean "just ordinary folks." Indeed these are precisely the people for whom Bess Streeter Aldrich felt the greatest affinity, and for whom she wrote.

Besides her writing, which seems to have been a real labor of love as well as a means of livelihood, she enjoyed activities in her church (Methodist), Order of Eastern Star, Nebraska Writers Guild (of which she was for a time president), the Nebraska Press Association, the Omaha Women's Press Club, Altrusa of Lincoln, and the honorary societies Chi Delta Phi (national literary fraternity) and Theta Sigma Phi (national journalistic sorority).

In 1934 she was awarded an Honorary Doctorate of Literature by the University of Nebraska for her achievements as homemaker, author, citizen, and one giving distinguished service to Nebraska. And in 1939 the Lincoln Kiwanis Club honored her with the Distinguished Service Medal as "Homemaker, Citizen, and Author."

After her death on 3 August 1954, 52nd Street, where her Lincoln home stood, was renamed "Aldrich Road." Eleven years later in the small town of Elmwood, a Nebraska Historical Marker sponsored by the Elmwood Library Board was dedicated to her. It stands in Elmwood Park, across the street from the house in which she lived for many years.

In 1973 she was elected to the Nebraska Hall of Fame, the second woman to be so honored; only Willa Cather preceded her. And in 1976, at the celebration of the nation's Bicentennial, she was named one of the Ten Mothers of Achievement from Nebraska.

An unusual honor was bestowed upon her as recently as 1984. The unique publishing company, Amereon House (Mattituck, New York) reprinted *The Home-Coming and Other Stories* and *Across the Smiling*

Meadows and Other Stories. Joanna Paulson, the editor, says in a preface to the latter volume that the purpose of the publishers is "to preserve and distribute the efforts of authors of quality and popularity that have fallen between the cracks [sic] in our modern, fast-paced society".

One cannot see Bess Streeter Aldrich as a "forgotten" literary figure. In 1987 Elmwood, her home town, honored her memory with an "Aldrich Day." The "Bess Streeter Aldrich Foundation," formed in 1977, seeks to promote her work and is ambitious to raise money for a "permanent memorial."

One of the most significant examples of the praise she has received may be found in the 1949 poll by a group of scholastic magazines. Asked to name the ten books which have done the best job of telling about American life, the readers included *A Lantern in Her Hand*—the only one of the ten not filmed.

Certainly Bess Streeter Aldrich's work is a faithful, if not a complete, picture of American life. Readers can turn with confidence to her richly detailed and authentic account of pioneering on the prairies, of everyday life in small towns, to restore their faith in the spirit of their country.

Carol Miles Petersen

SOURCE: An introduction to *The Collected Short Works, 1907-1919: Bess Streeter Aldrich,* edited by Carol Miles Petersen, University of Nebraska Press, 1995, pp. vii-xiii.

In describing how to write a short story, Bess Streeter Aldrich noted the author must "live the lives of his characters, crawling into their very skins. . . . He must be an actor. More than that, he must play all the parts."[1] In playing "all the parts," Bess Streeter Aldrich brought to her readers the pleasure of well-written stories that reflect her own personality: her positive outlook on life, her humor, her understanding of people. The stories further offer the pleasure of recognizing characters and incidents that reappear in Aldrich novels: the revised Mason and Cutter family stories became the books *Mother Mason* (1924), and *The Cutters* (1926); and Zimri Streeter appears as "Grandpa Stàtler" in the 1915 story of that name, in the 1925 novel *The Rim of the Prairie* in the 1939 *The Song of Years* and as the hero of the 1944 short story **"Soldier Vote of '64."** The character of the school teacher in **"The Madonna of the Purple-**

Dots" (1907) and in **"The Cat Is on the Mat"** (1916) appears as that of the protagonist in *The Rim of the Prairie.*

Many of these stories are reprinted for the first time since their original publication. I have included two that were sold but not published—one, **"The Madonna of the Purple Dots,"** because the magazine went out of business and the other, **"Concerning the Best Man,"** because of an editorial policy change. Aldrich wrote more than one hundred short stories and was able to claim the enviable record of never writing a story she did not sell. Many of her stories were syndicated after first publication and many were sold to British magazines; her readership was enormous. All of her novels are in print.

This book contains stories that Aldrich wrote from the start of her career through 1919. That year she turned thirty-eight, and had accomplished a great deal both in her personal life and in her writing. After graduating from college in 1901 she taught for three years, received a second teaching degree, married, moved three times, bore three children and was pregnant with her fourth child, was active in church work, organized the first Women's Club and helped start the first Public Library in Elmwood, Nebraska, and wrote and sold twenty-six stories plus miscellaneous articles. All of this demonstrates the truth of a comment in 1920 by one of her editors that hers was "a case of stored up energy."[2]

Bessie Genevra Streeter was born in Cedar Falls, Iowa, on 17 February 1881, the youngest of eight children. With ten years separating Bess from her nearest brother and fourteen from her nearest sister, Bess learned to rely on her reading and her own imagination for entertainment; she said that the characters she met in books became as familiar to her as the neighbors. Reading meant curling up in the large friendly armchair in the living room or tucking a book under her apron as she went upstairs in the morning to make the beds, knowing that if she got her chores done quickly she could then read until someone began to wonder where she was. Favorite authors included James M. Barrie, whose humor she enjoyed, and Charles Dickens, whose characterizations she appreciated. Along with her personal favorites, there was the Bible, a staple of her Scots-Presbyterian family. From it, she learned the moral principles by which she would live and which her writing would reflect. She also learned Bible verses, which occasionally surface in her novels, rephrased, but with cadences intact.

Relishing stories as she did, Bess began creating her own—sometimes in the playhouse that her father had built for her in the backyard. Probably from about the age of nine or ten and using a lead pencil as she always would for first drafts, Bess wrote fanciful stories; she knew even as a child that "when words are put together right they're just like singing."[3] Also in the playhouse, pedaling with furious speed on a broken treadle sewing machine, she transported herself on adventurous trips; playing with neighborhood friends, she wove tales of exciting balls, beautiful gowns, and handsome knights with their ladies. One of these friends, Grace Simpson, recalls how Bess would begin telling a story peopled by herself and all of her listeners; she would describe the setting, the dazzling people, and her own exquisite dress; then turning to Grace, Bess would say it was Grace's turn. Grace, lacking a flowing imagination, would respond, "Oh, I don't know, Bess, you tell me."[4] And Bess would describe Grace's and any of the other children's costumes in detail. In all likelihood Grace Simpson was reincarnated as Josephine Cutter's friend, Effie Peterson, in **"Josephine Encounters a Siren"** (*The American Magazine,* December 1922).

Bess won her first writing prize, a camera, at the age of fourteen, later admitting, "It was then I first tasted blood; for the intoxication of seeing my name in print was overwhelming." At seventeen she entered a contest with a story she later described as "heavy as a moving van. It oozed pathos. It dripped melancholy."[5] It won five dollars for her, which she used to purchase a showy umbrella she thought made her look sophisticated and which would later appear as a humorous object in her writing. She wrote articles throughout her college career at Iowa State Normal School, now known as the University of Northern Iowa, from which she graduated in 1901. She then went on to teach in Boone and Marshalltown, Iowa, and then Salt Lake City, Utah. She returned to Cedar Falls, Iowa, in 1906, working as Assistant Supervisor of the Primary Department on the equivalent of her master's degree, which she received the following year. While she taught and worked on her second degree, she wrote articles and published children's stories and had a story accepted for publication just weeks before her wedding.

However, after her 1907 marriage to attorney Charles Sweetzer Aldrich and their subsequent move from Cedar Falls to Tipton, Iowa, she found little time for writing. In 1909 the Aldriches, their two-month-old daughter Mary Eleanor, Bess's mother, and her sister Clara and brother-in-law John Cobb moved to Elmwood, Nebraska, where the Aldriches and the Cobbs had purchased the American Exchange Bank. For the next two years, Aldrich spent her time as wife and mother and became an active member of her new community. Then, in 1911, she saw an advertisement in the *Ladies Home Journal* asking readers to send in stories for a contest the *Journal* was sponsoring. Aldrich's desire to write resurfaced, and the next few afternoons while the baby napped, Aldrich wrote her story. She took it to the bank to type, and when one of the clerks needed to use the typewriter, Bess took out her story, waited until he was done, and then sat down to pick out the letters again until the next interruption. The contest attracted more than two thousand entrants, apparently exceeding what was anticipated, for the magazine dropped the contest idea and instead purchased six of the submitted stories. Aldrich**'s "The Little House Next Door"** was one of those. When the $175 check came, her mother, who was living at the Aldrich home at the time, said, "Look again, Bess, it must be a dollar seventy-five!"[6] It was, indeed, one hundred seventy-five.

Bess Streeter Aldrich then began the transition from occasional to full-time author. With the excitement and impetus of this important sale, she began immediately on another story, sandwiching writing time between the tasks of caring for her husband, her children, and her home. She explained that "the blood that had come from the people who crossed the Mississippi on the ice with oxen began to assert itself, and I determined that if keeping constantly at writing would eventually land one somewhere, I would begin writing in earnest. From that time on I had a manuscript on the road" almost constantly. The next story "wandered around from magazine to magazine making twenty-three trips before it found an editor who would buy it, and it brought only twenty dollars." Because some of her stories went out so often, they became dog-eared, and Aldrich would retype the first and last pages to create the impression that the story was on its first trip. She said that she was "selling one just often enough to encourage me."[7]

In order to sell, Aldrich knew she had to work on the details and techniques of writing; thus she did whatever gave her the opportunity to practice. She entered and won a few newspaper contests, submitted a recipe to *Armour Cookbook* that was accepted, sent a couple of comments to *The Delineator* and received one dollar for each, and wrote some other miscellaneous materials, only two of which are included in this collection. The first is **"My Life Test"** and the second is **"How I Knew When the Right Man Came Along."** These both have the Aldrich cadence and character types, and, to the best of my knowledge, are Aldrich's writings; however, they were published anonymously, and no conclusive evidence proving they are hers has come to my attention. Both are recorded in her financial journal.

Every acceptance, whether it garnered one dollar or many times that amount, was recorded in Aldrich's financial journal. In four years, she had earned a total of $638 for her writings; only three sales had exceeded $100. She continued to work at her craft by taking correspondence lessons from a writing school whose director told her that inasmuch as she had already had some success in publishing, he would take her on as his private pupil and read her work himself. It was not long before he told her that she was a born writer and that her work was so good there was little he could teach her, although he would be glad to continue to read and critique any material she might choose to send him. Acceptances for her work increased.

The year 1918 was an important one for Aldrich. Until this time, describing it as a form of writer's print fright much like an actor's stage fright, Aldrich had written as Margaret Dean Stevens, a combination of her two grandmothers' names. She was now confident enough to use Bess Streeter Aldrich. Proof of her increasing success came in 1918 when *McCall's* accepted **"The Box behind the Door,"** and *The People's Home Journal,* another solid magazine of the time, bought **"Their House of Dreams."** The letter from *The American Magazine* for **"Mother's Dash for Liberty"** must have been the most exciting acceptance since the *Journal* had published **"The Little House Next Door"** in 1911. Aldrich felt this sale was her turning point, for she had long been trying to break into the highly regarded *American,* which had rejected some of her stories that other magazines, such as *McCall's,* had subsequently accepted. *The American* reflected the optimistic ideals of its editor, John M. Siddall, who chose only well-written and upbeat stories. Evidently Siddall understood his subscribers, for by November of 1919 *The American*'s paid circulation was more than 125 million.[8] **"Mother's Dash"** appeared in the December issue. Shortly thereafter, a soldier stationed in Germany wrote that his buddies had worn out his copy of *The American* because **"Mother's Dash"** reminded them so much

of home and their own mothers; he asked for more of these stories. Aldrich already had the next one at the editor's office.

In 1920 her fourth and last child was born, giving Bess and Charles one daughter and three sons. Fortunately, Charles gave Bess "help and encouragement . . . pressed [her] to take more time for writing, encouraged [her] in every way." Continuing to find the time to write was not easy, however, and she struggled with obstacles: "I wrote when the meals cooked, when babies tumbled over my feet, and while I was ironing, in the old days. The hand that rocked the cradle was often the left one, while the right was jotting down a sentence or two. I have had the first draft of many a story sprinkled liberally with good old sudsy dishwater."[9] Nor did the writing itself necessarily come easily, and Aldrich speaks of "walking the floor" in distress over an idea as she would of walking the floor with a baby in distress, and in so doing she reveals how for her the private and the professional, the domestic and the literary, were one.[10]

Not surprisingly, Aldrich's principles for her fiction were those by which she lived. Her writing must be acceptable to everyone, she determined. Her stories are about decent people saying and doing decent things. There is no swearing in Aldrich stories, no sex, no divorce, none of the seamy side of life; indeed, "decent" and "seamy" are Aldrich's terms. She wrote,

> Why quarrel with a writer over realism and idealism? After all, an author is a glass through which a picture of life is projected. The picture falls upon the pages of the writer's manuscript according to the mental and emotional contours of that writer. It is useless to try to change these patterns. If one writer does not see life in terms of dirt and grime and debaucheries, it is no sign that those sordid things do not exist. If another does not see life in terms of faith and love, courage and good deeds, it does not follow that those characteristics do not exist. . . . I claim that one may portray some of the decent things about him and reserve the privilege to call that real life too.[11]

By similar principles, Aldrich chose to write of domestic rather than of political conflicts. As a granddaughter, a wife, and a writer she knew of war: during the Civil War her grandfather, in his sixties, had gone to Atlanta to bring the Iowa soldiers' votes back to their state to be counted in the 1864 presidential election, and, because all contact with the

North had been cut, he had had to endure with Sherman's troops the terrible march to the sea. Her husband had served in the Spanish-American War and had almost died; and Aldrich wrote and published stories during World War I. War was the single topic for which Aldrich expressed unequivocal hatred, and in her own way she devoted herself to eradicating it. As if willing a future free of war, she joined others in believing that World War I would end all wars; and as if erasing it from the present, she expunged it from her fiction. The **"Rosemary of Remembrance,"** published in the *Black Cat Magazine* in 1917, contains no direct mention of the conflict—nor do any of her stories. Only in the subtext of metaphors does armed violence erupt: words are "like a hand grenade" and "shrapnel."[12] The "hand grenade" metaphor also appears in a 1918 story and rain is compared to "shrapnel" in another 1918 story. Perhaps the metaphors took her unaware, for Aldrich consciously dedicated herself to the belief that people read to escape, and that as a writer she should offer an enjoyable respite from war's horrors. It was a principle of literary nonviolence, one might say—a principle Aldrich retained throughout her career. Years later she explained to an editor that she could not believe that during a war people wanted to read about conflict in their leisure time.[13]

An observer of life and people, Aldrich recognized that much of life is lived through feelings. She said that "my type of story is a story of emotion rather than of the intellect. I try to make the reader feel."[14] She also wanted to promote understanding of rural lives by her urban readers. Aldrich lived and wrote in a village, and her stories ring with the life of small towns: the kensingtons (church women's groups), the school activities, the functions and celebrations that were combined efforts of all the townspeople, and the sense of personal history they had about each other. In her stories, Aldrich is protective of and supports those who remain on the farms; her message is that farmers are becoming well educated and often may be college graduates and that the wives are becoming chic and up to date, much as their urban sisters. One reason her work was so in demand was that she offered to her readers the feel of the country, the best of their memories of rural homes known or imagined. As one editor wrote to Aldrich, he and his wife were "small town folks—the big cities are full of us. . . . You don't merely create characters, you create people with whom we are familiar."[15] Aldrich was a fighter for what she believed in, although something of a velvet-gloved fighter, and there was little

that could raise her ire as quickly as someone insulting her beloved Midwest, which she inevitably defended. Aldrich believed in the farmers and villagers and in their lives, knew that they experienced the same emotions as their urban relatives, and, while recognizing that they were not perfect, wrote of them with respect and affection.

Always conscious of the distinctions that a choice of language makes, she rejected academic classifications and described herself as a realist, explaining that "sentiment" (that is, emotion), was part of reality:

> Sentiment doesn't lie in soil, or in climate, or latitude, or longitude. It lies in the hearts of people. Wherever there are folks who live and work and love and die, whether they raise hogs in Iowa or oranges in California or the sails of a pleasure boat at Palm Beach, there is the stuff of which stories are made.[16]

My own label for Aldrich's writing is "romantic realist," for she was a writer who affirmed the goodness that exists in everyday living.

Even in these early years as a writer, Aldrich was firm in her principles, but she never felt it her duty to force her ideas on others. She offered her thoughts and words as possibilities or examples, but let each choose her or his own path. She was consistent in her ideals.

Notes

1. Bess Streeter Aldrich, cards on how to write a short story, Box 10, archives of Nebraska State Historical Society, Lincoln, Nebraska, hereinafter NSHS.

2. John M. Siddall to Bess Streeter Aldrich, 22 June 1920, Box 4, NSHS.

3. Bess Streeter Aldrich, *The Cutters (New York: D. Appleton & Company, 1926), p. 110.*

4. Julie Bailey, "Bess Streeter Aldrich, Her Life and Work," May 1965, p. 7, Cedar Falls Historical Society, Cedar Falls, Iowa.

5. Bess Streeter Aldrich, "How I Mixed Stories with Do-Nuts," *The American Magazine,* February 1921, p. 33.

6. Item 20, n.p., n.d., NSHS.

7. Bess Streeter Aldrich, Box 10, NSHS. Box 10, File Misc. and Mss., p. 5, NSHS.

8. John M. Siddall to Bess Streeter Aldrich, 19 November 1919, Box 4, NSHS.

9. "Nebraska Woman Gains Fame as Author," *Fillmore County (Neb.) News,* 12 May 1926.

10. Box 10, File Misc. and Mss., p. 4, NSHS.

11. "There Are Two Viewpoints . . . ," Box 10, File Misc. and Mss., p. 2, NSHS.

12. Bess Streeter Aldrich, "The Rosemary of Remembrance," *The Black Cat Magazine,* 1917.

13. John L. B. Williams to Bess Streeter Aldrich, 18 September 1941, Box 7, Bus. Corres. File 1941, NSHS.

14. Draft of talk "And There Are Times When . . . ," Box 10, File Misc. and Mss., p. 1, NSHS.

15. John M. Siddall to Bess Streeter Aldrich, 22 January 1920, Box 4, NSHS.

16. Lillian Lambert, "Bess Streeter Aldrich," *Midland Schools* (Des Moines, Ia.) 42:8 (April 1928), University of Northern Iowa Archives, p. 299.

Eleanor Estes
1906-1988

American author of books for elementary graders.

Major works include *The Moffats* (1941), *The Middle Moffat* (1942), *Rufus M* (1943), *The Hundred Dresses* (1944), *Ginger Pye* (1951).

For further information on Estes's life and works, see *CLR,* Volume 2.

INTRODUCTION

Eleanor Estes's well-loved classics of children's literature, *The Moffats*, *The Middle Moffat*, and *Rufus M*, are poignant and funny stories about family life as viewed from the perspective of one of its children. The episodic nature of the chapters that comprise the books about the Moffats reflect the unstructured patterns of real life leading from one present moment to the next. Critics have commented on the circuitous episodes that lead the Moffat children into an ever widening world, made safe because it is rooted and centered in the security of a strong family. Beginning with short forays near to home, the children travel further and further away in successive stories and books, until they achieve adulthood and the ability to establish their own homes. Caroline Hunt describes Estes's books as "an ongoing chronicle. . . . punctuated as in real life by the cycle of the seasons and by such rites of passage as a new school, a new baby, and so on . . . Events may be arranged so as to have a narrative structure that makes sense, but there is no hint that the family's *life* has a neat pattern."

Estes's detailed recall of a child's vision lends an innocent and honest perspective to events occurring both within and outside of the family. Scenes such as Joey dancing with the dog, the "ghost" in the attic frightening its creators, and Jane looking at her street upside-down through her legs are compelling evocations of childhood. Louisa Smith remarked in *Touchstones: Reflections on the Best in Children's Literature*, "What singles out *The Moffats* as an important book is Jane's particularly flawed vision of the events of the book, a child's vision captured by Estes as well as any author has done. . . . Estes reaffirmed the

tradition of the American family story in which every child remains an individual and has a life independent of the family, and yet in which the family remains central. . . . *The Moffats* is a touchstone book because it so cleverly integrates its family situations with a carefully evoked sense of a child's vision." Estes also uses this vision to address a serious philosophical dilemma in *The Hundred Dresses*. Maddie is troubled because of her honest assessment of how her own fears prevented her from defending Wanda from being victimized. This is especially clear at the end of the book, when Maddie remains unsatisfied with the conclusion of events because she understands very well what her own failure has been.

David L. Russell suggested that many serious critics have neglected Estes work because of their inability to appreciate her accomplishments. "It is surprising that these books, having achieved the status of minor classics, have attracted so little critical attention," he wrote. "Among the reasons for this critical neglect we may suggest the lack of philosophical depth (although the works are psychologically genuine); the flirtation with a rose-colored view of reality (although Estes generally eschews sentimentality); and the apparent absence of a sophisticated literary design bringing unity to the books (although one of the great achievements of art is to make the work seem artless.) . . . Estes has more than just sympathy with the child's viewpoint; she has an implicit trust in that viewpoint to speak faithfully and honestly for itself. Therein lies much of her success."

BIOGRAPHICAL INFORMATION

Estes was born and raised in West Haven, Connecticut, which she renamed Cranbury and used for the setting of the books featuring both the Moffat and Pye families. Her illustrator, sculptor Louis Slobodkin, recalled how, after working with Estes on detailed floor plans and street designs for the first Moffat book, he was astonished to see his "imaginary" town laid out before him when his train stopped briefly for a layover at a Connecticut station.

Estes's books about the Moffats and the Pyes have many autobiographical elements. It has been noted that although the Moffat books take place during World War I, the children come into little actual contact with the effects of the war. This was Estes's own experience as a child during the war, growing up at a time when children were shielded from the harsh realities of life for as long as possible.

Estes attended the Pratt Institute Library School in New York, and after graduation became a children's librarian at the Free Public Library in New Haven. Many episodes from her books were based on experiences she had had, or observed, and noted down. One such is Rufus Moffat's determination to get his library card. This episode was inspired by a little girl whom Estes, in her capacity of children's librarian, helped learn to spell her name so that *she* could get a library card, much like Rufus in the story.

Estes's husband, Rice, was also a librarian. They married in 1932 and had one child.

MAJOR WORKS

Estes's best-known work is her series of stories about the Moffat family. Each of these books is a collection of stories with an underlying theme that holds them together in a particular time frame. Although they take place during World War I, told as they are from the point of view of the two youngest Moffat children, the war has little acknowledged effect on the Moffats' lives. The family is poor and without a father, but, again, this is treated as a matter of course, and if there is any strain in their poverty, Mama shields them from it. Held together in time, the books follow the family as the children grow, mature, and venture into circles outside their home and family. The first book, *The Moffats,* centers on the yellow house they live in being put up for sale and ends with the family moving to a new home. *The Middle Moffat* focuses more on Jane, the second youngest child, as she adjusts to her new home, makes new friends, and establishes herself as an individual apart from her family. *Rufus M* follows the youngest Moffat into the world as he reaches out to a stranger and the family reaches out into the community. Estes wrote and illustrated the last of the Moffat books, *The Moffat Museum* in 1983, forty years after the publication of *Rufus M.* In it, she tied up loose ends. Sylvie gets married, Joe drops out of school to help support the family, and Jane hovers on the verge of adulthood as the family puts together a museum of personal memorabilia in their barn.

Estes also used the child's perspective in *The Hundred Dresses*, her short but compelling portrait of prejudice and persecution in the school yard. Maddie is the observer and commentator on the events, told in flashback, as they unfold around Wanda, the Polish immigrant girl. Motherless and poor, Wanda comes to school every day in the same dress, always newly washed and indifferently pressed. This, plus her difficulty with English and her consignment, because of her muddy shoes, to the section of the room where the rough boys sit, sets her apart from the other girls in her class. When she speaks one day of the hundred dresses she has in a closet at home, she becomes the subject of harassment, led by the most popular girl in the class and Maddie's best friend. Their constant persecution forces Wanda's father to move his family to the city, but this news coincides with the announcement that Wanda has won an art contest with one hundred beautiful drawings of dresses. Maddie, whose views speak to us, is not only filled with remorse, but acknowledges that although she felt that her abetting the treatment of Wanda was wrong, she was too afraid of bringing that treatment upon herself to defend her view; and while Peggy, her friend, is satisfied in the end with the letter written to and received from Wanda, Maddie is not.

Estes's *Ginger Pye* was inspired by an incident from her childhood. Ginger is the beloved puppy of the Pye family, bought with hard earned money. Much to the family's grief, Ginger is stolen, and the book details the children's pursuit of the perpetrators. Ginger is finally restored to them, older and much abused, and takes his place in their attractive, affable, and loving family again. *Pinky Pye* (1958), written as a sequel, follows the Pye's cat and centers on the little pet owl lost by a visiting ornithologist.

AWARDS

Three of Estes's books were named Newbery Honor books by the American Library Association—*The Middle Moffat* in 1943, *Rufus M* in 1944, and *The Hundred Dresses* in 1945. *Ginger Pye* received the American Library Association's Newbery Medal and the Spring Book Festival Award from the New York Herald Tribune in 1952. In 1961, *The Moffats* won the Lewis Carroll Shelf Award. Estes was honored with the Pratt Institute Medal in 1968.

AUTHOR COMMENTARY

Eleanor Estes

SOURCE: A speech delivered at a meeting of the International Reading Association in New York, in *A Sense of Story: Essays on Contemporary Writers for Children,* by John Rowe Townsend, Longman, 1971, pp. 86-7.

To many people, including myself, it is provocative to try to unravel the threads that might throw light upon the mystery of the writing of a book. In the beginning there was nothing. How on the bare, blank, beguiling paper did words appear, join together in a right, harmonious, and sometimes beautiful fashion until, behold! the writer and the reader find themselves with a brand-new book, nonexistent a short time ago, and different from any other?

Like bees who by instinct go from flower to flower gathering honey, writers, merely by being alive, are constantly gathering ideas and impressions—their honey—which eventually will lodge somewhere in some book. To bees, some honey is sweeter than other, and some quite bitter. Yet, bitter or sweet, it is all gathered, and so it is with the born writer that all ideas and impressions are his potential nectar and must be gathered and stored by him, either to be used in a book, rejected, or held in reserve.

There are probably as many ways of writing a book as there are writers, and each individual has his own means, stemming from his own personality, of conveying ideas and impressions, so no two people could write the same book. Today I speak only for myself when I speak of how a book gets written. Sometimes I feel I am a blindfolded person and groping my way toward a book. Then I pick up the scent of the book and happily I am on my way, the trail of the book having become clear, direct, and straight. I am the sort of writer who would like to have plenty of time in which to do nothing. Time just to sit, or to stand at the window, or watch the ocean, or people, or to wander up the street or about the house, to pace. For often it is in these do-nothing times that the best honey is gathered. "How many hours a day does the writer write upon his book?" is a question often asked. "Twenty-four," the answer could be, for does not the writer call upon his dreams? And unlike the bee, who has to go and get his honey, the writer need never stir from one spot; his honey comes to him.

Sights, smells, sounds, and impressions often enter the mind in its most do-nothing time and take root. One may overhear a wonderful remark—"David's dog had expeditis" (for "hepatitis"), and, "There's a dragon in Gretchen's yard. It was in my yard, tomorrow"—remarks which etch themselves in the mind. A good sentence may simply hop into one's mind, a first sentence to a book or a chapter. "The way Mama could peel apples!" seemed a good way to begin a book and so it was I began *The Moffats.*

Do-nothing time must be coupled with do-something time, however, in which the real mechanics of writing must take over. Discipline, patience to go over one's work again and again, improving and refining, definite hours in which to write are all essential. Otherwise a writer might end up only with shelves of unwritten books. His books might be "air books" like the "air food" the family of shipwrecked dolls ate in Anne Parrish's famous classic, *Floating Island:*

> "Another cup of this delicious air, if you please, my dear," said Mr. Doll, passing his shell to Mrs. Doll.
>
> "But, my dear, you've had two already. I'm afraid you won't sleep a wink!"
>
> However, she poured him another shellful.

"When do we start?" asked William.

"Don't speak with your mouth full, my son."

William swallowed the air.

"Use your napkin, William," said Mrs. Doll.

Air food is all right for dolls and children at play, but people need more substance than air for nourishment, and happily writers have the need to turn their "air" books into real books, and have them savored, read, and cherished. A writer, lacking discipline, may spend more and more of his time in the do-nothing hours and may end up with not even as much of a book as our same Mr. Doll in *Floating Island* did. Let's see how Mr. Doll went about writing a book:

> He took a swim every morning to clear his brain.
>
> Then he took a sun bath.
>
> Then a brisk walk along the beach.
>
> Then he sat by the waterfall to collect his thoughts.
>
> Then a nap, because his brain was tired.
>
> Then a swim to wake himself up.
>
> Then it was suppertime.
>
> Then he watched the stars.
>
> And then it was bedtime.
>
> This went on until Mrs. Doll said: "My dear, that isn't the way to write a book! Go into your study after breakfast and write. Dinah will bring your lunch on a tray, and you'd better not work later than five o'clock every day . . . ."
>
> So, Mr. Doll, not very eagerly, tried Mrs. Doll's way.

By the end of the week Mr. Doll did have a very pretty page, ornamented and attractive, and even though it was not a book, it was more than air.

To many writers, as it is to me, keeping notes is practically a compulsion. Notes refresh the memory with thoughts that may get too deeply stored in the innermost portion of the mind, and be lost. Most people, including writers, have ideas that slide, un-asked for, into the forepart of the mind, lightly, noise-lessly as a fleck of dust floats by in a sunbeam before our eyes. Sometimes the idea is not held, not nur-tured, not invited to stay so that one may become ac-quainted with it; and it slides back into the dark from whence it had emerged.

Writers, artists, teachers, and all who are creative in their vision, must welcome the elusive thought, ex-amine it, turn it around, consider whether it has value

or not, and then, either reject it as useless, or round it out and use it. The same applies in fact to all readers. Indeed, it applies to all people who strive to live cre-atively, to "those of them," as Plato said, "I mean, who are quick-witted, and like bees on the wing, light on every flower and out of all they hear, gather influences as to the character and way of life which are best for them. . . . "

To the writer, his memory and his impressions are insistent. He finds he must get them down on paper, enhance them in the light of his own imagination, use them as a springboard. This happens often years and years after the impression has been made.

Where, for instance, did those moths come from that flew out of the organ in the chapter of "The Organ Recital" in *The Middle Moffat?* They flew out of a bank vault from which a little old lady in front of me asked to have some jewelry removed. They fluffed all over the bank and all over us. They had had a nice breeding place in the green velvet linings of the little jewelry boxes. And I'm sure that once I saw one moth fly out of our little old pump organ, from the felt paddings somewhere. So that one moth and the bank moths combined for "The Organ Recital" chapter.

And how did the first chapter of *Rufus M.* get writ-ten, the chapter in which Rufus learns to write his name, an accomplishment which he achieved in the public library? One day, many years ago, when I was a children's librarian in the George Bruce Branch Li-brary in New York, a very little girl who could not see over the desk arrived in the children's room. She wanted to take home a book. When she understood that to do this she must have a library card, and that to have a library card she must print her name, which, not being quite old enough for school yet, she did not know how to do, she was not deterred. She spoke little and she did not say that she could not write her name, which was, I remember, Barbara Cooney. She bravely jabbed great symbols on the application blank, which she made up for the occasion. Most little children see little difference between their kind of imitative jagged lines up and down and grownups' writing.

I told Barbara Cooney that her writing was nice, but that it did not spell her name. And I suggested that she go home and have her sister teach her how to print her name. She did not budge; she said nothing, but she was not going to go home. So I undertook to teach her to print her name. As I recall it—once a book has been written it is impossible for me to sever the imagined portions from the remembered portions of any incident—her whole day and mine were entirely devoted to her great achievement. For before closing time, she did have her card and her book and she knew how to print her name—B A R B A R A C O O N E Y. Years later, in telling how Rufus learned to write the "offat" part of Moffat, Barbara Cooney came back, unasked for, into my mind, asking to be transfused into the chapter about Rufus' learning to write his name.

So, in writing, inventiveness and imagination become partners of remembered impressions, and all skip along together. "Now you, now me," they seem to say, none of them alone being sufficient for creating a book. In revising a book, which I do many times, sometimes a thought or an incident is taken out and put back into storage. If it is worth writing about, it will emerge again some other time while writing some other book and insist upon being included. With each writing of his book, the writer is like a singer striving, pushing, reaching higher for a still higher, and more eloquent, note. Now the intellectual concept, the conscious thinking about what has been emerging, outweighs the first outpouring. The writer must survey his work critically, coolly, and as though he were a stranger to it. He must be willing to prune, expertly and hardheartedly. At the end of each revision, a manuscript may look like a battered old hive, worked over, torn apart, pinned together, added to, deleted from, words changed and words changed back. Yet the book must retain its initial freshness and spontaneity.

It is only after the fourth revision that I feel I know my book. It takes a while to get used to the new book. The writer is a little shaken and uncertain for a time. Is the book, most of all, a good one? Was the best, most flavorsome honey put into it? How much a writer needs to be told now, "How beautiful!" when, finally, his book is off to the press; how lost he feels without it, having grown now to love it.

Sometimes the time is not ripe for the writing of a certain book. But, if certain ideas or a group of ideas and impressions keep bubbling to the front of the mind, then most likely the time is ripe to include them in a special book. In this light we may consider *Ginger Pye* and *Pinky Pye*. Initial drafts, notes for both of these books, were made about ten years before the actual books as we know them now were written.

Ginger was a dog we had when I was a child. After *The Moffats,* my first book, was finished, I wrote a story about this dog, Ginger. But my heart was not completely in it, for I was still preoccupied with Moffats. So I put these first sketches about Ginger away in my notes. There they stayed for ten years, while I wrote other books.

Then I began to think about Ginger again, for we had acquired a new and different dog, who reminded me of him. At first I thought I would put Ginger into a fourth book about the Moffats. But in the end I decided to place him merely in the same town and time.

So *Ginger Pye* is about our old dog, Ginger. Mr. Pye is based partly on my husband and partly on my childhood remembrance of a certain man, the father of a friend, who was an ornithologist, very well-known nationally but a modest, humble man whose importance the town did not suspect. Mr. Pye is also partly based on another ornithologist whom we met in the west in later years. And this man happened to be the owner of a pygmy owl.

Now this pygmy owl, out west, did not get into the book *Ginger Pye,* for it sometimes takes me years to realize that I have seen a good thing. And it was lucky he did not, for he belongs in *Pinky Pye,* where indeed he is. Have you ever seen how fierce a pygmy owl can look, and how beguiling? I remember how avariciously he ate up a bright green grasshopper his owners caught for him. This pygmy owl stored himself away in my mind, and the great intensity, owl intensity, that was his personality, engraved itself on my mind, too.

Mrs. Pye is based on many people, too: partly my mother, partly my sister, partly myself—that is the timid, over-anxious, have-you-got-your-sweater part—and partly made up. Rachel and Jerry are two children based on all the children I've known. Uncle Bennie, who is an uncle from the moment he came into the world, is based on all little uncles—my brother, for instance, who was a little uncle, and a little boy who used to come into the Seward Park Library, whose name was Uncle Henry, and who was an uncle, though only six.

The search for Ginger is the theme of *Ginger Pye.* Our dog, Ginger, really was stolen on Thanksgiving Day when he was a few months old, still a very little puppy. And he did return, full grown, dragging a ragged long rope behind him and with terrible scars on his face, in the month of May. This book, being a search, permitted me to include in it many impressions that I had not yet been able to get into any other book, such as those of tramps and sunny fields, and walking along behind a cow switching its tail to get rid of flies, and the eerie sound of a certain whistle, a sort of wailing siren, that blew each evening at five o'clock, usually, it seemed to me, when I was in the sunny field. It always frightened me unbearably, and my sister told me it was the gypsies' whistle, summoning them home, at five o'clock. Usually when an impression finally finds a home in some book, one can forget about it.

The perpendicular swimmer in **Ginger Pye** is based on a boy I knew who seemed to me to prefer that mode of swimming to the horizontal. The unsavory character is based on all unsavory characters. Bit-nose Sam is based on a man who had his nose bitten off him by another man, a far-distant relative—the biter not the bitee—of my cousins. As children, we really had bought Ginger for one dollar. I don't remember how we earned *that* dollar, but the dollar that Rachel and Jerry earned is based on a fifty-cent piece that a friend and I earned dusting the pews of our church for her big brother Sam. Now this big brother Sam is the Sam Doody of both Pye books. The chapter "Dusting the Pews" was first written for a Moffat book, but I felt that it did not fit, put it aside, until years later, when it seemed right for Ginger's dollar.

Many of the characters of the Pye books, as well as the Moffat books, are based on my childhood memories, with much gathered in later years, and with embellishments of the imagination—memories of people who used to inhabit that town named, in my books, Cranbury. Mr. Tuttle, who looked like a tall man when he was sitting down but a short man when standing, is based on a man I used to study in church, whom we called the tall and short man.

The manner in which Mr. Pye first met Mrs. Pye, his future bride—that is, he knocked her down while running up a down escalator—is based on an incident related to me by my husband. One morning, years ago, my husband chanced, upon entering a deserted subway station, to witness his very dignified, rather severe boss, who wore a Vandyke beard, running up a down escalator to the top, thinking the station was empty and suitable for the fullfillment of an ancient wish. Wouldn't you know that my husband would come along at that moment and encounter his panting boss? And wasn't this fortunate for Mrs. Pye, because otherwise, years later, in my book, Mr. Pye might not have run up a down escalator that day, knocked down the future Mrs. Pye, who was on her way home, enthralled from having attended her very

first opera, *Tannhauser*—which happens also to have been my very first opera, and married her? Mr. Pye might even have married somebody else, if my husband had not seen his boss run up the down escalator.

Well, ten years after the original notes about our cat, Pinky, had been made and set aside, notes which had nothing to do with the Pyes, for the Pyes had not yet been invented and put into a book, I thought to myself, "Now, since the Pyes are such a family for pets, why not give them Pinky? Pinky Pye." So I examined the early notes. I liked the string-bean game I found among them, and also the account of how Pinky had typed the word "woogie," thus becoming a typewriting cat. And so I was right on the trail, now, of **Pinky Pye**.

Where did that big fish come from that Mr. Bish caught bare-handed, when he was hot on the trail of finding little Owlie in the home of his brother ornithologist, Mr. Pye? Well, that fish really was a fish another dear friend of ours, not an ornithologist at all, had really caught bare-handed as it lay floundering at the edge of the ocean, much to the chagrin of the real fishermen, red-faced and broiling in the sun, who had not had a nibble all summer. So, that chapter I dedicate to the friend who caught the fish bare-handed, and other bits and parts of all my books I dedicate to this person and to that person from whom I have been given some compelling and individual impression.

And so, as you see, for all the muddling explanation one tries to give concerning the creating of a book, that creation still remains as mysterious and inexplicable as life itself. But we all enjoy pondering it. Here are my heartfelt thanks to all who have liked the honey I've gathered so far.

Eleanor Estes

SOURCE: "Gathering Honey," in *The Horn Book Magazine*, Vol. XXXVI, No. 6, December, 1960, pp. 487-94.

Like bees who by instinct go from flower to flower gathering honey, writers, merely by being alive, are constantly gathering ideas and impressions—their honey—which eventually will lodge somewhere in some book. To bees, some honey is sweeter than other, and some quite bitter. Yet, bitter or sweet, it is all gathered, and so it is with the born writer that all ideas and impressions are his potential nectar and must be gathered and stored by him, either to be used in a book, rejected, or held in reserve.

There are probably as many ways of writing a book as there are writers, and each individual has his own means, stemming from his own personality, of conveying ideas and impressions, so no two people could write the same book. Today I speak only for myself when I speak of how a book gets written. Sometimes I feel I am a blindfolded person and groping my way toward a book. Then I pick up the scent of the book and happily I am on my way, the trail of the book having become clear, direct, and straight. I am the sort of writer who would like to have plenty of time in which to do nothing. Time just to sit, or to stand at the window, or watch the ocean, or people, or to wander up the street or about the house, to pace. For often it is in these do-nothing times that the best honey is gathered. 'How many hours a day does the writer spend upon his book?' is a question often asked. 'Twenty-four,' the answer could be, for does not the writer call upon his dreams? And unlike the bee, who has to go and get his honey, the writer need never stir from one spot; his honey comes to him . . .

To the writer, his memory and his impressions are insistent. He finds he must get them down on paper, enhance them in the light of his own imagination, use them as a springboard. This happens often years and years after the impression has been made . . .

In writing, inventiveness and imagination become partners of remembered impressions, and all skip along together. 'Now you, now me,' they seem to say, none of them alone being sufficient for creating a book. In revising a book, which I do many times, sometimes a thought or an incident is taken out and put back into storage. If it is worth writing about, it will emerge again some other time while writing some other book and insist upon being included. With each writing of his book, the writer is like a singer striving, pushing, reaching higher for a still higher, and more eloquent, note. Now the intellectual concept, the conscious thinking about what has been emerging, outweighs the first outpouring. The writer must survey his work critically, coolly, and as though he were a stranger to it. He must be willing to prune, expertly and hardheartedly. At the end of each revision, a manuscript may look like a battered old hive, worked over, torn apart, pinned together, added to, deleted from, words changed and words changed back. Yet the book must retain its initial freshness and spontaneity.

It is only after the fourth revision that I feel I know my book. It takes a while to get used to the new book. The writer is a little shaken and uncertain for a time. Is the book, most of all, a good one? Was the best, most flavoursome honey put into it? How much a writer needs to be told now, 'How beautiful!' when, finally, his book is off to the press; how lost he feels without it, having grown now to love it.

GENERAL COMMENTARY

Louis Slobodkin

SOURCE: "The Caldecott Medal Acceptance," in *The Horn Book Magazine,* Vol. XX, No. 4, July, 1944, pp. 307-17.

But for a certain bend in the road, the little princess, if I were destined to do her in some art form, might have been created in polished brass and perched on top of some memorial flag pole, or perpetually blowing a trumpet from a limestone church corbel, or reposing benignly carved in marble and tucked securely into the corner of a pediment of some building. The bend in the road which brought the Caldecott Medal and me together in Cleveland on May 11, 1944, began some six years ago.

I had taken my family up to Cape Ann where we usually summer, and there we met two nice young people, sunning themselves on an old stone wall. They were the Estes, Eleanor and Rice, and the strangest thing about them was—they were librarians. Now I don't know why that should have seemed strange, but I have had the same reaction when I met my first anthropologists and again when I met my first professional wrestlers. Come to think of it, maybe sculptors seem strange to people, too, these fellows who stand hacking away at stone or building a lump of clay for a long, long time. Anyway, I met the Estes, and since then I've met so many librarians and they're all such nice people.

By the next summer or the summer after that, Eleanor Estes had written her first manuscript, and it had been accepted. Since these were long summer afternoons, we all sat around and talked. We talked of books, of type, of the principles of illustration. Eleanor had definite ideas on how she wanted her book to look, and I, with the wisdom of an armchair strategist, talked with great authority on the relation of line to type, etc. If the talk had shifted to toe dancing, I would have talked with equal easy assurance on *pas de deux* or something else I knew little about.

Later that fall when Eleanor asked if I would illustrate her book, *The Moffats,* I said yes, indeed, but frankly I was not as brave as I sounded. I was told to make a few drawings, ink ones, and take them up to Mrs. Elisabeth B. Hamilton, juvenile editor at Harcourt, Brace, to make sure they could be reproduced. I studied the manuscript, made my drawings, and took them up. I was told to go ahead. I did and returned some time later with about 130 ink drawings and 20 or 30 pencil drawings I wanted to finish for that book. Then I discovered there were limitations to bookmaking. After many consultations between Eleanor and me, we eliminated drawings by the democratic procedure of voting them in or out by a show of hands and left about 100 line cuts in that book.

And so I was launched, a little late in life, along this new road towards a new form of expression, and into a completely new world, where, to paraphrase Mr. Melcher's excellent *P.W.,* you meet such interesting people, authors, publishers, librarians, printers, pressmen. And I learned a new language: picas, overlays, slash vignette strip-ins, print and turn, and print and tumble. To one who has spent his life with flying buttresses, bull points and cabbage modelers, that sounded like a bit of *Finnegans Wake* and, although I was hardened to dying plaster and feather-edged granite, I was a little shocked to hear of a bleeding page and that a book has a spine.

That first book was not as easy as it sounds. Having devoted my life to sculpture, I needed to establish a new æsthetic logic on how to approach this problem of doing a book. It was not so much the difference of the scale of the work because all sculpture of any importance, I might venture, all major architectural works and monuments, usually start by being pencil-sketched on the back of some old envelope from somebody's pocket. The idea is jotted down in scale and usually preserved carefully through the enlarged sketches to the full-sized work. No, it's the demands that books make on the mental processes which were the points of departure.

When you start a sculpture composition, you develop one main thought; all sketches and primary indications tend towards developing that idea with all its ramifications. Say it's a colossal figure or composition of a couple of sculpture units. After your primary sketches and mechanical preparations are complete, you settle down to work, five months, seven months, a year or more, on one shape, one movement, and one thought. Of course, you develop and

clarify and carry through essential *nuances* of good sculpture. But a change in the composition, a deviation from this one idea, the mere movement of a ponderous clay arm, a few inches in any direction, is a major operation, an engineering feat. There's the readjustment of the weight, the sawing through of the armature, the risk of destroying all the work you've done in the past six months and throwing that much of your life into the clay bin. You don't often change from your first idea: you compromise. And that's true, too, of changes in a stone carving.

Now, moving from this one-composition and one-idea way of a sculptor's life, to the crackle of thinking of hundreds of compositions within a short space of time was the main difficulty. For each drawing was a complete composition in itself. Every Moffat was an individual sculpture unit. Then there was another element, space, and the shape of space, limited by the requirements of the book. Sculpture makes its own space. It pushes its way into existence.

Movement, and there is plenty of that in the Moffats, was no problem. Sculpture has movement, subtle and restrained. The problem of the "yellow house" suggested a theory that might be the solution.

This drawing for books might be another variation of architectural sculpture. A manuscript may be considered a blueprint. The author was the architect. There was this house with a number of rooms in it, a front yard, and a back yard, a little landscaping there, set on half-moon shaped New Dollar Street, the railroad tracks at one end and a trolley line at the other. That's city planning on a small scale.

I consulted with Eleanor and actually drew floor plans and elevations of the yellow house and of all the other houses around and the brick lot, the street, and the surrounding territories that had something to do with the action of the story. It was so clear in my mind that sometime later, after the book had been printed, when a train I was traveling on one summer afternoon stopped on a trestle outside of New Haven, I looked down at a small town which was strangely familiar. It was the actual town of Cranbury out of that book!

Of course, this architect had done a very unusual thing. She had not only laid out a house and street, in her manuscript, she provided the tenants. That's something blueprint architects wish they could guarantee. I didn't know whether to consider the Moffats and their friends and enemy (that was the

Frost boy, you know) tenants or mobile units of sculpture. But, in short, this architectural theory worked, for books, or seemed to.

I went back to my sculpture and, of course, there was a flurry on the publication day of this first book—thousands of reproductions of my mistakes—and then, along came *The Middle Moffat,* I worked *The Middle Moffat* at the same time that I was carrying through three large sandstone panels in their final stage in my studio. What with stone dust in my ink-pots and ink spots on my stone—then finding as I smashed a fine chisel with my stone mallet it had become a quill pen and ripping my paper with the lost stone chisel found again in the ink—I don't remember the æsthetic theories involved.

The system I used was a very simple one. I read and reread the manuscript. I kept making notes and notes of the pictures I'd like to do, indicating them roughly on the typewritten sheets transferred to my dummy, and then taking one chapter at a time I did the drawings. I drew a good deal at home in the evening and late into the night, and it was only natural that our boy, Michael, who was just beginning to talk—that's putting it mildly, getting quite loquacious—would be shushed by his mama or his big brother Larry, "Papa's making Moffats." Since through all that period of his articulate life this went on, drawing in our house was not drawing, it was making moffats.

Some of the chapters in *The Middle Moffat* struck me so funny as I read them on subway trains instead of a newspaper, I'd guffaw out loud and people would gather themselves together for a quick exit, in case anything else developed. The Three Bears, and that basketball game when Janey took up sports. Not only the chapter itself but the situation was really this. Janey knew nothing about basketball, neither did that sports expert, Eleanor Estes, and I knew less than either of them. I was never any good at anything like that—basketball, baseball, or any sport. I used to box and wrestle a little. There was a time I swam long distances—very slowly—so when we all got together, Janey, Eleanor and I, over a bit of basketball, what happened happened. I had remembered vague things about basketball courts, baskets, and girls in bloomers, but I never felt those drawings were really adequate. From the couple of hundred drawings made, 130 line cuts got into that book. It might be a little crowded. Anyway, I finished it, and I finished and installed my sandstone panels at about the same time, and that theory about the relation of architectural sculpture to books, what with the activity of

Janey in *The Middle Moffat,* and all those other goings on, that theory wasn't finished, but it had received an awful kick in the cornice.

Now, speaking of theories, recently I've had a curious thought not a theory, that designing and illustrating a book is something like cooking. I might enlarge on some of the principles of how to cook a book.

First, there is the author's manuscript. It is to be prepared for public consumption. A mimeographed copy of the typewritten pages would be pretty raw and perhaps indigestible. You carefully study the main motive of this manuscript, pinch, sniff, and sample it a bit. Whenever I receive one (always a cold blue carbon copy) I quickly ask: May I make some penciled notes as I read? I scribble over every page just a little; that's just to thaw it out and get rid of the ice-box chill. By that time, I've sensed whether this manuscript is meat, fish, or fowl, and have come to some conclusion as to how it might be handled.

Now, how and what to do, to enhance sympathetically, enrich, and bring out the maximum flavor, texture, color, and quality is the problem. Seasonings and embellishments must be in character with the main motive. Whipped cream on roast beef is no more foolish than flippant drawings on a solid bit of writing or *vice versa;* a heavy curried gravy on custard—maybe that's good! What herbs, relishes, garnish, and side dishes will be used to complement the flavor of the meat, fish, or fowl manuscript is now decided. You think of the potentialities and taste of the manuscript. Is it rich, mild, subtle, dry, sweet, or like veal that's too young, and certain river fish so bland in flavor that it must depend on a clever, overpowering sauce and decoration to hide its shortcomings?

I hold no brief for cooks or book designers who drown all their work in the same kind of sauce and ruin the natural flavor of any manuscript with the tiresome monotony of commercial capers and whirligigs. You must consider the limitations, production, and capabilities of the oven (the printing press). Then your budget. You can't use truffles, sherry, or heavy cream—or five or six colors, special type, trick margins, and costly board covers on work that is expected to sell for a small sum and in a limited market. You might have to confine yourself entirely to black pepper, salt, a bit of garlic—just a few line cuts—and it's not to be scoffed at if it's properly done. Garlic is called *la fleur de cuisine* by the *cordons bleus.*

So after you've seasoned, stuffed, dressed and tied your roast neatly with the type, drawings, colors, and, of course, allowed for shrinkage by keeping your color high-keyed and your drawings so they will reproduce, you pop it into the oven or the press, and pray everything blends together nicely, and that there's some gravy.

Then—there is hash—and stewing a book and not to mention just unadulterated pot-boiling. . . .

This can go on and on, but before I leave this dissertation on how to cook a book, I'd like to register my indignation as a father and a taxpayer concerning one form of our American cuisine and bookmaking. There is the chilled lime gelatine, garnished with brilliant little bits of pimiento—nestling in a few leaves of lettuce and tenderly resting on nothing—school of cooking and bookmaking. These literary feasts, tasteless, dainty, precious, and unnutritious, are being served up to our healthy little girls and boys, served up, rammed down their throats as pure literature, beauty and art. But getting back to the main road after this culinary digression:

We just began to swing into *The Sun and the Wind and Mr. Todd.* It was a nice contrast from the hundreds of pen drawings I had done. Eleanor and I had talked now and again about this book. The manuscript had a swirly spaciousness and I liked the thought of working with my elbows free in sanguine again. That is the usual medium I used around the studio, and the type of drawing gallery and museum people expected from me, in their invited shows. Pen drawing, no matter how free the technique, still demands precision, and there is a lot of nervous tension. The book was to be something grandiose with a counterpoint sort of meek and mild—a tongue in the cheek symphony of deep bass—interposed with the timid piping of a piccolo—a gentle victim of an Olympic battle. Of course, Mr. Todd was really a grown-up Moffat, and I delighted in the idea of working him against the great baroque hulks of the Sun and the Wind, particularly that boasting windbag, the Wind. Those drawings were finished up on Cape Ann. That summer I shocked all my painter friends by working right through. I had expected to take it easy the last week of the season, but it turned cold, or perhaps the momentum of the Sun and the Wind was still with me, and I spent that last week dashing about wildly, splashing huge water colors all over the place. We returned to New York with portfolios jammed with the results of that water color binge, and the drawings and data for *The Sun and the Wind and Mr. Todd.*

So it was only natural, after watching the drawings through the offset process which was a new experience for me, that when Elisabeth Hamilton offered me Mr. Thurber's manuscript for *Many Moons,* to get started all over again. It was to be printed in offset lithography, in color, and I was to do my own color separation and have complete liberty. Now, I knew absolutely nothing about color separation. That didn't bother me. I could find out. What I did not know was—what do young people think about color? I mean people about ten. I had had definite reactions about their thoughts on drawing.

It is my conviction that people of ten and younger have a keener sense of appreciation of those qualities that make good drawing than any of us beyond that age. Drawing is the most lyric of all the plastic arts, the most closely related to poetry. A well-indicated line should, like a line of poetry, suggest things, stir the imagination, and start a fount of ideas. With their keen imagination, children react quickly to the emotional intention of a line. They see as much, and more, than you can suggest in your drawing. And by drawing I don't merely mean dexterity in the sense of that story that's told about Giotto in response to someone who had questioned his ability:—he silently picked up a long pencil and, with a simple turn of the wrist, he drew a perfect circle on a sheet of paper. That was a good trick, but I believe the story was untrue. I am certain Giotto was too great an artist to waste his time on a circle that meant nothing. And by drawing I don't mean mere factual representation, and there's a story equally false that might illustrate that too, of Raphael, who, being in the customary condition of an artist, broke, drew a perfect coin on the table in a tavern after he'd finished his meal and thus fooled the tavern keeper.

Our brilliant young under-ten-ers have little concern with mere dexterity or factual drawing, and I believe not at all with photographs. We would all have spent more time with the family album instead of with *St. Nicholas Magazine* and the Katzenjammer Kids, when we were young, if that were true. Any kind of drawing attracts their attention. They disregard it if it's bad, and return to it if it is good.

Now about sculpture—I know they have a delightful indifference to sculpture, yet a fine appreciation for the elements that make good sculpture—a plastic consciousness. You must all know little boys and girls who treasure beautifully shaped pebbles and stones, or curiously formed pieces of wood, or collections of sea-shells. These are the purest forms of sculpture without laurel leaves or buttons—abstract shapes which influence our best sculptors.

But, the only articulate expression I've ever heard from those under ten years old about color was the very audible "Ah" that is heard on a Fourth of July night when glorious purple, green, gold, and red rockets burst in the darkened skies. And, too, their admiration for the primitive clashing colors they dress up in on Hallowe'en and similar occasions. I thought of colors like that as I worked.

Well, the technique and the theories for *Many Moons* were all set.

Since I had no contact with the author and worked only from the manuscript, I then had to conclude and interpret my characters, background, etc. The manuscript was short, there were no descriptions of the main personalities or the settings.

Take our princess—she was little, and ate too many raspberry tarts and went to bed, stayed there except once when she went out to play in the garden. Overeating and such indolence might suggest a fat little glutton—or an only child, imperious—nothing less than the moon would suit her, and she kept a number of grown-ups racing about to satisfy her whim. One might draw a nasty little brat.

But then she might be just a little girl (incidentally a princess) who ate just a little too much, say half a tart. A little girl, a little stomach, a little spoiled, and timidly being just a little difficult—because she already knew the answers—with the traditional golden tresses of a princess (blondes seem to get green around the gills quicker than others due to overindulgence). I felt that, since she was our heroine and heroines should arouse sympathy, it was best to present her so.

Then there was the problem of movement. There were two main sets: the princess's bedroom, and she sat there; and the throne room, and the king sat there. There had to be some movement. We couldn't have people just sitting around, or keep repeating the jester going up and down the stairs. I hoped with strongly contrasting colors turning a page of blue and purple to the next of bright yellow and so on, and in handling the subjects of conversation as animated things and a little free interpretation of the script, I could suggest an illusion of movement in the book.

Then when I finally got down to doing my drawing and water colors, I had to get some actual ideas on structure and some convincing data on palaces, etc. I raked my memory for palaces and all things royal. I remembered the palaces I'd seen in Europe. They would never do. It seemed to me that no child would accept any of these huge ornate warehouses, I recalled that real kings and princesses lived in, as a real palace. That's true, too, of the thrones, throne rooms, royal bedrooms, and other regal paraphernalia one saw on a sight-seeing tour in Europe, in the old days, for a few francs here or a couple of pfennigs there.

So I tried to imagine a palace, a princess's bedroom, a throne, and all that, as they would look had I never been contaminated by actually seeing them. In other words, trying to see them as children, with their vivid and rich imagination, might, in the brilliant colors, the all silk, and satin, velvet and gold, and luminous marble they seem to feel is part of the everyday life of a princess.

And as I've indicated in my drawings and water colors in *Many Moons,* the king, come what may, always wears full court regalia and is never seen in his shirt-sleeves, and a little princess always wears a golden crown, even to bed, just a little one.

So, with a few more technical this and thats, the drawings were made, the separations finished, the book was printed—and *this* happened. I feel it my duty to tell you in what direction I am going, bearing very proudly this Caldecott Medal which you have so generously awarded me.

After some years of working at sculpture, theory and procedure become simplified. If someone were to catch me unawares and ask quickly what I am trying to do with architectural sculpture, I might unwittingly shout, incidentalism. I'd like to do my sculpture on buildings or in a setting so that when one sees the building one realizes, incidentally, there's a piece of sculpture there, that it relates so well to the wall and its surroundings, it looks as if it belonged there, and functions as a horizon or focal point to the eye. It serves best that way.

If I were questioned about sculpture for exhibitions, museums, etc., I'd say quickly, if I were off-guard, apples and a good tree trunk, for I'm trying to get the strong, plastic life of apple shapes, and the growth and supple movement of a tree trunk.

Now about books—and I'm very grateful to you for having let me talk about them.

Among my friends, there are some who collect books and when they show their treasures, their most sacred possessions are not always the beautifully bound, finely printed volumes, but often some lesser book by a lesser author, a first edition which on page 177 has a misprint. The presses were stopped, corrections made, and there are only a few of these books extant.

Somehow, a mistake happened, and a bit of human frailty got through the rolls of the press, and this bit of warm humanity has become a precious book exhibited by the Grolier Society.

If someone were to ask me, now that I've worked just a few years on books for children, what am I trying to do, what is my ambition, I might say "humanism" and explain that I'm trying to get as much humanity through the rollers of a press, with all its mistakes and frailties, that I can, deliberately and intentionally. It may clog the presses, but it's worth trying.

Eleven years ago last night, there was a big bonfire started by a tyrant who had wanted to be an artist but could only become an assistant paperhanger. That fire was fed by books. Those books were burned for many reasons. One of the main reasons was that they were concerned with humanity and human relations—of course, those books weren't lost. They were printed on indestructible truths, with the fireproof blood from the heart. My ambition is to do work that will have that much reason to exist.

Mabel F. Rice

SOURCE: "Eleanor Estes: A Study in Versatility," in *Elementary English*, Vol. XLV, No. 5, May, 1968, pp. 553-57.

Could I ever kick myself! The editor of *Elementary English* offered me a choice of eight or nine authors and illustrators of children's books as a subject for this article, and I had to choose Eleanor Estes! It looked so easy! Beginning with the first Moffat in 1941, I had read all the Estes books, used them in children's literature classes, county institutes, state conventions; taken wide swaths from one or another for storytelling; laughed with some, cried with another; cussed the author for one; grown old along with the Moffats, the Pyes, Wanda Petronski, and Mr. Todd. And I do mean old, for the Moffats celebrated their Silver Anniversary in 1966. Finally in my old age I meet up with Billy Maloon. Now to try to crystalize that enduring friendship; to capture on paper the magic that is Eleanor Estes! Oh me!

Eleanor Estes didn't begin with magic. She began with the simplest family story in the world, the Moffats. Mrs. Moffat, a widow, is the community seamstress with four nice uncomplicated children—Sylvie and Joey, Janey and Rufus. They live in a yellow house on New Dollar Street in Cranbury, a small town in Connecticut that wasn't on the map until the Moffats put it there and the Pyes moved in.

The Moffats slipped quietly on to the literary scene of the children's book world, but soon to children and their grateful parents; to librarians and teachers the Moffats were as familiar as the family next door or down the street. One thought of them as a typical American family. Now a quarter of a century later, it develops that the Moffat books have been translated into numerous foreign languages which bespeaks a universality of appeal.

The experiences of the Moffats are no more unusual than those of most lively families, but in the hands of Eleanor Estes they take an unexpected twist. Who hasn't known a small boy who had to be dragged kicking and screaming on his first day of school? But who but Rufus Moffat would challenge the struggling Hughie with this clincher: "Everybody has to go to school. Even God had to go to school." Joey Moffat is characterized in one sentence: "And whereas Joey was rarely in a play, he was often in charge of switching the lights on and off."

Most of the humor of the Estes books is implicit in the situations as the reader sees them. Often they are not at all funny to the characters in the story. The hair of most mothers would whiten at the very thought of the escapade, unpremeditated and undetected, of Hughie and Rufus as they board and ride a switching box car. Right after morning recess on that first day of school Rufus glimpsed the fleeing Hughie as he boarded the sidetracked car on the tracks near the school. Rufus slipped out of the room in hot pursuit, climbed into the car after Hughie; the switch engine bumped the car and it began to move. The two five-and-a-half year youngsters were several towns away when they were discovered by a kindly member of the track crew who inveigled the engineer of the passing flyer to take them into his cab and back to Cranbury. In a thirty second stop, the two vagrants were dropped off and Rufus had them back in their seats in Room One just in time to be dismissed with the class for noon lunch. No one had missed them, no one was the wiser,—but the reader, who if it isn't a mother, will find it amusing.

Rufus M. and his adventures in obtaining a library card appears at least once in every course in Storytelling, usually as a "final story." Lifted from its setting, it loses none of its unity. Now Mrs. Estes reveals the fact that the original library card episode centered about a little girl named Barbara Cooney—long before she was to become the recipient of a Caldecott Medal.

Like the Moffats, the town of Cranbury, Connecticut, is the setting for the Pye Books, *Ginger Pye* and *Pinky Pye.* Cranbury is actually West Haven where Eleanor Estes lived as a child in a family which, like the Moffats, had four children, two boys and two girls. Since Cranbury is a small town, the Pyes know the Moffats. Mr. Pye is a famous ornithologist who is called to Washington. Their dog named Ginger is the Newbery Medal winner, *Ginger Pye.* Eleanor Estes says that Ginger Pye is the one character in all her books that is taken entirely from life. Her own family had a dog named Ginger who was kidnapped and recovered six months later with scars on his face.

Father and Mother Pye met at the top of an escalator in a subway station where Mr. Pye, age thirty-five, was fulfilling a long cherished desire by racing madly up the down escalator. He ran smack into his future bride and knocked her down. Jerry, Rachel, Uncle Benny, age three, and their old cat Gracie complete the family until Pinky was abandoned in the midst of the group. Many a family has a young uncle or aunt, younger than the children. The Pye activities are not more unusual than those of most families, except that the Pyes like the Moffats have been touched with the Estes wand.

Pinky Pye is actually a mild mystery with the clues planted early in the book. The little typewriting kitten, Pinky, is a brat of a cat but like many a brat is completely lovable. Her antics provide much of the humor along with those of the rare pygmy owl, Owly Pye.

In the same folksy small neighborhood tradition of the Moffats and the Pyes is a newer Estes book, *The Alley* (1964). In *The Alley,* Eleanor Estes attains new heights in character delineation. One feels that somewhere the author must have known or heard of a small boy like Billy Maloon who put on his dry clothing over his wet bathing suit because, he said, it was the easiest way to carry the suit home; who donned his snow suit in the morning because the forecast was for snow, but who refused to take it off when the sun boiled down before noon. When Billy Maloon dressed for the day he stayed dressed. Billy Maloon it was who listened with attention and respect whenever another child was speaking. Did Billy Maloon spring full grown, fully clothed from the brain of Eleanor Estes? If so, what a brain!

The Alley is actually "Faculty Row" in Brooklyn, a lovely little street on which are the faculty homes of Grandby College. These are faculty children. Their mothers are faculty wives. When Katy Starr presides as judge at the trial of the burglars she wears her father's academic gown. One would expect to find few dumbbells among the faculty row children. There are none. The setting is a natural for the author whose husband, Rice Estes, is chairman of the Library School of Pratt Institute in Brooklyn.

The main character in *The Alley* is Connie Ives who at age ten is too shy to use the telephone, even to answer it. The story features Connie, her family, and her home. Billy Maloon is her "best friend." Katy Starr is that embryo club woman, author of Katy's Laws which govern child life in the Alley. Katy who is rather rude is fair and respected by the other children, but her manners irritate Connie.

The robbery of the Ives' home takes place early in the story. The detection of clues runs throughout the book. Billy Maloon is the avid detective who finally solves the mystery and helps the police to catch the burglars.

By the end of the book, Connie Ives has assumed new poise and confidence and can use and answer the telephone. Katy Starr's manners are improving and Connie sees a new pattern of friendship dawning for herself and Katy. *The Alley* lacks some of the humor of the Moffats and the Pyes, but for its insight in child character and personality it has few peers.

Toward the end of the morning session of a huge summer school course for teachers at Whittier College the visiting lecturer, Dr. Paul Witty, put down his papers and picked up a thin colorful book, Sometimes he ended the period with a poem or a book review and the class looked forward to them. He stood silent for a moment, looking at the book before he announced the title. *The Hundred Dresses* by Eleanor Estes. Without preface or comment, he began to read. The large group sat silent, all eyes fixed intently on the reader. No proverbial pin dropped. People scarcely seemed to breathe. When he finished, he closed the book softly. No zipper zipped. No one rushed to the doors. People sat staring at the reader or straight ahead, looking, one suspects, beyond the end of the book. Why had Maddie said that she would never see Wanda again? Of course she would see her someday. She *had* to see her . . . at some art exhibition where Wanda's work would be on display . . . but no . . . that wasn't in the book or even hinted.

The class filed out silently, almost reverently. They must have scattered to libraries and book stores in their home towns across Southern California. The next morning one saw at the top of many a pile of notebooks and papers *The Hundred Dresses.* Teachers smiled at one another as they displayed their books. Some were library books, some new books. One woman walked up to Dr. Witty who stood waiting to open the class, the usual crowd clustered around him. She thrust a new copy of *The Hundred Dresses* and a fountain pen into his hands. "Please autograph it for me," she said. He hesitated, started to speak. "You sold it to me," she said. "Sign it!" He signed.

Since 1944 readers and listeners alike have been sold on *The Hundred Dresses* Reviewers have exhausted their stock of adjectives and had to repeat. Poignant, compassionate, tender, lovely, different, charming, original, subtle, unforgettable, always unforgettable. . . . This delicate story of child snobbery toward the underprivileged pupil is all too familiar to most of us. It may bring unsettling memories, but if you haven't read it, run, don't walk, to the nearest library or bookstore, get it, and make your own list of adjectives.

The Estes books are a never-ending source of material for the storyteller. *The Sun and the Wind and Mr. Todd* (1943) is a storyteller's find. It is the first effort of Eleanor Estes to break into the field of fantasy. Mr. Todd is the weatherman and like most weathermen, his lot is not entirely a happy one. When Mr. Todd predicted sun and the people prepared for a picnic, sure enough it rained. When Mr. Todd said rain and people carried their umbrellas, the sun shone down in a fiery blast. Mr. Todd started out for a weatherman's convention with high hopes for help in his problems. But, of all things, that was the day, the very day, that the Sun and the Wind had that titanic contest to see which was the stronger. As you remember the Aesop fable, the object of their efforts was a lonely traveler plodding along the highway. Which of the two celestial contestants could make the traveler remove his coat? And wouldn't you know it? That hapless traveler was Mr. Todd on his way to the weatherman's convention. The story follows the Aesop pattern. The Wind in all his fury could not budge Mr. Todd but under the Sun's torrid blaze, Mr. Todd removed his coat.

Up to this point, *The Sun and the Wind and Mr. Todd* makes a good reading-aloud book, but now the story becomes a little involved. The child audience becomes restive. The skillful storyteller can delete and streamline the tale, bringing it to a rollicking close. The book is out of print but it deserves preservation in more than one type of anthology.

Three fanciful tales are bookmates under the title of the first: *The Sleeping Giant* (1948). The other two are **"The Lost Shadow"** and **"A Nice Room for Giraffes."** These gentle, humorous stories tickle the childish sense of the utterly ridiculous.

The Witch Family (1960) is a downright serious attempt to make a modern novel on the witch theme. It is similar in effect to the combination of fact and fancy that has proved so enormously successful on television, in series that appeal equally to the adult and the young audience.

In *Miranda the Great* (1967) Mrs. Estes uses the classical background of ancient Rome for her account of a noble cat who rescues all the cats and kittens from the historic fire. Miranda preserves them to become the ancestors of the Roman cats of today.

The Echoing Green (1947) is Mrs. Estes' one book for the adult reading audience. Here again is the background of small town New England, but gone is the humor of the Moffat and Pye chronicles. Parts of the book are too earthy for comfort. However, so powerful is the writing that the word pictures once printed on one's consciousness remain there to rise again, to haunt and to plague. That in itself is a tribute to superb writing. Frances Clarke Sayers in a *Horn Book* article says that the novel suffers from too close adhesion to reality. It is the reader who suffers. To say that the story is well written is an understatement. It is too well written. One closes the last page with a sigh wondering, "Was this book necessary?"

Her experience with her own small daughter, Hilda, must have been the author's inspiration for a venture in a new type of book for her, the picture book for the young child. Hilda was born in 1948 to Eleanor and Rice Estes. *A Little Oven,* story and pictures by Eleanor Estes, was published in 1955. The title and the theme are based on an adult's misinterpretation of a small child's language. When Herena was tired her mother took her in her arms for "a little lovin'." The little French girl, Genevieve, watched with round eyes and went home to tell her mother that she, too, wanted "a little 'ovin." The mother searched far and wide for a little oven before she discovered the real meaning of Genevieve's request. If one could over be justified in calling a book "sweet," that book is *A Little Oven,* unless of course it is *Pinky Pye.*

Few indeed are the Estes books that have been permitted to go out of print. Few are the writers who have succeeded in producing books destined to be classics in such a wide variety of areas.

John Rowe Townsend

SOURCE: "Eleanor Estes," in *A Sense of Story: Essays on Contemporary Writers for Children,* Longman, 1971, pp. 79-85.

Writing for children does not always, or even usually, require the author to take a child's-eye view. The mark of the tenth-rate story for children is often a creaking attempt to get down to child level, like an uncle on hands and knees playing games on the carpet. It is ineffectual and undignified. Children, on the whole, prefer adults to behave as adults, and to talk to them as adults talk. Yet the story of family life, which can be weighed by the child against his own experience in a way that the fairy tale or adventure story cannot, does require of its author a lively sense of what it is like to be a child in a family.

Although most of us see children from outside on most days of the week, I believe it is true that to *feel* as a child we must usually rely on the still-existent child within ourselves. It was not by accident that Louisa Alcott, and even E. Nesbit, who had several children of her own, went back to memories of their own childhood. Among living writers, Meindert DeJong and Noel Streatfeild have drawn on similar resources. And Eleanor Estes, in her books on the Moffats and the Pyes, went back to the place and period, and many of the details, of her own youth in a small Connecticut town. The quality of the three Moffat books which makes them exceptional is, I think, an unusual purity of the childish vision. This is not to say that the books themselves are childish. The author has the gift of selective recall, combined with adult experience of work with children, and with the mature qualities of perception and perspective. She has also a limpid, apparently effortless style which suggests a natural writer.

A natural writer; not, I think, a born novelist. Mrs Estes's books for children have been artistically successful in inverse proportion to the extent to which they employed, or needed to employ, the novelist's technique.

The three Moffat books are not novels. Yet although they seem artless they are perfectly formed. Each book consists of a chain of episodes, linked unobtrusively by a theme which requires little development and imparts little tension; and this is exactly the construction which allows the author to make the best use of her talents. In *Ginger Pye* and *The Alley,* however, there are plots of mystery and detection which call for a dramatic build-up, a logical progression towards climax, which the author is infuriatingly unable or unwilling to provide.

Ginger Pye (1951) is the story of the kidnapping and recovery of Ginger, the 'pure-bred, part fox-terrier and part collie' pup whom Jerry and Rachel Pye have saved up to buy. And as a story it hangs fire for chapter after chapter. Even the climax is more of an anticlimax, since Jerry's and Rachel's attempts at detection are hardly relevant and Ginger escapes by his own efforts, aided by the quickness of Uncle Bennie, aged three. Similarly in *The Alley* (1964) the investigation of a double crime, committed by burglars and by supposed policemen, proceeds so slowly that the reader experiences impatience rather than suspense. As stories of detection by youngsters, these do not begin to compare with the work of such writers as Erich Kästner and Paul Berna.

But *Ginger Pye* at least is not to be judged as a failed mystery story. It is a much-liked and likeable book whose merits have little to do with its plot. (The trouble probably is that the plot is not of a *kind* which can be successfully faded into the background; it demands to be developed.) The real interest of the story lies in the characters of the Pye family and in the irrelevant or barely-relevant episodes which are forever pushing the story-line aside.

Mrs Estes has said that Rachel and Jerry, who are nine and ten at the start of the story, are based on 'all the children I've ever known', which seems to suggest that they are composite characters rather than individuals. This may be true of Jerry, a sturdy small boy who is quite credible but has no marked personality of his own. But it cannot be true of Rachel, who has an interesting, quirky mind and an endearing habit of slipping away into byways of reminiscence. And there are oddly memorable incidents: no reader of *Ginger Pye* will surely ever forget how Mr Pye met Mrs Pye by knocking her down when he was trying to run up the down escalator, or how Rachel and Jerry polished the pews in church with three-year-old Uncle Bennie's help:

> Rachel had quite a long duster, and she tied it around Uncle Bennie's pants. 'Whee-ee,' she said, sending him sliding down the long pew . . .

And, 'Whee-ee,' said Jerry, picking him up, putting him on the next pew and sending him sliding back.

This was great fun for everybody and particularly for Uncle Bennie, who thought it almost as good as tobogganing. He did not mind at all being turned into a duster.

The characters of the mild ornithologist Mr Pye and of poor worried Mama are rounded out in a sequel, *Pinky Pye* (1958), which brings two new members to the Pye family: a small clever kitten and a small fierce owl. And there are further engaging glimpses of Uncle Bennie, cherishing his pet the dead locust, or conversing with God and obligingly replying to himself on behalf of the Almighty. Uncle Bennie and Pinky Pye herself, the kitten who can type—for did she not produce before witnesses the word *woogie* on the typewriter?—make the book worth while, although the meditations of Pinky with which we are presented do not strike me as kittenlike.

Among Mrs Estes's books of the 1960s, *The Witch Family,* in which two small girls become more and more involved in an imaginary world which they themselves have created, is an interesting conception but it doesn't come off; one feels that even in fictional terms nothing is really happening. *The Alley*—in the intervals between the author's attempts to make something of its burglar-catching plot—is more successful, perhaps because it is closer to the kind of thing she can do best. The Alley is a small Brooklyn backwater occupied by academic families; and in it Mrs Estes creates a whole community of children, every one distinct. The characters include a charmingly loquacious ten-year-old heroine, Connie, and the formidable, law-giving Katy who keeps the whole place in order. There is a splendidly funny chapter—quite irrelevant to the story—in which Connie sets up the Alley Conservatory of Music and offers piano lessons to the other children. Her first pupil is Winifred.

'Now,' said Connie, plunging right into lesson one, not to lose any time. 'You see those gold letters in the middle of the piano. They say, "Ludlow". Now, middle C is just a little bit to the left of the centre of those gold letters. That is the way to find C, the most important note of the piano. If you have that, you have everything. Now, I will play the scale of C major.'

Connie played the scale of C major. She decided that she might be a piano teacher when she grew up, because she enjoyed teaching so much.

The next pupil is Nicky, who is only three but comes in for some praise:

'You have a very good ear,' said Connie.

'Yes,' he said. 'I can wiggle it.'

In spite of its unsatisfactory story-line, I am sorry that *The Alley* has not so far been published in England. There are several episodes which prove that the author has by no means lost her touch. Yet it is still the three Moffat books which show Mrs Estes at her best. She has never surpassed them; they are the heart of her achievement.

The Moffats, The Middle Moffat and *Rufus M* were published in the United States in the early 1940s but did not reach England until nearly twenty years later. They tell of incidents in the life of a hard-up family in the New England town of 'Cranbury'—very close to New Haven—just before and during the First World War. When written they were already period pieces, with their references to horse-drawn wagons and early, spluttering automobiles, old-fashioned clothes and furnishings and habits. But their appeal is not a period appeal: it is the enduring essence of childhood.

At the start, Sylvie Moffat is fifteen, Joey twelve, Jane nine and Rufus five and a half. Mama, a widow, is a dressmaker. Some three years appear to pass during the three books. The point of view is almost always that of the younger members of the family; neither Mama nor Sylvie is ever the central character of an episode, and Joey stars very rarely. The threat of sale hanging over the family home is the thread that holds the episodes of the first book together; the second book, *The Middle Moffat,* is loosely threaded by Jane's efforts to see the Oldest Inhabitant safely through to his hundredth birthday; the third, with Rufus as hero, has the First World War as its background.

The style is simple, never arch or facetious. But the author is not afraid to make her hero or heroine the victim of gentle humour, so that, at the same time as identifying, the child can also stand outside and patronize. The humour has even a slight dryness. When we learn that 'My Country, 'Tis of Thee' was all Rufus could play on the organ, we are also told, casually, that he could play it like lightning. And 'Fine! Fine! Just what I've always wanted,' says the Oldest Inhabitant, on being told his fortune, which is, 'The world is your oyster. You will be a fireman.' Again and again there is the contrast between children's wild ambitions and what they can actually do; and the details they worry about in their grandiose schemes are—convincingly—mere gnats to be strained at when the camel is already swallowed.

Thus Rufus, convinced that with a little practice he can become an expert ventriloquist, plans to project Harold Callahan's voice into Harold Callahan's inkwell at school and shout 'Let me out!'; but he feels he will have to be sure the sliding lid on Harold's inkwell is open, 'because he was not certain a ventriloquist could throw his voice into an inkwell if the top was closed'.

The small, precise touch, evoking at once the response that 'yes, it was like that', is a recurrent feature of all three books, beginning with the first sentence of *The Moffats,* which shows Jane marvelling at the way Mama can peel apples so rapidly into long ringlets. The title of *Rufus M* derives from Rufus's attempt to fill out a library card; the M was as far as he could get in the available space, and every child and parent knows just how that happened. Joey Moffat, we are told, 'always had a good pencil with a fine sharp point in his pocket. He could whistle and he could whittle.' Yes, of course, he would. He was that kind of boy. 'But he was not good at dancing school and he did not like it.' No, of course, he wouldn't.

A fact seldom emphasized but often indicated is that the Moffats are poor. For Mama—and, increasingly, big sister Sylvie—family life means work and worry as well as love. This is a feature in common with *Little Women* and with E. Nesbit's Bastable stories and *The Railway Children.* The efforts to save or earn a few pennies, the horror when a five-dollar bill seems lost, are serious matters; the solidarity of the family counts for a great deal when the wolf is not all that far from the door. Against a background of material poverty, the wealth of family affection can be seen at its true value.

Two episodes, both in *Rufus M*—the last of the three books—stand a little apart from the rest. One is Rufus's end-of-season visit to the mist-wreathed pleasure-ground, which has an air of wistful strangeness. The other is the final chapter, in which the Moffats' plans and dreams float up the chimney on scraps of charred paper. This last is one of the very few occasions on which I think an ending is acceptable for children which one might not offer to adults. To a grown-up person this scene seems slightly contrived and sentimental. But grown-ups are sophisticated in the matter of story design; also, we are afraid of our feelings. In this case, the occasion is the farewell to a family whom the reader has come to know well in the course of the three books, and to love greatly. The note is a proper one on which

to end; it rings true. If it is embarrassing to grown-ups, that may be a reflection on grown-ups rather than on children or on the author.

The Moffat books are, I believe, outstanding among family stories. On them, with a little support from the Pyes and *The Alley,* Mrs Estes's reputation rests. It is quite a small base. But in the last analysis a writer's distinction does not depend on the number of his books, or even on the number of his good books. It depends on the quality of his best. Three like those about the Moffats are sufficient.

Carolyn T. Kingston

SOURCE: "The Tragic Moment: The Hundred Dresses," in *Tragic Mode in Children's Literature,* Teachers College Press, 1974, pp. 21-2.

Wanda, daughter of a poor Polish immigrant, lives on the wrong side of town in an ugly shack. Motherless Wanda owns only one dress, which she scrupulously washes each night. Her efforts to make a good appearance are almost useless, however, because she has no iron. The other girls tease her mercilessly, urged on by the leader of their group, who has lovely clothes and comes from a socially prominent family. Only one little girl does not wish to follow suit, but does not have the courage to befriend Wanda and so risk being excluded from the "in" segment of the class.

One day, teased beyond endurance, the Polish girl states that she has a hundred dresses at home, but the girls laugh and taunt her all the more.

Although a regular attendant at school, Wanda is very quiet, and so it is several days before anyone notices her absence. Shortly after, a note comes from Wanda, saying that she has moved to another town but leaves as a present to her classmates one hundred beautifully-drawn pictures of various costumes. She has not only been scrupulously clean, but scrupulously honest. Now the girls realize their mistake in thinking Wanda an empty braggart, but as she has given no forwarding address, they cannot apologize. Except for the group leader, who shrugs Wanda off, the girls are sorry, but it is the child who longed to help who suffers deeply, learning at first hand the bitterness of having made a mistake that can never be righted.

The Hundred Dresses is a study of exteriors and interiors in disharmony, and as such it makes a statement about life that has universal implications.

Wanda, the heroine, has integrity, honesty, and talent—shimmering qualities—hidden beneath a crumpled dress and a stolid manner.

The other girls have lovely appearances and are socially adept but their pleasant exteriors cover shallow and even ugly natures. The group leader is little touched by the schoolroom tragedy. Shrugging off the dark glimpse of herself, she goes on in her old ways. Her friends are somewhat stirred, but the knife turns in the heart of the child who wanted to help Wanda all along. For this girl, the catharsis caused by Wanda's tragic sojourn and departure is deeply moving and changes her whole manner of thinking. Wanda herself does not change. She is the catalyst precipitating the clarification of her world. Had she not appeared, the placid surfaces of her schoolmates might have remained unruffled, but Wanda's being highlighted the latent hubris of her milieu. Without conscious effort she showed those whose lives she touched devastating views of themselves, and so became to them "insufferable."

But the story is neither sermon nor editorial—it is song—mournful, timeless, haunting. The simple Anglo-Saxon words tell a momentous story just as the unpretentious heroine casts a mighty shadow. The author makes no effort to shuffle events to bring happiness into the Polish girl's life, nor to give her would-be friend a chance to make amends. Wanda's conflict with her group is inevitable. "This is the situation," says the author, and so ends her tragic song.

The Hundred Dresses is complete tragedy, told in the manner of the ancients, event by event irresistably building toward the final tragic end. Wanda does not die, but she is as unreachable as if death had claimed her, and perhaps the effect upon the others is more tragic than actual death would have been, for then she might more easily have been forgotten.

Darlene Kelly

SOURCE: "Alice Munro's *Day of the Butterfly*: An American Source," in *Ariel: A Review of International English Literature,* Vol. 29, No. 2, April, 1998, pp. 115-27.

In his autobiography, *A Sort of Life* (1971), Graham Greene gives an amusing account of how, years after it was written, he was startled to find in his short story "Under the Garden" an unlikely source: Beatrix Potter's *Squirrel Nutkin.* Quite unconsciously, as he

explains, he had reworked into his own murder story that terrifying moment in Potter's miniature thriller when the hapless Tom Kitten is being "trounced up by the rats behind the skirting board and the sinister Anna Maria covering him with dough" (52). Clearly there is no way of predicting how and when in an author's mature writings material from the slagheap of childhood reading may assert itself.

Certainly in the case of Alice Munro, works she read as a child would seem to have infiltrated her stories. As her family and friends have noted, reading was an "addiction" to her (Ross 15). And she read widely and eclectically. Emily Brontë's *Wuthering Heights,* Tennyson's poetry, Dickens's *Child's History of England,* and L. M. Montgomery's novels, especially *Emily of New Moon,* captured her youthful imagination (Ross 14-16). Just as influential, however, were writers of a kind that clever people rarely mention when furbishing the child-prodigy part of their critical reputations:

> . . . behind all those childhood books I've mentioned, I was just reading anything and everything. When people talk about their reading, they tend to mention [only] the respectable books. I mentioned Tennyson, for instance, but at the same time I was reading *Gone with the Wind* compulsively. . . . I read everything we happened to have in the house, and the books that came into our house all came in by accident. So my reading was just here and there, and all over. I [also] read what was in the Sunday school library. (Ross 19)

Elsewhere she points out that authors "who have never become very well known" because they wrote only "a few marvellous stories" are unfortunately excluded from a writer's list of literary mentors. "One tends not to think of them," Munro told one interviewer, "when you're on the spot with a question like this" (Struthers 11). The reason, then, for omitting such writers is not their unimportance, but memory's inevitable gaps.

Difficult as it can be to remember what we read as adults, it is harder yet to retrieve the name of every book familiar to us in childhood. Yet these stories, though immature, cannot be denied; they too leave their mark. The persistent impression made by books read in youth may account for the striking similarity between Alice Munro's "Day of the Butterfly," written in 1953, and *The Hundred Dresses* (1944) by American juvenile writer Eleanor Estes, best known for her award-winning books about the Moffat family. Munro may have deliberately emulated Estes, a good possibility given her habit of staging "imitations" of successful narratives in her head, sometimes committing these works of dual authorship to paper (Ross 20, 22). She defends this early activity as a kind of apprenticeship: "There's nothing wrong with writing imitations. It's the only way, I think, to learn" (Ross 22). Whether a writer is or is not aware of copying others, Munro considers the practice to be greatly beneficial:

> I'm not very often aware of influences, but I'm sure they're happening all the time. . . . I'm probably using things that other people have used first without even realizing I'm doing it. I think many of us do that. Or we pick up a tone that seems appropriate to a certain kind of material, and we try out that tone. Or perhaps we're given courage to go on using a kind of approach or material when otherwise we might worry that too much had been done of this. (Struthers 17)

Munro's admission that in the early stages of her career she modelled her work on that of others makes her use of *The Hundred Dresses* entirely plausible. Or perhaps she wove strands from Estes's compelling tale into her story all unconsciously, much as Graham Greene without realizing transposed elements of Beatrix Potter's *Squirrel Nutkin* into his short story. In any case, if Munro had not read Estes's minor classic before writing "Day of the Butterfly," then it is by an extraordinary coincidence that two stories written less than a decade apart should be almost mirror images of each other.

During the early 1940s, when the young Alice Munro was reading all manner of books, Estes's novels were a staple in North American libraries. Because Estes is not a writer of the same rank, say as C. S. Lewis or Frances Hodgson Burnett, a few words should be said about her place in children's literature. In 1943, she won the Newbery Honor label for *Rufus M* and, in 1952, the Newbery Medal for *Ginger Pye,* two awards which established her reputation as one of America's finest children's writers. Her books about the fatherless Moffat children were a perennial favourite with young readers, but adults were quick to see the greater sophistication of *The Hundred Dresses,* a sombre account of how children of mainly Anglo-Saxon descent so persecute a Polish classmate that her family has to move away.[1] In a survey of children's books written between 1920 and 1950, Ruth Hill Viguers notes that "Among the few fine stories of a child who is 'different,' one stands out for its subtlety, its good writing and its perfect understanding of childhood. Eleanor Estes, in her *The Hundred Dresses* (1944), has accomplished what only an artist

in the portrayal of children can do" (551). Critics writing in another survey of children's literature make a case for the book's uniqueness, saying that "Eleanor Estes's *The Hundred Dresses* (1944) has some claim to be the first story to deal with prejudice, [one which] is all the more distinguished by its downbeat ending" (*Children's Literature* 250). Estes can hardly be credited with having written the first story to deal with prejudice among children—Mark Twain's *Huckleberry Finn* (1884) and Katherine Mansfield's story "The Doll House" (1922), for example, both preceded *The Hundred Dresses*—but her sombre theme was indeed uncommon in literature written expressly for children at that time.

Estes's controversial subject no doubt piqued the interest of Munro, whose stories often explore the dark side of human motivation. She might also have been inclined to expose the evil of racism by her own dislike of it, a dislike made clear by her remarks on the bias of a juvenile encyclopedia called *The Book of Knowledge,* which she had read uncritically as a child: "These books have glaring faults—they're quite racist—and I would never give them to children to read" (Ross 14). But Estes's skilful treatment of her subject in *The Hundred Dresses* could alone have inspired Munro's respectful imitation of it in "Day of the Butterfly." Mastering fictional techniques which had worked well for others was very important to Munro in her days as a fledgling writer. Her first stories, "Day of the Butterfly" among them,[2] she herself compared to "paintings that are said to be 'in the school of,' [or] 'after the manner'" of another artist (Struthers 23). Just how closely Munro emulated the "manner" or art of Estes in "Day of the Butterfly" can be inferred from its compelling resemblance to *The Hundred Dresses.*

This paper documents the main parallels between the two works. Both Munro and Estes convey the foreign girl's suffering from a classmate's perspective. The two stories begin the same way: the girl through whose eyes we see events (a central consciousness in Estes, a first-person narrator in Munro) first describes the victim as a person who, before being harassed, was thought beneath everyone's notice, a subtle form of discrimination; then, noting those details which set the unfortunate child apart, this same observer makes clear to us, if not to herself, just why it was a young foreigner who was treated so cruelly. Estes's memorable character types will be shown to inhabit Munro's story as well, notably the immigrant friends and relations of the tiny pariah who worsen her social status, and also the young bullies who like a pendulum swing from abusing their strange classmate to doting on her. In Munro as in Estes, teachers accidentally initiate the youngster's misery and later preside over the group's act of collective restitution. The most remarkable similarity, however, is the shocking recognition by both Munro's narrator and Estes's observer that they are the victim's alter ego.

The Hundred Dresses opens with deceptive simplicity: "Today, Monday, Wanda Petronski was not in her seat. But nobody, not even Peggy and Madeline, the girls who started all the fun, noticed her absence" (1). The "fun" turns out to be the ritual mockery of Wanda for having once claimed to have one hundred dresses in a closet at home, despite her obvious poverty. This taunting is called the "hundred dresses game" and also "having fun with Wanda" by Madeline, or Maddie,[3] the girl who witnesses the events. Before the game ever started, no one had even noticed Wanda; outside of those moments when she is being persecuted, the children continue to ignore her; and when she stops coming to school altogether, no one remarks upon her absence for several days. In her understated way, Estes has captured society's attitude to the people it marginalizes. Neglect eventually gives way to persecution when Maddie's friend Peggy sets out to expose Wanda as a liar. Peggy daily cross-examines her in a "mock polite" voice (17), ostensibly to establish the truth of the matter: "Why did [Wanda] want to lie? And she wasn't just an ordinary person, else why would she have a name like that?" (16-17). The last line points to Wanda's ethnicity as the real irritant. Most of the children in the class do not have an unusual name like "Petronski," but rather "names [that were] easy to say, like Thomas, Smith, or Allen" (10). It comes as no surprise later that in a letter to the teacher Wanda's father should cite discrimination as the reason that he and his family are moving away: "Dear teacher: My Wanda will not come to your school any more. Jake also. Now we move away to big city. No more holler Polack. No more ask why funny name. Plenty of funny names in the big city" (47).

Mr. Petronski's broken English recalls details given earlier in the story that set Wanda herself apart. She too has trouble with English, as is shown by her painful failure to read aloud when called upon to do so and by her classmates' impatience with her on these occasions (36). She makes herself noticeable by wearing the same worn, if clean, blue dress every day. Then there is the greasy sheen of her forehead. Maddie, herself a poor girl who wears other people's cast-off clothing, is very thankful that at least her own "forehead didn't shine the way Wanda's round one did. What did she use on it? Sapolio? That's what all the girls wanted to know" (17). In part, Wanda is reviled by others simply because of her greasy look, a stigma that Alice Munro's child-victim in "Day of the Butterfly" bears as well.

Wanda is also derided for living in a strange, rundown neighbourhood, a place made worse by its nearness to the house of another immigrant, an unemployed Swede who is known as "old man Svenson." Svenson's dilapidated house and property show the effects of his being out of a job. Maddie has heard people speak of him at best as an "'old good-for-nothing,'" at worst as someone who once shot a man (54). Yet these harsh judgements are based on nothing more substantial than poor Mr. Svenson's foreignness—he mumbles unintelligibly when addressed—and his offputting appearance, with his "drooping mustache and tangled hair, his hound loping behind him, and the long streams of tobacco juice [which] he expertly shot from between his scattered yellow teeth" (59). The book's illustrations reinforce this benign reading of Mr. Svenson's character.[4] The soft outlines of Louis Slobodkin's two sketches of him—seated innocuously on his porch in one and looking startled at the questions put to him by Peggy and Maddie in another—predispose us to see Mr. Svenson as a harmless man who has been badly treated by his American neighbours, and to regard Wanda the same way.

Like the young Polish victim in *The Hundred Dresses,* the foreign child in Munro's "Day of the Butterfly" at the outset is entirely ignored, confirming her status as a non-entity. The narrator Helen recalls barely noticing the girl whom she would later torment: "I do not remember when Myra Sayla came to town, though she must have been in our class at school for two or three years" (100). Prior to harassing her, the schoolchildren "had not paid much attention to Myra" (102); and when Myra stops coming to school, Helen cannot even say whether it was "the day . . . or the week after" another incident that Myra vanished, inconsequential as she was (106).

At first glance, the group's cruelty to Myra seems arbitrary, but Helen's careful noting of all the things that set Myra apart makes its own statement about why she is hounded, the same technique found in *The Hundred Dresses.* Even the minor details used to establish Myra's strangeness mimic those of Estes. Like Wanda, for example, Myra has trouble with English, being unable to spell and, when she speaks, sounding as if she were "wetting her lips with her tongue" (104-05). Her clothes are also as ill-fitting as those of her counterpart in *The Hundred Dresses.* Wanda always wore the same blue dress "that looked like a piece of the sky in summer" (24) but that "didn't hang right" (12), two details which are fused together in the reference to Myra's "glimmer[ing] sadly in sky-blue taffeta, in dusty turquoise crepe, a grown woman's dress made over, weighted by a big bow at the V of the neck and folding empty over [her] narrow chest" (106). In short, she looks ridiculous.

Just as Wanda's social status suffers because of her proximity to the suspect Mr. Svenson, so too Myra's unfortunate connections make her lose caste in the eyes of her ruthless young critics. Deliberate mention is made of the fact that her aunt is a nun, for example, a reference that might seem innocent except that, in Munro's world, people's religious affiliation is so often a lightning rod, making them the object of discrimination.[5] Also, the unappetizing sight of Myra's father, a Svenson-like character who sits idly in his store all day chewing garlic, "with his shirt open over his swelling stomach and tufts of black hair showing around his belly button" (103), hardly enhances her social position. Significantly, the children find the daughter's own appearance as repellent as the father's. One compelling detail in Estes's work which becomes even more arresting when duplicated by Munro is the greasy look which stigmatizes both foreign girls. Myra's turban of "oily" hair recalls Wanda's forehead which looks as if she had rubbed Sapolio on it, in each case perhaps an oblique reference to their nationality, since many ethnic groups use creams and pomades to make skin supple and hair lustrous. This sign of obvious difference inspires Helen and her classmates to devise a "game," as they call it (103), a euphemism that also appears in *The Hundred Dresses:*

> . . . now a game developed; it started with saying, "Let's be nice to Myra!" Then we would walk up to her in formal groups of three or four and at a signal, say together, "Hel-lo Myra. Hello *My*-ra!" and follow up with something like, "What do you wash your hair in, Myra, it's so nice and shiny, Myra." "Oh she washes it in cod-liver oil, don't you Myra, she washes it in cod-liver oil, can't you smell it?" (103)

The songs and chants of childhood, as Iona and Peter Opie famously demonstrated in such books as *The Singing Game* (1985), *The Lore and Language of*

Schoolchildren (1959), and *Children's Games in Street and Playground* (1969) are a universal part of growing up. As both Estes and Munro show, so is taunting.

What gives special interest to each author's depiction of schoolyard bullying is her emphasis on ritual. The teacher in both works, for example, like a shaman leads the group from guilt to atonement. In *The Hundred Dresses,* Miss Mason, in other respects a decent person, is the first to discriminate against Wanda by relegating her to a corner of the room "where rough boys who did not make good marks on their report cards sat" (3), presumably because Wanda like the boys had mud on her shoes—in her case picked up from a long trek to school along country roads. The teacher no doubt simply wanted to keep the floor clean, but her segregation of Wanda still sets an unfortunate precedent. Similarly, in "Day of the Butterfly," Myra's trials are also begun by her teacher. When Myra asks permission to take her little brother home because he has "wet himself" (100), Miss Darling forces her to put her request more euphemistically, making her ridiculous before the class. From that moment on Myra and her brother stand alone at recess on the school's back porch. In their isolation, they are strikingly like Wanda, who, while other children congregate in the playground, remains in her solitary place "by the ivy-covered brick wall of the school building" (14). Perceiving the misery of Myra and her brother, Miss Darling tries to scold the children into treating them better, a ploy that backfires with the invention of the taunting game. In the end, each girl finds asylum from the torture of school, Wanda in a larger city and Myra in a cancer ward.

The process of atonement in *The Hundred Dresses* begins when the teacher announces that Wanda has won an art contest with one hundred sketches of beautiful dresses, drawings which substantiate her once preposterous claim. This proclamation is followed by the news contained in Mr. Petronski's letter. Upon reading this document Miss Mason first adjusts her glasses, then removes and wipes them, a sign of clearer moral vision and perhaps even of regret for her part in Wanda's suffering. She is now fitted for the task of inspiring a similar change of heart in her students. Gently she tells them that their hurtful comments were probably made "in thoughtlessness" (48), but that they must examine their conscience all the same. Maddie and Peggy visit Wanda's house, hoping that she might still be there and that they might congratulate her; on finding it vacant, they send her a friendly letter praising her drawings (65). Wanda sends them a gracious (if unidiomatic) reply which the teacher reads aloud to the whole class. The children are now delighted to hear from the celebrated artist whom before they had mistreated. At the time of the class Christmas party, the ballet student Cecile, whose lovely red dress months earlier had provoked Wanda's boast, performs the "Passing of Autumn" for her classmates, a dance which becomes their favourite. This detail makes its point unobtrusively: the vile behaviour of the previous autumn is now a thing of the past for the children, who here undergo a ritual purgation.

In "Day of the Butterfly," Munro enlarges upon Estes's idea of the teacher-guided ritual, giving it several complex twists. Miss Darling's attempted defence of Myra and her brother makes them into living fetishes, or "small figures carved of wood, for worship or magic with faces smooth and aged" (101). Myra is later said to be "set apart for legendary uses" (103), but Miss Darling is incapable of understanding the scapegoating and victim worship that this term implies, far less her own role in expediting them. Like Miss Mason in *The Hundred Dresses*, she too is bespectacled, although her glasses are "fragile" and their rims "thin" (100, 101), two epithets which also describe her vision. Without realizing it she provokes the children into taunting Myra; with like incomprehension she inspires their collective atonement by organizing a fake birthday party for Myra in March in case she dies before her actual birthday in July. The idea of the party greatly appeals to the young bullies for whom Myra now becomes oddly enviable. Although she does not dazzle her classmates with a hundred beautiful drawings, Myra exudes all the same "the excitement of sickness and hospitals," within which context she is "impressively set free of all the rules and conditions of [her classmates'] lives" (107). The girls plan the party as if it were a "cause" (108) and decide that their gifts should exceed the twenty-five cent limit imposed by Miss Darling. In a striking phrase, they are said to discuss Myra "as if she were something [they] owned" (108). The earlier comparison of Myra to a small figure carved of wood now acquires a new, chilling significance: a human being must become an object, this time of worship, before the group can absolve itself.

The real awakening in each story, however, is not experienced by the group at all; rather, this improved moral vision is attributed solely to the girl from whose perspective the story is told, and then only when she comes to see herself as the victim's alter

ego. Maddie's recognition of her kinship to Wanda begins on a bright October day when everyone seems more brightly arrayed than usual and even "Wanda looked pretty" (106). She sees that Wanda's claim on this occasion to have a hundred dresses is based on a simple desire to be like all the other girls who at that moment are admiring Cecile's red dress. With a piece of broken glass Maddie flashes a rainbow of the October colours onto nearby houses, trees, and telephone poles (23), a perfect symbol for herself as a reflector or mirror image of the bullied girl. Maddie always feels ill at ease when others harass Wanda, but her one attempt to stop Peggy from doing so ends abruptly when she perceives how much a target like Wanda she herself is:

> Suddenly she paused and shuddered. She pictured herself in the school yard, a new target for Peggy and the girls. Peggy might ask her where she got the dress she had on, and Maddie would have to say that it was one of Peggy's old ones that Maddie's mother had tried to disguise with new trimmings so that no one in Room 13 would recognize it. (35)

In Wanda's predicament, Maddie sees an image of her own. The very names "Wanda" and "Maddie— their capital letters an inversion of each other, and the rest a trochaic assembly of likesounding vowels and consonants—underline this identity. In the final analysis, Maddie's sense of kinship with Wanda impels her to make amends. Restitution takes the form of fantasies in which Maddie rescues her other self from various perils and, more concretely, of the friendly letter that she and Peggy write. Yet as the last paragraph of the novel makes clear, Maddie remains troubled by the memory of the persecuted girl:

> . . . she blinked away the tears that came every time she thought of Wanda standing alone in that sunny spot in the school yard close to the wall, looking stolidly over at the group of laughing girls after she had walked off, after she had said, "Sure, a hundred of them—all lined up . . . ." (80)

In "Day of the Butterfly," the narrator retraces the journey to self-awareness made by Estes's Maddie. With adult hindsight, Helen presents at the story's end all the clues of her kinship with Myra, recalling uneasily, just as Maddie had done with Wanda, how her ostracized double used to stand alone against the school. Although not foreign like Myra, Helen has other liabilities. She lives outside the city limits, for example, which is presumably why her boots are encrusted with mud, a stigma in Estes's fictional world as well. Just as Maddie fears becoming the next Wanda, so too does Helen sense that her poverty will make her as inviting a target for bullying as Myra:

> I was the only one in the class who carried a lunch pail and ate peanut-butter sandwiches in the high, bare, mustard-coloured cloak-room, the only one who had to wear rubber boots in the spring, when the roads were heavy with mud. I felt a little danger, on account of this; but I could not tell exactly what it was. (103)

As a child Helen cannot entirely decipher her kinship with Myra, but she clearly senses it, as we see in the passage just quoted. This awareness of a common bond is reinforced by Helen's learning that Myra reads the same comics and popular fiction that she herself does (105). That Helen finally grasps what Maddie had plainly stated in *The Hundred Dresses*— that in her resemblance to the victim she herself might become the object of the next schoolyard game—is evident from her reaction when, in giving Myra the tin butterfly from her cracker jack box, she grazes Myra's hand: "I flushed but Myra did not. I realized the pledge as our fingers touched; I was panicky, but *all right,* I thought, I can come early and walk with her other mornings. I can go and talk to her at recess. Why not? *Why not?*" (106). She is relieved that Myra does not wear the butterfly and that she vanishes shortly afterwards into the hospital. Helen and her classmates write Myra a letter (just as Peggy and Maddie write to Wanda) and give her lavish presents. Helen refers to these gifts as "guilt-tinged offerings" (110), and she resolves to get rid of the one that Myra gives her. Like Maddie, Helen cannot escape the "treachery of [her] own heart" (110). The story ends exactly like *The Hundred Dresses,* with the sometime persecutor haunted by the image of the victim standing solitarily against the school:

> Did Myra ever say goodbye? Not likely. She sat in her high bed, her delicate brown neck, rising out of a hospital gown too big for her, her brown carved face immune to treachery, her offering perhaps already forgotten, prepared to be set apart for legendary uses, as she was even in the back porch at school. (110)

In the first published version of "Day of the Butterfly," which appeared in *Chatelaine* (July 1965) under the title "Good-by Myra," the story had ended far more lamely: "At the door I had to pause once more and look back at her sitting in the high hospital bed. I thought that soon I would be outside. So I called back quickly, treacherously, almost gaily, 'Good-

by!'" (58). In keeping with her early practice of imitating works she admired, Munro improved this conclusion by emulating Eleanor Estes's dramatic return to the time of past injury, an effective reminder in both works that the memory of cruel acts is not easily annulled.

To see *The Hundred Dresses* as the source of Munro's "Day of the Butterfly" heightens our appreciation of both texts, since each one casts a helpful light on the other. Such a study also illuminates the process by which texts are made of other texts. Finally, a comparison of the two works proves John Rowe Townsend's point that the boundaries between children's literature and adult fiction are shifting and elusive. Many books written for a mature audience— such as *Gulliver's Travels* and *Robinson Crusoe*—are often appropriated by youngsters, whereas children's works such as the Alice books and Tolkien's *The Lord of the Rings* can be popular with adults. No writer in any genre has a monopoly on the truth; and the truth buried deep in a child's heart, as Eleanor Estes and Alice Munro so movingly show, only the skill of a genuine storyteller is needed to reveal.

Notes

1. In "Eleanor Estes: A Study in Versatility," Mabel F. Rice tells of how a group of teachers taking summer school were held spellbound by their professor's reading of *The Hundred Dresses:*

> Toward the end of the morning session of a huge summer school course for teachers at Whittier College the visiting lecturer, Dr. Paul Witty, put down his papers and picked up a thick colorful book. Sometimes he ended the period with a poem or a book review and the class looked forward to them. He stood silent for a moment, looking at the book before he announced the title. *The Hundred Dresses* by Eleanor Estes. Without preface or comment, he began to read. The large group sat silent, all eyes fixed intently on the reader. No proverbial pin dropped. People scarcely seemed to breathe. When he finished, he closed the book softly. . . . The class filed out silently, almost reverently. They must have scattered to libraries and book stores in their home towns across Southern California. The next morning one saw at the top of many a pile of notebooks and papers *The Hundred Dresses.* (555-56)

In "Therapeutic Reading," Matilda Bailey recounts how a teacher of a racially mixed group of children saw in *The Hundred Dresses* a means of preventing discrimination:

> In an Anglo-Saxon community, the influx of "foreigners" often presents a problem in the school.

One teacher wisely anticipated difficulty by reading aloud to her class Eleanor Estes's *The Hundred Dresses.* The pupils quickly recognized that the little girl in the story with her strange and almost unpronounceable name, was a very nice little girl made extremely unhappy by the Browns and Smiths and Joneses in her class.

One girl said after the reading of the story, "I wish she were in our class. We'd be nice to her." (32)

2. Munro admits that certain early stories, including "The Day of the Butterfly," were imitations of other works. At the time of her interview by Tim Struthers, she said that she couldn't recall just whom she was imitating in "Day of the Butterfly" because it was "*such* an early story" (Struthers 23). As she also said in the same interview, writers who have never become famous but who wrote one or two splendid stories are often forgotten when a writer is "put on the spot" with questions about influences (11).

3. This unusual nickname also appears in "The Peace of Utrecht" in *Dance of the Happy Shades,* a minor detail but one that nonetheless strengthens the case for Estes's influence on Munro.

4. Estes's book is made greatly appealing by Louis Slobodkin's whimsical sketches and watercolours. The smudged impression of his characters' faces, for example, is a perfect screen onto which young readers can project themselves; and his avoidance of period detail gives the story a timeless quality.

5. In "Friend of My Youth," the mother of the narrator dismisses the Cameronian sect as a "freak religion from Scotland" (*Friend of My Youth* 5), a lofty judgment delivered from the "perch of her obedient and lighthearted Anglicanism" (5). One woman in "Accident" tells another of how a priest gave the last rites to, or "did the business" on, a Catholic boy after he died, a comment that elicits a censorious cluck from her listener: "There was not much hostility to Catholics in this disapproval, really; it was a courtesy Protestants were bound to pay to each other" (*The Moons of Jupiter* 93). The narrator of "Privilege" echoes this idea in observing that people of the town were "Catholics or fundamentalist Protestants, honour-bound to molest each other" (*Who Do You Think You Are?* 24). Such molestation sometimes took the form of preventing religious intermarriage. In "Walker Brothers Cowboy," a man's family rejects his sweetheart because she is a Catholic, or a person who "digs with the wrong foot" (*Dance of the Happy Shades* 14, 17). Similarly, in "Jesse and Meribeth,"

Floris had been courted by the local druggist, "but Aunt Ena objected to him: he drank (that is, he drank a little), and was a Catholic" (*The Progress of Love* 186). Clearly, to Aunt Ena, the druggist's being a Catholic was as bad as his being a drunkard.

Louisa Smith

SOURCE: "Eleanor Estes' *The Moffats*: Through Colored Glass," in *Touchstones: Reflections on the Best in Children's Literature,* edited by Perry Nodelman, Children's Literature Association, 1985, pp. 64-9.

In the typescript of her Newbery acceptance speech, Eleanor Estes wrote, "One remembers sitting on curbs, looking at the world through a bit of broken glass, red or green or blue, but one cannot write a whole chapter on this pleasant and wondrous sensation, so one imagines and writes the trolley car chapter in '*The Moffats*'" (Kerlan Collection, University of Minnesota). It is just this memory that infuses not just one chapter, but the entire book of *The Moffats,* and to some extent its sequels, *The Middle Moffat* and *Rufus M.,* creating a vision delivered through a child's colored-glass perspective. Time and again, the reader is reminded that the view of the Moffats' life is that of a child's, not an adult's.

Commenting on Estes' books in the 1952 *Horn Book* article that introduced Estes' Newbery acceptance speech, Frances Clark Sayers predicted that Estes' books were "destined to become part of the glad heritage which parents share with children, remembered from childhood, through adulthood, and returned to childhood again through one's children, and their children's children" (258). Perhaps the world moved too quickly. In short order, it became much different from the New Dollar Street on which the Moffats lived, and today's grandparents are more likely to be the candidates for sharing the remembered Moffat experiences with grandchildren. But that change should not diminish Estes' contribution to children's literature, and it does not explain her rather faded reputation.

All three Moffat books have a quiet, wry tone. Nothing momentous happens—but then, childhood life in the forties was a protected one. A world war was being fought, but American children were spared the details and indeed, beyond the inconvenience of ration stamps, the consequences also. Estes has captured this quality beautifully, even though it may not be a quality that children want to read about today. What is important to bear in mind is that Estes reaffirmed the tradition of the American family story in which every child remains an individual and has a life independent of the family, and yet in which the family remains central. The reader will recognize this tradition in the Alcott books, and in the Cleary books which followed Estes' books. *The Moffats* is a touchstone book because it so cleverly integrates its family situations with a carefully evoked sense of a child's vision.

Jane Moffat, whose perspective is the focusing one in *The Moffats*, is an observer, a child who, although involved in the adventures in the story, watches and contemplates what she watches. Other writers have mentioned Jane's upside-down viewing position as a familiar childhood occupation; in fact, the reader's first glimpse of Jane's street is presented through this posture: "It was wonderful to look at things from between her legs, upside down. Everything had a different look altogether, a much cleaner, brighter look" (9-10). Most children have experimented with distorted views of their world, whether upside down, or on their backs, or spinning around, stopping and watching the world spin, or looking through pieces of glass or mirrors, to the enhancement of the ordinary and the encouragement of the imagination. What would it be like to live on the other side of the looking glass? What if the city were made entirely of emeralds? To Jane, New Dollar Street looks brighter in reverse.

But Jane is established as an observer with the very first sentence of the book. She is watching her mother peel an apple, in such a way that the peel comes off in one long curl. Next, Jane climbs onto the hitching post in front of the yellow house, ostensibly to look for her brothers, Joey and Rufus, but mostly just to look up the street to the trolley line and down the street to the railroad. The reader, of course, gets the positioning of the yellow house as center in this setting; but more important the reader learns that this is a posture that Jane will keep throughout the book—the posture of the watcher.

The For Sale sign for the yellow house, hammered up in the first chapter, foreshadows the eventual move by the Moffats, but it also changes the demeanor of the yellow house. As Jane observes,

> the sign made the house strange and unfamiliar. It was like looking a long time at Mama's face and thinking 'This is Mama'; looking and looking and thinking, 'Who is Mama?' And the longer she'd look at Mama's face the stranger and more unfamiliar it would seem to her (19).

A strange perspective indeed for a child's book, but one every child could relate to—at least every child who has spent a long period of time gazing at one object.

While some of Jane's observations are almost metaphysical, others lead to amusing situations. For example, Jane has constructed an entire mythology about Chief Mulligan, the Chief of Police, even to the point of seeing the two small trimmed mulberry trees on either side of the stoop of his house as sentries guarding him. The Chief is a person worthy of her respect and fear, so that when Jane learns that, because she was mimicking the new Superintendent of School's walk, she could be arrested and sent to jail for her deed, she truly believes it possible. When sent to the store for sugar, she checks out the street first to make sure it is safe. When faced with the prospect of meeting Chief Mulligan, Jane chooses to hide in the breadbox rather than risk the danger of being apprehended.

In addition to Jane's unusual perspective on reality, she also has a dream world, which is quite private. In it, she is a princess with golden curls, a not-entirely-original dream but one which fortifies her, especially since her hair is brown and resists curling. She also rides a white horse and is met by a prince on a black horse. As she falls asleep in the breadbox, the dream vision becomes extended and distorted. She is pursued by the Chief of Police "on a stout red steed belching fire and smoke from his nostrils" (44). One isn't quite sure who is doing the belching, the horse or the Chief of Police. Jane is not caught; at her urging her horse leaps over the lake, leaving the Chief on the other shore. She does, however, wait for the prince to show up afterwards. Usually princesses are saved by princess, so this is another manifestation of Jane's somewhat singular vision. It is this dream vision which serves to establish the bond of friendship between Nancy Stokes and Jane at the end of *The Moffats.* Nancy also has a dream, that of being an opera singer and being applauded, and as the two girls share their visions, Jane experiences an "incredible feeling of happiness." She is going to have a best friend.

Underlying the premise of the book is the idea of poverty. A widow with four children, renting a house which could be sold at any moment and making a living sewing clothing, had not too many prospects, even if she is the best dressmaker in Cranbury. No rich uncle appears to bail the family out, nor does an appreciative customer who turns out to be rich set

Mama up in business. Mama must keep up appearances. Whenever she goes to deal with a situation, she always wears a hat and gloves. "Mama was the only housewife on New Dollar Street who put on her hat and gloves even when she was only going down to Elm Street" (18). Respectability is an important asset for a widow, especially a poor one. Independence and self-sufficiency appear to be values in this book. No charity is ever mentioned, not even when Rufus, the youngest, has scarlet fever.

The possibility of poverty especially intrudes during the chapter about the dark of winter. While Joey sifts the ashes for possible good coals, Jane asks if they are poverty-stricken and Mama replies, "Just poor." Jane had visualized having to go into the street to sell matches, so she is relieved to find out that they are only poor. Money, however, is carefully rationed, as evidenced by the trip to the coal yard. Along the way Jane and Joey look at oranges, apples, tangerines, and grapefruit with much the same desire as the little match girl viewed the dinners of the more fortunate. When they reach the coal yard, they find that the $5.00 is missing. "No money, no coal," they're told—and, the reader senses, no compassion either. All the way home the children search the street for the money, to no avail. They are met by men coming home from work, which underscores their fatherless state. Fortunately, the money is discovered at home and no pity is wasted on the situation as, indeed, it never is, throughout the book. But the facts remain; Mama cannot afford to buy the yellow-house, they must move to a smaller one. Mama remains dependent on whether or not she can satisfy her customers. One can also notice that the children go to their events such as dancing school, school, or church on their own, while Mama presumably stays home to work. Other children are escorted by their parents.

As Virginia Wolf points out in her article on Eleanor Estes in *American Writers for Children,* **The Moffats** is "a collection of episodes resulting in a celebration of a way of life" (148). Not all these episodes feature Jane. The reader learns of Rufus' first day of school, Joe's performance at a dancing school recital, Rufus' scarlet fever. In fact, Jane shares equal billing with her two brothers throughout. But Jane's perspective begins and ends the book. We see the new house which the Moffats move to at the conclusion of **The Moffats** as Jane sees it: "Jane was rather charmed with the long green carpet at the end of which was their tiny little house. It was somehow like looking through the wrong end of a telescope" (274). The

others complain of the long front yard and the lack of apple trees, but the reader knows that Jane's view will eventually be the dominant one, once the others adjust.

As promised in the end of **The Moffats,** Jane does acquire a new friend, Nancy, whose backyard touches on the Moffat property. This friendship is quite satisfactorily developed in the next Moffat book, **The Middle Moffat.** The attraction between the two girls is their shared imagination; and it is one of the few areas that they do share, which makes the friendship really remarkable. Unlike Jane, Nancy has only one other child in her family, lives in an enormous house with servants, and takes music lessons. But the difference in social status makes little difference to this friendship. Jane does not appear envious, only curious, and Nancy is not condescending, apparently pleased to have found such an inventive friend. When they do have a falling out, both girls are unhappy. Nancy eventually admits she was wrong.

Aside from the addition of a best friend, Jane also gains the friendship of the oldest citizen, Mr. Buckle. In an attempt to establish her identity in the family, to have a label for her mother to use in introductions, Jane decides to become the Middle Moffat, although when she tries out the new title on the oldest citizen, she says she is the mysterious middle Moffat. Mr. Buckle takes the introduction in stride, playing Hawkshaw, a movie detective, to her mysterious Moffat. This relationship continues throughout the book, as each takes special interest in the other, Jane because she thinks it her mission to help Mr. Buckle live to be a hundred, Mr. Buckle because he finds Jane amusing. He attends her organ recital (she can't play the organ), and she entertains him while his daughter is at the Browning Society meeting (he beats her at her favorite game, double solitaire). The book ends with Mr. Buckle's birthday celebration and Jane's ride in the dignitaries' automobile as his guest.

Like **The Moffats, The Middle Moffat** is also a series of stories, but this time, most feature Jane. Perhaps the most revealing story about childhood perception involves Jane's attempt to make her mother a brocaded bag for Christmas. She embroiders MAMA with white thread on blue calico. She continues to see it, however, as "brocaded and sparkling with gold and silver threads, all embroidered together into a gorgeous pattern" (154), until she finally looks at it in a mirror and sees it for what it is, "a very plain blue calico bag with a crooked MAMA embroidered on one side and a humped-back daisy on the other" (166).

The last book of the Moffat series features Rufus, the youngest child. World War II intrudes slightly more here than in the other two books. Sylvie works for the Red Cross, Jane knits scarves, and Rufus struggles over a washcloth for the soldiers. When a trainload of soldiers leaves town, Rufus presents his washcloth to one of them personally, with his name attached. Eventually he receives a thank you note from the soldier. The book also contains a section on planting a victory garden. Rufus' beans are wildly successful. In the last chapter, the Armistice is signed and the Moffats look forward to better times.

The shift to Rufus' perspective makes this last book less enjoyable. Rufus' viewpoint is not as insightful as Jane's, perhaps because Rufus seems more straightforward and determined, whereas Jane has the element of the dreamer about her.

Estes has been cited for her full development of characters, and for her contribution to the family story; but other writers could have the same comments written about them. In fact, comments like these do not distinguish *The Moffats* from other books of this type, and have perhaps even led, in part, to the book's dismissal as dated. What singles out *The Moffats* as an important book is Jane's particularly flawed vision of the events of the book, a child's vision captured by Estes as well as any author has done.

Underwritten to the point of being almost unobserved, the humor of most of the situations, which is the saving grace of the book, is anchored in the visual. Joey dancing with the dog, the movement of the ghost in the attic so that even its creators are terrified, the hated sign on the house, the intrusive Murdocks, are all carefully detailed.

Repeatedly people would ask Estes if she were Jane Moffat. Like most authors, she claimed that her characters were composites; but in **"Gathering Honey,"** she admitted that when Jane was "not winning games," when she was "standing on the side-lines, doing nothing, alone" then they were similar (Typescript in the Kerlan Collection). The emphasis should be on "the side-lines," because Jane does have that special gift of observation, and her creator shares it. In the same manuscript, Estes said.

> Sometimes I feel I am a blindfolded person and groping my way toward a book . . . I am the sort of writer who would like to have plenty of time in which to do nothing. Time just to sit, or to stand at the window, or watch the ocean, or people, or to wander up the street or about the house, to pace.

Jane has that kind of time, and that makes *The Moffats* a refreshing change from the fast pace of school and television and lessons and extra-curricular activities into which children are plunged. Sometimes people need that time, especially for contemplation, and it is just that tone of quiet, contemplative observation that *The Moffats* provides for its readers, children and adults alike. People need time to sit on a curb and look through colored glass occasionally.

David L. Russell

SOURCE: "Stability and Change in the Family Saga: Eleanor Estes's *Moffat* Series," in *Children's Literature Association Quarterly,* Vol. 14, No. 3, Winter, 1989, pp. 171-74.

Eleanor Estes's endearing stories of the Moffat family of Cranbury, Connecticut, are much like a charming patchwork quilt, each of its various fabrics evoking in us some fond childhood memory—grandmother's paisley party dress, Uncle Arthur's silk robe, grandfather's nightshirt. As with such a patchwork quilt, the pleasures of Estes's works are derived from the evocative richness of their color, the multiplicity of their designs, and their familiar warmth, rather than from any artfully interwoven grand design. John Rowe Townsend calls Estes "a natural writer; not . . . a born novelist . . . Each [Moffat] book consists of a chain of episodes, linked unobtrusively by a theme which requires little development and imparts little tension . . . " (*A Sense of Story* 80). Caroline Hunt has also pointed out that the episodic structure may, in fact, be most aptly suited to the family story:

> The family's saga is an ongoing chronicle and is punctuated as in real life, by the cycle of the seasons and by such rites of passage as a new school, a new baby, and so on. . . . Events may be arranged so as to have a narrative structure that makes sense, but there is no hint that the family's *life* has a neat pattern. (10)

But the real danger with which episodic chronicles flirt may be the failure to produce the necessary tension requisite of great art. Paul Murray Kendall observes, "All great art achieves much of its force from tension, the exciting state of balance or reconciliation achieved among opposing elements" (16). In literature, this tension is represented by the essentially random and chaotic nature of life juxtaposed against the demand for structure and pattern imposed by the work of art. Consequently, we fault clever and contrived plots, as well as those without any cohesive order or direction.

Estes's reputation as a writer may rely upon a relatively small handful of works, but that reputation is unquestionably solid and the popularity of the Moffats has endured for over forty years now. It is surprising that these books, having achieved the status of minor classics, have attracted so little attention from literary critics. Among the reasons for this critical neglect we may suggest the lack of philosophical depth (although the works are psychologically genuine); the flirtation with a rose-colored view of reality (although Estes generally eschews sentimentality); and the apparent absence of a sophisticated literary design bringing unity to the books (although one of the great achievements of art is to make the work seem artless). Individually, the four books of the Moffat series (*The Moffats* 1941, *The Middle Moffat* 1942, *Rufus M* 1943, and *The Moffat Museum* 1983) suggest a rather casual fragmentation, but viewed together they present a more tightly-knit piece, and somehow the whole is greater than the sum of the parts.

The Moffat Museum, while lacking some of the magic of the earlier books, seems almost to have been written out of necessity, as if Estes felt a driving need to tie up loose ends, to put the edging on the quilt. Estes's pattern, however, was clearly established in the first book, *The Moffats.* In this book we are introduced to the four Moffat children—Sylvie, Joe, Jane and Rufus—and their widowed mother. They are a poor family, but "not poverty stricken," Mama assures them (*The Moffats* 190). And, as Virginia Wolf points out, "the family's lack of money provides what conflict there is in the novel" (148). They live a contented life in their yellow house on New Dollar Street.

One of Estes's greatest strengths is her ability to create a sense of place, deftly weaving colors, sounds, shapes, and smells, settling upon the most salient features:

> New Dollar Street was shaped like a bow. That is it was not a straight street put out by a measuring rod. It had a gentle curve in it like one half of a parenthesis, the first half. Exactly halfway down New Dollar Street was the yellow house where the Moffats . . . lived . . . the yellow house was the best house to be living in in the whole block because it was the only house from which you could see all the way to both corners. (*The Moffats* 5)

The imagery exudes security—the gently curving street reaching to embrace the warm yellow house set comfortably in the middle, from where one may safely survey the happenings in the outside world. At one end of the street are the trolley tracks and the way to the markets; at the other end are the railroad tracks and the way to the wide world. However, we quickly learn that this comfortable and apparently secure world is, in fact, illusory, for in the first chapter we learn that the owner of the yellow house (for the Moffats are renters) has put it up for sale. The sale of the house would force the Moffats to move, and it is the threat of this impending change that provides the unifying focus for the entire book.

Typically of children, the four Moffat siblings react with trepidation to this imminent menace—a reaction resulting partly from the natural need for security that all children have and partly from the natural fear of the unknown. (We must also acknowledge that the Moffat children may have more than the normal need for security since they have lost their father, an event only briefly alluded to in the entire series, but nevertheless very real.) The image of the family, as initially conveyed through the eyes of the children (and it is through their eyes that the events of the novel are revealed), is very much like that of Wordsworth's child in "We Are Seven": the family is a constant and the family unit as they know it always has been and always will be. But Estes knows better, and the need for the family's adaptability becomes an important theme as this book—and indeed the whole series—progresses.

At the outset, the Moffat children see themselves at the center of everything—all roads converge on Cranbury and lead to New Dollar Street, and the simple events of their lives take on heroic proportions. Rufus, the youngest, for example, feels personally responsible for the irascible Hughie Pudge on the first day of school. Jane, in *The Middle Moffat,* imagines herself to be personally responsible for seeing to it that the oldest inhabitant makes it to his one hundredth birthday. That they never feel insignificant or unimportant is a testimony to their mother's loving care. They do, however, posses the uneasy self-consciousness of children, persuaded that the eyes of the world are upon them, and events in their lives become historic occasions.

Estes's style further conveys the childlike point of view in its deceptively naive simplicity and its free, almost rambling, chapter organization. The chapter entitled, "Share and Share Alike," in *The Middle Moffat,* opens with Joe and Rufus playing on stilts and Jane making a daring dash beneath the grocer's horse (much to Mama's displeasure). Mama then sends Jane on an errand to run the sleeve of a bridal gown to the Cadwalladers' for a fitting. Jane watches as the seven Cadwallader sisters titter with excitement and then they give her a five-cent tip. Jane wrestles with the dilemma of how to split five cents equally among the four Moffat siblings. She finally solves the problem by spending the whole lot on a treat for herself. (A less perceptive and more sentimental writer than Estes would undoubtedly have had Jane spend the leftover penny on Mama or perhaps to have had the child buy something for all to enjoy—but how uncharacteristically altruistic of children that would have been.) Then, on Jane's arrival home, the Moffat children engage in a traditional game to divide up the four kittens of Catherine the cat. Jane wins the kitten she had hoped for, although her joy is clouded by the guilt she feels for not having shared her five-cent tip. And thus ends the chapter.

Such a series of loosely-connected events punctuated by modest peaks of excitement, wonder, delight, and worry is typical of Estes's style. As Frances Clarke Sayers has aptly observed, "the vitality of Eleanor Estes derives from the fact that she sees childhood whole—its zests, its dilemmas, its cruelties, its compassion. She never moves outside that understanding, because she never needs to lean upon the crutch of adult concepts or explanations" (258). Estes has more than just sympathy with the child's viewpoint; she has an implicit trust in that viewpoint to speak faithfully and honestly for itself. Therein lies much of her success. And so, the individual chapters wander rather casually from occasion to occasion, but each is tied in a very clear way to the dominant theme—finding comfort, security, and stability in the midst of continual, unpredictable change.

In *The Moffats* these wanderings typically assume the form of circular journeys—Rufus's inadvertent train trip as he seeks to retrieve the runaway Hughie Pudge; the great circle made by Joe, Jane, and Rufus on their adventure with the Salvation Army captain, his wagon and horse; Jane's disastrous errand to Mr. Brooney's delicatessen, which results in her hiding in the bread box to avoid the chief of police, whom she mistakenly believes wants to arrest her; Jane's and Joe's difficult journey to the coal yard in the bitter winter; Rufus's special journey on "his" trolley. The journeys always end at home and that arrival is always depicted as a pleasant experience: "[Joe] pulled down his cap, jerked up his coat collar, stuck his hands in his pockets, and walked home in the rain, whistling" (*The Moffats* 166). Not even the rain can

dampen the spirits when the journey's end is home. However, the most crucial journey in this first book of the series is the last one the family undertakes, and it is, significantly, the only one that is not circular. This, of course, is their departure from the house on New Dollar Street as they head to their new home on Ashbellows Place. That the children at last have the strength to make the journey they had so long dreaded is the result of the accumulated experience of their previous journeys, the ever-widening circles away from home and the venturing into the world abroad.

This pattern of circular journeys is continued in the chapters of the sequel, *The Middle Moffat.* In this book we see the family at the beginning of a new stage in its progress—specifically the adjustment to a new home. The episodes of this work, as the title suggests, focus on Jane and her adjustment to the new house on Ashbellows Place. It is usually noted that Jane's obsessive desire to ensure that the Oldest Inhabitant, Mr. Buckle, reach his one hundredth birthday is the thread that loosely ties the episodes together. The final chapter does bring events full circle with the long-awaited centenary celebration for Mr. Buckle, but the great majority of the book does not concern Mr. Buckle at all. Instead, the chapters are primarily devoted to Jane's efforts at adapting to her life outside the family circle—an adaptation that both Sylvie and Joe have already successfully made. This theme is, in fact, suggested in *The Moffats* when Jane muses that Sylvie scarcely has any time for the family and

> [Jane] was thinking that some day she too would be too old to run up the street and race with the trolley cars. She would have to walk like Mrs. Pudge. How could she bear that? . . . Jane had a feeling that just as surely as that they, the Moffats, were moving away from the yellow house that day, time would take these other keen delights from her, too. (*The Moffats* 277-78)

What we discover in *The Middle Moffat* is that while Jane is correct about the facts—some of these delights are taken from her—she is mistaken about her interpretation. Growing up and putting away childish things can be wonderful adventures in themselves, not to be met with regret, but to be welcomed with zestful anticipation. To realize this, Jane must prove to herself that she has an existence, an individuality, of her own. (She calls herself "the Middle Moffat" in an attempt to define her uniqueness, to give herself identity.) But Jane's adventures into the wide world are careful and measured—in other words, typical of a young child's.

In *The Middle Moffat,* we find the same circular motif as we found in its predecessor. The concluding passages of over half the chapters of this second work of the series make either implicit or explicit references to Jane's returning happily home after some adventure—whether it be returning from her first meal as a guest in a friend's home or from an afternoon of gaming with the Oldest Inhabitant. One of the most notable of these references to a homecoming is to be found in the chapter entitled "Eclipse over Cranbury." Jane has induced her new best friend, Nancy Stokes, to accompany her to desolate Gooseneck Point where they might better observe the solar eclipse. They discover, to their amazement, that they were the only Cranbury residents to brave the cold and journey to the Point. That knowledge brings Jane a great sense of satisfaction—"She had not just watched it from her own front yard" (*The Middle Moffat* 214). This experience becomes an expression of her merging independence, of her growth as an individual. But, we are not surprised to be told that, after this adventure, the two friends "hurried home" (214), an expression of her still equally strong need for a sure and safe harbor. Likewise, in the same book, the chapter describing the performance of "The Three Bears" concludes with a reminder that because of the snug costumes Mama had made for the children, "[They] had nice warm bear pajamas to sleep in for the rest of the winter" (187). The imagery of the comfortable security of the home permeates the children's every action. Consequently, when she is invited to ride in a seat of honor next to Mr. Buckle in the celebratory parade, Jane has indeed made a place for herself outside the family circle. Nevertheless, the family and the home remain central to the end, for Mr. Buckle invites all the Moffats into his fancy parade automobile, and "slowly the limousine rolled home" (290). The clear message is that growing up and change are made more palatable by the presence of the stable anchorage provided by the family and the home. Jane has, over the course of the first two books, developed into a young girl with self-confidence, one who can be entrusted with responsibility, and one who has learned to reach beyond her own family for fulfillment. She is much less solipsistic than when we first met her, and much wiser.

The third book of the series, *Rufus M,* has generally been regarded as less interesting than its predecessors because "Rufus' viewpoint is not as insightful as Jane's, perhaps because Rufus seems more straightforward and determined, whereas Jane has the element of the dreamer about her" (Smith 68; see also Wolf 149). Estes may have realized this, for when she returned to complete the series some forty years later, she returned to Jane's viewpoint. However, *Rufus M* is significantly different from the other books of the series in a number of ways. Not only did Estes experiment with another character's point of view, she chose as her unifying thread an historical occasion—the American involvement in the First World War. It is because of this that we can actually pin dates to the fictional events of the whole series—and even establish the years of the Moffat children's births (they, in fact, closely correspond with those of Eleanor Estes and her siblings).

It is possible to view each successive book of the series as representing a further expansion of a single governing theme: the reaching out and the embracing of increasingly larger worlds on the parts of the Moffat children. The family remains a close unit, but the inevitable sweep of time is changing its nature, first as the family must adapt to a new dwelling place and then as the individual family members begin to discover their own separate identities and forge new extra-familial relationships. In the second book, for instance, Jane finds a new best friend in Nancy Stokes and she develops a friendship with Mr. Buckle. In *Rufus M,* Rufus takes an even bolder step in reaching out to a stranger completely unknown to the family—the soldier for whom he knits a wash cloth. Also in this book, the entire family reaches outside the community—most notably in the planting of the victory garden, thus realizing a national duty, and in the final wishes they make for world peace.

Unfortunately, *Rufus M* also contains some of the more disappointing chapters of the series. In "The Invisible Piano Player," we see a seven-year-old Rufus rather incredibly gullible as he is convinced that an invisible man is the pianist making music at a neighbor's player piano. In "Eyes in the Pipes," both Moffat boys imagine that two gleaming eyes in the unlaid sewer pipes are those of some exotic wild animal. Almost too predictably, the eyes turn out to be those of the Moffats' own Catherine the cat. In the two preceding books, Estes relied on an old familiar pattern for her chapter design, and that is the common folktale pattern of departure, adventure, and homecoming, with each chapter revealing a new experience in the process of the children's growing up. Estes largely abandoned this pattern for much of *Rufus M* and failed to find a satisfactory substitute; consequently, the chapters of this book often seem shallow or fatuous, nor do they so readily fit into a larger scheme.

The conclusion of *Rufus M* is marked by Armistice Day and we are left with the hope of better times to come. Regrettably, where we have been in the course of this book is not so clear—at least in regard to the title character. Rufus seems not to have developed in the course of the year; we see him in the first chapter already an admirably altruistic child, ambitiously knitting a generous wash cloth for a soldier. The events of the book do not alter his character or even significantly expand on it. Virginia Wolf correctly notes that if it were not for Rufus's generally delightful and engaging personality, the book would have little to recommend it (149). Much more than any of the other books, *Rufus M* is a loose collection of only mildly amusing anecdotes about a child in Connecticut in 1919.

The Moffat Museum was not published until 1983—forty years after *Rufus M*—and it is tempting to see this book as having resulted from Estes's need to tidy up loose ends. The four decades separating the writing of this book from that of the other three allowed ample time for nostalgia to develop and there is a pervasive sense of a stroll down memory lane in this latter book. The gathering of Moffat memorabilia for the museum, Sylvie's wedding, Straw Hat Day (a sort of coming-of-age ritual for Cranbury's young men, who now include Joey), and Joey's determination to continue his education despite the fact that economic conditions forced him to drop out of public school at 16 to help support the family—all are events dangerously flirting with sentimentality.

One of the central concerns in *The Moffat Museum* is the marriage of Sylvie. Of all the Moffats, Sylvie plays the smallest role in the books. From the very beginning she is almost too old to possess any real interest for the child reader (or for her brothers and sister through whose eyes we are permitted to observe the family). Sylvie is a typically busy teenager with "Choir rehearsals, plays at the Town Hall, her dances, her friends, her diary, drawing! . . . She was hardly ever at home" (*The Middle Moffat* 39). Of course, what is happening, unbeknownst to Jane who makes these observations, is the widening of Sylvie's circle beyond the home and the family, the inevitable and necessary business of growing up. *The Moffat Museum* is the conclusion of this saga in which change and the passage of time are ameliorated by the constancy of familial love. This notion is interestingly explored when the children establish a museum in their barn with the implicit assumption that their personal possessions and memorabilia are indeed artifacts of general public interest. Their bicycle, affec-

tionately termed "Bikey," for example, becomes "This famous bike! Every member of the family beginning with Sylvie, the real owner . . . a Christmas present when she was ten . . . had learned to ride on it!" (*The Moffat Museum* 9). What the Moffats have come to realize is that their past requires a conscious effort at preservation, that things do change with the passage of time.

The title of this final book carries a double meaning. Literally, of course, it refers to the makeshift museum in the barn containing the family's relics. But for any fan of the Moffat books, to open the pages of this book and enjoy once more the adventures of the exuberant Moffat children is like a visit to a museum of sorts—where memories are recaptured and preserved. The past looms over this book as it does not over its predecessors, and its poignancy results from our realization that, with the Moffats growing up—and leaving home—this is, indeed, the end of the Moffat series. John Rowe Townsend once prematurely defended the sentimentality of the final chapter of *Rufus M* as acceptable for a "farewell to the family whom the reader has come to know well . . . and love greatly" (84). Perhaps we could adapt this justification more appropriately to *The Moffat Museum,* which is the true farewell.

The Moffat Museum is characteristically rich with sensory references suggesting warmth and sweetness: the smell of roses, honeysuckle, coffee, tobacco, hop vines, and double mint, all exuding the memories of a simpler, fresher time. The poignancy of the final chapter of *The Moffat Museum* was inevitable given the direction Estes chose to take. But despite her flirtation with sentimentality, she does not completely succumb. For if the past is evident in this volume, so is the reality of the future. Joey must drop out of school to help support the family. He will attempt to earn his diploma through correspondence courses, but it is clear that this will be no easy task. Joey, like Sylvie just before him, has reached adulthood, and Jane's own rite of passage is not far behind as time carries them all forward in its relentless march.

Estes's message of time and change and adaptability prevented her from creating interminably youthful children with inexhaustible adventures (such as Nancy Drew and the Hardy Boys). At her best, Estes does not write in loosely-connected episodes, but rather in subtle patterns and rhythms, the whole work growing richer and the design growing clearer with each addition. But like the best of artists, she knows the virtue of restraint; she knows when to quit.

In her decision to create a series of the Moffat family stories, Estes also had to decide whether to write each book as a self-contained entity, independent of its predecessors, or to build each new book on the foundations of the preceding one. The former choice (which is, of course, the choice of the lucrative syndicated series represented by Nancy Drew, the Bobbsey Twins, the Hardy Boys) fairly prohibits any meaningful growth—physical or intellectual—in the main characters, lest soon they outgrow their *raison d'etre*. These characters function in a vacuum unaffected by the vicissitudes of life that touch the rest of us, and they remain oblivious to the essence of life. These perpetually youthful protagonists can even be brought up to date, swept into a new era, with virtually no damage to the credibility of their stories. But Estes's choice—that is, to build each book upon the last and to fix it in time—creates the family saga, and while the miscellaneous adventures of the various family members may provide occasional plot intrigue, the reader's ultimate interest is in the growth and maturation of the characters, the nuances of their personalities, and their commentaries on life itself. It is easy to confuse which Moffat episodes belong to which book, but it is impossible to forget the exhilarating characters themselves, just as it is impossible to avoid a strong and affectionate attachment to each of them.

Estes's series has naturally limited the number of books she could reasonably produce about the Moffats (at least without shifting audiences as Louisa May Alcott essentially did with her chronicles of the March family). But the rewards of Estes's series amply compensate for this small sacrifice. Her series allowed her to explore the nature of the family and its peculiar role, in the midst of its own essential transience, in guiding each of us safely and surely through those most difficult and profoundly influential times of our lives—our childhood and our adolescence.

Additonal coverage of Estes's life and career is contained in the following sources published by the Gale Group: *Contemporary Authors,* **Vols. 1-4 Revised, 125;** *Contemporary Authors New Revision Series,* **Vols. 5, 20, 84;** *Dictionary of Literary Biography,* **Vol. 22;** *Junior DISCovering Authors; Major Authors and Illustrators for Children and Young Adults; St. James Guide to Children's Writers; Something about the Author,* **Vols. 7, 56, 91.**

Der Struwwelpeter

Heinrich Hoffmann

(Full name Heinrich Hoffmann-Donner) German physician, poet, and illustrator of picture books.

Major works include *Der Struwwelpeter* (1845), *König Nüssknacker und der arme Reinhold* (1851), *Im Himmel und auf der Erde* (1858), *Prinz Grünewald* (1871).

The following entry presents criticism on Hoffman's *Der Struwwelpeter* (1845).

INTRODUCTION

Hoffmann is remembered as the author of *Der Struwwelpeter*, one of the best-known children's works of the nineteenth century. Originally a scrapbook of rhymes and simple drawings that Hoffmann used to placate the young patients he examined, the work created a sensation among friends who encouraged Hoffmann to publish it. The work comprises ten cautionary tales in verse with accompanying illustrations depicting the terrible fates that may befall naughty children, including Struwwelpeter, who refuses to trim his hair or nails, Harriet who plays with matches, and Konrad who sucks his thumb. The work gained international fame through translation and spawned numerous parodies.

BIOGRAPHICAL INFORMATION

Hoffmann was born in Frankfurt in 1809, the only child of architect Phillipp Jakob Hoffmann and his wife. Hoffmann's mother died soon after his birth, and his father married his late wife's younger sister when Hoffmann was three. Hoffmann attended a succession of schools and ultimately pursued a medical education. In 1829 he left Frankfurt for Heidelberg, where he passed his state examinations and completed his thesis. He returned to Frankfurt in 1834 and finished his doctoral studies. Hoffmann then settled into his profession, lecturing at the Senckenberg Institute of Surgery and developing a private medical practice. In 1840 he married Thérèse Don-

ner, and together they had three children. Shortly after the birth of the youngest, Lina, Hoffmann made a gift of the "Struwwelpeter" scrapbook to his three-year-old son, Carl, for Christmas 1844. Enthusiastic friends and relatives soon begged Hoffmann to publish it, but he insisted that he was not an author of children's books—he was a physician and the author of medical treatises. When the picture book came to the attention of local publishers Rütten and Löning, an agreement was reached to release the work commercially. It was an immediate hit, running into four editions within two months of publication. By 1847 *Der Struwwelpeter* was available in twelve languages, including English, French, Italian, Norwegian, Swedish, and Russian. Following the success of *Der Struwwelpeter*, Hoffmann published adult works, including plays, poems, and songs. He returned to children's literature in 1851 with the picture book

König Nüssknacker und der arme Reinhold (King Nutcracker and the Dream of Poor Reinhold), a Christmas story centering on an ill and impoverished boy who wakes from a fever to find that Christmas trimmings, toys, food, and warm clothing have been provided by more prosperous citizens of the town. Hoffmann used the proceeds of these works to fund the Affenstein, a psychiatric hospital that was his life's dream. The hospital opened in 1864, utilizing the most modern and humane concepts of treatment then available. Hoffmann remained the director of the Affenstein for the balance of his career. He retired in 1883 having been named a senator and *Geheimer Sanitaterath*. He died in 1894.

MAJOR WORKS

Der Struwwelpeter contains rhymes and accompanying illustrations that outline the fates of naughty children. At a hospital for the poor, Hoffmann would entertain his young patients with humorous pencil sketches and stories to relieve anxiety during painful procedures. The sketches include the story of "Johnny-Head-in-the-Air," who never watches where he is going, Harriet, who plays with matches and is consumed in flames, Augustus, who starves after stubbornly refusing to eat his soup, Konrad, who sucks his thumb and ultimately has his thumbs cut off by a tailor, and "shock-headed Peter," who refuses to groom himself and ends up with long, curling fingernails and wild, unruly hair. The book has been criticized for its severity, for punishments that do not fit the crimes. One story, in particular, is condemned for embedded racism, in what was likely intended as an anti-racist message. In the story, the "inky boys," who refused to stop mocking a black youth, are themselves dipped in ink and made even blacker than their victim. Critics charge that making a punishment of being black simply perpetuates the negative racial views that lie at the root of racism, and they point to the stereotypical depiction of the black character in the illustration as further evidence of Hoffmann's racism.

CRITICAL RECEPTION

Initial response to *Der Struwwelpeter* was enthusiastic. In reaction to the bland, moralistic tales that typified German children's literature of the mid-nineteenth century, *Der Struwwelpeter* offered a refreshing approach in its nonsense and exaggeration. The work became a standard in children's libraries for several generations. However, by the late twentieth century, approaches to child-rearing had altered significantly, and many of the situations depicted in *Struwwelpeter* were deemed too harsh or too politically incorrect to share with young children. Taking a sociological approach to the work in "*Struwwelpeter* at One Hundred and Fifty: Norms, Control, and Discipline in the Civilizing Process," Joachim J. Savelsberg noted that while a late-twentieth-century observer might identify many dissimilarities between the stories of *Struwwelpeter* and modern trends in early childhood education, such principles as cultural and racial pluralism, non-violence, and cautions regarding dangerous activities remain constant. According to Savelsberg, "The stories of *Struwwelpeter* are stories about deeds defined as evil deeds and about punishment. Just like overall ideas about crime and punishment, the ideas of *Struwwelpeter* reflect the changing social conditions of its time." Another commentator, Eva-Marie Metcalf assessed the lasting value of *Struwwelpeter* in *The Lion and the Unicorn*, Vol. 20, and noted "Hoffmann created a book . . . that introduced two concepts fundamental for modern children's books, namely child orientation (i.e., an eye to the psyche of the child reader) and high entertainment value (an eye to the desires of the child reader), and he put both in the service of education."

TITLE COMMENTARY

📖 *DER STRUWWELPETER* (1845)

Donald MacAndrew

SOURCE: "The Man Who Invented *Struwwelpeter*," in *The Saturday Book*, Vol. 23, edited by John Hadfield, Hutchinson, 1963, pp. 190-209.

In 1844, as Christmas approached, Carl, only son—as yet—of Dr Heinrich Hoffmann-Donner, a Frankfurt physician, grew giddy with excitement. He was going to see his baby sister Lina for the first time. Also he had been told that this year King Nutcracker would give him something extra special. *Etwas wundervoll!* Something only he would get.

Christmas Eve came at last and, after Carl had been introduced to the fortnight-old Lina in his mama's room, and the curtains were drawn, and the oil lamps lit, he, three-year-old Carl, in his best petticoat, escorted by a big strapping red-armed nursegirl, two maids, and a knifeboy joined the company in the drawing-room. Through all his days this, his earliest memory-picture, was to hang in Carl's mind, a brilliantly lit window in the night of the past.

From the upper branches of the candle-lit tree, which nearly touched the ceiling, hung gilt walnuts, alecampaine, marzipan fruit; from the lower branches hung parcels innumerable; while round the trunk were ranged wonderful Nurenberg toys—a gilt knight on horseback, a pasteboard castle, a Jack-a-dandy. Dominating all was a wooden idol with huge painted head and articulated jaws.

> This was King Nutcracker, King of the Toys,
> Monarch beloved of Good Girls and Boys.

And at King Nutcracker's feet, tied with pink ribbon, lay the surprise.

Scarcely had the long Christmas hymn ended when Carl ran to untie the mysterious parcel. We must hope for his papa's sake that its contents sent him into the required raptures. For Carl's present was a scrapbook containing some drawings that Dr Hoffmann had scribbled for a little boy patient, plus the verses which he used to read aloud in the half-hour before Carl's bedtime.

Neither Carl's joy on discovery of the scrapbook, nor perhaps his chagrin, is recorded. The picture blurs, leaving him a shimmer of anticipation. Our subject is not Carl, but the perennial, exorbitant acclaim that posterity has bestowed upon the crudely coloured scrapbook.

Every *Saturday Book* reader of thirty or over must remember Struwwelpeter—remember at least his strange figure on the cover of the book. There Shock-headed Peter stands, his hair circling his head like a halo, his nails as long as porcupine quills. Wearing a loose collar, a red belted blouse, and green gaiters, he bestrides a pedestal ornamented with scissors and combs. Stamped on our minds at the age of four or thereabouts his image is unerasable.

A minute's reflection will recall the pretty title-page too. Here in a starry paradise an angel with a golden crown and crimson wings sits reading **Struwwelpeter.** On either side of her German child-angels pour trays full of toys on the earth-children below: upon good children who play quietly with their toys, sit properly at table, accompany Mama to church. Framed like an illuminated text by these vignettes is Dr Hoffmann's stern little preface, declaring that his pretty picture book is eligible only as a Christmas gift:

> *Wenn die kinder artig sind*
> *Kommt zu ihnem das Christkind.*

Pretty Stories and Funny Pictures is the subtitle of **The English Struwwelpeter.** And now that this has come back to us fragments of the gay jingly rhymes may start to sing in our heads and the pictures take form in our minds. We must, we feel—after however many decades—reopen the book. How familiar it all seems! Of the ten poems eight tell of naughty little boys, one of a naughty little girl, while set in the midst is the tale of the Green Sportsman who shoots the hares with his long duck-gun. What sticky ends some of these troublesome infants come to! Harriet, disobeying Mama, lights a match and is burnt to a cinder. Augustus, that 'chubby lad', with his 'fat ruddy cheeks', won't drink his soup and very soon starves. And Conrad—if Conrad *will* suck his thumbs, says Mama, 'the great long-red-legged Tailor Man' will come and cut them off. Oh, that nightmare drawing of the Tailor flying through the doorway!

> Snip snap snip! the scissors go,
> And Conrad cries out oh, oh oh!

And, oh, the bland cruelty of the poem's apologue!

> Ah, said Mama, I knew he'd come
> To Naughty little Suck-a-thumb.

Why do these *Pretty Stories* (of little girls being burnt alive) *and Funny Pictures* (of little boys having their thumbs cut off) still attract? Other contemporary books of 'morally useful' children's verse, *The Cowslip, The Daisy,* etc., have, in the past eighty years, been read only by sophisticated adult dabblers in Georgian and Early Victorian antiquariana. No modern child would look at them, or, indeed, be allowed to look at them, for the dire consequences of such modes of preaching to the young have long been stressed. Yet **Struwwelpeter,** the most sanguinary of all babies' books, is reissued each year. Why?

Two reasons occur. One is Dr Hoffmann's superb gift of nonsense. Whether or not he intended to write orthodox children's books—'ethics in popular garb'— the moment he took up pencil or pen his nonsense-logic governed him. Take the three poems just cited. The lady who wrote *The Cowslip* would certainly have caused Harriet to be incinerated for her folly, but she would never have provided two Cassandra-like kittens who by their reiterated wail play Greek chorus to the tragedy:

> 'Tis very, very wrong, you know
> Me-ow Me-ow. Me-o Me-o.
> You'll burn to death if you do so.

One cannot see her allowing her illustrator to draw those same kittens in tears over Harriet's little scarlet shoes, holding big yellow handkerchiefs to their eyes and wearing black crape bows on their tails. One cannot see her letting him put a porcelain tureen marked 'SUPPE' on Augustus's grave. Her Conrad would, of course, get punished. But not by that horripilant tailor. No, no. He would be birched by Papa.

In the didactic literature of the day it is Papa and Mama who distribute awards, the nice kind boy getting the cakes while the cruel boy is beaten. But *Struwwelpeter* contains no nice children. Nor is there any dunce's cap, back-board, or birch. Papa's or Mama's role is, firstly, to raise an admonitory finger; later, serenely to say 'I told you so'. The naughtiness of Harriet and Augustus brings down its own punishment. So, too, with Johnny Head-in-Air, Fidgety Phil, Robert.

Only when Dr Hoffmann treats of nigger-baiting does he let retribution come by external agency. The woolly-headed blackamoor—you remember?—walks abroad in the noonday sun. He unfurls his green umbrella. Suddenly three small boys run on to the scene and begin to jeer. A stentorian voice bids them desist. We turn the page and, lo! tall Agrippa, 'so tall he nearly touched the sky' looms up, another Spring-heeled Jack, with his beard and his dressing-gown. He lifts the three boys like puppies and dips them in his 'mighty inkstand'. The blackamoor has the last laugh. For his tormentors are now blacker than he.

Thus Heinrich Hoffmann's two claims to originality merge. He removed those conventional prigs, the stern papa and the saintly child, and replaced them with such feats of his frolic imagination as the Magus of the inkstand and Good Dog Tray. The picture of the brown water-spaniel Tray, seated in his young master's chair, wearing his young master's bib, and wolfing his young master's supper, while Cruel Frederick upstairs gets dosed with 'nasty physic', fully satisfies the child's natural hunger to see the biter bit.

But was this planned? Or did Heinrich—as distinct from Dr Hoffmann—sometimes see with a child's eyes, see a child's world of primary colours, of fun, of fear, of pity, of ruthlessness? To decide that we must glance at the Herr Doktor.

Three childhood influences went to the make-up of Heinrich Hoffmann: the cold rectitude of his father, his stepmother's gaiety and love, and, much more potent, the character of his birthplace, Frankfurt-am-Main, the Free City, which marked and moulded all its sons.

Let us begin with his father. Philipp Jakob Hoffmann, son of a cabinet-maker, was an architect. He won early fame with his designs in the Ionic style for the Rothschild Bankhaus at Frankfurt, and later, when the Romantic Movement suddenly flowered, and the Middle Ages became a cult, he restored some of the city's Romanesque and Gothic churches. At thirty-six he took a house in the Bochenheimerstrasse and married a rich wine-merchant's daughter; he was, he felt, decidedly a Frankfurt notable.

Heinrich, their only child, was born, a seven-month baby, on June 21, 1809. His mother died shortly afterwards. When Heinrich was three his father married his late wife's younger sister, Nettchen. It was for both a marriage of convenience; but little though Nettchen might love her husband, she idolized her stepson, in whose eyes she seemed—and all his days was to seem—a picture-book angel.

By his schoolmasters—he was sent in all to five schools—and by his grave, touchy, hyper-conscientious papa, Heinrich was imbued with every correct principle, while Mama Nettchen, whose cosy charm and playfulness were the joy of her select coffee circle, added sweetness to the diet.

But what of Frankfurt, the birthplace, the environment? Goethe, another native, had called the Frankfurters 'pig-headed' and 'Philistine', and Bismarck, their Prussian representative from 1851 to 1858, groaned over the 'dreary skittishness of their attempts at humour'. Still, this is the verdict of Titans. Middling people coming to the Free City from Germany's toy kingdoms, princedoms, duchies, grand duchies, and margraviates were favourably impressed. This community of stock-jobbers, they found, displayed the most unlooked-for contrasts of character.

That the Babel of beaver-hatted and drab-coated brokers and share-pushers who thronged the Frankfurther Börse each midday should consist mainly of church-going and church-parading family men one might expect; also that their wives' attire in *Dom* church or synagogue should be of a stupefying richness: but not that the churches they attended should for choice be bare, whitewashed, Lutheran: not that their domestic lives should be dowdy and philosophical. *Non*-Sabbath ostentation was in Frankfurt a cardinal sin. Even the big banking families, the Von Bethmanns, Metzlers, Rothschilds, recognized that. By 1830 the Rothschilds were Europe's Kings of High Finance. They had branches in London, Vienna, Paris, Naples. Yet even they, when not contracting ten-billion-mark foreign loans, were living frugally, philanthropically.

Frankfurt's history was written on her town face. The city centre upheld the old patriarchal way of life, a medieval backcloth that had seen the Antwerp merchants of the sixteenth century. But with the increase of trade the world's money mart had expanded. Fringing the zone of steep-stepped red sandstone gables and winding cobbled lanes was now an area of broad streets and neo-classic mansions, offices, exchange buildings, banks. Architecturally, old and new Frankfurt were centuries apart. Yet they were blended by an overall tone: a lack of ornament, a plainness, evident alike on house-front and on hearth, which spoke of the proud egalitarianism that was the citizen's birthright. Here everybody mingled. Catholic dined with Lutheran, Gentile with Jew, merchant senator and banker prince with humble schoolteacher, pastor, medico. With this magnificent heritage for ballast how should a young Frankfurter not pity the natives of all towns but his? Or, having made his pile, not aim at joining the bead-roll of Frankfurt's benefactors and win local immortality by endowing a hospital or a school?

Such posthumous fame had been desired, passionately desired, by Philipp Hoffmann. But he saw now that it could not be. No *strasse gasse haus allee weg* would ever bear his name. The municipal authorities who had lately appointed him Inspector of Roads and Waterways would see to that. Besides, younger architects had supplanted him. Still, there was Heinrich. A civic edifice might one day commemorate his son. Let Heinrich hack away at the glum rock-face of life till public honour, most glittering of all life's prizes, should rain on him.

Heinrich, at twenty, was studying medicine at the Burg-hôpital. The next step, if he got his certificate, would be Heidelberg. But here his papa demurred. Philipp had heard stories of Heidelberg student morals, and he feared for his son. For Heinrich, though intellectually brilliant, was pleasure-loving. A keen dancer, figure-skater, and guitar-player, he was in demand at all parties and balls. He had not his papa's fine ascetic good looks, but his tall forehead, his funny mobile face, and his agile body: these, shot through with a tearing zest for life, made him, as all Frankfurt said, captivating. Far better, then, that Heinrich should pursue his studies and qualify here at home. Hadn't scores of the first doctors done so? Didn't the curriculum at the Burg-hôptial cover all medical, surgical, and obstetrical knowledge? Didn't . . . ?

But to Heidelberg, of course, Heinrich went. Mama Nettchen, defying her husband by abetting Heinrich, as was her wont, paid half his fees, and then, through her influence with the trustees of the Von Bethmann grant to help poor medical students, procured him the other half. Thence-forward Frankfurt saw nothing of young Hoffmann for five years. Nothing till his father's death in 1834, when he returned to the city crowned with glory. At Heidelberg he had passed his *Staatsexamen.* At Hallé he had written his thesis *de Phlegmasia Alba,* which got published and was at once acclaimed. Now, home in Frankfurt, he quickly took his doctorate. He then lectured on anatomy at the Senckenberg Institute of Surgery, and started building a practice.

After her bereavement Mama Nettchen shared a small apartment with Heinrich. They were poor, laughter-loving, sociable. She, who for the past ten years had had to forgo all entertaining owing to the sardonic remarks of her husband, again frequented whist parties and *Kaffee Klatsches.* Heinrich was all over the city. For him Frankfurt was a townscape limned in bright paint-box colours. He inaugurated the Tutti Frutti Club, the membership of which included his particular friends, Eduard and Gustav Passavant, plus doctors, jurists, university professors, Fröbel instructors, and teachers from the Stadtiches gymnasium and the New Model School. To qualify for election one had to be a poet. Every self-respecting youth in every German state had scribbled poetry for the past twenty years, but not till after Heinrich's departure for Heidelberg did the mode catch on in Frankfurt.

Each summer vacation, with satchels and notebooks, the club went for a tramp on the Taunus Mountains. The stage props of late German Romanticism were all there. True, Heinrich chiefly sang of forest inns, their hosts, their Hebes, their *Schweinfleisch,* their hock. But midnight crags and ruined towers could also inspire him. Occasionally, too, he would affect the half-humdrum, half-fairy-tale, Biedermeier convention.

Reading parties had also come into vogue. After school and office hours the young poetasters would flock to the *salon* of an imperious bluestocking lady, who, when the heel-clicking, hand-kissing ritual was done, would allot each one a part in a Schiller tragedy, or some stanzas from a metaphysical bard, or a chapter from a Scott or Miss Edgeworth novel. It was at a Maria Edgeworth reading that Heinrich met his wife. Hardly had the session started when the hostess introduced some newcomers to the town, a brother and three sisters named Donner. All three fräuleins were beauties, but the youngest, true to fairy-tale form, was a ravishing beauty.

Thérèse Donner, when she distracted a whole roomful's attention from *Ormond,* and enslaved Heinrich, was seventeen. She had lately come from Brussels, where her father, a native of Rosenfeldt, was partner in a firm of cloth-merchants. Her mother was dead. Settled now in Frankfurt, the young Donners were caught in an eddy of boating parties, reading parties, aesthetic teas, and musical evenings. At these symposia Heinrich had eyes only for lovely moon-faced Thérèse. Three years passed. The *jünges mädchen*'s long golden plaits were looped up and coiled in a *jüngfrau*'s braided coronet. And Heinrich was still courting.

Then, in the fourth year, Papa Donner died, and at last the nuptials of Frankfurt's best-liked young man and loveliest girl could be solemnized in the Katherinen Kirche, on March 5, 1840. The Hoffmanns then took a first-floor apartment fronting the Main. Thérèse's married sister lodged beneath, and Mama Nettchen overhead.

This is the period of *Struwwelpeter.* Early each Monday in 1844 the general practitioner Dr Hoffmann-Donner (as he now styled himself) left the house carrying a stout carpet bag that ordinarily held rhubarb, senna pods, and squills, but which today bulged with surgical instruments. He entered the great horse-market in the Göetheplatz. Here were carriages for hire. Here for twenty groschen was leased to Heinrich each Monday a battered old shandrydan with an ancient flea-bitten screw between the shafts. Down the aristocratic Zeil, and through the outskirts, he rattled in this conveyance, pulling up finally before the Kästenhôpital (poor-box hospital). *Struwwelpeter*'s 'onlie begetter' was a child patient at this institute. To coax the small dim face into a smile before the hot poultice was applied, or the castor-oil gulped, Dr Hoffmann would produce pencil and paper and tell a story in pictures. Portrayals of the dreadful fates of disobedient children would, he found, provoke squirms of half-fearful delight. Home in his consulting-room he would invent rhymes to accompany the drawings.

Genius is said to be a supreme capacity for taking pains. Now the book whose manuscript Dr Hoffmann gave to his son Carl on that memorable Christmas Eve has, beyond question, achieved a certain immortality. Yet it is doubtful if the composition of his *chef d'œuvre* gave this good paterfamilias a single headache. What happened, then, when he sat down to scribble? Was deathless verse turned out by some sort of heavenly fluke?

However it was, his tutelary angel at once took control. At Lina's christening party Mama Nettchen showed the scrapbook to the bluestocking lady. She commanded Heinrich to publish it. Heinrich laughed. '*Nein, nein,* gracious lady, I do not write for children.' Nor could his colleagues at the Senckenberg persuade him. But when Rütten and Löening, editors of the *Literarische Anstalt,* approached him, and assured him he had written a probable best-seller, he yielded. In the end he became enthusiastic. 'I visited the lithographer daily', he records, 'to see that my drawings were not "artistically improved". I made him copy them line by line, and I checked each one of the stones'; a statement inexpressibly droll when one remembers the naive chromo-lithograph illustrations to the first impression.

In cardboard covers—then a novelty—and priced at fifty-nine Kreuzer, the book ran into four editions in Frankfurt within two months of publication. This was in 1845. In 1846 *Struwwelpeter* must have adorned Christmas tables in every city, town, and village in Germany. In 1847 a Leipzig publisher brought out editions in twelve different languages. For Britain, **Shock-headed Peter;** for America, **Slovenly Peter; Pierre Ebouriffé** (France); **Pierino Porcospino** (Italy); **Busteper** (Norway); **Pelle Smusk** (Sweden); **Strepka Rastrepka** (Russia); **Joáo Felpudo** (Portugal); etc. Heinrich had, by accident, produced what an English obituarist was fifty years later to call 'The King of Nursery Books for the children of Europe and America'.

Heinrich was now a public figure. Every Sunday at noon all Frankfurt's public men, the high officials of the *Stadt,* the senators, their wives, children, governesses, tutors, and footmen, were on view on the Wallenlagen Promenade. In this setting of splendid liveries, rich Turkey shawls, green or red gingham gamps, suave lawns, and blazing parterres, the Hoffmann family made a modest showing. They had only three children, attended by one nursemaid. Little Carl and Eduard, moreover, wore orthodox peaked caps, belted smocks, and pantaloons; little Lina, pigtails and pantalettes. Yet it was at these unostentatious Hoffmanns that Frankfurt's visitors—in 1851—chiefly gaped. In their eyes the Frau Doktoren's dark Raphaelesque draperies, worn to enhance her fair madonna-style beauty, if slightly eccentric, made the Sabbath weeds of the Oberburgmeister's wife and the Hof Marshal's wife look frumpy and provincial. The Herr Doktor, in his chimney-pot hat and plain black coat, appeared more urbane than the bigwigs who were continually saluting him. Well might he smile, that little forty-two-year-old doctor. Had not his one book conquered half the world?

Heinrich, in fact, was far from pleased. Throughout two continents, and in Brazil, it seemed he was known as '*Struwwelpeter* Hoffmann'. He, an anatomist, pathologist, psychiatrist, and alienist; he, whose dissertations **On the Pituitary Gland** and **Concerning the Physiology and Nature of Hallucination** were standard works; he, who had done so much to aid the city's suffering humanity; he was, apparently, to figure in the *Stadt* annals as the creator of a nursery book.

But wait. That same year—1851—the Kästenhôpital produced a daughter institute, the new Nervenklinik. Hoffmann, as specialist in nervous ailments, was appointed Herr Direktor. Looking about him, the Herr Direktor could not but see that the place needed thousands of gulden spending on it. How to raise them? Half the royalties of *Struwwelpeter* he put by for the children: the other half Thérèse spent on dress. Still, spurious *Struwwelpeter*'s now crammed all the bookshops. And Rütten and Löening were imploring him to do another book. Why not comply, then, and let whatever accrued be the foundation stone of his ideal clinic?

In the five years that passed between Heinrich's first and his second *Kinderbuch*—or *Struwwelpeterbuch* as the new genre was at once called—Rütten and Löening had issued some more, professedly adult, literature from his pen: poems, plays, fables, a political squib, and a book of songs, **The Breviary of Marriage.** Each of these had made a short fizz and then died. They are written to specifications: goody-goody-baddy moralistic soup thickened with some extremely lumpy farce. Heinrich Hoffmann was no writer for grown-ups.

However, Christmas 1851 saw his second juvenile picture book. **King Nutcracker and the Dream of Poor Reinhold** was to enjoy for twenty years in America and Britain a popularity that rivalled that of *Struwwelpeter.* Three English translations were made, the best being by J. R. Planche, the famous deviser of burlesques, extravaganzas, and pantomimes for Drury Lane Theatre. Indeed, **King Nutcracker** IS a Christmas pantomime in verse.

The curtain rises on the Frankfurt shops at Christmas Eve. The author reminds us that not all children at this holy-tide get sweets and toys. In Scene Two a poor widow's son tosses on his pallet in a high fever. Midnight strikes and an angel floats into the hovel.

Follows the Transformation Scene. The angel gives Reinhold a box of bricks wherewith to build a model town, and this, while the hovel disappears into the flies and the wings, takes on the dimensions of a real town. Scene Four: A Square in Toy Town. Taran-tara! Taran-tara! A scarlet trumpeter struts by announcing that King Nutcracker will pay a visit of state. King Nutcracker enters and calls a review of his household troops. Whereupon the Royal Footguards, the Dragoons, the Artillery in the form of a pastry cook dragging in a nine-pounder cannon loaded with bull's-eyes, a Noah's Ark, and a ballet of *Struwwelpeter* characters successively take the stage. At last, the play done, His Majesty summons his charger, a gaily bedight rocking-horse, and gallops away, while Reinhold wakes—Scene Five—to find that food and warm clothes have been brought to the hovel, likewise a Christmas tree hung with all the toys of his dream. The poem concludes with the smug reflection that whatever may now be the joy of mother and son, thrice blessed are the supposedly rich neighbours who have left these gifts.

Yes, it is pi stuff. And derivative too. The concept of the poor boy and the angel has a distinct flavour of Hans Andersen and Grimm; and Heinrich's great namesake, Amadeus Hoffmann, had, some fifty years earlier, written of King Nutcracker and the Land of Sweets. Nevertheless, Heinrich's version has an undoubted charm. And his illustrations had enormously improved. He himself deemed it his masterpiece, and the book is still popular in Germany.

His next nursery book, **Im Himmel und auf der Erde,** found him still in angelic vein. Its principal poem, **'Saturday in Heaven',** shows child-angels beating their cloud mattresses, polishing up the moon, giving an extra lick of gold paint to the stars, and milking cows on the Milky Way, prior to singing in the Heavenly Choir on Sunday morning. Admirably suited for wet Sunday mornings here below in 1854.

Bastien the Lazybones, 1858, is more fun. Space forbids our following that big idle galoot Bastien through his many misadventures between our first sight of him playing truant from school, and his burial in the same cemetery as the naughty *Struwwelpeter* children. But they are delightful, and since Heinrich, as children's author, was to produce nothing else for thirteen years, young readers must have feared that his tomb also lay thereabouts. Well, it didn't. The reason for his silence was that another vision now filled the Doctor's sky.

Dr Hoffmann used to call 1851, when he became senior consultant of the Kästenhôpital's new nerve clinic, 'the deciding date in my career'. This was true. But not on account of his new job. What decides an imaginative man's career is, surely, a sudden compelling change of vision, and some time in 1851 there glimmered in Hoffmann's imagination the frail scaffolding of a project that was, in a remarkably short time, to develop walls, windows, roof, porches, and doors, and to dilate till it filled his mind's eye. Frankfurt's ideal asylum stood entire in its author's mind eight years before the first brick was laid.

That summer Hoffmann spent his vacation travelling about Germany and Austria looking at the latest thing in mental homes. He returned laden with notes, jottings, ideas. No high wall round the institute at Mecklenberg Schwerein, Illenau's barred windows disguised by filigree ironwork. Each inmate to be given a ploy suited to his abilities, whether cooking, tailoring, shoemaking, carpentry, gardening. Handcuffs and strait-jackets to be used only in extreme cases. Therapy to be based on friendship and trust between doctor and patient, co-operation, encouragement in self-expression, individuality, love. Naturally when, glowing with enthusiasm, he poured out these wildcat schemes to the Board of Health there were inevitably the usual jokes about whether he oughtn't himself to be inmate of a home.

Neither the Board of Health nor the *Stadtrat* positively refused this romantic doctor permission to build his mad-house. They simply said he must raise the money first. Then they dismissed the matter, confident that by making him no grant they had dispersed his mirage. But they were reckoning without the doctor's radiant optimism. Also his tremendous popularity in Frankfurt. The next thing they heard was that he was holding a public meeting at which he spoke of the cramped quarters and obsolete treatment at the city asylum. Then came his series of articles in the *Frankfurter Intelligenzblatt*. Then he distributed five thousand pamphlets. Then he called on the wealthier burgesses with his collecting-box. Then he organized a public collection. But only when they learnt that a neighbouring *Freiherr* had given 100,000 gulden to his scheme, and the Heiliggeist hospital another 100,000, did these rather bovine officials take alarm.

What with bequests and subscriptions, the revenues of **King Nutcracker,** and those of the *Frankfurter Hinkenden Boten* (a humorous journal he had edited from 1849 to 1851), Heinrich amassed in a wonderfully short time the 380,000 gulden postulated by the

authorities. It was for them now to purchase a site. As might be expected, they prevaricated. They dithered, not saying yes or no for five years. Meantime Heinrich met opposition from another quarter. Thérèse had heard that in his perfect asylum the doctors and their families were to live on the premises. Propinquity to madmen, life in an institute, was, apparently, expected of *her!* In vain did her brother and sister advise her that Heinrich was of those who build cloud castles all their days: *she* descried about him the aura of one whose vision would materialize. He seemed so utterly immune. Her rages, and the hubbub created by his in-laws on her behalf, were, she surmised, for Heinrich a disturbance in remote outer space.

In 1859 appeared his **Observations upon and Experience of Mental Disease and Epilepsy,** 175 closely written pages with graphs, case-histories, and tables, covering every form of psychosis from mild imbecility to blaring madness, and incorporating diagnoses of hysteria, melancholia, megalomania, religious mania, nymphomania, etc. Let it be said at once that this exhaustive encyclopaedia brought nothing new to medical science. Though Hoffmann had by now a large empirical knowledge of his subject, he made no discoveries, and does not consequently figure in medical history. Here were collated, however, for the first time, the revolutionary findings of certain French, Swiss, and German psychiatrists, with special regard to the interaction of mental and physical states, a phenomenon which, though more or less accepted everywhere else, still aroused hostility in Frankfurt. All innovations would be howled down in Frankfurt for some ten years, and then, in the eleventh year, overnight, the wind would change. Dr Hoffmann's book effected such a change. 'A new asylum! The new science! Lunacy reform!' became the cry.

That year the Municipality purchased nearly thirty acres to the north of the city. 1863 saw the first hundred patients erecting a wattle fence round the garden of an establishment built to house two hundred. In 1864 Hoffmann's vision was realized. 'The Affenstein' had been planned as a theatre for that system of healing which its founder had advocated from the beginning, with one wing devoted to workshops, one to recreation rooms, a concert hall, and so on. Structurally the interior was a synthesis of some ten up-to-date sanatoria which Dr Hoffman and the architect had visited while touring north Europe in 1860. They had decided upon a plain old-fashioned frontage. Here the Municipality jibbed. We provided the ground, it said, therefore we ought to have a say. As a result, the Affenstein was encumbered with a fussy neo-German-Gothic façade, which all Frankfurt deplored.

Hoffmann's flair for organization, joined to the intuitive sympathy which won him the confidence of every stricken person and every child, gave a distinctive hue to his reign at the Affenstein. Throughout those twenty-four years, it is said, only three people incurred his displeasure: two students who professed to be Darwin disciples, and a votary of Schopenhauer. To the superintendent of the Affenstein—sane, progressive, bonhomous, whose entry into a ward was 'like a sunrise', and who had embellished the main corridor with holy pictures—Darwinism and the new philosophy were sores erupted from that rank mid-century dogma of free thought, which, if not checked, would bring down fire from heaven.

Other glimpses of the superintendent in asylum hours, however, reveal the practical Dr—as opposed to simple Heinrich—Hoffmann: Dr Hoffmann in his sanctum preparing the monthly clinical report; Dr Hoffmann in the big dayroom ordering his stretcher-bearers to carry a man who has collapsed, kicking and vomiting, while playing bagatelle, to the isolation wing, *not* the violent ward; Dr Hoffmann, with the victim's hellish laughter still ringing in his ears, discussing bromides with his house apothecary. When the Affenstein opened, Dr Hoffmann was a *Sanitaterath Zeit*. Imperial Germany was to make him *Geheimer Sanitaterath*.

In 1866, the year of the Affenstein's inaguration, the Prussian Federals had annexed Frankfurt, and in 1871 the city became part of the German Empire. As senator, and *Geheimer Sanitaterath,* Hoffmann now stood on the top-most peak. But he was lonely. His children had long since grown up: Carl was a doctor of law, Eduard was studying law, and Lina had married one of her brothers' lawyer colleagues. Thérèse now received fashionable poets at her coffee parties . . . he still had Thérèse, but . . . Then, suddenly, he again felt the pull of literature. Lina's children, he would write something for them. So it was that in 1871, at the age of sixty-two, Heinrich produced his fifth, last, longest, and incontestably his loveliest, *Kindermarchen.*

How briefly to describe ***Prinz Grunewald and Perlensein, with her Dear Donkey:*** its poetry, its oddity; the broad grin which, like the face on a kite, intermittently dances above the characters, now sailing into the King's council chamber, now penetrating the forest deeps, now drawing its face close to ours as if to share the joke? No adumbration could do the story justice. Enough, then, to say that the tale is of its kind perfect; that the author's illustrations are by far his best; that the telling owes much to Heinrich's great friend Berthold Auerbach, a famous children's author; but that it is not lit by genius, and so has been forgotten.

The Affenstein was Dr Hoffmann's real bid for immortality. On October 9, 1877, the Emperor Wilhelm I paid Frankfurt, as part of his kaiserdom, a state visit, and all the senators were invited to dinner at the Main Post Office: demi-uniform, or tails and white tie: official. On the great evening the Emperor, passing down an avenue of boiled shirts, stopped and addressed Heinrich thus: 'We so admire your work.' Heinrich construed this as a compliment on the Affenstein. As the guests sat at coffee, the Imperial President of Police approached him. Heinrich faced this functionary with some misgivings, fearful that his popping sugar-plums into his pocket for his grandchildren had been detected. But no, he was ushered into the Imperial presence. 'When,' asked the Kaiser, 'will you give us another children's book?' 'Majesty, my duties at the Affenstein——' But Kaiser Wilhelm waved the Affenstein aside. '***Struwwelpeter*** now . . . we have so enjoyed ***Struwwelpeter.*** . . . '

Six years later Dr Hoffmann's professional jubilee was celebrated. Five years after that he retired.

On leaving the Affenstein, Heinrich and Thérèse took an apartment in the nearby Gruneburgweg. There, on September 20, 1894, Heinrich died. His German obituarists, while doing the *Geheimer Sanitaterath* proud, hinted that the therapeutic art as he expounded it had served its turn. They were right. The nineteenth century was ebbing fast. Practices that Heinrich had sternly discountenanced—such as the analysis of hysteria by hypnotism—had lately been adopted at the Affenstein, while from Vienna and Zürich came tidings of new bizarre suns metamorphosing the psychopathic sky. Leipzig, moreover, could boast an ultramodern lunatic asylum, a pattern for all future establishments. Soon the entire house that Heinrich built would be as Gothic as its façade.

When in 1928 the Affenstein was demolished, few could say who was its founder. Yet in another context his name was known to all the world. Sixteen years earlier the Frankfurt papers had recorded the passing, at the age of ninety-two, of 'Thérèse Hoffmann-Donner, widow of the world-renowned children's author'.

Dr Hoffmann's memorials, scattered about Frankfurt, are a graph of his posthumous fame. His grave in the Hauptfriedhof is inscribed *Geheimer Sanitaterath,* and when, rather later, it was decided to give his name to a street, a lane running alongside the Frankfurter Nervenklinik was chosen. But today the little Heinrich-Hoffmann-Straasse skirts a clinic all steel, glass, and reinforced concrete, as different from anything Dr Hoffmann knew as its regimen is from his prescriptions. Psycho-therapy, psycho-analysis, the Unconscious—these have thrown into obscurity the once progressive nineteenth-century psychiatrist, just as the American Army H.Q., built on its site, has effaced his life's dream, the Affenstein. Only Struwwelpeter-Hoffmann lives on. The plaque on the house in the Gruneburgweg, unveiled in 1957, has *Hier wohnten der Schopfer von Struwwelpeter* written on it, and when, that same year, a worthier monument was bespoken, the graceful Struwwelpeter fountain in the Niederrad Stadeon was erected.

In Britain, for twenty years after his creator's death, *Struwwelpeter* continued, a hardy perennial in every bookshop. Then, one night, suddenly, he disappeared. D.O.R.A. had come into force. The Kaiser Kruhn tulips were uprooted from the Corporation Gardens, the German bands quitted the esplanades, and the words 'Made in Saxony' were struck off the toys in the sixpenny bazaars. As to *Shock-headed Peter,* a usurper stood on his plinth: *Swollen-headed William,* E. V. Lucas's lampoon on Wilhelm II.

The Kaiser was defeated. And though for some time people with German names were still sent to Coventry, *Struwwelpeter* at once returned to the children's counter.

In March 1944 the old medieval Frankfurt, with the high peaked roofs and timbered façades, was consumed in a holocaust of ashes. But no incendiary bomb hit *Struwwelpeter.* Even today, when the bookshops are crammed with space-and-sputnik annuals, two English publishers reissue *Struwwelpeter* regularly each autumn.

Heinrich Hoffmann achieved immortality with twenty-four pages of jingly rhymes and amateur drawings. Was ever Mount Parnassus so easily scaled?

L. Mosheim

SOURCE: "*Struwwelpeter*: Yes or No?" in *The Junior Bookshelf,* Vol. 27, No. 6, December, 1963, pp. 330-32.

When I was selling children's books, long years of experience taught me always to have *Struwwelpeter* in stock, but to keep it safely on the shelves and to avoid any conspicuous display.

Sooner or later I would be asked for it by someone who remembered *Struwwelpeter* fondly from his childhood and was delighted that it was still in print. On the other hand, if the book was on the display stand, I could be sure that a customer would pick it up and exclaim: "O that awful book, I would never, never give it to my child!"

I have been wondering what is so special about this picture book, written in 1845 by a German doctor, that it should arouse so much controversy still.

One thing is certain: the book still has a strong attraction for very young children. The situations are taken from everyday life and so are familiar to them, and the illustrations are understood without any difficulty. Children accept the picture of Mother with long skirt and bonnet and Father with whiskers as figures of authority and are not troubled by their strange appearance. The text consists of ten cautionary tales, put into easily remembered rhymes, each telling of an adventure which happened to a child who misbehaved. Only once is an adult the chief character: The Man that went out Shooting. This is, by the way, the weakest of the ten tales.

The author never bores his readers with long descriptions. All the stories have a strong climax and a clearly indicated moral where naughtiness is punished and good behaviour rewarded.

Dr. Heinrich Hoffmann was a well known general practitioner in Frankfurt a. M. He designed the *Struwwelpeter* as a Christmas present for his three years-old son after having searched the shops in vain for a suitable book. He disliked the sombre and pious fare offered to him, because he wanted to amuse his child as well as to instruct him. Of course, the good doctor believed as did all his Victorian contemporaries, that children should be seen and not heard. He starts the book with: "When the children have been good, that is, be it understood, good at meal-times, good at play, good all night and good all day . . . "

Seht, ihr lieben Kinder, seht,
Wie's dem Philipp weiter geht!
Oben steht es auf dem Bild.
Seht! Er schaukelt gar zu wild,
Bis der Stuhl nach hinten fällt;
Da ist nichts mehr, was ihn hält;
Nach dem Tischtuch greift er, schreit.
Doch was hilft's? Zu gleicher Zeit
Fallen Teller, Flasch' und Brot.
Vater ist in großer Not.
Und die Mutter blicket stumm
Auf dem ganzen Tisch herum.

An illustration from Der Struwwelpeter.

The moral in these cautionary verses is the main point of the difference of opinion among customers. It has been said that the description of how bad boy Frederick tormented the animals could put ideas into a child's head, and that most of the punishments are much too severe compared with the crime committed. I do not think that there is any danger that a child would imitate cruel Frederick, but the second point cannot be easily disregarded.

Children are often tougher than we think. The picture of Shock-headed Peter will probably just make them laugh, and they will not worry about the outcome of Robert's involuntary flight into space. Of course, it may well be against all modern principles to make children eat what they dislike, and sensitive children could be frightened by the fate of soup-hating Augustus. The picture of foolish Harriet being burnt to death might well produce nightmares, but it cannot be denied that the habit of playing with matches could have a far more disastrous result! A warning of such severity is often needed.

There is one story which even the most devoted admirer of **Struwwelpeter** cannot defend—the hideous picture of the tailor cutting off the thumbs of little

Conrad, who sucked his fingers. I know some parents who approved of **Struwwelpeter,** but father thought it wise to paste the story of Suck-a-Thumb together with the result that his little daughter pried at the hidden pages till she could see the original pictures! Even though Dr. Hoffman did not know Freud, he was certainly aware of the fascination children derive from being a little frightened.

The author also indulges in "Schadenfreude." Dog Tray laughs as he enjoys the wonderful meal originally prepared for cruel Frederick, who gets nasty medicine instead. Even the harmless little fishes add insult to injury, when they are obviously delighted at the sight of Johnny Head-in-Air dripping all over.

Dr. Hoffman's sense of humour does not always show itself in such a crude way. He has a warm feeling for the underdog, who always comes out on top in the end. The hunter, not the hare, is shot, and the gang of naughty boys who paid no heed to Aggrippa's warning: Leave the black-a-moor alone, for if he tries with all his might, he cannot change from black to white "are dipped into an inkstand" till "they are black, as black can be."

The author certainly has a wonderful imagination and often his sense of fun overcomes his desire to preach a lesson. This is most often seen in the pictures. Augustus' grave is adorned with the despised soup dish. The delicious food, which was to make Fidgety Philip's dinner, is replaced by a pair of birches. Even the mourning cats, who cry till their tears make a little pool, have their tails decorated with poor Harriet's red hair ribbons, although we had just been told that only the scarlet shoes were found among Harriet's ashes.

Struwwelpeter right or wrong? Everyone must decide for himself—and I would not try to answer the question. Two English publishers (George Routledge & Sons Ltd. and Blackie & Son Ltd.) certainly think it worthwhile to keep the book alive. Both use the same excellent anonymous translation of the German verse, and they have never changed the original illustrations drawn by the author.

Jack Zipes

SOURCE: "Down with *Heidi,* Down with *Struwwelpeter,* Three Cheers for the Revolution: Towards a New Socialist Children's Literature in West Germany," in *Children's Literature,* Vol. 5, 1976, pp. 162-80.

The term "classical" is a difficult one to define, especially when discussing children's literature, since children do not determine what books they want to read, nor are they encouraged to evaluate and produce them. Classical children's books are essentially those standard works which have been selected by adults in part of a historical socialization process, and therefore they correspond greatly to the aesthetic tastes and moral standards of a particular adult world. For the most part, they convey a distinct image of the world to children and foster the ideological hegemony of ruling-class interests. Looked at from a historical-materialist point of view, classical children's books are vital instruments in the formation of class consciousness, aesthetic sensibility, and character structure.

It is clear that not every classical children's book serves repressive ends. Nor is there a conscious plan to produce books which nullify the potential for creativity and critical thinking in children. Every children's book must be looked at historically to determine its real aesthetic and ideological value. Here many factors must be taken into consideration. Generally speaking, a book for children should aim to render a clear and interesting picture of an epoch or topic with all its contradictions and speak to children's problems truthfully so that they can learn to master these problems and develop their own identity. The communicative function of the language and images should help the child improve his or her learning ability and creative potential. Restricted codes and closed reference systems should be avoided. Each new book should try to incorporate the most recent pedagogical and psychological discoveries about education and society in order to increase the emancipatory value of the book. By this I mean that the structure and contents of a children's book should be geared, no matter how fantastic the subject matter and style, toward helping children understand how to work together to free their own individual talents and to overcome obstacles which may be preventing their free development. In this respect the entire question of book production and the reception of a book must be reconsidered to include the participation of children in the entire process. Ultimately, if this is done, the term classical will take on another, more authentic meaning.

No doubt, some classical books deserve their status because they were written to speak, and continue to speak, to children's *real* needs. Most have unfortunately retained classical status because they are still useful in the indoctrination of children to the standards of a ruling class and also serve the market needs of the book industry. It is from this historical-materialist perspective, then, one which corresponds to the socialist critique of the New Left in West Germany, that I shall be using the term classical, and here the two books **Struwwelpeter** and *Heidi* are perfect models of the classical German children's book. Not only have all children in German-speaking countries from the late nineteenth century to the present been predominantly influenced by these two books, but children in America as well.

Struwwelpeter was written in 1844 by the physician Heinrich Hoffmann, who could not find an appropriate book for his three-year-old son and decided to write his own, based on stories he used to tell his young patients to prevent them from becoming disruptive and getting upset. Soon after the book was published in 1845, it grew in popularity. Up through 1974 there have been over six hundred different German editions and numerous translations, not to mention the hundreds of imitations and parodies. There is hardly a German adult or child who does not know that Struwwelpeter is everything one is not supposed to become, the model of the disobedient child who never cuts his fingernails and lets his hair grow wild—in short, a barbarian. The rhymed, illustrated stories which follow our introduction to him present a composite picture of Struwwelpeter: evil Peter, who tortures animals and people with a whip, and who is finally bitten by a dog and put to bed; little Pauline, who plays with matches and burns herself to death; three boys who make fun of a Negro and are then dipped in black ink as punishment by a stern adult; the wild hunter, who loses his rifle and is shot by a rabbit; Konrad the thumb-sucker, who has his thumbs cut off because he persists in sucking; Kaspar, who wastes away to nothing because he refuses to eat his soup; Phillip, who is smothered by a tablecloth because he will not sit still at the table; Robert, who goes out into a storm and is carried away forever by a huge wind; Hans, who never watches where he walks and almost drowns while walking near a pond. All the stories are written to frighten the young reader, and the illustrations are correspondingly gruesome and terrifying. (Adults generally find them comical.) Only one of the stories involves a little girl. As always, the assumption is made that little girls are more docile and obedient than little boys, who are terrors. Hoffmann's picture of what a little boy is and how he should be treated is an accurate reflection of the general *Biedermeier* (Victorian) attitude toward children: "Little children are to be seen, not heard," and if they are heard, they are to be punished severely.

The danger of *Struwwelpeter* and its imitations stems from the fact that it can be easily comprehended by children from age two on and has indeed stamped the consciousness of German children for generations. To a great extent, it reflects a peculiar hostility to children (what Germans call *Kinderfeindlichkeit*) which has been a disturbing element in the history of German civilization. *Struwwelpeter* glorifies obedience to arbitrary authority, and in each example the children are summarily punished by the adult world. No clear-cut reasons are given for the behavior or the punishment; discipline is elevated above curiosity and creativity. It is not by chance, then, that this book has retained its bestseller, classical status to the present. Whether it will be superseded by the most recent parody, *Der Anti-Struwwelpeter* by Friedrich Karl Waechter, will depend on the general development of the new socialist children's literature.

Susanna Ashton and Amy Jean Petersen

SOURCE: "Etching the Jingle Along: Mark Twain's *Slovenly Peter,*" in *Children's Literature Association Quarterly,* Vol. 20, No. 1, Spring, 1995, pp. 36-41.

Der Struwwelpeter, which has been variously translated as *Slovenly Peter, Shock-headed Peter,* and *Tousle-Headed Peter,* is a collection of eleven children's poems written by Dr. Heinrich Hoffmann in 1844. In its assorted translations, *Struwwelpeter* is arguably the best-known children's book of the nineteenth century. Few nurseries in Europe or North America were without a tattered copy of it, although the work was not originally intended for a public audience. Indeed, Hoffmann was always somewhat embarrassed by its great success: "Those bad boys got further around the world than I did. . . . They learned all kinds of languages that even I don't understand. . . . it is quite natural that one would reprint them with enthusiasm in North America," he wrote. As a doctor who frequently had to make house calls on children, Hoffmann created a repertoire of rhymes and pictures to distract them during his visits. One Christmas, discouraged by the selection of children's books available to him, he wrote out his own verses as a gift for his young son. At the urging of friends, Hoffmann published 1,500 copies of his Christmas book under the title *Lustige Geschichten und drollige Bilder (Jolly Tales and Funny*

Pictures), although it soon became known simply by the name of its most famous character. Within four weeks the first edition was completely sold out. Hundreds of authorized and unauthorized versions began to appear around the world, and the success of *Struwwelpeter* was born.

Nearly fifty years later, in 1819, these morbidly humorous poems caught the attention of America's foremost humorist, Mark Twain, who translated the collection as *Slovenly Peter* while visiting Germany with his family. Some investments having recently failed, the family was short of funds, and translating *Struwwelpeter* may have seemed an excellent way to earn money fast. These hopes were reasonable, for despite his financial ups and downs, Twain's name was renowned throughout Europe and the United States. *The Adventures of Tom Sawyer* (1876) had been a great success, and Twain had become well known as a children's writer. Combining his name with *Struwwelpeter* must have sounded like a sure thing. On 27 October 1891 Twain wrote to his publisher, "I have worked myself to death the last 3 days and nights translating . . . the most celebrated child's book in Europe." He had hoped to publish *Slovenly Peter* in time for the Christmas shopping season, but was quickly frustrated by copyright problems. Twain's *Slovenly Peter* was not published until it appeared in a limited edition in 1935, twenty-five years after his death.

Commercial considerations aside, Twain's interest in *Struwwelpeter* is not surprising. Hoffmann's poems focus upon and perhaps even glamorize bad children, a theme that had a lifelong fascination for Twain. Hence Twain highlighted aspects of *Struwwelpeter* that had gone unremarked in earlier English-language versions, added some of his own embellishments, and succeeded in creating a work of energy and wit that may have better reflected the tenor of the original Hoffmann poems than did many of the more widely published translations.

Full of graphic illustrations and grim humor, Hoffmann's poems are cautionary tales with a twist. Unlike the standard Sunday School morality so commonly found in nineteenth-century American children's works, *Struwwelpeter* features violence and gore in conjunction with what might be termed black humor. Moreover, Hoffmann's illustrations gave *Struwwelpeter* a surreal, even loony, quality. Occasionally categorized as nonsense and sometimes placed in the realm of cautionary tales, *Struwwelpeter* has consistently been hard to define. Even so, it has been repeatedly hailed as Germany's greatest contribution to children's literature since the Brothers Grimm. In her exhaustive analysis of *Struwwelpeter,* critic Marie-Luis Könneker addresses the debate surrounding the effect of this book on German culture; some have argued that because of the large number of people who had contact with the text at an impressionable age, Hoffmann's bad children might have had a greater influence on German consciousness than *Faust* or even the *Communist Manifesto.*

In Hoffmann's poems, misbehaving children meet with fates generally construed as disproportionate to their crimes. The "Daumenlutcher Bub" (thumbsucking boy) who disregards his mother's warnings has his thumbs cut off by a mysterious tailor who wields a giant pair of scissors. The colorful accompanying illustration features blood spurting from the little boy's hands. Little Pauline plays with matches and thus burns to death. In another instance, pudgy young Kaspar refuses to eat his soup, and the illustrations show him withering into a stick figure. The depiction of a grave with his name on it indicates his final fate.

Not all the poems are so grim. Hanns Stare-in-the-Air, for example, simply fails to look where he is walking and falls into the water. He emerges wiser and wetter, but none the worse for wear. The title poem does not even have a clear story; it merely describes a victim of bad grooming. Underneath the famous illustration of a defiant boy with foot-long fingernails and wild bushy hair, Twain writes:

> See this frowsy "cratur"—
> Pah! it's Struwwelpeter!
> On his fingers rusty,
> On his tow-head musty,
> Scissors seldom come;
> Lets his talons grow a year,
> Hardly ever combs his hair,—
> Do any loathe him? Some!
> They hail him "Modern satyr—
> Disgusting Struwwelpeter."

But the overall tenor of the collection is indeed one of crime and punishment. Bad things happen to bad children. This circumstance does not necessarily mean that Hoffmann intended his book to be didactic. As Charles Frey and John W. Griffith argue in *The Literary Heritage of Childhood,* "Hoffmann's attitude toward the moral lessons of his poems is difficult to locate." On the one hand, it seems too simplistic to read the poems as a strict mockery of nineteenth-century morality, for however absurd the consequences of misbehavior, in each case a child is punished. Indeed, Hoffmann's introductory poem states that good children shall be rewarded with "picture books" and that "naughty, romping girls and boys" deserve no gifts at all. This introduction, if taken as a guide for approaching the poems, suggests the standard bourgeois approach to nineteenth-century child rearing. For all its nonsense humor and subversive qualities, it seems probable that many adults purchased *Struwwelpeter* thinking it a straightforward albeit unusually entertaining example of didactic literature. On the other hand, Hoffmann's own writings explicitly deny the didactic intent. He thought the stories were funny and belonged to a greater tradition, one that also included the Grimms' fairy tales.

As might be expected, contemporary critics take different positions on the intent and effects of these stories. Margaret Higonnet, for example, posits Hoffmann as a parodist. She argues that since the purpose of writing *Struwwelpeter* was to keep children entertained and distracted during the doctor's visits, a strictly didactic text would not serve his purposes. Thus the pictures in particular were "designed to link him to children" and "to enable him to cross the barrier erected by punitive adults." This alignment of child and Hoffmann against the adult world suggests to Higonnet a carefully posed text that works against the didactic tradition. Several critics share this view, notably Helmut Müller, who finds that children notice the "surreality" of the figures and thus appreciate the humor Hoffmann intended.

In contrast, Thomas Freeman admits that it is "surprising that a doctor interested in psychiatric medicine would produce a book which would deliberately frighten young children and increase their anxiety." Nevertheless, Freeman concludes that this is indeed what occurred, even though Hoffmann's sympathetic view of his own patients might suggest—erroneously—that he "opposed the popular Victorian practice of using threats to scare children into their 'proper' place, where they are to be seen and not heard." Freeman even argues that if Hoffmann's patients were quieted by the pictures he drew for them, it was only because they were probably "shocked" into "a state of stupified horror." This view chimes with Alice Miller's well-known stance on pedagogy of any kind: "My antipedagogic position is not directed against a specific type of pedagogical ideology but against all pedagogical ideology per se, even if it is of an anti-authoritarian nature. . . . all advice that pertains to raising children betrays more or less clearly the numerous, variously clothed needs of the *adult.*"

But if we consider Hoffmann's own version of what happened, we see the likelihood that the children were indeed entertained, because they were able to follow the story as it visually unfolded. Hoffmann would take a notebook out of his bag, tear out a page, and quickly sketch a small boy, telling his young patient the story of how the rascal would not let anyone cut his hair or his nails. Hoffmann would keep drawing until nothing was left to be seen of the original figure but strands of hair and long clawlike nails. That would enthrall and confuse the little patient into an awed and watchful silence. In the meantime, Hoffmann would have measured the patient's pulse and temperature. He professed to thus "attain [his] goal" (calming down the child), which was "achieved" not by terrorizing children, but by capturing their interest. Hoffmann himself believed that his was a playful process: "The wild malcontent becomes calm, the tears dry and the doctor can playfully fulfill his obligations." It is not until later in the nineteenth century that these stories begin to seem morbid to a German audience. Müller tells us that nineteenth-century children experienced "unadulterated glee" when looking at Hoffmann's figures, that they were able to recognize easily the exaggeration in the figures, and that therefore they did not read them as a serious threat.

Struwwelpeter's appeal to Twain may have lain precisely in this ambiguity. If it was a collection of subversive poetry, it was supremely entertaining. If solely a collection of cautionary tales, it deserved attention for its shameless techniques. That it was not clearly in one camp or the other likely contributed to the "mysterious fascination" it exerted upon him (see Twain's "Translator's Note"). Moreover, Twain further complicated the issue of *Struwwelpeter*'s didactic intent (or lack thereof) by emphasizing much of the violence skimmed over in the anonymous earlier English translation used in most legitimate and illegitimate editions. Twain's version is starkly unlike that found in so many British and American nurseries. In the popular English version, for instance, the dog is "whipp'd" until "sore." Twain, however, emphasizes Frederick's nasty behavior with gusto, writing:

> He whacked him here, he whacked him there,
> He whacked with all his might and main,
> He made him howl and dance with pain.

Although full of awkward rhymes and structures, Twain's renditions may be seen as far more faithful to the *spirit* of the original illustrations and text than the previous translations had been; his difference from the standard English version will strike many

readers as all to the good. The language of Twain's work, however, often differs dramatically from the German. He elaborates extensively on scenes that receive little, if any, treatment in the original German version, presumably a reason for his decision to describe his version of Hoffmann's poems as "freely translated." Indeed, one critic has gone so far as to accuse Twain of having written verses using the illustrations, rather than the German, as his guide. Twain's self-proclaimed poor command of German—he pokes fun at his own linguistic deficiencies in his essay "The Awful German Language"—makes this criticism believable, but the illustrations are so compelling that one can hardly condemn him for having leaned so heavily upon them.

In Hoffmann's original version, each poem was accompanied by a series of pictures, usually framed or connected by borders and lattices that would weave themselves in and around each poem. These frames were occasionally omitted from pirated versions, but their fanciful use of vines, twigs, and in one case an actual picture frame, served to integrate the poems vividly with the images. This integration was so important to Hoffmann that he tightly controlled the reproduction of his work within Germany and, as far as he could, in other countries. (It was this firm copyright control that presumably frustrated Twain's plans for publication.) Fortunately, most pirated versions recognized the significance of Hoffmann's illustrations. Pirates tampered with his drawings and did occasionally omit the carefully designed borders, but rarely replaced the artwork wholesale. In fact, *Struwwelpeter* was probably successful in its many translations precisely because of its vivid images. Verses may have faltered, but the pictures could speak for themselves.

"The Story of Ugly Frederick" provides a typical example of how Twain would infuse life into his translations, using the illustrations as a guide. Frederick is a cruel and violent child who beats a dog. The dog, in revenge, finally bites Frederick. Frederick is put to bed, and the dog sits downstairs eating all of Frederick's dinner. Hoffmann writes:

> Der Hund an Friedrichs Tischchen saß,
> wo er den grossen Kuchen aß;
> a auch die gute Leberwurst
> und trank den Wein fur seinen Durst.
> Die Peitsche hat er mitgebracht
> und nimmt sie sorglich sehr in acht.

A literal translation of the first four lines would read: "The dog sat at Friedrich's little table, / where he ate the big cake; / [he] also ate the good liverwurst / and drank the wine for his thirst." In the popular English version we hear the story rhymed:

> But good dog Tray is happy now;
> He has no time to say "bow-wow"
> He seats himself in Frederick's chair
> And laughs to see the nice things there;
> The soup he swallows, sup by sup,—
> And eats the pies and puddings up.

As Philip Hofer points out in his introduction to Twain's *Slovenly Peter,* "as anyone can see, in the picture [are] a fine liver sausage, a big cake, and red wine glowing in a carafe and glass!" The anonymous Victorian editor/censor/translator apparently decided to water the wine down and substitute pies and puddings. Twain, as might be expected, had no such scruples about using the illustrations as his guide. He describes the triumph of the dog with enthusiasm, if not with grace:

> He hangs the whip upon the chair,
> And mounts aloft and seats him there;
> He sips the wine, so rich and red,
> And feels it swimming in his head,
> He munches grateful at the cake,
> And wishes he might never wake
> From this debauch; while think by think
> His thoughts dream on, and link by link
> The liver-sausage disappears,
> And his hurt soul relents in tears.

The comparative forcefulness and vivid imagery of Twain's translation may be a reflection of the more American nature of his work, his own artistic inclinations as a writer, or more progressive ideas about what children were and were not equipped to handle. Of course, his concerns were not always consistent. Twain suggested to his publishers that they might want to remove the illustration of the chamber pot from under Frederick's bed: "It is too frank . . . though I don't see any real harm about it," he wrote, perhaps meaning too frank for prudish Americans, although perfectly acceptable by European standards and his own.

In the popular translation circulated within the United States and Britain, the narrator is unobtrusive. In Twain's version, however, the storyteller and/or translator are continually intruding and involving themselves in the reader's experience. Alongside excruciatingly painful couplets, such as "The dog's his heir, and this estate / That dog inherits, and will ate," Twain adds paratextual explanatory notes that were published on the same page as the poem in the 1935 edition. On the "will ate" problem Twain instructs,

> My child, never use an expression like that. It is utterly unprincipled and outrageous to say ate when you mean eat, and you must never do it ex-

cept when crowded for a rhyme. As you grow up you will find that poetry is a sandy road to travel, and the only way to pull through at all is to lay your grammar down and take hold with both hands. M.T.

In another poem, after writing "He took his game-bag, powder, gun / And fiercely to the fields he spun," Twain remarks, "Baby, you must take notice of this awkward form of speech and never use it. Except in translating. M.T."

These notes do more than extricate Twain from grammatical culpability while entertaining his audience; they also introduce a warm and personal element, picking up Hoffmann's intimate tone and exaggerating it still further. Although Twain speaks, as Hoffmann does, directly to the child/(adult) reader, Hoffmann speaks to a general, informal "you" ("Du siehst hier, wie schwarz sie sind") or to a group of "dear children" ("Seht, ihr lieben Kinder, seht, wie's dem Philipp weiter geht!"). Twain, on the other hand, addresses what seems to be a *specific* child, taking the adult/child relationship beyond the text and into the world of real actions and consequences. His humorous and self-reflexive critique adds verisimilitude and intimacy. Thus instead of leaving it in the "nursery rhyme" genre, Twain's margin notes place the work in a category all its own. Twain's narrator's voice is personalized—he even adds his own initials. Hence the Twain voice seems more real than the generic adult advice-giver/storyteller tone Hoffmann uses. Furthermore, there is the implication that the child reader was one of Twain's own children. Since Twain presented this book to his children on Christmas day (just as Hoffmann did) in 1891, the direct address takes on an authenticity, which does not at all diminish its charm. As *Slovenly Peter* was intended for the very young—Twain guessed "3-7 years old"—it also seems likely that Twain envisioned adults reading it aloud to their children, while privately enjoying the ironic humor aligning the translator's frustrations with those of parents in the age-old problem of reconciling words with actions: "Do as I say not as I do." The "My child" and "Baby" would have created, in any case, an interactive reading experience for adult and child.

To other poems Twain added cultural and period references. These references may have been designed to make the work more contemporary, more American, or perhaps just more funny. As Dixon Wecter points out, Twain "improves" on the German. Wecter does not elaborate on this issue, but it is clear that among Twain's innovations are amusing and distinctive American literary references. In German, Konrad's thumbs are cut off and "Hei! Da schreit der Konrad sehr." (Literally, "Hei! Thus Konrad screams very much.") Twain tells us that "While that lad his tongue unfurled / [he] fired a yell heard 'round the world." As might be expected, this is in stark contrast to the pallid "Snip! Snap! Snip! the scissors go / And Conrad cries out—Oh! Oh! Oh!" of the popular nineteenth-century version.

Similarly, Twain**'s "The Tale of the Terrible Hunter Man"** incorporates American slang. This story differs from the others in that no particular child is involved and no particular misdeed is punished, although as it involves active and punitive animal players it bears a strong family resemblance to verses such as **"Ugly Frederick."** Here a rabbit steals the glasses and gun of a sleeping hunter and chases him simply because he is a hunter. In German the story explains:

> Er legte sich ins grüne Gras;
> das alles sah der kleine Has.
> Und als der Jäger schnarcht' und schlief,
> der Has ganz heimlich zu ihm lief,
> und nahm die Flint' und auch die Brill',
> und schlich davon ganz leis' und still.

The popular version, **"The Story of the Man That Went Out Shooting,"** describes the scene as follows:

> And, while he slept like any top,
> The little hare came, hop, hop, hop,
> Took gun and spectacles, and then
> On her hind legs went off again.

Far more vibrant are Twain's hunter and rabbit, described in colloquial American:

> And as he dreamed and snored and slept,
> The furry rascal to him crept,
> And stole his gun and smooched his specs,
> And hied him hence with these effects.

In **"The Tale of Soupy Kaspar'** (which the popular translation calls **"The Story of Augustus Who Would Not Have Any Soup"**), Twain does not even attempt to find equivalents for emphatic terms such as "gar." Instead, he constructs his own playful references, and concludes:

> The fourth day came, and here you see
> How doth this little busy bee
> He weighed perhaps a half a pound—
> Death came and tucked him in the ground.

The "busy bee" from the famous poem "Against Idleness and Mischief" (1715) is obviously another inside joke for the English-speaking audience. Most nineteenth-century English or American children would have recognized the busy bee poem as the didactic and often satirized work that it was. Twain's jab here is thus especially appropriate in the context of *Slovenly Peter.*

Twain's translations are easily criticized for their inaccuracy and general awkwardness. Nevertheless, they retain a charm evocative of Ogden Nash or Hilaire Belloc. Some of his rhymes are quite clever, or at least mischievous (modern satyr/Struwwelpeter; unfurled/around the world; smeller/umbrella; pawses/lawses). He occasionally manages to incorporate German (Waves his shears, the heartless grub / And calls for Dawmen-lutscher-bub), onomatopoeia (ker-slam, ker-blam, ker-blim), alliteration (hied him hence), and internal rhyme. His version also exploits the typeface to hyperbolic effect (And fled; and *fled!* and FLED! and FLED!). The popular version is frequently included in anthologies of nonsense, but Twain's version would be even more appropriate. Compare the cries of the cats in the popular version of the story of the child who played with matches with those in Twain's rendering. The popular reads:

> The pussy cats saw this,
> And said: "Oh, naughty, naughty Miss!"
> And stretch'd their claws
> And rais'd their paws:
> "Me-ow, mee-o, me-ow, me-o,
> You'll burn to death, if you do so."

While Twain writes:

> And Mintz and Mountz, the catties,
> Lift up their little patties,
> They threaten with their pawses:
> "It is against the lawses!
> Me-yow! Me-yo! Me-yow! Me-yo!
> Drop it or you are ashes, O!"

Twain's poetry may not have been as controlled as the more popular verses, but it was in keeping with his stated goal: maintaining the "jingle" of the work. As Twain wrote in his introduction,

> It was Dr. Hoffmann's opinion that the charm of the book lay not in the subjects or the pictures, but wholly in the jingle. That may be true, for rhymes that jingle felicitously are very dear to a child's ear. In this translation I have done my best to fetch the jingle along.

The *Slovenly Peter* venture may have been Twain's major foray into the world of translation, but it was nowhere near his sole attempt at poetry. The author of more than 120 poems, he wrote verse throughout his life, some comic, some serious. His novels are full of characters who write or recite poetry (the Duke's version of Hamlet's Soliloquy in *Huckleberry Finn* [1885] is just one memorable example). Twain also wrote parodies of Shakespeare, Swift, Poe, and others, with the sentimental poets being his favorite target. In a survey of Twain's poetry, Arthur L. Scott observes that in Twain's later years, "there was scarcely a major theme of his prose which did not find a voice in his poetry." The verses of *Slovenly Peter* share many traits with his other poetic works: the humor, the difficult moral stances, the penchant for explanatory or pseudo-apologetic notes, and the imaginative manipulation of grammar. Nevertheless, *Slovenly Peter* stands alone as a collection of poetry Twain intended for publication. Despite its frivolous nature, this translation featured themes and ideas that Twain had been toying with for years.

In 1865, Twain wrote a series of short articles and stories for various publications while he was in California, several of which exhibit a Struwwelpetrian humor. A pair of these articles, titled "Advice for Good Little Boys" and "Advice for Good Little Girls," featured cynical guidance such as "You ought never take anything that don't belong to you—if you can not carry it off" and "You ought never to 'sass' old people—unless they 'sass' you first." These sketches, along with "The Story of the Bad Little Boy That Bore a Charmed Life," have been described as a "faint but intriguing anticipation of Clemens' lifelong interest in satirizing 'Sunday School Fiction.'" *Slovenly Peter,* coming after *Tom Sawyer* and *Huckleberry Finn,* may thus be seen as another manifestation of Twain's determination to show that bad boys are more interesting than good ones. The final poem in the collection, **"The Story of Flying Robert,"** is a particularly telling example. This poem tells the story of a boy who goes outside in the rain and is carried away in a storm. Frey and Griffith sensibly ask why flying is seen as a punishment when in most children's literature "flying away is a distinct privilege." Flying Robert, like Huck Finn, gets to escape social institutions: we see a church receding in the distance as he is carried farther and farther away. Robert may be miserably wet, but he is having an adventure, one that would greatly have appealed to Twain himself.

English-language *Struwwelpeter*s have been reprinted again and again in nonsense anthologies, often alongside Edward Lear's limericks. In most cases, it is the anonymous earlier version that has been disseminated. It seems a pity that the Twain translation, with its distinctly idiosyncratic and American nature, has never been given much of an opportunity to educate, entertain, or corrupt young—and old—readers.

Christa Wolf

SOURCE: "Parting from the Phantoms: The Business of Germany," in *PMLA,* Vol. 111, No. 3, May, 1996, pp. 395-407.

Everything about Germany has been said. I make this claim after wearily pushing aside the stacks of recently published books, the piles of fresh newspaper articles that I have read, skimmed, or left unread. What a giant gruel Germans have been cooking up, talking and writing and analyzing and arguing and polemicizing and pontificating and lamenting, even satirizing themselves and Germany, in the past four years. We have stirred this gruel ourselves, put the pot on the fire, watched it simmer, bubble, sizzle, boil over; we have tasted it, eaten it up like good little children. But the gruel cannot be consumed, nor can it be held in check any longer. It is spilling over the stove and kitchen, out from the messy house onto the road, onto all the streets of our German cities, apparently bringing no nourishment to the homeless Germans who huddle there. And if we well-housed Germans want to be honest—and what do Germans today want more urgently than to be honest!—we must admit that we no longer like the taste of this German millet gruel. We are sick of it. We are fed up with it.

"No!" cries the German Suppenkaspar, the Boy Who Won't Eat His Soup, who along with his friend Struwwelpeter is just this year celebrating his 150th birthday in blooming health (that is, their story is still being printed in great numbers): "O take the beastly soup away / I won't eat any soup today!" The question arises how a child raised to be antiauthoritarian can be forced to eat up the soup he has cooked himself, to swallow something he doesn't like. Normally he prefers to stuff himself to the gills with Italian food; he is definitely no anorexic, unlike the earlier soup rebel that the Frankfurt doctor Heinrich Hoffmann gave his little son Karl for Christmas 1844 and who died on the fifth day of his hunger strike.

What can we do but laugh at that, since we know better about practically everything, including hunger strikes? How long did the hunger strikers hold out in the Bischofferode potash plant? Twenty days? Yet they are still alive. And it all happened just because they did not want to eat the soup that others had cooked for them but that they too in their gullibility had helped to cook for themselves. You must make allowances for them because the party for which the majority of them voted, as Christians, in March 1990 did not tell them that their plant would unfortunately have to be closed down as part of achieving the level playing field demanded by a market economy. So we saw on our TV screens the image of faithful Christians, some of whom were still fasting, giving union speeches in their church, and we heard them singing hymns like battle songs along with their priest, and we saw many of them crying, men and women both.

Where am I headed? First, I just want to ask what really has become of good old Struwwelpeter, whom the well-known German psychoanalyst Georg Groddeck compared to Goethe's Faust for the depth of his effect on the German psyche. Is he still the same old Shock-Headed Peter, after five changes of government and society—the same whose hair (his creator admits) may have been "wickedly pulled" in the revolution of 1848? And who then, no doubt, cut off his unkempt mop and marched against France wearing a Prussian military haircut; who surely did not stand in the way of Bismarck's founding of the empire; who has tried out a number of different coiffures since then; and who confronts us today with a managerial fringe or a bald pate? Is he still the same old Peter, adaptable to anything?

And what about his friend Little Konrad? Is he still sucking his thumb or chewing his fingernails down to the quick the minute his mommy turns her back or leaves the house for a bit—for her husband does not dispute her right to a job (he is out of work, incidentally, and hangs out in a bar, so what is she supposed to do at the stove all day)? Then the little boy gets bored, and, "zoom, his thumb's in his mouth!" I would like to know in how many German families children are still told that little boys who suck their thumbs get them cut off—snip snap snip. The Institute for Applied Social Science fails to give us the dope on this. On the other hand, it does inform us that as of November 1993, ninety-two percent of Germans feel they are not a united people. Seventy percent in the East and sixty percent in the West reportedly feel that divisive factors predominate, so perhaps it is all the more useful to remind ourselves of something we have in common: the book *Struwwelpeter,* with its "merry tales" and "funny pictures" that all Germans read as children and that has affected even those who have not read it. This is what distinguishes a true book of popular literature: it springs from the national soul and pours its spirit back into its source, flowing back and forth, and—this is another thing we have learned—is hard to replace with a tradition of rational thought.

Alas, we shake our heads when we read *Struwwelpeter.* Even back in the 1840s, no sooner did the "coal-black crow-black blackamoor" "stroll past the door" than Ludwig came "running over," "waving his little flag"; and when Kaspar and Wilhelm joined him, "They shrieked and laughed all three / As the little moor went by / Because black as ink was he!" Those really were the good old days! All they did was shriek and laugh; they didn't throw the nigger off the commuter train, didn't put a knife to his throat, didn't even kick him with their hobnailed boots. How can that be? Dad and Mom actually smile at black people on the street, and at Turks and refugees, too, and think even Jews are human, and they are slightly taken aback if Sonny Boy doesn't share their opinions. But when they are on their own and stir the embers of their piety, they pray, "Dear God, I thank thee that I am not like those people!" Thanks to German unification, they are now free at last to accompany Frederick the Great to his ancestral resting place at Sans Souci in Potsdam, no matter what anyone may think. And Kaiser Wilhelm is being hoisted back up on his high horse, where from the elbow of the Rhine he can now cast his baleful gaze on France—at the moment when, as it happens, we Germans are once again struggling to find our identity, which after all we must be allowed at last, mustn't we? And how much nicer it would have been—yes, it would have been *even nicer*—if at Schinkel's New Guard House in Berlin we had been allowed to remember not only the victims of wars caused by Germans and their tyranny but, at the same time, those who have these victims on their conscience. But you can't have everything at once, can you, and isn't moderation a splendid German virtue? But now I remember why I brought up the subject of German history.

Incidentally, a victim sometimes gets to turn the tables, as the folktales of *Struwwelpeter* acknowledge. In the tale of the wild huntsman, the hare grabs the musket from the hunter, sets his spectacles on her own nose, and boldly aims the gun at her persecutor: "And now she makes the gun to fire. / The hunter is in deadly fear."

We ought to be familiar with this kind of fear. I felt it as a refugee at the start of May 1945, somewhere on a highway in Mecklenburg, when German prisoners from the Sachsenhausen concentration camp who had been abandoned by their German guards and driven off by the advancing Soviet troops started to arm themselves with the cast-off weapons of the defeated German Wehrmacht—a sight that caused my muted uneasiness to cross the threshold into guilt, although it could not yet cross the far higher barrier into language. That took years to happen. The closer your ties to a guilty system, the greater your share in the guilt and the longer you need before you can express it. And as we know, many Germans, very many Germans, never acknowledged their guilt or their complicity by a single word or made any apology. On the contrary, first they suppressed any guilt feelings that might have arisen, and then they suppressed the dull underlying discomfort as well. They let it sink down to the dregs of the unclarified and the unexpressed in the German temper, which are cultivated in many German families—in how many? I ask again. The same people now hear it said that the gas chambers that exterminated the Jews never existed and read in the newspapers that in Berlin the names of Communists murdered by the Nazis are to be removed from street signs. So I shall say their names here: Hans Beimler, Katja Niederkirchner, Heinz Kapelle. And I shall ask what signal the German mind will receive and no doubt is meant to receive from this elimination of history, which confirms us in our innocence. I almost hesitate to say the other names that are now at risk, because I can hardly believe it: Marx, Engels, Rosa Luxemburg, Karl Liebknecht. But Berliners are allowed to keep the names of German fighter pilots on their street signs.

All coincidence, no doubt. Yet the coincidences are beginning to mount up, and coincidentally they all are heading in the same direction: to the right. This is a moment of opportunity, and people are taking advantage of it. The German woman too can be put back in her proper place. In Heinrich Hoffmann's tales she already lacked the power of speech, for "Upon the table all around / The mother looks and makes no sound." But the *Struwwelpeter* book also tells us the story of Little Pauline, who clearly has too good a time when she is left alone at home, jumping around the room "light of heart and full of song," a silly little thing, easily led astray, who cannot resist playing with matches and gets her just deserts: she goes up in flames, so that nothing is left of her but the frivolous red shoes she liked to dance around in, no doubt with lewd intentions. Burning up spoils her fun entirely, which may well be the secret message of the auto-da-fé. One little girl in a book among so many little boys, and she is the one who has to burn. That is striking, because setting fires, burning up houses and people, has always been boys' work and still is.

J. D. Stahl

SOURCE: "Mark Twain's *Slovenly Peter* in the Context of Twain and German Culture," in *The Lion and the Unicorn,* Vol. 20, No. 2, December, 1996, pp. 166-80.

Both Germany and the United States have moralistic traditions of childhood instruction reaching back to the formative periods of their cultural origins. The interest Mark Twain showed in Heinrich Hoffmann's **Struwwelpeter,** and his editorial and creative decisions in translating the popular German original, represent revealing intersections of two related but distinctly different cultural traditions. Mark Twain was drawn to the orderliness of German culture, but his interpretation of violence, alcohol, and racial prejudice in the anecdotes of Hoffmann's ironically cautionary work is more indebted to the American context than to the German "culture of restraint" or "Kultur der Zurückhaltung." Hoffmann's **Struwwelpeter** embodies a German cultural theme of conflict over "Zucht des Körpers" or "discipline of the body," which clearly fascinated Mark Twain, but which in his translation he shifted to emphasize American themes.

A brief examination of the backgrounds against which Hoffmann's and Twain's works emerged may be useful to the understanding of both more fully. Punishment made vivid by its violence is a didactic theme that spans the centuries. The volume titled *Poetischer Bilderschatz der vornehmsten Biblischen Geschichten des alten und neuen Testamentes, zum erbaulichen Vergnügen der Jugend ans Licht gestellet [Poetic Image Treasury of the Most Noble Biblical Stories of the Old and New Testament, Brought to Light for the Instructive Pleasure of Youth]* published in 1758 in Leipzig by an anonymous author, included the following illustrations:

> Adonibesek werden die Daumen und Zehen abgehackt,
> Gericht der Sündfluth,
> Isaacs Opferung,
> Pharaoh ersäuft im Rothen Meer,
> Der gestrafte Flucher,
> Die Rotte Korah wird verschlungen,
> Der Tod der füni Könige,
> Sauls Söhne gefangen,
> Die Bären fressen die spottenden Knaben, u.a.

> Adonibesek's thumbs and toes are hacked off,
> the judgment of the flood,
> the sacrifice of Isaac,
> Pharaoh drowns in the Red Sea,

the punishment of the one who curses,
the band of Korah is devoured,
the death of the five kings,
Saul's sons captured,
the bears eat the mocking boys, etc.

The verses in this work were accompanied by moral lessons that drew pointed conclusions for young readers about the application of the stories to their life and conduct.

Similarly, in the American Puritan tradition, James Janeway illustrated the need for children's spiritual repentance and moral vigilance through his horrific "Happy Death" stories, which invariably ended with the death of his young protagonists. Janeway, Isaac Watts, and other Puritan writers shared a moral passion for the reform and redemption of the young that issued in such frightful warnings as the one contained in a stanza of Watt's poem "Obedience to Parents":

and ravens shall pick out his eyes
and eagles eat the same.

In the German tradition, this moralistic and religious strain was counterbalanced somewhat in the nineteenth century by a more scientifically-oriented informational genre, the "Sachbuch," or informational book, which originated in the works of Johann Amos Comenius (*Orbis Pictus*) and Johann Bernhard Basedow (*Ein Vorrath der basten Erkenntnisse*). It was this factual tradition, though, in a particularly pedantic and unimaginative form, that, at least according to one of Hoffmann's accounts, provided the impetus for his critical and creative departure.

As he told the story,

Ich hatte in den Buchläden allerlei Zeug gesehen, trefflich gezeichnet, glänzend bemalt, Märchen, Geschichten, Indianer- und Räuberszenen; als ich nun gar einen Folio-Band entdeckte, mit den Abbildungen von Pferden, Hunden, Vögeln, von Tischen, Bänken, Töpfen und Kesseln, alle mit der Bemerkung 1/3, 1/8, 1/10 der Lebensgrösse, da hatte ich genug. Was soll damit ein Kind, dem man einen Tisch und einen Stuhl abbildet? Was es in dem Buche sieht, das ist ihm ein Stuhl und ein Tisch, grösser oder kleiner, es ist ihm nun einmal ein Tisch, ob es daran oder darauf sitzen kann oder nicht, und von Original oder Kopie ist nicht die Rede, von grösser oder kleiner vollends gar nicht. . . .

I saw all sorts of things in the bookstores, expertly drawn, glowingly painted, fairy tales, stories, scenes of life among Indians and robbers.

When I finally saw a folio volume with reproductions of horses, dogs, birds, and of tables, benches, pots and kettles, all with the remark 1/3, 1/8, 1/10 of life size, I had had enough. What is a child supposed to do with the reproduction of a table or a chair? What the child sees in the book is a table and a chair, whether it is larger or smaller; it just is a table, whether the child can sit at it or on it or not. And to talk of original or copy, greater or smaller, is simply out of the question. . . . (my translation)

Hoffmann's dissatisfaction with the slickly-produced children's books of his day, coupled with his disgust at the dry scientific approach, unsuited to children, in his opinion, of a particular type of Sachbuch, culminated in his determination to make a better effort himself. What his brief critique of the folio volume reveals is his imaginative capacity to envision how a child is likely to perceive objects represented in a book. Perhaps the most revealing phrase of Hoffmann is "was es in dem Buche sieht, das ist ihm ein Stuhl und ein Tisch . . . ob es daran oder darauf sitzen kann oder nicht." His interpretation of the child's consciousness focuses on the child's imaginative relationship to the object pictured, whether that relationship be physical or mental. He insists that, to the child, the object is not an abstraction or a concept, but rather a real object: "es ist ihm nun einmal ein Tisch."

Mark Twain's dissatisfaction with the prevalent juvenile literature of his time bears some similarities to Hoffmann's. Twain objected to the sentimental and didactic abstraction of much literature available to or aimed at young audiences in the American republic. In the "Ode to Stephen Dowling Bots, Dec'd" in *Adventures of Huckleberry Finn,* he juxtaposed the mundane, physical reality of death with the high-flying ethereal rhetoric of sentimental religious poetry:

They got him out and emptied him;
Alas, it was too late;
His spirit was gone for to sport aloft
In the realms of the good and great.

By doing so, he deflated the pretentiousness of a didactic tradition that ignored the concrete realities of children's lives in favor of a kind of transcendental nonsense, or hogwash, as he would have called it.

Mark Twain's relationship to the moralistic tradition was, like Hoffmann's, a highly paradoxical one. He cannot be said to have been free from it so much as to have made a radical departure within it. In savagely humorous parodies such as "The Story of the Good Little Boy" and "The Story of the Bad Little Boy," Twain inverted the pieties of Sunday School fiction. The good little boy is Jacob Blivens, and he is destroyed by a nitroglycerine explosion. Mark Twain's counter-moral (or anti-moral) is directed against the tradition that taught Jacob Blivens that "the good little boys always died. He loved to live, you know, and this was the most unpleasant feature about being a Sunday-School book boy. He knew it was not healthy to be good."

Mark Twain was contemptuous about most of the genteel children's literature of his time, and his goal in writing was always to write for adults and young people simultaneously, or for adults who could remember what it was like to have been a child. Like Hoffmann, he was somewhat embarrassed by the enormous success of some of his works and would have preferred to have acquired a more serious reputation for the work he considered his best and most important.

Certainly, when Mark Twain chose to devote time and energy to the project of translating Hoffmann's *Struwwelpeter* in Berlin in October of 1891, he had some commercial goals in mind and was keenly aware of the popularity of the book. As he wrote, "*Struwwelpeter* is the best known book in Germany, and has the largest sale known to the book trade, and the widest circulation." In a time when the members of the Clemens family, as his daughter Clara later wrote, "were compelled to spend every German mark as if it were an American dollar," "owing to financial losses," any scheme to turn a quick profit was appealing.

However, at least two further motivations for Twain's efforts are easily discernible. One was the prospect of giving pleasure to his children, which he succeeded in, as Clara's account reveals. She tells how she and her sisters witnessed their father's dramatic rendition of Slovenly Peter that Christmas morning in 1891. Samuel Clemens placed his translation of *Struwwelpeter,* carefully wrapped and adorned with a huge red ribbon, beneath the Christmas tree. Clara recounts:

> He seated himself near the tree and read the verses aloud in his inimitable, dramatic manner. He was a good actor! He knew the verses by heart and required only the uncertain light of the candles to prevent his getting off the rhythmical path. Jean and Susie and I were very youthful and susceptible. We responded almost with tears to Father's graphic gestures in describing Pauline's conflagration. And how we laughed when he eloquently pictured the careless Hans walking straight into the pond among all the little fishes! All because the poor boy could not remove his eyes from the sky!

Clara's adult analysis of why the verses appealed to Clemens reveals the other evident facet of his attraction to Hoffmann's work:

> There is an impious spirit of contrariness in the verses of this work that appealed to Father, suffering as he was from the blue Berlin mood of those first few weeks. He could sympathize with Kaspar, who wouldn't take his soup, because Father did not care for German soup either. The man who dipped the recalcitrant boy into the ink-bottle was after his own heart. How often had Father wanted to dip interrupting intruders into his own ink-bottle and watch them slink away in a black garb of shining fluid!

Significantly, Clara finds the "impious spirit of contrariness" in both child and adult in *Slovenly Peter.* This accords with Mark Twain's powerful insistence that children and adults are subject to the same temperamental impulses, hypocrisies, and contradictions. In a pivotal scene of *The Adventures of Tom Sawyer,* Tom doses Peter the cat with the Pain-killer his Aunt Polly has been dosing on him. The Pain-killer "was simply fire in liquid form," but Aunt Polly is convinced that it is good for Tom, until Peter goes on a wild rampage after receiving a treatment of it.

> Peter sprang a couple of yards in the air, and then delivered a war-whoop and set off round and round the room, banging against furniture, upsetting flower pots, and making general havoc. Next he rose on his hind feet and pranced around, in a frenzy of enjoyment, with his head over his shoulder and his voice proclaiming his unappeasable happiness. Then he went tearing around the house, again spreading chaos and destruction in his path. Aunt Polly entered in time to see him throw a few double somersets, deliver a final mighty hurrah, and sail through the open window, carrying the rest of the flower-pots with him.

Aunt Polly interrogates the boy about what he has been doing:

> "Now, sir, what did you want to treat that poor dumb beast so for?"
>
> "I done it out of pity for him—because he hadn't any aunt."
>
> "Hadn't any aunt!—You numskull. What has that got to do with it?"
>
> "Heaps. Because if he'd a had one she'd a burnt him out herself! She'd a roasted his bowels out of him thout any more feeling than if he was a human!"
>
> Aunt Polly felt a sudden pang of remorse. This was putting the thing in a new light; what was cruelty to a cat might be cruelty to a boy too.

Here Mark Twain has reversed the customary didactic relationship. The child teaches the adult a lesson, but unlike most instruction of children by adults, Tom's lesson is humorous, ironic, and mischievously pragmatic. Lewis Carroll achieved a similar purpose in *Alice in Wonderland* when he satirized stories in which "friends" (the Rationalist euphemism for adult authority figures) taught children lessons such as "if you cut your finger *very* deeply with a knife, it usually bleeds." However, Mark Twain dramatized the conflict, not merely as a battle between pedagogical styles, but as a question of perspective and values. Tom's prank raises the questions of who should have the inherent right to teach whom, and why.

Similarly, Hoffmann in **"Die Geschichte vom Wilden Jäger,"** or **"The Story of the Wild Hunter,"** reversed a relationship of power and oppression. The hunter is near-sighted, like Aunt Polly. He goes out "to have some fun," as the 1848 translation glosses his intention. Hoffmann was more blunt: "Er . . . wollte schiessen tot den Has"—he wanted to shoot the hare to kill, or, as Evan K. Gibson translates it in **Der Struwwelpeter Polyglott,** "to see the hare and shoot him dead." But the hare mischievously "sits in his house of leaves and mocks" the hunter. The hunter succumbs to his weaknesses as a human being: under the influence of the heat of the sun and the weight of his gun, he falls asleep.

What follows is a carnivalesque comedy: the hare becomes the hunter, the hunter becomes the hare. In an absurd sequence of events, the hunter plunges down a well, foreshadowing Alice's plunge down the rabbit-hole, the cup of coffee of the hunter's wife is shot out of her hand and the nose of the hare's child is burned by the hot coffee. (Incidentally, perhaps the figure of the hare with the spectacles and gun also foreshadows, though it is probably too audacious to assert that it inspired, the character of the imperious White Rabbit with his white kid-gloves, coat, and watch on a chain in *Alice in Wonderland*.)

Here, as elsewhere in *Struwwelpeter,* the density and intensity of physical sensations is noteworthy: a nose being burnt by coffee, a shattering cup, the explosion of the gun, the cries of the hunter fleeing for his life, and before that, the drowsiness induced by the heat, the hopping of the hare—all vivid sensations or actions children can readily imagine, unlike, perhaps, the abstraction of proportionate sizes. The theme of Hoffmann's stories is frequently the comedy of simple sensations. This comedy of simple sensations ("Am Brunnen stand ein großer Hund, trank Wasser dort mit seinem Mund" 18—"At the fountain stood a large dog, drinking water with his mouth") is linked to the inversions and distortions of ordinary relationships: the boy beats the maid; cats warn of disaster; the hare hunts the hunter; a boy flies away in a storm, carried by an umbrella, which is ordinarily an object of protection from storms; and the tailor, who ordinarily sews clothes to protect human bodies, snips off thumbs with giant scissors. Hoffmann extrapolates familiar sensations and figures into grotesque exaggerations that are still linked to the familiar through elements of the mundane.

Though many of Hoffmann's stories appear to teach clearly defined lessons, their didactic stance is not easily defined. Jack Zipes points out in an essay published in 1976 that "no clear-cut reasons are given for the behavior or for the punishment" in *Struwwelpeter,* and he indicts the book for glorifying obedience to arbitrary authority. Some critics have recoiled from the violence of these tales, as Thomas Freeman does in an essay in the *Journal of Popular Culture,* in which he states "I do not agree that these poems can be justified as suitable reading material for small children. Both the stories of Conrad and Paulina play upon some of the worst fears which can torment a child." Freeman attacks the lessons of the stories as he sees them: "We are not told to be moral for morality's sake. Instead we are told to behave—or else." Other critics, such as Dyrenfurth-Graebsch, have defended the stories as reflecting "the child's simple desire for justice," while still others have regarded the book primarily as satire or comedy and have pointed out that the exaggeration of the stories is readily recognizable as such by children.

My own assessment of the didactic purpose and method of Hoffmann's enduringly popular work is as follows. While the stories—verses and pictures— have undoubted cautionary and instructional content, they are also suffused with a wry combination of humor, extravagance, and pragmatism. The world of Hoffmann's imagination as revealed in this book is a harsh and abrupt one, but it is also vigorous and fascinating. There is an undercurrent of anarchic energy running through this work that is not entirely contained by the moralistic frame. Thus, while some of the stories have obvious morals such as "eat your soup," "don't play with matches," "look where you're going," and "don't rock back on your chair at the table," other stories and scenes, such as **"The Wild Hunter," "Flying Robert,"** and the eponymous Struwwelpeter himself, immortalized upon a pedestal, are less transparent and univocal. Even the stories with the clear, unquestionable morals have an odd, distinct quality that transcends their teaching purpose.

One way of examining this odd quality is to say that there are two conflicting, yet equally valid ways of regarding this book. The first is that Hoffmann evokes, through a vivid exploration of its opposite, a comfortable childhood world in which children do not burn to death, are not dipped in ink or bitten by a dog until they bleed, do not have their thumbs cut off, do not starve to death, or even normally pull tablecloths onto the floor, fall into canals, or fly away in storms—except in their imaginations.

The other, perhaps complementary way of regarding this book is to see it as a work in which children are the central actors. This is not a realm of dry, factual information, nor is it a realm in which adults are in the foreground. It is an active stage, with energetic, assertive figures, starkly outlined, sometimes surprisingly alone. In existential isolation, boldly disobedient characters defy authority and suffer the consequences. Whatever else one may say about Hoffmann's characters, what they *do* matters. If one were to imagine the improbable fiction of a child reared entirely upon a diet of *Struwwelpeter* and nothing else, it would be more likely to say, as an adult, "Here I stand, I can do no other," or "Give me liberty or give me death" than "Life has no meaning" or "Hell is other people."

Putting these two somewhat incompatible descriptions of Hoffmann's work together, namely its indirect evocation, through its opposite, of the normal, less violent, less threatening world many bourgeois children inhabit, and its representation of bold if bad existential martyrs of childhood self-assertion, we arrive at a paradoxical vision of a work in which the instincts of self-preservation and the allure of rebellion do battle. The drama of this battle is given sensory shape in the bodily inflictions and pleasures endured and enjoyed by characters in this book—and we should not forget that Hoffmann emphasizes physical pleasures as well as the punishments that are so often the cause of unsympathetic critics' revulsion.

Children are promised the pleasure of "Gut's genug, und ein schönes Bilderbuch" if they behave, but more vivid is the dog's pleasure in the "große Kuchen, gute Leberwurst," and the "Wein für seinen Durst" in the story of Cruel Fredrick, the spectator's voyeuristic pleasure, redeemed by participating in moral instruction, in seeing the child burning "lichterloh," the boys "viel schwärzer als das Mohrenkind," and the humorous pleasure of the visual joke of a soup tureen adorning Kaspar's grave.

If German culture is indeed the "Kultur der Zurückhaltung," *Struwwelpeter* is its psychomachia as much as *Faust* or *Magister Ludi* might be said to be.

What, then, does Mark Twain, the archetypal American author, do with this very German set of stories? Mark Twain's relations with Germany and the Germans of his time were generally cordial. The tone of the relationship was set by Baron von Tauchnitz's voluntary payment of royalties to Samuel Clemens for the German translations of his works at a time when international copyright laws did not yet exist or were entirely ineffective. Mark Twain's writings were well received in Germany, and his popularity made him a literary lion by the 1890s, as Clara's comment about her father's steady stream of visitors indicates. Samuel Clemens devoted considerable energy to learning the German language and chronicled some of his frustration with the complexities of German grammar in his essay "The Awful German Language," published as an appendix to *A Tramp Abroad* in 1880. He was confounded by the many cases and difficult declinations, but he turned his frustration into comedy, coining some of the most hilarious descriptions of German linguistic practices ever.

> In German a young lady has no sex, while a turnip has. Think what overwrought reverence that shows for the turnip and what callous disrespect for the girl. . . . I translate this from a conversation in one of the best German Sunday-school books:
>
> "Gretchen—Wilhelm, where is the turnip?
>
> Wilhelm—She has gone to the kitchen.
>
> Gretchen—Where is the accomplished and beautiful English maiden?
>
> Wilhelm—It has gone to the opera."

To continue with the German genders: a tree is male, its buds are female, its leaves are neuter. Horses are sexless, dogs are male, cats are female—tomcats included, of course. A person's mouth, neck, bosom, elbows, fingers, nails, feet and body are of the male sex, and his head is male or neuter according to the word selected to signify it and not according to the sex of the individual who wears it—for in Germany all the women wear either male heads or sexless ones. A person's nose, lips, shoulders, breast, hands and toes are of the female sex and his hair, ears, eyes, chin, legs, knees, heart and conscience haven't any sex at all. The inventor of the language probably got what he knew about a conscience from hearsay.

Twain was one of the great cultural interpreters of his time, writing widely-circulated books that influenced how Americans saw Europe and Europeans. In *A Tramp Abroad* and elsewhere, he represented German culture with a mixture of reverence, irreverent comedy, satire, and frustration. He described romantic scenes such as the Lorelei and the castle at Heidelberg with relish, but he was particularly fascinated by the elaborate rituals of the Burschenschaften (student fraternities) at the university, and described their duels in great detail. He pretended to raft down the Neckar as one would raft down the Mississippi River, and he wrote a brief burlesque of a Black Forest novel, which turns on the question of whose manure pile is the largest.

The great difficulty that Twain faced in translating *Struwwelpeter* was to retain some of the idiomatic flavor of the original while still writing rhyming verse. Translating poetry is a notoriously difficult enterprise, and it is no surprise that translation is often equated with betrayal (the famous Italian pun *traduttore = traditore* illustrates this perception). One can think of the effort of translation as a scale of choices, from literal on the one side to highly interpretive and inventive on the other. The dangers of the literal approach include woodenness, incomprehensibility, or awkwardness because of idioms, metaphors, or phrases that are not used in the target language. Word-for-word translation tends towards lifelessness and artificiality. The perils at the other end of the scale are obvious: departure from the meanings and stylistic qualities of the original, betrayal of the spirit of the source work.

Mark Twain's *Slovenly Peter* is far more interpretive and inventive than faithful. As Susanna Ashton and Amy Jean Petersen have emphasized in their excellent recent article in *Children's Literature Association Quarterly,* Twain attempted to "fetch the jingle [of the original] along" in his interpretation. As Mark Twain himself stated, "Poetry is a sandy road to travel, and the only way to pull through at all is to lay your grammar down and take hold with both hands." This he does, with a vengeance, in *Slovenly Peter.* Twain loved to dramatize intellectual labor as struggle and conflict, as is evident in his violent metaphors throughout his humorous essays and speeches about the German language.

Ashton and Petersen make a largely positive assessment of Twain's interpretation of *Struwwelpeter:* "Although full of awkward rhymes and structures, Twain's renditions may be seen as far more faithful to the *spirit* of the original illustrations and text than the previous translations had been; his difference from the standard English version will strike many readers as all to the good. The language of Twain's work, however, often differs dramatically from the German. He elaborates extensively on scenes that receive little, if any, treatment in the original German version, presumably a reason for his decision to describe his version of Hoffmann's poems as 'freely translated'." This thoughtful judgment has much truth in it, but it perhaps underemphasizes the degree of Mark Twain's interpretation in the process. As in his writings about Germany in *A Tramp Abroad* and elsewhere, Twain puts a selective and distinctly American spin on the material. By intensifying certain elements that are present in the original, he estranges them from their culture of origin and puts a specifically American and Twainian stamp on them.

In particular, Twain uses a range of American references, intensifies the violence, makes himself as translator/interpreter a subject of his writing, and shifts the morals idiosyncratically. Ashton and Petersen point out Twain's use of American slang, such as when the hare "stole his gun and smooched his specs / And hied him hence with these effects." They do not mention that Twain calls the hare "Brer Rabbit," a name that immediately invokes the wealth of American stories dealing with the trickster rabbit who has connections to Anansi, the trickster god of West Africa, and who was popularized for white readers by Joel Chandler Harris. They also do not mention that Twain does not mitigate the implicit racism of **"The Story of the Black Boys,"** which represents the Moor's darkness as something to be pitied. Twain translates the description of the "kohlpech-rabenschwarzer Moor" rather literally as the "coal-pitch-raven-black young Moor." If anything, Twain increases the racism of the episode, for he refers to the Moor as "that poor Missing Link," making an obvious reference to the Darwinian controversy of his time. He also calls the boy "that poor pitch-black piteous Moor," and, most offensively, "that Niggerkin." Where Hoffmann wrote, "Du siehst sie hier, wie schwarz sie sind, viel schwärzer als das Mohrenkind," Twain wrote: "You see them here, all black as sin—Much blacker than that Niggerkin."

Similarly, Twain intensifies the violence of the story in American frontier fashion. Whereas Hoffman's Friederich "schlug den Hund, der heulte sehr, und trat und schlug ihn immer mehr," (he "beat the dog, which howled greatly, and kicked and beat it more and more"), Twain's Fred'rick "whacked him here, he whacked him there, He whacked with all his might and main, He made him howl and dance with pain." Where Hoffmann stated that wicked Friedrich "peitschte seine Gretchen gar"—"even whipped his Gretchen," Twain uses the vastly more suggestive "He banged the housemaid black and blue." When the hare chases the hunter across the landscape, in German he "läuft davon und springt und schreit: 'Zu Hilf', ihr Leut'! Zu Hilf', ihr Leut'!" (He "ran away, and leaped and cried, 'Help, People, Help, People!'") In Twain's burlesque, Brer Rabbit "drew a bead, the hunter fled, And fled, and *fled!* and FLED! and FLED! And howled for help as on he sped, howled as if to raise the dead; O'er marsh and moor, through glade and dell, the awful clamor rose and fell, And in its course where passed this flight, All life lay smitten dead with fright."

Twain does well with some of the onomatopoeic qualities of Hoffmann's original, as in the story of the thumb-sucker: "Bang! here goes the door ker-slam! Whoop! the tailor lands ker-blam! Waves his shears, the heartless grub, And calls for Dawmen-lutscher-bub. Claps his weapon to the thumb, Snips it square as head of drum," and, as Ashton and Peterson note, he intensifies the boy's cry of pain: "While that lad his tongue unfurled And fired a yell heard 'round the world.'" Some of Hoffmann's bizarre details become more bizarre in Twain's interpretation: the little fishes that laugh at Hans Guck-in-die-Luft "lachen, daß man's hören tut, lachen fort noch lange Zeit; und die Mappe schwimmt schon weit"—they "laugh audibly, continue laughing a long time, and the satchel swims far away already." But for Twain, "Those little fish go swimming by And up at him they cock their eye, And stick their heads out full a-span, And laugh as only fishes can; Laugh and giggle, jeer and snort—How strange to see them thus cavort! Meantime the atlas, gone astray, Has drifted many yards away."

What I am suggesting is that Twain adds a strong flavor of fascination with the absurd, grotesque, and violent to his rendition, going considerably beyond the "spirit of the original." This tendency is rooted, I believe, in the frontier tradition of the tall tale, the brag, the burlesque, of the kind that surfaces in his writings again and again, and that reflects the American experience of conflict, isolation, and the overwhelming forces on the frontier. Furthermore, an undercurrent of Puritan theology is visible in certain

details, such as the already-mentioned phrase "black as sin," and, in reaction, in the glee with which Twain dwells on the drunkenness of the dog at Fred'rick's table: "He sips the wine, so rich and red, And feels it swimming in his head, He munches greatful at the cake, And wishes he might never wake From this debauch; while think by think His thoughts dream on, and link by link The liver-sausage disappears, And his hurt soul relents in tears." This is clearly a Presbyterian, not a Lutheran dog.

Hoffmann mentions the wine as a matter of course; Twain, coming from a society in which alcohol was a subject of religious controversy, emphasizes it with libertine pleasure in the violation of taboo. In *A Tramp Abroad,* he pursued a similar theme when he wrote about relations of German professors with their students:

> There seems to be no chilly distance existing between the German students and the professor but, on the contrary, a companionable intercourse, the opposite of chilliness and reserve. When the professor enters a beer-hall in the evening where students are gathered these rise up and take off their caps and invite the old gentleman to sit with them and partake. He accepts and the pleasant talk and the beer flow for an hour or two, and by and by the professor, properly charged and comfortable, gives a cordial good night, while the students stand bowing and uncovered. And then he moves on his happy way homeward with all his vast cargo of learning afloat in his hold. Nobody finds fault or feels outraged. No harm has been done.

Twain's final comments here suggest that he is writing pointedly to an American audience that would not take professors drinking with their students, or perhaps any form of drinking of alcoholic beverages, for granted, or approve of it at all.

Ashton and Petersen have emphasized the friendliness and personableness of Twain's persona as he makes himself visible as translator and narrator in the story, addressing an individual reader: "*You* see them here . . . ." But I wish to add that his asides to the reader seem to me either condescending to the child or meant as jokes aimed at adults. When he writes "The dog's his heir, and this estate That dog inherits, and will ate.*" he adds in the footnote: "*My child, never use an expression like that. It is utterly unprincipled and outrageous to say ate when you mean eat, and you must never do it except when crowded for a rhyme." Similarly when he comments about the phrase "He took his game-bag, powder, gun, And fiercely to the fields he spun,*" he writes in the footnote: "*Baby, you must take notice of this awkward form of speech and never use it. Except in translating."

In a curious way, the American quality of Twain's *Slovenly Peter* contrasts with the communal or collective German quality of *Struwwelpeter.* Hoffmann's classic work is a complex instruction book, not so much in the manners as in the *Sichtweise* or social perspective of German society, with its conflicts about control of the body and of its impulses: issues of Mäßigung, Zucht, Anstand, all common words in German childrearing that have few or no equivalents in American English, at least in idiomatic conversation about childrearing. Mark Twain emphasizes himself as the interpreter and teller of the tales, which he embellishes with themes that are preoccupations of the frontier. He succeeds in making vivid renditions, particularly of the stories of the girl with the matches and **"Cruel Fred'rick."**

Yet Mark Twain misses something essentially German in the original, and substitute something quintessentially American in the process. Perhaps his subtly eccentric interpretation of the **"Story of Flying Robert"** provides an aptly epigrammatic conclusion symbolic of this transposition. Hoffmann concludes with the cryptic image of an unknowable fate that befalls boy, umbrella, and hat as they are carried away:

> Schirm und Robert fliegen dort
> durch die Wolken immer fort.
> Und der Hut fliegt weit voran,
> stößt zuletzt am Himmel an.
> Wo der Wind sie hingetragen,
> ja! das weiß kein Mensch zu sagen.

In Evan Gibson's translation:

> Robert and umbrella there
> still upon the gusty air,
> while his hat blows far ahead;
> from the earth it now has fled.
> Where the wind blew them away
> no one here below can say.

Though Hoffmann emphasizes universal limits: the hat finally hits heaven, and no human being can tell where the three were carried. But Twain describes it thus:

> And so he sails and sails and sails,
> Through banks of murky clouds, and wails,
> And weeps and mourns, poor draggled rat,
> Because he can't o'ertake his hat.
> Oh, where on high can that hat be?

When you find out, pray come tell me.

Both Hoffmann's and Twain's poems are images of human fate in the universe; but Hoffmann's has a stoic agnosticism, a recognition of limits to human knowledge. Twain's "poor draggled rat" is a pitiful soul, absurdly grieving for a lost hat while flying through the vast unknown, and the question Twain wants to have his listeners answer him is not what becomes of the boy, but where the hat has gone. Just as he misses the subtly melancholy yet resigned tone of Hoffmann's flight, the thing he should perhaps have been "auf der Hut" for, Twain misses something of the German quality of *Struwwelpeter,* and substitutes for it a new hat, though not old hat, to be sure.

Gerhard Weiss

SOURCE: "'Tricky Dick': *Struwwelpeter* and American Politics," in *The Lion and the Unicorn,* Vol. 20, No. 2, December, 1996, pp. 217-29.

When in 1845 the newly founded "Literarische Anstalt" in Frankfurt, Germany, printed a little book entitled *Lustige Geschichten und drollige Bilder mit 15 schön colorierten Tafeln für Kinder von 3 bis 6 Jahren,* neither the author, who hid behind the pseudonym Reimerich Kinderlieb, nor the publishers, Messers, Rütten and Loening, suspected that they had made history. For the publishers, it was a children's book like many others, intended for local consumption. Its author, the Frankfurt physician Heinrich Hoffmann, was a complete dilettante as a writer and illustrator, whose sole ambition had been to create an entertaining and wholesome book to give his little son Carl for Christmas. Nobody expected that these *Lustige Geschichten,* known as *Der Struwwelpeter* since their 3rd edition in 1847, would go through countless more editions and become a text that rivals in popularity with the fairy tales of the Brothers Grimm. Even for those who may never have read a line of the book, the image of "Struwwelpeter," the messy fellow with his unkempt hair and uncut fingernails, has become an icon of popular culture, competing with Mickey Mouse and Donald Duck. Today, his image can be found on orange wrappers, coffee mugs, paper napkins, and sundry other paraphernalia.

The publication of *Der Struwwelpeter* was a spark that lit fires all over the world. Almost immediately the book was translated into English and other languages. A number of these translations actually were printed by the "Literarische Anstalt" in Frankfurt and became an important export item for the city. The *Struwwelpeter* franchise turned out to be excellent business. In the early 1880s, the Frankfurt *English Struwwelpeter* "based on the 125th edition of the celebrated German work," reached its 29th edition. As an extra selling point abroad, the color lithographs of the export editions were prepared with particular care.

What is of special interest to us today is not so much the commercial success of *Der Struwwelpeter,* but the miracle that this little book, with its simple verse and its rather dilettante illustrations, almost immediately turned into a worldwide hit, leading not only to a multitude of translations, but also to innumerable adaptations, parodies, and imitations. This is particularly surprising, since German children's books traditionally have had a difficult time being accepted—as has German literature in general—beyond the German language borders. German literature simply does not translate well. Yet, *Der Struwwelpeter* obviously struck a responsive cord abroad, especially in the Anglo-Saxon world. Outside of Grimm's *Märchen,* it has become the only German children's book of world renown. It also has taken on a life of its own, as a spoof work for adults. There even exists a *Großer Struwwelpeter* (written by Richard Schmidt-Cabanis and published in 1877), which was dedicated to "children from 17 to 77."

The many parodies and adaptations that have evolved outside the German speaking countries are a matter of particular fascination. After all, to be effective, these works presuppose a close acquaintance with the prototype to which they allude. Since some of these versions have appeared in substantial editions, one can conclude that the publsihers could count on a reading public well acquainted with the original. These adaptations—many of which are quite sophisticated—predominantly address an adult audience. Almost all have a strong political slant. In Great Britain, where the earliest translation of Heinrich Hoffmann's work became available in 1848, a whole series of parodies and adaptations reached the market around the turn of the century. As far as can be ascertained, the earliest has been Edward Harold Begbie's *The Political Struwwelpeter,* published in London in 1899. It uses the *Struwwelpeter* theme to satirize the British political scene of the day; its messy fellow is the "neglected" British Lion, with unkempt mane and uncut claws:

> See the British Lion pose
> Wildly groping for his foes!
> Men who tinker up the laws
> Never manicure his claws:

> And you will observe with pain
> No one ever crimps his mane;
> Seeing that he's so neglected
> Do you wonder he's dejected?

Another work by the same author, the *Struwwelpeter Alphabet,* was published in 1900. It shows Queen Victoria towering as a Christmas angel over the problems of the British Empire. Individual public figures appear in alphabetical order and in mostly unflattering ways. Under "G", for example, we find the German Emperor, decked out in military glory with a tankard of beer in one hand and a German flag in the other. The letter "Z" is occupied by Emile Zola, drawn in the image of Hoffmann's "großer Nikolas" in the process of dunking the naughty boys into the big inkwell. Zola's "naughties," of course, are the culprits of the Dreyfus trial, and "Into the pot by one and twos, He plunges all and cries—'J'accuse'!"

With the exception of the portrait of William II, there was no connection to anything specifically German in these adaptations. This changed in 1914 when, two months into the war, Edward Lucas published his *Swollen Headed William,* "painful stories and funny pictures. After the German!" Within one month, the book reached four editions and a total volume of 50,000 copies. The British tradition of *Struwwelpeter* adaptations continued through the Third Reich. In 1933, *Truffel Eater. Pretty Stories and Funny Pictures,* was printed in London by an author who used the pseudonym "Oistros," i.e., Horse Fly. Its Struwwelpeter is Adolf Hitler himself: "Look at Adolf where he stands / With his Nazi hair and hands." The last of the great British adaptations is *Struwwelhitler: A Nazi Story Book by Doktor Schrecklichkeit,* a book authored by Robert and Philip Spence and published in London in 1941. The authors call it "a parody on the original Struwwelpeter" (1), and the "Führer" appears in all his horror:

> Just look at him! There he stands
> With his nasty hair and hands
> See the horrid blood drops drip
> From each dirty finger tip.

We do not know how many copies of this book were actually sold and to what extent it contributed to the Allied war effort. Its profits, in any case, were dedicated to the "*Daily Sketch* War Relief fund, which supplies wireless sets, games, and woolen comforts to our Fighting Services, and clothing, bedding, boots and food to air raid victims."

While the British excelled in their political adaptations of *Der Struwwelpeter,* we find nothing of similar quality in America. To be sure, Heinrich Hoffmann's book reached the shores of the United States soon after its initial publication in Europe. In addition to the imported Frankfurt and London copies, actual American translations are recorded as early as 1849. James Taylor Dunn points out that the Philadelphia edition of 1851, entitled *Slovenly Peter, or Pleasant Stories and Funny Pictures,* in fact is an 1849 translation by Annis Lee Furness. It was this book which became a favorite at the house of Ralph Waldo Emerson. Today, a picture of Slovenly Peter by Emerson's son Edward graces the *Struwwelpeter* Web site on the Internet. Mark Twain's translation, completed in Berlin in 1891 as a Christmas present for his children (the Hoffmann tradition repeats itself), was not put to print until 1935. To be sure, there were a number of other American translations, and—from the 1930s to 1954—one copy of Hoffmann's original manuscript (Manuscript #2), found a home in New York. The New York Public Library is the holder of a copy of one of the very few surviving first editions of the book. There also can be no question that copies of *Der Struwwelpeter* were brought over from Germany and were a staple in the libraries of middle-class German immigrants. German bookstores in New York, Milwaukee, Cincinnati, St. Louis, and other "German" centers had their *Struwwelpeter*s in stock. However, as far as we know, no "authorized" German version was ever printed in the United States. Nevertheless, *Der Struwwelpeter* remains well known among people of German descent—even if an inquiry solicits nothing more than "Ah, yes, *that* book! My grandfather loved to read it to me. Grandpa was very authoritarian."

It must be admitted that *Der Struwwelpeter* never had the intellectual impact on the United States that it once had on Britain. In America, it remained for the most part a book for children. However, even in the United States, Hoffmann's book was the impetus for at least one major political satire, Dr. Joseph Wortis' *Tricky Dick and His Pals.* It is a book of "comic stories . . . and funny pictures. . . . All in the manner of Dr. Heinrich Hoffmann's *Der Struwwelpeter.*" The twenty-six page work was published in 1974 by Quadrangle/New York Times Books in New York and simultaneously in Canada. In many ways, this book is a maverick and it is very difficult to trace its publishing history. Although issued by a major publishing house, it apparently was never reviewed, and it has also been impossible to ascertain how many copies of it had actually been printed. Neither the original publisher nor its successor, Random House, could furnish any information. Even the Library of Congress was at a loss regarding the number of cop-

ies contained in the book's one and only edition. All indications are that the number must have been quite small, most likely because the book appeared on the market when the Nixon presidency had already become history. *Tricky Dick* remained listed in *Books in Print* until 1982, at a price of $3.95.

While Dr. Wortis' book was not a political bombshell, it nevertheless shows an intriguing use of the *Struwwelpeter* theme in a contemporary American setting. However, before we examine the work itself, we need to say a few words about its author, and how he came to write his *Struwwelpeter* derivative, the cautionary tale of *Tricky Dick and His Pals.* Dr. Joseph Wortis was a New York psychiatrist. In 1934, he had spent some time in Vienna in order to learn psychoanalysis from Sigmund Freud by having himself psychoanalyzed by the master. Twenty years later, Wortis published his copious notes from these sessions under the title *Fragments of an Analysis with Freud.* This elegantly written book was well received, even by the general public. It offers a fascinating view of Freud's way of operating and reveals quite a bit about Dr. Wortis himself. Dr. Wortis, whose mother was Alsatian, spoke German well. In the preface to the Freud book he writes: "Our conversations were all in German, but I kept my notes in English, with frequent inclusion of the German words and phrases that Freud used." In the spring of 1956, the *New Yorker* published a parody of this book which, as Dr. Henry Wortis said, left his father "not amused." An earlier publication by Joseph Wortis was a treatise on *Soviet Psychiatry,* which appeared in 1950, at the height of the Cold War. It resulted in a citation before the Senate Internal Security Subcommittee in 1953. When Wortis was asked whether he had any Communist affiliations, he responded "I must say that my mother always brought me up to feel that it was extremely impolite to ask people what their political views were." While Dr. Wortis' obituary in the *New York Times* (February 28, 1995) lists his many publications and accomplishments, *Tricky Dick and His Pals* is not mentioned at all.

The family environment which Dr. Wortis had created in his home was one in which the arts and a liberal political activism played a major role. In the immediate family, there were authors, poets, composers, and painters. His wife Helen published a book and articles on women's rights. His younger son, Avi Wortis (now a well-known writer of children's books, publishing under the pseudonym "Avi"), speaks of a "house full of books," where it was a tradition that the children would be read to every night, and where the grandparents were known to be "excellent story tellers."

Dr. Joseph Wortis knew the German *Struwwelpeter* from his German-speaking mother and he later read English versions to his own children. The book held a special fascination for him, and he considered it "very moral, teaching children not to be cruel to animals, not to be racist, not to play with fire, etc." Perhaps he saw a certain kinship between himself and Dr. Heinrich Hoffmann. In 1988, he dedicated an editorial to Hoffmann in his own journal, *Biological Psychiatry,* in which he writes: "the crimes of Hitlerism have given Germany a bad name, but we need to remember that Germany has its great progressive traditions, too, of Goethe, Heine, Bach, Beethoven, and many others. It is within this great tradition that Hoffmann has his modest place, an enlightened psychiatrist who advanced the humane reforms of his time, an early enemy of racism, sexism, and reaction, who embraces the whole broad culture of his period, and who brought joy and humor to countless millions of children and adults."

We do not know what exactly brought Wortis to write his *Tricky Dick* in the *Struwwelpeter* style. His own moral outrage at the Nixon capers obviously played a major part. He maintains that he had not been aware of any previous *Struwwelpeter* adaptations and parodies and that, therefore, none had served as his model. He saw Hoffmann's book as a cautionary tale with a set of negative examples from which children could learn moral lessons. In his own text, he tries a similar deterrent approach by presenting "some more stories about children today who got into trouble" (Preface). It is a *reductio ad absurdum,* in which Richard Nixon and his associates are shrunk to ill-behaving boys in small-town America, the supposed epicenter of morality. The language is deliberately simple, keeping with the author's proclaimed intent that this is actually a book for children: "Look at this child so clean and slick / He's called Obnoxious Tricky Dick" (introductory episode). The reader soon realizes that this is not a book designed for a "Children's Story Hour," but that the real addressee is the sophisticated adult who can understand the allusions to the political events. In many ways, these stories are akin to the critical cartoons of the Nixon era, like those of Herblock, for example. For the reader today, more than twenty years after Watergate, the work has become a *roman a clèf,* written in a code that requires some effort to decipher.

As a work in the *Struwwelpeter* tradition, the illustrations are an integral part of the text. In the Preface, Joseph Wortis directly refers to this: "Over a hundred years ago Dr. Heinrich Hoffmann would draw funny pictures and tell comical stories to children who were sick. The children liked the stories so much that they didn't mind taking their medicine." On the inside cover, we find many examples of actual *Struwwelpeter* images ("Philip Flips," "Pauline Plays with Matches," "Frightful Freddy," "Poor Connie," "Kaspar won't Eat his Dinner / Kaspar gets Thinner and Thinner," etc.).

The illustrations for *Tricky Dick* were prepared by David Arkin, Wortis' brother-in-law. Arkin had made a name for himself as author and illustrator of a children's book *Black and White,* "a song that is a story about freedom to go to school together." Although the book was published in 1966, Arkin's poem "Black and White" actually dates back to 1956, the early days of the Civil Rights movement.

While some of Arkin's colourful illustrations are *Struwwelpeter* inspired, the iconography is strictly American. The images have no foreign accent. The setting seems to be America's heartland, with a distinct 1920s-1930s flavor. It is the world of Norman Rockwell, or of the Hardy Boys. This makes the actions of the "Pals" appear even more outrageous and, to put it simply, "un-American." As in *Der Struwwelpeter,* the figures are drawn with simple strokes, showing exaggerated gesticulations. Dick, of course, is always recognizable by his conspicuous nose, his prominent ears, and his hairline. Two pictorial leitmotifs remind us of the making and unmaking of the political Nixon: the dog and the tapes. On the title page, Nixon stands on top of the doghouse, resting securely on the political foundation of his "Checkers Speech." Behind him is the empty tape-reel, the eighteen minute gap that he hoped would save his presidency. In the last episode, however, Dick is himself in the doghouse, and the tapes unravel around him.

The twenty-six unnumbered pages of the book contain an Introduction that defines Dick's character, twelve episodes describing various pranks committed by Dick and his gang, and a Conclusion showing Dick's just punishment. In the first episode, we encounter "Dick the Snooper":

> Dick loved to sneak, he loved to pry
> And peep through keyholes on the sly. . . .
> He liked to do these things, but UGH!-
> Especially he liked to bug.

Dick becomes so obsessed with bugging that he finally bugs himself and then finds that his friends are also listening in, leading him to cry out "You snoop on me, it isn't fair!" The second episode, entitled "Dick goes Shopping" is the story of Little Dick being sent by mother to "buy some milk and sugar quick." The naughty boy tries to cheat his mother out of the change, but in the end has to pay back every cent. This leads to the moral conclusion: "Children who try to fool their mothers / Will never tell the truth to others." The reference here, of course, is to the allegation that Nixon abused public funds, as was claimed in the case of the $17 million spent on his private estate, and in his tax audit which resulted in an additional tax bill of $300,000. In the third episode, we deal with "Uncle Sam's Illness." This turns out to be an interesting adaptation of the **"Friedrich"** and the **"Hunter"** tales of the original *Struwwelpeter* with a Nixonian twist:

> When Dicky's Uncle Sam was ill
> And saved to pay the doctor bill,
> Dick took the money just for fun
> So he could buy a great big gun.

Friedrich gets bitten by the dog, Dicky shoots himself with his own gun—they both end up having learned a lesson and taking bitter medicine. The subtext, of course, is the claim that President Nixon diverted money badly needed to address social ills in order to increase the military budget.

Episode four introduces us to Dick's pals: We meet "Jan and Hans," who follow Dicky through thick and thin: "They'd mess in things that weren't theirs / and poke in other folks' affairs." One night, they sneak into a doctor's house, to look at "dirty books." The reference here is to Nixon's aids Ehrlichman and Haldeman who broke into the office of Dr. Fielding, Daniel Ellsberg's psychiatrist. In the fifth episode, we meet the "Katzenjammer Big Parade," a spoof on the Committee to Re-elect the President. The kids march down Main Street, blindly following the banner of "Dick's the One" (cf. the campaign slogan: Nixon's the One), until they fall into a sewer hole. Episode six, the "Nasty Tongue" recalls the capers of Spiro Agnew, now re-named "Kid Spagno." His nasty tongue and shady business deals finally catch up with him: "But this time he was in the soup / And landed in the chicken coop." He is exposed as a "Phony Fake" and put away for good. The seventh episode conjures up the shades of Donald Segretti, the "Dirty Tricks Man" of the 1972 Nixon campaign. He appears as Dicky's pal Confetti and does what Segretti had done: he plants stink bombs (here at a church

affair), and he writes fake letters ("He'd send mean letters out to Eddie / And sign them with the name of Freddie"). In the end, of course, justice prevails, and as punishment he loses his girlfriend Kate, because he had "messed things up so horribly."

Episode eight continues the "Dirty Tricks," now focusing on the "White House Plumber" Howard Hunt, who here appears as "Howie the Rat." He is a rat that tries to appear as a sweet pussycat. In due course he is found out for what he really is, and is laughed back into his rathole. Gradually, Dicky and his pals run into difficulties as other children begin to resist them. For example, in episode nine, "Dick gets Burned," Dick uses jelly-gasoline (napalm?) against his enemies, but in the end is himself "ignited." There is an interesting iconography here, for the children whom Dick and his pals are trying to beat up are obviously people of color. Indeed, one could read this episode as a reference to the war in Viet Nam, or to American involvements in the uprisings in Latin America. The text leaves this open:

> Some other children, girls and boys
> Agreed to share their games and toys,
> But Tricky Dick called them bad names
> And took their toys and stole their games.
> He and his pals began to fight
> To force those kids with all their might
> To change their ways and play like him. . . .

In the brief episode ten, we find a portrayal of "Martha and Mitch"—i.e., U.S. Attorney General John Mitchell and his wife Martha. Like the real Martha Mitchell, little Martha of this episode is so upset with "this dishonest rotten mess" that she "spills the beans" of Mitch's crimes: "She told her parents what he did / While frightened little Mitchell hid." Episode eleven, entitled "Cops and Robbers" draws on Nixon's friendship with the wealthy Bebe Reboso, here appearing under the name of "Babe."

> Dick liked Babe best of all the boys,
> Because he owned a lot of toys,
> A boy who could help him in his aim
> To get more power and more fame.

The boys get into all kinds of trouble. They rob and steal and even snitch Havana cigars from Babe's father. When they smoke them in secret, they, of course, get horribly sick and are punished with a "great big whack."

Episode twelve presents us with the penultimate Watergate. In the story of Tricky Dick, it becomes a real floodgate installed in a drainage ditch, where Dick's sister Ella is happily floating her toy-boat.

Dick together with his friends Stan (Maurice Stans) and Mitch (John Mitchell), up to no good as usual, open the watergate "and almost drowned that ship of state. / Some plumbers tried to stop the tide / But they were all just swept aside." While Dick is saved at the last moment "all covered up with mud so high / His mother thought he'd nearly die," he does receive his just reward in the Conclusion, "Dick's Punishment." Now the children all turn against him, and he ends in the doghouse,

> . . . alone in his disgrace
> And no one wants to see his face.
> And nobody will trust him now
> As far as you can throw a cow.
> For trust is earned, it seems to me,
> Only by truth and decency.

This brief overview can give the reader only an inkling of what *Tricky Dick* is all about. As with *Struwwelpeter,* its illustrations form an integral part of the text and need to be considered to appreciate the book fully. It certainly is not a parody, because Wortis moves far afield from the original German story. Yet, Hoffmann's old tale definitely had inspired him. Wortis himself acknowledges this ancestry. It is the *Struwwelpeter* technique that has shaped *Tricky Dick,* a moral tale "for children," but with an even more important subtext that can only be appreciated by fairly sophisticated adults. Did Dr. Wortis' *Tricky Dick* actually influence American politics? Of course not. The book has remained a sleeper and is known only to *Struwwelpeter* friends. Richard Nixon most likely never read this cautionary tale, and the book has in no way improved the ethics in political Washington. But, then, it shares such a lack of political effectiveness with all the other *Struwwelpeter* adaptations, wherever they may have appeared. They are intellectual exercises for the connoisseurs, printed in the main by respected publishing houses and not by firebrand clandestine presses. Their subversion is not really subversive. Yet, though they have not toppled any governments, they are one more testimony to the remarkable universal appeal of Dr. Heinrich Hoffmann's *Lustige Geschichten,* which were first published 150 years ago, and which, in the oldest tradition of booktitling, became known by their incipit, *Der Struwwelpeter.*

Thomas Freeman

SOURCE: "Heinrich Hoffmann's *Struwwelpeter*: An Inquiry into the Effects of Violence in Children's Literature" in *Journal of Popular Culture,* Vol. 10, No. 4, Spring, 1997, pp. 808-20.

One of the all-time best sellers in German children's literature is Heinrich Hoffmann's *Struwwelpeter,* a short collection of illustrated verses which achieved unprecedented popularity almost immediately after its publication in 1844. For several generations almost every German child has read the *Struwwelpeter.* While today some parents consider it too violent for their children, and replace it with milder fare, five German publishers currently keep it in print, despite the fact that over 600 editions have already been printed. Cheap paperback editions are widely found in bookstores, newsstands, and department stores. Among the translations into many foreign languages is a Latin version after the manner of *Winnie the Pooh.*

The author of *Struwwelpeter* tells us that he was forced to write the book himself because he was unable to find what he considered suitable reading material for his three year old son. In the winter of 1844 Hoffmann was looking for a picture-book to use as a Christmas present. He was not satisfied with what he found in any of the primers he examined—especially those with abstract moral pronouncements like "Good children must be honest, must keep themselves clean," etc. He believed that children are more responsive to simple visual presentations than to verbal exhortations. He decided to create a primer in verse of his own, and to illustrate it himself with pictures which would be appropriate, simple, and which would delight a child. Although he had published some of his poetry previously, he did not originally intend the *Struwwelpeter* to circulate beyond his immediate family. However, when several of his friends persuaded him to publish the book, he took enough pride in his creation to stipulate that his illustrations be printed just as he had drawn them and not be touched up or altered by professional artists.

Hoffmann was neither a professional artist nor a writer. He was a private physician, who also devoted part of his time to caring for patients in an insane asylum. It is indeed surprising that a doctor interested in psychiatric medicine would produce a book which would deliberately frighten young children and increase their anxiety. According to Hoffmann's own account, he had already sketched little episodes such as we find in the *Struwwelpeter* to distract and "comfort" the frightened young children he treated in his medical practice. These children, particularly those between the ages of three and six, were terrified of doctors, because when they misbehaved their parents would use the threat of the doctor to intimidate them: "If you don't eat your spinach the doctor will come and get you and give you bitter medicine and let his leeches loose on you!"

Hoffmann describes the fears of his little patients with such sympathy and sensitivity that one might almost think he opposed the popular Victorian practice of using threats to scare children into their "proper" place, where they are to be seen and not heard. The children had merely to catch sight of Dr. Hoffmann and they would burst into tears, fight him off and kick. But the doctor's little sketches can only have made the children more frightened than ever, since they replace one fear with many others. And if they were as effective in quieting the children as he says they were, then this was not because they comforted the children, but rather because they probably shocked them into a state of stupefied horror. Now they were no longer worried that the doctor would "get them"—they were much more terrified by Hoffmann's tailor and his scissors.

> And above all Conrad listen—don't be dumb.
> You must no longer suck your thumb.
> If you do the tailor will come
> And cut it off before you can run.
> Like a piece of paper, the scissors will sever,
> And you'll never have another. Never. Never.
> Mommy leaves: Is Conrad disconcerted?
> Not at all: slurp-whoop the thumb's inserted.
> Bang goes the door,
> And then before
> Conrad can run away,
> The tailor comes and cuts and cuts.
> The thumbs are gone—they do not stay.
> And when Mommy comes home, Conrad is sad.
> The thumbs are gone from this boy who's been bad.

Quite a few writers on German children's literature have sought to rationalize away the potential harm of the *Struwwelpeter.* In her well-known book on European children's literature, Bettina Hürlimann praises the wonderful deep blue color of thumb-sucking Conrad's coat. She is not quite so enthusiastic about the deep red of his spattering blood. Hürlimann confesses that the story and the picture still give her cold shivers, as they did when she was a child. She recalls that when she was little she used to quickly skip over the page with the skinny tailor and the big scissors with all the blood dripping down—and Conrad screaming. But she could never resist glancing at it either. She knows that other critics have disapproved of Hoffmann's violent method of breaking the habit of thumb-sucking, but she herself concludes that the means he employs to break this "evil practice" are justified. After all, she says, modern psychology has

not been able to come up with any better way of eliminating thumb-sucking, and Dr. Hoffmann was willing to try anything to cure children of the offensive habit.

Another unforgettable figure from the *Struwwelpeter* is Paulina, the little girl who plays with matches. Hürlimann also finds this story justified. For although the child's fate is "terrible," the reader is only subjected to one "little" picture of her burning up. Moreover, the picture of her reduced to a small pile of smoldering ashes has more of "symbolic" than a "realistic" effect.

> **"The Sad Story of the Matches"**
> Paulina was alone all day
> Her parents both had gone away.
> And so with happy cheer she sprang
> Through the room, and sang and sang.
> Then suddenly right near her kitty
> She saw the matches neat and pretty.
> "Oh," she said, "how nice and fine,
> This toy will be mine, all mine!
> I'll light this little wooden stick,
> Just like Mommy, sure and quick."
> And Minz and Maunz the cats both grey
> Lift their paws as if to say:
> Meow Me-oh Meow Me-oh.
> Your daddy always told you no.
> Hands off or up in flames you'll go!
> Paulina does not hear the cats say no,
> The lighted matches brightly glow . . .
> Alas alack—her dress is aflame.
> Her apron burns—this is no game.
> Her hand burns and then her hair
> And soon Paulina isn't there.
> And Minz and Maunz, they scream; how pitifully they
> 　cry.
> Help! Help! Oh me! Oh my!
> The whole child's burning clear up to the sky!
> Everything is burned away.
> The little child: her skin, her hair.
> We cannot find them anywhere.
> A pile of ash is all that's there.
> And two little shoes—so red, so fair.
> And Minz and Maunz they sit in tears,
> And cry though no one ever hears.
> Meow, Me-oh, Meow, Me-oh.
> Where did the poor child's parents go?
> And as they cry their tears do flow
> Like a brooklet through the meadow.

I do not agree that these poems can be justified as suitable reading material for small children.

Both the stories of Conrad and Paulina play upon some of the worst fears which can torment a child. Not only is Paulina burned up, but also she is abandoned by her parents, when she needs them desperately. Psychoanalysts would no doubt tell us that the loss of Conrad's thumbs suggests children's castration fears. It is not merely because of the possible lasting impact of these scenes that the *Struwwelpeter* can be harmful.

One of the poems which exemplifies best what I think is wrong with the book is the story of "naughty Frederic." This may be taken as an attack on cruelty to animals, as Hürlimann maintains; even so, it does not present the right reasons for being kind to them. In the poem and illustrations we are shown bad little Frederic, who tears the wings off of flies, beats birds to death with a chair, and kills a cat with a brick. However, when he attacks a dog with his whip he meets his match. After being beaten and kicked until he yowls terribly, the dog turns on Frederic and bites his leg deep "into his blood," (which we see spurting out). Now it is Frederic's turn to howl and cry, and the pain is so great that he has to go to bed and take bitter medicine, administered by a doctor who bears an unmistakable resemblance to Dr. Hoffmann himself.

We see that in this poem we are not told to be kind to animals because they have feelings and suffer, but rather because the torture may backfire and the victim may strike back at us and hurt us in turn. We are not told to be moral for morality's sake. Instead we are told to behave—or else. Still, despite the distortions and exaggerations there is a certain sense to what happens. It is not true, as Zipes has maintained in a recent article, that no clear-cut reasons are given for the behavior of any of the characters in the *Struwwelpeter* or for the punishments they are subjected to. Paulina plays with matches because she thinks they are pretty toys, and what happens to her follows as a logical and perfectly possible consequence of what she does. Similarly the death of another figure, little Caspar, who refuses to eat because he does not like his food, is not exactly a capricious punishment doled out without explanation by arbitrary authority. The reason for his death is simple He does not eat. And the character who gives the book its name, the *Struwwelpeter* ("Struwwel" means "in disarray"), is a little boy who has refused to cut his hair or nails for almost a year. The result is that he is considered disgusting and is rejected for his claws and his long hair. (Little did Hoffmann suspect that what he depicted as the horror of horrors would come to be a "chic" hair style of the future.)

One of the most striking episodes in the *Struwwelpeter* is the **"Story of the Black Boy,"** which Hürlimann condones as an "enchanting" "childish comedy" preaching "racial tolerance." It is, in fact,

nothing of the sort. The first illustration shows a little black boy with huge lips, dressed only in short pants and carrying an umbrella. He looks very much like little black Sambo. The text tells us that he is a "tarcoal-raven" black Moor, as "black as ink." We also see three little German boys pointing at him and laughing because he is black. Bearded "big Nicholas" then brings his "big ink pot" and angrily warns them that they should leave the black boy alone. Nicholas explains that it's not the boy's fault he is black; he can't help it that he is not as white as they are. Despite the warning, the boys laugh even harder at the "poor" black Moor. Then, Nicholas seizes the white boys, and ignoring their struggles and screams, immerses them in his big ink pot, making them "even blacker" than the Moor. Hoffmann was trying to advocate racial tolerance by punishing the white boys for laughing at the black child. Unfortunately, his own racism was so deeply ingrained that he considered being black itself to be a punishment.

Many writers on German children's literature besides Hürlimann, have overlooked or rationalized away the potential harm of the *Struwwelpeter.* Dyhrenfurth for example, believes that the severe punishments in the book satisfy the child's simple desire for justice. But do children really think that thumb-sucking is a crime of such magnitude that the offender should have his thumbs amputated? Does another figure in the book, called little Robert, deserve to be blown away forever simply because he goes out in the rain with his umbrella when he is not supposed to? The punishments are indeed disproportionate to the offense.

Wiegand calls the *Struwwelpeter* "harmless satire," an example of "comic epic poetry," full of the grossest exaggerations, but nevertheless "well-intentioned." He approves of the *Struwwelpeter* as a "classic" for preschoolers, but he finds some of the imitations of the original book by other writers so brutal that they turn his stomach.

Merget writes that although some children have been frightened by the pictures, the book is original; furthermore, children like it since they love exaggerations. Rümann also praises the "original, fresh" quality of Hoffmann's illustrations, and the "charm" of the first edition with its excellently printed colors.

Critics disagree as to whether or not children will take the pictures literally, as depictions of reality. Dyhrenfurth stresses that the pictures, which are now old-fashioned, are removed from daily reality, conveying the atmosphere of fairy tales, which makes the book less realistically brutal. By contrast, Köster says that Hoffmann, who knew just what interests children, wrote from their point of view and created episodes which relate to their daily lives. Schneider agrees: since young children fail to grasp fairy tales whose heroes are far removed from everyday experience they prefer stories that relate to daily life. According to Schneider, the **Struwwelpeter** is a "typical and charming" example of this kind of relevance.

Recent critics of the book have objected not to its violence but to its authoritarian method. Halbfas says the **Struwwelpeter** is the prototype of many books that reflected the prevailing attitudes of the nineteenth-century German nursery. Fathers expected their children to obey them without question or qualification; and severely punished any deviations from their socially acceptable code. According to Zipes the **Struwwelpeter** is indeed a "children's classic," not only because of its vast and continual sales, but also because it upheld the values of the "ruling class." Zipes claims that various elites have foisted so-called classics on children to make them fear God, adults, and governments, and thus become passive obedient subjects. By stating that the book is "a primer on how to cultivate the authoritarian personality which has been stamped on the consciousness of German children for generations," Zipes implies that the book contributed to producing the kind of mentality that made the Third Reich possible. One immediately thinks of Adorno's study *The Authoritarian Personality*. It seems to me, however, that one does not produce, or undo authoritarian personalities with primers. The **Struwwelpeter** is not so much a "cause," as it is a reflection of what already exists in a society. Zipes singles out the **Struwwelpeter** as a symbol of the manipulation of children by today's "unscrupulous publishers, librarians, educators and parents' organizations," who seek to "stifle creativity and curiosity," but are opposed by recent anti-authoritarian and socialist children's literature. Zipes's view is an exaggeration bordering on caricature. I see no improvement in replacing authoritarian indoctrination with its socialist analogue glorifying the joys of collective life-styles. The **Struwwelpeter** as the symbol of the indoctrination and exploitation of children reminds me of the parodies of literary techniques in the *Pooh Perplex*. By contrast Brinkmann, a Jungian, interprets the **Struwwelpeter** as an archetypal manifestation of the destructive aspect of the god Shiva and of figures from Germanic and Greek mythology. Thus we now have conflicting interpretations of the mystique of the **Struwwelpeter** which run the gamut from

mythological, to Marxist, Jungian, Freudian, and Christian interpretations. Perhaps what we still need is a grand synthesis in the manner of Aristotle or Hegel!

In *Der Struwwelpeter von Heute,* a little-known work published in 1914, and intended both for parents as well as for children, Friedrich Stern sought to undo what he claimed was the psychological damage caused by the **Struwwelpeter.** Stern presented a new set of verses and pictures based on the old ones, but systematically contradicting them. He dedicated the book to Hoffmann and the many children whom he had frightened with his book. Stern's new poems teach that children should be allowed to let off steam, and have a good time while they can, since the rest of life is so serious. The "Struwwelpeter" should be allowed to wear his hair however he likes. After all, composers and artists and other adults have long hair. Besides, the external appearance of the "Struwwelpeter's" head is not important if his thoughts are good. Stern denies that Frederic was really wicked; his parents and the adult world were responsible for his naughtiness. Similarly, Paulina was not to blame for her unfortunate fate, her mother should never have left the matches where she could reach them. Conrad should not be reprimanded for sucking his thumb, since adults are satisfying the same impulse when they smoke pipes and cigars. Stern urges Conrad to return as an adult, form a fist with his mutilated hand, and "really bash" that tailor for what he did to him. Caspar, says Stern, was no doubt justified in refusing to eat his watery soup; he should have been given something good to eat.

Stern thus places the blame for children's bad behavior on their parents, who are too busy amusing themselves to pay attention to the little ones. His anti-authoritarian position is summarized in his declaration that we should resist all people, "whether master or knave" who seek to rob us of our "freedom to think and believe as we choose." This noble sentiment makes his treatment of the story of the little black boy all the more disappointing and disconcerting. To be sure, the illustration shows the ink-pot spilled over, Nicholas retreating into the background, and a little white boy shaking hands with the little black boy. But the text tells us that stark naked little "nigger boys" (the English words are used) are indeed rarely seen in Germany. If they stay in the Congo that's one thing, but in Germany it's only natural for children to laugh, and adults too. It's no crime against the state to laugh, so there is no need for Nicholas to inflict any punishment. The "punishment" of using the ink-pot to turn the little boys into blacks was too severe. The best thing is to bring the little boys some goodies to eat, and get the little black boy dressed in some proper clothing as quickly as possible. Ironically, in view of the fanatical development of German racism later in the twentieth century, this one "crime" in the *Struwwelpeter* should have been severely condemned, not rewarded with "goodies."

Conclusion: How Harmful is the **Struwwelpeter?**

The *Struwwelpeter* has been frightening and horrifying children for generations, but has it inflicted any long-term psychological damage on young readers? I think the book may in fact be potentially harmful to children, but its effect really depends on the total context in which a child grows up. In other words, its effect depends primarily on parental attitudes towards punishment and violence, and on the way the book is presented or read to the child. The eminent child psychiatrist Bruno Bettelheim believes that if a child is already "happy and well-adjusted" the long-term effect of the *Struwwelpeter* will not be significant. For these fortunate children, the book is "like water running off a duck's back." However, according to Bettelheim, if a child already has trouble dealing with his anxieties, the *Struwwelpeter* can reinforce them, though it does not create them. They are already there. Thus seeing the tailor cutting off Conrad's thumbs can reinforce castration fears. Similarly the violence in the *Struwwelpeter* can reinforce the aggressiveness which is already there in a child. This does not mean, however, that *all* violence should be removed from *all* children's literature. The fact is, that even before they encounter literature, children have already inevitably and unavoidably been exposed to influences which make it impossible for them to be "innocent." On the contrary, as Bettelheim has written, their imaginations are "violent, anxious, destructive, even sadistic." Given the fact that regardless of what they read or see children are troubled by "formless, nameless anxieties . . . chaotic, angry, and even violent fantasies," there is really no point in trying to shelter children by censoring all possible violence and fear out of their lives. The important thing is to help children deal with the "violent beast" already in them. And here the *Struwwelpeter* fails dismally. It uses violence negatively. It sets out deliberately to frighten children into obedience. Fairy tales also attempt to shape children's characters and they also contain a considerable amount of brutal violence. In fact, Hoffmann cited the violence in fairy tales as a justification for the violence in the *Struwwelpeter.* By contrast, as

Bettelheim has shown in his most recent book, fairy tales use violence in a positive, constructive manner, to reassure children that the violence within them is not unique and to suggest to them ways of coping with it. Instead of merely accusing children of being bad and making them guilty as the *Struwwelpeter* does, fairy tales are often symbolic representations of the process of psychological growth which children of various ages are able to grasp semiconsciously and even unconsciously. They offer to children a vehicle for fantasizing about their problems, for venting their hostilities and working through their conflicts (many of which are repressed into the unconscious) without the damage and pain of a direct, conscious, explicit confrontation.

Not long ago I was in a movie theater filled with young children watching a film where screaming victims were being mutilated and eaten alive by giant rats. Although these ghastly scenes showed every possible detail of color and sound, the little children did not appear to suffer from what they saw. Quite the contrary, they were laughing with delight. Bettelheim has written that to deprive a child of monsters and violence and horror in literature is to leave the child "helpless with his worse anxieties—much more so than if he had been told fairy tales which give the anxieties form and body and also show ways to overcome these monsters. If our fear of being devoured takes the tangible form of a witch, it can be gotten rid of by burning her in the oven!" The crucial point is that the fairy tales show children a way out: the heroes overcome obstacles and emerge victorious; problems are solved; monsters are vanquished; and evildoers are violently punished. These punishments reassure the child that the world is just, and the violence of the punishments does not disturb him, since he is aware that *he* is not the evil one who will suffer. Children watching a horror film can enjoy it because they can anticipate the destruction of the monsters. The "good" heroes with whom they identify emerge victorious. But some children who read the *Struwwelpeter* are exposed to the devastating experience, of seeing children with whom they identify subject to guilt without forgiveness and punishment without reprieve.

What then are the long-term effects of violence in the *Struwwelpeter?* At best it has no lasting effect on children, but at worst it can reinforce already existing fears and violent tendencies. How then, do violent tendencies originate in children? Konrad Lorenz has postulated the existence of an innate aggressive instinct in man, which would account for these tendencies, but Lorenz draws unfounded analogies between the behavior of lower animals and man, and his theory has been thoroughly discredited. If man's violence is not predetermined, but *learned,* then we must indeed acquire violence and aggression from our surroundings.

It seems to follow that the impact of violence not only in literature but especially in the other media must be truly profound. Could it be that nations raised on a fare of constant violence as "entertainment" are prone to outbreaks of violent crime? Or are they more likely to be caught up in the irrational frenzy of war with its inevitable attrocities? Is it possible that violence in the media desensitizes us and lowers our resistance to violence so that we accept it and take it for granted?

Alternatively, is it also possible that the media are a kind of steam valve that allows us vicarious participation in violence? Up to this point, studies of the effect of violence in the media on behavior have offered contradictory conclusions. Perhaps this is because questions such as these cannot be answered with certainty. It seems to me, however, that there are other factors which take precedence over exposure to violence in the media. Among these are the child's early relationships to people rather than to books and films and TV. It has been shown, for instance, that:

> aggressive children are likely to come from homes where the expression of aggression is not regulated by family rules. By the age of twelve, however, such children show less aggression than those from permissive homes with neither rules nor punishment. The least aggressive children come from homes which confront them from infancy with strong rules to prevent aggression but in which bad behavior is controlled in a nonpunitive manner. In such homes praise and affection are balanced against the withdrawal of love when the child behaves badly. It appears that such treatment is effective in eliciting a strong conscience.

Thus it would appear that a child's anxieties and violent tendencies are determined above all by the attitudes and practices which prevail in his home, and not by the books he reads. Even so, books like the *Struwwelpeter* may be potentially harmful to certain children, because they can reinforce already existing anxieties and aggressions.

Winfred Kaminski

SOURCE: "Destroying the Plot," in *Canadian Children's Literature,* Vol. 25, No. 93, Spring, 1999, pp. 75-6.

There are only a few German books which are recognized as worldwide children's classics—one of them is Heinrich Hoffmann's picture book *Struwwelpeter.*

In 1844, H. Hoffmann, a former medical doctor, became a children's book author. When, just around Christmas, he started to look for a present for his son and couldn't find anything he bought a little empty booklet and started to write and paint the verses and drawings which would later become so well-known. In 1845, when the book was published, a classic was born.

Hoffmann has succeeded in creating something of an archetype—his *Struwwelpeter* has something for everyone. He has been, at various times, forced into uniform as a *Militärstruwwelpeter,* or has metamorphosed into the German Emperor William II, "Swollen-headed William;" he has even changed into *Struwwel-Hitler,* and a little girl, *Struwwellotte.* Not long ago, Struwwelpter got to be gay and at last, very successfully, became Anti-Struwwelpeter.

Very recently, Canada's Iolair Publishing has produced another variation—Struwwelpetriade—translated by Seanair and published as *Struwwelpeter Tales of Hoffmann.* From Seanair's long preface we learn:

> My translations are not word for word translations. Instead, they try to give the exact original stories in modern English. It would be criminal to alter or try to 'improve' these classics: the words and surroundings are changed only slightly, just enough to bring the REAL stories to the late 20th century North American reader.

Well, let us examine whether he is right.

Seanair honours H. Hoffmann very much in that his stories generally leave things uncertain and undetermined. They are short and simple and invite the reader to follow the pictures. But Seanair also tends to make those things clear and evident which have been left open-ended by Hoffmann. His sequels to the stories result in there being only one meaning left. I must disagree with Seanair in this, because it is the power of Hoffmann's picture book that it offers only short moments without reference to anything that has happened either before or after the story is told.

Hoffmann shows dramatic episodes, and he reveals strong emotions—hate, anxiety, anger, violence, and loneliness. Seanair attempts to put "observed facts" in the place of those emotions. Seanair's ideas concerning the stories' endings tend to demonstrate "friendly possibilities." But by changing Hoffmann's tales in this way the drama and the grotesque get lost. For example, Seanair invites the reader to discuss whether the hunter has been drowned, and proposes that the reader accept that help arrived just in time to save the hunter's life. This attempt to suggest new endings to the stories and to change the settings in order to make them fit for twentieth-century North America seems to me a failure.

What Seanair seems to perceive as wrong in these stories in reality is not wrong at all; the "mistakes" are part of the power of the story: they affect our feelings and they attract our minds. H. Hoffmann's pictures and verses are not perfect, but they aren't boring either. Nevertheless, after a long life of many trials and tribulations, *Struwwelpeter* is still vital enough to survive even Seanair's attack.

Brian Alderson

SOURCE: A review of *Struwwelpeter,* in *Books for Keeps,* No. 119, November, 1999, p. 32.

Well, how do you pronounce it to start with?

Most people here say 'strewel' (to rhyme with 'crewel') and then plain 'Peter'; but it really needs to be given a rich German pronunciation as it were: Sh-truvelpeter, with a guttural 'r' and a strong short first 'e' in 'Peter'.

What does it mean?

The usual translation is 'Shock-headed Peter' but (as you may guess) 'Struwwel' has more force to it than that, implying hair tangled up like barbed wire. The word refers to the figure who usually appears on the cover and the first page of the book: Peter, standing on a plinth and glowering at us from under his hair. His finger-nails are a foot or so longer than those of even the most fashionable of today's teenagers.

Who wrote it, and when?

Heinrich Hoffmann (1809-1894), a physician in Frankfurt a.M., didn't care for the heavy moralism and the over-realistic illustration of contemporary children's books. His original manuscript was con-

cocted in 1844 for the enjoyment of some friends and as a Christmas present for his 3-year-old son Carl. One of the friends was a publisher (who also published Marx and Engels's *Die Heilige Familie!*) and he and Hoffmann organised publication of the first edition of what was then called **Lustige Geschichten und Drollige Bilder** for Christmas 1845: six stories occupying fifteen pages, illustrated and decorated by Hoffmann himself, with the text printed letterpress and the pictures lithographed and then coloured by hand. The book was an immediate success and with publication of the fifth edition in 1847 it attained its canonic form: ten stories on 24 pages, with the title now changed to **Der Struwwelpeter,** and with the youth himself no longer at the back of the book but presiding over everything immediately after the title-page.

When did it come to England?

In 1848 under the title **The English Struwwelpeter; or pretty stories and funny pictures for little children. After the Sixth Edition of the celebrated German work.** Since it was printed for Hoffmann's publisher, who sold it through agents, it naturally followed the German sequence of stories and used the author's illustrations, which were now printed from wood-blocks with hand-colouring. No one knows who translated the verses, but whoever it was did a very passable job and his text is still found in current editions. These are merely the latest reprints of a work which has appeared in uncountable numbers in this country (often with several publishers putting out editions at one and the same time), which has been translated into at least thirty languages, and which must hold a world record as the most widely-disseminated text to have been consistently accompanied by versions of its author's original illustrations.

What is pretty about the stories?

Well may you ask. Most of them have to do with foolish, stroppy or unbiddable children who meet various come-uppances: Bullyboy Frederick, bitten by a dog; Harriet, playing with matches and burning herself to ashes; three yobbos who taunt a black boy and get dunked in a large inkwell by tall Agrippa; and—most famously—Conrad Suck-a-Thumb who is de-digitized by the Red-legg'd Scissor-man. One story has no children in it and concerns a hunter after hares who falls asleep and is then chased and shot at by his quarry. Opinions differ about all this, with doubts expressed (especially by congenital thumb-suckers) over Hoffmann's motives, and with nods and winks at the fact that he was German.

A case for the defence.

Sky-larking, m'lud. The whole thing was conceived as a joke and a send-up of the *moralités* inflicted on child readers (then, as now) and Hoffmann relishes his chance to have a go at stupidity and pomposity. There is too the graphic beauty admired by Sendak. This has nothing to do with the surface gloss of fashionable painter-illustrators, but stems from Dr Hoffmann's wonderful versatility in giving visual life to his various texts—the more powerful perhaps because of its very amateurishness. **Struwwelpeter** makes play with half a dozen graphic devices never before found together in so short a book: strip cartoons, sequential events in a single picture, personified objects, symbolic decorations etc. all cleverly patterned around each page of text.

An inspiration to plagiarists and parodists.

Simple in structure and widely popular among generations of readers **Struwwelpeter** has proved a rich source for imitators and satirists. The former are usually hopeless, proving Hoffmann's naive surrealism to be inimitable, but the latter can turn his cautionary episodes to good, if transient, effect (see for instance *The Political Struwwelpeter,* 1899; *Swollen-headed* [Kaiser] *William,* 1914; *Struwwelhitler,* 1941; and *Tricky Dick* [Nixon] *and his Pals,* 1974.) Musical settings have also been made, the most recent of which, *Shockheaded Peter: a junk opera,* with music by The Tiger Lillies, is still touring around and is not to be missed.

E. Nesbit
1858-1924

(Full name Edith Nesbit Bland; also wrote under the pseudonym Fabian Bland) English author of books for elementary school children.

Major works include *The Story of the Treasure Seekers* (1899), *Five Children and It* (1902), *The Railway Children* (1906), *Harding's Luck* (1909).

Major works about Nesbit: *E. Nesbit: A Biography* (Doris Langley Moore, 1933, revised 1966), *Magic and the Magician: E. Nesbit and Her Children's Books* (Noel Streatfeild, 1958), *E. Nesbit* (Anthea Bell, 1960), *A Woman of Passion: The Life of E. Nesbit* (Julia Briggs, 1987).

For further information on Nesbit's life and works, see *CLR,* Volume 3.

INTRODUCTION

Called "the first writer of modern fiction for children," E. Nesbit created a new form of the genre by fusing fairy tale with reality and telling her stories from a child's perspective in a child's voice. Influenced by Charles Dickens, Kenneth Grahame, and George MacDonald, as well as traditional folk and fairy tales, her innovative approach to literature for children influenced in turn many other writers, including C. S. Lewis, Edgar Eager, and H. G. Wells. Declaring, "I make it a point of honour never to *write down* to a child," Nesbit wrote stories about groups of spirited and imaginative children engaged in activities apart from adults, whose antics usually landed them in some kind of trouble.

Nesbit is especially appreciated for her sense of fun and for her ability to recall in vivid detail the experiences of childhood. In an article in *Junior Bookshelf*, M. S. Crouch wrote of Nesbit's work, "No books have been so frank, so patently honest and so colloquial. She gave a vigorous kick to the departing pedant, drew back the curtains of adult prejudice, and let the sun shine on children who were responsible, thoughtful and courageous, and who yet remained essentially young. Her books are of their period; they breathe the spirit of the new century which,

in a very different way, fills the contemporary work of her friend [George Bernard] Shaw, but they speak in a highly personal and quite modern way to any child of today who cares to listen."

BIOGRAPHICAL INFORMATION

Nesbit's childhood was an insecure one. Her father died when she was four, and her widowed mother moved frequently and at random around England and back and forth to the continent. Nesbit attended a variety of different schools in Germany, France, and England, and is reported to have departed from one French Catholic boarding school at the age of 11 leaving two empty wine bottles under her bed for the nuns to discover. The family finally settled in a large country house in Kent when Nesbit was 13 years old. She loved living there, and roamed about happily with her two brothers, generally free from adult supervision and school, much like the children in her books. This house and its environs inspired the settings for several of her books.

When she was 21, and seven months pregnant, Nesbit married the charming Hubert Bland, famous as much for his womanizing as for his politics and journalistic skills. Shortly after their first child was born, Bland came down with smallpox, and was defrauded by his business partner during his illness. Forced to support her family, Nesbit did recitations, painted greeting cards and, increasingly, sold poems and stories to newspapers and magazines.

With her husband, Nesbit helped to form the Fabian Society, a group of socialists and free-thinkers who included H. G. Wells, George Bernard Shaw, and Annie Besant. She flaunted her unconventionality by cutting her hair short, wearing flowing "aesthetic" wool garments and knickers, riding a bicycle, jumping fences, and smoking incessantly, even in public. In her middle age, she persuaded the officials at the French Opera to open all the windows (something *never* done before) by pretending to faint and gasping for air in various strategic points in the building. She kept, as well, an unconventional household, running a sort of country salon, not only for her Fabian friends, but for many artists of the time, including G. K. Chesterton, Laurence Houseman, and Rudyard Kipling, a great fan of hers, who enjoyed reading her stories to his children. H. G. Wells once said that the Bland house was "a place to which one rushed down from town at week-end to snatch one's bed before anyone else got it." Nesbit bore three children and adopted two others, fathered by her husband upon her housekeeper. She mothered them so well that it was only through a family crisis (her youngest son, Fabian, died of a tonsillectomy at home) that the children discovered their true parentage. Nöel Coward called her "The most genuine Bohemian I ever met," but she had a strong conservative side, as did her husband, writing for and about middle-class children, defending traditional ideas about a woman's place, and opposing women's suffrage.

Nesbit, who wanted to be accepted as a poet and serious author, wrote all the books for which she is best known after she was forty years old. *The Story of the Treasure Seekers* first appeared in 1898 as a series of stories in the *Pall Mall* and *Windsor* magazines and was published in book form the following year. The stories that would become *Five Children and It* and *The Book of Dragons* (1900) were first published in the *Strand*, as was *The Phoenix and the Carpet;* and *The New Treasure Seekers* was serialized in *London Magazine*. Bland died in 1914, and Nesbit felt herself to be "broken off short" by his death. During the next few years she suffered ill health and poverty, taking in lodgers to maintain her large house and selling fruit and flowers from her garden. Shaw paid for her son John's university education, and she was awarded a small pension in recognition of her services to literature, but she was unhappy and lonely. In 1917 she married Thomas Terry Tucker, a marine engineer and old friend of the family. Nicknamed "Skipper," he provided Nesbit with stability and affection at a time when she most needed it. When asked by an admirer if she was going to write more children's books, she replied. "Publishers tell me that children don't want my sort of books any more." She died in 1924, at the age of 65, of heart and lung disease, possibly the result of her constant smoking.

MAJOR WORKS

Victorian stories for children tended to feature children who were excessively sweet and moral, whereas Nesbit began with a self-conscious preference for writing imaginative, not moral, stories for children. In her first children's books she created memorable child narrators. In *The Treasure Seekers,* ostensibly written by the eldest of the Bastable children, Oswald addresses the audience in its own idiom. Nesbit continued this device in the succeeding Bastable books, *The Woodbegoods* (1901), and *The New Treasure Seekers* (1904). These three books document the children's experiences as they try to improve the family fortunes and perform good deeds, each time finding that events do not unfold as they intended.

Nesbit next introduced the element of magic into this formula. Many critics consider *Five Children and It* to be the pinnacle of Nesbit's innovative skills. *Five Children and It* chronicles the experiences of a family of children who are granted wishes by a peculiar being that calls itself a sandfairy, or Psammead. When they unearth it from its sandpit refuge, it agrees to grant the lot of them one wish per day, but despite good intentions, the wishes always backfire. These experiences help the children grow and mature, a process that continues in the two succeeding volumes, *The Phoenix and the Carpet* (1904) and *The Story of the Amulet* (1906). In these two books, the children engage in travel through time and space and meet other magical creatures, but the stories become more intense and more philosophically complicated, especially when Nesbit began to include scenes expounding socialist principles, thereby politicizing her writing.

The Railway Children has always been one of Nesbit's more popular books and was made into a film in 1970. It follows the formula of *The Story of the Treasure Seekers* telling stories of a family of unsupervised children and the experiences that befall them as they venture into the world.

Harding's Luck, sequel to *The House of Arden* (1908), was a true departure for Nesbit in that its protagonist was not a middle-class child, but one who was of the "lower class," crippled and poor. In this blending of fantasy and reality, young Dickie Harding, a lame orphan boy from the slums of Deptford, not only travels back in time, but inhabits the body of his ancestor, a seventeenth century aristocrat, both rich and healthy. He eventually makes the decision to remain in the past, living as his own ancestor, in a complete rejection of the present with interesting philosophical implications.

CRITICAL RECEPTION

Nesbit had been supporting her family with her writing for many years before the publication and critical success of her children's books. When *The Story of the Treasure Seekers* came out, many critics thought that she had at last hit her stride, and she enjoyed great success that continued for many years. Toward the end of her life, there was a decrease in her popularity as works of fantasy went out of style, and she died ill and impoverished; but succeeding generations have rediscovered her work, and many of her children's books have been in print consistently for the last 100 years.

GENERAL COMMENTARY

J. B. Priestley

SOURCE: "E. Nesbit: An Appreciation," in *Bookman,* Vol. 67, No. 399, December, 1924, pp. 157-59.

Anyone between the ages of nine and ninety ought to be able to enjoy E. Nesbit's stories for children. But some of us are specially privileged in this matter because we are just old enough and young enough to have been children when the early stories were appearing as serials in the *Strand Magazine,* and we can remember the fascination they exercised upon us month by month, and how we were entranced by Mr.

H. R. Millar. (It was delightful to see those illustrations again in the pleasant collected edition; for nobody can illustrate tales of magic like Mr. Millar, whose enchanted castles, hairy savages and beautiful queens are beyond the pen and pencil of any other artist.) And more than once when I have been gossiping about books with my contemporaries and the talk has veered round to old delights, E. Nesbit's name has suddenly turned up, and then the years have vanished like smoke, everybody has talked at once and we have renewed our acquaintance with the Psammead, the Phœnix and the Magic Carpet. Well, our children will never have the pleasure of following such adventures month by month (even if Mr. Douglas Fairbanks and his friends should leave them either time or inclination for it), for E. Nesbit has left us, and left us very much poorer, for she was, I gather, a remarkable woman in half a dozen ways; but happily the books are still with us, so that we can renew our acquaintance with them and watch them weave their old spell over a new generation of little readers.

Fortified by Mr. Fisher Unwin's new edition, I have been renewing my acquaintance with these stories, and I do not mind confessing that I thought it a hazardous undertaking. It probably meant stripping the bloom from scores of delicious memories, bringing E. Nesbit and all her works down to earth with a bang, for it is one thing reading a book when your imagination is aflame at a touch and everything is magical, and another thing reading it when the years seem to be closing door after door and you are a harassed payer of taxes and only a masterpiece quickens you. But these stories came through triumphantly. Without a doubt they are immensely good, touched with a kind of genius, and certainly unsurpassed in their own field. Indeed, they are so good that not only will they ravish any fairly imaginative child, but they will also enable any fairly sensitive adult to recapture some of his childhood, bringing back those summer days that seemed as long then, in their spaciousness, their loitering sunlit hours, as whole months do now.

The first thing to be said about E. Nesbit is that she understood children as few authors, even among those who have written constantly about children, have understood them. The little girls and boys of her stories are not the little girls and boys of a sentimental dream, but the actual occupants of our nurseries, sometimes a little more brisk and bright and imaginative perhaps, but still the same girls and boys. And as she wrote for children, she did not look down upon her little protagonists from some adult Olympus; but even when she did not make a child the narrator (as she frequently did) she always contrived that the ideal spectator who tells the story should look at things as a child does, should see the world from a height of four feet and not of five feet and so many inches. For the adult, a great deal of the fun in these stories comes from the piquancy of the child's point of view. It is a pleasant change, to say the least for it, to see life from a small boy's angle of vision and so to have any love episode that may inevitably turn up thoroughly scamped. "And that," remarks one of these small boys, "is all the story of the long-lost grandmother and Albert's uncle. I am afraid it is rather dull, but it was very important (to him), so I felt it ought to be narrated. Stories about lovers and getting married are generally slow. I like a love-story where the hero parts with the girl at the garden-gate in the gloaming and goes off and has adventures, and you don't see her any more till he comes home to marry her at the end of the book. And I suppose people have to marry. Albert's uncle is awfully old—more than thirty—and the lady is advanced in years—twenty-six next Christmas." And all these children are realistically treated; they are not superlatively good or brave or poetical, but are the restless, irritating, delightful creatures, now snapping at one another, now swearing eternal friendships, that may be discovered lurking in little gangs round any corner.

So excellent is her account of children's normal pastimes, scrapes, quarrels, reconciliations, hopes, fears and delights, that three of her stories, and these not the weakest, namely, *The Story of the Treasure-Seekers, The Would-Be-Goods* and the *New Treasure Seekers,* are concerned with nothing else, and have not that fantastic element in them which we usually connect with her name. All three describe the adventures of the six Bastable children, a motherless crew who are really very good but have an unusual capacity for those enterprises tersely characterised by unsympathetic and unimaginative adults as "mischief," so great a capacity indeed that they band themselves into the society that gives its name to the second book. These stories are so good that some judges have considered them the best, on the grounds that the absence of magic is a limitation that the author triumphantly overcomes. In one sense this is true, but if a wider scope in the narrative, the introduction of magic here, gives an author a better opportunity for good writing, it also gives him or her a better opportunity for bad writing: these things cut both ways. And for my own part I do not hesitate to prefer the more fantastic stories, for it is in these sto-

ries that we have the real E. Nesbit, who invented a kind of tale that owes little or nothing to past masterpieces—"Alice in Wonderland," "The Water Babies" and the like—and contrived that such tales should express every side of a child's mind and life. Some writers can deal justly with humorous or poetical fantasy, but cannot handle children realistically; other writers can handle the children but would be all at sea with the more imaginative pieces of invention: our author was at home with both, and that is her triumph.

Who, having once read them, does not remember with delight the adventures of Jane, Anthea, Robert and Cyril, those fortunate children who were always stumbling upon magical things? It was they who found the Psammead, that strange sand-fairy who could grant wishes (by blowing itself up), but was always grumbling about it. It was Robert who in an unguarded moment, forgetting that there was magic about, wished that he were bigger than the baker's boy (that objectionable youth), and suddenly found himself some ten or eleven feet high, and an object of some interest in the landscape. What an embarrassing situation it was when someone wished that there were Red Indians in the neighbourhood, and the wish was immediately granted. And how deftly all this magic is managed, so that we slip into it gradually and never for a moment remain incredulous, unlike the adults in the stories, who never believe anything. What adventures these four had with the Phœnix, the vainest but most polished and polite of all fabulous creatures, and with that carpet, which mother bought so cheaply in the Kentish Town Road, that turned out to be a Magic Carpet and took the children to all manner of queer places. How awkward it was when the carpet, under the wear and tear of so many journeys, began to be worn and had to be repaired with ordinary material, which not being magical had the effect of making the person standing upon it half in and half out of the magic. That is why the curate, who was brought hastily from his study in East London to marry the cook and the burglar (the cook had been taken to an island, where she became queen of the cannibals, and then the burglar was taken there to be her consort), the unfortunate curate was very misty all the time he was on the island and really thought he was still in his study but in some kind of insane fit, poor man. What invention and genuine high spirits there are in that chapter in which the Phœnix searches for its temple and at last comes to the central offices of the Phœnix Fire Insurance Company, introduces itself there and is honoured by the whole staff. After speeches have been made in its honour, some homemade incense is burnt, and then the manager begins his hymn:

> "Absolute security!
> No Liability!
> All kinds of property
> Insured against fire . . . "

And the whole staff, managers, secretaries and clerks, join in the chorus:

> "Class one, for private dwelling-house,
> For household goods and shops allows;
> Provided these are built of brick
> Or stone, and tiled and slated thick . . . "

A glorious adventure.

The later stories, *The Story of the Amulet, The Enchanted Castle, The House of Arden* and *Harding's Luck,* are more ambitious, and there is in them, besides a knowledge of children and a power of inventing amusing and fantastic incidents and the rest, a real power of the imagination, a genuine sense of atmosphere and poetry. Many of the scenes in the amulet story, and particularly the description of Atlantis and its final destruction, are sufficiently powerful to catch the adult imagination. And in *The Enchanted Castle,* which contains some of our author's best invention and writing and is perhaps her best all-round story, there are not only all the good things we have had before—the childish humour and play—but also some genuine passages of the horrible, the grotesque and the beautiful. Thus, the chapter in which the Ugly-Wuglies (creatures made out of old clothes, golf-clubs, hockey and walking sticks and painted masks—we have all made them) come to life, or at least come as near to life as they can, is really horrible. And some of the later chapters, that in which the statues of the gods and goddesses came to life in the moonlight and sat with the children, and Phœbus sang to his lyre so that "it seemed that the whole world lay like a magic apple in the hand of each listener," or that chapter in which the four children and the two adults (who are reunited lovers) watch the magic moonrise over the ancient flat stones of sacrifice and great beasts, mammoths, dragons and stone gods of Egypt and Assyria, bull-bodied, bird-winged, cat-head, and uncouth idols and lastly the ancient gods and goddesses take on a magic life of their own and move silently into the circle of moonlight; such chapters as these have a beauty and significance that make most of our grown-up fiction seem a tawdry affair and that can hardly be matched in the whole range of children's literature. And now that the time has past when any praise of ours can mean anything to the writer, we can only hope that the creation of such happy and innocent fables brought as much pleasure to her as a knowledge of them has brought to us, and that there were once children about her knee whose eloquent bright eyes and eager faces long ago anticipated and expressed our gratitude.

Edward Eager

SOURCE: "Daily Magic," in *The Horn Book Magazine,* Vol. XXXIV, No. 5, October, 1958, pp. 349-58.

It is customary, in writing of E. Nesbit, to begin by telling how one first read her stories in *The Strand Magazine,* either devouring the installments one by one as they appeared, or perhaps even better, coming upon them unexpectedly in old bound volumes in some grandmotherly attic.

This did not happen to me. My childhood occurred too late for the original Nesbit era, and too soon for the revival sponsored in this country by William Rose Benét, Christopher Morley, May Lamberton Becker, Earle Walbridge and others (not to mention the firm of Coward-McCann, which earned everlasting honor by beginning to reissue her books in 1929, and has continued to do so ever since).

I was dimly aware of the renewal of interest in Nesbit in the early thirties, but since I was then entering my own early twenties, with no thought of ever again having anything to do with the world of children's books, it all seemed very remote.

It was not till 1947 that I became a second-generation Nesbitian when I discovered a second-hand copy of *Wet Magic,* while casting about for books to read to my son. I have not got over the effects of that discovery yet, nor, I hope, will I ever.

Probably the sincerest compliment I could pay her is already paid in the fact that my own books for children could not even have existed if it were not for her influence. And I am always careful to acknowledge this indebtedness in each of my stories; so that any child who likes my books and doesn't know hers may be led back to the master of us all.

For just as Beatrix Potter is the genius of the picture book, so I believe E. Nesbit to be the one truly "great" writer for the ten-, eleven- and twelve-year-old. (I don't count Lewis Carroll, as in my experience the age when one stops being terrified by, and begins loving, *Alice* is about thirteen and a half. And Kenneth Grahame, whose *The Golden Age* had an undoubted influence on the Nesbit style, is an author to wait for, too, I think. As for Mrs. [Juliana Horatia] Ewing, so sadly forgotten of late, she is best come upon a bit earlier, except for *Mary's Meadow,* which might almost have been written by E. Nesbit herself.)

How to describe the Nesbit charm for those who don't yet know it? Better for them to stop reading this article and read the books themselves. I have read all I could find of those that matter (she wrote countless potboilers that are not worth searching for). And I have read the excellent biography by Doris Langley Moore, never published in this country but still obtainable, I believe, from England.

From this book the real Edith Nesbit Bland emerges lifesize and unforgettable, stubborn, charming, wrongheaded, parading in flowing gowns, scattering ashes from her omnipresent cigarette. One finds her plunging ardently into Fabian socialism, handling unconventionally but with childlike directness the problems presented by a philandering husband (a whole novel could be written about her marriage with Hubert Bland). Later one grows impatient, watching her waste valuable time and energy trying to prove that Bacon wrote Shakespeare.

Then there is the charming interlude of what might be called her intellectual flirtation with H. G. Wells. Wells, whom she admired immeasurably (he is the "great reformer" in chapter twelve of ***The Story of the Amulet***), had read some of her writing, decided (incomprehensibly) she was a man, and named her Ernest in his mind, a nickname that was to remain through their friendship. One day, after they had met, he appeared at Well Hall unexpectedly, bag and baggage, announcing, "Ernest, I've come to stay." E. Nesbit was delighted. In the words of Mrs. Langley Moore, "nothing could have gratified her more than this frank confidence in her Bohemianism." And of course we see plainly that nothing could have. It was such an ungrown-up thing to do. So unconventional an arrival must have gone straight to the heart of the child Edith, still very much alive somewhere inside the fascinating, unconventional Mrs. Bland.

Elsewhere in the book we are told that E. Nesbit resented the time taken up by her children's stories, and yearned to be free of them in order to devote herself to writing novels and poetry. We may be forgiven for not believing it. Maybe Mrs. Bland felt like

that, or pretended to, but not E. Nesbit. Naturally, moving in the circle that she did, among all those witty people doing and saying such grown-up things, she must have known times when she pined for recognition on an adult plane. Recognition, and the very much needed money that went with it, were always important to her.

But her books for children were never the mere potboilers she claimed they were. Every page shines with the delight the writer took in fashioning it, and this is a thing that cannot be faked. I know. In truth it is her "adult" writing that bears a synthetic stamp. Her poems and novels are mere self-conscious attitudinizing, the little girl playing "lady" in borrowed clothes, and all of them have long been forgotten. It was when the child in her spoke out directly to other children that she achieved greatness.

I do not mean to equate genius with arrested mental or emotional development. But there are lucky people who never lose the gift of seeing the world as a child sees it, a magic place where anything can happen next minute, and delightful and unexpected things constantly do. Of such, among those of us who try to write for children, is the kingdom of Heaven. And in that kingdom E. Nesbit stands with the archangels.

Of course there are other people who plainly have never known what it is like to be a child at all, who would suppress fairy tales and tell children "nothing that is not true." (I once knew a lady who denied her children Santa Claus, till they rebelled and forced her to relent. And when one year she so far relaxed as to say that he had been there and brought *one* of the presents, her little girl cried, "And did he wear a red coat and a white beard?" "No," said the lady, stubbornly progressive to the end. "He wore a business suit!")

Tragically, toward the end of E. Nesbit's life, the fantasyhaters were in vogue (again)! One of the saddest chapters in Doris Langley Moore's book is the one that tells of her sending stories to publishers, only to have them returned with the comment that there was no longer any demand for "her sort of books."

The thought of these lost, unpublished Nesbits is enough to make the reader weep. "Bitter unavailing tears" indeed! It is true that the books of her later years are not so strong as her first work, but who knows? She might have found a second wind and finished in a burst of triumph, like Verdi. And if not, even second-rate E. Nesbit is better than no E. Nesbit at all. Which is my justification for having dared to write second-rate E. Nesbit myself.

Still, even without these forgotten manuscripts (what one would give to know even the titles!) there remain in print today, on one side or the other of the Atlantic, fifteen books. And fifteen books of such golden quality are a priceless treasure for any child.

First in any listing of E. Nesbit's works always must come the three books dealing with the Bastable children, delectably titled *The Treasure Seekers, The Wouldbegoods* and *The New Treasure Seekers.* (There is a fourth book, *Oswald Bastable and Others,* obtainable in England, which contains four additional Bastable adventures, as well as eleven other short pieces.)

Who could forget the Bastables, particularly the noble Oswald? One sees them as perpetual pilgrims, marching forever down the road with peas in their shoes and a brave plan in mind to save the family fortunes, stopping by the way to dam the stream (and later cause a nearly-disastrous flood), forgetting in their zeal the cricket ball left lodged in a roof-gutter (which still later is to cause a flood of another kind).

And yet, so short are the memories of critics that one frequently sees the Bastable books listed as fantasies, or among "magic stories." They are of course nothing of the kind, but belong firmly in the realistic tradition of heroic naughtiness, or naughty heroics. And surely of all the naughty children in literature, none were ever so heroic as they, nor any heroes so (unintentionally, of course) very naughty!

Nevertheless, in spite of all the fun, in spite of the unforgettable, endearing Oswald, I question whether the Bastable stories are the best introduction to E. Nesbit today, at least for American children. Because they are realistic books, the details seem more dated, the "Britishness" more marked, than in the Nesbit magic stories. The things these children do are too different from the things children do today for them to qualify as "easy reading." Thus the very elements which make these books unique may be the elements which stand in the way of their acceptance.

If there is resistance to E. Nesbit on the part of some American children in these days, I think it may well be because they encounter the Bastable stories first. Certainly every child should know the Bastables, but if on first exposure he doesn't see their charm, let him meet E. Nesbit instead in the world of fantasy,

where background counts for less and once the story gets going, all is gas and gaiters. Then, if he is a right-minded child, he will be won to her forever, and Oswald and his brothers and sisters can follow later.

Before passing on to the Nesbit magic stories, there are two more "realistic" books, one of which must be ordered from England, to be mentioned briefly. *Five of Us and Madeline* is a collection of E. Nesbit's last stories, published after her death and edited by her daughter, Rosamund Sharp. Ten of the stories introduce a new family modeled on Bastable lines, and very nice, too. And "the fell Madeline," pale and mousy and sniffing and cowardly, yet capable of great moments when hard pressed, is a personage to remember. Interestingly, this is the first book illustrated by Nora S. Unwin. The drawings were done when she was still a girl in her teens and, frankly, their interest is purely historic.

Of *The Railway Children* it is the accepted thing to say that it is too sentimental, and perhaps it is, though the sentiment is never false and often touching. And if the story is unbelievable, still the things that happen to Roberta and Peter and Phyllis are just the things that any child would know *ought* to happen to a family that moves to a house near the railway tracks. Yes, *The Railway Children* deserves wider circulation.

With *The Wonderful Garden* one comes close to the very best of E. Nesbit, yet it is a book hard to define. Is it "real"? Is it fantasy? It is either or both. Here is a book in which every event *could* have a prosy, dull, boring, logical explanation. Or there could be magic at work, and of course the children in the book, Caroline and Charlotte and Charles, know that there is. This "magic or not?" formula is one oddly challenging and tempting to the writer, and devilish hard to bring off. I know, because I've just finished trying it, myself. E. Nesbit handles it with consummate skill, to make an almost perfect book. *The Wonderful Garden,* with its incidental and fascinating flower-magic lore, is a book peculiarly attractive to the adult reader, and for this reason I would hesitate before pressing it over-enthusiastically on any non-Nesbit-inoculated child. Again, let him meet her first in the purely "magic" books. Then he will demand all the rest.

Of these magic books there are eight, and of these eight two, *The Magic City* and *Wet Magic,* are late works and, authorities agree, inferior to her best writing. Perhaps. But who could forget Philip waking in the night and walking over the bridge and into the city he has built himself, of blocks and books and bric-a-brac? Who could forget those engaging dachshunds, the cowardly Brenda and the heroic Max? Who could forget the languishing mermaid in **Wet Magic** ("We die in captivity!") and, later, the battle of the books, with its picture (by H. R. Millar, of course) of Boadicea vanquishing Mrs. Markham and the Queen of the Amazons dealing with Miss Murdstone? (Here again, however, adult appreciation may be different from a child's.)

We are left with a golden half-dozen. There are the "five children" books (**Five Children and It, The Phoenix and the Carpet** and **The Story of the Amulet**). There are the Arden stories (**The House of Arden** and **Harding's Luck**). And, shining proudly by itself, there is **The Enchanted Castle.**

Who can choose among them? Who can describe perfection? Given only one choice, I would take **The Enchanted Castle** for *my* desert island, but Doris Langley Moore would not agree, though Roger Lancelyn Green (in *Tellers of Tales,* Edmund Ward, England) feels as I do.

But why make comparisons? Read them all. Step up, step up and meet the Psammead and the Mouldiwarp (and the Mouldierwarp and the Mouldiestwarp). Learn how to make Ugly-Wuglies (and *then* see what happens)! Find out how it feels to own a magic carpet *and* a phoenix at the same time. And what takes place when the magic carpet begins to wear out and develops a hole in the middle? Explore the lost kingdom of Atlantis. Go seeking for the real head of the house of Arden and follow the adventures that begin when a crippled boy in a London slum plants strange seeds in his back garden.

And always remember that magic has a mind of its own and will thwart you if it can. So that if you wish, for example, to be invisible and the magic ring you happen to have on you is geared to twenty-four hour cycles (or twenty-one, or fourteen, or seven; you never can tell with magic), invisible you will remain till the time is up. Or four yards high, as was poor Mabel's fate on one historic occasion. And think of the complications, as you go about your daily round.

For if there is one thing that makes E. Nesbit's magic books more enchanting than any others, it is not that they are funny, or exciting, or beautifully written, or full of wonderfully alive and endearing children, all of which they are. It is the *dailiness* of the magic.

Here is no land of dragons and ogres or Mock Turtles and Tin Woodmen. The world of E. Nesbit (except for some elaborate and debatable business with magic clouds toward the end of **The House of Arden**) is the ordinary or garden world we all know, with just the right pinch of magic added. So that after you finish reading one of her stories you feel it could all happen to *you,* any day now, round any corner.

The next time you pick up what you think is a nickel in the street, make sure it *is* a nickel and not a magic talisman. And don't go scrabbling about in sandpits unless you want your fingers to encounter a furry form and your startled ears to hear the voice of a Psammead begging to be allowed to sleep undisturbed for another thousand years.

But of course you *do* want your fingers and your ears to encounter just that; all right-minded people do.

The next best thing to having it actually happen to you is to read about it in the books of E. Nesbit.

Mavis Strange

SOURCE: "E. Nesbit, as I Knew Her," in *The Horn Book Magazine,* Vol. XXXIV, No. 5, October, 1958, pp. 359-63.

It seems incredible that it is now more than half a century since, as a small girl on her ninth birthday, I received my first "E. Nesbit" story, **The Five Children and It.**

These delightful tales came out originally in *The Strand Magazine* in serial form, with H. R. Millar's strikingly good illustrations, and were published later, in the familiar red and gold covers, in time for Christmas which, needless to say, was incomplete unless one of these treasures was numbered amongst one's presents.

Three of us children (a favorite cousin, a younger sister and myself) decided one rainy day that we must write to E. Nesbit a "Thank you" letter for all that her stories meant to us, in inspiration, delight and adventure. The first letters went astray, and daring greatly we wrote again. This time we received a prompt reply written in her own broad, generous but difficult-to-read handwriting that I was soon to know so well.

"My dears," she wrote, "I *did* reply to your first letters. I wonder what happened to mine? Perhaps it got put in a drawer and slipped over the edge and was lost forever, or perhaps bad boys put lighted fuses in the pillar box in which it was posted." She went on to say that "its fate would remain forever a mystery, like that of the Man in the Iron Mask, or what became of the little Dauphin?"

To Cecily, who with youth's frankness had written giving a list of those classic authors whose work she had preferred to E. Nesbit's, she replied that she was right to declare this preference and added, "Oh, there's one other—Mrs. [Juliana Horatia] Ewing"; to Kathie, youngest of the trio, that she wished she had a Magic Carpet to send her so that we could all visit her; and to me she said that perhaps one day she would name one of her book children "Mavis" (see *Wet Magic*).

After this we wrote to her annually on her birthday, August 15th ("same day as Julius Caesar's and Napoleon's!" she told us), and when in 1910 I went to boarding school in Folkestone, she invited me to lunch with her at "the Other House," Dymchurch, where she had a holiday retreat. Dymchurch in those days was comparatively unspoilt country by the sea, with miles of sand.

I remember well driving from Folkstone along the coast, punctuated by the old Martello towers erected in the days when Napoleon was expected to invade our shores. The old horse clip-clopped along and my heart was beating in anticipation.

We (my mother and I) arrived at a shabby lovable house near the sea, and she stood at the door to welcome us. I can see her still so vividly—of medium height and fullish figure, her brown untidy curly hair piled up and held with tortoise-shell combs. Her kind and beautiful brown eyes looked at one, over spectacles tilted to the very tip of her well-shaped nose— they looked with such penetration I remember. She wore flowing frocks of "Liberty" browns and flames, hanging from a yoke with flowing sleeves, and I rather think amber beads; and a longish cigarette holder completed the picture, for she was always smoking.

Her welcome set the tongue-tied school girl at ease. Kittens in a basket completed the homely atmosphere in that old paneled room where lunch of roast chicken and chocolate pudding was served to complete the conquest of a child's heart. "Oh dear," she said, "I'm *so* sorry but they've left the chicken's boots on!" as the "help" bore in the fowl with his scaled feet and claws erect in splendor, and after that sally I was at

home with her then and forever. So began our strange friendship which lasted until she died when I was in my mid-twenties.

We met on occasions when she visited the Midlands but we continued to write. Once as a teen-ager I wrote to her in desperation about my temper. She replied with eight pages by return of post. "My dear, *I* know what it is to have a temper, I've had a long and hard struggle with mine." She advised me firmly to have the courage to "stop the row," to say I was "sorry," even if I felt strongly that I was in the right. In this letter she spoke very simply of God (the only time she ever mentioned religion in all our friendship) and advised me to go to Him in prayer, and not only to ask for help but also to tell Him when I had been good. She wrote rather humorously of how "we can tell our friends that we had got a 'blue' at Oxford, or taken a First Class Honours, yet you can't say to your friend I *have* been good today—can you? but you *can* say it to God and I'm sure He likes to hear it and understands. . . . Forgive me, Mavis, if this sounds a 'preachy' letter, but you *did* ask me . . . ." Her serious undivided attention given immediately to this childish problem was so typical of her whole-heartedness and sincerity.

Our friendship continued, mainly on paper. Once she wrote and asked me to write frankly saying what parts of her stories I "skipped," also anything I "disliked," as she had been asked to write some articles for children and wanted them to be a success. I am told she resented criticism, but this does not seem to show it to be the case. My reply was not helpful, as I could *honestly* say I had never "skipped" anything that she wrote, I enjoyed it all too much!

She was quick-tempered, kind, generous, impatient, and noble-hearted as her relationship with her first husband, Hubert Bland, demonstrated. He died before I could meet him but I saw his striking portrait. He was a journalist and they were both members of the early Fabian Society where their friends included Shaw, Chesterton and Wells—E. Nesbit was an ardent and romantic Socialist. She spoke of Hubert with great affection, but *she* was the family breadwinner. It was ironic that she hoped to be remembered for her verse and her novels, and yet it was the children's books that made her famous and paid the household bills.

We met again when World War I brought me to London for war work and I used to visit her occasionally at Well Hall, Eltham, Kent (now destroyed by fire).

This was another lovely shabby old house with three ghosts and a moat. It is fully described in her novel *The Red House* (in which the whole tribe of the Bastable family visited it as a Society of Antiquaries). A notice on the gate stated that E. Nesbit sold Fruit and Flowers (she was very hard up at that time), but if I know her generous heart, the flowers would have been made up in enormous bunches and the fruit would be heavily overweight!

I remember well one happy Sunday at Well Hall when I arrived to find all and sundry making jam—a glorious mixture of improbable people from every walk of life, all stirring away, while E. Nesbit, who had invited me to lunch, said gaily, "We've settled *not* to have any lunch as it's war-time!" and handed me instead a spoon for stirring. Oh how hungry I was! Later we all ate by candlelight and adjourned to the paneled drawing room where she sat at the grand piano and played little old-fashioned lilting waltzes while we young things danced or sang songs of her inventing set to the traditional old tunes, and her son John, aged about seventeen (the lamb of *The Five Children and It*) gave his celebrated imitation of Sir Henry Wood conducting his orchestra at the Queen's Hall "Proms" (how little one knew that in another and more terrible war the old Queen's Hall would be demolished).

E. Nesbit often told me of her loneliness after her husband's death; her children were grown up and John, who later became a doctor, seemed to be the only one at home and her devoted slave, so when she wrote to tell me she had married again I was glad that she had someone to care for her. Some of her friends were disapproving, as she made a choice that seemed strange after her first brilliant erratic husband. Her second marriage was to a character straight from a novel by W. W. Jacobs. He was small, bearded, elderly, and known as "the Skipper"—T. T. Tucker by name and Master of the Woolwich Ferry boat. He addressed her as "Mate," and this warmth and love in the evening of their lives was a very real and living force. I was fond of this kind, cockney little man.

After the war, I went back to the Midlands and E. Nesbit and her "Skipper" went back to Dymchurch where they lived in two converted Army huts which were adapted to suit their simple needs and christened "The Long Boat."

I had received occasional joyous letters from E. Nesbit about her new home and how "The Long Boat" was taking shape—the place "full of shavings and carpenters," so that as I happened to be in Folkestone I decided to take the bus to visit her (no clip-clopping cab horse this time). I had not heard from her for quite a long time, but had no idea that anything was amiss and thought that it would be great fun to pay her a surprise visit.

After some difficulty I found the place. I remember a farm gate that led to a low building, not far from the sea, but on the edge of Romney Marsh. I knocked at the door, and a grave-faced little friend admitted me, and explained that E. N. was "very ill," but when E. Nesbit learned that I was there she insisted on seeing me.

She lay wrapped in a robe on her throne-like fourposter. (Later she was to dictate a letter to me, for we had much correspondence at the end, in which she said that she lay "like a queen on her fourposter" and looked at her beloved Romney Marsh.)

Her face was like ivory, the dark eyes full of pain; we talked but the whole thing seemed to me unreal. Young, awkward, gawky and broken-hearted, I sat on a stiff chair and twisted my legs in desperation around its rungs, while I sought vainly for the right words. Suddenly in the old characteristic manner she scolded me violently, telling me to sit up and take Queen Mary for my model who "always crosses her right foot over her left." Crestfallen, I pulled myself into a more becoming posture, when with her old sweet smile she said, "Forgive me, my dear, I'm cross and fretful because I really am so very ill."

The "Skipper" was present, and I felt I must go, as I could see she was too ill to talk, though talk she did with her old brilliance. I rose to depart when, to my horror, she turned to him and said firmly, "Help me up, I want to stand at the gate and see Mavis on her way." Nothing would stop her. She got up from her bed and, leaning heavily on him, dragged herself to the gateway where she stood holding on to the post and her husband's arm.

As I hurried down the lane, each time I looked back she stood there with her little home and beloved Romney Marsh as background—a frail and indomitable figure, blowing me kisses, waving me "farewell."

Noel Streatfeild

SOURCE: "Oswald Bastable," in *The Horn Book Magazine,* Vol. XXXIV, No. 5, October, 1958, pp. 366-72.

Amongst all the characters authors have invented to tell their stories in the first person, Oswald Bastable holds an honourable place, if for nothing else than for his original approach to his story.

From the moment he introduces himself Oswald is no character in a book, but the most amusing of all the boys the reader knows. He never describes his looks clearly, a hint here and there but no more, yet he is quietly confident, and rightly, that everybody who reads about him would recognise him instantly, should they have the fortune to meet him. He is like the child who, when asked what they were drawing, replied "God." "But you can't draw God, darling," their mother said, "nobody knows what He looks like." "They will," the child answered, "when I've finished." By the time Oswald lays his pen down at the end of *The New Treasure Seekers,* it would be a dense reader indeed who did not know Oswald as well as they know the members of their own family.

"It was Oswald who first thought of looking for treasure. Oswald often thinks of very interesting things. And directly he thought of it he did not keep it to himself, as some boys would have done, but he told the others."

Having made this clear statement about the subject of his book and given his readers their first hint of his quality, though of course remaining the anonymous writer, Oswald then gives quickly and clearly the reasons why treasure is needed, and small fragments of news to help the readers get to know his family. Dora was trying to mend a large hole in one of Noël's stockings: "Dora is the only one of us who ever tries to mend anything." What a picture that gives of the Bastables, with their uncared-for look, and incidentally of Dora. In describing Alice's efforts to make things he draws another picture of the family's appearance: "Most of our things are black or grey since Mother died." Poor children, it was hard enough for them getting on without their mother, and it cannot have made it easier that they had the constant reminder of being dressed in mourning. And what a picture of a date that description of the blacks and greys gives. The children were still in mourning, because "Father does not like you to ask for new things." Yet when Mother died, though Father was ill, that the children, even little H.O., should not be clothed in suitable mourning was unthinkable, as E. Nesbit remembered only too well from the days when she, a small thing of four, was dressed in mourning, quite possibly black with crape on it, for her father.

E. Nesbit, having conceived Oswald, was able to use him to speak for her. Except for Lewis Carroll in his opening of *Alice in Wonderland* no author has been able to lay down so clearly as E. Nesbit what in their opinion a children's book should be. "The best part of books is when things are happening. That is the best part of real things too. This is why I shall not tell you in this story about all the days when nothing happened. You will not catch me saying, 'thus the sad days passed slowly by'—or 'the years rolled on their weary course'—or 'time went on'—because it is silly; of course time goes on—whether you say so or not. So I shall just tell you the nice, interesting parts—and in between you will understand that we had our meals and got up and went to bed, and dull things like that. It would be sickening to write all that down, though of course it happens."

Lovers of the E. Nesbit books may disagree with her, and wish sometimes less happened, as her families are at their best when pausing before a new adventure, but it is interesting to know through Oswald how her mind worked when she was brooding on an idea for one of her books for children.

None of the Bastables are so young for their age as Oswald. He cannot have been less than twelve and could have been thirteen. Even allowing for the fact that children were far younger for their ages when E. Nesbit wrote about the Bastables, Oswald is allowed to be downright childish on occasion. It is impossible to believe, and I am sure E. Nesbit did not, that a boy of twelve or thirteen, let alone a girl of perhaps fourteen, could be fooled into thinking they had found the half-crowns which had so palpably come out of Albert-next-door's Uncle's pocket, yet they did, for Oswald records: "We looked at each other, speechless with surprise and delight, like in books." The answer is probably in the customs of the time of which she was writing. Small children would not have been allowed to roam about alone, but would have been confined to the garden unless someone adult could go with them. But of course almost none of the adventures she planned could have taken place had there been an adult around, so she resorted to a neat trick, and gave only the ages of the twins and H.O.; the ages of the others she leaves in the air. If there are readers so prosaic they must know every detail, let them work out the ages of Dora, Oswald and Dicky for themselves, but do not let them hope E. Nesbit is going to spoil her book for such as they. Her children are the ages she wants them to be for the purposes of her story, and that should be enough for anyone.

One reason why E. Nesbit's books are not dated is that she understood the essence of childhood. "But H.O. did not care about waiting, and I felt for him.

Dora is rather like grown-ups in that way; she does not seem to understand that when you want a thing you do want it, and that you don't wish to wait, even a minute." Oswald was always properly indignant of delays. "Some people have no idea of the value of time. And Dora is one of those who do not understand that when you want to do a thing you *do* want to, and not to do something else, and perhaps your own thing, a week later." E. Nesbit was one of the fortunate who remain young in heart, or even her blottingpaper memory might have failed her, for how things spoil by being kept is easily forgotten by grown-ups.

E. Nesbit, although she might play about with her children's ages, never writes down to an imagined age group. She uses the words that feel to her right, and if her readers did not know them, then there was always the dictionary. "We laughed—because we knew what an amphora is. If you don't you might look it up in the dicker. It's not a flower, though it sounds like one out of the gardening book, the kind you never hear of anyone growing." It would have been easy for Oswald to have said what amphorae were, but apart from the fact that E. Nesbit believed in looking things up in the dictionary, it was not the way her mind worked. She wrote about intelligent children for intelligent children, for even when her children were doing something foolish, they remained good thinkers.

Oswald draws a remarkable picture of himself. "My Father is prompt and decisive in action, and so is his eldest son." "Oswald did not feel quite sure Father would like us to go asking for shillings and sixpences, or even half-crowns, from strangers, but he did not say so. The money had been asked for and got, and it couldn't be helped—and perhaps he wanted the pudding—I am not able to remember exactly why he did not speak up and say, 'This is wrong,' but anyway he didn't." "Oswald (this has more than once happened) was the first to restore his manners. He made a proper bow like he has been taught." "Alice was knitting by the fire; it was for Father, but I am sure his feet are not at all that shape. He has a high and beautifully formed instep like Oswald's." "Oswald is a very modest boy, I believe, but even he would not deny that he has an active brain. The author has heard both his father and Albert's uncle say so. And the most far-reaching ideas often come to him quite naturally—just as silly notions that aren't any good might come to you." "And I was glad I'd owned up, for Father slapped me on the back, and said I was a young brick, and our robber said I was no funk anyway, and though I got very hot under the blanket I liked it, and

I explained that the others would have done the same if they had thought of it." "But Oswald tries to make allowances even for people who do not wash their ears."

There is scarcely a page of the Bastable books which has not some gem on it which shows the Oswaldishness of Oswald. Few could argue that he is by far the most original of the children in the Nesbit portrait gallery.

It is interesting to speculate why, having discovered how brilliantly she could tell a story through the mouth of one of her characters, E. Nesbit deserted the idea for direct story telling. To-day when even the best children's writers seem to find a formula and stick to it, her various ways of telling her story and her complete change in type of story are refreshing. It is of course possible, and indeed it seems likely, that book selling was less commercialised then than it is at the present time and so she did not suffer from publishers both at home and in America who asked incessantly for more about the Bastables, or another book about the Psammead, or, if she did, she paid no attention. She was of course far better placed financially than our present-day writers. She is said to have made £2,000 a year out of her children's books, which would be roughly £6,000 to-day, and of course by to-day's standards income tax was very low so she was able to keep most of her earnings. Even so it is interesting that she was able to abandon her characters at the height of their success and invent a new set, and a new way of telling their story, and to move from the everyday world into fantasy and back again, gathering a new public as she went. Whatever the reason, either because E. Nesbit flouted the publisher's wishes or because her inventive mind refused to be trammelled, she told whatever story it was in her mind to tell, and for that reason she is the most exhilarating writer to study.

Except for *The Railway Children,* the Bastables are the most solid family group E. Nesbit gave her public. This is partly due to the fact already mentioned that her children clung to each other because they had no one else to cling to, for their father was absorbed in business and their mother was dead. There is too the feeling of permanence, again already mentioned, given by the family words. The children do not begin when the book begins, for they have had a past to which words and jokes belong. As an example, quite unexplained there is this charming expression: it is in relation to the booby-trap hamper sent to the porter and the shame when the porter's old father-in-law came to call: "It was hard. But it was ginger-ale and seed cake compared with having to tell Father . . . ." To what does the gingerale and seed cake relate? When had the children had a meal of ginger-ale and seed cake, which had stayed in their memories to such an extent it was an understood family expression? And in all three books there are casual mentions of events which happened before the readers began to know the children. H.O., for instance, is not christened in the book. He was named after an advertisement long before the story starts. In *The New Treasure Seekers,* without any tiresome footnote saying "Read *The Wouldbegoods,*" Oswald says he always liked Denny to have ideas of his own, "because it was us who taught him the folly of white-mousishness." This is typically E. Nesbit. The Bastables are real, they do not belong to one book or another book. Denny, as E. Nesbit had first known him, did suffer from white-mousishness and it was the Bastables who cured him, and she takes it for granted that her readers know this and if they do not and would wish to, then they can find out about Denny and Daisy for themselves.

Perhaps nothing shows E. Nesbit's gift for writing for children more clearly than the ability she has for making her children live. It is not possible to find out how long she existed with her characters before she put pen to paper. The time this takes varies from author to author, but one thing is certain, she never wrote a word of the Bastables until she knew them better than the children around her, for only by knowing everything about her characters, infinitely more than she had any intention of using, could she have made them live and breathe to such an extent that when Oswald wrote at the end of *The New Treasure Seekers* that this was the last story that the present author was going to write, it did not mean for her readers that the Bastable Saga had come to an end. It was more as if a family of children who lived next door, and were so well known they were like part of the family, had moved to another place where, though you might not see them, they were still enjoying their vivid and exciting lives. To be able to do this is a quality possessed by the very few, and so it is no wonder that E. Nesbit's books still live and will live for countless children yet unborn.

Barbara Smith

SOURCE: "The Expressions of Social Values in the Writing of E. Nesbit," in *Children's Literature,* Vol. 3, 1974, pp. 153-64.

Edith Nesbit Bland would no doubt have been considered an unconventional personality regardless of the era into which she happened to be born. She

reached adulthood during the late Victorian age, however, and in that age she appeared remarkably advanced in her personal behavior and values. The most comprehensive biography—by Doris Langley Moore—traces Nesbit's strong individualism from her childhood to her death. Moore spices her chapter about the Blands' involvement in the early Fabian Society with details about E. Nesbit's personal appearance and habits which might lead one to believe that she was indeed the prototype of today's liberated woman. E. Nesbit cut her hair short in the 1880's, wore "aesthetic" loose-fitting dresses, and smoked in public. Moore further promotes the image of the Blands' Bohemianism by stressing the radical nature of their socialist politics:

> These views were then regarded as little less than seditious: one needed as much moral courage to confess to them as one might need today to confess to an out-and-out belief in the most extreme form of Communism. The outrageous young Blands were Socialists.[1]

Socialism in the general sense was perhaps an "outrageous" idea in comparison with the more conservative and staid beliefs of Englishmen of the same social stratum as the Blands, yet the Fabian Society itself was by no means a group of political firebrands.

In *The History of the Fabian Society* by one of its original founders, Edward Pease, the types who were initially attracted to Fabian ideals are described as being comfortably middle-class intellectuals:

> the seed sown by Henry George took root, not in the slums and alleys of our cities—no intellectual seed of any sort can germinate in the sickly, sunless atmosphere of slums—but in the minds of people who had sufficient leisure and education to think of other things than breadwinning.[2]

In the introduction to the 1963 reprinting of Pease's history, Margaret Cole points out the exclusiveness of the early Society membership, despite the fact that its primary goal was to "abolish poverty." And in the political spectrum of that period the Fabians were comparatively moderate in their radicalism.

The words "gradualist," "evolutionary," and "practical" attached to Fabian doctrines indicate the non-revolutionary methods of which the Society generally approved. There were, nevertheless, left-wing and right-wing factions within the society itself. In a letter to a friend E. Nesbitt explains these divisions:

> There are two distinct elements in the F.S. . . . The practical and the visionary—the first being much the strongest—but a perpetual warfare goes on

between the parties which gives to the Fabian an excitement which it might otherwise lack. We belong—needless to say—to the practical party, and so do most of our intimate friends . . . (Moore, p. 107)

Hubert Bland was in fact one of the most conservative members of the Society and seemed to have had much influence on his wife's political commitments. H. G. Wells, who was at one time a member of the Society and a frequent visitor to the Bland household, makes a case for an innate difference in the couple's political natures. In his *Experiment in Autobiography* he writes:

> It was, I am convinced, because she, in her general drift, was radical and anarchistic, that the pose of Bland's self-protection hardened into this form of gentlemanly conservatism. He presented himself as a Tory in grain.
>
> She acquiesced in these posturings. If she had not, I suppose he would have argued with her until she did.
>
> But a gay holiday spirit bubbled beneath her verbal orthodoxies and escaped into her work. The Bastables are an anarchistic lot. Her soul was against the government all the time.[3]

All of this must be remembered in considering the political and social views in E. Nesbit's works. As a member of the Fabian Society, she was by association more politically unorthodox than most people in her social and historical context. Yet the organization was itself middle-class and moderate, and her background was middle-class. Her husband's powerful personality may have had the effect of diluting her commitments, and the domestic conflicts between them may also have tempered these enforced beliefs with an undercurrent of resentment.

The families in the three Bastable books and in the magic series are unmistakably middle-class, although their parents' financial statuses have the tendency to fluctuate. The family in *The Railway Children* is also only temporarily poor, because of their father's absence. All of these children often come into contact with persons whom they consider poor, however, and a frequent result of these encounters is initial if not long-term misunderstanding.

One character, Oswald, is the principle mouthpiece for E. Nesbit's satire of existing conditions. As a part of the program of their newly formed society for doing good deeds the children in *The Wouldbegoods* try to befriend a Mrs. Simpkins, who has a son in the war. Oswald in his humorously embellished style explains the children's fascination with soldiers as the partial reason " . . . why we sought to aid and abet the poor widow at the white cottage in her desolate and oppressedness."[4] They finally arrive at weeding her garden as a means of helping her, but by mistake pull up turnips and cabbages which her son had planted before he left. Mrs. Simpkins reaction to their good deed is quite emotional:

> "You wicked, meddlesome, nasty children!" she said, "ain't yo got enough of your own good ground to runch up and spoil, but you must come into *my* little lot? . . . Dratted little busybodies . . . " (p. 57)

Although everything turns out well in this episode, the children are often the victims of antagonisms which are tinged with class-resentment, perhaps because they so often put themselves into the position of trying to be charitable to those they consider less fortunate than themselves.

In another episode in *The Wouldbegoods* the children get the idea of providing lemonade for "poor and thirsty" travelers at a roadside "Benevolent Bar." The Bar has mixed success since some of the people who pass by seem not to think too much of the youngsters' philanthropy. One mutters: "Bloomin' Sunday-school treat." And Oswald recalls that:

> One man told us he could pay for his own liquor when he was dry, which praise be, he wasn't over and above at present; and others asked if we hadn't any beer, and when we said "No," they said it showed what sort we were—as if the sort was not a good one, which it is.
>
> And another man said, "Slops again! You never get nothing for nothing, not this side of heaven you don't. Look at the bloomin' blue ribbon on em! Oh Lord'!" (p. 214)

Finally the children get into a row with three "big disagreeable men" and some rough boys from the village, but they are rescued by two previously made friends. Oswald sums up the failed venture by deciding:

> I really think we shall never try to be benevolent to the poor and needy again. At any rate not unless we know them very well first. (p. 220)

By making these encounters fail, E. Nesbit shows the tensions and inequalities which exist in a class-ridden society.

The children's own perspective about what it means to be poor is forgivably naive, yet E. Nesbit herself makes invidious distinctions between them and the lower-class characters they meet. The really poor people and inevitably the villainous ones speak broken or Cockney English. In *The Story of The Treasure Seekers* a robber and a burglar invade the Bastable home during the space of one evening. Oswald says of the robber (who is really a friend of their father). "I did feel so sorry for him. He used such nice words, and he had a gentleman's voice."[5] The real burglar speaks in a slangy dialect:

> "All right, governor! Stow that scent sprinkler. I'll give in. Blowed if I ain't pretty well sick of the job, anyway." (p. 166)

Oswald notices, " . . . his face was red and his voice was thick. How different from our own robber!"

Another characteristic of certain poor people is that they are not as quick as the Bastables, who are of course very bright and inventive. Oswald suspects that the poor widow Mrs. Simpkins "would not understand poetry," so they decide not to make her a gift of one of Noel's poems (*Wouldbegoods,* p. 55). Mrs. Pettigrew, the cook at Moat House, lacks the most rudimentary literary understanding. Oswald remarks:

> She thinks Albert's uncle copies things out of printed books, when he is really writing new ones. I wonder how she thinks printed books get made first of all. Many servants are like this. (p. 69)

In *The New Treasure Seekers* the Bastables meet some poor children while they are on a picnic with some adult friends. Oswald notes "they did not seem to be very clever children, or just the sort you would choose for your friends, but I suppose you like to play, however little you are other people's sort."[6] At first the children wonder why the village children have not been taught to play rounders, but they soon realize it is "because it is most awfully difficult to make them understand the very simplest thing" (p. 283).

Joan Evans de Alonso lived at Well Hall, Eltham, in the E. Nesbit household from 1916-1920. The Evans family spent all their school vacation there and knew the author and her family very well. Mrs. Alonso pointed out in a conversation with me that an English upbringing was a class-conscious matter, and that the E. Nesbit children are true to the English upbringing of that period. She added, "Children were very sure of their standards in behavior and taste."[7] It is problematic, then, whether E. Nesbit unwittingly stereotypes the poor or points out differences that did in fact exist.

In the last book of the series the Bastables continue their efforts to aid the poor with the usual unsuccessful results. They make a disgustingly soapy "conscience pudding" for Christmas and do not seem to realize that they are not really performing a service by trying to give it away to someone who is needy. The Cockney accented ire they inspire in the strangers they insult by trying to give away their gift is, by this time, familiar. An incident in which they play a trick on a porter with a fake gift basket of food again points up the difficulty of interacting beneficially and without misunderstanding with one's social inferiors.

At the end of *The Wouldbegoods* Oswald remarks:

> "If anything in these chronicles of the Wouldbegoods should make you try to be good yourself, the author will be very glad, of course. But take my advice and don't make a society for trying in. It is much easier without." (p. 282f)

Perhaps E. Nesbit herself would agree with this advice after her experiments with social work and giving mammoth Christmas parties for one thousand poor children at a time.[8] Certainly the Wouldbegood Society is generally unsuccessful and merely serves to get the children into more trouble rather than to keep them—or get others—out of it. With their mischief the children also antagonize adults who are not poor, but the fact that English poor people are also proud makes it difficult for the Bastables to "help" them without prompting resentment.

An exploration of adults' involvement in activities of social uplift occurs in *The New Treasure Seekers.* Eustace Sandal and his sisters Miss Sandal and Mrs. Bax have interests very much like some of E. Nesbit's own friends. It is amusing to see the Bastables' childish interpretations of this family's social ideals and to speculate whether E. Nesbit is having some fun with the dedicated types she was familiar with in the Fabian Society. Oswald's descriptions of the Sandals are certainly tinged with a kind of humorous misunderstanding and skepticism:

> Father knows a man called Eustace Sandal. I do not know how to express his inside soul, but I have heard father say he means well. He is a vegetarian and a Primitive Social Something, and an all-wooler, and things like that, and he is really as good as he can stick, only most awfully dull. I believe he eats bread and milk from choice. Well, he has great magnificent dreams about all the things you can do for other people, and he wants to distill cultivatedness into the sort of people who live in Model Workmen's Dwellings, and teach them to live up to better things. This is what he says. (p. 193)

When the youngsters visit Mr. Sandal's sister, who lives by the sea, they discover that she is much like her brother. Miss Sandal lives in a very bare white house and she tells the children upon their arrival that "The motto of our little household is 'plain living and high thinking'" (p. 188). She is also a vegetarian and does not keep a servant. Oswald observes pointedly, "She was kind, but rather like her house— there was something bare and bald about her inside mind" (p. 190).

When Mr. Sandal has an accident, Miss Sandal leaves them in the care of a cook and the children hatch several plans to earn some money for their absent hostess. To their young minds the only reason for enduring such a "cold rice pudding" existence is that one is poor and does not have the resources to do better. Mr. Sandal's accident, incidentally, is the result of climbing up on some scaffolding to give a workman a tract on temperance. He manages to make both of them fall off, and it is only a dust cart passing underneath that saves their lives. The workman, it turns out, is a teetotaler. Mr. Sandal's benevolent efforts are in this case just as ineffectual as the children's. Fortunately the Sandal family is redeemed by a third member, Mrs. Bax, who smokes cigarettes and has short hair. The Bastables like her very much after they discover that she does not particularly appreciate them acting like "Sunday School children" just for the sake of maintaining quiet in the house. Oswald asserts, "Mrs. Bax, now that her true nature was revealed, proved to be A1" (p. 275). Obviously this "advanced woman" and the Bastables are kindred spirits.

Although some older women win the admiration of Oswald and the others, Oswald as narrator is a remarkable, if juvenile, "male chauvinist" in the comments he makes about his sisters and about girls in general. His criticisms are perhaps more grating to the sensibilities of a contemporary woman reader than they might have been to a young reader of past decades. However, it is still curious to consider why a woman writer would be so consistently anti-female unless her motive was to be subtly satirical of sex-role stereotypes. If Oswald is E. Nesbit's vehicle for expressing dissatisfaction with women's position in late Victorian society, his anti-female declarations are so similar in tone to those made by actual male supremacists that few readers would realize that she was not supporting the *status quo*. Certainly the intended satire would completely escape her young audience. There are so many references of this type that only a few of them can be included here as examples.

In *The Story of the Treasure Seekers,* after capturing the "robber," Oswald shares a celebration feast with his father and his robber-friend. Oswald remarks:

> We sat up till past twelve o'clock, and I never felt so pleased to think I was not born a girl. (p. 172)

During one of the children's councils they smoke the pipe of peace using an old bubble pipe:

> We put tea-leaves in it . . . but the girls are not allowed to have any. It is not right to let girls smoke. They get to think too much of themselves if you let them do everything the same as men. (p. 141)

Since E. Nesbit herself smoked, one can assume she intended to satirize sex role stereotypes.

In *The Wouldbegoods* Oswald's attitude is that of pained and superior benevolence towards the weaker sex. He tolerates girls at the same time that he criticizes them, always mindful that his duty as a brother is to be patient with the stupid feminity of his sisters. It is the girls who arrive at the idea of a society for doing good deeds, and Oswald and Dicky immediately realize its potential for inhibiting their plans for having fun (p. 43). Oswald subscribes to the theory that there are particular roles which males and females are best fitted for and that each sex has its particular nature. When girls cry about killing rats, Oswald reasons:

> Girls cannot help this; we must not be waxy with them on account of it, they have their nature, the same as bull-dogs have, and it is this that makes them so useful in smoothing the pillows of the sickbed and tending wounded heroes. (p. 109)

When Alice, the more tomboyish of the two sisters and therefore Oswald's favorite, balks at baiting her fishing hook, Oswald observes in the same vein:

> Girls are strange, mysterious, silly things. Alice always enjoys a rat hunt until the rat is caught, but she hates fishing from beginning to end. We boys have got to like it. (p. 151)

Oswald undoubtedly feels some pressure as the eldest boy in the family to set a manly example for the others, and his view of girls is no doubt typical of a preadolsecent in the early 1900's. Girls faint, are naturally inclined towards giggling, and even the best of them have the habit of crying, but boys must transcend these failings even if it means hiding their feelings.

At least one adult agrees with Oswald's opinions about the position of women. In *The New Treasure Seekers* an old sailor tells the children a story about a man who is arrested for smuggling on his wedding day. Alice asks what his wife did about this and the sailor explains, "*She* didn't do nothing, . . . It's a woman's place not to do nothing till she's told to . . ." (p. 212).

The old man's values are also properly Victorian, but E. Nesbit herself knew that there were alternative and less passive ways for women to conduct their own lives. Moore points out that E. Nesbit was always a tomboy and that this influenced her attitudes as well as her actions:

> She was not a masculine woman, but neither was she, in the full sense of the term, a feminine one. Strange paradoxes were everywhere apparent in her. she gloried in material independence, but spiritually, as her relations with Hubert Bland must show, she exemplified dependent womanhood. She loved children, but was not . . . maternal. (p. 219f)

In analyzing the general weaknesses of E. Nesbit's adult poetry, Moore points out that she made an effort not to reveal her inner feelings in what she wrote:

> No one can suspect that she had any marked partiality for her own sex; she seldom attempted to conceal her preference for the other; yet, again and again, she wrote love poems as if addressed by a man to a woman. Her motives, it may be assumed, were connected with the shrinking from reality which she has described; she wanted to write love poetry, but not to expose her heart. (p. 225)

Perhaps she adopted Oswald's perspective in the children's books for the same reason.

Noel Streatfeild in his semi-critical work about E. Nesbit, *Magic and the Magician,* attributes her preference for her male characters and the accuracy with which they are depicted to the pleasure she derived from the companionship of her own two brothers as a child.[9] Whether her motivations for preferring male characters were simple or complex, only in one work, *The Railway Children,* does she allow a female character to take decided precedence over her brother. Roberta, the oldest of the three children, is obviously the author's favorite. Nesbit writes:

> I hope you don't mind my telling you a good deal about Roberta. The fact is I am growing very fond of her. The more I observe her the more I love her. And I notice all sorts of things about her that I like.[10]

Streatfeild believes that Roberta is really a kind of emotional surrogate for E. Nesbit's son, Fabian, who died suddenly at the age of fifteen, several years before the writing of this work. Although Bobbie has many qualities which E. Nesbit admires, she protects herself from too painful an involvement with her character by making her a girl (Streatfeild, p. 122).

Paradoxically, despite E. Nesbit's obvious bias in favor of men in her own group of acquaintances and in her literary creations, she did not support the movement for women's suffrage. Moore indicates that her stance against women's rights was greatly influenced by her husband:

> The behavior of certain feminine agitators was exciting derision at that time all over the country, and E. Nesbit showed no greater sympathy towards them than was felt by women whose political views were less advanced than hers. Nevertheless, two or three of her friends were of the opinion that she was by no means opposed to the breaking down of sex barriers on principle, and might have taken part in the movement herself had it not been for Hubert Bland's influence. (p. 266)

Something of Bland's influence must be indicated by the painful domestic situation which he imposed upon her. Not only did he carry on a series of affairs throughout their marriage, he also required that she accept as her own the children of her companion-housekeeper—children of whom he was the father. H. G. Wells emphasizes the subterfuge that pervaded life at Well Hall during the time that he visited the Blands:

> Then gradually something else came into the *ensemble.* It came first to the visitor at Well Hall as chance whispering, as flashes of conflict and fierce resentment, as raised voices in another room, a rush of feet down a passage and the banging of a door. . . . You found after a time that Well Hall was not so much an atmosphere as a web. (p. 516)

The ambivalences which these arrangements aroused in E. Nesbit's psyche must have been great. Perhaps the pro-masculine attitudes in her fiction served as an escape from the constrictions of her own situation. An early poem must reflect her real attitude; in **"The Wife of All Ages"** Nesbit writes:

> Suppose I yearned, and longed, and dreamed, and fluttered,
>   What would you say or think, or further, do?
> Why should one rule be fit for me to follow,
>   While there exists a different law for you?[11]

At the end of the poem the wife admits that she will still willingly accept whatever part of his affection her husband allots to her. In her children's books this serious issue is only indirectly present: E. Nesbit usually insures free reign for the children's adventures by eliminating one or both parents from their midst.

The most obvious stereotypes in E. Nesbit's writing are not of poor people or of women, but of minority groups. Jews, Indians, "savages," and Blacks all merit a derogatory phrase or two. In *The Story of the Treasure Seekers* the children visit a moneylender, Z. Rosenbaum, whom they believe to be a generous benefactor. Mr. Rosenbaum has "a very long white beard and a hookey nose—like a falcon" and he says that he can lend the children a pound at sixty per cent interest, payable when they are twenty-one (p. 105). Oswald remarks, "And all the time he was stroking the sovereign and looking at it as if he thought it very beautiful." Whatever the author's opinion, the children believe in Mr. Rosenbaum's kindness and Alice asks why he is not invited to the party at their Uncle's mansion after the family's fortunes have changed:

> But everybody laughed, and Uncle said—"Your father has paid him the sovereign he lent you. I don't think he could have borne another pleasant surprise." (p. 206)

Of course Jewish moneylenders are not appropriate party guests.

In *The Story of the Amulet,* which makes the most positive statement of any of the works about the need for social reforms, there is nevertheless an adventure in the financial district in which Old Levinstein and another Mr. Rosenbaum are portrayed as being selfish, usorious, and incapable of speaking "decent" English.[12]

The expression "nigger" is used indiscriminately in several of the works. In *The Story of the Treasure Seekers* the Indian uncle compliments Oswald by saying " . . . he's a man! If he's not a man, I'm a nigger! Eh!—what?" (p. 198). In a recent edition of *The Conscience Pudding,* excerpted from *The New Treasure Seekers,* the word nigger is deleted. Obviously it had little negative significance to white people at the time that E. Nesbit was writing, but merely expressed the attitudes that she and her audience shared about the negligibility of dark-skinned people.

In *The Phoenix and the Carpet,* one of the children suggests that they can escape from a band of savages by going into the water, because, as he explains,

"I've—heard—savages always—dirty."[13] In this case the children have been negatively indoctrinated, whereas in the case of the first Mr. Rosenbaum, they were innocent about the attitude they were expected to hold.

These incidents and phrases are hardly essential to the total conceptions of the works as a whole, yet they do indirectly reflect the attitudes of the society in which Nesbit did her writing, if not her personal opinions. Indeed, it is very difficult to pin down E. Nesbit's attitudes on any of these matters. Is she serious or satirical in her statements about the role of women? Is she in fact more sympathetic toward her bungling wouldbegoods' efforts to alleviate the sufferings of the poor than she is toward the poor themselves? To what degree are her attitudes affected by her own experience of social reform movements and by her husband's encouragement of her commitment to certain causes? Do any of these matters bear consideration when it is known that E. Nesbit usually wrote under the constraint to earn money and therefore to please her publishers and the public, if not always herself?

These questions are partly answered in her later works, in which, as Moore points out, she is much less subtle in expressing her personal views, often to the detriment of her story (p. 266). In *The Story of the Amulet* (1906) there is, however, a skillful blending of a children's magical adventure and a clear-cut statement of E. Nesbit's social concerns. This is the most philosophical of the three magic books about the children Cyril, Anthea, Robert, and Jane, and it is also the most fascinating on an adult level. Her magical plot device, the idea of travel through time, enables her to explore themes which go beyond a mere fantasy for children. The amulet, which transports the children to different civilizations of the past, is much more complex in its magic than the Psammead or the Phoenix and the carpet, because it requires a highly abstract understanding of the dimension of time. The children gradually learn to think of time in unconventional ways, following the advice of the Psammead that "Time and space are only forms of thought" (p. 61). Not only does their understanding of the particular concept grow, but in all the three magic books they seem to increase in wisdom as a result of their magical adventures.

In the first of the series, *The Five Children and It,* the children are quite thoughtless in the wishes they ask the Psammead to grant them and they usually suffer more than they benefit from the magic they have at their disposal. In *The Phoenix and the Carpet* the children get into just as much trouble, although there is the added excitement of being instantly transported in space to a new setting. The Phoenix has the role of a semi-adult figure and provides both instruction and entertainment for the children. In both these works they learn to take into account the feelings of others, since the Psammead as well as the Phoenix are demanding and self-centered. In *The Story of the Amulet* the children have reached the stage at which they can appreciate the lessons of "history" and carefully follow the directions which safe use of the amulet requires.

At the beginning of the novel the children are walking in a district where there are several pet shops. They feel sympathy for the animals who are in cages, because they had once been trapped in a besieged castle themselves. There is the implication that their magical adventures provide experiences which help them to mature and become better persons.

Two of the things which E. Nesbit emphasizes in her depictions of the ancient civilizations the children visit are the dispensation of justice and the condition of the working or slave classes. She also compares the level of past civilizations with the state of affairs in England, and often the present is seen as being little better than the past. When the Babylonian Queen visits the children, she is amazed at the state of the working classes. E. Nesbit provides biting social commentary in this scene:

> "But how badly you keep your slaves. How wretched and poor and neglected they seem," she said, as the cab rattled along the Mile End Road.
>
> "They aren't slaves; they're working people," said Jane.
>
> "Of course they're working. That's what slaves are. Don't you tell me. Do you suppose I don't know a slave's face when I see it? Why don't their masters see that they're better fed and better clothed? Tell me in three words."
>
> No one answered. The wage system of modern England is a little difficult to explain in three words even if you understand it—which the children didn't.
>
> "You'll have a revolt of your slaves if you're not careful," said the Queen.
>
> "Oh, no," said Cyril; "you see they have votes—that makes them safe not to revolt. It makes all the difference. Father told me so."
>
> "What is this vote?" asked the Queen. "Is it a charm? What do they do with it?"

I don't know," said the harassed Cyril; "it's just a vote, that's all! They don't do anything particular with it."

"I see," said the Queen; "a sort of a plaything . . . " (pp. 168, 170)

Through her fantasy E. Nesbit expresses criticism about real social wrongs. The children have social consciences themselves. In Egypt they hear the workers protesting their wretched conditions and when they are able to confront the Pharoah, Anthea takes the opportunity to ask him to grant the workers' demands as a condition of their continuing with their magic exhibition (p. 238).

In the chapter entitled "The Sorry-Present and the Expelled Boy" E. Nesbit makes her most serious indictment of the present by having the children travel into the future. In its details E. Nesbit's picture of what is to come is very much influenced by the Fabians' social ideals. Everything is clean and beautiful. Littering is a major offense. The little boy the children meet is named Wells, after the "great reformer" and he actually likes school, where he is able to pursue an independent project each year. The people dress in soft clothes and although the little boy's house is bare of ornaments, it is to these children very beautiful. From their comments the little boy's mother assumes that the children come from a very backward country and she is miserably upset when she is whisked into the present and sees the horrible conditions which the children take for granted.

This may seem heavy-handed for a child's book, but the clear statement of E. Nesbit's views on serious matters does not detract from the adventure, and at least one gets the satisfaction of seeing that indeed E. Nesbit's political commitment did extend to her fiction. The magic books are altogether more sophisticated because a third-person adult narrator is used. Although these children are less well-defined and less real than the Bastables or the Railway Children, there are more ideas to get hold of in the fantasies. In the last work in the magic series there is sincere concern for the poor, and even the issue of male superiority is finally counterattacked. At a lecture which the children attend with the Psammead the speaker wishes that the boys in the audience will grow up to be "noble, brave and unselfish," and the wish comes true because it is said in the presence of the magic creature, who grants all wishes. Anthea remarks that it is too bad that the lecturer did not include girls, because she and Jane will have to try to attain these qualities on their own. Jane replies that the girls no doubt have these traits already "because of our beautiful natures. It's only boys that have to be made brave by magic" (p. 295). ***The Story of the Amulet*** ends on a note of reconciliation between the past and the present with the joining of the souls of the Egyptian priest and the learned gentleman, and hope for the future has already been provided, as seen through the children's own eyes when they visit it themselves. How such an ideal world is to be made reality is not specifically explained, but E. Nesbit has at least stated ideals in which she believes. In a letter to H. G. Wells, E. Nesbit admits that she wishes that she could write books like his *Modern Utopia*.[14] ***The Story of the Amulet,*** which was perhaps influenced by Wells' *Time Machine*, is undoubtedly E. Nesbit's attempt to write a highly idealistic work for children. It corroborates Joan Evans de Alonso's summary assertion about her commitments:

> She foresaw an ideal future. In spirit she was definitely a social thinker.

In conclusion, the question should be raised whether the matters which have been discussed here are important to the children who read the E. Nesbit books now. If E. Nesbit's purpose was to satirize the attitudes of her contemporaries toward women and the poor, she does it so subtly that few children would be able to see through the stereotyped images she presents to the protest underneath. It is likely that the very delicacy with which she pokes fun at establishment values is the result of her own ambivalence about these values and also of her doubts about using writing for children as a platform for adult ideas. E. Nesbit's magic books are less dated and also less negative in the social images which they promote than the works in the Bastable series and have much to offer contemporary readers. ***The Railway Children*** is the best of the non-magic books because of its successful depiction of real children, both female and male. All the novels, however, have elements in them which are entertaining both to children and to an adult reader who enjoys travelling back through time to the consciousness of childhood.

Notes

1. Doris Langley Moore, *E. Nesbit, A Biography,* rev. ed. (1933; rpt. London: Ernest Benn, 1967), p. 102.

2. Edward R. Pease, *The History of the Fabian Society,* 3rd ed. intro. Margaret Cole (1918; rpt. Liverpool: Frank Cass & Co., 1963), p. 19.

3. H. G. Wells, *Experiment in Autobiography* (1934; rpt. Philadelphia: J. B. Lippincott, 1967), p. 515.

4. E. Nesbit, *The Wouldbegoods* (1901; rpt. London: Penguin, 1971), p. 54.

5. E. Nesbit, *The Story of the Treasure Seekers* (1899; rpt. London: Penguin, 1971), p. 163.

6. E. Nesbit, *The New Treasure Seekers* (1904; rpt. New York: Coward McCann, n. d.), p. 283.

7. From an interview, May 31, 1972, in Cambridge, Massachusetts.

8. Moore, p. 141.

9. Noel Streatfeild, *Magic and the Magician, E. Nesbit and Her Children's Books* (London: Abelard Schuman, 1958), p. 66.

10. E. Nesbit, *The Railway Children* (1906; rpt. London: Penguin, 1971), p. 114.

11. E. Nesbit, *Lays and Legends* (London: Longmans, Green & Co., 1886), p. 82.

12. E. Nesbit, *The Story of the Amulet* (1906; rpt. Clinton, Mass.; Colonial Press, n.d.), pp. 172-174.

13. E. Nesbit, *The Phoenix and the Carpet* (1904; rpt. London: Penguin, n.d.), p. 70.

14. Moore, p. 228

Colin N. Manlove

SOURCE: "Fantasy as Witty Conceit: E. Nesbit," in *Mosaic,* Vol. 10, No. 2, Winter, 1977, pp. 109-30.

> [Fancy] has no other counters to play with, but fixities and definites. The Fancy is indeed no other than a mode of Memory emancipated from the order of time and space; while it is blended with, and modified by that empirical faculty of the will, which we express by the word CHOICE.
>
> Coleridge, *Biog. Lit.* ch. XIII
>
> It is sometimes said in intended praise of a story of magic and fantasy that it created an atmosphere in which the reader felt that 'anything might happen.' The truth is that if the story were really like that it would be a very bad one; for to be convincing it must, like every other kind of writing answer to laws of logic, even though this may not be everybody's logic. It may take its own rules, but it must obey them scrupulously.
>
> "Magic and Make-Believe," *TLS* (28 May, 1954), p. xii col i

The fantasies or fairy-stories of E. Nesbit were all published, one might say with chronological neatness, between 1900 and 1913,[1] starting with **The Book of Dragons** (first serialised in 1899) and ending with **Wet Magic.** Naturally, given such dates, the commentator is drawn to see them as significant: to find Nesbit's work 'modern' rather than 'Victorian,' and rather less modern than Edwardian.[2] In this aim he will not be frustrated, for it is true that Nesbit's stories are often much less didactic in final intent than those of her forbears, Mrs. [Juliana Horatia] Ewing and Mrs. [Mary Louisa] Molesworth, in their reworkings of traditional fairy tale;[3] and true too that the class assumptions and clear values on which many of them depend vanished with the Great War. Yet such an account requires qualification. One might point to the fact that Nesbit wrote for children, and the relation between delighting and instructing a child is a perennial issue in children's literature, since the adult of any age stands at least partly in the role of instructor in relation to the child. Thackeray's *The Rose and the Ring* (1855) may have a light moral frame, but the primary object is the delight of a child through fantastic incongruities. A given author may equally write highly didactic and non-moral tales: the same George MacDonald who wrote *The Lost Princess* also wrote "The Light Princess"; and Nesbit could with equal facility set about the purely witty **"Melisande"** (*NUT*) as the more instructive **"Whereyouwantogoto"** (*NUT*) or **"Justnowland"** (*MW*). Then again, there must always be an element of 'class structure' in children's literature, not only because the adults who write them or appear as actors in the stories have to be leaders and repositories of value, but also because the child's mind is inveterately hierarchical, and his mental outlook is founded on rules, orders and stations. Nor, one could add, was Nesbit the first to write her kind of fantasy. Her primary literary debt was to the work of F. Anstey (pseudonym of Thomas Anstey Guthrie) who, in such stories as *Vice Versa, or, A Lesson to Fathers* (1882), *The Tinted Venus, A Farcical Romance* (1885) and *The Brass Bottle* (1900), had developed the comic possibilities of fantasy beyond those exploited by Thackeray, Dickens or MacDonald:[4] though written within the 'Victorian' period, not one of his books attempts to be moral, and indeed in one of his stories, "The Good Little Girl,"[5] he gives us a young female prig who is cured of her penchant for making improving remarks by means of a spell which makes every 'sentence' she utters be accompanied by the dropping from her lips of jewels which are subsequently found to be fakes.

Nevertheless it is true that Nesbit is one of the first children's writers whose books, particularly her comic ones, are not largely concerned with moral issues and the instruction of a juvenile readership. Nesbit had an extraordinary gift for remembering her own childhood, and for putting herself inside the minds of her child-characters: she once said,

> You cannot hope to understand children by commonsense, by reason, by logic, nor by any science whatsoever. You cannot understand them by imagination—not even by love itself. There is only one way: to remember what you thought and felt and liked and hated when you yourself were a child. Not what you know now—or think you know—you ought to have thought and liked, but what you did then, in stark fact, like and think. There is no other way.[6]

If one is going to write from a 'child's eye' point of view in this way, the distance necessary for moral instruction is to a large degree removed. "I make it a point of honour never to *write down* to a child," Nesbit once declared (Moore, 178). A vast gulf separates her from earlier writers who began with a *self-conscious* preference for imaginative rather than moral stories for the young: Nesbit simply does not work from the outside like this, and it shows; she is not *giving* the child reader anything, for in a sense she is that reader. As her biographer has said, "she understood children with a fellow-feeling rather than with the detachment of a psychologist."[7]

This special power of recall cannot readily be explained: certainly it has nothing to do with literary tradition or the time at which she wrote. To some extent it must be related to the vividness of her own childhood and character: yet the evidence here does not always point to a rosy youth. Her father died in 1862 when she was only four, and her mother took the family abroad for the sake of Edith's sister Mary's health (she was consumptive). It was not until she was fourteen, and after a variety of not often pleasant boarding schools in France, Germany and Britain,[8] that Edith had a lasting home again, at Halstead Hall in Kent. Longing for the return of a father, and a child's remote sense of the precariousness of the family fortunes are themes in many of her children's books—particularly **The Story of the Treasure Seekers** (1899), **The Would Be Goods** (1901), **The Railway Children** (1906) and **The Story of the Amulet** (1906). Nesbit was, however, a 'tom boy' as a child, and had endless games and 'scrapes' with her brothers Alfred and Harry, of which only a few mentions have survived[9] apart from those which doubtless found their way into her books. Without a father, and with her mother trying to carry on the agricultural school he had previously run, her early childhood must have been unusually free; and to this must be added the fact that her mother was far from strict.[10] What her early experience certainly did enforce on Nesbit was her sense of a family, and particularly of *children:* she hardly ever writes about the solitary child, but about the interactions of brothers and sisters, and always from a position of involvement, from the children's point of view (she was one of the first to do this).

Nesbit is not a writer with a definite philosophy or moral code which unifies or gives 'purpose' to her books. She herself flouted the conventions of her time, smoking cigarettes in public, wearing outrageous 'Aesthetic' clothes (and making her children do so too),[11] and bringing up in her own family two of the children of her husband's extra-marital affairs.[12] Here again the lack of distance on her part in her children's books is explained. But the important point here is that she never committed herself to one thing in life (except her family), and had no fixed and narrow point of view.

One of the keys to an understanding of Nesbit is her passionate delight in life, and her wish to experience it to the full, to 'spread' herself in every direction. She threw herself with enthusiasm into everything she did. She was a prominent foundation member of the Fabian Society. She became a dedicated 'Aesthete' in the eighties.[13] She made herself an accomplished hostess, and held many 'open house' weekends at Well Hall, her house in Sussex. She wrote articles as a poetry critic for the *Athenaeum.* For years she tried to identify Bacon with Shakespeare by means of logarithms.[14] She became fascinated with the construction of model cities out of household objects, writing a book, *The Magic City* (1910), on the subject, and exhibiting one of her cities at a stand at Olympia in 1912. And she was a writer of a vast number of books both for adults and children: of 'real life' novels, melodramas poems, magic books, horror tales and stories of childhood.

The range of her friendships and reading shows the same love of variety. She herself declared that she had read Hume, Locke and Berkeley, Percy's *Anecdotes* in 39 volumes, Burton's *Anatomy of Melancholy,* Buchner's *Man,* Mill's *Subjection of Women,* Louis Blanc's *Historical Revelations* and Sinnet's *Esoteric Bhuddism.*[15] She was influenced by writers as diverse as Dickens, Mrs. J. H. Ewing, Henry James, Kenneth Grahame, George Eliot, Mrs. M. L.

Molesworth, Thackeray, Wells, Anstey, Kipling, Charles Reade, George MacDonald and E. M. Forster; and she had a passion for drama, particularly Ibsen.[16] Laurence Housman actually assisted her with plots—and gave her the Phoenix.[17] Her 'sampler' of English poetry, *Poets' Whispers* (1895), speaks for itself of the breadth of her love for poetry; she and her husband Hubert Bland were members of the Browning and Shelley Societies. In 1908 she helped launch and edit the quarterly periodical *The Neolith:*[18] three of the contributors, with whose work she was at least partly familiar, were Lord Dunsany, Arthur Machen and Richard Middleton. Nesbit was influenced by the 'Decadent' mode too,[19] and herself contributed some work to the *Yellow Book.* Her circle of friends and acquaintances was vast: for example with Shaw, Wells, Kipling, Laurence Housman, Forster and Chesterton she was a particular friend, and she also knew William Morris, Yeats, Baron Corvo, Conrad, W. E. Henley, Wilde and Rider Haggard.[20] It has been said in description of her character and reading that:

> Few writers have had a wider range of tastes than E. Nesbit or cultivated friendships with other writers so different in outlook and in accomplishments. A fervent Ibsen enthusiast . . . she could shed tears over *Jessica's First Prayer;* a disciple of Kipling, she still perceived all the charm and delicacy of Henry James; she read the most advanced and challenging literature of the nineties and managed to appreciate it without any infidelity to her earlier loves—Dickens, Thackeray, George Eliot, and Charles Reade; fairy stories, adventure stories, contemplative poetry, political and religious works, anything in short that was good of its kind was capable of providing entertainment for her. And when there was nothing better to be had, she was glad enough even of what was not 'good of its kind.' As she once told a friend, she would rather at any time in her life have read a railway timetable than nothing. As for her friendships, she seemed as she grew older to become rather more than less sensitive to the attractions of new intimacies, and the interesting possibilities of strangers. (Moore, 163)

Nesbit's character—her child-likeness, her refusal to be fixed on one activity or code in life, her sheer zest—is portrayed in the character of her books. It emerges in the form of episodic narratives organized not by 'themes' or deep meanings but by comic schemata which make witty conceits out of magic.

There is no recurrent theme or motif running through the variety of stories that she wrote (it has been said of the disparity between her adult and her children's books that "it is almost impossible not to believe there were two Nesbits"[21]): and there is rarely a central idea in any single one of her works either. Her long stories often fall apart naturally into narrative vignettes. *Five Children and It* (1902) begins with the discovery by a family of children of a strange sand-fairy called a Psammead, which grants them a wish each morning with the proviso that the effects of the wish vanish at sunset. The book is thereafter a series of episodes, each centred on a wish granted, but all quite unrelated to one another. One day the children wish "'to be rich beyond the dreams of something or other'" (p. 44) and the Psammead fills the gravel pit near where they are standing with gold. But it is gold in the form of spade-guineas, which no shopkeeper will accept; and finally the children are taken to the police station to be charged with unlawful possession. Just as the worst is about to befall, however, the gold vanishes at sunset, and they are released, with reprimands. On another occasion they wish for wings, and are on the top of a church tower at sunset (chs. 4,5); on another Robert, who has just been unfairly beaten by the local baker's boy, wishes to be bigger than him, and the Psammead makes him a giant—by sunset he is being exhibited at a fairground (ch. 8). A similar technique is used in *The Phoenix and the Carpet* (1904). Several of Nesbit's magic books are simply collections of tales—*The Book of Dragons* (1900), *Nine Unlikely Tales* (1901), *Oswald Bastable and Others* (1905), *The Magic World* (1912). In other stories there is a general narrative frame binding a series of episodes: thus in *The Story of the Amulet* the objective of the children is the search, by time-travelling, for the other half of a section of a magic amulet which they have found in a shop (the recovery of the whole will grant them their "heart's desire"): but much of the story is a series of visits to different civilizations, and the entertaining effects to be derived from bringing a family of Edwardian children together with people from Stone Age, Babylonian, Roman or Phoenician cultures. Nesbit uses the same framing method in her 'domestic' children's novels: the general aim of the children in *The Treasure Seekers* is the restoration of the fortunes of the Bastable family by finding or making money, but the various attempts are complete and individual in themselves; and similarly with the general objective of *The Would Be Goods.*

Nesbit's books do not ask more than a literal level of reading. The search for the "heart's desire" in *The Story of the Amulet* could conceivably have been made into a metaphor of spiritual pilgrimage, but, apart from one hint, the Amulet is treated merely as

an object to be secured; and at the end, when it has been restored, the heart's desire thus gained is simply the return of the children's parents from abroad. One can extend this point to Nesbit's more adult imaginative works. Where the subject of her "modern melodrama," *Salome and the Head* (1909), would have been to a writer such as George MacDonald one rich in symbolic possibilities, it offered Nesbit simply the opportunity to exploit the full horror of the story by giving it a modern setting. In *Dormant* (1911) one of the characters, Antony Drelincourt, discovers through magical experiments the elixir of life, and with it wakes the beautiful Eugenia, who has been in a state of suspended animation for forty-five years. Alchemy is only the background for the romantic concern of the novel: Drelincourt, formerly pledged to one Rose Royal, abandons her for Eugenia; but later, while he is trying by means of the elixir to make himself more acceptable to Eugenia by becoming immortal, both of them are drowned. Charles Williams, who wrote numbers of fantasies concerned with the use and misuse of magic, would have made a theme out of Antony's blasphemy in his perversion of man's condition (as he does with Gregory Persimmons in *War in Heaven* (1930);[22] MacDonald might have made the opposition of the two women a symbol of the waning subconscious; but Nesbit is more interested in using alchemy here simply as an exciting mechanism for the precipitation of amorous reversals.

Similarly, the supernatural characters in Nesbit's work have forms determined purely by the fancy of the creator.[23] This is the shape of the Psammead, the strangest of all:

> Its eyes were on long horns like a snail's eyes, and it could move them in and out like telescopes; it had ears like a bat's ears, and its tubby body was shaped like a spider's and covered with thick soft fur; its legs and arms were furry too, and it had hands and feet like a monkey's. (*FCI*, 14)

The Psammead's appearance is in no way symbolic, or expressive of a spiritual condition, as it would have been if George MacDonald had been writing the story. In his *The Princess and Curdie* (1882), for example, MacDonald gives us a creature called Lina, which is similarly a "mass of incongruities," but here the form is the projection of an inner state (the boy-hero Curdie is told that "'Shapes are only dresses . . . and dresses are only names'"):

> She had a very short body, and very long legs made like an elephant's, so that in lying down she kneeled with both pairs. Her tail, which dragged on the floor behind her, was twice as

long and quite as thick as her body. Her head was something between that of a polar bear and a snake. Her eyes were dark green, with a yellow light in them. Her under teeth came up like a fringe of icicles, only very white, outside of her upper lip. Her throat looked as if the hair had been plucked off. It showed a skin white and smooth.[24]

Nesbit's description is simply additive: the Psammead is formed of a mingling of attractive and repulsive elements. We move from the snail's eyes to the more pleasing suggestion of a 'gadget' in the analogy with telescopes; thence from bats to tubbiness, from spiders to thick soft fur, and then, in different order, from furriness to monkeys. In MacDonald's account there is nothing very attractive in the portrait, unless we are determined over the tail: the "skin white and smooth" might be pleasing but for the fact that it occurs where the hair has been removed, thus reminding one of the lividness of scar tissue. What MacDonald juxtaposes here is the unfamiliar or displeasing with the familiar. Elephants, polar bears, snakes and icicles are not common to our experience. Nor of course do polar bears and snakes belong together, except in the one particular of shape of head, and the same goes for elephants and icicles. The picture is one of a body perverted: we are aware of a proportion which has been everywhere upset. The body is too short, the legs too long and thick; she cannot lie down properly; the tail is an unwieldy encumbrance; the bottom teeth are useless, except for rending; her throat hair is missing. The whole picture gives us the sense of a mixture of laughable ungainliness, enormous power, ferocity (the mixture of dark green and yellow light in her eyes is peculiarly effective) and gentle, helpless innocence (the white skin)—precisely the spiritual state the form expresses. Where Nesbit's fusion of discordant qualities is a product of fancy, MacDonald's is one of the imagination. MacDonald himself described fancy as "hunting after resemblances that carry with them no interpretation," and, one imagines, would probably have spoken of Nesbit as he did of Shelley: "the evidences of pure imagination in his writings are infrequent as compared with those of fancy; there are not half the instances of the direct embodiment of idea in form, that there are of the presentation of strange resemblances between external things."[25]

There are other points of difference between Nesbit's and more 'philosophical' fairy-tales. For instance, her magic creatures are not inaccessible, and do not require, as they do in MacDonald's fantasy, some spiritual qualification on the part of the person who wants

to meet them. Pure accident often throws up the supernatural in her books. In *Five Children and It* the Psammead is discovered while the children are digging a hole ("through to Australia") in the local gravel pit; and in *The Story of the Amulet* the fairy is found again, by accident, while the children are looking at a pet shop; and, once rescued, it takes them to the shop where the half-Amulet is to be found. In *The Phoenix and the Carpet* the Phoenix egg is found rolled up in a carpet the children's parents have just bought, and it is a blunder of Robert's which knocks the egg off the mantelpiece into the nursery fire, thus ensuring the appearance of the bird.[26] The children rarely have to be 'good' in order to meet the magic creatures; nor do they have to be gifted with imaginative vision: in fact they can explain their peculiar intimacy with magic only as the possession of luck, or of some inexplicable attractive force on their part:

'Do you know, sometimes I think we are the sort of people that things *do* happen to.'

'It's like that in history,' said Jane: 'some kings are full of interesting things, and others—nothing ever happens to them, except their being born and crowned and buried, and sometimes not that.' (*PC*, 12)

There are occasional exceptions: in *The House of Arden* (1908) the children have to avoid quarrelling for first one and then three days before the door to the room with magic chests will appear. Particularly in her later magic books, Nesbit tried to move towards a more mystical and 'poetic' treatment of the supernatural, and this involved spiritual considerations: but she was a little out of her element in so reaching for the 'significant' and the portentous, and these stories are not the expression of her peculiar genius.

Nesbit's fairy-tales are perhaps not unlike other fantasies in that they usually end with the reversal of the magic. In *Five Children and It,* as we have seen, every wish ends at nightfall and the effects, whether they be a heap of gold, wings, or a baby suddenly becoming a grown-up, are removed. In *The Phoenix and the Carpet* the magic bird may burn down the Garrick Theatre, but the audience escapes, and the theatre is restored by the phoenix that same night. The magic is often made public, but people are made to think they were temporarily mad or dreaming, or even to accept the magic as one of nature's freaks (the giant Robert in ch. 8 of *Five Children and It* is taken on as one by a showman at a fair). In this way, too, the magic can disappear without trace. Occasionally it may leave concrete effects, like the mass of gold which Edward and Gustus make out of a half-sovereign with the magic telescope in **"The Mixed Mine"** (*MW*, 52-6): but there the enlarging takes place underground and is made by the children to appear like the discovery of a gold mine; so that the magical may be passed off as the real.

This removal of the supernatural happens at the end of many fantasies. All the disturbed magic in a Charles Williams novel returns to its origin; Tolkien's Ring is destroyed; MacDonald's Anodos and Vane return to their castles to wait. However, in these fantasies there has been one permanent change which is not generally to be found in Nesbit's tales—a change in the sould of the hero, whereby the supernatural enters and alters his spirit. But Nesbit is not usually concerned with writing fantastic *Bildungsromanen*. In her work there is rarely a permanent spiritual change, or portrayal of continued growth, in the characters: Whereyouwantogoto in the end is Whereyoustartedfrom. Certainly her characters do gain and learn from their experiences, but the gaining and learning have nothing to do with transformation. A story may end with material profit, as in the case of the gold of **"The Mixed Mine"** or the valuables that Tavy finds thanks to the magic china cat in **"The White Cat"** (*MW*); with 'intellectual' benefit, as in the case of the fusion of the minds of the "learned gentleman" and Rekh-mar at the end of *The Story of the Amulet,* or Edwin's development as a mathematician thanks to the Arithmetic Fairy in **"The Sums that Came Right"** (*NUT*). Parents return to children at the end of **"Justnow-land"** and *The Story of the Amulet.* Annabel's dislike for her aunt is removed by her experiences in **"The Aunt and Annabel"** (*MW*). But however one regards them, these are not *spiritual* benefits, particularly not that entry into and transformation of the soul by the supernatural implied in the notion here.

Even in those few of Nesbit's tales where moral education is at the centre of interest the morality is often curiously linked with material values. In **"Wherey-ouwantogoto"** (*NUT*, 51-84) the children are taken by a magic ball to a sunny, sandy beach with rocks and caves, shells, seaweeds, a friendly dog and a seal and a huge picnic lunch lying waiting for them. They have only to be good, and they will have these things as long as they wish. But on the fourth day they quarrel over who is to make the fern-bed, and a housemaid appears to inform them that it is her place to make the beds, and that she will make sure the children are in them by seven every evening. A fur-ther quarrel turns the delicious food with which they are supplied into the kind of fare they have at home; and another brings a bathing machine, with a notice on it saying, "'You must not bathe any more except through me.'" And so on, until they have turned the delightful beach into a hideous seaside resort. Their last act is to cut into the magic ball to see "'what makes him bounce'": upon which the scene is metamorphosed into the surroundings of their home, where they are punished by their aunt and uncle and sent to bed. The morality of this story is simply that being good is practical politics: there is no sense that it is a delightful experience in itself, only that it is a precondition. A story with a similarly 'materialistic' effect is **"The Cat-Hood of Maurice"** (*MW*), where the ethics of putting oneself in another's position are worked out in the very physical terms of Maurice's transformation into the cat he has so thoughtlessly bullied and teased, and the cat's temporary assumption of Maurice's body.[27]

One would not wish to be moral on this issue, but there is some sense in which Evelyn Underhill's distinction, in her book *Mysticism* (1911), between attitudes to the unseen can be applied to Nesbit. Miss Underhill terms the two attitudes "the way of magic" and "the way of mysticism." Magic is selfish, whether individually or socially: the magician wants to use the supernatural for his or humanity's ends. Mysticism, however, involves the struggle to remove the self through submission to an ultimate reality "for no personal gain, to satisfy no transcendental curiosity, to obtain no other worldly joys, but purely from an instinct of love." In short "magic wants to get, mysticism wants to give."[28] This polarity at least provides an interesting analogy for an understanding of Nesbit's fairy tales. The Amulet in *The Story of the Amulet* has the promise of goodness without effort:

> 'The complete Amulet can keep off all the things that make people unhappy—jealousy, bad-temper, pride, disagreeableness, greediness, selfishness, laziness. Evil spirits, people called them when the Amulet was made. . . . And it can give you strength and courage. . . . And virtue. . . . And it can give you your heart's desire.' (*SA,* 51-2)

It is interesting to remark, in relation to Miss Underhill's phrase 'transcendental curiosity' that in many of Nesbit's fairy tales magic is used to satisfy curiosity. Like Mrs. De Ward in **"Accidental Magic,"** Nesbit was fascinated by esoteric knowledge, by "'all the things that people are not quite sure about—the things that are hidden and secret, wonderful and mysterious—the things people make discoveries about'"

(*MW*, 58-9). Thus, in *The Story of the Amulet, The House of Arden* and *Harding's Luck* (1909), part of the interest involves the 'discovery' of the unknown springs of action determining historical events, and the bringing-to-life of civilizations otherwise known only through fragmentary evidence. For instance, one of the episodes in *The Story of the Amulet* involves a visit to Atlantis, at the end of which the children watch the destruction of the civilization by volcano and tidal wave; and in *The House of Arden* (ch. 8) the children are unwitting agents in the discovery of the Gunpowder Plot in 1605: here the "unknown springs of action" are given to, rather than discovered in, the past.[29]

So far we have said what Nesbit's fairy tales are not: it is time to say rather more of what they are. The method and end of most of her fantasy is the exploitation of comic incongruities. There are several forms that this takes. For example, there is the gap between what one expects the supernatural to be, and what it turns out to be. The appearance of the Psammead is hardly one's notion of a fairy. Nesbit also plays against our notion of the remoteness of the supernatural: her magic creatures often have the hard definition and idiosyncrasy of realistic characters. The origin of the Psammead is within time, in the prehistoric past, and that past is made no more strange and remote than the everyday present:

> 'Why, almost everyone had Pterodactyl for breakfast in my time! . . . I believe they were very good grilled. . . . People used to send their little boys down to the seashore early in the morning before breakfast to get the day's wishes, and very often the eldest boy in the family would be told to wish for a Megatherium, ready jointed for cooking. . . . when people had dinner-parties it was nearly always Megatheriums; and Ichthyosaurus, because his fins were a great delicacy and his tail made soup.' (*FCI*, 18-19)

The 'day's wishes' is a marvellous piece of witty reduction: it shows something that we will consider more later—that is, how Nesbit's imagination works inwards to the brilliant *aperçu* rather than outward to large structures and themes. Both the Psammead and the Phoenix belong to a definite 'species,' and though the Phoenix has semi-mythical origin, it is treated almost as a household pet. Such familiarity, with the Psammead in its paper bag, or sleeping in its bath of sand, and the Phoenix roosting "on the cornice supporting the window-curtains of the boys' room" (*PC*, 23) is calculated deflation of mystery. As for their personalities, the Psammead hates water, and is bad-tempered, highly practical, cynical, contemptuous

and jealous of being loved;[30] the Phoenix loves anything to do with fire—including Fire Insurance Offices—and is aristocratic, conceited and pompous; and the Mouldiwarp is slow, rustic and tetchy.

The magic creatures are also given everyday speech. Shortly after the magic bird in *The Phoenix and the Carpet* has hatched from its fiery egg after a two-thousand year sleep, it flies round the living room and, alighting on the tablecloth, scorches the material: at which, "'It's only a very little scorched,' said the Phoenix, apologetically; 'it will come out in the wash'" (*PC*, 17). The Phoenix can use London slang when called upon, and despite its long absence from the world, can converse in perfect French (*PC*, 94-5, 121, 124). Similarly, when the Psammead sees its new travelling bag,

> 'Humph,' it said, sniffing a little contemptuously, yet at the same time affectionately, 'it's not so dusty.'

> The Psammead seemed to pick up very easily the kind of things that people said nowadays. For a creature that had in its time associated with Megatheriums and Pterodactyls, its quickness was really wonderful. (*SA*, 176)

Few writers can have mentioned the actual *feel* of a supernatural creature as Nesbit does. When Anthea first discovers the Psammead burrowing away from her in the sand, what she feels is its fur (*FCI*, 13). The Psammead is 'to be felt' also in the bites it inflicts on the cruel shopkeeper and on the "learned gentleman," and through its weight in Anthea's arms or in its waterproof bag.[31] Similarly the reader is made almost to feel the bulge of the Phoenix hidden beneath Robert's coat when he takes it to the theatre, where it emerges "crushed and dishevelled" (*PC*, 208-10).

The method here is the comic marriage of the strange and the familiar. In the shorter fairy tales we find genii which appear from magic rings in the forms of footmen and butlers, a princess who falls in love with a royal lift operator, a dragon which swims in a sea of treacle, another which, supposedly fierce, is won over with sugar-lumps, a dispossessed princess who is restored by an enchanted hedgehog, the transformation of an entire country's population into mussels, and a king who is metamorphosed by the laughter of a cockatoucan into "a villa-residence, replete with every modern improvement."[32]

At the same time the children in the magic books remain very real and intensely human.[33] It is one of Nesbit's strengths as a writer of fantasy that in the midst of magic nothing is lost of realism.

'Now I've been thinking'—

'Not really?' whispered Robert.

'In the silent what's-its-names of the night. It's like suddenly being asked something out of history—the date of the Conquest or something; you know it all right all the time, but when you're asked it all goes out of your head. Ladies and gentlemen, you know jolly well that when we're all rotting about in the usual way heaps of things keep cropping up, and then real earnest wishes come into the heads of the beholder'—

'Hear, hear!' said Robert.

'—of the beholder, however stupid he is,' Cyril went on.

'Why, even Robert might happen to think of a really useful wish if he didn't injure his poor little brains trying so hard to think.' (*FCI*, 198)

Cyril is a literary relative of Oswald Bastable: the sudden lapse from high-flown diction into child vernacular is superb, but even better is the complete mixture of metaphors which turns the children into decomposing vegetables and thoughts into fungi—not to mention, of course, the "*heads* of the *beholder.*" Nesbit is fond of such linguistic interplay. When the children have succeeded in wishing themselves into being besieged in a castle by a troop of soldiers, Robert tries to address the leader in what language he can recall from his knowledge of historical romance: "'Sir Wulfric de Talbot,' he said slowly, 'should think foul scorn to—to keep a chap—I mean one who has done him no hurt—when he wants to cut off quietly—I mean to depart without violence'" (*FCI*, 166). In *The Story of the Amulet,* when the children are rescued from a Babylonian dungeon by the supernatural Nisroch, Servant of the Amulet, he asks them:

'Is there aught else that the Servant of the great Name can do for those that speak that name?'

'No—oh, *no,*' said Cyril. 'It's all right now. Thanks ever so.'

'You are a dear,' cried Anthea, not in the least knowing what she was saying. (*SA*, 167)

Of course one of the main types of comic interplay in the magic books is that between the children and the difficulties that magic makes for them. When they ask the Psammead to make them "'as beautiful as the day'" (*FCI*, 22) they become unrecognizable to one another, and their baby brother the Lamb, who has remained unchanged, does not know them and breaks into screams. When at last they reach home, Martha

the nursemaid seizes the Lamb and bids the strangers be off, "'Go along with you, you nasty little Eyetalian monkey[s]'" (*FCI*, 30). The children are reduced to standing in a dry ditch, waiting for sunset and the end of their beauty. Perhaps the most amusing episode of this type is the one in which Cyril, irritated at the Lamb's having accidentally broken his watch, wishes without thinking that the Lamb were grown up. The subsequent struggles of the children to look after the now adult Lamb and prevent him from escorting a lady friend home on his bicycle are beautifully handled; the finest moment occurs when Martha, who, thanks to the Psammead, has now been made blind to any of the magical transformations of the children, picks up the slight but adult figure of the Lamb:

'Come to his own Martha, then—a precious poppet!'

The grown-up Lamb . . . struggled furiously. An expression of intense horror and annoyance was seen on his face. But Martha was stronger than he. She lifted him up and carried him into the house. None of the children will ever forget that picture. The neat grey-flannel-suited grown-up young man with the green tie and the little black moustache—fortunately, he was slightly built, and not tall—struggling in the sturdy arms of Martha, who bore him away helpless, imploring him, as she went, to be a good boy now, and come and have his nice brem-milk! (*FCI*, 250)

In Nesbit's finer magic books the strangeness of the creatures, places or peoples that the children see is always to some extent reduced. This is not done by evasion, or 'drawing a veil,' because Nesbit will not insult the intelligence of her readers. Instead she often uses a technique which could loosely be called 'metaphoric' in its blending of the potentially frightening with the familiar. The strange city in which Philip and Lucy find themselves in *The Magic City* is an enlarged and animated version of the one they themselves previously built in their house out of books, finger-bowls, vases, cabinets, chessmen, pepper-pots and a host of other domestic objects, and the people in it are Philip's toys.[34] The same 'identification game' is the motif of the stories **"The Blue Mountain"** (*NUT*), and **"The Town in the Library in the Town in the Library"** (*NUT*).[35] When the children in *The Story of the Amulet* are watching the terrifying destruction of Atlantis, and the "learned gentleman" puts everyone's lives at risk by refusing to return home through the Amulet till the last moment, we are suddenly brought back to the immediate scene when the enraged Psammead leaps out of its bag and bites his hand (*SA*, 229). Again, the music at the Babylonian banquet

> reminded Anthea of the band she and the others had once had on the fifth of November—with penny horns, a tin whistle, a tea tray, the tongs, a policeman's rattle, and a toy drum. They had enjoyed this band very much at the time. But it was quite different when someone else was making the same kind of music. Anthea understood now that Father had not been really heartless and unreasonable when he had told them to stop that infuriating din. (*SA*, 159)

The two contexts are married in Anthea's mind: Babylonian minstrelsy and policemen's rattles meet like the two halves of the amulet.[36]

What we have in this interplay of natural and supernatural in Nesbit's magic books is in part the fusion of two personal and literary impulses in her life. On the one hand she was what we may call a realist. Enough perhaps has been given of her biography to show how much she was a lady of her time, thoroughly involved with life both socially and intellectually. She wrote many poems on the folly of artistic or religious asceticism: one ends, "Still there's the wisdom that wise men call folly, / Still one can go and pick daisies with Molly!"[37] Though professedly Catholics, neither she nor her husband Hubert Bland often attended church, and they seemed to take little account of whether they were in a state of grace (Moore, 210-11). Occasionally in her poetry Nesbit set out the possibilities of a life of contemplation, but only to return to 'this world' in the end.[38] She once wrote, on the Fabian Society, to a friend, "There are two distinct elements in the F.S. . . . The practical and the visionary—the first being much the strongest. . . . We belong—needless to say—to the practical party" (Moore, 107). Several of her poems concern the choice between town and country, and end by preferring to face the former: "We fight for freedom and the souls of men—/ Here, and not there, is fought and won our fight."[39] The emphasis of her religious poetry is on the Incarnation,[40] and the theme of motherhood runs through all her verse.[41] Her poem **"Jesus in London"** (1908)[42] is a description not of Christ's divinity, but of how he would deal with the Mammon of the Victorian age, and with the misery and repression of the lower classes.

Nesbit could be quite honestly materialistic: though her writing must have given her considerable pleasure, she was also very concerned to use it to provide money, not so often for the essentials of life, but to make comfort more comfortable. Thus, thinking of a boating holiday on the Medway, she points out how such joys have to be paid for in "hard coin," by writing another chapter, "And I will earn, working like mad, / The Medway, with the Psammead."[43] Again, in her lines, **"To a Young Poet,"** she writes, "Write for sale, and not for use. / This is a commercial age!" and

> If your soul should droop and die,
> Bury it with undimmed eye.
> Never mind what memory says—
> Soul's a thing that never pays![44]

These various types of involvement with the 'real' world are to be contrasted with another side of her nature. The supernatural "always had a strange fascination for her."[45] For example, she believed in ghosts all her life, partly owing to an early experience in Dinan. She had gone for a ramble with her brothers, and they came across a dilapidated, locked chateau. The children found a boarded-up doorway at the back, and through the planks they could see a bare room with a heap of straw; but as they looked, the straw began to gather itself up and spun until it made a rope almost touching the ceiling. In their flight, the children passed a cottage, whence emerged an old woman who said, "'Je vois, mes enfants, que vous avez vu la dame qui file'" (Moore, 66-7). They never found the castle again. There were many other traumatic experiences in Nesbit's childhood. Perhaps the most harrowing was her visit with her sisters to the "mummies of Bordeaux" (she had wanted to go, because the name 'mummy' seemed so pleasant): the mummies turned out to be two hundred skeletons arranged in standing positions round three sides of a vault, skeletons with the flesh hardened to the bones and with long dry hair round their faces. As she put it later, "The mummies of Bordeaux were the crowning horror of my childish life . . . the shock of that sight branded it on my brain, and I never forgot it."[46] For a girl who "had no defence against the most cruel sensibility" (Moore, 54), the effects of these early experiences were particularly far-reaching on her work.[47] In addition she lived for most of her life in a series of reputedly haunted houses, which in itself must have been stimulus to a native morbidity of temperament, her fascination for "searching into subjects which she herself found terrifying":

> Like a little girl fascinated with ghost stories whose after-effects she well knows to be disastrous, she would sit up at night writing tales of violence and death until she was afraid to go to bed. And she would read books and see sights which, as she was fully aware beforehand, were certain to upset her nerves. (Moore, 236)

Having been terrified at the thought of skeletons when she was a child, she tried the quaint and quite counter-productive expedient of familiarizing her own children with such items by keeping a skull and a pile of bones to which she would introduce them (*ibid*).

"[Nesbit's] sufferings ultimately resulted in an extraordinary dichotomy in her creative work" (Moore, 54). The fascinated terror of the supernatural and the horrifying found expression in many of the stories she wrote:[48] it is there in **Salome** and in **Dormant,** and in a number of shorter ghost and terror tales collected in **Grim Tales** (1893), **Man and Maid** (1906), **Fear** (1910) and **To the Adventurous** (1923).[49] While it is true that there was a *fin de siècle* vogue for such tales, and that Nesbit was one among such contemporary writers as Richard Middleton, Arthur Machen, Algernon Blackwood, M. R. James and W. H. Hodgson, her stories sometimes have a neurotic character all their own. For instance, **"The Power of Darkness"** is set in a waxworks filled with grisly scenes of violence done in wax: one man lays a wager that another cannot spend a night there, and the one who accepts the challenge goes mad during his vigil.[50] In **"The House of Silence,"** a thief robs a wealthy but strangely silent house, and loses himself in tunnels leading off one of the rooms, until at the end of one tunnel he comes to a little sunlit courtyard where he sees a lady in green lying dead with a great black swarm of flies buzzing round her.[51] There is a peculiarly obsessional quality in these stories.[52]

The other, the 'realistic' side of Nesbit, went both into her Bastable children's books and into a range of adult novels and stories such as **Thirteen Ways Home** (1901), **The Literary Sense** (1903), **The Red House** (1903), **The Incomplete Amorist** (1906), **Daphne in Fitzroy Street** (1909), **These Little Ones** (1909), **The Incredible Honeymoon** (1921) and **The Lark** (1922). Of the adult books only the first two named are well-written: the others are mostly on romantic themes well-worn by popular novelists of the time. **The Literary Sense** is a series of stories, most of them on the slightly Jamesian theme of self-dramatization and its consequences, and **The Red House** describes family life in an idyllic manner, and, unusual for its day, married love. Its uninviting title Nesbit felt was probably the main cause of the poor sales of the former, but **The Red House** was a considerable success (Moore, 198, 212-3).

These two sides of Nesbit—the 'realist' and the 'supernaturalist'—are brought together in her magic books, where magic is given a colloquial and comic face, and is brought into contact with very human children. One would not claim that this makes the magic books the summit of Nesbit's achievement—the Bastable stories are as finely done[53]—but it does show that in those books she united opposed impulses in her own nature; or that, to put it more theoretically, there "the most heterogeneous ideas are yoked by violence together." This last phrase was applied by Dr. Johnson to the method of the metaphysical poets of the seventeenth century, and indeed the character of Nesbit's more successful work could be called 'conceited'. It is true that whereas a poet such as Donne compares constancy in love to a pair of compasses, that is, joins two opposed contents, to bring out his meaning more fully, Nesbit has no such meaning to clarify, and she wishes us to attend to incongruity rather than likeness between the terms. One should perhaps in these respects liken her more to Cleveland than to Donne: she is, as we have said, more a fanciful than an imaginative writer. None the less, in all Nesbit's more characteristic magic books the central aim, and the one on which her strength depends, is the production of situations or images in which maximum comic energy is generated by a clash of contents. When she veers, as she does in the later books, into a belief in the reality of the magic, the balance is upset, and we have the would-be mysticism of **The House of Arden** or **Harding's Luck,** or the mingled mysticism and horror of **The Enchanted Castle** (1907).

At its best, this method is not purely random: it is nothing so simple as taking one context and throwing it together with one as far opposed as possible, for there is always a law which gives the bringing together of the terms a certain inevitability; "her magic was governed by inexorable rules of logic."[54] For example, the purely superficial kinship between the Phoenix and the Phoenix Fire Office is sufficient to justify the bird's considering the latter a temple erected to its fame. Thus the stage is set for the ludicrous events which take place when it visits the office and asks for the High Priest. When, also in **The Phoenix and the Carpet,** the children ask the magic Persian carpet to revisit its native land, "'and bring back the most beautiful and delightful productions of it you can,'" the carpet is only being true to the laws of its own vision in returning with one hundred and ninety-nine very hungry and vocal Persian cats (*PC*, 137, 140-1). There is a simultaneous centripetal and centrifugal movement which gives a special pleasure: we see what thinly justifies bringing the terms together at the same time as they drive one another apart. The story **"Uncle James, or The Purple**

Stranger" has behind it a law of reversal. We are told that the island of Rotundia was created when a pointed piece of rock impaled a lump of soft clay and both, spinning in the opposite direction to that of the earth, fell into the sea and came to rest. Thus it is that on the island elephants are tiny while guinea-pigs and rabbits are enormous; and thus too, "all the things we have to make—buns and cake and short-bread—grow on trees and bushes, but in Rotundia they have to make their cauliflowers and cabbages and carrots and apples and onions, just as our cooks make puddings and turnovers" (*BD*, 50).

Nesbit is as fond of the use of arithmetic and logic in magical contexts as the metaphysical poets were in writing of love.[55] One of her best-known stories is **"Melisande, or, Long and Short Division"** in which a Princess, doomed at birth by her wicked fairy god-mother Malevola to be bald, uses a wish she is given when she is grown up to have golden hair a yard long, which will grow an inch every day, and twice as fast every time it is cut. The result is that she is soon growing balefuls of hair every minute, and the family have to advertise for "a competent Prince" to try to find a way round the problem. Eventually Prince Florizel appears. He tells Melisande that when her hair has filled the room in which she is, she should climb on to the window-sill and tie her hair three times round a large iron hook in the outside wall. Then, standing by her, he bids her jump, and while she is suspended, he cuts the hair and lowers her by the remainder gently to the ground. Thus, in-stead of cutting the hair off the Princess, he has cut the Princess off the hair. Unfortunately, by the logic of magic it is now not the hair that grows, but the Princess. She grows so large that eventually she has to leave the country and stand in the ocean. Florizel manages to climb to her ear and tell her to use her scissors to cut off her hair. As soon as she does so, she shrinks to her normal size, and swims home. Now once more the hair grows at a prodigious rate. The King writes to his fairy godmother Fortuna ask-ing for help, and she hints—she can do no more—at the use of scales. Florizel grasps the point. He has a pair of scales made large enough to accommodate the Princess on one side, while her growing hair is piled on the other pan, and then, when the weight of the hair equals the weight of the Princess, he cuts cleanly through the hair above the fulcrum. In this way "'nei-ther you nor your hair can possibly decide which ought to go on growing.'" Of course, as the Princess says, it would be possible for *both* to do so, but the Prince, with a shudder, replies, "'Impossible . . . there

are limits even to Malevola's malevolence'" (*NUT*, 187-8). Here the rules of logic give way to those of fair play, and we accept the point.

"Melisande" is probably the finest example of this method. Nesbit also uses arithmetic in **"The Sums That Came Right,"** in which the Arithmetic Fairy appears to Edwin when he looks inside his schooldesk, and offers to help him with his sums. A nice touch occurs when Edwin tells her she is beauti-ful and "She looked down and played shyly with the bunch of miscellaneous examples in vulgar fractions which adorned her waistband" (*NUT*, 228). Edwin has just been complaining that lessons produce noth-ing concrete: the Fairy's magic is such that every sum he makes is mirrored in real life—so that when he sets about one beginning, "'If seven thousand five hundred and sixty-three white rabbits . . . ,'" he finds on returning home "the whole of the front garden, as well as most of the back garden . . . a seething mass of white rabbits." After much extravagance of this sort, Edwin tries to recall the Fairy—in vain, until he uses the logic of magic in this way: "'If 7,535 fairies were in my desk at school and I subtracted 710 and added 1,006, and the rest flew away in 783 equal gangs, how many would be left over in the desk?'" (*NUT*, 229, 236). In another story, **"The Island of the Nine Whirlpools"** (*BD*), a Princess is impris-oned on an island guarded by a dragon and sur-rounded by nine whirlpools. Every enchantment has a loophole: the whirls are calm for five minutes in every twenty-four hours, and this period of calm be-gins five minutes earlier every day; and the dragon turns to stone and sleeps for five minutes each day and begins its sleep three minutes later every day. Prince Nigel, who comes to rescue the princess, has to calculate when the quiescence of the whirls and of the dragon will interlock in such a way that if he lures the dragon into the water when the whirls are quiet it will begin its slumber just as they start again, and will be unable to save itself.

Sometimes a species of punning provides the 'yoking-together' element of Nesbit's tales. In **"Belinda and Bellamant,"** the Princess is doomed by a family of wicked bell-people to "'grow uglier every day except Sundays, and every Sunday she shall be seven times prettier than the Sunday before'" (*MW*, 164), until she can find a bell "'that doesn't ring, and can't ring, and never will ring, and wasn't made to ring.'" Mean-while, the wicked fairy godmothers of the corre-sponding Prince have rendered him quite physically incompatible by making him handsome all week and unbearably ugly on Sundays, until he can manage to stay underwater for more than two minutes. The requirements for the removal of the two curses seem to have no connection with one another, and we also expect something that *looks* like a ringing bell to be the salvation of the Princess: but in the end it is a diving bell which removes both curses. This story is a particularly fine example of Nesbit's method, for it can be seen that though the curses are opposed, they fit in with or are complementary to one another, in the same way that the Prince and Princess belong to one another. The situation is as neat as that in Marvell's "The Definition of Love"—their love "so truly parallel, / Though infinite, can never meet." They do join forces to try to remove their curses ("the conjunction of the mind") but they cannot *marry* until that removal ("And opposition of the stars"). Best of all perhaps is the way that one object answers both curses: the witty fusion in the form of the diving bell joins the Prince and Princess in a shared release which itself effectively marries them. Another, if slightly less brilliant story in this manner is **"The Princess and the Hedge-Pig,"** in which the Princess is doomed to be turned out of her kingdom, to have to face her enemies without a friend to help her and to be unable to return to her own again until she finds "'A thousand spears to follow her to battle'" (*MW*, 104). In the end a Prince who has been transformed into a hedgehog answers the requirement with his thousand spines.

There are of course degrees of appositeness in Nesbit's method. In **"The Cockatoucan"** the magic bird has the power to change people into *anything* when it laughs. Sometimes the transformation is apt, as in the case of Pridmore, Matilda's grim nursemaid, who is turned into an automatic machine "such as those which you see in a railway station" (*NUT*, 19): but one has moved away from this when the bird laughs on a public holiday meant to celebrate the return of the King's victorious army:

> The Cockatoucan laughed just as the reception was beautifully arranged. It laughed, and the general holiday was turned into an income tax; the magnificent reception changed itself into a royal reprimand, and the Army itself suddenly became a discontented Sunday-school treat, and had to be fed with buns and brought home in brakes, crying. (*NUT*, 33)

This is superb, but not because of the sheer disparity of the terms, particularly the last (notice how the sentence gathers itself for it, and how also the transformations in the first two cases are less ambitious, making full weight fall on the third): it is partly the interplay of abstract and concrete—'holiday' to 'income tax,' 'reception' to 'reprimand,' 'Army' to 'treat' and then back to a crowd of children. But it is only locally successful, and by the time the Cockatoucan has laughed again we are in the realms of unmitigated fancy:

> 'There's your dear father—he's a desirable villa—the Prime Minister was a little boy, and he got back again, and now he's turned into a Comic Opera. Half the Palace housemaids are breakers, dashing themselves against the Palace crockery: the Navy, to a man, are changed to French poodles, and the Army to German sausages. Your favourite nurse is now a flourishing steam laundry, and I, alas! am too clever by half.' (*NUT*, 41)

Although this is great fun, it has no element of rule or logic behind it. Here too, one could go into the twisting of the rules or the faulty causality in such tales as **"The Blue Mountain"** (*NUT*), **"The Prince, Two Mice, and Some Kitchen-Maids"** (*NUT*), **"Fortunatus Rex & Co."** (*NUT*) or **"The Princess and the Cat"** (*OBO*). But the point should be sufficiently clear: the skill that goes into the better stories is a real one, requiring considerable subtlety and artistic discipline, and this can be seen by comparison with those tales in which it is not so fully brought to bear.

E. Nesbit's fantasy is not what one would call great literature: it is at its best without any deeply-felt spiritual meaning, and it could be argued that the sensibility behind it is not particularly sophisticated—even that it is at times materialistic. To repeat our classification, her work is fanciful rather than imaginative. But fancy has its place: and one could claim that in Nesbit's work it reaches a high point of wit and ingenuity. She had her literary forebears—Thackeray, MacDonald, Carroll, Mrs. Molesworth and particularly F. Anstey, all of whom played magic against humdrum real life for comic effect; but she gave the 'realistic' side more vitality by her special understanding of a child's mind, and the magic more scope by her use of rules and logic. The result is that the bringing-together of opposites in her magic books is of a variety, skill and comic potential unequalled before her or since.[56] But these books are also a picture of Nesbit's zest for life in almost any form: the 'conceited' method of juxtaposing opposites returns us to the lady who was as happy with logarithms as with Ibsen, with Shaw as with Chesterton, with Fabianism as with the *Yellow Book*. Inventive powers and wit of the kind that she shows are not often recognized by literary criticism: perhaps there might be a healthy diminution of gravity if they were.

Notes

Abbreviations (throughout, numbers after abbreviations are page references).

(Except where it is explicitly stated otherwise, all books mentioned in this article were published in London.)

BD—Nesbit, *The Book of Dragons* (1900)

BVSL—Nesbit, *Ballads and Verses of the Spiritual Life* (1911)

FC1—Nesbit, *Five Children and It* (1902)

LL1—Nesbit, *Lays and Legends* (1886)

LL2—Nesbit, *Lays and Legends, Second Series* (1892)

Moore—Doris Langley Moore, *E. Nesbit, A Biography* (rev. ed., 1967)

MV—Nesbit, *Many Voices, Poems* (1922)

MW—Nesbit, *The Magic World* (1912)

NUT—Nesbit, *Nine Unlikely Tales for Children* (1901)

OBO—Nesbit, *Oswald Bastable and Others* (1905)

PC—Nesbit, *The Phoenix and the Carpet* (1904)

PV—Nesbit, *A Pomander of Verse* (1895)

RR—Nesbit, *The Rainbow and the Rose, Poems* (1905)

SA—Nesbit, *The Story of the Amulet* (1906)

1. That is, when she was aged between 42 and 55. She had as many publications (if most of them were hack-work) before this period as during it; so that she had a long apprenticeship, though little of it hinted at the imaginative powers in reserve.

2. See *e.g.* Frank Eyre, *20th Century Children's Books* (1952), p. 12; "What Makes a Good Book?," *TLS* (23 Nov., 1956), p.i., col. iii; Marcus Crouch, "The Nesbit Tradition," *Junior Bookshelf* XXII, no. 4 (Oct., 1958), 195; Anthea Bell, *E. Nesbit* (1960), pp. 12-13.

3. For accounts of the development of children's literature in the nineteenth century, see Gillian Avery, with Angela Bull, *Nineteenth Century Children, He-*

roes and Heroines in English Children's Stories 1780-1900 (1965); Cornelia Meigs, and others, *A Critical History of Children's Literature, A Survey of Children's Books in English* (rev. ed., New York, 1969).

4. The 'method' of Anstey's fantasies generally involves the comic impact of the supernatural on everyday life. In *Vice Versa,* the mind of a thoughtless and heartless father is made to change places with that of his son: the father goes to the boarding school of which the son has complained and learns all too painfully that the boy's misery was well-founded; and meanwhile the son ruins his father's business. In *The Tinted Venus,* the goddess Venus comes to life in the form of a statue which represents her, and attempts to win the love of a Victorian hairdresser from his fiancée, first by clumsy guile and later by force. *The Brass Bottle* describes a genie called Fakrash who is accidentally released from confinement in a brass bottle by a poor London architect, whose affairs suffer thereafter from the ignorant eagerness to please of the genie. (It is an interesting fact that much of Anstey's magic is 'confinement' magic). Both Nesbit and Anstey expressed their admiration for each other's work (Moore, 194). Nevertheless Anstey differs from Nesbit in two ways: he does not write from a child's point of view, and he does not use rules and logic in his fantasy in the way that, as we shall see, Nesbit does.

5. First published in Anstey, *The Talking Horse and Other Tales* (1892); reprinted in Anstey, *Paleface and Redskin, and Other Stories for Boys and Girls* (1898).

6. Nesbit, *Wings and the Child, or, The Building of Magic Cities* (1913), p. 20. See also pp. 3, 74; and letter of 10 Dec., 1913, quoted in Moore, 280.

7. Moore, 264. It is a strange fact, however, that Nesbit often lacked sympathy with her own children: see on this Moore, 43, 146-7, 219-20, 258-62.

8. Moore, 73-7. On Nesbit's earlier schools, see Nesbit, "My School-Days," *The Girl's Own Annual,* XVIII (1896-7), 28, 106.

9. For some of these see "My School-Days," pp. 375, 575, 635-6, 711, 788; Moore, 39.

10. See Moore, 68; Noel Streatfeild, *Magic and the Magician, E. Nesbit and Her Children's Books* (1958), p. 22.

11. Moore, 105, 111, 156, 237-8, 239; the last describes how at Dymchurch "E. Nesbit had been known in earlier years to cycle down to the sea front

in a billowing garment bearing some resemblance to a tea gown, and even now she could be seen holding conversation with the Vicar from a seat on her rain-barrel, her long quill cigarette-holder between her lips, or walking about arm-in-arm with the humble woman who did her housework." Nevertheless, Nesbit followed the *sexual* conventionalism her husband preached: she opposed the Women's Suffrage movement, even introducing, in the Pretenderette of *The Magic City* (1910) a direct mockery of it (Moore, 266-7).

12. A daughter in 1886, and a son in 1899 (Moore, 130-1, 184-5).

13. Moore, 114, 126, 147, 150.

14. This despite limitations as a mathematician (Moore, 248-52).

15. See *Wings and the Child,* p. 91 (for the first five of these authors); and letter of March, 1884, in Moore, 106.

16. Moore, 160-1, 163, 164, 175, 193-4, 202, 228, 248, 270-2. She was one of the first to recognize E. M. Forster's talent.

17. Moore, 143, 194, 211. On her difficulties in inventing plots, see Moore, 109.

18. Moore, 240-7. It proved too costly, and ended with the fourth number.

19. See e.g. her 'precious' *A Pomander of Verse* (1895), with its obsession with lilies, and its division into sections entitled 'Ambergris,' 'Lavender,' 'Rose,' 'Rosemary,' 'Myrrh,' 'Musk,' 'Bergamot.' One of her tales, "The Ice Dragon, or, Do As You Are Told," is written largely for the sake of the 'Decadent' image of the dragon curled and frozen round the ice-pillar of the North Pole: "though he was very terrible he was very beautiful, too . . . with his deep, clear Prussian blue-ness, and his rainbow-coloured glitter. And rising from the cold coil of the frozen dragon the North Pole shot up like a pillar made of one great diamond, and every now and then it cracked a little, from sheer coldness. The sound of the cracking was the only thing that broke the great white silence in the midst of which the dragon lay like an enormous jewel, and the straight flames went up all round him like the stalks of tall lilies" (*BD,* 131).

20. One of the ways by which Nesbit became acquainted with other writers was by her practice of sending out copies of her books for (hopefully enthusiastic) comment (Moore, 121-2, 160-1, 201-2).

21. Streatfeild, *op. cit.,* p. 22.

22. Williams knew Nesbit's work, as one of the entries in his Commonplace Book of 1912-16 shows: "Knowledge that Time and Space are only modes of thought 'is not this the beginning of all magic?' (E. Nesbit.—*Amulet)*" (quoted in Charles Williams, *The Image of the City and Other Essays,* ed. Anne Ridler (1958), p. 171). The first part of this is a reference to the Psammead's comment, "'Time and space are only forms of thought'" (*SA,* 69).

23. There is only one exception to this rule—the crows in 'Justnowland,' who were once human beings and were warned "'that if we didn't behave well our bodies would grow like our souls. But we didn't think so. And then all in a minute they *did*—and we were crows, and our bodies were as black as our souls. Our souls are quite white now . . . .'" (*MW,* 193). This idea of soul making body (moral (d)evolution) Nesbit probably took from Kingsley or MacDonald, though it is also reminiscent of Blake's "The Little Black Boy." Kingsley set out in *The Water-Babies* to show "that your soul makes your body, just as a snail makes his shell" and gives as one instance of this the birds called molly-mocks who are "the spirits of the old Greenland skippers" who were lazy and greedy, and are so transformed till they have worked out their repentance (1863 edition, pp. 88, 275).

24. *op. cit.* (2nd edition, 1888), pp. 56, 76.

25. MacDonald, *Orts* (1882), pp. 41, 279.

26. Similarly with the discovery of the mermaid in a fairground in *Wet Magic,* or the many 'accidents' of the shorter fairy tales.

27. This story is based directly on the method of Anstey's *Vice Versa;* as also is "The Twopenny Spell" (*OBO*).

28. *op. cit.* (revised edition, 1930), pp. 71, 70.

29. Nesbit is careful to give a more historical reason which would equally explain the discovery—Mr. Tresham's letter to his relation Lord Monteagle, revealing the plot. But of course we are not to *know* that by itself this would have been sufficient to unearth the conspiracy: and Elfrida, who inadvertently 'gave the game away,' certainly feels guilty at her betrayal (*The House of Arden* (1908), pp. 206, 212, 212-3).

30. It has been suggested that Nesbit drew on the character of the (more gently) recalcitrant cuckoo in Mrs. M. L. Molesworth's *The Cuckoo Clock* (1877)

for that of the Psammead (J. R. Townsend, *Written for Children, An Outline of English Children's Literature* (1965), pp. 71, 80).

31. *SA,* 33, 34, 44 (where we are told it weighed "about three pounds and a quarter"), 128, 175-7, 202, 229, 266.

32. Respectively, "The Ring and the Lamp" (*OBO*); "The Charmed Life; or, The Princess and the Lift-Man" (*OBO*); "Billy the King" (*OBO*); "Justnow-land" (*MW*); "The Princess and the Hedge-Pig" (*MW*); "Septimus Septimusson" (*MW*); "The Cocka-toucan" (*NUT*).

33. This is not so much the case in the shorter magic tales, where the emphasis tends to be much more on the almost rococo possibilities of magic rather than on its interaction with real life. The bulk of these stories in fact take place wholly within fairylands.

34. *The Magic City* (1910), pp. 54-5. Similarly the dragon the children have to destroy as one of their tasks as saviours of the city is "'the clockwork dragon that had been given [to Philip] the Christmas before last'" (p. 121); the waiters at the victory banquet are matches and the food itself is made of wood (pp. 137-42); and the terrible carpet the children have to unravel is "'a little crochet mat I'd made of red wool'" as Lucy explains, and all they have to do is find the end and pull (p. 155).

35. E. M. Forster particularly liked this story of all those in *NUT* (Moore, 271).

36. Indeed this junction of time is at once the object of the search and the method of the book. Thus the past is made often as familiar as the present, as, for example, when a Babylonian queen talks with unaffected familiarity (*SA,* 141, 144-59). This 'marriage' can be accomplished in other ways, as in the episodes where Anthea presents a "Lowther Arcade bangle" to a Stone Age girl; Caesar is taught how guns work by means of a cappistol; Pharoah is entertained by the 'magic' of striking matches; and the Phoenician captain Pheles steers his ship by night using Robert's shilling compass (*SA,* 83, 251, 270, 277, 338).

37. "The Will to Live" (*RR,* 15). See also "Tekel" and "Absolution" (*LLI,* 1-17, 119-33); "A Tragedy" (*LL2,* 81-3); "At the Gate," "The Monk" and "Earth and Heaven" (*BVSL,* 7-14, 15, 71-8).

38. "The Will to Live" and "The Star" (*RR,* 13-15, 89-90).

39. "Here and There" (*LL2,* 55-6). See also "August" (*LL1,* 142-4); "London's Voices" (*BVSL,* 97-8); "Saturday Song" (*MV,* 33-4). Contrast, however, "Town and Country" and "The Choice" (*PV,* 80, 85).

40. See "Lullaby" (*LL2,* 51-2); "Magnificat," "Evening Prayer" (which rejects the notion of a transcendent and 'other' God) and "The Three Kings" (*BVSL,* 19-20, 21, 30-3); "Mary of Magdala' (*MV,* 60-1).

41. See "Lullaby" (*PV,* 17); "Two Lullabies," "Baby Song" and "Mother" (*LL2,* 45-8, 49-50, 57); "Mother Song" and "Death" (*RR,* 69-70, 137-8); "The Crown of Life," "Evening Prayer" and "Submission" (*BVSL,* 17-18, 21, 101); "From the Portuguese—II," "In Trouble" and "The Mother's Prayer" (*MV,* 68-9, 74-5, 88-91).

42. This was reprinted as "Inasmuch As Ye Did It Not" in *BVSL,* 102-5 and *MV,* 91-4.

43. Unpublished poem of 1902, quoted in Moore, 196.

44. "To a Young Poet" (*LL2,* 111).

45. Moore, 134. See also p. 268, "she was superstitious to an extreme degree."

46. Nesbit, "My School-Days," *The Girl's Own Annual* XVIII (1896-7), 314, col. iii.

47. For others see "My School-Days," pp. 184, 264-5.

48. Nesbit's first extant prose composition, written when she was six or seven, was a story set in Rome about Mira, daughter of Agrippa and Claudia, who discovers a secret meeting of Christians in a catacomb-cavern, the corridor leading to the cavern being lined "with dead bodies"; the manuscript broke off at this point (Moore, 79-80).

49. *Fear* contains thirteen horror tales, five of which are reprints from the seven in *Grim Tales. Man and Maid* and *To the Adventurous* have only scattered tales of terror.

50. This story originated in a visit of Nesbit's to the grisly wax-work show in the Musée Grévin in Paris in 1905 (Moore, 236).

51. Both of these stories appeared in *Man and Maid.*

52. Her biographer remarks, "Her horror stories were probably more disturbing to her than to her readers. They fail to capture the emotions that she is so pal-

pably bent upon arousing, for the same reason that an actor will fail to capture the emotions of his audience when he is so much moved by it that he loses control of it. The terrors she wrote of were all actively her own. A great many of the stories, for example, concern cataleptic trances and premature burial—a subject which it always distressed her to contemplate; yet she never succeeded in conveying the fear which she is known to have felt herself" (Moore, 236-7).

53. There the fun is often generated by bringing together reality and children's illusions about life. (One source for this theme in Nesbit's own childhood experience is described in "My School-Days" (see note 45), p. 436, where she had romantic expectations of a shepherdess her sister took her to see, only to find the reality a disappointment—an episode reminiscent of Nekayah's pastoral hopes in Johnson's *Rasselas*, ch. XIX.)

54. Marcus Crouch, *Treasure Seekers and Borrowers, Children's Books in Britain, 1900-1960* (1962), p. 15.

55. Which makes quite strange her biographer's statement that "She was seldom either precise or logical in her mode of thinking" (Moore, 272).

56. On her would-be imitators, see Marcus Crouch, "The Nesbit Tradition," *Junior Bookshelf* XXII (Oct., 1958), 195-8.

Stephen Krensky

SOURCE: "A Second Look: *The Story of the Treasure Seekers*," in *The Horn Book Magazine,* Vol. LIV, No. 3, June, 1978, pp. 310-12.

E. Nesbit's popularity was founded on more than twenty children's books written near the turn of the century, but such is her present reputation in this country that mentioning her name elicits either a passionate sigh or a puzzled stare. Her influence, of course, has never been questioned; later writers—from C. S. Lewis to Edward Eager—have acknowledged their considerable debt to her. Among Nesbit's followers some argument may exist over which is her finest book, but undeniably it was **The Story of the Treasure Seekers** that first brought her lasting prominence.

And rightly so. The book chronicles the efforts of the Bastable children—Nora, Oswald, Dicky, Alice, Noël, and H. O. (Horace Octavius)—to reestablish the fam-

ily fortunes, sadly depleted since their father became ill and his business partner absconded to Spain with the firm's money. This blow was preceded by the death of their mother. Her passing is barely mentioned, but as Oswald pointedly remarks: "If you think we don't care because I don't tell you much about her you only show that you do not understand people at all."

Though Nesbit was later inclined towards fantasies like **Five Children and It** and **The Enchanted Castle** no magic reigns in **The Treasure Seekers;** instead, the action flows from the rather happy conspiring of people and events that dooms most of the Bastables' schemes to failure. Their experiences are narrated by the ostensibly anonymous Oswald, the spiritual twin of every child longing to trade places with Jim Hawkins or Huckleberry Finn. Together, he and his brothers and sisters concoct projects for their financial betterment. In our own day inflation may have wreaked havoc with the value of buried treasure, but the Bastables' attempt to find it will always be priceless. As for flushing out burglars, selling Noël's poems, or rescuing pedestrians from a fierce dog (their own beloved pet Pincher), each episode engagingly blends amiable mayhem and sensitive insights, even if the results add little to the family coffers. Inevitably, perhaps, it is only when the Bastables—with self-effacing charm—help someone they think is worse off than they are that their luck finally changes.

Admittedly, the book is more a collection of episodes than a single evolving story, a condition reflecting its earlier serialization, chapter by chapter. The essentially independent adventures could be extended at will, a lucrative situation the prolific Nesbit clearly found to her liking. And for her contemporary readers, who could closely identify with the characters, there could hardly be too many installments. Modern children, however, accustomed to tighter narratives with a discernible thrust, may find the pace too leisurely. But such fidgety readers might well enjoy the book piecemeal, like nibbling at a dessert too rich to eat all at once.

Serialization is no longer a common practice, the magazines that supported it having mostly disappeared. No doubt, some critics consider **The Story of the Treasure Seekers** similarly out-moded, conceived in an age of sentimental didacticism that is presently unfashionable. Many Victorian authors did serve up great spoonfuls of moral porridge, and Nesbit probably swallowed hearty doses of them in her youth; but her own offerings, heavily flavored with humor and irony, remain fresh and palatable even now. Unlike her more dated peers, whose plot-centered books could not survive the passing years, Nesbit was chiefly concerned with her characters. With the Bastables, she captured the curious mingling of ignorance, innocence, and pluck that children possess in full measure, displaying their sense and sensibility in a way unmatched at the time and rarely matched since.

Stephen Prickett

SOURCE: "Worlds within Words: Kipling and Nesbit," in *Victorian Fantasy,* Indiana University Press, 1979, pp. 198-239.

[Not] all the influences on Kipling's fantasy were from the past. Among the most immediate stimuli for the Puck stories had been Edith Nesbit's ***The Phoenix and the Carpet,*** published in 1904. As was her habit with authors she admired, Nesbit had sent Kipling a copy on publication and it had been received with delight by the children at Bateman's. His influence is no less marked on her. As early as ***The Wouldbegoods*** in 1901 she had made the Bastable children act out stories from *The Jungle Books* and even try to talk in the language of Kipling's characters. The parallels and contrasts between the two writers show us the final flowering of the Victorian tradition of fantasy—even though the best work of both falls strictly into the Edwardian period. In spite of the fact that she was seven years older than Kipling, Nesbit had shown none of his precocious development, and she did not begin to write any of the books she is now remembered by until the early years of the twentieth century, when she was over forty. Like Kipling, she was a natural fantasy writer, and her late start was due as much as anything to her difficulty in discovering her true bent in face of the overwhelmingly 'realistic' conventions of the Victorian novel. Her now-forgotten novels for adults failed partly because of their tendency towards the fantastic.

Like Kipling, Nesbit, had had a disturbed and somewhat insecure childhood. Her mother was widowed when she was four, and thereafter they moved frequently, and seemingly at random. She was sent to a variety of more or less unsatisfactory schools in England and France. Her career as a professional writer was more or less forced upon her by circumstances. A hurried marriage at the age of twenty-one when she was seven months pregnant had left her as the bread-winner for a family when, within a few months,

her husband, Hubert Bland, contracted smallpox. While he was ill his partner in business made off with the funds.[1] This shaky start to the marriage set the pattern that was to continue. In contrast with the order and stability of the Kipling household under the beneficent dictatorship of Mrs. Kipling (who held the purse-strings and even gave Rudyard his 'pocket money'), the Nesbit/Bland household, even in its later years of prosperity, was disorganized, unstable and bohemian. Hubert Bland's two great hobbies were socialism and womanizing. To H. G. Wells, whose tastes were much too similar for friendship, he boasted that he was 'a student, and experimentalist . . . in illicit love'.[2] Like many compulsive seducers, he combined promiscuity with a strong sense of the conventions he defied. He was a staunch, if not strict Roman Catholic, and relations within the Fabian society were severely strained when he found Wells making advances to his daughter Rosamund while she was still a teenager. All Shaw's acid but calculated tact was needed to heal the breach.[3] The quarrel was the more ironic since Rosamund was not Nesbit's child at all, but one of Bland's by Alice Hoatson, her companion-cum-housekeeper—and Bland's mistress. It says much for Edith Nesbit's character that she adopted both the illegitimate children of this union, and brought them up with her own. It was many years before they found out the truth. Commenting on this often strained *ménage-à-trois,* Wells observed 'all this E. Nesbit not only detested and mitigated and tolerated, but presided over and I think found exceedingly interesting.' Moore agrees, but adds that 'It had taken her many years to reach that comparative detachment.'[4] In the meantime, Nesbit herself indulged in a number of love-affairs, perhaps partly compensatory, with (among others) Shaw, Richard le Galienne, and even Dr. Wallis Budge of the Egyptian section of the British Museum. Yet the marriage endured, and in a strange way Nesbit and Bland were deeply dependent on each other. When he died in 1914, she was heartbroken.

If the nonsense fantasies of the mid-Victorians, Lear and Carroll, had been the product of inhibition, it would scarcely be possible to argue the same of Nesbit, who made a point of matching the unconventional state of her private life with equally unconventional public behaviour. Noël Coward described her as 'the most genuine Bohemian I ever met.'[5] She dressed in long loose-fitting flowing dresses, very far removed from the elaborate tightly-corseted costumes of late Victorian and Edwardian fashions, and smoked heavily, even in public,—a habit which almost certainly contributed to her death of lung and heart disease in 1924. Moreover, she had begun her scandalous ways early—long before she met Bland. When she was removed from a French convent school at the age of eleven, she left behind her, for the nuns to discover, two empty wine-bottles of which she had presumably drunk the contents, and in middle age she persuaded officials at the Paris Opera to open all the windows (an unheard of thing) by pretending to faint and gasping for air at various strategic points in the building. As she herself seems to have recognized by her frequent references to him, if she had an affinity with any of the earlier fantasy-writers it would be with Kingsley. To some child fans she wrote:

> I am very pleased to have your letters, and to know that you like my books. You are quite right to like Kingsley and Dickens and George MacDonald better than you like me . . . [6]

The modesty was not assumed. Nesbit always thought of herself primarily as a poet, even after the great financial success of her children's books. While her serious poetry is scarcely remembered, it is the poetic sensibility in her prose that links her with Kipling, and makes her, with him, one of the great fantasists.

It is this quality too that marks off so unmistakably the great writers like Nesbit and Kipling from other late Victorian fantasists, such as F. Anstey,[7] probably best known today as the author of *Vice Versa* (1882). Anstey's novel *The Brass Bottle* was published in 1900, and several critics have noted the similarities between it and *The Phoenix and the Carpet.* The brass bottle of the title contains an Arabian Jinn which had been imprisoned there thousands of years before by Solomon for various misdeeds. His effusive gratitude to his rescuer in modern London is, of course, a menace, and provides the setting for a series of comic magical disasters. As do so many of the nineteenth-century fantasies, the story draws heavily and in some detail on *The Arabian Nights.* Nevertheless, clever as much of it is, it remains at the level of situation-comedy, lacking the sharpness or depth of character to be found in either Nesbit or Kipling, or any of the wider social and philosophical concerns. As in most light comedy, Anstey's world is a thinner simpler place than the one we all know.

The sense of an extra poetic richness and depth in the worlds of both Nesbit and Kipling was helped by a common illustrator of remarkable talent. H. R. Millar. He worked closely with both authors, and with Nesbit in particular he became adept at translating her slightest hints into substantial visual images—sometimes a matter of necessity when she was so late with her copy that he had to work from scrawled chapter précis rather than the finished text. Nevertheless his results so delighted her that she used to insist there was telepathy between them. His picture of the Psammead, was, she declared, 'exactly like the creature she had in her own imagination.'[8] Certainly it was Millar who gave form to so many of her most dramatic images. We have already seen what he did with her prehistoric monsters, the Great Sloth and the 'Dinosaurus'. He captures no less successfully the table-top architecture of the Magic City, at once grandiose and exotic in design, yet familiar and domestic in detail and materials. As with all the great illustrators of fantasy, Cruikshank, Doyle, Lear, or Tenniel, it is the meticulous attention to details where every article tells a story that brings the pictures to life. Behind that ability to add 'something more' to a scene than we might perceive in real life lay a visual tradition stretching back to Hogarth, and beyond. Millar was to Nesbit's fantasy what Tenniel was to Carroll's.[9]

As both Nesbit and Kipling developed as writers it is clear that it is this 'poetic' element, the desire always for something *more,* that made the confines of conventional realism increasingly unsatisfactory. Dobrée writes of how Kipling's 'broodings on life', his family disasters, and his own ill-health led him more and more towards 'adding a fourth dimension to the pictures he presented of human beings, their actions and reactions.'[10] Nesbit's work in the early 1900s shows a remarkably similar tendency. The world of *The Wouldbegoods* and *The Treasure Seekers* gives way to that of the Phoenix and the Psammead and the Three Mouldiwarps, and the more complex supernatural of *The Magic City* and *The Enchanted Castle.* Like Kipling, Nesbit came to need a larger stage for her 'realism' than reality permitted. Just as Dan and Una, growing up in a Sussex village, could only come to understand the complex tapestry of their cultural inheritance through the 'magic' of Puck, so Nesbit's children needed 'magic' to see their suburban London society in perspective.

The Story of the Amulet, for instance, is built around a series of visits to the remote past, or, in one dramatic case, the future. But given the superficial framework, the resemblance to *Puck* is slight. As has been pointed out, Kipling's children themselves stay in the present. As a result their view of history is personal: it is essentially a series of deeds, great or small, performed by unsung heroes. There is cumulative progress, but it is made up of the actions of brave individuals who played their cards as they had been dealt them. 'What else could I have done?' is the refrain of *Rewards and Fairies*. Nesbit, the socialist, is less concerned with individuals than with societies. She wants to show not the similarities with our own time, but the enormous differences between the outlook of other ages and our own. C. S. Lewis records how, as a child, it was his favourite Nesbit novel for this reason. 'It first opened my eyes to antiquity, the dark backward and abysm of time.'[11] But the resulting picture, as it is slowly built up, incident by incident, is a devastating critique of her own society. We have already had hints of this from the Phoenix, but his open disapproval of the drab dreariness of Edwardian London might well be dismissed as the natural nostalgia of a creature more accustomed to an Egyptian temple of its own than the modern, Fire Assurance Office. But *The Amulet*'s message is more insistent. The children find a dirty little girl crying in St. James's Park. Her parents are dead, and she is about to be taken into the Workhouse. With an ironic echo of Shakespeare's *Cymbeline*—shortly to be explained—she is called Imogen. The children take her to see their lodger, the 'learned gentleman' from the British Museum,[12] who wishes sadly that they 'could find a home where they would be glad to have her'—and the Psammead, being present, is at once forced to grant his request. They find themselves in ancient Britain. The children are amazed. 'But why *here*?' says Anthea in astonishment, 'Why *now*?'

> 'You don't suppose anyone would want a child like that in *your* times—in *your* towns?' said the Psammead in irritated tones. 'You've got your country into such a mess that there's no room for half your children—and no one to want them.'[13]

Then the little girl meets a woman who resembles her mother, and who has lost a child just like her—and there is a joyful reunion. As in Kipling, there are hints here either of reincarnation, or of the recurrence of certain types in every generation—but the Psammead refuses to be drawn. 'Who knows? but each one fills the empty place in the other's heart. It is enough.'[14]

Twentieth-century progress is such that it no longer has a place in anyone's heart for the unwanted child. But this is in turn symptomatic of a much wider inhumanity. By means of another unguarded wish in the Psammead's presence, the Queen of Babylon is enabled to visit London. The children proudly show her the sights.

> And now from the window of a four-wheeled cab the Queen of Babylon beheld the wonders of London. Buckingham Palace she thought uninteresting; Westminster Abbey and the Houses of Parliament little better. But she liked the Tower, and the River, and the ships filled her with wonder and delight.
>
> 'But now badly you keep your slaves. How wretched and poor and neglected they seem,' she said, as the cab rattled along the Mile End Road.
>
> 'They aren't slaves; they're working-people,' said Jane.
>
> 'Of course they're working. That's what slaves are. Don't you tell me. Do you suppose I don't know a slave's face when I see it? Why don't their masters see they're better fed and better clothed? Tell me in three words.'
>
> No one answered. The wage-system of modern England is a little difficult to explain in three words even if you understand it—which the children didn't.
>
> 'You'll have a revolt of your slaves if you're not careful', said the Queen.
>
> 'Oh, no,' said Cyril; 'you see they have votes—that makes them safe not to revolt. It makes all the difference. Father told me so.'
>
> 'What is this vote?' asked the Queen. 'Is it a charm? What do they do with it?'
>
> 'I don't know,' said the harassed Cyril. 'it's just a vote, that's all! They don't do anything particular with it.'
>
> 'I see,' said the Queen; 'a sort of plaything . . .'[15]

In a society brought up on the Bible, Babylon has always had a bad press. To compare twentieth-century London, with all its tourist attractions, unfavourably with Babylon, not merely in terms of architecture, but even in morals and general humanity was a final calculated insult. The condemnation of the present is rounded off by a visit to the future. The first thing they notice in comparison with the 'sorry-present' is the cleanliness and lack of pollution.

> As they came through the doors of the (British) Museum they blinked at the sudden glory of sunlight and blue sky. The houses opposite the Museum were gone. Instead there was a big garden, with trees and flowers and smooth green lawns, and not a single notice to tell you not to walk on the grass and not to destroy the trees and shrubs and not to pick the flowers. There were comfortable seats all about, and arbours covered with roses, and long trellised walks, also rose-covered.[16]

In view of the recent fight by conservationists to preserve the buildings opposite the British Museum, the passage has an un-intentionally ironic ring today. The general picture of a clean London with gardens and flowers everywhere inhabited by people with long flowing clothes and happy faces is an amalgam of the vague Fabian day-dreams of the time about the coming socialist paradise. Though there are sharper typical Nesbit touches, such as men being in charge of babies, and playing with them, the overall picture is similar to the sort of optimistic view of the future being painted by H. G. Wells. The similarity is deliberate: the children meet a small boy named Wells, after the 'great reformer'. The real parallel, however, is with Imogen. This boy too is crying in the park, but, it turns out, this is because he has been punished for the dreadful crime of dropping litter by being expelled from school for the day—'for a whole day!' Having explained the joys of his project-centred curriculum to the children, he takes them home. His house has no need of ornaments because every single thing in it is beautiful. For safety, it is centrally-heated, and the furniture in the nursery is padded to prevent children hurting themselves. To show their gratitude for the hospitality they have received, the children offer to take his mother with them through the amulet to see *their* London.

> The lady went, laughing. But she did not laugh when she found herself, suddenly, in the dining-room at Fitzroy Street.
>
> 'Oh, what a *horrible* trick!' she cried. 'What a hateful, dark, ugly place!'
>
> She ran to the window and looked out. The sky was grey, the street was foggy, a dismal organ-grinder was standing opposite the door, a beggar and a man who sold matches were quarrelling at the edge of the pavement on whose greasy black surface people hurried along, hastening to get to the shelter of their houses.
>
> 'Oh, look at their faces, their horrible faces!' she cried. 'What's the matter with them all?'
>
> 'They're poor people, that's all,' said Robert.
>
> 'But it's *not* all! They're ill, they're unhappy, they're wicked . . .'[17]

The parallel with the Queen of Babylon is complete.

Nesbit's hatred of the sorry-present is taken to its logical conclusion in one of her last books, *Harding's Luck* (1909). Dickie Harding, a little lame orphan boy from the slums of Deptford, acquires by magic another 'self' as his own ancestor, Richard Arden, in James I's reign. No longer a cripple, in this other life he lives in a great house with servants and friends among the green fields and orchards of Deptford. As always, Nesbit is not above loading the

dice: just as it was sunny in the future and wet in the present (not *all* fog and rain is due to pollution!), so it helps to be rich and an aristocrat if you are to live happily in the early seventeenth century. Nevertheless, the comparison is a serious one. The 'welfare state' of the great Jacobean house, where everyone has his place but all are looked after, is contrasted with the misery of *laissez-faire* Edwardian England with its ugliness and unemployment and neglect of its children. The men of the twentieth century seem to be all manipulators of people or money: con-men or pawnbrokers; the men of the seventeenth century (who closely resemble some of the twentieth-century characters in looks) are craftsmen of skill and integrity.

The possibilities of time-travel are exploited for their own dramatic value, however, and not merely for social comment. One of the most effective scenes is where Dickie's cousins, Edred and Elfrida, who are the central characters in an earlier Nesbit story, *The House of Arden,* nearly get the whole family executed for High Treason by singing 'Please to remember the Fifth of November/Gunpowder treason and plot . . . '*before* the Gunpowder Plot has happened. But even here the opportunities for social comment are not altogether wasted. Dickie's nurse, who mysteriously seems to understand about time-travel, warns him to be very careful what he says, or she will be 'burned as a witch.' He urges her to come back with him to the twentieth century—for 'they don't burn people for witches there'.

> 'No,' said the nurse, 'but they let them live such lives in their ugly towns that my life here with all its risks is far better worth living. Thou knowest how folk live in Deptford in thy time—how all the green trees are gone, and good work is gone, and people do bad work for just so much as will keep together their worn bodies and desolate souls. And sometimes they starve to death.'[18]

Eventually Dickie makes the choice to return for ever to the seventeenth century, where he is not crippled (both literally and, we presume, metaphorically) and can be happier than he ever will in the present. Though it is done partly as a sacrifice, to allow the other Arden children to inherit, it is the most complete rejection of the present in any fantasy of the period.

In an argument with Edred and Elfrida in *The House of Arden,* Richard makes use of the nurse's argument himself for rejecting the twentieth century.

> 'Why don't you want to come with us to our times?'

'I hate your times. They're ugly, they're cruel,' said Richard.

'They don't cut your head off for nothing anyhow in our times,' said Edred, and shut you up in the Tower.'

'They do worse things,' Richard said. '*I* know. They make people work fourteen hours a day for nine shillings a week, so that they never have enough to eat or wear, and no time to sleep or be happy in. They won't give people food or clothes, or let them work to get them; and then they put the people in prison if they take enough to keep them alive. They let people get horrid diseases, till their jaws drop off, so as to have a particular kind of china. Women have to go out to work instead of looking after their babies, and the little girl that's left in charge drops the baby and it's crippled for life. Oh! I know. I won't go back with you. You might keep me there for ever.' He shuddered.[19]

As a book *Harding's Luck* is uneven. With its companion volume, *The House of Arden,* it forms a separate group from either Nesbit's earlier fantasies, which, like *The Phoenix,* or the Psammead books, centre on Edwardian London and are fairly episodic in structure, or the late ones which involve totally 'other' worlds. They are in some ways her most ambitious experiment in that they tell essentially the same story from two points of view, and involve some of the basic problems of science-fiction: time-travel, for instance.

This was one of the questions that always puzzled the children—and they used to talk it over together till their heads seemed to be spinning round. The question of course was: Did their being in past times make any difference to the other people in past times? In other words, when you were taking part in historical scenes, did it matter what you said or did? Of course it seemed to matter extremely—at the time.'[20]

They are told by the nurse that they can, in fact, leave no trace on times past—from which we, if not the children, may be intended to glean some theory (Hegelian or Marxist?) of the inevitability of history.[21] But the difference between Dickie's journeys into the past and those of the children in *The Amulet* is that they always remained physically *themselves*—visibly visitors to another time or place—whereas Dickie *is* somebody else. In Jacobean England he is not lame, for example. He is a different physical person, Richard Arden. This raises an even more puzzling problem—which Nesbit herself is aware of—that if Dickie has 'become' young Richard

Arden of 1606, what has happened to the boy who was previously 'Richard Arden'? Indeed, if we read the text closely it is not clear that the 'Richard' who refuses to come to the twentieth century with Edred and Elfrida is in fact Dickie. His comment that 'in *your* time nobody cares' is, to say the least, ambiguous. The nurse in *Harding's Luck* suggests that the 'missing' Edred and Elfrida from 1606 are 'somewhere else—in Julius Caesar's time, to be exact—but they don't know it, and never will know it. They haven't the charm. To them it will be a dream that they have forgotten.'[22] But this system of interchanging personalities has to be endless, if it is to work at all. Moreover, the more people that are doing it, the less remarkable it becomes—unless we are to assume that, as in *The Finest Story in the World,* we all carry within us the memories of every life that we have 'lived'. The very strengths of fantasy are in danger of becoming weaknesses—the 'rules' are in danger of being lost.

Nevertheless *Harding's Luck* has some of the best descriptions to be found anywhere in Nesbit, such as the opening passages which set the tone of the whole book.

Dickie lived at New Cross. At least the address was New Cross, but really the house where he lived was one of a row of horrid little houses built on the slope where once green fields ran down the hill to the river, and the old houses of the Deptford merchants stood stately in their pleasant gardens and fruitful orchards. All those good fields and happy gardens are built over now. It is as though some wicked giant had taken a big brush full of yellow ochre paint, and another full of mud-colour, and had painted out the green in streaks of dull yellow and filthy brown; and the brown is the roads and the yellow is the houses. Miles and miles and miles of them, and not a green thing to be seen except the cabbages in the greengrocers' shops, and here and there some poor trails of creeping-jenny drooping from a dirty window-sill. There is a little yard at the back of each house; this is called 'the garden', and some of these show green—but they only show it to the houses' back windows. You cannot see it from the street . . . there were no green things growing in the garden at the back of the house where Dickie lived with his aunt. There were stones and bones, and bits of brick, and dirty old dish-cloths matted together with grease and mud, worn-out broom-heads and broken shovels, a bottomless pail, and the mouldy remains of a hutch where once rabbits had lived. But that was a very long time ago, and Dickie had never seen the rabbits. A boy had brought a brown rabbit to school once, buttoned up inside his jacket . . . So

Dickie knew what rabbits were like. And he was fond of the hutch for the sake of what had once lived there.

And when his aunt sold the poor remains of the hutch to a man with a barrow who was ready to buy anything, and who took also the pail and the shovels, giving threepence for the lot, Dickie was almost as unhappy as though the hutch had really held a furry friend. And he hated the man who took the hutch away, all the more because there were empty rabbit-skins hanging sadly from the back of the barrow.[23]

As a child's view of the world, this movement from the general to the particular, with its trains of association about the rabbits, is among the best things she ever wrote. But alongside this kind of acute observation are passages of slack writing and hackneyed themes. The nurse wavers between 'Odds Bodikins!' and modern English—not wholly to be accounted for by her time changes! For many modern readers the discovery that little lame Dickie of Deptford is really the rightful Lord Arden in the twentieth century does not give quite the thrill that this unwearied theme, with its echoes of Curdie's hidden royalty and *Little Lord Fauntleroy,* clearly gave Nesbit's contemporaries. Yet, this said, *Harding's Luck* does display at its best a quality that gave Nesbit's fantasy its enduring greatness, and sets her beside Kipling as one of the giants of the genre.

This is the underlying sense of a stable and ordered moral world. Her magic is often mysterious, and occasionally perfunctory, but it never gives the impression of being arbitrary or meaningless. In part, this is achieved by a network of literary cross-references to other writers—particularly, as we have seen, to fellow writers of fantasy. Just as Kipling's Puck knows his *Midsummer Night's Dream* and is steeped in English literature, so we get the impression from Nesbit that her magic is not her creation, but belongs to a much deeper and older world than can be conjured up by any single writer alone. Her work is studded with allusions of this kind. Dickie Harding reads Kingsley when he gets the chance. The children in *Wet Magic* are reading from *The Water Babies* at the beginning, and when the mermaid wishes to convince them that they really will be able to come under the water with her, she too makes reference to it.

'someone once told me a story about Water Babies. Did you never hear of that?'

'Yes, but that was a made-up story,' said Bernard stolidly.

'Yes, of course,' she agreed, 'but a great deal of it's quite true, all the same.'[24]

On the page before there had been casual references both to Heine and Matthew Arnold. Even the invocation that summons up the mermaids is a quotation from a master of fantasy on a cosmic scale: Milton himself.

> Sabrina fair,
> Listen where thou art sitting,
> Under the glassy green, translucent wave . . .
> (*Comus,* 859-61)

More delightfully zany is the parrot in ***The Magic City*** who is disinclined to 'ordinary conversation' and will only quote from Dryden's translation of *The Aeneid*—which sends everyone to sleep (p. 171). In both ***The Magic City*** and ***Wet Magic*** buildings or caves are actually made of books, and characters, both pleasant and unpleasant, are constantly leaking out of them into the respective magic worlds. The symbolism of literature as itself constituting a 'magic world' is obvious. All literature is a way of enriching our reality and enabling us to discover in it more than we knew.[25] Fantasy is the extreme example by which we understand how the rest works.

Yet mere references alone are not sufficient to establish continuity with the tradition. As MacDonald had clearly seen, an invented world may have any set of rules the writer chooses, provided they are consistent with each other, but the moral law 'remains everywhere the same'. There is no hint of Nesbit's own unconventional life-style in her writings: indeed, her stories may be seen as a tribute to the order that she personally so much lacked. But, if so, the 'order' is not that of the Victorian conventions. Like her predecessors, and like Kipling, she lays stress on the permanent values of honour, truthfulness, fair-mindedness, loyalty, love, and self-sacrifice. At their most limited these need be no more than the virtues of the tribe or in-group against the rest, but, as with Kipling at his best, Nesbit is also aware of the limitations of the tribal code. Beyond what Kipling called 'the Law', but not superseding it, are other qualities of reconciliation and forgiveness whose roots are religious. This is a fact that it is easy to overlook. It is only when we meet their contemporaries like Ballentyne or Rider Haggard who lack this other dimension that we begin to see what differentiates the fantasy of a Kipling or a Nesbit from mere adventure stories or excursions into the exotic. In the twentieth century it marks the difference between the great fantasy writers, such as Tolkien or Lewis, and a host of science-fiction writers who, however good they may be as story-tellers, seem in the end to inhabit an arbitrary and simplified world rather than one richer and more complex than our own. Writers will often show more of themselves in their books than to their friends, and it would have come to less of a surprise to many of her readers than to her circle of Fabian friends when, in 1906, just after she had begun her great series of magical fantasies, she was received into the Roman Catholic Church. It was a quest of a different kind for another world that would enrich her own. Though she later became sceptical about the exclusive claims of Catholicism,[26] Nesbit never lost her religious faith. From her letters, and from accounts of close friends it seems clear that towards the end of her life it grew increasingly important to her.

From her books we have a surprising amount of evidence of a philosophical kind. It has often been noticed that Plato and the Bible are the two greatest philosophical influences on English literature; it has less often been observed how great their influence has been specifically in the direction of fantasy. Nevertheless, their pull is obvious. Both suggest the existence of 'other worlds' impinging on this, but of a greater reality, as part of a greater metaphysical and moral whole that is ultimately beyond man's understanding. We have already seen something of the Biblical influence. The writers Nesbit seems to mention most often, Kingsley, MacDonald, and among her contemporaries, Kipling, all owe much to the Christian Platonic tradition, but in many ways Nesbit was possibly the greatest Platonist of them all. It is the side of her work most frequently misunderstood even now. Ever since her biographer, Doris Langley Moore, placed *The Magic City* and *The Enchanted Castle* among her least successful books, they have been largely ignored or dismissed by critics. She herself finds the construction of the former 'loose and rambling',[27] and another writer on children's books, Anthea Bell, is even more forthright. 'Not much need be said of *The Magic City*,' she declares, 'For once, she had an excellent idea and never rose to it; she develops it in rather a prosaic, plodding manner foreign to the other fantasies.'[28] Nor has *The Enchanted Castle* fared any better, being 'not quite in the same rank with the works which preceded it.'[29] The problem with any writer who worked as quickly and, often, as carelessly as Nesbit did is that peculiarities in her work can be plausibly dismissed as bad workmanship. In fact, Nesbit is very rarely a bad workman in her children's books. *The Magic City* and *The Enchanted Castle* present us with a very different kind of fantasy from stories like the *Phoenix* and the *Amulet* which, for all their serious social awareness, are essentially humorous and episodic. Both have quite a

complicated cumulative philosophical structure. They involve the discovery not so much of magic creatures in this world, as of the existence of other worlds alongside this one.

The Magic City is in a world of art—in its widest sense. It is only entered by an act of creativity of some kind. Not merely is Philip's table-top city there and all his other models, but so is Mr. Perrin, the carpenter who made his first set of bricks—'true to the thousandth of an inch'—and so is every other person who helped to make any part of the materials. 'D'you see,' asks Perrin, '*Making*'s the thing. If it was no more than the lad that turned the handle of the grindstone to sharp the knife that carved a bit of a cabinet or what not, or a child that picked a teazle to finish a bit of the cloth that's glued on to the bottom of a chessman—they're all here.'[30] Even the evil 'Pretenderette', the steely-eyed nurse, is there, who absent-mindedly rebuilt a few bricks of Philip's city she had knocked over with her sleeve. Through Mr. Noah Nesbit goes to unusual trouble to explain the rules of her universe.

> . . . you see, you built those cities in two worlds. It's pulled down in *this* world. But in the other world it's still going on.
>
> . . . Everything people make in that world goes on forever.[31]

If we had met this in a serious adult novel we would most probably recognize it at once. The underlying Platonism is obvious. Moreover, the idea that our created works of art have a timeless existence in an ideal order is a common twentieth-century critical notion[32] with roots in the nineteenth century as far back as Coleridge.[33] and Nesbit goes out of her way specifically to include literature in the artistic forms of her magic world. People and animals are constantly escaping from books. We have already mentioned the Great Sloth in an earlier chapter. Others include the Hippogriff, or flying horse, and even finally Barbarians and a Roman army under Julius Caesar. Though Plato, of course, denied works of art a place of his world of ideal forms,[34] the appeal of his ideas has, paradoxically, always been greatest among artists—who have traditionally emphasized that his was primarily a mystical vision rather than a carefully worked-out system.

As always, Nesbit is inclined to present her beliefs in the form of parody—often, even, as self-mockery. Her obsessional and quite irrational belief that Bacon wrote Shakespeare's plays makes its appearance in the form of the gaoler, Mr. Bacon-Shakespeare, who has written twenty-seven volumes all in cypher on the subject of a crocheted mat that no one can unravel, but unfortunately forgotten the key. The structure of her ideas, however, is significant: though the construction of the book is complicated, it is the very antithesis of 'loose and rambling'. Philip's *official* task is to perform a series of heroic deeds to prove himself the 'Deliverer' and not the 'Destroyer' (the only two options open to him). Each is presented as a further stage of initiation and is marked by an ascending order of chivalry. When the Pretenderette, mounted on the winged Hippogriff, kidnaps Philip and flies away with him Lucy protests that Mr. Noah had told her that 'the Hippogriff could only carry one'. 'One ordinary human being,' said Mr. Noah gently, 'you forget that dear Philip is now an earl.'[35] In fact, of course, Philip's *real* task is to learn to love Lucy, the daughter of the man his sister has just married, and whom he deeply resents. The tasks are an opportunity for them to work together. In the first, Philip has to rescue Lucy from a dragon. In the second they have to unravel a carpet which is not woven, but crocheted—a fact which Philip cannot see until Lucy points it out to him. As they proceed, the tasks become progressively more psychologically 'unravelling' as they deal with personal renunciation, self-sacrifice, and finally the Great Sloth and the Pretenderette herself—who had become unlovable from being unloved. By a device faintly reminiscent of *The Brushwood Boy*, Philip's sister Helen, who has created with him as a game a secret and forbidden island, is found to be on the island—because it is part of her dream as well as his. In giving the island away, Philip has to renounce her, since that is her only route into the magic world. Again, the symbolism of their changing relationship is obvious. Later, in real life when she has returned from her honeymoon she admits to remembering dimly her 'dream'.

In both *The Magic City* and *The Enchanted Castle* there are repeated hints that all knowledge is but a recognition of what we have known all along. This Platonic 'recognition' theme[36] is central to the growing maturity of the children. Many of Philip's deeds are in fact performed first, as the thing which needed to be done, and then discovered to be the next stage afterwards. The giving of the forbidden island to the homeless islanders is done simply because they *are* homeless, and must be found somewhere to live. It is immediately after this act that the reconciliation of Philip and Lucy takes place. Similarly, in *Harding's Luck,* long before Dickie has first been into the past, he finds that he recognizes the interior layout of

Arden Castle when he helps to burgle it, although he has never been there before. Being a burglar in what is, unknown to you, your own 'home' is a typical Nesbit twist of irony—but as a symbol it can be seen at a number of levels. Much of the story can in fact be taken as an experiment in *déjà vu*: the feeling of having 'been here before'. Sometimes, as in Kipling, this is specifically linked with notions of reincarnation. Dickie, for instance, meets people in Jacobean England who are apparently 'the same' as people he knew in the slums of Deptford, but the way in which the device is used suggests that Nesbit is more interested in the way the same people will behave under different circumstances, than she is in actual reincarnation—although this, too, of course is a Platonic theme.[37] Much more specifically Platonic is the nurse's question to Dickie, when she has been trying to explain what has been happening: 'Dids't never hear that all life is dream?'

Nesbit certainly had, and it is in her treatment of this central notion of so much Victorian fantasy that she stands most clearly in the Platonic Christian tradition of James Hogg, Novalis, MacDonald, and Kingsley. The unreal or illusory nature of time, which comes in almost every one of these later fantasies, is part of a wider feeling that life itself is but a dream into which we bring reports, like the poor shepherd girl Kilmeny, of a greater reality beyond. In *The Enchanted Castle* there is a magic ring that—disconcertingly—is just what its possessor *says* it is. Much of the story is taken up with a series of comic misadventures similar in kind to those with the Psammead in *Five Children and It*. The ring can be used to create things, to become rich, to become invisible, and even to grow—all with equally confusing and disastrous consequences. At the same time, however, the ring also initiates its wearers into another world where statues become alive and monsters roam the grounds of Yalding Castle. The statues of Greek gods scattered around the grounds become the real Greek pantheon, and the children join them in a feast—a literal symposium. In the final chapter the children with Lord Yalding and his fiancée are present at a vast mystical vision of the great dance of creation:

> The moonbeam slants more and more; now it touches the far end of the stone, now it draws nearer and nearer the middle of it, now at last it touches the very heart and centre of that central stone. And then it is as though a spring were touched, a fountain of light released. Everything changes. Or, rather, everything is revealed. There are no more secrets. The plan of the world seems plain, like an easy sum that one writes in big figures on a child's slate. One wonders how one can

ever have wondered about anything. Space is not; every place that one has seen or dreamed of is here. Time is not; into this instant is crowded all that one has ever done or dreamed of doing. It is a moment, and it is eternity. It is the centre of the universe and it is the universe itself. The eternal light rests on and illuminates the eternal heart of things.

. . . Afterwards none of them could ever remember at all what had happened. But they never forgot that they had been somewhere where everything was easy and beautiful. And people who can remember even that much are never quite the same again. And when they came to talk of it next day they found that to each some little part of that night's great enlightenment was left.

. . . Then a wave of intention swept over the mighty crowd. All the faces, bird, beast, Greek statue, Babylonian monsters, human child and human lover, turned upward, the radiant light illumined them and one word broke from all.

'The light!' they cried, and the sound of their voice was like the sound of a great wave; 'the light! the light—'[38]

There is an extraordinary, yet significant, parallel to this scene in a minor key at the end of *The Magic City.* To rid the city of Barbarians who have escaped from Caesar's *Gallic War,* Caesar himself is summoned from the same book. He and his legions are clearly meant to stand for order and civilization against chaos and barbarism. After a night of fighting the barbarians are safely driven back between hard covers, and as dawn breaks Caesar passes judgement on the Pretenderette. Though he had been called up originally for a limited military objective, he now seems to have taken over the role of lawgiver. But the 'Law' is that of love. In a 'Last Judgment' scene the loveless Pretenderette is condemned to serve the people of Briskford, newly released fom the Great Sloth, until they love her so much they cannot bear to part with her—at which point, of course, her 'punishment' ceases to be one. Any possible theological implications of this judgement of Caesar are rapidly passed over because as he speaks both children now see an extraordinary resemblance between him and Lucy's father (now to be Philip's also). At the same moment the sun rises and they are dazzled by the light on his armour. When they open their eyes he is gone. The justice transmuted into love, the glimpse of a father in this (for Philip a new discovery), and the dazzling light are all familiar images. The whole incident is important in that it is not necessary in any way to the plot, but presents a sudden, and slightly incomprehensible twist to the

story. Though we can recognize in the 'light' echoes of Plato's Sun myth in *The Republic,* there are also nearer and more immediate references here to the European mystical tradition. As Kingsley did at the end of *The Water Babies,* Nesbit is harking back here (and even more in the passage from ***The Enchanted Castle***) to the consummation of space and time in the contemplation of the 'Light Eternal' at the end of Dante's *Paradiso.*

Finally, in such scenes as these there is the hint (it is no more) of that odd metaphysical *frisson* that links Dante with this minority tradition of Victorian children's writers, and that transforms fantasy from simple escapism into something much more enduringly rooted in the human psyche. It is present in Canto III of the *Paradiso* when Dante suddenly discovers that the faces he thought were either reflections or figments of his own mind were, in fact, more real and alive than he could easily comprehend. It is present (as Keats saw) in Adam's dream in *Paradise Lost,* where he awakens and finds his dream is truth. It is present, as we have seen, tantalizingly and fleetingly in Carroll, Kingsley, MacDonald, and Kipling— and again here with Nesbit as Philip discovers that what he has glimpsed for a moment, after so much moral struggle, within the 'magic city' has become part of the reality of his everyday life. The uncompromising Platonism of Anselm's ontological proof of God owes something of its curious magnificence to this same basic human desire for the dream that comes true. Keats had boldly attributed this power to the 'Imagination', but by mid-century the allimportant shock of this transformational view of the imagination had been lost—and largely replaced by theories of aesthetics. In 'Art' the mystery and urgency of other worlds had largely faded or become dissipated. it was left to children's writers such as Nesbit to create anew, and at a different level of experience, the 'high fantasy' of a world too rich and complex to be contained by the conventions of Victorian naturalism.

Notes

1. Since Bland was also a near-pathological liar, it is difficult to be sure of any facts that depend on his unsubstantiated word. He certainly seems to have deceived Nesbit about his family of 'ancient North Country stock' which is referred to by Doris Langley Moore (p. 88). He was born in Cable Street. His business ventures seem equally obscure.

2. Doris Langley Moore, *E. Nesbit: A Biography,* Revised edn., Ernest Benn, 1967, p. 15.

3. Norman and Jeanne MacKenzie, *The Time Traveller: The Life of H. G. Wells,* Weidenfeld and Nicolson, 1973, Ch. 14.

4. Moore, p. 18.

5. *Ibid.* p. 221.

6. *Ibid.* p. 255.

7. The pen-name of Thomas Anstey Guthrie (1856-1934), author of many novels and shorter pieces, mostly of a fantastic nature. He was a great admirer of Nesbit.

8. Moore, pp. 191-3.

9. But without the clash of personalities that always threatened to wreck that brilliant partnership. Millar accepted Nesbit's unpunctuality with calmness and resource, and never wavered in his admiration for her as a writer. But this did not mean uncritical agreement. On one occasion he pointed out to her that her passionate hatred of the vast new housing developments was quite inconsistent of her, since it was what she, as a socialist, had been fighting for for years.

10. Dobrée, p. 167.

11. *Surprised by Joy,* Fontana, Collins, 1959, p. 17.

12. He is of course based on Dr. Wallis Budge of the British Museum who Nesbit met while researching background for *The Amulet.* It was he who steered her away from ancient Egyptian legends, explaining that they were too full of sex to be useful in a children's book. He became her confidant, and possibly her lover. *The Amulet* is dedicated to him.

13. *The Story of the Amulet,* Puffin Books, 1959, p. 183.

14. *Ibid.* p. 187.

15. *Ibid.* p. 148.

16. *Ibid.* p. 223.

17. pp. 231-2.

18. *Harding's Luck,* Seventh Impression, Ernest Benn, 1947, p. 183.

19. *The House of Arden,* New edition, Ernest Benn, 1958, pp. 240-41.

20. *The House of Arden,* p. 166.

21. In what is, technically, much the most interesting of his fantasies, *Tourmalin's Time Cheques* (1891), F. Anstey had already suggested an ingenious way of breaking this seemingly inflexible rule. Peter Tourmalin is irritated by the prospect of gaining hours of boring extra time as he sails westwards on his way back from Australia to England. A mysterious stranger on the ship suggests that he deposits the 'extra' time with him in his 'Time Bank', and cashes the cheques as he wants them later. All he has to do is to write a cheque for so many minutes and place it under the nearest clock. He will instantly find himself back on board the *SS Boomerang* enjoying in sunlit southern seas the time he has so prudently 'saved'. The following winter Tourmalin does so. To his mingled delight and horror he finds that though on his voyage home he had, to the best of his knowledge, avoided any shipboard romances and remained true to his Sophia, his fiancée who was to meet him at Gibraltar, in the 'saved' time he has apparently become romantically entangled with *two* extremely attractive girls from the ship. Each time he returns it is clear that things are getting more and more out of hand—with passionate scenes and threatened suicides in a style not unworthily anticipating P. G. Wodehouse. In England, in the 'present', he is now married to the earnest and virtuous Sophia, and the hard-pressed Tourmalin clearly relishes these 'past' romances, in spite of their threatening complexities. When Sophia finds out, she explains that it is his duty to 'return' to the ship and clear up these entanglements—which are clearly 'real' since they have happened in the past. Protesting, Tourmalin eventually does so, only to plunge deeper and deeper into the toils so that by the time he reaches Gibralter both girls believe him engaged to them. Sophia, joining the ship at Gibralter, discovers all and breaks off their engagement forthwith. His protest that he is already *married* to her, and that it is because of her that he is in this mess, is, of course, treated by the Sophia of the past with the contempt it deserves. Unfortunately, having set up this fascinating situation, in which the key events are only happening because of other events in the future which now cannot happen, Anstey hastily breaks off the story by declaring it was a 'dream'. Nevertheless, the basic paradox is one that deserves further and better treatment in science-fiction.

22. *Harding's Luck,* p. 180.

23. pp. 1-3.

24. *Wet Magic,* Seventh Impression, Ernest Benn, 1945. pp. 121-2.

25. The amulet is a good example of how Nesbit can take classic metaphors of literatureand give them a visual and concrete form. It grows into an enormous arch for the children to step through into 'other worlds'—past or future. We recall Tennyson's Ulysses:

> ' . . . all experience is an arch wherethrough
> Gleams that untravelled world whose margin fades
> For ever and for ever when I move.' (19-21)

26. Moore, p. 307.

27. Moore, p. 265.

28. Anthea Bell, *E. Nesbit,* Bodley Head Monographs 1960, Collected as *Three Bodley Head Monographs* 1968, p. 146.

The one dissenter from this chorus of disfavour was Noël Coward, who hoarded his pocket money as a child in order to buy a whole year's worth of the *Strand Magazine* and so read Nesbit's stories right through without a break. There were a few numbers missing of the year that had *The Magic City,* and so, he tells us, 'I stole a coral necklace from a visiting friend of Mother's, pawned it for five shillings, and bought the complete book at the Army and Navy Stores . . . In later years I told E. Nesbit of this little incident and I regret to say she was delighted.' (*Ibid.* pp. 146-7.)

29. Moore, p. 324.

30. *The Magic City,* Ernest Benn, 1958, p. 106.

31. p. 84.

32. See for instance T. S. Eliot's 'Tradition and the Individual Talent' in his *Selected Essays,* Faber, 1951 and W. B. Yeats's poem, *Sailing to Byzantium.*

33. See Stephen Prickett, *Coleridge and Wordsworth: The Poetry of Growth,* pp. 115-20.

34. *Republic,* Book 10.

35. p. 218.

36. *Phaedo,* 72B. Plato, *The Last Days of Socrates,* Translated Hugh Tredennick, Penguin, 1954, pp. 94-5.

37. Again, see *Phaedo.*

38. pp. 346-9. It is interesting to compare this passage with the parallel one at the end of C. S. Lewis's *Perelandra,* which also draws on Dante. Though Lewis had read a great deal of Nesbit, I do not know if he had ever read *The Enchanted Castle.*

Anita Moss

SOURCE: "The Story of the Treasure Seekers: The Idiom of Childhood," in *Touchstones: Reflections on the Best in Children's Literature,* edited by Perry Nodelman, Children's Literature Association, 1985, pp. 188-97.

As Oswald Bastable would put it, E. Nesbit's **The Story of the Treasure Seekers** is "A1" by anyone's standards. All the critics agree. The book is the first truly modern book for children. It is delightfully subversive. It captures a genuine sense of the child's "voice" for the first time in children's fiction. In the distinguished series of novels which **The Story of the Treasure Seekers** began, E. Nesbit accomplished much more: she first introduced time travel to children's fantasy in **The Story of the Amulet, The House of Arden,** and **Harding's Luck.** She created those vain and crotchety magical creatures—the Psammead, the Phoenix, and the Mouldiwarp. Finally, she re-invigorated the tradition of British literary fairy tale, which had grown precious and decadent by the end of the nineteenth century. E. Nesbit was herself a fascinating woman, the kind men (and women too) fall in love with and never forget. An unconventional Bohemian who refused to wear corsets, E. Nesbit went about in flowing, aesthetic gowns with bracelets to her elbows, wore knickers, rode the bicycle, jumped fences, smoked in public, adopted two of her husband's illegitimate children as her own, and tolerated a highly unconventional household.

But her first children's novel, **The Story of the Treasure Seekers** is the focus of this essay. E. Nesbit had been writing sentimental novels and poetry, gothic thrillers, and some highly derivative stories for children for approximately twenty years before its publication in 1899. After she had published a series of articles on her own childhood in the 1896-97 issues of *The Girl's Own Paper,* Nesbit apparently recovered much of her own vivid childhood experience, and hence, a powerful source for her great children's stories. Drawing upon her earlier story for children, **"The Play Times,"** which had been published in *Nister's Holiday Annual of 1894-96,* Nesbit began writing **The Story of the Treasure Seekers,** which first appeared serially in the *Pall Mall Magazine* and the *Windsor Magazine* in 1898. Later, Nesbit continued to write about the adventures of the Bastable children in *The Wouldbegoods* (1901) and *The New Treasure Seekers* (1904). She also included some tales about the Bastables in *Oswald Bastable and Others* (1905). Affectionate readers refer to these volumes collectively as "the Bastable tales."

The Story of the Treasure Seekers can be considered a touchstone of children's literature for several reasons. First, it popularizes an important tradition in modern children's literature: a group of spirited and imaginative children engaged in adventures apart from adults. At a time in British children's literature when the Romantic child of Charles Dickens and George MacDonald had lost much of its vitality as a symbol, having become excessively sweet in such works as Lewis Carroll's *Sylvie and Bruno* and Frances Hodgson Burnett's *Little Lord Fauntleroy,* Nesbit gave new life to children's literature. Nesbit is also given credit for creating one of the first child narrators in children's literature and hence, for addressing her child audience in its own colloquial idiom. Structurally, *The Story of the Treasure Seekers* fuses conventions of the fairy tale and those of the realistic story in ways that offer new possibilities for subsequent writers. Nesbit also explores the place of writing, publication, and reading in the child's imaginative life, and suggests ways that children use reading and writing to make sense of their experience and to survive both pain and benumbing boredom.

E. Nesbit was well-prepared to write a children's book which represented a breakthrough in her own career and in the history of children's literature. She had read the works of Lewis Carroll, George Mac-Donald, Charles Kingsley, Mrs. Ewing, and Mrs. Moleworth carefully. She had internalized the conventions of fairy tale, romance, and such popular forms as detective fiction and adventure stories. Moreover she had read the major nineteenth-century novelists, and was particularly influenced by the works of Charles Dickens. Among her contemporaries, Rudyard Kipling and Kenneth Grahame were important influences.

Probably the most immediate influences on *The Story of the Treasure Seekers* were Kenneth Grahame's *The Golden Age* (1895) and *Dream Days* (1899), and Dickens' children's book *A Holiday Romance* (1868). In Grahame's two books for adults, he recounts the adventures of several children, often in a green natu-

ral setting. Grahame characterizes the adults as slow, ignorant, restrictive "Olympians," who prefer to be indoors, while the children are lithe and light-hearted "Arcadians," who find release and identity when they are free from the supervision of these adults. Nesbit knew these books quite well. In fact, Oswald Bastable notes that *The Golden Age* is "A1 except when it gets mixed-up with adult nonsense." Nesbit no doubt escapes this sentimental "adult nonsense," the nostalgia expressed by a grown-up narrator looking back upon the pastoral pleasures of a lost childhood, by adopting the rhetorical device of the child narrator.

Charles Dickens had used child narrators in *A Holiday Romance;* he also had coyly half-hidden and half-revealed the identity of the narrator, as Nesbit does with Oswald Bastable. But the voice in Dickens' story (actually four different stories narrated by different children) is silly, affected, and self-consciously cute; the voice in *The Story of the Treasure Seekers* is much closer to the authentic voice of childhood. While Oswald pretends to hide his identity, he soon gives the secret away through his glorification of "the noble Oswald" or by lapsing into first person narration when recounting Oswald's adventures. The narrator also freely admits that he knows more about Oswald's thoughts and experiences than he knows about the other Bastable children. The character of Oswald, his presiding voice, becomes an important aesthetic feature of the three volumes devoted to the adventures of the Bastables, since it is the element which unifies the episodic stories.

The Story of the Treasure Seekers begins with the attempts of the Bastable children to restore "the fallen fortunes of the ancient House of Bastable". As in fairy tales, the children's mother has died, and the father, having been ill and having been the victim of an unscrupulous business partner (just as Nesbit's husband, Hubert Bland, was) seems to be rather weak and ineffectual. Though a loving parent, Mr. Bastable is besieged by bill collectors, plagued by a troubled business and the threat of poverty, and essentially unable to provide emotionally or materially for his children.

The Bastable children attempt to find treasure by digging for it, by selling Noel's poetry, by peddling a foul-tasting sherry, by being bandits, editors, and would-be rescuers of a generous benefactor. Finally they try to use a divining rod to locate treasure. Each of these attempts, an idea of one of the children, ends in comic disaster. The Bastables accidentally "plant" Albert-next-door up to his neck while digging for treasure (an episode inspired by a similar incident in Nesbit's childhood). They are successful at selling Noel's poetry, but get into trouble when they try to sell sherry fortified with generous doses of sugar to a stern and humorless clergyman. At the end of *The Story of the Treasure Seekers,* the fallen fortunes of the Bastables are at last restored through the generosity of the children's maternal uncle. Moved by the innocence and generosity of the Bastable children, their "poor Indian" uncle provides money to rescue the father's floundering business, and moves the family from the shabbily comfortable "semi-detached house in Lewisham" to his stately mansion.

Nesbit thus draws upon a familiar nineteenth-century literary convention: the frozen emotions of the crusty-hearted old gentleman are melted by the goodness of spirited and imaginative children. Intensely aware of her debt to fairy tales and to Dickens, Nesbit has Oswald defend the ending of his narrative: "That was a wonderful day. It was a treasure and no mistake . . . like things out of a fairy tale . . . ". And, "This ending is like what happens in Dickens's books; but I think it was jollier to happen like a book, and it shows what a nice man uncle is. . . . Besides I can't help it if it is like Dickens because it happens this way. Real life is often something like books".

Oswald might well have added that in any event, he needed the over-arching fairy-tale structure to unify the disparate episodes of the narrative. An even more significant unifying element is the presence of the "implied" author, who is vibrantly present through the voice of Oswald Bastable. Just as Mark Twain's use of Huck Finn as narrator enables him to create dramatic irony, a tension between the narrator and the tale being told, so Oswald as narrator permits Nesbit not only to create a more convincing rendering of childhood experience, but also to discover her own voice as a children's author.

Oswald as narrator in Nesbit's first classic for children functions to alleviate a difficulty often present in children's books—the split between the adult writer and the child reader, as well as the split between the adult narrator and the child character. Nesbit speaks to the child reader and makes her authorial presence manifest in the tension between Oswald as narrator and the story he tells. Nesbit often wants the reader to know more than Oswald knows; yet she does not wish to turn too much irony against her narrator. And in some important ways, Oswald as narrator does represent Nesbit herself.

Just as Nesbit was at the time of composing *The Story of the Treasure Seekers* a novice author for children, so Oswald portrays himself as new to the craft of writing fiction. Nesbit dramatizes Oswald throughout the Bastable stories in the process of discovering his technique. Like Nesbit, Oswald is not interested in presenting dreary daily routine. As he confidently assures his readers, "The best part of books is when things are happening. That is the best part of real things too". Oswald's principle literary advisor, Albert's uncle (a writer himself) affirms that Oswald's practice here is sound, "Quite right. That's what we [writers] call selection, a necessity of true art".

Oswald reflects a self-conscious awareness that he is writing for children and remarks, "I have often thought that if the people who write books for children, knew a little more, it would be better. I shall not tell you anything about us except that I should like to know if I was reading the story and you were writing it". Throughout the Bastable stories, Oswald continues to display his awareness of making rhetorical choices and of experimenting with narrative technique, a device which seems to reveal Nesbit's own awareness that she is also making choices as she experiments with writing her first significant book for children. Oswald as narrator and as novice writer thus allows Nesbit to draw a sharp distinction between the kind of children's book she is writing and more conventional Victorian children's books.

Wayne Booth has argued that an author may speak to a reader by creating a center-of-consciousness in a novel. One important way that Nesbit addresses her child audience is through her child narrator; his language and his ways of knowing issue from Nesbit's vivid memory of her own childhood experience, but they are nevertheless shaped and created by the adult author. Oswald's narration allows Nesbit not only to present the facts, set the scene, and control the reader's expectations, but also to manipulate mood; she can create a lighter comic mood, even when she presents such serious, even painfully sad, family problems as the death of the mother and the father's severe financial difficulties.

At other places in the narrative Nesbit makes her authorial presence known through the distance between what Oswald knows and the significance of what he narrates. Nesbit gently deflates Oswald, for example, by allowing him to give away the identity of the narrator long before he thinks he has revealed the secret. Also, in the episode, "Digging for Treasure," the reader knows that Albert's uncle has dropped the coins into the garden, though Oswald does not. The device of the child narrator thus permits Nesbit to narrate the scene without appearing to condescend either to the child reader or her own child characters. Similarly, at the end of *The Story of the Treasure Seekers* the reader perceives that the "poor Indian uncle" is in fact wealthy, though Oswald does not guess. Thus Nesbit as implied author assures the child reader that all will at last be well with the Bastables.

Nor does Nesbit always share Oswald's views of the other Bastable children. Oswald often puffs and glorifies himself at the expense of others. He is particularly hard on his older sister, Dora, whom he resents because she is apt to talk "like the good elder sister in books" and often reminds her brothers and sister that they are about to embark upon an adventure which is wrong. Oswald is astonished when Dora breaks down, cries, and admits that she had promised her dying mother to care for the others. The reader and the implied author, however, are not surprised at this revelation; they have known Dora far better than Oswald has, even though he is telling the story.

Oswald, then, plays a double role in Nesbit's Bastable stories—as dramatized narrator and as dramatized author. Nesbit shows him making such rhetorical choices as selection of detail and diction. As Nesbit's own rhetorical device, Oswald-as-narrator molds the child reader's beliefs by endorsing the childhood values of honesty, courage, and imagination, and reprehending excessive piety, sneakiness, lying and lack of imagination. Oswald's narration allows Nesbit to maintain a holiday mood throughout *The Story of the Treasure Seekers.* When too much pain or danger threatens to intrude and to shatter this atmosphere, Oswald refuses to talk further about it. His self-consciousness as novice author, particularly his awareness of what kind of story will please a child reader, undoubtedly reflects Nesbit's awareness that she too is writing for a new audience. Even so, the authorial presence is evident in *The Story of the Treasure Seekers* when Nesbit subjects Oswald to gentle irony.

Oswald has commented that life is often "something like books," and indeed most of the Bastables' adventures are "something like books," since the children incorporate the language and conventions of books into their play, and even feel sorry for Albert-next-door because he has not read much and therefore does not know how to play. The Bastables have read the books and know how to play; what is more,

they are given the freedom to exercise their imaginations to the fullest because of their circumstances.

Like Harry and Laura Graham of Catherine Sinclair's *Holiday House* (1839), and Mark Twain's Tom Sawyer, the Bastables enjoy much freedom from adult supervision. Too poor to go to school, the children appear free as well from adult institutions. They live in a safe community, so they can go on picnics, go exploring, and even ride into the city on the train by themselves. Although their house in Lewisham has grown shabby, the Bastables nevertheless preside regally in their own nursery, establish their own rules (the Bastable code of honor), and generally remain free of adult intrusion. The Bastables get into trouble, not through real naughtiness, but through excess exuberance and inventiveness. They never intend to do wrong, and when they do, they are quick to "own-up."

Since they do not go to school, the Bastables often invent their own games, usually based upon the books they have read. In *The Story of the Treasure Seekers,* games and adventures pass from the realm of make-believe into comically catastrophic reality because of the Bastables' urgent financial need. Given their circumstances, the children's exceptional freedom is credible, since their father is simply too preoccupied with business and worry to watch over them.

In any event, Nesbit is interested in revealing the social interaction among children at play, on holiday, and unconstrained by adult presence. In *The Wouldbegoods,* Oswald explains that he and his siblings were not neglected, that they often had very good times with adults:

> In some ways the good times you have with grown ups are better than the ones you have by yourselves. At any rate they are safer. . . . But these secure pleasures are not so interesting to tell about as the things you do when there is no one to stop you on the edge of a rash act. It is curious, too, that many of our most interesting games happened when the grown-ups were all away.

In the interest of telling a good story, Oswald (and Nesbit) choose to tell about holiday adventures. This convention of literary childhood, which Nesbit helped to create, depends, however, upon the presence of a secure family. Children genuinely neglected must confront painful abandonment and isolation, not the joyous liberation to play and to imagine in a world of their own, which is nevertheless sponsored by caring adults.

Just as this myth of literary childhood in *The Story of the Treasure Seekers* depends upon a secure family or guardian, so it seems also to require a sense of home, a secure and stable place as a shelter to the imagination. Nesbit was keenly aware of the importance of the material world in shaping the minds and imaginations of children. As Noel Streatfeild has remarked, Nesbit is always careful to give her child characters a specifically described house. Hence in the Bastable tales, the "semi-detached house in Lewisham," the "Moat House," and "the Red House" all receive much attention. They are the centers from which the children may venture out and to which they may safely return.

In the sketches Nesbit wrote about her own childhood, her mother usually rescued her from the cruelties of adult institutions. Likewise, benevolent adults, usually Albert's uncle, rescue the Bastables when they encounter situations too difficult for them to master themselves. For example, the Bastables invent clever ways to restore their fallen fortunes, but providing economic security for the family is finally too much for them. Only an adult can provide for such extensive material needs.

While adults may rescue children and sympathize with them, Nesbit believed that childhood was profoundly separate from adulthood. In her study of childhood, *Wings and the Child,* she explains this conviction:

> There is a freemasonry between children, a spontaneous confidence and give-and-take which is and must be forever impossible between children and grown-ups, no matter how sympathetic the grown-up, how confiding the child. Between the child and the grown-up there is a great gulf fixed, and this gulf, the gulf between one generation and the next, can never really be bridged.

Because of this gulf Nesbit believed that adults could only sympathize with children by remembering their own childhood experience. Nesbit further distinguishes between two kinds of adults: those who have forgotten what it is to be a child and those who remember. In *The Story of the Treasure Seekers,* most of the adults have forgotten. The children's father clearly loves them, but in his conversations with them, Mr. Bastable is always the grown-up speaking to children. Albert's uncle, however, possesses the capacity to reach across the gulf between himself and the children, as does the Bastables' "Indian uncle," who knows well enough that the way to enjoy an otherwise unsavory pudding is to pretend that it is a wild boar.

Albert's uncle also possesses a vivid imagination, which puts him in touch with his own childhood and hence with the children. Oswald explains the quality in *The Story of the Treasure Seekers:* "That's one thing I like Albert's uncle for. He always talks like a book, and yet you can always understand what he means. I think he is more like us, inside of his mind than most grown-up people are. He can pretend beautifully . . ."

In *The Story of the Treasure Seekers,* then, books become a mode by which adults and children may understand one another. Nesbit suggests that books may help to foster a genuine community in which humanistic sympathy may occur. As Oswald remarks in *The Wouldbegoods,* "I always like people who know the same songs we do, and books and tunes and things". Thus the most famous woman poet of her day, Mrs. Leslie (clearly modeled on Nesbit herself), is immediately attracted to Oswald and Nöel on the train, when she hears them shout, "Good Hunting!" from Kipling's *The Jungle Books.* After giving the boys a few shillings and learning that they intend to try to sell Nöel's poetry to a newspaper, she suggests that they use her name in the interview. Books are not only a way to make new friends, but also to establish important literary contacts.

Though not all of the adults in the Bastable stories possess the keen sense of childhood that Albert's uncle and Mrs. Leslie do, critics have rightly commented that Nesbit rarely creates a truly unsympathetic adult or child character. Through forthrightness and good manners, Oswald can usually reach a seemingly unapproachable adult. And when he fails, Alice usually succeeds. When Oswald unwittingly disturbs the privacy of the young ladies next door in *The Story of the Treasure Seekers,* he apologizes in so open and honest a manner that he wins not only the young ladies' forgiveness, but also their admiration. Likewise, when Lord Tottenham determines to take Nöel and Oswald before the magistrate, Alice successfully beseeches him to reconsider. Finally Nesbit implies that adults fail to respond to children because they are preoccupied, not because they are truly cruel or unsympathetic.

Now and again, however, Nesbit does create an adult clearly frozen into an alienated attitude towards children. The "Murdstone" aunt in *The Wouldbegoods* and the dour clergyman in *The Story of the Treasure Seekers* are telling examples. Oswald can quickly and accurately judge the character of an adult by the books they prefer and the foods they prepare.

Of the "Murdstone" aunt, Oswald remarks scornfully, "I don't suppose she has ever read anything but *Markham's History* and *Mangnall's Questins*" (*The Wouldbegoods*).

Nesbit's subversively anarchic spirit and her deep suspicion of social institutions are expressed in the Bastables rebellion against adult institutions. The most sympathetic adults in the Bastable stories are writers. The least sympathetic adults are associated with bureaucracy: the clergyman and Lord Tottenham, M.P., in *The Story of the Treasure Seekers,* and the rude policeman and sour missionary in *The Wouldbegoods.* Association with bureaucracy, Nesbit implies, may cause adults to forget what it is to think, feel, and imagine as children and hence, to lose a vital part of themselves.

In *The Story of the Treasure Seekers* the community of childhood remains undisturbed. The children are perpetually on holiday, and the book ends with the joyous Christmas gathering at the Bastables' "Indian uncle's" mansion. Painful events are kept at a distance. In *The Wouldbegoods* and *The New Treasure Seekers,* Nesbit indicates that the community is about to be broken. The children, for one important thing, have entered school. Being rescued by the Indian uncle means that the children must leave the amiable freedom of the shabby house in Lewisham and move into a complex mansion, where they inevitably encounter servants who say, "No." The holiday, make-believe world of *The Story of the Treasure Seekers* begins to fade. Oswald comments in *The Wouldbegoods,* "Then Midsummer holiday came, and we breathed again—but only a few days. We began to feel as if we had forgotten something and did not know what it was".

In the latter two volumes of the Bastable tales, the children become much more concerned about social and conventional morality and less able to follow their own natural impulses. At the end of *The Wouldbegoods,* Oswald and the other Bastables realize that Albert's uncle's impending marriage will necessarily change their easy relationship with him, that he is moving into a grown-up way of life. Oswald sadly admits that even he feels grown-upness creeping up on him. In the final volume, this sense that the childhood world must inevitably yield to the demands and constraints of the adult world becomes yet more pronounced. *The Story of the Treasure Seekers* is a better book than the other Bastable books at least in part because this sense of nostalgia for a lost childhood has not yet crept into the narrative.

The final volume of the Bastable stories marks the end of Oswald's writing career, as he stands poised and ready to leap from childhood into weary grown-upness; but it was just the beginning for E. Nesbit. In the Bastable stories, she had discovered, or more precisely, rediscovered, childhood and its power as an imaginative source for her writing. She had recaptured the language of childhood with its own special ways of seeing, feeling, and knowing the world. She had discovered some important features which were to reappear later in her great books for children—a family of children set free from the supervision of adults, and the blending of the structures and themes of fairy tales with those of realistic fiction. She had experimented with a dramatized narrator, and apparently felt confident enough to abandon the device in subsequent books.

U. C. Knoepflmacher

SOURCE: "Of Babylands and Babylons: E. Nesbit and the Reclamation of the Fairy Tale," in *Tulsa Studies in Women's Literature,* Vol. 6, No. 2, Fall, 1987, pp. 299-325.

> How many miles to Babylon?
>   Three score and ten!
> Can I get there by candlelight?
>   Yes, and back again![1]

Children's fairy tales resulted from the male usurpation of a female country. When writer-collectors such as Perrault and the brothers Grimm chose to establish an imaginative realm for the benefit of that new species "Children," they resorted to folk-tales that had once been the pre-eminent possession of women story-tellers. Though acknowledging the origins of these tales, male writers also palmed off as their own the imaginative powers they had appropriated. Charles Perrault may admit to having borrowed his materials from *contes de vieilles* told by his son's nurse; Jakob and Wilhelm Grimm may even be lavish in crediting informants such as Dorothea Viehmann, the *Märchenfrau.* But their very attraction to a quasi-maternal source seems to compel these writers to de-feminize many of the stories they had impounded, often going even so far, as Ruth Bottigheimer has convincingly shown, as to silence the voices of their female protagonists.[2]

Yet, even when enlisted to serve a male ideology, the traditional fairy tale inevitably manages to retain its female terrain. Whether a story empowers the disenfranchised female or whether it constricts her yearning for a wider sphere of action ultimately matters less than the story's fluid traffic between gender-spheres. The traffic depicted in "Cinderella" and "The Fisherman's Wife" moves in exactly opposite directions. Cinderella's progress from hearth to palace becomes a paradigm for many a woman writer eager to counteract her own marginalization. On the other hand, the story of the fisherman's wife (which Virginia Woolf placed at the center of *To The Lighthouse*) denies this desire for expansion by transporting its heroine back to the confines of the hearth. Still, whether the emphasis falls on dilation or on contraction, the female wish to obtain power is spatially rendered as the restoration of a domain of her own. And by dramatizing that wish the fairy tale always contains imbedded within it an implicit response to the male appropriators of its outer husk. It thus not only counters a Perrault or the Grimms but also those fantasists who, like Lewis Carroll and George MacDonald, devised fairy-tale-like structures in order to feed on the energies of an Alice, a Sylvie, or a mighty North Wind.

Indeed, when Lewis Carroll, in his prefatory poem to *Alice in Wonderland,* casts Alice Liddell as the most influential of the "cruel Three" who steer his story-teller's boat, he is calling attention to the very etymology of the genre to which his own "poor voice" has contributed. The English words *fairy* and *fay,* like the French *fée* and the Spanish *hada,* are all derived from the Latin *fata,* or Fates. Thus, as Andrew Lang noted at the end of the nineteenth century, the *Fées* were the latter-day equivalent of the Greek *Morai* or Roman *Parcae,* weavers and spinners, the Weird Sisters. The fairies who foretold the fate of children were cast as prophetesses with portentous powers. And these powers were those of language, something that E. B. White remembered in our own century when he chose a female weaver called Charlotte, "a true friend and a good writer," to preserve the life of a male pig. Charlotte greets Wilbur with the world "Salutations." Her Latinism helps us recall that the Latin *fata* is derived from the word *fari,* to speak.

Yet, at the very same time that their male counterparts adopted the mode of the fairy tale, women writers spoke out against it. Given the provenance of the form, it seems surprising to find so many influential female authors of the late eighteenth and early nineteenth centuries proclaim their emphatic objections to returning to a country once essentially their own. Not only the oft-cited Mrs. Barbauld and Mrs. Trimmer expressed their opposition to fantasy, but even a

writer as inventive as Maria Edgeworth voiced her fervent hope "that the magic of Dr. Johnson's name will not have the power to restore the reign of fairies." Citing Johnson's contention that "babies" should not merely "hear stories of babies like themselves" but rather have "their imaginations raised by tales of giants and fairies, and castles and enchantments," Edgeworth challenged "his authority" as forcefully as possible:

> The fact remains to be proved: but supposing that [children] do prefer such tales, is this a reason why they should be indulged in reading them? It may be said that a little experience in life would soon convince them, that fairies, giants, and enchanters are not to be met with in the world. But why should the mind be filled with fantastic visions, instead of useful knowledge? Why should so much valuable time be lost? Why should we vitiate their taste, and spoil their appetite, by suffering them to feed upon sweetmeats?[3]

Edgeworth's rationalist and utilitarian position continued to be maintained even by those Victorian women writers who guardedly reintroduced the supernatural into their tales for children. Thus, despite its title, a story like Mrs. Gatty's 1851 "The Fairy Godmothers" still valorizes the Governess or "mentoria" figure whom Mitzi Myers rightly places at the center of the "resilient and purposeful maternal discourse" that runs from Sarah Fielding through Mary Wollstonecraft to Mrs. Sherwood.[4] In Mrs. Gatty's handling, the Governess carries a far greater authority than the Fairy, whose "unlucky" interest in a girl called Aurora has led that child to assume that she could somehow grow up unencumbered. The Governess, who "had just been reading the old French fairy tales of 'Les Fées'" with her ward, swiftly rebukes Aurora for wishing that her Fairy Godmother might have given her at birth "the gift of growing up to be a young lady very quick, and of learning everything without any trouble at all." Such a desire for ready-made powers, the Governess holds, is unnatural. Moreover, it is impossible. Fairies can not help their godchildren bypass the limits and constraints placed on all of human life. The Governess therefore insists on the essential impotence of such magical agents: "Fairies have no power to counteract what God has ordained; and He has ordained that we enjoy but little what we get at without labour and trouble."[5]

Although, as the century proceeded, women gradually began to reclaim the wonderlands appropriated by the male writers of fairy tales, their attitude towards the genre continued to be guarded. Writers such as Jean Ingelow, Juliana Horatia Ewing (Mrs. Gatty's daughter), and Christina Rossetti introduced alluring dreamscapes and fairylands into their prose stories for children. At the same time, however, these domains are presented as dangerously anarchic, at odds with restraints that male imaginations might evade with impunity but that women must recognize as binding. The fantasies of these and similar late-Victorian authors who still acted as Christian "mentorias"—Mrs. Molesworth and Mrs. Mulock, for example—may involve a transportation into exotic herlands that release a dormant female imagination, but the final emphasis falls on the safety of the quotidian. The child-voyager (often a female dreamer, like Carroll's Alice) must return chastened to take her place in the everyday world. Fantasy thus serves an ideology that remains essentially anti-fantastic.[6]

E. Nesbit is occasionally regarded as the first woman writer of children's books able to free herself from the realistic conventions that had still bound fantasists like Ewing, Molesworth, and Mulock.[7] On the surface, E. Nesbit appears to be a "New Woman," far removed from her more strait-laced Victorian sisters: in 1880, she defied conventionality by being seven months pregnant when she married Hubert Bland, a womanizer who later regaled her with two children whom she nurtured along with her own, though they were born to another woman; she helped found the Fabian Society; she supported other radical causes and esoteric cults such as the theosophy espoused by Madame Blavatsky and Annie Besant. And yet, as a closer look at "Daisy" Nesbit's early life suggests, she was shaped by forces that made her as susceptible to various sorts of colonization by men as Mary Ann Evans had been, several decades earlier, before she became George Eliot. Nesbit's fiction for children, therefore, much like Eliot's fiction for adults, neither radically challenges a patriarchal order nor sharply departs from the more pronounced moralism of earlier nineteenth-century women writers. Her powerful comic imagination, always enlisted in the service of a social superego, relies on irony to thwart immature child-wishes. *Five Children and It* (1902), a book in which such child-wishes result in a series of comic mishaps, and its much more ambitious sequel, *The Story of the Amulet* (1906), to be examined closely later in this essay, thus bear a decided family resemblance to such paler works as Molesworth's *The Cuckoo Clock* and *The Tapestry Room*, from which, as Roger Lancelyn Green has noticed, Nesbit borrowed her own substitute for a fairy, the deliciously grumpy Psammead.[8]

Nesbit, then, is hardly as different from her Victorian peers as she might seem.[9] She, too, remains an anti-fantastic fantasist who derives much of her power from her ambivalence about the female imagination she sets out to reappropriate. Yet, in one significant respect, Nesbit does differ from the "mentorias" before her. Her resistance to the magical realms she domesticates and controls through irony does not stem from the moral inhibitions that had weighed so heavily with earlier women writers. If their incursions into fairylands terrified them because they released pleasurable wishes at odds with the moral order they had agreed to uphold as "the real," her own flights of fancy raised more personal fears about abandonment and dissolution. These fears were rooted in the traumas of an early childhood that she dramatically revived in **"My School-Days,"** the twelve-part series of autobiographical vignettes she published in *The Girl's Own Paper,* from October 1896 to September 1897, just before her first major success as a children's author with *The Treasure Seekers* (1899).

"My School-Days" opens with the narrator's act of relation not just to the child she once was but to all children: her words, she explains, are written "not because I have anything strange to relate" but "the other reason rather—that I was a child as other children, that my memories are their memories, as my hopes were their hopes, my dreams their dreams, my fears their fears."[10] The identity of the extraordinary child who will emerge from her narrative, she therefore insists, is not at all special but wholly representative. Sincere and yet also disingenuous, her plea helps to explain an important feature of *The Story of the Amulet.* It is no coincidence that the child-voyagers in that book (and in its immediate two predecessors, *Five Children and It* and *The Phoenix and the Carpet* [1904]), should form a group of four, composed of two boys and two girls, rather than the singular child or complementary girl/boy pair who embark on strange voyages in other Victorian books of fantasy.

E. Nesbit always sought her identity in groups, whether in units formed by children, parents-and-children, or Fabian Socialists. As a six-year-old, the youngest of the four surviving Nesbit children, she joined her two older brothers in an abortive attempt to run away from her mother's home after the death of their educator-father.[11] Thereafter, even when she rebelled, she needed to feel part of a family, though it was one made up of her philandering husband's illegitimate children. As **"My School-Days"** indirectly demonstrates, Nesbit was forced to replenish the vacuum left by her father's death and by her mother's subsequent blindness to the emotional needs of the younger children whom she shuffled to different boarding schools. Just as George Eliot's art bears the traces of a mother's emotional neglect, so Nesbit's imaginative writings for children spring from her "most clear and vivid recollection" of the marks left on her psyche by her mother's repeated "travel and change of scene."[12] For only by sharing this "book of memory" with her can we also come to understand the ambivalence that marked her reclamation of the province of the fairy tale.

I

Doris Langley Moore, who mined **"My School-Days"** for important factual information in the early chapters of her biography of E. Nesbit, finds the vignettes "rambling and disorganized." And it is true that Nesbit soon veers away from the ostensible subject of her education to what Moore calls "the much more congenial subject of her wanderings" in a narrative that itself strays from the chronology the narrator professes to be following.[13] Yet it is precisely this free-associating vein that makes **"My School-Days"** so rewarding a text. Though, as a biographer rather than textual critic, Moore is content to reproduce materials that demand considerable interpretation, she shrewdly senses that the memories Nesbit tried to master, the events she selected, "the dialogues with her brothers she had reconstructed," even the personal and familiar tone she had adopted, would all lead directly into her subsequent fairy tales for children.[14]

Besides the portrait of the impressionable and precocious "Daisy" Nesbit whose acute terrors and yearnings **"My School-Days"** so powerfully evokes, the series yields two other constants: a delineation of the various physical settings into which the child is transported and an account of the appearances and disappearances of a mother who seems distant even when she occasionally shares the same setting. In the very first installment, the mother never understands her daughter's seemingly irrational aversion to a "Stuart plaid frock" the child is asked to wear. She does not know that Daisy has come to associate the skirt with the attire of a hated tormentor, an older girl who "tortured me unremittingly" in the very first school to which her mother had sent her. The despised frock is finally torn when it cushions the bold little Eve's fall off an "apple-tree." Having "saved my life at the expense of its own," it can now be further rent into

pieces as Daisy celebrates "its internment in the rag-bag." The mother remains oblivious. She is privy neither to the miseries suffered at school nor to the joys the erstwhile "prisoner" experiences on burying the frock. (As in Nesbit's later fantasies, images of imprisonment and of burial-places abound throughout the series.)

The first installment thus ends on an important note of dissociation: Stuart plaid frocks will always hold a special meaning that a mother who failed to inform herself of her child's denigration will never be allowed to penetrate. The account ends with an attempt to minimize the estrangement that has been exposed. That gap, however, will only widen in the subsequent installments. As the child continues to be removed, the mother in whom she had wished to confide is identified as the prime agent of her ostracism. In the first installment, while still at the nearby boarding school, Daisy periodically manages to pass by "our own house, where always someone might be at the window, and never any one was." Her disappointment explains why, in retaliation, she must exclude the figure she had yearned for:

> I have often wondered what it is that keeps children from telling their mothers these things—and even now I don't know. I only know I might have been saved many of these little-big troubles if I had only been able to explain. But I wasn't; and to this day my mother does not know how and why I hated that Stuart plaid frock.[15]

The reader is allowed to see more in this cautious summation than the narrator is willing to disclose. Like the fetish doll on whom George Eliot's Maggie Tulliver vents her forbidden anger at adults, the frock that is rent into pieces acts as an outlet for the child's resentment. Precisely because the mother never knows that she unwittingly asked her daughter to wear a garment that the child came to identify with maternal absenteeism, Daisy finds a measure of compensation by clinging to a private space of her own. In the eleven installments that follow, this imaginative space will either adapt itself to the contours of those settings that Daisy can gratefully share with figures more nurturant than her mother—her brothers, for instance; a kindly boy-waiter; an equally kindly colleague of her father's; the truly maternal Madame Lourdes and her daughter Mimi—or it will be peopled by terrifying figures of ghosts, skins, mummies, and the specter—formed by "a big black bonnet and a hideous mask"—of an "old woman" that "haunted my dreams for years—haunts them still indeed" (IV, 264).

The same pattern that shapes the first installment recurs in what is surely the most gruesome of the emotional experiences presented in **"My School-Days,"** the encounter with the mummies of Bordeaux, promised in Part IV, yet delayed by a series of flash-backs recounting earlier terrors of night-lights, imagined skeletons, a two-headed calf (stuffed), and the "black skin of an emu" (IV, 264). Yet in Part V, when the memory of the mummies is finally confronted, this "crowning horror of my childish life," so much more damaging than the hateful plaid skirt, again proves to be something the child cannot share with her mother. The terrifying memory, she confides in her last paragraph, could be "banished" only after she herself became a mother and firmly resolved that her own children "should never know such fear." Yet if her "babies, thank God, never have known" that secret terror, nor did her mother: "It was a dark cloud that overshadowed my childhood, and I don't believe my mother ever knew how dark it was, for I could not tell anyone the full horror of it while it was over me; and when it had passed I came from under it, as one who has lived long years in an enchanter's castle, where the sun is darkened always, might come forth into the splendour of noontide" (V, 314).

Still, in this episode, the child's inability to share "the full horror" with her mother stems from reasons very different from those leading to her earlier secrecy in the matter of the plaid frock. In the earlier event, the act of exclusion became an exercise of power that allowed her to retaliate against the parent who had excluded her. In this instance, however, the encounter with the desiccated bodies of "about two hundred" men, women, and children unleashes a sardonic mockery of the expectations of the trusting child—the child who had asked her equally naive sisters to take her to "see the mummies" because, as the narrator explains at the outset, "To me the name of a mummy was as a friend's name" (V, 313). Why should the little girl, tired of the "strange babble of foreign tongues," somehow have associated a mummy with "home"? The answer she provides seems disarmingly suited to the innocent mini-tourist: "I longed to see them as I longed to see home," she confides, because she hoped to be reminded of their cousins in the British Museum, back "in dear, dear England," where they had been safely encased in well-lit corridors, protected by "kindly curators" (such as the Egyptologist Dr. Wallis Budge, to whom Nesbit would later dedicate *The Story of the Amulet*). But the girl's "vision of dry boards and white light and glass cases" vanishes as soon as she descends into the musty catacombs. There, a grotesque array of

skeletons in varying states of decomposition "seemed to reach towards me," while nearest to the exit through which she flees she is forced to behold "the dried body of a little child hung up by its hair" (IV, 313, 314).

It is her obvious identification with that discarded child that leads us to share Daisy's need for comforting by a "mummy" we expect to be reassuring and loving. Yet the mother who allowed her girls, unaccompanied, to go on this ghastly expedition still fails to intervene. In the paragraph that follows the description of Daisy's staggering flight away from "those charnel-house faces," we find her all by herself in a cavernous hotel room waiting for her dinner: "for my mother did not approve of late dinners for little people, and I was accustomed to have my bread-and-milk alone while she and my sisters supped" (V, 314). A moving curtain, a sudden noise startle the screaming child, and she rushes into the outstretched arms of "a young waiter, hardly more than a boy," whose familiar face she gratefully recognizes. He now proceeds to soothe her, even though, like the maternal surrogate celebrated in the next installment, Madame Lourdes, he "spoke no English and I no French." Significantly enough, the waiter assumes the role apparently never discharged by the mother, who continues to sup with an obliviousness that allows her child's fright to go as "unnoticed" as before:

> I hope he did not get into any trouble that night for neglected duties, for he did not attempt to leave me till my mother came back. He sat me down on his knee and petted me and sang to me under his breath, and fed me with the bread and milk, when by-and-by I grew calm enough to take it. All good things be with him wherever he is! . . . I like to believe that now he has little children of his own, who hold out their arms when he opens the doors, and who climb upon his knees clamouring for those same songs which he sang, out of the kindness of his boyish heart, to the little frightened English child, such a long, long time ago.

Yet for all his willingness to remove Daisy's fear this male nurturer cannot be told the causes of that fear. The horror at what had seemed a "friend's name," the dissolution of a familiar "home" into an unfamiliar charnel-house, where dried children can hang by their hair, must be kept private until at last aired in print.

The twelve vignettes of **"My School-Days"** try to overturn the process of defamiliarization Edith Nesbit experienced as a child. By repositioning the remembering adult among the now familiar settings of her childhood past, these sketches can control the past and overcome its traumas. Simultaneously, however, **"My School-Days"** tries to replace the mother, whose absence is so repeatedly stressed, with other surrogates, whose interaction with Daisy is gratefully remembered. The boy-waiter must be awarded an imaginary family "of his own," because Nesbit, now a mother herself, needs to believe in the primal fusion denied to her as a child. In this sense, **"My School-Days"** also constitutes an attempt to regain the mother and, thus, to vanquish the fear of the chasm left by her removal, a chasm that the child's mind can only fill with similarly dissolving substitutes—a frock interred in a rag-bag, a mummy whose drying skin has drawn itself back from "gleaming teeth and empty eye-sockets" (V, 314), the moldering feathers of an emu, or, at the very end of the series, the rotting pelt of a fox killed and skinned by Daisy's fellow-outcast, her brother Alfred, whom she joins in secretly burying the skin "beside the body it had covered" (XII, 788).

Nesbit finds it easier to come to terms with these alien settings than with the mother, to whom, in the next-to-last installment, she still writes "a frantic letter . . . begging her to take me away" (XI, 711). On only one occasion can the mother remove some fears Daisy feels far more intensely than her older sisters; but even then this protectress makes "light of the adventure" (VIII, 534). Finally, however, the mother, whose whereabouts are usually mysterious, allows the children to settle, first in a French countryhouse, and, later, in Kent. Though no longer absent, she continues to maintain her aloofness. Still, a maternal neglect is now regarded as beneficial, for it allows Daisy and her brothers "to run wild" in a pastoral world sentimentalized in the last installments (X, 635). The garden plots celebrated in those last sketches thus achieve the solace the mother failed to produce. The hyper-imaginative child, who, much earlier, had come perilously close to a nervous breakdown (III, 184), is now conducted by her brothers into "a network of lanes, fringed with maiden-hair," which lead her "away into fairyland" (IX, 575).

Still, therapeutic as they turn out to be, the idealized gardens at the end of **"My School-Days"** dull the over-active imagination the reader finds so compelling. The closure seems forced. For in her sentimental paean to the "Kentish home, dearer to me than all," Nesbit tries to effect a double reconciliation that remains unconvincing. This final setting is meant to displace all the earlier ones through which the child had been hurried. And, since it is supposed to erase all memories of the discomforts caused by her abandonment, it is also meant to act as an emblem of a long-delayed fusion with her mother. The narrator, who had informed us, a few paragraphs before, that at the age of fifteen she "ventured to show some verses to my mother," now chooses to cap her twelve-part reminiscences by shifting from prose into a lyric celebration of a recovered Eden, better far:

> There is a grey-walled garden far away
> From noise and smoke of cities where the hours
> Pass with soft wings among the happy flowers
> And lovely leisure blossoms every day.

It was with mawkish verses such as these (and with delicate water-colors of flowers and garden-plots) that the young Mrs. Bland tried at first to support her husband and herself. The poem that concludes **"My School-Days"** may even be the one a fifteen-year-old had actually presented to her mother. But even if it is not, this attempted return to a coveted plot of ground seems to foreclose the imaginative energies so powerfully released in the earlier sketches. The "pleasant fields of memory" that the writer now superimposed on her itinerant past seem as arbitrary as the "daisied fields" that George Eliot invoked for the wandering Maggie Tulliver at the end of *The Mill on the Floss.* George Eliot, however, could detach herself in her subsequent fictions from the unsatisfied childhood self she called Maggie. E. Nesbit, on the other hand, would continue to explore her anger, fear, and flight in books addressed to child-readers whom she envisioned as replications of the resilient wanderer she had been herself. Fairyland was not to be found in garden-plots with flower beds. It had still to be reclaimed.

II

By the time she wrote *Five Children and It and The Story of the Amulet,* E. Nesbit had come to understand that such a process of reclamation demanded more than the flowery poems and animal tales she had produced in the 1890s before the composition of **"My School-Days."** Her authorial self-awareness, still in abeyance in collections with coy titles like *Sunny Tales for Snowy Days, Pussy Tales,* and *Doggy Tales,* now quickly sharpened. It came into its boldest relief with *Nine Unlikely Tales for Children* (1901). There, in a comic story like **"Fortunatus Rex & Co.,"** she not only wonderfully subverts the staples of the traditional fairy tale but also provides a self-mocking commentary on her own imaginative enterprise by thematizing a female impostor's magical recovery of a threatened girlhood world. Although **"Fortunatus Rex & Co."** appeared one year before *Five Children and It* and five years before *The Story of the Amulet,* it almost can be said to allegorize—albeit through caricature and indirection—what Nesbit undertook more overtly, in far greater detail, and with increasing seriousness, in her two longer books. We should therefore look at these two full-scale efforts first. For both *Five Children and It* and *The Story of the Amulet* must be read as defensive structures against the very fear of abandonment defused through reminiscence in **"My School-Days."**

Five Children and It opens in a setting similar to the one celebrated at the end of **"My School-Days"**: here, too, excited children are conducted by their mother to "a white house in a green garden and an orchard beyond."[16] But the mother who seems "in no hurry to get out" of the carriage that has brought them to this place is just as uneager to join them in a "first glorious rush round the garden and the orchard and the thorny, thistly, briery, brambly wilderness beyond the broken gate and the dry fountain" (p. 19). Moreover, she soon altogether deserts her four children and the male baby they call "the Lamb." Leaving them in the care of Martha the housekeeper, she rushes "away to stay with Granny, who was not very well" (p. 22).[17]

Although the mother will return in the last chapter of the book, the children's father remains even more numinous. Away on "business," he seems remembered mostly by the children as a purveyor of scientific knowledge, much as Nesbit's own father, John Collis Nesbit, a chemist and geologist, must have been recalled by the girl who was not yet four at the time of his death. It seems significant, therefore, that the father should be invoked by the daughter Anthea, as the four children set out to explore not the lush garden-wilderness celebrated in **"My School-Days"** as a feminine space of recovery, but rather the gravel-pit, which, like the chalk-quarry, also adjoins the house. When Cyril, the oldest boy, proposes that they take their spades to dig in the gravel-pit, which they can "pretend" to convert into the "seaside," Anthea reminds them that "Father said it was once" part of the sea itself: "he says there are shells there thousands of years old" (p. 23).

It is in this primordial gravel-pit that the children unearth the "It" of the book's title, the Psammead whose unreliable powers they try to tap both in this story and in its sequel. Discovered as soon as the mother has left, removed immediately upon her return, the

Psammead acts as a dubious parental substitute for both mother and father. If, like that more traditional surrogate, a fairy godmother, the Psammead has the power to grant wishes to powerless children, it does not regard them solicitously as its wards. Indeed, as soon as the children touch the fur of the still half-buried creature they unearth, it demands to be left alone. Throughout the story, it will treat them "coldly" and "crossly" (pp. 169, 153), "almost" snarl at them (p. 153) and even try to bite them (p. 212). Crosser and crosser in each of its appearances, it clearly prefers, as the children note, "its own company to theirs" (p. 212). Indeed, when only one of the children, Robert, comes to see it after the ill-fated adventure in which they had sprouted wings, the Psammead greets the boy with the undisguised hope that the others might have shared the fate of a Ninivite boy whose wings turned to stone at sunset: "Where are the rest of you? Not smashed themselves up with those wings, I hope?" (p. 120).

"The thing" or "it," as the Psammead is called before it volunteers its identity, is a composite creature in more ways than one (p. 27). A zoological amalgam, combining the features of snail, bat, spider, and monkey, it is neither distinctly feminine nor masculine. Just as the unit of two girls (Anthea and Jane) and two boys (Cyril and Robert) is referred to as an "it,"[18] so does this "It" seem to be an androgyne. In giving birth to wishes, it must swell and swell; yet its fear of water and all forms of moistness remove it from conventional femininity. The creature "sharply" explains that its name, Psammead, should indeed be Greek to children who do not know that the word *psammos* comes from the Greek name for sand: it is, "in plain English, then, a *Sand-fairy*" (p. 27). But the name Nesbit has concocted, which the children pronounce "Sammyadd," seems itself a strange hybrid. In either of its forms, it seems to combine the names of father ("pa," "dad") and mother ("ma," "mom," "mammy") with the notion of absence or death. This notion is reenforced by the Psammead's obsessive digging into the gravel-pit, which acts both as a grave-pit for marine life that once teemed in a "wet sea" and as the dry protective enclosure it needs to keep "alive" (pp. 24, 25).

"My School-Days" ended with the Nesbit children's burial of the rotting fox fur; the action of *Five Children and It* begins with the disinterment of a shape "covered with thick fur" (p. 27). Before uncovering the creature with "long rat-like whiskers," Robert assumes that it will be a pesky rodent: "father says they infest old places" (pp. 29, 25). The story is indeed designed to rid old places of troublesome infestations that might otherwise continue to gnaw away. Comical and engrossing in its grotesqueness, yet at the same time distinctly unpleasant, the Psammead represents an effort to defuse some of the unsettling associations that Nesbit had begun to unearth in **"My School-Days."** There, the parental void created by a dead father and a remote mother had also been invaded by animated "things" that needed to be dug up only to be buried again: the frayed frock, the decomposing mummies, the moldering feathers of an emu (a bird Robert curiously happens to recall just as the children start to dig in the gravel-pit).

The narrative of **"My School-Days"** presented the unfulfilled desires of a childhood self forced to seek some sort of replacement for a buried father and the mother who kept herself out of reach. In *Five Children and It,* both of these figures have become combined into the fantastic Psammead who wants to stay asleep by burrowing back into the ossified geological strata associated with a removed father and who, when awakened, responds to the children's demands much in the manner of a distancing mother by saying, "I'm tired of you" (p. 32). Still, as a magical creature, the Psammead cannot evade its role as a fulfiller of desire. He thus is obliged to grant, no matter how reluctantly, child-wishes denied to an unsated "Daisy" Nesbit. Why, then, are its powers so persistently misused?

Thwarted again and again in the outcome of the wishes so grudgingly granted to them, the children come to mistrust not only the Psammead itself (p. 65) but also their own unreliable desires. Like the protagonists of earlier didactic tales, they soon find wishfulness an untoward burden. It literally weighs them down. Not only do wished-for golden guineas disappear at sunset, but even when they first materialize, their weight makes them dangerous. When the Psammead fills the gravel-pit with coins, the younger two children treat the heaps of money as if they were the sand-piles into which the Psammead likes to burrow. As Robert "began to bury" Jane "as you bury your father in sand when you are at the sea side," she soon shrieks out in pain, "'Oh, stop, it's too heavy. It hurts!'" When he disregards her plea and goes on, Jane, "very white, and trembling a little," has to be lifted out by her older siblings: "'You've no idea what it's like,' said she; 'it's like stones on you—or like chains'" (p. 47). Although, like "Daisy" Nesbit, Jane is the youngest of the band of four, she will become the first to recognize the need for wishes more "useful" than wings, or castles, or Alice-like exten-

sions in size. Nonetheless, Jane's own naive wish in the book's last chapter proves to be the most troublesome of all. Her wish is more reality-oriented and more directly aimed at the mother whom the other three children found easier to forget.[19] But her desire to please her returning mother by rewarding her with the missing jewels of Lady Chittenden, a figure introduced earlier in the book as a child-hater, creates complications that can be resolved only by granting the Psammead its own desire to terminate its wish-giving activities.

Jane "dreamily" thinks it would be "jolly" for mother to find all the "lovely" jewels stolen from Lady Chittenden (p. 204). Her wish seems a natural, if naive, expression of a little girl's eagerness to please a parent who owns few ornaments beyond her engagement ring and a "little pearl brooch with great-grandpapa's hair in it" (p. 204). But the wish is also a bribe of sorts, an attempt to make the mother's return worth her undertaking. In this sense, Jane's wish recalls the first "private wish" of Anthea's and Jane's, "which they had never told the boys," articulated by Anthea in the opening chapter of the book: "I wish we were all as beautiful as the day" (p. 32). Jewels of extraordinary value and children of extraordinary beauty may cause a straying mother to want to stay at home. Yet, as the children realize, estrangement rather than a strengthened fusion results from both of the wishes that frame the book's structure of desire.

In the first instance, the desire for greater beauty, granted by the Psammead, proves immediately alienating: only by detecting a few still-familiar flaws in their unaltered attire (the hole in Jane's pinafore; Anthea's "dirty handkerchief")—flaws that, normally, would evoke an adult's censure—can the children themselves gradually manage to recognize each other. But they remain unfamiliar to all others. Their picture-card beauty only estranges them from the other family members. Baby still whimpers for "my Panty" even when Anthea, his "favourite sister," responds to his plea by holding her arms towards him, much as a mother would beckon her child (pp. 35, 34). And Martha the housekeeper, who so proudly invokes the authority of the "ma" she has been delegated to represent during the matriarch's absence, violently slams the door in the face of the children who have trudged home for their expected dinner. These most certainly are not "our children," Martha decides. To add insult to injury, she empties a jug of cold water on an especially foreign-looking Robert.

Maternal nurturance is not to be wasted on outsiders. Martha feeds the starving foursome only after they have recovered their familiar, "nice and ugly," features (p. 38).

The pleasure that Jane expects to produce by having the Psammead place Lady Chittenden's stolen jewelry on her mother's dressing table results in an alienation that seems far less remediable. Eight "loving arms" greet the "mummy darling" who holds Baby upon her long-delayed return. But when those eight arms clasp her in order to prevent her from entering her room, the mother is made to feel "as if she had only two children, one the Lamb and the other an octopus" (p. 206). And when truthful Jane tries to tell her mother that the jewelry was deposited there by "a Fairy," she is "sharply" reproved (p. 209), as is Martha, who had hoped to surprise her mistress with the news of her own impending betrothal. Instead, Martha now finds that her groom is unfairly suspected of being a burglar. The children assess the "awful" situation brought about by "that silly wish of Jane's" (p. 209). Separation, rather than the strengthened bonds they had expected—their family bonds and Martha's bond with a man they too have come to like—now seems inevitable. An "innocent man" is being accused of robbery; "mother and father" will themselves be implicated and "put into prison"; and, as the children of felons, Jane and Anthea and Robert and Cyril (and the Lamb, too) will all "be branded outcasts" (p. 211). Though childish and exaggerated, these fears are more intense than all their wishes put together. To allow the Psammead its own wish for a release from wish-giving thus strikes them as a small price to pay for a final restoration of the old order.

Oblivion becomes a cure. By making mother and Martha forget the whole incident of the stolen jewels and by having Lady Chittenden recover what "had not been lost at all," far greater losses can be averted (p. 215). The Psammead need no longer be awakened; it can return to enjoy "a good long sleep" (though it will be forced to reappear in *The Story of the Amulet*). It is last seen, burrowing back into unconsciousness, "scratching fiercely to the last, and the sand closed over it" (p. 214). Immediately upon its disappearance, "mother walked in, hot and dusty," sprinkled by some of the same sand perhaps that had provided the Psammead with its dusty cover. As Jane happily notes: "She doesn't remember" (p. 215). Just as Nesbit's mother was kept in the dark about feelings the child chose to conceal, so is this mother blind to a Psammead on whose dubious powers her children were forced to feed during her absence. As

in **"My School-Days,"** so, too, in *Five Children and It,* secrets are a form of retaliation. The children will not tell the mother who finds everything "so natural and pleasant" that the Baby she embraces had, earlier, been carted off by the child-scorning Lady Chittenden, transformed into a child-worshiper by the Psammead's unnatural magic. They are willing to share her conventional delight with "the flowery-boweryness of the house" and to allow her to replace an account of their fantastic adventures with trite anecdotes "about Granny, and Granny's pigeons, and Auntie Emma's lame donkey" (p. 206).

Even after their mother insists on protecting them against robbers they know to be non-existent, the children admire "the dashing and decided way" in which she takes control; somewhat pathetically, they think "how useful she would have been" in helping them escape "some of the tight places in which they had found themselves in consequence of their ill-timed wishes" (p. 210). But the figure who strikes them as "a born general" is more suspect than they are willing to allow. By awarding Lady Chittenden's jewels to a mother who has entrusted the safekeeping of the jewels who are her children to a servant, Nesbit creates an ironic sub-text that yokes the two women in ways unperceived both by the children in the story and by child-readers.

The children rightly distrust Lady Chittenden's infatuation with the Lamb, knowing it to be artificial and exaggerated. When the vapid lady vows to be overwhelmed by the "dear darling duck of a baby!" she had never before noticed, she asks Anthea: "Oh, I *should* so like to adopt it! Do you think its mother would mind?" (p. 73). Exhibiting her mother's own decisiveness, Anthea sharply retorts, "She'd mind very much indeed" (p. 73). And yet, both Lady Chittenden and the absent mother are pointedly contrasted to a female figure who is truly eager to nurture. That figure is a gipsy woman, Amelia, who has lost all of her own babies. (Nesbit suffered several miscarriages herself.) Whereas the other gipsies are attracted to the Lamb only by virtue of the same magic that endeared him to Lady Chittenden, Amelia continues to stare "affectionately" at the baby even after the magic has worn off. When she leans toward the Lamb, he "unexpectedly" offers no resistance but tenderly strokes her face:

> "Poor, poor!" said the Lamb. And he let the gipsy woman kiss him, and what is more, he kissed her brown cheeks in return—a very nice kiss, as all his kisses are, and not a wet one like some babies give. The gipsy woman moved her finger about

his forehead, as if she had been writing something there, and the same with his chest and his hands and his feet; then she said: "May he be brave, and have the strong head to think with, and the strong heart to love with, and the strong hands to work with, and the strong feet to travel with, and always come safe home to his own." Then she said something in a strange language no one could understand. (p. 84)

To Robert, the gipsy woman's behavior seems "silly"; Cyril finds it "rather decent," an expression Anthea changes to "very nice" and Jane further amends to "too frightfully nice for anything" (p. 85). But child-readers who might identify with any one of these escalating responses to the stranger's benediction would still miss Nesbit's double self-inscription. For Nesbit here becomes both the woman "writing something" for a child and that child itself. The author who dedicates her book to the infant John Bland, whom her prefatory poem addresses as "My Lamb," was willing to nurture this adopted child as if it had been her own. She thus displayed the feelings valued in Amelia but satirized in Lady Chittenden.

Yet, if the adult Nesbit cast herself as the blesser of another's child, she also recast her childhood self in the Lamb who responds so lovingly to a surrogate mother. She would intensify this primal desire, still unsatisfied in *Five Children and It,* in the book's sequel. There, Imogen, an abandoned modern child, can find a mother only by being transplanted into a different historical era, while Anthea, Jane, Robert, and Cyril, separated from both Mother and Lamb, must rely on more than a Psammead to recover their own threatened family unit.

In *Five Children and It,* however, Nesbit still feels compelled to undercut the desire for union glimpsed briefly in the short-lived symbiosis between Amelia and the Lamb. Only by placing severe restrictions on the very wishfulness that propels her book can Nesbit come to terms with her own lack of satiety as a child. Although her narrator often sides with her child-readers against the unimaginative strictures imposed by adults, she is also Psammead-like in derogating child-wishes repeatedly shown to be most futile and "very foolish" (p. 88). If the cross and sleepy Psammead wants above all to be left alone, the narrator, too, has little patience with a juvenile readership whose expectations and tastes in fiction (especially boys' adventure stories) she impishly mocks. Siding with neither adult nor child, the narrator thus maintains her distance from both the grown-ups satirized in the story and from the children whose

hunger she needs to exorcise. That hunger would at last be fully acknowledged in *The Story of the Amulet.* Although the narrator's ironic voice is still maintained in the later book, it will give way, at the end, to "the voice of glorious sweetness" that speaks to the children and leads them to recover the double arch of a perfect female Amulet offering a "perfect union, which is not of time or space."[20]

III

Read superficially, *Five Children and It and The Story of the Amulet* appear to be pendants, much like *Alice in Wonderland* and *Through the Looking-Glass:* the same protagonists are carried into a new series of adventures, each of which, once again, fails to yield its wished-for object. Yet the two books are radically different in conception. Whereas the episodic ventures of *Five Children and It* were cast as diversions to fill up the space emptied by a mother who had left her children, the trans-historical voyages undertaken in *The Story of the Amulet* are prompted by the desire to recover the mother herself. Nesbit's later book thus depicts a quest for the maternal. In *Five Children and It,* the mother had merely left to tend "Granny." Now, however, she has been removed (and taken the Lamb with her) because she has herself become "very ill" (p. 13). The children's sense of desertion thus seems far more justified than before: while "Mother, poor dear Mother," is trying to recover her health in Madeira, Father has had to go to Manchuria to cover the Sino-Russian war. The "summer holiday" the children had hoped to repeat has turned into something "different," potentially ominous, "very horrid" (p. 12). Instead of being once more placed in the countryside and briefly entrusted to a caring young Martha, they have been deposited in London, at "Fitzroy Street, near the British Museum," for an indefinite stay with what strikes them as a less satisfying stand-in: an aged former nurse, who now rents out rooms to solitary lodgers. Although the children will befriend one such lodger, the Egyptologist bachelor who will accompany them on some of their expeditions through time and space, their new surroundings make them feel "perfectly wretched" (p. 13).

Still without the "It" they are about to rediscover in London, a Psammead very much in danger of its own life, the children give vent to a grief that had never perturbed them in the earlier book: the girls break down and weep, while the two boys "pretend that no boy would be such a muff as to cry." Such denials notwithstanding, all feel the same pain of desertion: "everyone felt as if it had been trying not to cry all its life, and that it must cry now, if it died for it" (p. 13). *The Story of the Amulet* confronts the intense emotions masked through comedy in *Five Children and It,* a text the narrator now derogates for having ended "in a most tiresome way" (p. 12). Near the end of the earlier book, the children's fear that they might become "branded outcasts" as the result of Jane's final wish was mocked for its hyperbole. Their present predicament, however, is hardly laughable. The possibility of permanent loss seems as real to them as it had seemed to the little girl in **"My School-Days."** Mother and Lamb, the children fear, may never return. Father may well perish in the war-zone. War, slaughter, and male conquest will soon punctuate adventures that thrust them into a history capable of causing far greater harm than the damages that, in the earlier book, could be erased daily at the onset of dusk.

In *Five Children and It,* the children could easily return home even when carried away by their most extravagant wishes: in their farthest excursion, they could still be brought back by the vicar onto whose tower-roof they had flown. No such guarantee is possible in *The Story of the Amulet,* where a safe return to the present always seems in doubt. History is a nightmare from which the over-confident young travelers may never awake: they may forever linger in the subterranean dungeon into which they have been cast by a furious king of Babylon. Nor is banishment into some remote past the only threat they must face. Death stalks each of the places they visit; it disrupts havens they assume to be secure. The primitive, pastoral village in predynastic Egypt that they visit on their first journey is suddenly overrun by superior invaders armed with copper spears and knives. To the children who manage to retreat to London in the nick of time, the "cruel, dark, big-nosed face, with the red, wet knife in its gleaming teeth" (p. 86) lingers as an afterimage far more unsettling than their memories of the caricatures of medieval knights and Red Indians who had stepped out of juvenile books to attack them in *Five Children and It.* Real and palpable, history can house terrors every bit as powerful as those that had shaken the child in **"My School-Days."**

Given the magnitude of the obstacles arraigned against them, the children require more than a Sand-fairy to bring about the realization of their "wish" for fusion (p. 31). They are glad to retrieve the Psammead after having considered the release of some ordinary animal captives, "chained or caged" in Lon-

don's pet-shops (p. 18). But the Psammead is not extraordinary enough. Their own confinement cannot be cured by the creature who reminds them that it cannot "give you any more wishes" (p. 31). A new vehicle for the gratification of the more primal desire activated by this book is now needed. And that new agent, appropriately enough, is itself an emblem of maternal generativity, the womb-like Amulet through the enlargement of which the children must pass in their various transmigrations.

Anthea, whose role is far more prominent in this book than in its predecessor, not only brings about the Psammead's liberation but also is soon charged by it to obtain the services of a more powerful and regenerative "It." Anthea's election by the Psammead follows a significant precedent. For Anthea's mother, too, had asked the girl to act as her chosen delegate. This transference of power enables Anthea to dry her tears and proudly cling to "what Mother had said, the night before she went, about Anthea being the eldest girl, and about trying to make the others happy" (p. 14). Soon, she presents the other three children with the "red, smooth, softly shining stone" of the female *ankh,* which, all agree, "would make the owner of it perfectly happy" (p. 35).

The androgynous Psammead explains that the *ankh*'s greater potency stems from female fecundity: "This thing is half of an Amulet that can do all sorts of things; it can make the corn grow, and the waters flow, and the trees bear fruit, and the little new beautiful babies come" (p. 39). Yet Anthea is quick to recognize that only the fusion of both halves of the Amulet can bring about the single wish uniting all four children: the restoration of their parents and the Lamb. Since the half-amulet in their possession can merely transport them to places in which "to look for the other half" (p. 40), its integration is as much in their interest as the restoration of their family's wholeness. But even the power of the half-amulet cannot be released unless the children and the Psammead manage to decode the cuneiform inscription that strikes Cyril as a representation of "chickens and things" (p. 40).

In *Five Children and It* the gipsy woman Amelia crowned her maternal blessing with an incantation worded "in a strange language no one could understand." Though just as unintelligible, the words inscribed on the Amulet now need to be chanted by the children themselves as an expression of their own desire for fusion. Once again, it is Anthea who takes the initiative. She remembers the "poor learned gentleman upstairs," a scholar-figure such as the one who defused "Daisy" Nesbit's fears in her father's cabinet of wonders. Led by Anthea, the group ventures into the room in which their first sight is of "a mummy-case—very, very, very big—painted in red and yellow and green and black, and the face of it seemed to look at them quite angrily" (p. 43).

The ensuing scene reactivates yet significantly transforms images and associations that Nesbit had presented in the episode of the Bordeaux mummies in Part V of **"My School-Days."** There, the little girl who ventured into the charnel house with her siblings had clung to a memory of the "kindly curators," who guarded the mummies of the British Museum, before she was shocked by the terrifying experience that followed. Here, however, after similarly referring her child-readers to the exhibits in the British Museum, Nesbit further removes potential horror by introducing Jimmy, the gentle but absent-minded scholar, who decodes the inscription of the charm. Daisy's fears of abandonment had to be overcome by the boy-waiter who fed the child in the Bordeaux hotel; now it is a girl who nurtures an adult male. Sensing Jimmy's child-like loneliness, Anthea coaxes him to eat the congealed mutton chop he has forgotten. She remembers that "Mother always" had told her to remind her father to eat his regular meals when "not at home to do it herself." And, glancing at the scowling mummy-case, Anthea concludes that "*it certainly did not look as though it would ever think of reminding people of their meals*" (p. 49).

Once again, two different kinds of "mummies" are ironically juxtaposed. But whereas in **"My School-Days"** that juxtaposition was to the detriment of the flesh-and-blood mother, here the Mother whom Andrea has internalized can be privileged. Like the Psammead, Jimmy helps the children recover energies from which he will himself benefit. He provides them with the words that, intoned as soon as they have left him, permit them to hear, faintly at first, and then more powerfully, a primal female voice. Accompanied by a "beautiful light" emanating from the oval of the *ankh,* "greeny," growing in strength "as though thousands and thousands of glow-worms were signalling to their winged sweethearts from the middle of the circle," the voice also grows, "not so much in loudness as in sweetness (though it grew louder, too), till it was so sweet that you wanted to cry with pleasure." The source of that pleasure is unmistakeable: "It was like nightingales, and the sea, and the fiddle, and the voice of your mother when you have been a long time away, and she meets you at the door when you get home" (pp. 50-51).

Such lyricism would have been unthinkable in the ironic mode of *Five Children and It.* Now, however, the yearning for a recovery of that sweet maternal presence is no longer treated defensively. Nesbit's mother had died, at the age of eighty-four, after the publication of *Five Children and It.* Though removed forever now, she also became, paradoxically, more accessible as an object of desire for her daughter's imagination. The mother eagerly awaiting a child is a figure Nesbit repeatedly introduces in *The Story of the Amulet.* Mothering has ceased to be restricted to biological mothers, to time and place, or, for that matter, to the living. Thus, a "sad-eyed woman" who lost her Imogen to wolves in ancient Britain can be supplied with the deserted little Cockney girl whose mother "don't live nowheres" in modern London (p. 179). The gipsy Amelia could not be allowed possession of the Lamb, but here, surrogate mother and surrogate child blend "so strongly that they stood an instant like a statue carved in stone" (p. 186). This reunion sets a pattern for more ordinary ones. In a future Britain, the expelled boy Wells (named after Nesbit's fellow-Fabian and Hubert Bland's fellow-philanderer)[21] is hugged by the woman with a "good, bright mother-face" who welcomes him back home and informs her visitors about the wonders of child-care in her Utopian world (p. 227). Babylon, too, its despotic king notwithstanding, offers abundant female nurturance: Jane is cosseted both by the "kind-faced woman" who dresses her in her daughter's attire and by the queen herself. Indeed, the mother-queen, who slightly resembles Lady Chittenden, becomes so fond of British children that the Psammead must grant her a visit to London, where the children disguise her in "Mother's old theatre cloak" and hat (p. 141).

Nesbit's freeing of maternity in *The Story of the Amulet* enabled her at last to reclaim a fairy-tale mythology from its male appropriators. It is hardly a coincidence that the magic of the "perfect" Amulet should have been progressively reduced, throughout history, by a succession of male ravages. As the female voice tells the children, the "strange men with strange weapons" who "destroyed my shrine" were followed by priests who "enslaved" the charm and rendered it passive well before its further mutilation. And the half-amulet itself was wrested away by the followers of still another invader, "a small man, a conqueror with an army," whom Nesbit's narrator helpfully identifies as Napoleon (p. 53).

Again and again, Nesbit sets such acquisitive male predators in opposition to the maternal wholeness that she now seeks to relocate through time and space. Among these foils are imperialist figures such as Caesar, Napoleon, and the long-nosed Semitic conquerors whose greed and cruelty Nesbit identifies (in a racist touch that one would never find in her friend Kipling's work) with the Jewish merchant who had sold the Amulet to the children.[22] Male tyranny takes other shapes as well: the suicidal traders who dash their ship against the rocks shouting, "Tyre for ever!" (p. 256); the Pharaoh who oppresses "working-men" who "nowadays," we are told, "would have lived at Brixton or Brockley" (p. 201). Only the Queen of Babylon is an exception in this panorama of male history. She can rule in favor of a female petitioner caught between the conflicting narratives of two males whom the Queen finds equally guilty. But such an exercise of her power can be undertaken only when the Queen's husband is on one of his forays. Currently away "to fetch home his fourteenth wife," the monarch has "set his heart on an Egyptian to complete his collection" (p. 117). The Queen's attempt to buttress her own position ("I am the Queen; they are only the wives") sounds very much like the justification of a more modern wife forced to wink at Hubert Bland's open infidelities.

That Nesbit wanted to free fairy-tale "magic" from its dependence on male power is evident from still another self-inscription in *The Story of the Amulet.* Separated by the returning King of Babylon not only from Jane and the Queen, but also from the Psammead and the Amulet, the children try to rely on the agency of an alien wish-giver, "the great Nisroch," whom the Queen found missing from the list of the seven great ones of England that Cyril recites with male pride (p. 116). But Cyril has forgotten the name of this creature:

> "What was the name the Queen said?" asked Cyril suddenly. "Nisbeth—Nesbit—something? You know, the slave of the great names?"
>
> "Wait a sec," said Robert, "though I don't know why you want it. Nusroch—Nisrock—Nisroch—that's it."
>
> Then Anthea pulled herself together. All her muscles tightened, and the muscles of her mind and soul, if you can call them that, tightened too.
>
> "UR HEKAU SETCHEH," she cried in a fervent voice. "Oh, Nisroch, servant of the great Ones, come and help us!" (p. 127)

The "strange and terrible figure," whose male body sprouts an eagle's head and wings, materializes in "a cold, blue light" unlike that of the Amulet; he embodies all the magic that "Nisbeth-Nesbit" now wants to transcend, much as she wishes to go beyond her previous incarnation as Psammead.

In her desire to activate a female mythology, Nesbit availed herself of the theosophical writings of Helena Petrovna Blavatsky and Annie Besant. Whether she had fully mastered the cosmogony that Blavatsky scattered through the seven "stanzas" of the first volume of *The Secret Doctrine* (1888) remains doubtful; nor do the seven localities visited by the children correspond to the seven Races detailed in Blavatsky's second volume (though the children do visit the fabled Atlantis, the dwelling place of the Fourth Race, just before its destruction by a tidal wave).[23] Yet Nesbit drew from Blavatsky and from Annie Besant's more tempered *The Ancient Wisdom* (1897) the notion that a desire for fusion could be transcended by a process of reincarnation that allows "the loves of old [to] reappear in the loves of today."[24] The seven "Logoi," planets, or globes on which Theosophy based its chain of being, had led to many numerological permutations. In her fairy tale, Nesbit, too, toyed with such materials. Through the hieroglyph of the *ankh,* itself an emblem for the unity of life like the Hebrew letter *chaj,* seven travelers (the four children, the Psammead, Jimmy, and the priest Rekhmarā) visit seven localities (pre-dynastic Egypt, Babylon, Atlantis, pre-Roman Britain, Pharaoh's Egypt, future London, Tyre) before they can reach that primordial place (Blavatsky's Third Root Race?) in which the amulet is still in its pristine state of perfection.

Before the children can at last become a unit of seven by having Father, Mother, and Lamb restored to them, two other fusions take place. The half-amulet on which the children have relied becomes reincorporated into a perfect whole: "and then, as one drop of water mingles with another when the panes of the window are wrinkled in rain, as one bead of mercury is drawn into another bead, the half Amulet that was the children's and was also Rehk-marā's, slipped into the whole Amulet, and, behold! there was only one—the perfect and ultimate Charm" (p. 275). Yet still another transmigration is needed. When the "beautiful, terrible voice" of the Amulet informs Rekh-marā that no imperfect men can now pass through the perfected oval, the Egyptian priest—adult, male, treacherous—is invited to seek a soul "so akin" to his own "as to offer it refuge . . . that thus they two may be one soul in one body" (p. 277). The kindred soul is that of Jimmy, the child-man. Under the glowing arch, "Rekh-marā, Divine Father of the Temple of Amen-Rā, was drawn into, slipped into, disappeared into, and was one with Jimmy, the good, the beloved, the learned gentleman" (p. 279). A horrid centipede, the evil in the soul of Rekh-marā, can be quickly squashed by Robert. Like the horrid Nisroch and like the Psammead that is allowed to disappear forever, the centipede is a dispensable reminder of a world unintegrated by love. Even the grumpy Psammead is at last capable of bestowing "one last lingering look at Anthea"—a look she will always consider to have been "a loving look" (p. 280).

IV

Despite the earnestness of her desire to recover something like the Imperishable Sacred Land postulated by Theosophy, Nesbit never succumbed to the temptation of converting her fairy tales into pseudo-religious tracts. At one of the most comically anarchic moments of *The Story of the Amulet,* Nesbit manages to wink at the book's machinery of transmigration. The Queen of Babylon, aided by the Psammead, has caused all the "Babylonian things" held captive in the British Museum to float out into the Museum yard. A reporter blames this chaotic situation on the latest female cult:

> A journalist, who was just leaving the museum, spoke to Robert as he passed.
>
> "Theosophy, I suppose?" he said. "Is she Mrs Besant?"
>
> "Yes," said Robert recklessly.
>
> The journalist passed through the gates just before they were shut. He rushed off to Fleet Street, and his paper got out a new edition within half an hour.
>
> MRS BESANT AND THEOSOPHY
>
> IMPERTINENT MIRACLE AT THE
>
> BRITISH MUSEUM
>
> People saw it in fat, black letters on the boards carried by the sellers of newspapers. Some few people who had nothing better to do went down to the Museum on the top of omnibuses. But by the time they got there there was nothing to be seen. (pp. 145-46)

By juxtaposing magic to the ordinary world of newspapers, Nesbit mocks the impertinence of her own miracle-making. In her wishful attempts to repair her sense of incompleteness and loss through the agency of a new female magic, the writer often saw herself as an impostress of sorts. Her ability to view her own enterprise with absolute clarity is evident in her 1901 story of **"Fortunatus Rex & Co, or, The Mystery of the Disappearing Schoolgirls."** In that wonderfully clever tale, she blended theosophy with humor as a commentary on her inventive efforts to reclaim a territory for the female imagination.

"Fortunatus Rex" playfully recombines some of the same ingredients found in **"My School-Days,"** *Five Children and It,* and *The Story of the Amulet.* The disappearance of Princess Daisy, the youngest of the seven princesses at Miss Fitzroy Robinson's "Select Boarding Establishment for the Daughters of Respectable Monarchs," is mourned by her inconsolable father King Fortunatus, though not at all by the matter-of-fact Queen whose housekeeping chores do not leave her "much time for weeping."[25] Yet if Princess Daisy's magical disappearance and restoration involve a comic fantasy that reprocesses the narratives relied upon by "Daisy" Nesbit to account for her own separation from a too busy mother, the emphasis of the fairy tale falls neither on her nor on the six older princesses who have been similarly abducted, but rather on the figure of their deliverer, Miss Fitzroy Robinson herself. It is this updated version of a fairy godmother that gives **"Fortunatus Rex"** its delicious vitality.

A composite of the pompous schoolmistresses of Nesbit's youth, of the mother who vainly tried to run the school John Nesbit had set up, and, most importantly, of E. Nesbit herself as a money-making, Psammead-like dispenser of illusions, Miss Robinson profits from her ability to make others believe in her fictions. Though little actual teaching goes on at her permissive educational establishment, she has so impressed "all the really high-class kings" with her phony credentials that they "were only too pleased to be permitted to pay ten thousand pounds a year for their daughters' education" (p. 127). But if, as an educator, Miss Robinson seems far more interested in investing "in land" than in her pupils, her powers as an illusionist nonetheless prove to be deservedly impressive. It is as a magician who can command more powerful spells than her former male instructor in white and black magic that she manages to reclaim the princesses from her rival's enchantment and to demand that, in recompense, King Fortunatus make "green again" the land that his building company has ruthlessly cut into squares for ugly housing developments (p. 144). Secluding herself in seven acres—which she wanted to be walled in a circular structure much like the one housing the Amulet—Miss Robinson zealously guards her orchard. There, she preserves the seven golden apples that imprison Daisy and her six fellow-princesses until each is kissed seven times by six eager princes and Daisy's loving little brother. Just as the green light of the Amulet can mend broken halves, so does Miss Robinson extend her greening powers beyond her seven acres of garden. The male magician that she has cut and placed into two separate geographical globes can fuse his severed halves as soon as the six princesses join their grooms.[26]

Miss Robinson, then, whose name "Fitzroy" would reappear in the city address of the children in *The Story of the Amulet* and whose watch-dog "Martha" bears the name of the children's rural guardian in *Five Children and It,* becomes the preserver and re-storer of a female terrain. She is, simultaneously, an impostress and a figure of enormous power, laugh-able yet awesome. If her momentary negligence causes her wards to disappear, it is Miss Robinson's activation of a magic misused by males that makes her superior to her chief foils—the enchanter who tries to possess her school and its female inmates, and the King whose acquisition of more and more land becomes just as much an act of possession that she must resist.

By asserting Miss Robinson's superiority to these two male rivals, Nesbit signifies her own reappro-priation of a literary province. That reappropriation is made possible by the balance she asks us to value in a figure that is neither as power-hungry as the magi-cian who tries to wrest away her pupils nor as senti-mental as the King who must mutilate the country-side in order to find compensation for the loss of little Daisy. As enamoured of little girls as Lewis Carroll and other male child-lovers, Fortunatus finds little comfort "in the fact that his other child, Prince Denis, was spared to him. Denis was all very well and a nice little boy in his way, but a boy is not a girl" (p. 134). Nesbit enlists Miss Robinson to re-claim the King as much as his daughter. He must learn that material power cannot compensate him for emotional loss.

Nesbit's shrewd correction of the male fantasists who had adopted forms not their own to sustain their loss of the feminine could come only from one who had achieved a full understanding of the compensatory nature of her own art as a fantasist. As she realized, only the wishful structures of a fully balanced, ma-ture woman could bring home a little girl lost.

Notes

1. The nursery rhyme both opens and occurs twice within "The Way to Babylon," the sixth chapter in which Nesbit's four child-travelers meet the "splen-did dreamlady" who will return their visit, in *The Story of the Amulet* (Harmondsworth: Penguin Books, 1973), pp. 90, 93, 95, 107. The song is sung by Jane

who, as the youngest, corresponds to Edith or "Daisy" Nesbit, the last (and, apparently, the most neglected) of her widowed mother's children.

2. Ruth Bottigheimer, "Silenced Women in the Grimms' Tales: The 'Fit' Between Fairy Tales and Society in Their Historical Context," in *Fairy Tales and Society: Illusion, Allusion, and Paradigm,* ed. Ruth B. Bottigheimer (Philadelphia: University of Pennsylvania Press, 1986), pp. 115-31. See also Bot-tigheimer's "The Transformed Queen: A Search for the Origins of Negative Female Archetypes in Grimms' Fairy Tales," *Amsterdamer Beiträge,* 10 (1980).

3. Maria Edgeworth, Preface to *The Parent's Assis-tant, or, Stories for Children* (New York: James Miller, n.d.), p. x.

4. Mitzi Myers, "Impeccable Governesses, Rational Dames, and Moral Mothers: Mary Wollstonecraft and the Female Tradition in Georgian Children's Books," *Children's Literature,* 14 (1986), 31-59.

5. Mrs. Alfred [Margaret] Gatty, *The Fairy Godmoth-ers and Other Tales,* 2nd ed. (London: Bell and Daldy, 1858), pp. 16, 17.

6. See, in this connection, my "Avenging Alice: Christina Rossetti and Lewis Carroll," *Nineteenth-Century Literature,* 41 (1986), 299-328.

7. Alison Lurie, "Riding the Wave of the Future," *New York Review of Books* (25 October 1984), pp. 22, 19.

8. Roger Lancelyn Green, "Introduction: E. Nesbit and the World of Enchantment," *Five Children and It* (Harmondsworth: Penguin Books, 1978), p. 15.

9. Lurie's efforts to dissociate the "radical features" of Nesbit's art from the work of Mrs. Molesworth and Mrs. Ewing, moralists whose books presumably "are gathering dust on the shelves of secondhand bookshops," strike me as most unconvincing. She praises Nesbit for somehow returning to "the oldest sort of juvenile literature, the folk tale," even though it was actually Ewing whose far more overt con-sciousness of an oral tradition of female story-tellers led her to adapt an Irish folk-tale in her comic "Ame-lia and the Dwarfs" (Lurie, p. 22). For a discussion of the relation between "Amelia" and the folk-tale of "Wee Meg Barnilegs," see my "Little Girls Without Their Curls: Female Aggression in Victorian Chil-dren's Literature by Women Writers," *Children's Lit-erature,* 9 (1983), 14-30.

10. "My School-Days," Part I, *The Girl's Own Paper,* 18 (1896-1897), 28.

11. Doris Langley Moore, *E. Nesbit: A Biography* (Philadelphia: Chilton Company, 1966), p. 8.

12. "My School-Days," p. 28.

13. Moore, p. 42.

14. Moore, p. 33.

15. "My School-Days," p. 28. Subsequent references to this work will be cited in the text by installment number and page.

16. All subsequent references to the Penguin edition of *Five Children and It* will be cited in the text.

17. Nesbit's eighty-four-year-old mother, who died in 1902, the year in which *Five Children and It* appeared in book form, had been ill for some time; her dependence on her only surviving daughter, herself now a mother of five children, including the recently adopted John Bland, the infant "Lamb" to whom the book is dedicated, clearly once again aroused for the writer the issue of maternal nurturance.

18. See, for instance, p. 100: "Everyone now turned out its pockets on the lead roof of the tower"; Nesbit deliberately shuns using either "their" or "his or her."

19. Although all four children compose letters in which they try to tell their mother about the Psammead, only Jane's gets mailed (Robert accidentally spills ink on Anthea's letter and has no time to compose his own; Cyril misplaces his own "long letter"). And Jane, unable to spell "Psammead," is content to write: "We found a strange thing" (pp. 87-88). In "My School-Days," Daisy, too, conceals her real feelings in her letters home.

20. *The Story of the Amulet,* p. 276. Subsequent references to the Penguin edition will be cited in the text.

21. The mother of Wells tells the children that he is named after "the great reformer" who "lived in the dark ages," who saw "that what you ought to do is to find out what you want and then try to get it" (p. 231). That Nesbit's good friend and admirer H. G. Wells may have wanted her (and her teenage daughter Rosamund, as well) is strongly suggested by some of her biographers (see Moore, for instance, pp. xiv-xv, 178-79).

22. Further anti-Semitic touches mar the scene in which the Queen of Babylon's bodyguards behead Jewish members of the London Stock Exchange, in chapter eight (pp. 152-53). Nesbit admired Kipling (though not, apparently, his philo-Semitism). She mentions him in *Five Children and It* and has Cyril include him in his list of the seven "great ones" he presents to the Queen of Babylon. That list, done with tongue-in-check, includes two political leaders, one of whom is Semitic himself (Alfred the Great and Lord Beaconsfield), two military leaders (Nelson and Gordon), two authors (Shakespeare and "Mr Rudyard Kipling"), and a fictional character whom Cyril regards as living ("Mr Sherlock Holmes").

23. Marion Meade, *Madame Blavatsky: The Woman Behind the Myth* (New York: G. P. Putnam's Sons, 1980), pp. 414-15.

24. Annie Besant, *The Ancient Wisdom: An Outline of Theosophical Teachings* (Madras: The Theosophical Publishing House, 1949), p. 267.

25. *E. Nesbit's Fairy Stories,* ed. Naomi Lewis (London: Hodder and Stoughton, 1980), p. 134. Subsequent references to this edition will be cited in the text.

26. In keeping with her interest in the mystical number seven, Nesbit devises a scheme in which each of the six princes picks a mate with a name that, when fused with his, adds up to seven: Prince Secundus, thus, instead of picking the apple that held Secunda, as intended, finds himself with Quinta; "Tertius held Quarta, and so on" (p. 143). Although these choices seem "wrong" and defy the expectations of their parents, Miss Robinson, still in the shape of an old crone, asks all to "be contented with what you have" (p. 143). If numerology is here enlisted to subvert the conventions of romantic love, so does Nesbit undercut the fairy-tale convention in which an aged crone turns into a blooming beauty: "While she was speaking the old woman got younger and younger, till as she spoke the last words she was quite young, not more than fifty-five. And it was Miss Fitzroy Robinson!" (p. 143).

Alison Lurie

SOURCE: "E. Nesbit," in *Writers for Children: Critical Studies of Major Authors since the Seventeenth Century,* edited by Jane M. Bingham, Charles Scribner's Sons, 1988, pp. 423-30.

Victorian literary fairy tales tend to have a conservative moral and political bias. Under their charm and invention is usually an improving lesson: adults know best; good, obedient, patient, and self-effacing little boys and girls are rewarded by the fairies, and naughty, assertive ones are punished. In the most widely read British authors of the period—Frances Browne, Dinah Craik, Juliana Ewing, M. L. S. Molesworth, and even the greatest of them all, George MacDonald—the usual tone is that of a kind lady or gentleman delivering a delightfully disguised sermon.

In the final years of Victoria's reign, however, a writer appeared who was to challenge this pattern so energetically and with such success that it makes sense now to speak of juvenile literature as before and after E. Nesbit. Though there are foreshadowings of her characteristic manner in Charles Dickens' *Holiday Romance* (1868) and Kenneth Grahame's *The Golden Age* (1895), Nesbit was the first to write at length for children as intellectual equals and in their own language. Her books were also innovative in other ways: they presented a modern view of childhood, they took place in contemporary England and recommended socialist solutions to its problems; and they used magic both as a comic device and as a serious metaphor for the power of the imagination.

The woman who overturned so many conventions of children's literature was herself a very unconventional member of the Victorian upper middle class, into which she was born in 1858. Edith Nesbit was the youngest daughter of John Collis Nesbit, the head of a London agricultural college, who died in 1862, when she was three. After his death, his wife first tried to keep the college going and then spent the next six years traveling from one European city to another in search of inexpensive lodgings and a healthier climate for her invalid daughter, Mary. As a child, Edith was a rebellious, hot-tempered tomboy, and no doubt a trial to her gentle widowed mother. She hated most of the schools she was sent to in England and on the Continent, and declared later that she had "never been able to love a doll." Her passions were reading, riding, swimming, and playing pirates with her older brothers during holidays. She began to compose poems and stories in early childhood, and already at twelve dreamed of becoming a writer; her verses were first published in newspapers when she was only fifteen.

In 1880, at twenty-one, Edith Nesbit married a handsome young businessman named Hubert Bland; she was seven months pregnant at the time. Shortly after the wedding, disaster struck: Bland became seriously ill with smallpox, and his partner disappeared with all the capital of the firm. Somehow Edith had to support herself, her new baby, and her convalescent husband. She did it by painting greeting cards; giving recitations; and turning out a flood of ephemeral verses, stories, essays, and novels. After he had recovered, Hubert Bland also took up the pen, eventually becoming a well-known political journalist; yet throughout their marriage Edith, and not her husband, remained the economic mainstay of their large family.

The work Nesbit produced between the ages of twenty and forty gives almost no sign of what was to come; it is conventional and often, to the modern taste, sentimental. Then suddenly, in 1898, the "Bastable" stories began to appear in the *Pall Mall* magazine; they were published as a book, **The Story of the Treasure Seekers,** the following year. The lively, comic adventures of six modern London children who try to restore the family fortunes were instantly popular and soon became famous. Two equally successful sequels followed: **The Wouldbegoods** (1901) and **The New Treasure Seekers** (1904). What seems to have released Nesbit's genius was the decision to tell her story through the persona of Oswald Bastable, a child much after her own pattern: bold, quick-tempered, egotistic, and literary.

The success of **The Treasure Seekers** made it possible for the Blands to leave London and move to Well Hall in Kent, a large, beautiful eighteenth-century brick house, which was to be Nesbit's home until almost the end of her life; it became the Moat House of the later Bastable stories. Over the next ten years she produced the books for which she is known today, books full of wit, energy, and invention, far superior to anything she had written before. Nesbit herself, however, seems to have been unaware of her own achievement. She never spoke of her best work as different from the rest, and she continued to turn out pedestrian stories and verses. To the end of her life she regretted that she could not afford to devote herself to what she mistakenly believed to be her real talent, serious poetry.

Throughout their life together the Blands kept open house for their many friends, including famous painters, writers, and politicians, as well as poor relations, abandoned and illegitimate children, and penniless would-be authors, artists, and cranks. H. G. Wells described Well Hall as "a place to which one rushed down from town at the week-end to snatch one's bed before anyone else got it." Though most of their guests did not know this, the Blands' marriage as well as their house was what today would be called "open," especially at the husband's end. Hubert Bland was constantly unfaithful; his wife, though hurt by his love affairs, usually ended by taking a sympathetic interest in the women involved. She also passed off two of his illegitimate children as her own and raised them along with her three.

As time went on Nesbit also now and then formed romantic attachments—although most of them probably never went beyond enthusiastic friendship. Even in late middle age she was the sort of woman men fall in love with: tall, good-looking, impulsive, charming, and completely unpredictable. Part of her charm was that in some sense she had never quite grown up. As her biographer Doris Langley Moore reports, she "had all the caprices, the little petulances, the sulks, the jealousies, the intolerance, the selfishnesses of a child; and with them went a child's freshness of vision, hunger for adventure, remorse for unkindness, quick sensibility, and reckless generosity." Nesbit's children remembered her as a delightful playmate but a less than perfect mother. Her quick temper and sudden whims made their life interesting but insecure, and her unconventional costume and manner sometimes caused them embarrassment. Her appearance was untidy and strikingly bohemian: she wore loose, trailing, "aesthetic" dress (and sometimes, for bicycling, pantaloons); her arms were loaded with silver bangles; and her abundant dark hair was bobbed. And, in an era when only "fast women" smoked, she was never without tobacco and cigarette papers—a defiance of convention that may have been responsible for her recurrent bronchial troubles and eventually for her death.

Both the Blands were socialists, founders and lifelong members of the Fabian Society. At one time or another Nesbit supported most of the radical causes of her day—and many of its radical fads, including dress reform, psychic research, and the claim that Francis Bacon had written the plays of Shakespeare.

In 1914 Hubert Bland died, and the next few years were a low point in his wife's career. She was frequently ill and unable to work, and many of her friends and relatives were away in the war. Sales of her books fell off, and she had to take in boarders to keep Well Hall going. In 1917, however, she remarried; her new husband was an old friend, Thomas Tucker, a retired marine engineer who also had been recently widowed. Though she wrote comparatively little, her last years with him were very happy.

Nesbit, it seems, remained emotionally about twelve years old all her life. Perhaps this is why she found it so easy to speak as one intelligent child to another, in a tone now so common in juvenile fiction that it is hard to realize how radical and even shocking it would have seemed at the time. In the late nineteenth century most writing for children was formal, leisurely, and gently didactic. Many writers still used the sort of artificial literary diction that Oswald makes fun of on the first page of *The Story of the Treasure Seekers:*

> I have read books myself, and I know how beastly it is when a story begins, "'Alas!' said Hildegarde with a deep sigh, 'we must look our last on this ancestral home'"—and then some one else says something—and you don't know for pages and pages where the home is, or who Hildegarde is or anything about it. Our ancestral home is in the Lewisham Road. It is semi-detached. . . .

Nesbit's tone is direct, humorous, and fast-moving, and her children are modern and believable. They are not types imagined by an adult, but individuals coolly observed by their peers, each with his or her faults and virtues and passions. Though she tries to be fair and give everyone an equal chance at adventures, Nesbit clearly prefers boys and girls of her own sort: bold, quick-tempered, egotistic, and literary, like Oswald Bastable. In all her stories the sort of serious, diffident, well-behaved children who would have been the heroes and heroines of a typical Victorian fairy tale are portrayed as timid and dull—though a few of them can, with proper encouragement from their peers, improve, as the "white mouse" Denny does in *The Wouldbegoods.*

The Treasure Seekers and its sequels are firmly rooted in the contemporary world. The Bastable children need to restore the family fortunes because their father's business partner has taken advantage of his illness to abscond to Spain with all the capital of the firm, just as Hubert Bland's partner once did. The children's attempts to earn money by selling patent medicine, starting a newspaper, rescuing an old gentleman from danger (their own pet dog), or finding and marrying a princess tend to produce comic disaster. The story, however, in the tradition of juvenile fiction, ends happily. In the two sequels the Bastables' intended good deeds have a similar effect. By proper Victorian standards they behave badly—often disobeying their elders, digging up gardens, trespassing, and playing practical jokes—but though they are sometimes scolded and punished, they are always forgiven.

The Treasure Seekers was followed by two volumes of humorous fairy tales, *The Book of Dragons* (1900) and *Nine Unlikely Tales* (1901). They differ from most earlier literary fairy stories in that though they may contain magicians and dragons and kings and queens, they clearly take place in the present. The language in which they are told is also contemporary. Discarding the romantic diction of the traditional literary fairy story and its conventional epithets, the golden hair and milk-white steeds, Nesbit uses Edwardian slang and draws her comparisons from the Edwardian child's world of experience. The dragon in **"Uncle James"** has "wings like old purple umbrellas that have been very much rained on," and the court officials wear "gold coronets with velvet sticking up out of the middle like the cream in the very expensive jam tarts." And when there is a magical transformation, it often produces very modern results. In **"The Cockatoucan"** (*Nine Unlikely Tales*) the unpleasant nursemaid Pridmore becomes an Automatic Nagging Machine like the candy dispensers in London railway stations, "greedy, grasping things which take your pennies and give you next to nothing in chocolate and change." What comes out of her are little rolls of paper with remarks on them like "Don't be tiresome."

Though she does not use a first-person child narrator, Nesbit's tone in these literary fairy stories is much like that of Oswald Bastable—contemporary, informal, direct; even today her wholehearted espousal of the child's point of view is striking. In **"The Cockatoucan,"** for instance, she explains why Matilda doesn't want to visit her Great-aunt Willoughby:

> She would be asked about her lessons, and how many marks she had, and whether she had been a good girl. I can't think why grown-up people don't see how impertinent these questions are. Suppose you were to answer, "I'm top of my class, Auntie, thank you, and I'm very good. And now let's have a little talk about you. Aunt, dear, how much money have you got, and have you been scolding the servants again, or have you tried to be good and patient as a properly brought up aunt should be, eh, dear?"

Nesbit's next important book, *Five Children and It* (1902), combines the magical invention of her short tales with the realism and social comedy of the "Bastable" stories, creating a new and influential model for juvenile fantasy. The typical Victorian fairy tale, though it may begin in the real world, soon moves into some timeless Wonderland or country at the back of the North Wind. One of Nesbit's most brilliant moves was to reverse the process, and bring magic into modern London. In this she may have been following the lead of a contemporary writer of adult fantasy, F. Anstey, whose *Brass Bottle* (1900) had brought a genie into the life of an ordinary, contemporary young man. But whatever her sources, Nesbit was the first to imagine for a child audience what would be the actual consequences of magic happenings in the modern world: for example, the delivery by magic carpet of a hundred and ninety-nine Persian cats to the basement dining room of a house in Camden Town, or the transformation of one's brother into a ten-foot boy giant.

Nesbit's other original invention in *The Five Children and It* was the replacement of the traditional good fairy who grants wishes by an ill-tempered, monkeylike creature called the Psammead, who has extendable eyes like a snail's and a horror of water. Other authors of fantasy, of course—notably Lewis Carroll—had already invented strange ill-tempered creatures, but Nesbit was the first to invest such a figure with magical powers and make it central to an otherwise realistic narrative.

The Five Children and It is not only an amusing adventure story but also a tale of the vanity of human—or at least juvenile—wishes. The children in the book want to be "as beautiful as the day"; they ask for a sand pit full of gold sovereigns, giant size and strength, and instant adulthood. Each wish leads them into an appropriate comic disaster. When they become beautiful, for instance, their baby brother does not recognize them and bursts into howls of distrust, and they begin to quarrel among themselves—a not unusual result of such transformations in real life. When the spells end at sunset, the children are always greatly relieved. The reader, of course, has the pleasure of living out these granted wishes in imagination, plus the assurance that his or her unattainable desires are not so desirable after all.

The Phoenix and the Carpet (1904) continues the adventures of the five children, maintaining the comedy and imaginative invention of the original. It introduces another magical creature, the Phoenix, who is better looking and better tempered than the Psammead, but rather vain and self-centered. The central magic device is a secondhand flying carpet that takes the children to France, India, and the South Seas, with humorous consequences.

In the last volume of the series, *The Story of the Amulet* (1906), the Psammead is rediscovered in, and rescued from, a London pet shop. With its help the five children travel in time rather than space, visiting ancient Britain, Egypt, Babylon, and the lost island of Atlantis. *The Story of the Amulet* is unique among Nesbit's books in that it was carefully researched, and each chapter checked by an expert—Dr. Wallis (later Sir Ernest) Budge, the keeper of Egyptian and Assyrian antiquities at the British Museum. In the opinion of many critics, it is Nesbit's best work. It is also the one in which her political beliefs are most evident.

As a Fabian socialist, Nesbit was greatly concerned about the living conditions of the urban poor. One of her recurrent themes is the aesthetic unpleasantness and threat to health of modern cities in general and especially of London, which she called that "hateful, dark, ugly place." Many of us are now so accustomed to the nostalgic, prettified BBC version of Edwardian London that we have forgotten, if we ever knew, that in the early years of this century much of the city was filthy and many of its inhabitants sick or starving, its streets fouled with horse manure and urine, its river polluted, and its air often unfit to breathe. (The peasoup fogs that lend mystery and charm to the adventures of Sherlock Holmes were in fact a damp, poisonous smog.) In *The Story of the Amulet,* a rash wish brings the Queen of Babylon, whom the children have met in the past, to London. It appalls her:

> "But how badly you keep your slaves. How wretched and poor and neglected they seem," she said, as the cab rattled along the Mile End Road.

> "They aren't slaves; they're working-people," said Jane.

> "Of course they're working. That's what slaves are. Don't you tell me. Do you suppose I don't know a slave's face when I see it? Why don't their masters see that they're better fed and better clothed? . . . You'll have a revolt of your slaves if you're not careful," said the Queen.

> "Oh, no," said Cyril; "you see they have votes—that makes them safe not to revolt. It makes all the difference. Father told me so."

> "What is this vote?" asked the Queen. "Is it a charm? What do they do with it?"

> "I don't know," said the harassed Cyril; "it's just a vote, that's all! They don't do anything particular with it."

> "I see," said the Queen; "a sort of plaything."

Later in the same book the Amulet takes the children into a future in which England has become a Fabian Utopia, a city of parks and flowers, with clean air and an unpolluted Thames. People live in beautiful, uncluttered houses and wear loose woolly clothes of the sort favored by William Morris and by the Aesthetic Movement. There are no idle rich: everyone works, and no one goes hungry; the schools are progressive and coeducational; and both men and women care for babies.

With *The Railway Children* (1906) Nesbit returned to the realistic story, producing a work that in some ways anticipates the juvenile "problem novels" of today. The families in all of Nesbit's books tend to be in difficulties, just as the Blands so often were. Sometimes one of the parents is dead; but even if both survive, the father is out of the country, or ill, or has lost his job. The mother too may be ill (in *Five of Us—and Madeline* [1925] she has had a nervous breakdown), or she may be away caring for a sick relative. Often, as a result of these domestic disruptions, Nesbit's children have to leave their family home with the remaining parent, or go and stay with unsympathetic strangers in bleak, unattractive lodgings. Even when the family is intact, they are usually in cramped economic circumstances. The situation is most depressing when they live in town, for, as Nesbit remarks in *Five Children and It,* "London is like a prison for children, especially if their relatives are not rich."

In *The Railway Children* the protagonists not only have fallen upon hard times but also are in serious trouble: their father is in prison. It turns out that he has been mistakenly accused, but the resulting social shame and isolation of the family is real, and the children's efforts to adjust to their changed circumstances and even enjoy themselves are both ingenious and courageous. The tale is unique among Nesbit's family stories in that it is dominated by one child, Roberta, who is almost—but not quite—too good, brave, and kind to be true. *The Railway Children* has proved to be one of the most enduringly popular of Nesbit's books; it has been made into a television play and, more recently, a successful feature film.

In 1907 Nesbit published what may be, next to *The Story of the Amulet,* her most interesting and sophisticated fantasy, *The Enchanted Castle.* Here magic is not so much an imaginative projection of possibilities and the source of amusing adventures as an intensified image of reality. For example, it makes literal the perception that many adults have no idea of what is going on with the children who are living with them, and possibly don't even care. One of the children in the story, Mabel, finds a ring that makes her invisible, but it is soon clear that she was already more or less invisible to the aunt with whom she lives. Mabel's aunt feels not the slightest anxiety about her niece's disappearance, and readily swallows a made-up story about her having been adopted by a lady in a motor car. The other children are shocked by this insouciance, but Mabel explains that her aunt's mind is clogged with sentimental fantasy: "She's not mad, only she's always reading novelettes."

In the most striking episode of *The Enchanted Castle,* Nesbit's Fabian convictions, her comic sense, and her use of magic as a metaphor work together. Mabel and the other children decide to put on a play, and because there are only three grown-ups to watch it, they construct an audience out of old clothes, pillows, unbrellas, brooms, and hockey sticks, with painted paper faces. A magic ring brings these ungainly creatures to life, and they are transformed into awful caricatures of different types of contemporary adults. Eventually, most of the "Ugly-Wuglies" (as Gerald calls them) are disenchanted and become piles of old clothes again, but one remains alive. He is the sort of elderly gentleman "who travels first class and smokes expensive cigars," and Jimmy, the most materialistic of the children, is rather impressed by him: "'He's got a motor-car,' Jimmy went on, . . . 'and a garden with a tennis-court, and a lake, and a carriage and pair. . . . He's frightfully rich, . . . He's simply rolling in money. . . . I wish *I* was rich.'" Since Jimmy has the magic ring, his wish is instantly granted:

> By quick but perfectly plain-to-be-seen degrees Jimmy became rich. . . . The whole thing was over in a few seconds. Yet in those few seconds they saw him grow to a youth, a young man, a middle-aged man; and then, with a sort of shivering shock, unspeakably horrible and definite, he seemed to settle down into an elderly gentleman, handsomely but rather dowdily dressed, who was looking down at them through spectacles and asking them the nearest way to the railway-station. . . .
>
> "Oh, Jimmy, *don't!*" cried Mabel, desperately.
>
> Gerald said: "This is perfectly beastly," and Kathleen broke into wild weeping. (*The Enchanted Castle,* pp. 185-186)

In his new persona Jimmy no longer knows the other children and is very unpleasant to them. But he turns out to be well acquainted with the elderly Ugly-Wugly, and they travel up to London together, fol-

lowed by Jimmy's desperate brother, Gerald. There it appears that both Jimmy and the Ugly-Wugly have offices in the City complete with "a tangle of clerks and mahogany desks." An office boy tells Gerald that in spite of their apparent friendship, the two stock-brokers "'is all for cutting each other's throats—oh, only in the way of business—been at it for years.'" The whole episode plunges Gerald into a kind of existential crisis:

> [He] wildly wondered what magic and how much had been needed to give history and a past to these two things of yesterday, the rich Jimmy and the Ugly-Wugly. If he could get them away, would all memory of them fade—in this boy's mind, for instance; in the minds of all the people who did business with them in the City? Would the mahogany-and-clerk-furnished offices fade away? Were the clerks real? Was the mahogany? Was he himself real? (ibid., p. 195-196)

Since Gerald is a character in a book, the answer to this last question is no. He is literally no more real than the elderly Ugly-Wugly—he too is a creature composed playfully out of odds and ends and brought to life by a kind of instant magic. But however unreal Gerald may be, Nesbit seems to be suggesting that there is something even more unreal about the average successful businessman. In spite of the pomp and circumstance of his exterior life, the City man is essentially, as Gerald puts it, "only just old clothes and nothing inside." He is an empty assemblage of expensive tailoring—or a greedy little boy who has grown up too fast.

The House of Arden (1908) and *Harding's Luck* (1909), though imperfect, are among Nesbit's most interesting and innovative works. The two stories, in both of which contemporary children travel back into the past, are interlocking rather than consecutive. In the first, Edred and Elfrida, searching for a lost family treasure, take over the bodies and lives of two children who were their ancestors; in *Harding's Luck* Dick does the same. This device is now so common in juvenile fantasy as to have become almost a cliché, but to Nesbit's readers it must have seemed new and exciting.

Another original feature of these two stories is the widening of Nesbit's social range. Before *The Enchanted Castle* all her central characters had been middle-class. Working-class children had been portrayed as aggressive and rude—like the threatening regamuffins of *The Phoenix and the Carpet*—or else as ignorant and pathetic. The upper class often fared no better. Most of Nesbit's fairy-tale kings and queens were comic bunglers, and her court officials tended to be two-faced frauds with an up-to-date command of smarmy rhetoric. The real-life princess whom Noel had discovered in *The Treasure Seekers* turned out to be a dull, overdressed little girl who was afraid to play in the park.

The children in *The House of Arden,* however, are aristocrats—Edred is the future Lord Arden. He is unusual among Nesbit's heroes in that at the start of the story he is extremely disagreeable: cowardly, mean, and rather stupid. Victorian juvenile literature, of course, is full of children whose characters need improvement; Edred is notable mainly in that it isn't suggested that he should learn to obey and respect his elders. Also, his reformation is not achieved with the help of surrogate parent figures, but through experience and the example of his peers. (Nesbit here anticipates by three years one of the central themes of Frances Hodgson Burnett's masterpiece, *The Secret Garden.*)

Dickie Harding, the crippled hero of *Harding's Luck,* is also a new sort of character. He is almost uneducated and comes from the worst slums of South London, yet he is the most wholly admirable of all Nesbit's child heroes. Dickie not only is intelligent, imaginative, and courageous, but also is capable of self-sacrifice. In his past life he is not a poor, lame orphan, but privileged, healthy, and much loved. Yet he chooses to return to modern times for the sake of Beale, a tramp and part-time thief, and the only person who has ever been kind to him.

After *Harding's Luck* Nesbit's books are less impressive as a whole, but all of them contain good moments, and they continue to exhibit her remarkable sense of how children think, speak, and feel. *The Magic City* (1910), though perhaps the thinnest of her later works, is interesting because it reflects Nesbit's hobby of building miniature towns out of blocks, boxes, china, and all sorts of household bric-a-brac. (She was so successful at this pastime that one of her towns was exhibited to the public.)

The Wonderful Garden (1911) describes the adventures of three children who discover what they believe to be enchanted seeds and a portrait that comes to life. It is marred by a condescending attitude toward her characters rare in Nesbit: she lets the reader know that there is no magic, only kindly adults who are indulging the children's fantasies and practicing a theatrical deception on them. In *Wet Magic* (1913) the magic is real, but though the book begins well,

with the rescue of a mermaid from a seaside side-show, Nesbit's imagination flags later on, and here too the end is spoiled for many readers by the casting of a spell that causes the children to forget all their adventures.

Several of the short tales in Nesbit's later collections, *The Magic World* (1912) and *Five of Us—and Madeline,* live up to her earlier standard. They also contain some of the most direct expression of her social views—radical in her own day, but today part of the democratic creed. One striking feature of Nesbit's tales is their implicit feminism. In deference to her husband's views, she never openly supported female suffrage, but her books are full of girls who, though they weep more easily, are as brave and independent-minded and adventurous as their brothers. And the heroines of her short fairy tales seldom sit around waiting to be rescued. In **"The Last of the Dragons,"** for instance *(Five of Us—and Madeline)* the Princess remarks: "Father, darling, couldn't we tie up one of the silly little princes for the dragon to look at—and then *I* could go and kill the dragon . . . ? I fence much better than any of the princes we know." In this story Nesbit also strikes a blow for what is now called male liberation: the princess falls in love with "a pale prince with large eyes and a head full of mathematics and philosophy" who has completely neglected his fencing lessons.

Nesbit's Fabian socialism is also evident in these late stories. **"The Mixed Mine"** *(The Magic World),* for example, reverses the standard Victorian plot in which a poor child is befriended and reformed by a more privileged one. Here it is the shabby Gustus who shows Edward how to get the best out of a magic telescope that enlarges whatever you look at with it; and it is Gustus who jollies Edward out of his fear of the consequences, remarking finally that his friend is "more like a man and less like a snivelling white rabbit now than what you was when I met you." The implicit Fabian moral seems to be that intelligent artisans can show a scientifically illiterate and scientifically nervous middle class how to use the new technology and increase resources for the good of the whole society. (At the end of the story Gustus and Edward share a treasure and an Oxford education, and plan to start a school for slum children.)

Modern and innovative as Nesbit's books were for her time, in a way they look back to the oldest type of juvenile literature, the traditional folktale. They recall the simplicity and directness of diction, and the physical humor, of the folktale rather than the poetic language, intellectual wit, and didactic intention of the typical Victorian fairy tale.

In Nesbit's stories, as in the traditional tale, magic often seems to be a metaphor for imagination. In the folktale, imagination can turn a cottage into a castle or transform an ugly girl into a beautiful one with a kiss. In the same way it is imagination, disguised as magic, that gives Nesbit's characters (and by exension her readers) the power to journey through space and time: to view India or the South Seas, to visit Shakespeare's London, ancient Egypt, or a future Utopia. Nesbit seems aware of this metaphor in at least some of her tales. **"The Book of Beasts"** *(The Book of Dragons),* for instance, can be read as a fable about the power of imaginative art. The magic volume of its title contains colored pictures of exotic creatures that become real when the volume is left open. The little boy who finds it releases first a butterfly, then a bird of paradise, and finally a dragon that threatens to destroy his country. If any book is vivid enough, this story says, what is in it will become real to us and invade our world for good or evil.

True imaginative power is strong enough to transform the most prosaic contemporary scene. In the folktale, straw becomes gold, and a pumpkin is changed into a coach. Nesbit's magic is as much at home in a basement in Camden Town as on a South Sea island, and like that of the folktale, it is seldom merely romantic. Though it grants the desires of her characters, it may also expose these desires as comically misconceived.

Socially, too, Nesbit's stories have affinities with folklore. Her adventurous little girls and athletic princesses recall the many traditional tales in which the heroines have wit, courage, and strength. And there is also a parallel with her political stance. The classic folktales first recorded by scholars in the nineteenth century tend to observe the world from a working-class perspective—not unnaturally, since most of them were collected from uneducated farmers, servants, and artisans. The heroes and heroines of these tales are usually the children of poor people. When they go out into the world to seek their fortunes they confront supernatural representatives of the upper class: rich, ugly giants and magicians and ogres. Many of the traditional tales, like Nesbit's, make fun of establishment figures. And as has often been pointed out, the good kings and queens of the folktale seem from internal evidence to be merely well-to-do farmers. (Literary retellings of these stories, however, from Charles Perrault to the present, usually give their royalty a convincingly aristocratic setting.)

There is no way of knowing whether Nesbit went back to these traditional folktale models consciously, or whether it was her own instinctive attitude to the world that made her break so conclusively with the past. Whatever the explanation, she was riding the wave of the future. And today, when most of her contemporaries are gathering dust on the shelves of secondhand bookshops, her stories are still read and loved by children, and echoed by adult authors. Almost every writer of children's fantasy in this century is—directly or indirectly—indebted to her.

Anita Moss

SOURCE: "E. Nesbit's Romantic Child in Modern Dress," in *Romanticism and Children's Literature in Nineteenth-Century England,* edited by James Holt McGavran, Jr., The University of Georgia Press, 1991, pp. 225-47.

Had E. Nesbit (1858-1924) written no children's books at all, her life would fascinate the student of social history. With her quick wit, lively sense of humor, keen intelligence, commitment to social issues on one hand and attraction to aesthetic escape on the other, as well as her famous friendships and love affairs, Nesbit's life reflected many of the best and worst traits of her era. Her ideas and her life often contradicted one another. Her commitment to social change, for example, did not always mesh with her taste for elegance. Her interest in children of all social classes did not quite square with her frank admission that she wrote for middle-class children and usually about them as well. Although she posed liberated identities for children, she was sometimes guilty of cruel and unjust treatment of her own children. Despite her advanced social views, she could not support women's efforts to secure essential rights because of her somewhat domineering husband, Hubert Bland. Nor did Nesbit's desire for social justice and a humane order quite coalesce with her sometimes conservative idealization of the past.

The trait that seems most abiding in Nesbit's children's books and in her interesting life is her vitality, her enormous zest for living and being in a world that her humor, imagination, and spirit allowed her to experience as a continuing and compelling adventure. Nesbit's passionate attention to life, to books, people, games, and creative work of all kinds, her close observation of the natural world, as well as her generosity and capacity for friendship, remained with her all of her life. As Nesbit grew older, her sensibility was marked with an increasing spirituality even as she continued her avid interest in the social and material world.

An heir to Romantic conceptions of nature, art, imagination, and the child, Nesbit celebrated creative activity of all kinds and stressed the imagination's capacity to infuse life with meaning and value. Hostile to the industrial invasion of England, Nesbit often expressed nostalgia for the past. She explored the limits of time and space, dimensions which take an inward turn in her children's stories, just as they do in many Romantic works of literature. While Nesbit abhorred the ugliness of industrial England and praised the value of life close to nature, she nevertheless exhibited an enduring fascination with science and a decided taste for a sophisticated cultural life available only in great cities.

Despite the numerous oppositions readily apparent in her life and children's stories, Nesbit managed to liberate herself and children's books from Victorian constraints. She became the most famous Edwardian writer for children and breathed new and vital life into the Romantic child with the publication of her "Bastable Stories"—*The Story of the Treasure Seekers* (1899), *The Wouldbegoods* (1901), and *The New Treasure Seekers* (1904). *The Story of the Treasure Seekers* stands squarely between Victorian and modern children's literature and has been acclaimed by critics as ushering in the "Nesbit Tradition" in twentieth-century children's literature, a vision that owes much to Romantic conceptions of childhood and imagination. By the end of the nineteenth century, however, the Romantic child had found expression in many fine children's stories and in novels for adults as well and had begun to lose much of its vitality in overly sentimental works such as James Barrie's *Peter Pan*, Frances Hodgson Burnett's *Little Lord Fauntleroy*, and countless ephemeral children's stories in which the Romantic child had become escapist and regressive. At the same time another Romantic vision of the child emerged, one that did not idealize the capacity of the child to redeem and to reconcile a community of adults but that celebrated childhood as a time of special, Pan-like vitality and pleasure. In this Romantic idealization of the child, the attitude represented was much more emphatically modern, as it stressed that children may realize themselves most fully when free from adult intrusions. Childhood in such works was itself a community,

one often located in a free green setting in which adults are regarded as enemies. In this vision of childhood, to grow up was to be forever severed from its joyous freedom except through memory.

Memory and imagination were for Nesbit the only vehicles which could enable the sympathetic adult to reach across the gulf of childhood. To write about "the Child" would inevitably lead the adult writer to nostalgic sentimentality. Like William Wordsworth, Nesbit felt that vivid memory of one's own childhood experience could indeed enable the adult to renew both the spirit and the senses, as she explained in her book on childhood education, *Wings and the Child:* "Do you remember the world of small and new and joyous and delightful things? Try to remember it . . . try to look at the world with the clear, clean eyes that once were yours in the days when you had never deceived a friend. You will then be able to see again certain ideals, unclouded and radiant . . . Look back and you will see that you yourself were also able to distinguish these things—once". Nesbit, like many other Romantic writers and such Victorian writers for children as Lewis Carroll and George MacDonald, deplored the emphasis upon facts in education. She believed that "liberty of thought, word, and deed was one of the rights of children," and she inveighed against an older method of education designed to break the child's spirit, citing a *Punch* cartoon, the legend of which read, "Cissy, go and see what Bobbie's doing and tell him not to". She also wrote in ringing and urgent tones about the follies of modern mechanistic education which treated children as a class (or mob) rather than as individual human beings: "I would have every man and woman in whom the heart of childhood still lives, protest, however feebly and haltingly, yet with all the power of the heart, against machine-made education—against the instruction which crams a child with facts and starves it of dreams". Education should instead be the "unfolding of a flower"; yet she argued that the last three hundred years of education "has led, in all things vital and spiritual, downhill all the way. We have gone on frustrating natural human intelligence and emotion, inculcating false doctrine, choking with incoherent facts the soul which asked to be fed with dreams come true—till now our civilization is a thing we cannot look at without a mental and moral nausea. We have, in our countryside, peasants too broken for rebellion, in our cities, 'The mortal sickness of a mind / Too unhappy to be kind'".

In educating the child, Nesbit agreed with Wordsworth that nature is the best teacher. Since the "prime instinct of the child at play . . . is to create," natural playthings—clay, sand, acorns, shells, sticks, and stones—best nourish the creative imagination. While Nesbit argued that modern toys distorted the child's imagination and spirit, these natural playthings were "the thousand adjuncts to that play which is dream and reality in one".

The imagination, according to Nesbit, was the most important faculty to be encouraged in the child's education. Imagination and faith were closely related in her view. Like John Ruskin and George Mac-Donald, Nesbit believed that imagination promotes the development of virtue and uproots the worst sins: "Imagination, duly fostered and trained, is to the world of visible wonder and beauty what the inner light is to the Japanese lantern. It transfigures everything into a glory".

Nesbit was well aware that because most children's books were written, published, and purchased by adults, children were all too easily imprisoned in and by the text. Victorian writers for children tended to freeze the good pious child in a frail angelic image, a powerful sepia found in the works of adult writers as well. Charles Dickens's Tiny Tim, George Mac-Donald's Diamond in *At the Back of the North Wind*, Dinah Mulock's Little Lame Prince, even Louisa May Alcott's Beth March—such characters are legion in Victorian fiction, and they often earn the contempt of Nesbit's child characters, who refer to narratives featuring such characters as "goody books" since they are often given as school prizes. Nesbit's characters avoid such books whenever possible in favor of fairy tales, adventure stories, and detective stories.

If Nesbit's Bastable children broke free of the imprisoned pious child, Nesbit herself succumbed to that seductive image at least once in depicting the angelic character of lame Dickie Harding in *Harding's Luck* (1999), a plucky boy who inspires world-weary deceitful adults, rescues his uncle from incredible danger, and in a generous gesture surrenders his inheritance and title to his cousins before returning to another life as stalwart Richard Arden, the son of a wealthy nobleman in the court of James I. Despite her conventional use of the pious child figure in this fantasy, however, Nesbit manages to achieve a complex unified aesthetic and social vision in *The House of Arden* and *Harding's Luck.*

In her book *The Story of the Treasure Seekers,* however, Nesbit liberates her child characters and, by implication, her child readers from this static myth of childhood. Nesbit's Bastable children—Dora, Oswald, Noel, Dicky, Alice, and H.O.—express their liberation from adults' nostalgia and aggression in several important ways. Their mother's death and their father's struggles with bankruptcy and poverty afford the Bastables exceptional freedom. They cannot afford either school or a governess. They live in a seemingly safe community, where they can explore and enjoy picnics. They even ride the train into the city alone. Although their house has grown shabby, the children nevertheless preside in their own nursery, establish their own rules, and evade adult constraints. They learn most from experience in the natural world, but they also learn from books and from Albert-next-door's uncle, a writer who retains empathy for children because he remembers his own childhood so vividly and has managed himself to evade such adult institutions as marriage.

The Bastables are perpetually on holiday. Like young William Wordsworth, they revel in their "glad animal movements" ("Tintern Abbey" and in their own inventiveness. Unlike many Victorian child characters, however, the Bastable children are by no means persecuted by adults. Oswald, Nesbit's child author and narrator, explains the Bastable attitude towards adults:

> The author of these few lines really does hope to goodness that no one will be such an owl as to think from the number of things we did when we were in the country that we were wretched, neglected little children, whose grown-up relations sparkled in the bright haunts of pleasure, and whirled in the giddy what's-its-name of fashion, while we were left to weep forsaken at home. It was nothing of the kind, and I wish you to know that my father was with us a good deal—and Albert's uncle—And we had some very decent times with them; and enjoyed ourselves very much, thank you. In some ways the good times you have with grown-ups are better than the ones you have by yourselves. At any rate they are safer . . . But these secure pleasures are not so interesting to tell about as the things you do when there is no one to stop you on the edge of a rash act. It is curious, too, that many of our most interesting games were when the grown-ups were all away. (*The Story of the Treasure Seekers*)

Thus Nesbit liberates the child from its image as victim of adult cruelty. Her child characters have good parents who understand their children's needs for freedom to enjoy adventures on their own.

Nesbit also overturns the Victorian stereotype of pious childhood by imbuing her Bastable children with spirited naughtiness. They have all of the appeal Leslie Fiedler ascribes to the "good bad boy" and the "good bad girl." Although the Bastables (except for the elder sister, Dora, who behaves according to Oswald "like the good elder sister out of books") are in fact incurably naughty, they are not liars or sneaks. They are quick to "own-up" when they are wrong. Most readers can scarcely fail to respond with pleasure to Oswald's opening statement in *The Wouldbegoods:* "This is the story of one of the most far-reaching and influentially naughty things we ever did in our lives. We did not mean to do such a deed. And yet we did do it. These things will happen with the best-regulated consciences". Oswald concludes with an address to the reader: "If you have never done any naughty acts, I expect it is only because you never had the sense to think of anything". Thus Nesbit's presiding voice in the Bastable books marks a radical departure from the condescending tones of most adult narrators in Victorian children's books.

While the spirited naughty child eventually became a stereotype itself in children's books and in popular culture, it still allowed Nesbit to break free from stifling Victorian conventions for writing for and about children. *The Wouldbegoods* in fact contains a strong element of parody of the moral tale. When the Bastables set out to be "good children," they wind up outdoing themselves in naughtiness. "Goodness" for Nesbit, as for William Blake, Wordsworth, and MacDonald, was not a matter of following a narrowly conceived set of social and moral rules.

Oswald-as-writer-and-narrator is a narrative strategy enabling Nesbit to evade the Victorian looking-glass of childhood, to create new images of childhood, and to endorse new modes of being and knowing. Wordsworth and Coleridge had tried and perhaps failed to speak to men and women in their own language. Most children's books also displayed a false idiom of childhood speech. Nesbit, however, succeeds brilliantly in speaking to children in their own language. Oswald cannot speak like characters in a "goody book" even when he tries. As a novice writer in *The Wouldbegoods,* Oswald decides to imitate conventional Victorian children's writers, explaining his experiment:

> let me do my narrating. I hope you will like it. I am going to write it a different way, like the books they give you for a prize at a girl's school—I mean a "young ladies school," of course—not a high school. High schools are not nearly so silly as some other kinds. Here goes. "'Ah, me!' sighed a slender maid of twelve summers, removing her elegant hat and passing her tapery fingers lightly through her tresses, 'how sad it is—is it not?—to

see able-bodied youths and young ladies wasting the precious summer hours in idleness and luxury!' The maiden frowned reproachingly, but yet with earnest gentleness, at the group of youths and maidens who sat beneath an Umbragipeaous beech tree and ate black currants".

At this point Oswald breaks off his narrative and exclaims, "It's no use. I can't write like these books. I wonder how some authors can keep it up. What really happened was that we were all eating black currants in the orchard out of a cabbage leaf and Alice said, 'I say, look here. Let's do something. It's simply silly to waste a day'".

The Bastable children are steeped in fairy tales, adventure stories, and books by Charles Dickens, Rudyard Kipling, William Shakespeare, and other writers. They also read the newspaper, see plays, and read poetry. Noel writes and publishes poetry. The Bastables are altogether more literate and sophisticated than Wordsworth's rustic child characters. Like other late-nineteenth-century Romantics, Nesbit envisions nature as art. The sophistication and intelligence of her child characters are also features which allow them to escape entrapment in the text and to evade the adult writer's nostalgia as projected in many sentimental depictions of childhood. In the end, however, the Bastables do not break free. In *The New Treasure Seekers,* the last book about the Bastables, Oswald admits that he feels grown-upness creeping up on him, as he and his siblings must leave the green freedom of the country and submit to such adult institutions as school. As Oswald notes at one point in *The Wouldbegoods,* "We began to feel as if we had forgotten something and did not know what it was". Nesbit does not spell out what the Bastables are forgetting, but we can guess: that timeless ability of young children to play and to be without looking to past and future with regret and anxiety—eternity in the world of here and now.

If, like the Romantic poets before her, Nesbit was unable to sustain her revolutionary stance, if she did not entirely escape Victorian nostalgia for the lost golden age of childhood, she eventually found a solution to the dilemma by internalizing the child's quest for liberation. For Nesbit one solution to the problem—how to sustain the vision and to maintain the joy of childhood in a world of painful experience—lay in turning from the realistic to the fantasy mode.

Nesbit had always written and published literary fairy tales, some of which exhibit her best writing, defy deadening conventions, and advocate radically transformed modes of being and knowing. In 1901, though, she began to publish a series of tales under the title of "The Psammead," illustrated by H. R. Millar. Eventually these stories evolved into Nesbit's first series of full-length fantasies for children—*Five Children and It* (1901), *The Phoenix and the Carpet* (1903), and *The Story of the Amulet* (1905). In the first two of these fantasies Nesbit cleverly dramatizes the conscious wishes of children: the wish for wealth and beauty, the desire to fly, etc. In *Five Children and It* and *The Phoenix and the Carpet* Nesbit cleverly manipulates and parodies convention to create what C. N. Manlove describes as fantasy in which "narratives are organized not by themes or deep meanings but by comic schemata which make witty conceits out of magic". In these first two fantasies of the series Nesbit attempts to naturalize the supernatural. Magic becomes accessible for child characters through conscious acts of will. They may be seen as products of what Samuel Taylor Coleridge called "fancy" rather than the imagination (*Biographia Literaria*). Nevertheless, Nesbit reveals again her desire to free children from stereotyped images; her child characters in these books subvert stereotypes of childhood through their displays of wit and humor. Moreover, these two works of fantasy enable Nesbit to discover a richer ore to mine—a mode of fantasy which issues from a more expensive vision of art and society. In the first two books of the series, the children's wishes are obvious and material. In *The Story of the Amulet,* though, the child characters' concerns center not upon material gain and gratification but upon the mysteries of time and space.

In some significant respects *The Story of the Amulet* displays what Harold Bloom has described as the Promethean or socially active phase of Romantic rebellion. Nesbit ardently believed in social reform. She and her husband, Hubert Bland, were founding members of the Fabian Society and remained socialists all of their lives. In *The Story of the Amulet* the characters—Cyril, Robert, Anthea, and Jane—visit civilizations in ancient Egypt and Babylon; they even locate the lost continent of Atlantis. They have found one half of a magical amulet. The quest which organizes their adventures into past civilizations is to find the missing half of the magical charm and to reunite their family, as both parents have had to travel far away from home. Nesbit uses these visits to ancient civilizations to reveal social ills in Edwardian England. Eventually Nesbit proposes a Utopian vision of society when the children travel into the future. In this enlightened and humane society people

wear brief, comfortable clothing of bright colors and soft textures. Cities display the finest achievements of art and the best of nature as well. Architecture is functional as well as aesthetically pleasing. The institution of the family has been reorganized in order that both men and women participate in rearing children. Nesbit also envisions reforms in health care, education, and class structure.

The fantasy ends with a powerful vision. When the children at last find the missing half of the amulet and join the two halves, it becomes a brilliantly radiant arch through which the soul of the children's friend, an Egyptologist, unites with that of Rekh-Mara, a priest from ancient Egypt. Nesbit describes the union: "Then the great double arch glowed in and through the green light that had been there since the Name of Power had first been spoken—it glowed with a light more bright yet more soft than the other light—a light that the children could bear to look upon—a glory and splendour and sweetness unspeakable". While Nesbit describes this event in transcendent terms, she makes clear that the result will be enacted within the context of social reality. She also underscores the vital connections and potent links between the present and the past. Nesbit believed that human beings may participate in eternity, but this participation appears profoundly natural, rather than supernatural. *The Story of the Amulet* includes many such moments of vision which strongly resemble Wordsworth's "spots of time" (*Prelude* [1850]) or similar moments of vision in the poetry of William Blake and Percy Bysshe Shelley. Such moments, according to the children's old magical friend from *Five Children and It,* the wise and crotchety Psammead, allow us to "see everything happening in the same place at the same time".

One important way that Nesbit reveals significant connections between past and present is through story itself. The magical creatures in *The Story of the Amulet* all narrate their histories. Yet this story-telling capacity seems aligned with some larger creative power expressed in the amulet's exquisite music, light, and voice, just as Shelley's west wind, Coleridge's Aeolian harp, and Wordsworth's correspondent breeze (*Prelude*) seem to unite these Romantic poets' imaginations to some mysterious creative force.

We have noted that *The Story of the Amulet* is "Promethean" in exploring the child characters' penetration of time and space and in Nesbit's use of narrative to express revolutionary views on reforming her society, one which she increasingly viewed as destructive to imagination, beauty, health, and life. In *The Enchanted Castle* (1907) and *The Magic City* (1910), the quest turns increasingly inward. Northrop Frye has written "that the metaphorical structure of Romantic poetry tends to move inside and downward instead of outside and upward, hence the creative world is deep within, and so is heaven or the place of the presence of God". For Nesbit, as for her late-century Romantic contemporaries, this "center" was increasingly expressed in art itself—art as the reality, not art as the vehicle for apprehending a transcendent reality. During this period Nesbit had become increasingly interested in spiritual matters; for example, she was received into the Roman Catholic Church in 1906. Yet, unlike George MacDonald and C. S. Lewis, Nesbit does not express her religious faith and feeling through fantasy. Nesbit's mature fantasies—*The Enchanted Castle* (1907), *The House of Arden* (1908), *Harding's Luck* (1909), and *The Magic City* (1910)—celebrate the primacy of the human imagination and reveal the role of the arts as a center of value and meaning in human civilization. In all of these books creative acts of reading, writing, imagining, and building are all closely associated with magic. At such creative moments the child characters are at once their most totally human selves and also participants in eternity.

In *The Enchanted Castle* three siblings—Gerald, Jimmy, and Kathleen—remain at school with their French governess during the summer holiday because their cousin is seriously ill. The governess allows them to explore freely, and they soon discover an "enchanted castle," replete with a garden in which Greek statues and stone dinosaurs magically come to life. In this garden they find a "sleeping beauty," who turns out to be only Mabel, a servant's niece. Mabel plays tricks on the children but is shocked to find herself invisible because her ring really is magic. Nesbit structures several adventures and misadventures connected with the magical ring. A subplot concerning the French governess's longlost love, Lord Yalding, finally unifies the adventures and brings them to a close. When Lord Yalding and the young governess rediscover each other, they both wish "that all the magic this ring has wrought may be undone, and that the ring itself may be no more and no less than a charm to bind thee and me together forevermore".

Throughout *The Enchanted Castle* Nesbit links art, the imagination, nature, literature, magic, and belief. She describes nature as art and art as nature. Nesbit

also investigates the nature of fiction, lies, and truth. In contrast to Wordsworthian children who never seem to read, Gerald reads so much that he loses the vividness of actual experience by rendering it almost immediately into conventional and rather shallow literary language. Mabel's aunt has damaged her mind by reading too many novels in pink wrappers. The experience with magic, however, transforms Gerald's storytelling ability. He encounters radically new modes of being, knowing, and perceiving. Though Gerald believes his experience is merely a dream, he still makes good use of it as he narrates it to the other children: "As he told it some of the white mystery and magic of the moonlit gardens got into his voice and his words, so that when he told of the statues that came alive, and the great beast that was alive through its stone, Kathleen thrilled responsive, clutching his arm, and even Jimmy ceased to kick the wall with his boot heels and listened open-mouthed". Gerald's practice in using fictional language, his visionary experience in the castle garden, and his encounter with burglars clearly enliven and enhance his stories. Not only do Gerald's tales now resonate with mystery and magic; they also exhibit more exciting plots and more vivid concrete details. As Gerald's narrative skills develop, he blends literary conventions, practices his stories on a real child audience, and enlarges his plots with the mythic dimensions of dreams and fantasy.

One of the most potentially terrifying incidents in *The Enchanted Castle* occurs when the children find themselves transformed into stone. To become a stone statue, they learn, is not to become dead and lifeless but to be alive in a new and exciting way. Inside the stone dinosaur Kathleen was "just the same as ever, only she was Kathleen in a case of marble that would not let her move. It would not have let her cry, even if she wanted to. But she had not wanted to cry. Inside, the marble was not cold or hard. It seemed, somehow, to be softly lined with warmth and pleasantness and safety".

As living statues, the children swim on an enchanted island with other living statues. Significantly, these statues are characters from Greek and Roman mythology: Janus, Phoebus Apollo, and Hermes are among the mythological figures prominent in the scene. The higher reality in which the children participate, then, is not really a transcendent one, but profoundly human. The Greek and Roman characters seem to symbolize the best achievements of human civilization. Appropriately, the character of Phoebus Apollo plays a central role in this magical scene. The god of medicine, music, and poetry, the bringer of light, Apollo had conquered the dark unfathomable forces in the underworld and secured the basis of civilization. In juxtaposing the statues of Apollo and the dinosaur, Nesbit reveals opposing Apollonian and Dionysian dimensions in the human psyche. The children seem to experience magically these powers in their own imaginative lives and to integrate them through art. As they raptly listen to Apollo's music, the children enter a timeless realm of art:

> Then Phoebus struck the strings and softly plucked melody from them, and all the beautiful dreams of all the world came fluttering close with wings like doves' wings; and all the lovely thoughts that sometimes hover near, but not so near that you can catch them, now came home as to their nests in the hearts of those who listened. And those who listened forgot time and space, and how to be sad, and how to be naughty, and it seemed that the whole world lay like a magic apple in the hand of each listener, and that the whole world was good and beautiful.

This magical adventure within the protected oasis of the enchanted garden represents and celebrates artistic creation as a supreme value. The highly poetic texture of Nesbit's prose throughout the chapter emphasizes that the world of art and the creative imagination are the deep centers of magical enchantment. Mabel's human story, though shyly told, nevertheless exerts a hushing spell even upon the gods: "The marble Olympians listened enchanted—almost as enchanted as the castle itself, and the soft moonlit moments fell past like pearls dropping into a deep pool". Nesbit contrasts a highly realistic scene with this visionary garden of art. As the sun rises, the statues flee to their pedestals, and the children cease to be marble and become flesh. From an island of brambles and coarse grass, the children climb down into a passage ending in the Temple of Flora, "a great hall, whose arched roof was held up by two rows of round pillars, and whose every corner was filled with a soft, searching, lovely light, filling every cranny, as water fills the rocky secrecies of hidden sea-caves".

In this deep illuminated space, each child perceives a perfect vision differently; the narrator explains, "I won't describe it, because it does not look the same to any two people". The statue of Psyche presides over the cave and serves as the source of light. The secret of the magic, Nesbit implies, lies deep within the self, the creative center which enables each child to imagine "the most perfect thing possible". In Psyche's cave, the children enjoy viewing splendid artistic achievements from different cultures and eras,

all framed as if pictures in a gallery and each depicting "some moment when life had sprung to fire and flower—the best that the soul of man could ask or man's destiny grant". For Nesbit, as for the English Romantics before her, the arts are the center of civilization, just as the creative imagination is the center of the self. Her heavenly vision thus becomes profoundly imbued with the imaginative products of human culture, the only hope, Nesbit seems to imply, whereby her characters and her readers may sustain themselves in an increasingly mechanistic and materialistic world.

Between the publication of *The Enchanted Castle* and *The Magic City,* Nesbit turned her energies once more to writing about fantastic voyages in time with *The House of Arden* (1908) and *Harding's Luck* (1909). These two volumes exhibit Nesbit's outrage with the social conditions of Edwardian England, as well as her enduring fascination with the literary potential of fairy tales. In *The House of Arden* and *Harding's Luck* Nesbit experiments with fairy tale structures and the possibilities of time fantasy to pose a mature social and aesthetic vision. She also investigates the interpenetration of the past and present, while revealing the significance of the past and of place in the imaginative and emotional lives of children. Both of these splendid books resonate with the power of an imagination which can fuse dream and reality, the ordinary and the fabulous. Again Nesbit suggests that apparently transcendent realms may be apprehended through the creative acts of reading, writing, making, and imagining.

The House of Arden centers upon the time travels of Edred and Elfrida Arden, heirs to an ancient castle now fallen from former glory. When they move to Arden Castle, they learn from an ancient servant, Old Beale, that the last Arden treasure is hidden somewhere in the castle. Inspired by Old Beale's legend, the children search for and finally locate a fragile sheet of parchment on which is written a spell for finding the treasure:

> Hear, Oh badge of Arden's house,
> The spell my little age allows;
> Arden speaks it without fear,
> Badge of Arden's house, draw near,
> Make me brave and kind and wise,
> And show me where the treasure lies.

When Edred utters the spell, the "badge of Arden's House" appears in the form of a Mouldiwarp, a little animal resembling a mole whose emblem had been stamped in gold above the chequered shield on the cover of the white book in which the children had found the spell. This curious and comical creature initiates Edred and Elfrida into a series of magical journeys into the past: to the early nineteenth century when France is about to attack England in 1807; to the period of James I in 1605, when Elfrida inadvertently chants a rhyme about Guy Fawkes and the Gunpowder Plot and finds herself in the Tower of London, where she and Edred meet their cousin Richard Arden; and, perhaps the most perilous of all, to the sixteenth century in the period of Henry VIII's marriage to Anne Boleyn (1533-36). With the help of several characters from the sixteenth century—their old nurse, a wise woman, the Mouldiwarp, and Richard—the two children rescue their father and uncle from imprisonment in twentieth-century South America. Although this experience marks the end of their adventures into the past and their quest to find the treasure, Edred and Elfrida choose the true treasure—the happiness of a reunited family.

In the sequel to *The House of Arden, Harding's Luck,* Nesbit introduces Dickie Harding, a lame child who lives with a cruel woman in an impoverished little house in Deptford. (Nesbit knew the condition of such children well, as she devoted much time and energy to the poor children of Deptford.) Dickie amuses himself with a coral and bells and a seal, both bearing the image of a curious little mole-like creature. Dickie's father had instructed him never to part with these treasures, the emblems of his true noble identity. Dickie amuses himself by playing with these treasures and by reading. He also longs, like Mary Lennox in Frances Hodgson Burnett's *The Secret Garden,* to make a little garden of his own. From the cornchandler, Dickie purchases a packet of Perrokett's Artistic Bird Seed, which produces exotically beautiful moonflowers. Later Dickie attaches himself to a tramp, Beale, and travels about the countryside. Beale is a crook and uses Dickie to beg from passersby. Beale's true nature is clear to the reader, but not to the innocent Dickie. Eventually, however, Dickie reforms Beale and makes an honest man of him, and the two establish a household together.

In alternating chapters Nesbit creates Dickie's fantastic travels to the past. Arranging silver seeds from the moonflowers in crossed triangles, Dickie falls into a trancelike sleep and awakes in the reign of James I, where, no longer lame, he enjoys the privileged status as Sir Richard Arden's son. In this stately home Dickie studies Latin and Greek, learns to dance and to fence, and meets his cousins, Edred and Elfrida. He also learns the art of wood carving in this past life. When he returns to Beale, Dickie uses this craft to establish a business and an honest stable household for himself and Beale. Like many of Charles Dickens's characters, Dickie is quite literally father to the man. Later Dickie, who turns out to be the true heir of Arden Castle, finds the ancient treasure and relinquishes it all to his cousins in order to return permanently to his past life as the stalwart young Richard Arden. Nesbit clearly implies that the past is preferable in all ways to the present, though she also reveals the social problems of the past.

One of Nesbit's purposes in writing the Arden fantasies was clearly to enliven the study of history. Like Lewis Carroll's Alice, Nesbit had been forced to learn history out of a "horrid little book, called somebody's *Outlines of English History*" (Preface, *Children's Stories from English History*). She also wished to contrast the idea of "Arden" (actually a dense forest which covered the English Midlands in ancient times) with what Nesbit viewed as a corrupt and inhumane society. Nesbit's Arden suggests the values represented in William Shakespeare's comedy, *As You Like It*—the timelessness of the pastoral world, its unity of being, its sense of community where all social classes meet to bask in the green enchantment of the forest. Nesbit's Arden books ultimately celebrate literature itself as a living reality; it is therefore fitting that her Arden should resemble Shakespeare's more than it does the actual historical forest.

As Shakespeare's play is laced with verse and song, so too are Nesbit's fantasies. The timeless pastoral world of Arden is not only a green sphere of leisure; it is also the realm of creative energy and imaginative labor. Just as *As You Like It* simultaneously idealizes the pastoral life and calls it into question, so too Nesbit's Arden fantasies simultaneously idealize the past and reveal its flaws. Most important, both the play and Nesbit's Arden books end with a restored and revitalized order which offers hope for an ideal society. It is fitting, for example, that Lord Arden in contemporary times rescues ancient Arden lands from the Tallow King, a vulgar industrialist who abuses tenants and whose only concern is profit.

The Romantic elements of Nesbit's Arden fantasies owe much to such Victorian fantasy writers as Charles Kingsley, Jean Ingelow, Mary Louisa Molesworth, Dinah Mulock, and most especially, George MacDonald. Dickie Harding strongly resembles MacDonald's Diamond of *At the Back of the North Wind.* Dickie's goodness, innocence and resourcefulness transform everyone he encounters. His magical adventures are contrasted with chapters dealing with his poverty-ridden life in Deptford, just as Diamond's voyages contrast with his everyday existence in illness as the son of a poor cabman. The fantastic journeys of both Dickie and Diamond are presided over by strong, goddess-like maternal figures, who protect the children but who also teach them and help them to grow. yet both of these saintly children are finally too good for this world. As Diamond disappears into that mysterious place "at the back of the North Wind," so Dickie retreats into the time of James I. But Dickie does not retreat until he has transformed the present. Elfrida, Edred, and Dickie change the past; in turn those past actions transform the present. Thus, while Nesbit's Arden books do indeed reveal a conservative turn to the past somewhat at odds with her advanced social views, it is not merely an uncritical and idealized treatment of the past. The Arden books provide a thorough critique of both past and present. In so doing the books reveal Nesbit's sophisticated sense of history and the interpenetration of past and present.

In both Arden books Nesbit celebrates the activities of play, reading, composing, and creating. Literature in these books provides children with potent links to the past. The Mouldiwarp may only be summoned by an act of composing poetry. When Edred doubts his magical experience, the Mouldiwarp reminds him of the magical toadstools in Charles Kingsley's *Hereward the Wake,* and that less likely events had taken place in **The Story of the Amulet.** He chides Edred for not realizing that he is in a fairy tale, where anything is possible. Mouldiwarp himself can speak the languages of other creatures and control natural elements with the sweetness of his music and the power of his voice. In fact Mouldiwarp seems to be a powerful symbol of the creative imagination. As a mole, he is close to the earth but nevertheless summons pigeons and swans; hence he unifies heaven and earth, the physical and the spiritual. His abilities in fact resemble strongly Nesbit's own practice of blending the ordinary and the magical. A speaker of country dialect and a master of the most elegant French, Mouldiwarp dissolves social and cultural barriers and implies that art comes from folk and cultivated cultures. Although Mouldiwarp's relative, "Mouldierwarp," controls space and the "Mouldiestwarp" of all presides over some still higher and unattainable reality, Mouldiwarp remains the center of the magic and provides the vehicles for apprehending the other two levels.

In the course of his adventures Dickie Harding becomes a creative artist. Not only does he read, imag-

ine, and grow magical moonflowers; he entertains his friends with stories and steadily polishes his art of wood carving. Similarly, Edred and Elfrida become storytellers, and Elfrida's skill as a poet develops throughout the fantasies. In the Arden books, then, Nesbit integrates her social and aesthetic vision. She advocates careful analysis and imaginative immersion in the past in order to use one's creative gifts in the present and to make society itself a work of art—a garden where human beings may work, play, and love in joyous fellowship. In such an ideal society, Nesbit suggests, barriers of social class dissolve. Living itself becomes an art where greed, ugliness, and the indignities of poverty and social oppression have no place. Like William Morris, William Butler Yeats, and other late-century Romantics, Nesbit would unify labor and art in order that a true community could flourish. She was deeply aware of how alienated English workers were from their labor and how divided were the social classes; however conservative her books may appear from some perspectives, Nesbit never stopped dreaming that human effort and intelligence could establish a more just order of society. Thus Nesbit's child characters do not merely retreat into the past. She clearly intends for both her characters and her child readers to appropriate knowledge from the past, "lessons" in fact. In this sense Nesbit's later fantasies are indeed "didactic," but they are expansively, not narrowly, didactic.

In her last great fantasy for children, **The Magic City,** Nesbit expresses her natural supernaturalism most explicitly. In this complex book Nesbit explores the imaginary adventures of Philip Haldane. Through these adventures Philip adjusts to the marriage of his half-sister, Helen, to Peter Graham, her childhood sweetheart, now a widower with one daughter, Lucy. While the happy couple departs for an extended honeymoon in Europe, Philip remains with Lucy in Graham's spacious mansion. Fearful of a cruel and rather insensitive nurse, Philip amuses himself by building a magic city from books, toys, candle sticks, blocks, dominoes, and other common household items. This activity comforts him because it had been one of his favorite pastimes with Helen. At the Grange, however, Philip's creation results in punishment rather than the praise to which he has been accustomed. The unpleasant nurse accuses the child of being "naughty, wicked, and untruthful" and "whirled him off to bed" without supper.

Later in the night Philip awakens to brilliantly radiant moonlight and creeps downstairs for a last glimpse of his wonderful city. Instead he finds himself on a vast flat plain. He has entered his magic city. Soon Lucy joins him, and guardsmen apprehend both children. Lucy and Philip are told of an ancient prophecy foretelling that both a Destroyer and a Deliverer will enter the city by the route they have used.

Mr. Noah, apparently the ruler of the magic city, explains that one enters by building something. Philip also meets his old friend, Mr. Perrin, the master builder who made Philip's beloved and highly useful oak blocks. To be a Deliverer, Mr. Perrin explains, Philip must accomplish seven great deeds, the first of which is the slaying of an enormous green dragon. Philip's adversary arrives in the form of a "Pretenderette," though she is really only the unpleasant nurse who has also gotten into the magic city, perhaps in the act of trying to destroy it. In any event the nurse eventually proves herself to be the Destroyer, just as Philip, with the help of Lucy, becomes the Deliverer. Philip's most significant quest is not the seven brave deeds but the struggle to overcome his selfish and possessive feelings for Helen and to learn to love Lucy. The seven deeds serve this larger purpose.

Philip's first two heroic tasks are simple. He settles the dreadful dragon (only a windup toy) by removing the key. Nesbit hints that technology must serve humane purposes; to achieve this worthy end, Philip must be master of it. One of the most important events in the quest occurs when Philip is mysteriously kidnapped, since he joins Helen on an imaginary island during this episode. Helen explains that she had come to the island by walking in "at the other side of the dream". In an unselfish gesture, Philip yields his happy island to displaced islanders and also supplies the kingdom with fruit.

After Philip and Lucy have completed all the deeds, they return to the Magic City, where they must free the people from the Pretenderette, who has demolished the Hall of Justice, opened a book, and in the process released invaders into the magic city. To quell the invaders, Philip merely opens another book and calls upon Caesar to drive out the invaders. In the end the Pretenderette is condemned to make herself loved by someone, while Helen and Philip realize that they must return home. As in so many of Nesbit's children's books, the reunited family marks the end of the narrative. In building their own magical cities, Philip and Lucy not only solve their emotional problems but also create an order characterized by peace, satisfying labor, books, art, and the finest of cultural artifacts. Again, all barriers between people

dissolve, evil spells dissipate, and a new era is ushered in. Nesbit implies that Lucy and Philip will take these same values back to the primary world and that they will create such a beneficent world at the Grange.

Nesbit herself was famous for building magic cities, a process she describes in *Wings and the Child.* In the foreword to this book, Nesbit explains that it "took shape as an attempt to contribute something, however small and unworthy, to the science of building a magic city in the soul of a child, a city built of all things pure and fine and beautiful." The child will, she says, "use the whole force of dream and fancy to create something out of nothing".

In *The Magic City* Nesbit truly celebrates this human instinct to create something out of nothing. In discussing the complex philosophical structure of *The Magic City* Stephen Prickett has placed E. Nesbit in the Christian Platonic tradition of Charles Kingsley and George MacDonald, noting that *The Enchanted Castle* and *The Magic City* "involve the discovery not so much of magic creatures in this world, as of the existence of other worlds along-side this one". While Nesbit shared many spiritual and artistic convictions with Kingsley and MacDonald, *The Enchanted Castle,* the Arden books, and *The Magic City* do not celebrate the discovery of other worlds so much as the creation of an ideal human world. Hence, Nesbit, unlike Kingsley and MacDonald, stresses the human rather than the divine forces as the grounds of the magic world. Plato had felt that artists could only imitate shadows or reflections of the Ideas which existed in the mind of God. Plotinus and other Neoplatonists believed that the artist could through the creative imagination reach these Ideas and bypass the concrete world of objects. The English Romantic poets had in various ways attempted to "naturalize the supernatural and to humanize the divine". Nesbit's major fantasies show that she believes the way to create this human order is with creative acts within the context of the concrete world.

In *The Enchanted Castle* Gerald and Mabel appropriate visions and become storytellers. Even the Greek gods and goddesses listen to these stories. At the end of the fantasy, Lord Yalding yields supernatural magic for human love and determines to restore his castle through active human effort. Similarly in *The Magic City* the basis of Philip's magical world lies in the material world. The magic city's existence depends upon his creative labor. As Mr. Perrin explains: "All the cities and things you ever built is in this country. I don't know how it's managed, no more'n what you do. But so it is . . . *Making's* the thing. If it was no more than the lad that turned the handle of the grindstone to sharp the knife that carved a bit of a cabinet or what not, or a child that picked a teazle to finish a bit of the cloth that's glued on to the bottom of the chessman—they're all here". Similarly in the Arden fantasies the children use art and creative activities to enter the magical past and to restore the House of Arden; in so doing they establish a more progressive society for all who inhabit the estate.

Art and creative work, then, allow one to participate in a visionary city and to build an ideal community. The magic city is Nesbit's complex symbol for an ideal civilization. *The Magic City* thus resembles other Romantic expressions in making the highest claim for the place of art. Northrop Frye has written, "In the Romantic construct there is a center where inward and outward manifestations of a common motion and spirit are unified, where the ego is identified as itself because it is also identified with something which is not itself. In Blake this world at the deep center is Jerusalem, the city of God that mankind or Albion has sought all through history without success because he has been looking in the wrong direction, outside". In *The Magic City* and in her other fantasies, Nesbit suggests that the potential for magical creation, for making oneself a "Deliverer" rather than a "Destroyer," lies within each of us. Philip's quest involves his acceptance of help from Lucy and also reveals him on the boundary between the two worlds of the conscious and the unconscious, the ideal and the actual, the real and the imaginary. Just as magical creatures, rivers, and characters spill out of books in the magic city and profoundly affect events and characters, so art itself interacts with social and historical reality, at once reflecting and shaping it.

Towards the end of his adventures, Philip journies to Somnolentia with Lucy to awaken the Great Sloth. Here the children encounter a monstrous creature similar to the dinosaurs in *The Enchanted Castle*. This creature has put the people to sleep. They neglect their city and allow their clear stream to become clogged with gold (an analogy perhaps for what Nesbit saw happening to her own society). The sloth represents not just laziness, but a regressive refusal to create and thus to become fully human. It is humanity at an arrested state of development, since it only requires sleeping, eating, and soothing lullabies. One of the ways that Lucy and Philip awaken the Somnolentians and liberate them from the sloth's tyr-

anny is to remind the citizens of their true names and thus of their human identities. At Lucy's insistence, they work at restoring the buildings, gardens, and fields, just as Philip had worked to create his magic city. The city and the garden represent the human imagination at work on the mineral and vegetable worlds. The orderly beauty of the magic city is a heavenly vision against chaos. Such creative endeavor, Nesbit implies, requires both imagination and humanity. Thus Philip learns to share his adventure and his labor with Lucy. In the final scene Philip and Lucy cooperate as equals to build a model of the Grange and thus return home to be reunited with their family.

The most significant way that Nesbit's child characters liberate themselves from static myths of childhood is by seizing control of their own stories to become makers and creators. Unlike Wordsworth's child characters, Nesbit's are highly literate. Although they retain intuitive ways of knowing, the activities of reading, thinking, fabricating, and even artful lying help them to evade sentimentality, constraints, and aggressions of adults. While Wordsworth and MacDonald celebrate the simplicity and innocence of children, Lewis Carroll and Nesbit rejoice in their complexity, intelligence, and experience. Nesbit encourages her child characters and her readers to transcend literary and social convention, to speak in radically new voices, and to create new idioms and myths of childhood, just as Nesbit herself broke free of some rather stifling conventions of Victorian children's literature. We have seen that children in Romantic and Victorian children's literature have been entrapped in texts; it is a telling metaphor that Philip Haldane frees creatures from texts in *The Magic City*—frees both monsters and marvels, transforms them, and sends them back again. Similarly Nesbit releases her child characters and her child readers from such imprisonment. While Oswald Bastable had feared "grown-upness," Philip Haldane and Lucy of *The Magic City* and Gerald of *The Enchanted Castle* just grow. In her later fantasies Nesbit does not lock magic behind the golden gates of childhood but makes it available within the context of mundane reality. Her characters make the magic for themselves through the creative acts of storytelling and art. Finally, each of these fantasies ends with a reunited family experiencing a sense of renewal and anticipating a future of creative labors together. Implicit in all of Nesbit's children's stories is her profoundly optimistic belief in the human capacity for transformation. New societies may emerge from the ruins of the old, she suggests, just as new stories may be constructed from the worn-out fragments of literary convention.

Mervyn Nicholson

SOURCE: "What C. S. Lewis Took from E. Nesbit," in *Children's Literature Association Quarterly,* Vol. 16, No. 1, Spring, 1991, pp. 16-22.

For anyone who knows the Narnia books of C. S. Lewis, there is a story by E. Nesbit in her collection *The Magic World* that immediately stands out. It is called **"The Aunt and Amabel"**; it tells of a girl who damages a special flower-bed without meaning to. Her aunt punishes her by confining her to a "bedroom, the one with the wardrobe with a looking-glass in it" (228). The only furnishings described are a bed—and a wardrobe. Then Amabel finds a railway timetable that lists a peculiar destination: "the extraordinary name 'Whereyouwantogoto'." Its nearest "station was 'Bigwardrobeinspareroom'" (224). Intrigued, she opens the wardrobe door and steps inside, like Lucy in *The Lion, the Witch and the Wardrobe.* And like Lucy, Amabel discovers something in it besides coats—in her case a crystal cave. Lucy finds snowy woods, not a cave—but the faun Lucy meets immediately takes her to a cave. In Nesbit, Amabel finds a sumptuous place where she is lovingly welcomed by "The People Who Understand" (231). With their help she and her aunt are reconciled, exchanging forgiveness in a manner characteristic of Nesbit. The motif of *human* reconciliation is crucial. But the obvious point is that the motifs found in **"The Aunt and Amabel"** are also found in *The Lion, the Witch and the Wardrobe.* Lewis was deeply indebted to E. Nesbit, not only in matters of plot, character and image, but even in small details of phrasing. When he set out to write his *Chronicles of Narnia,* he though of them as being Nesbit books: as belonging to a type or genre practised by E. Nesbit.[1] In many respects the Narnia books begin where the Nesbit books leave off: *The Magician's Nephew,* the first of the series, begins with an allusion to Nesbit. Much has been said about Lewis's place in the tradition of Christian romance and apologetic and of his links to Christian writers like MacDonald and Williams, but this emphasis has obscured his debt to non-Christian and even anti-Christian writers. Of these, E. Nesbit is the most important. What is striking is that Lewis, a belligerently orthodox Christian, who saw his imaginative writing as performing a quasi-evangelistic function, should have so much in common with a writer like Nesbit, who was a Fabian Socialist with occult interests.[2]

In both writers, a division between two kinds of world is evident: the ordinary one of adult and childhood experience (the so-called "real" world), and an extraordinary world where impossible things happen—impossible by the standards of the "real" world at any rate. For convenience we may refer to them as, respectively, "This World," and the "Other World." This World is the realm of plausibility or actuality: the social context, normally the society of the author's time. The Other World is a realm of expanded possibilities: the place where anything may happen. Lewis uses the wardrobe as a threshold symbol to link This World with the Other World: the English countryside in 1940 with Narnia under Queen Jadis. E. Nesbit employs the wardrobe image in the same way, to link This World with the Other World, where This World is the realistic place of misunderstanding and punishment in turn-of-the-century England. By contrast the Other World is where such misunderstandings can be dissolved: here the desirable is the obtainable. The brevity of the short story form, however, dictates a very different use of the wardrobe image in Nesbit from what we find in Lewis, where the structure is far bigger and more elaborate. But that Lewis had **"The Aunt and Amabel"** in mind (however unconsciously) seems clear.

The links are too important to ignore. Both girls, separated from parents before the action begins, find a magic wardrobe. Lucy, under the stress of a competitive game, and Amabel, under the stress of punishment, go through the wardrobe into a world associated with desire (Narnia in one, "Whereyouwantogoto" in the other). Lewis adopts not only the image of the magic wardrobe but even the phraseology used by his predecessor. In Nesbit, Amabel finds that domestic furniture has expanded into a geographical location ("The name of the station was 'Bigwardrobeinspareroom'"). And while the room is called at first "the best bedroom," it is more often called the "spare room." Likewise, when Lucy tells Tumnus the faun how she came to be standing by the lamp-post in the snowy woods of Lantern Waste ("I—I got in through the wardrobe in the spare room" [9]), Tumnus turns her domestic landscape of rooms in a house into a geographical landscape ("if only I had worked harder at geography . . . I should no doubt know all about those strange countries" [9]), and when he says goodbye, he emphasizes this transformation: "I suppose you can find your own way from there back to Spare Oom and War Drobe" (10). "Wardrobe" becomes "War Drobe," and "spare room" "Spare Oom," altering the typography. Nesbit before him had also altered the typography:

"Bigwardrobeinspareroom." I emphasize this point because it reveals how thoroughly Lewis absorbed even a minor Nesbit story. He takes not only particular images—famous ones like the wardrobe—but particular words for building up his own mythical kingdom.

This is not all, either. When Amabel goes through her wardrobe, she enters a completely *white* world. Whiteness (of place, people, and things, even food) is repeatedly emphasized, reminding one of the white world, white witch, white reindeer, and white statues of the snowy Narnia that Lucy and soon Edmund happen into. Amabel boards a train with a marvelous system for meals: it supplies "Whatyouwantoeat" and "Whatyouwantodrink." In the blink of an eye she is given the very food and drink she likes best. Lewis withheld this detail from Lucy and kept it for Edmund. When Edmund blunders in and encounters the Queen, she invites him up into her sleigh—much as Amabel gets up into her magic railway carriage. She offers him a delicious drink, then adds: "It is dull . . . to drink without eating. . . . What would you like best to eat?" and, like the food Amabel prefers, Edmund's special food—Turkish Delight—appears instantly. In Nesbit, the theme of the instant gratification of desire is part of the human reconciliation that Lewis calls the "healing of harms" (*Silver Chair* 194). But in Lewis, it is the opposite: instant gratification is part of the wicked witch's temptation strategy to entrap a young male. By means of it he is made her instrument.

Before leaving *Wardrobe*, we may note another Nesbit link. In her profoundest tale, ***The Enchanted Castle***,[3] the statues in a castle garden come to life. The first of these magical beings to appear is a *faun*, who comes out of the woods past one of the children, like Tamnus the faun appearing to Lucy out of the woods—the first Narnian being to appear. The motif of statues coming to life is central to *Wardrobe*: the eponymous Witch turns people into statues that the eponymous Lion miraculously reanimates. This switching into statues and then back out of statues is the imaginative backbone of ***The Enchanted Castle***. In Nesbit, the living statues are Greek gods (reminding one of Narnia's Greek dryads, naiads, etc.); much is made of the fact that those who wake up as one of them find themselves incapable of being afraid: even if they want to, they can't. But as soon as they revert to ordinary mortality, they once more experience fear. This is exactly the condition of the saved in Lewis's apocalyptic *Last Battle*. As Lucy puts it, "Have you noticed, one can't feel afraid even

if one wants to? Try it" (156). The imagining of what life would feel like without the experience of fear forms a significant part in the profoundest visions of both writers.[4]

The Magic World (in which **"The Aunt and Amabel"** appears) is minor Nesbit. But it was major in its influence on Lewis, and other stories in the collection offer prototypes for Narnia, too. One, **"The Cat-Hood of Maurice,"** is crucial for *The Voyage of the Dawn Treader*. It tells of a boy named Maurice, who, like Lewis's Edmund and his unreformed Eustace, is a particularly obnoxious lot. Maurice is to be sent to a special school (the motif of the special school is prominent in *The Silver Chair* as "Experiment House"; it also turns up in *Wardrobe* as the cause of Edmund's nastiness). But after abusing a cat called Lord Hugh, Maurice is changed into the cat. He attempts to communicate with the humans about his dreadful predicament by using his saucer of milk: "He carefully dipped his right paw in it, for his idea was to make letters with it on the kitchen oil-cloth. He meant to write: 'please tell me to leave off being a cat and be Maurice again,' but he found his paw a very clumsy pen, and he had to rub out the first 'P' because it only looked like an accident" (18). Later he tries with ink, with unintelligible, even disastrous results. For example:

> It was not Mabel
> it was Maur
> ice I mean Lord Hugh (20)

One of the most memorable episodes of *The Voyage of the Dawn Treader* occurs when the self-centered Eustace turns into a dragon—because spiritually he is a dragon—and then tries to explain to the others, by writing in the sand, what had happened to him:

> But this never succeeded. In the first place Eustace (never having read the right books) had no idea how to tell a story straight. And for another thing, the muscles and nerves of the dragon-claws that he had to use had never learned to write and were not built for writing anyway. As a result he never got nearly to the end before the tide came in and washed away all the writing except the bits he had already trodden on or accidentally swished out with his tail. And all that anyone had seen would be something like this—the dots are for the bits he had smudged out—
>
> I WNET TO SLEE . . . RGOS AGRONS I MEAN DRANGONS CAVE CAUSE ITWAS DEAD AND AINIG SO HAR . . . WOKE UP AND COU . . . GET OFFF MI ARM OH BOTHER . . . (89)

Note the typographical attempt in each case to represent the unsuccessful message from the metamorphosed human (Lewis knew a similar episode in the myth of Io. Io, transformed into a cow, tries to communicate by means of hoofmarks in the sand of her father's river).

At the end of **"Cat-Hood"** Maurice regains human shape, having learned something from the experience of metamorphosis. Nesbit comments:

> Please dismiss any fears which you may entertain that after this Maurice became a model boy. He didn't. But he was much nicer than before . . . he is almost always nice to Mabel, for he cannot forget all that she was to him when he wore the shape of Lord Hugh. His father attributes all the improvement in his son's character to that week at Dr. Strongitharm's . . . Lord Hugh's character is unchanged, Cats learn slowly and with difficulty. (25)

With the same tone and ambivalence Lewis assesses the reforming Eustace:

> It would be nice, and fairly nearly true, to say that "from that time forth Eustace was a different boy." To be strictly accurate, he began to be a different boy. He had relapses. There were still many days when he could be very tiresome. But most of those I shall not notice. The cure had begun. (99)

> Back in our own world everyone soon started saying how Eustace had improved, and how "you'd never know him for the same boy"; everyone except Aunt Alberta (Eustace's mother), who said he had become very commonplace and tiresome and it must have been the influence of those Pevensie children. (210)

The dragon image itself in this episode of *Dawn Treader* is a Nesbit-style dragon—a dragon quite unlike those of other children's writers Lewis knew, such as Tolkien. Nesbit was something of an expert on dragons, with a book of dragon stories in 1899 (recently republished as **The Last of the Dragons and Some Others**). In his dragon story in *Dawn Treader* Lewis writes:

> Eustace nodded his terrible dragon head and thumped his tail in the sea and everyone skipped back (some of the sailors with ejaculations I will not put down in writing) to avoid the enormous and boiling tears which flowed from his eyes.

> Lucy tried hard to console him and even screwed up her courage to kiss the scaly face. (88-89)

Like Eustace the lonely dragon, the dragon in "Just-nowland," another *Magic World* story, is pathetically eager for human contact. One of Nesbit's many brave girls, a model for Lucy, comforts the dragon thus:

> The pinky sunset light fell on its face, and Elsie saw that it was weeping! Great fat tears as big as prize pears were coursing down its wrinkled cheeks.

> "Oh, don't," said Elsie, "*don't* cry! Poor dragon, what's the matter?"

> "Oh!" sobbed the dragon, "I'm only so glad you've come. I—I've been so lonely. No one to love me. You *do* love me, don't you?"

> "Give me a kiss, dear," said the dragon, sniffing. (200)

> It is no joke to kiss a dragon. But Elsie did it—somewhere on the hard green wrinkles of its forehead. (201)

Lewis emphasizes the paradoxical image of the crying dragon ("A powerful dragon crying its eyes out under the moon in a deserted valley is a sight and a sound hardly to be imagined" [85]): a dragon very unlike Tolkien's Smaug or the Fafnir of Wagner and Northern mythology—but one very like the human and vulnerable dragons to be found in Nesbit.

"Accidental Magic," another important story for Lewis in **The Magic World,** offers a prototype for *The Last Battle*. A boy named Quentin de Ward goes to sleep on the "altar" at Stonehenge. When he wakes up he has gone back in time, and is on a boat from Atlantis bound for England, carrying the altar stone for Stonehenge. He is inside a pavilion enclosing the stone. When he steps out he amazes and terrifies the crew—except for the priest on board, who welcomes him as "the Chosen of the Gods" (80). The priest then cows and terrifies the rest, using the boy's miraculous arrival to frighten them. But when he and the priest are alone together, the priest assails him angrily, wanting to know who he actually is: "'This Chosen of the Gods business is all very well for the vulgar. But you and I know that there is no such thing as magic'" (82). Thus he is a non-believing priest who uses religion to intimidate others: exactly the kind of figure to attract Lewis's attention. The non-believing leader who uses religion (=superstition) to control people is a favorite target of his. Later, the boy is sacrificed on the altar stone—and wakes up in his own time. Terror turns into joyous awakening, just as, earlier, the putative fiction turns into a reality.

This unbelieving priest reappears as Rishda Tarkaan, the Calormene invader in *The Last Battle*. He pretends that Aslan is hidden in a stable behind him, and even insists that Aslan is the same as the Calormene demon-god Tash. He parades a false Aslan out of the stable, who cows and terrifies everybody, just as the surprising appearance of the "Chosen of the Gods" astounds the crew in **"Accidental Magic."** Rishda assumes that belief is nonsense, good only for controlling others. Lewis emphasizes the motif of unbelievers manipulating those who do believe. Thus Rishda, to his horror, discovers the truth after all when Tash actually *does* turn up inside the stable. In **"Accidental Magic,"** the priest calls magic nonsense—but events prove him very wrong. Likewise, in *The Last Battle* the unscrupulous Rishda actually meets the god he doesn't believe in. Later the Calormenes sacrifice Narnians (just as Nesbit's Quentin is sacrificed) by casting them all into the stable. The Narnian king is thrown into the stable, but instead of dying, he finds himself in a totally different time and space—his true, proper home—exactly like Nesbit's Quentin, who wakes up not dead but free, in his proper time, and united with Nesbit's equivalent of heaven—his mother. Again, the nightmare dissolves into joyous liberation, just as, earlier, the unbeliever discovers his fiction to be the truth.

In **The Phoenix and the Carpet,** the four children transport their cook by magic to a paradisal South Sea Island, where she is made queen. Later, they bring a working-class Londoner who originally came from the country and prefers country work to the hand-to-mouth existence he has now, and the two are married. In *The Magician's Nephew,* a cabdriver, like the Londoner in Nesbit, originally came from the country and prefers country life; he is brought to Narnia suddenly by magic. Aslan makes him king. His wife, washing clothes back in England, is magically transported to Narnia to be queen. (Lewis, one notes, begins with a king and then gets a queen for him; Nesbit, a feminist, begins with a queen and then finds a king for her; see Wilson 226.)

Lewis drew upon Nesbit frequently, often in quite small details. For example when Uncle Andrew in *The Magician's Nephew* experiments with magic rings, he ties tape around a guinea-pig with a ring on top. But the guinea-pig is unable to return from the place to which the ring sends it, and it never comes back. Denis in Nesbit's **Would-Be-Goods** ties sashes around the middle of guinea-pigs, with "bows stuck up on the tops of their backs. One of the guinea-pigs was never seen again" (21). The guinea-pig disappeared in Nesbit and reappeared in Lewis. Her depiction of the attic in **The Would-Be-Goods** and her warning about stepping from rafter to rafter (90) is essentially repeated (warning included) in *Nephew* (13). In **The Phoenix and the Carpet** the children, trapped in a ruin, push away some debris against the wall and find a hidden door with steps leading down behind it (17 in all) to a treasure chamber. In *Prince Caspian,* the children, trapped on an island with a ruin, find a hidden door behind debris that they remove; again there are steps down (16 in this case) leading to a treasure chamber. Such echoes are common, even in phrasing. In *The Silver Chair,* the claustrophobic Jill panics when the children enter a tunnel. "'I can't go in there, I can't! I can't! I won't,' she panted" (130). In Nesbit's **The Railway Children,** the children must go into a dark tunnel; one girl has an identical panic: "'I don't like it. It'll be pitch dark in a minute. I *won't* go on in the dark. I don't care what you say, I *won't*'" (178). The importance of holding hands when there is magic about is emphasized throughout **The House of Arden** and by Lewis at the beginning of *Prince Caspian.* On a larger scale, the superb episode of the mer-people in *Dawn Treader* has a direct precedent in Nesbit's **Wet Magic.**

When he began the Narnia books, Lewis seems to have had Nesbit's important trilogy *Five Children and It, The Phoenix and the Carpet,* and *The Story of the Amulet* particularly in mind, especially *The Amulet,* the greatest of them. Thus just as there are four children in *The Amulet*—Cyril, Anthea, Robert, and Jane—there are four children, two of each sex arranged in the same age sequence, in *The Lion, the Witch and the Wardrobe.* But while *Wardrobe* has features typical of Nesbit, it is *The Magician's Nephew* that is perhaps closest to Nesbit. Lewis actually refers to her on the opening page. *Nephew* is set in her world: turn-of-the-century London. Nesbit's children are separated from their parents and must live in a house occupied by a single older woman; the topmost room of the house is occupied by a "poor learned gentleman," who is "very long and thin" (41, 42). *Nephew* similarly centers on the boy Digory, who is separated from his parents and must stay with a single older woman. In the attic of the house is the study of an eccentric old bachelor, who spends his time doing obscure research—exactly like the "very long and thin" bachelor upstairs in **The Amulet.**

In **The Amulet,** the children are guided by the supernatural Psammead to use a magic object—the amulet—to visit different places in history, including Atlantis on the day of its apocalyptic flood. The amulet, which they first see lying on a tray, in fact was made in Atlantis. Similarly, in Lewis's *Magician's Nephew,* Digory and his friend Polly, under the stimulus (compulsion might be more accurate) of his magician-uncle Andrew, visit other worlds by means of magic rings, which were created from material in a box made in Atlantis, and which are first seen lying on a tray. The **Amulet** children witness the total destruction of Atlantis and flee as they are about to be overwhelmed, just as Jadis (the future White Witch) and Polly and Digory barely escape Charn as it is being totally destroyed.

One of the most memorable visits in **The Amulet** is to Babylon. Nesbit's Babylon is the prototype of Lewis's Tashbaan in *The Horse and His Boy,* a huge, exotic city. Each is capital of a great empire; in each city, the children are dangerously separated from one another. The King of Babylon in Nesbit is ritually referred to with the invariant formula: "The King (may he live for ever!)" (103); the ruler of Calormen has the same ritual formula attached to his name: "the Tisroc (may he live for ever)" (16). The title Lewis invented for the Calormene king ("Tisroc") echoes the terrifying god of Babylon that Nesbit's children encounter—a god named "Nisroch."

Nesbit's depiction of Nisroch the Babylonian god, furthermore, is very like Lewis's demon-god Tash of Calormen. Nesbit says: "it had eagle's wings and an eagle's head and the body of a man." The cruel king swears by its *beak*. Its coming terrifies the children: "It came towards them, strong and unspeakably horrible" (**Amulet** 127). Lewis depicts Tash as "roughly the shape of a man [like Nisroch] but it had the head of a bird; some bird of prey with a cruel, curved *beak* . . . its fingers—all twenty of them—were curved like its *beak* and had long, pointed, bird-like claws instead of nails" (*The Last Battle* 77; my emphasis). Its loathsome appearance terrifies the Narnia group, just as the children in Nesbit are terrified and revolted. (Significantly, the pagan god in Nesbit, while horrible, also proves helpful; in Lewis, the pagan god is simply demonic.) In both Babylon and Tashbaan, the children are almost killed because they know a terrible state secret: the Word of Power in **The Amulet,** the Tisroc's invasion plan in *The Horse.* Nesbit's "Word of Power," moreover, is a prototype for Jadis's all-powerful "Deplorable Word" in *The Magician's Nephew*—her city of Charn being a kind of dead Tashbaan.

But the key point in **The Amulet** is the amiable Queen of Babylon. She appears to be the model for the chatty but otherwise harmless Lasaraleen in *The Horse and His Boy,* the Calormene princess who helps the heroine. Both talk about weddings. But it was another aspect of the Babylonian queen's character that interested Lewis: her imperious will. In this she is the model for Jadis in *The Magician's Nephew,*

the Queen of Charn. The episode of Jadis's visit to London is essentially a duplicate of the visit of the Queen of Babylon to London in **The Amulet.** In Lewis, Digory and Polly travel to Charn and inadvertently bring back with them Charn's Queen (Jadis) to London. There is a phase of separation and also a phase of tense waiting for the queen to appear. A dramatic confrontation follows between the queen, who has plundered a jewelry shop, and a crowd of working class Cockney types who taunt and jeer at her. The scene builds to a fight ("The Fight at the Lamp-Post," chapter 8), from which the queen and the children are suddenly, magically withdrawn. Separation, waiting, dramatic confrontation, sudden disappearance: these form the sequence of motifs.

In Nesbit an identical sequence occurs. After their adventure in Babylon, Nesbit's children remember one day that the Queen had acquired the power to visit them in their own city and time. There follows a period of tense *waiting* for the queen to turn up. Like Lewis, Nesbit emphasizes the inconveniences of having to wait around for someone who may show up any moment. When she finally arrives, the children borrow money to take the queen on an excursion (Uncle Andrew tries to borrow money for the same purpose in Lewis). They take her to the British Museum, and the children are *separated* (Anthea has to wait for the others). Like Jadis plundering the jewelry shop, the queen promptly appropriates all the Babylonian artifacts she finds in the museum. Later there is a sightseeing trip in a hansom cab (just as there is an excursion in a hansom cab in Lewis), and the Queen of Babylon soon finds herself in a dangerous *confrontation* with a crowd of lower-class types who laugh at—then attack—her. The rising tension explodes in a terrifying and bloody struggle that ends very suddenly (like waking from a nightmare) with the *magic exit* of both queen and children—exactly as in Lewis.[5] The conspicuous difference between these episodes captures the difference that defines each writer: Nesbit gives her scene a political message ("'You'll have a revolt of your slaves if you're not careful,' said the Queen" observing the impoverished workers of east end London [148]). Lewis picked up nothing of this socio-political emphasis; naturally, for him it is religion that is the way to human liberation, not social reform.

Many more examples could be cited, and I omit the whole area of style (Lewis's style in the Narnia books is extremely close to that of Nesbit) but perhaps the extent of Lewis's appropriation of Nesbit has been established sufficiently for me to consider why Lewis took so much from her—what it was about her vision that was so compatible with his own—and what was not assimilable. E. Nesbit's plotting technique is based, generally speaking, on a very simple formula. The typical Nesbit story begins with a group of children who are *separated* from their parents—sometimes from one parent, sometimes from both. The motif of separation from parents is often linked to one of two other, related motifs. The first of these is a *move* away from home, a change of living quarters that combines the fear of insecurity with the excitement of novelty and adventure. The other important motif used at the beginning of the Nesbit story is the *change of fortune:* somehow or other the family has lost its money or social status, and must now come to terms with "reduced circumstances." Separation has therefore three aspects: social, geographical, and financial. Thus separation sets the logical and natural goal of the plot: namely, to reunite parents with children; to return to the rightful home; and to restore the lost family fortune or status. In other words separation generates its opposite, unification, as the plot aim.

Between separation and reunification, we find a loose episodic sequence of events. Nesbit was essentially an episodic writer; several of her books are compilations of originally independent short stories. This series of adventures often works by bringing unfamiliar individuals into the original group of children, and, alternatively, by taking the children deep into a variety of unfamiliar social interactions. The action is designed to confront the child with the unfamiliar child (or adult or group), and to show that the alien being is really one of us. The strange is actually an aspect of oneself. The stranger may be as genuinely strange as the Psammead in *Five Children and It* or as painfully familiar as the troublesome Madeline in *Five of Us—and Madeline.* From a structural point of view, E. Nesbit is not a great craftsman of form. Her stories include episodes that are not vital; material could be added or subtracted without qualitative loss or alteration. She does not write the kind of snaptogether plot where every element in the narrative is essential to the final outcome and would be missed if it were absent, and where additions would be superfluous and even destroy the balance of the whole. There are exceptions—*Harding's Luck* (one of her best books) has a tight, formally satisfying construction. But for the most part her stories have a certain energy, freedom and spontaneity of creation in their narrative line indicating that perfection of form interested her less than concerns such as character and emotion.

Lewis took over the basic Nesbit framework. In *The Lion, the Witch and the Wardrobe,* the four children are sent away from home and parents (separation). In *Prince Caspian,* the action begins after the children have left home for boarding school, with a further separation imminent as they go to different schools. In *The Voyage of the Dawn Treader,* the parents (and two children) are separated from the two younger children, who are forced to stay with their uncongenial cousin Eustace, of dragon fame. In *The Silver Chair,* the two principals are at a boarding school ("Experiment House") more like a children's concentration camp than a school. In *The Last Battle,* Digory Kirke has mysteriously lost money and mansion, and lives in reduced circumstances, just as he and his mother do in *The Magician's Nephew,* again after a fall in family fortunes. *The Last Battle,* with its apocalyptic final vision of heaven, uses the drastic device of having the children actually killed in order to get them across the magic threshold from This World into the Other World of Narnia. Hence they are not merely separated from home, they never do return—but only because they are reunited with their true home, their true family, and their true fortune.

E. Nesbit was a Fabian socialist whose writing is secular, with the ethical values of an egalitarian social democrat. Her interest in the structure and functioning of society is completely absent from Lewis. Two features of her stories are conspicuous: (1) the emphasis on social interaction and (2) the vision of what she calls "heart's desire." Nesbit is fascinated by the dynamics of the social group, the spectacle of several very different people learning how to cooperate, how to compromise, how to help and sustain one another, how to lead and how to follow, how to face difficulty together. In her work, each individual, no matter how young or how strange, has something to contribute to the well-being of all. Nesbit's vision of "Heart's Desire" (a phrase Lewis uses in *The Magician's Nephew* for Digory's wish to have his mother healed) is the quest for a better society, one where everyone could fulfill his or her potential in a world of freedom, peace and plenty. This is the crowning vision of ***The Amulet:*** the visit to the utopian society of the future—a vision very like William Morris's *News from Nowhere* (or Eldorado in her own ***House of Arden***). Nesbit's Heart's Desire has to do with *human* creative power and wishes. It is emphatically not the fulfillment of God's will. Yet divinity is certainly present in Nesbit, notably in the court of heroism in ***Harding's Luck,*** in the Hall of Granted Wishes and the gathering of the gods in ***The En-***

chanted Castle, and in the Amulet numen, especially in its power to fuse/transform the identity of the Egyptian priest with that of the learned gentleman in *The Amulet.*

In Lewis, by contrast, the dynamics of group interaction are much less important. Lewis takes the basic Nesbit plot—children are separated from parents, travel or pass out of ordinary experience in quest of parents, and then at the end achieve restorative reunion—and attaches it instead to an enormous superstructure. This superstructure is a cosmic plot of divinely ordained creation, destruction and recreation. Everything in the world he invents is connected to this framework and to a divine creator. Everything that happens is part of a divine scheme. Whereas in Nesbit, the goal is to gain certain qualities and ideals, here the goal is to gain relationship with Aslan: this is the purpose of the seven chronicles and the reason why the children were brought to Narnia in the first place. Lewis's imagination is polarized: absolute Good (Aslan) on one side and beings very like absolute evil (Jadis, Tash, the Lady of the Green Kirtle, the cannibal giants) on the other. Nesbit's world is much less polarized; there are no totally evil beings—and no totally good ones, either. As in human society, people are a mix of good and evil: that is, they are capable of good and evil actions. The powerful and apparently wicked woman of *The Magic City* (one of Nesbit's feeblest books) turns out to be good and loving after all. The idea of the apparently bad authority figure revealed in the end to be good fascinated Lewis and forms the basis of his *Pilgrim's Regress.* But one is a family member; the other is an allegory of God.

In some ways Aslan is Lewis's most impressive and important creation, a being only remotely like Jesus in the Gospels. There is nothing like an Aslan—a coordinating creator who is all-powerful—in Nesbit. There are smaller figures: Psammead, Mouldiwrap (in *The House of Arden*), Phoenix (in *The Phoenix and the Carpet*), ghost (in *The Wonderful Garden*); but these are all fallible, intermediate. They correspond to—and provided models for—figures like Reepicheep and Puddleglum in Lewis (the two finest examples of his skill in creating character): not Aslan. The image of the furry little Psammead disappearing at the end of *The Amulet* (it gave "one last lingering look at Anthea—a loving look . . . and—vanished" to the place of its heart's desire, the temple of Baalbec [280]) lies behind the image of Reepicheep the Mouse at the end of *Dawn Treader:* Lucy embraces it—"Then it vanished" into the place of its heart's desire, Aslan's country (207).

Nesbit works episodically within a form that has a loose containing plot. Lewis, by contrast, was not comfortable with the leisurely, improvisational form that inspired Nesbit. It did not cohere with his belief in a providential, all-inclusive intelligence at work in the world. Lewis is characterized by an instinctive sense of formal harmony, as his literary-critical masterpiece *The Discarded Image* demonstrates. Only in *The Voyage of the Dawn Treader* do we find an episodic plot. In Lewis, there is an in-built teleological order; each part fits together in a totalizing structure; each event is a step toward the final consummation. Thus he concluded the series by writing a creation narrative (*The Magician's Nephew*) and an eschatological narrative (*The Last Battle*): that is he tidied up his creation. He answered the question of how Narnia got here in the first place and how it ends: he completes the unfolding of a divine plot of creation. He also explained smaller points—why there was a lamp-post burning in the middle of a wood, how the wardrobe came to be magical (and even why it sometimes opened into Narnia and sometimes did not), what the purpose of the sleeping dragons in Underland was, and so on. Nothing is accidental; no loose ends here. All that matters is following the will of Aslan, as Puddleglum makes clear in *The Silver Chair.* The ideal of duty to a hierarchical authority is basic to Lewis.

By contrast Nesbit is full of accidents, loose ends—and respect for personal impulse. That is because her worldview is one where fallible, struggling human beings are the final authority. In Nesbit, the driving energy is that of human desire—not God's will: respect for human wishes is thus central. As Oswald puts it in *The Would-Be-Goods,* repeating something he says in *The Treasure Seekers,* "when you want to do a thing you *do* want to, and not to do something else, and perhaps your own thing, a week later" (111). Hence the conflict of desire and frustration is a key theme in her writing. Learning how to handle frustration and bafflement without panic, without making things worse, is an essential skill in the struggle for a better world. The difference is between acting within a preordained framework determined by a superior power—and of human beings creating, or recreating, a framework for themselves. In one, human beings are responsible to God; in the other they are responsible to themselves and one another. Which makes more sense will depend on the worldview of the reader.

Yet on the deepest level the two writers do share a spiritual vision. Lewis, one notes, absorbs many elements of Nesbit's social concern; thus the heroine of

Nephew expresses outrage at the Queen of Charn's callous use of "her" people, "All the ordinary peope who'd never done you any harm" (61), in the manner of Nesbit. And Nesbit displays a reverence for a spirit beyond ordinary life, for example in the numinous amulet and its uncanny utterances. But in a deeper way what the two writers share is a spirituality of the imagination (hence their common concern with "reading the right books"): a perception of truth in human imagining, a value that has something infinite in it, what Lewis in *Experiment in Criticism* calls "the mythical." This heightening/expanding of experience typifies the closing scenes of *Dawn Treader* and the ecstasy of the gods in **The Enchanted Castle.**

Lewis integrated this heightened vision into his Christian system, of course, whereas Nesbit did not. And yet Lewis also powerfully articulates it in a non-Christian context. The profoundest moment in the Narnia stories occurs in *The Silver Chair* where the Queen of Underland or Lady of the Green Kirtle (metaphorically fallen nature, hence her green dress) attempts to put a spell on her visitors from above. Each in turn succumbs; each agrees with her that there are no stars or sky or sun or Aslan. There is only her dark realm under the ground: total alienation, with its machine-like workers glumly drudging for no real purpose, like the alienated laborers of Nesbit's London. Then Puddleglum stops the enchantment by putting out her magic fire; he makes a defiant speech to the Witch. This corresponds to the turning point in Lewis's adult fantasy *That Hideous Strength* when Mark refuses to degrade a crucifix—not because he believes in Christianity—but because human dignity does not allow him to degrade it, him, or himself, regardless of rewards, punishments, truth or untruth.

Puddleglum's words constitute one of the great passages in Lewis:

> All you've been saying is quite right, I shouldn't wonder . . . But there's one thing more to be said, even so. Suppose we *have* only dreamed, or made up, all those things—trees and grass and sun and moon and stars and Aslan himself. Suppose we have. Then all I can say is that, in that case, the made-up things seem a good deal more important than the real ones. Suppose this black pit of a kingdom *is* the only world. Well, it strikes me as a pretty poor one. And that's a funny thing, when you come to think of it. We're just babies making up a game if you're right. But four babies playing a game can make a play-world that licks your real world hollow. That's why I'm going to stand by the play-world. I'm on Aslan's side even if

there isn't any Aslan to lead it. I'm going to live as like a Narnian as I can even if there isn't any Narnia. (164)

This expression of the dignity of human imagination could not be stronger. This is, finally, what Lewis found in Nesbit: a spirit that does not depend on external deities but upon something infinitely valuable within us.

Notes

1. See Walter Hooper, *Past Watchful Dragons* (30).

2. She knew not only H. G. Wells and Eleanor Marx but Annie Besant. See the fine new biography of E. Nesbit by Julia Briggs; Knoepflmacher 320-23.

3. "The highest peak she was to reach, *The Enchanted Castle* (1907), the most completely satisfactory and most coherently plotted of all E. Nesbit's full-length books" (Green 212).

4. The experiencing of life without fear is a Shelleyan motif-in "The Cloud" and in one of the major influences on Lewis (and, less directly, on Nesbit), *Prometheus Unbound*.

5. Lewis's use of Nesbit here is especially evident, as noted by C. N. Manlove (73), who also suggests Chesterton as a source.

Sanjay Sircar

SOURCE: "E. Nesbit's "The Magician's Heart": From the Stage to the Page," in *Marvels & Tales*, Vol. IX, No. 2, December, 1995, pp. 171-206.

The existence of E. Nesbit's **"The Magician's Heart"** (summarised in the previous part of this project) as a pantomime/dramatic burlesque and as a prose narrative underscores the relationship between the stage fairy pantomime tradition and the nursery book, but the audience for the dramatic burlesque is automatically more inclusive than the audience for the burlesque Kunstmärchen, which is usually exclusively and *only* children's literature. Empirically, all children's literature is mediated to (bought for) children by adults. Normatively, however, a child may well choose or read a book for itself. Yet a child never goes to the pantomime by itself, it is always taken there accompanied by an adult (I refer to a period till at least 1960, children may have greater freedom today). Likewise, an adult reading a children's book without reference to a child or children is culturally an anomaly (and usually a despised one), but an adult "going to the panto" alone or with its peers is not. Going to the pantomime is also a much more important, expensive (and time-consuming) act than reading. Hence, the dramatic burlesque (pantomime) is associated with children (because of its sources in the Märchen, which are not invariably its sources), but it is *not* thought of as inherently children's literature.

Between 1888 and the early 1890s, Nesbit's family and circle enacted some entertainments for poor children (with a separate performance for adults) at the Deptford Board School at Christmastime, which grew from tableaux to pantomime/burlesques, including a version of **"Cinderella"** by Nesbit, followed by *The Sleeping Beauty* and *Aladdin,* in both of which Laurence Housman acted (Moore: [1933] 1967: 141-142). It seems that all these included either popular songs or original songs set to popular airs. In ***The Enchanted Castle,*** the children improvise and enact just such a pantomime version of "Beauty and the Beast." Nesbit's own pantomime version of **"Cinderella"** (possibly the one enacted at Deptford), which bears no resemblance to her semi-burlesque discursive retelling of **"Cinderella"** in *The Old Nursery Stories* (1908), was published as a separate text in 1909.

The play of **"The Magician's Heart"** was licensed on 3.12.06, and acted in January 1907. I think that I can claim to be the first person since the 1900s actually to have read the only known copy of the dramatic form of **"The Magician's Heart,"** a play in three scenes.[1] The typescript consists of thirty-one folio sheets renumbered to include the title page and dramatis personae. It is addressed "Well Hall, Eltham, Kent," where Nesbit lived, stamped "No. 48 Lord Chamberlain's Office," and marked British Library Catalogue No. 1906/35. The plot-outlines of **"The Magician's Heart"** remain the same in both versions. The play would seem adequately to fill Tolkien's "just bearable" form of pantomime, the sort in which the fairytale framework is a "vestigiary framework for farce" and no belief is expected or desire evoked, for it was devised to give the "celebrated conjurers" Maskelyne and Devant scope for the performance of "magic" at "London's Home of Magic and Mystery" (see Moore: 237).

It includes all the generic characteristics (or variations) indicated in accounts of dramatic burlesque. This form of dramatic entertainment often used Märchen plots (most popularly "Cinderella,"

"Aladdin," "Dick Whittington," and "Jack the Giant Killer"), and was often based on Märchen contaminatio, though not under that name, eg. "The Sleeping Beauty and the Beast" (1900, Booth: 379-449, see also quotation in Booth: 504). Its fantasy framework could equally well be a Kunstmärchen, as in **"The Magician's Heart".**[2] The other characteristics are stage enactment, irregularity of form (which allowed for the exotic, the irrational, the extravagant, the exuberant, the whimsical, the absurd, the topsey-turvey, the grotesque, the iconoclastic and the nightmarish), spectacle of all kinds, transvestism, audience participation, topical comedy, and wordplay.

Tolkien's Literary Belief (discussed previously) is a somewhat nebulous notion (presumably corresponding to Secondary Imagination), as is Desire, but both convey the sense that readers should be drawn or "carried away into" the world of the narrative. But the burlesque Kunstmärchen in general does not aim for this, for it contains constant reminders of its own syncretic construction out of the material and conventions of the Märchen, and it mockingly satirises Märchen magic. Hence the prose version of **"The Magician's Heart,"** like Thackeray's *The Rose and the Ring,* does not try to aspire to the condition of the true "fairy-story" or to conceal its origins in—and affinities with—dramatic burlesque. On the contrary, even more than *The Rose and the Ring,* it foregrounds its nature as "prosed pantomime," a sort of writing which corresponds to Tolkien's worst sort of pantomime, the "dramatised fairy-story."

A comparison of the two versions of **"The Magician's Heart"** shows Nesbit at work, and it shows how the opportunities and restraints of the two media result in differences in emphasis between the same author's versions of the same narrative. The differences between the two versions of **"The Magician's Heart"** show that Nesbit was actually quite a careful and thoughtful writer, for she alters and modifies her material in the rewriting, so that the printed version is more than the "book of the play." This goes against the received image of Nesbit the writer, which Doris Langley Moore was the first to construct. She emphasised that Nesbit at work was given to procrastination and delay, provided precis rather than finished work to the illustrator and was willing to alter a story to fitdrawings, did not plan or plot out her work before starting it, sought for plot materials from her friends and did not concentrate her efforts, was overprolix and frittered away her talent (Moore: 189-194, 215-216, 225-226).

More recently Julia Briggs reproduces this image (Briggs: 1987: 233-236), and Moore's statement that Nesbit revised at the end of a session but not as she wrote (Moore: 190), becomes with another writer "Often she wrote her individual stories at one go, with little revision" (Howes: 1989: 1). Moore and Briggs doubtless report factual observations, but they do not tell the whole story: even a cursory comparison of the serialised versions of Nesbit's fantasy novels in the *Strand Magazine* and their final versions in book form will show very careful alterations, deletions, elaborations, and ironing out of inconsistencies that do not amount to mere padding out for book publication, for the length of both versions is very similar (perhaps most interestingly in *The Enchanted Castle*). The prose recension of **"The Magician's Heart"** is tighter than the play, and the alterations are appropriate to the specific requirements of prose narrative. This evidence leads us to wonder whether the accepted view of Nesbit's writing process has been heavily influenced by a Romantic cultural stereotype of what the writer for children *should* be like: merrily flighty, inspired, disorganised and unconscious—in other words, "like a child" (as the same cultural stereotype assumes children to be).

The interest of *watching* a dramatic burlesque stems primarily from the *spectacle,* while the interest of *reading* a burlesque Kunstmärchen stems primarily from awareness of how the particular tale uses burlesque Kunstmärchen conventions and material in working with—and playing with—its Märchen prototypes. So the play of **"The Magician's Heart"** is more farcical, with more stress on the spectacle and broad and low-comic visual and aural elements, while the prose recension has more moral inflexions, sifts out or de-emphasises spectacle and sound, and enhances the comic, parodic relationship to the Märchen. The 30 pages of the play of **"The Magician's Heart,"** would take about an hour and a half on stage (allowing time for tricks and set changes). The 20 pages of the prose recension take about half an hour at most, to read aloud, less in silent reading. Nesbit obviously wrote the prose recension with the play in front of her, and most of the omissions are from the second and third scenes.

Spectacular and aurally striking elements in dramatic burlesque included music, dance and acrobatics, and impressive sets and machinery for special effects. The play of **"The Magician's Heart"** aims for both the spectacle and the comic incongruity of dramatic burlesque in its costumes. In the first scene, against a background of "Furnaces, alembics, crucibles," and the "Effect of mystery" created with "Eastern colours, draperies &c.," and a door with "iron bars, bolts and studs" (MH Mss: 3), the Magician starts out in black tights and ruff. This mystery is juxtaposed with the commonplace when he adds an incongruous frockcoat, hat and silk umbrella with which to go out (MH Mss: 14). Then, in the palace, the Magician is dressed as a cook (MH Mss: 16, 19), and he is finally brought into the throneroom in his frockcoat and high hat, but bound in chains (MH Mss: 25). The play also has the comic transvestism which was part of the carnivalesque spectacle of pantomime. There is no "principal boy" (an actress in a transvestite role), but whether or not a male acted the role, the Nurse is a standard transvestite "dame" part, with stock dame part insults—for example, when the Magician says to her, "You don't mean to say you ever think?" (MH Mss: 6).[3]

But even the most vivid written description cannot recreate the spectacle of drama, so the prose recension of **"The Magician's Heart"** omits all references to the furnishings of the tower and the Magician's dress. The sense of the grotesque conveyed by the stage transvestism of the dame is omitted entirely in the prose version, and the Nurse's part as a whole toned down. It omits the change into being "if possible, beautifully dressed" which accompanies the Apprentice's magic transposition in the play (MH Mss: 29), and turns the reference to the Princess's costume in the play, "very gorgeously dressed in white and silver" (MH Mss: 25) into the deadpan verbal jest of a "simple little morning frock of white chiffon and diamonds" (MH: 274). Here the prose recension adds to straight spectacle by an additional touch of comic parody (of Märchen and pantomime opulence), which requires greater sophistication to appreciate, and hence appeals perhaps to a more thoughtful (or even "grown-up") consciousness.

Spectacle in dramatic burlesque took in a good deal of visual comedy of a farcical knockabout kind, and the play of **"The Magician's Heart"** includes much comic stage business which Nesbit tones down on the page. So the Nurse tries to hug the reluctant Magician, her ham falls on his head, he dismisses the Apprentice's vaporous dream with a stamp, the ugly Princess's grimaces leave the group aghast, the Magician furiously hits out at the Apprentice when he sees the Princess has gone and is restrained by the Nurse. Then the Magician and the Apprentice drink a potion and "wildly" call out for a first single train-ticket by magic underground as they enter a cabinet to go to the Palace, while the Nurse "mildly" calls out the same words, the door opens and "She is still there, which ought to surprise the audience" because the trains are not running. In the palace they pull the stupefied Nurse out of a pie and set her aside to cool, the Nurse, "suddenly appearing from behind door screen," slaps the Magician as he threatens the Princess. Then the Magician presents "an enormous menu to the Princess," "so big that she cannot hold it," as he explains to the Nurse in dumb show that he is angry with her and she is never to "take such a liberty again" while the Apprentice and the Princess kiss each other over the menu, and plot to steal the heart. Finally, the Magician transfixes the Nurse who is about to strike him again (MH Mss: 3, 6, 8, 10, 14-15, 17, 19, 20, 21-22). None of this remains in the prose version.

Because the play of **"The Magician's Heart"** builds a plot around the stock repertoire of conjuring tricks, the spectacle in this dramatic burlesque mainly derives from the "magic" and the special effects. The manuscript shows that Nesbit was obviously given a list of the conjuring tricks, for the stage directions read "(*does the Lamp trick*)," "(*The pie trick*)" (MH Mss: 5, 16), etc. The tricks are woven round producing objects out of thin air, making things vanish and reappear, and transposing objects and people—presumably via trapdoors. All these were seen at children's parties and on stage—in India at least—till the end of the 1960s (perhaps an example of the contention that tradition survives longest on the periphery), but they are no longer a feature of children's entertainment today, when Steven Spielberg's movies and interactive video games provide far more impressive and overwhelming special effects.

To list only a selection, in the first scene in the Magician's tower, the Magician takes his heart out, produces eggs and apples from the Nurse's dress and bonnet, does the lamp trick (possibly making it fly around, for the prose version refers at another point to him making the lamp fly like a pigeon), and produces a handkerchief out of the air (MH Mss: 1,11, 4, 5 [cf. MH: 274], 5). The Apprentice sees a vision of the Princess in magic parti-coloured vapour, a special effect probably created by dry ice, the Magician changes from her ugly to pretty in his "consulting cabinet" (possibly a trick with a mask or a substitution of the actress), produces a chicken and a rabbit for a drugged pie with which to put his guards to sleep, and James and he vanish in the cabinet to follow the Princess to the palace (MH Mss: 7-8, 10, 14, 14, 15). There are many tricks connected with brewing the magic potion in the second scene (MH Mss:

16, 18, 21, 22, 22), and in the third scene in the throneroom, the rival princes are covered up and transposed, and Taykin is covered under the gallows and re-emerges as a child, with his large heart turned into a miniature detachable one, and there are showers of roses at the finale (MH Mss: 29-30, 31).

Equally entertaining, but perhaps not as conventional, is the way in which the dramatic burlesque indeed does away with any literary belief being required, as it foregrounds the correspondence between the stage-actor, who is indeed a conjurer with an assistant in real life, with his role in the drama as Magician with an Apprentice. The play focuses on his performance *as* performance, to include the audience participation characteristic of dramatic burlesque. So, the Magician tells his Nurse that he is a Magician by trade, and mourns (and presumably looks beyond her to the audience), "What's the use of being a Magician if you haven't got an audience. Oh, the audiences I've had!" and says sarcastically to the Princess that yes, he can do "a little" magic (MH Mss: 5, 8, 9, cf. MH: 266, 268). He gives the Princess his business cards advertising his wares, "assumes the manner" and the patter of a "drawing-room entertainer" as he nominally addresses his three interlocutors and actually the real audience as "Ladies and Gentlemen," as he refers to *not* having the pleasure of showing them the trick with the Princess, which alludes simultaneously to the convention that the audience is not there and to her being concealed in the cabinet, and as he says, "Here, James, roll it round three times to shew the audience she's there. (*To Nurse*) You're the audience." He enlists the Apprentice to display the empty sauce-pans, and finally, the Apprentice makes him "Promise not to work any more magic, except at children's parties" (MH Mss: 10, 22, 23).

The prose version omits much of this, *though all the stage "magic" could have been reproduced unchanged in prose*. Nesbit chooses instead *to reduce the amount of "magic" by omission and summary, but to retain the nature of Taykin's magic as comic, mocked-at, unbelieved-in conjuring—another instance of the substitution of parody for spectacle*. The eggs and apples and handkerchief from the play remain (MH: 266), and so does a much less drawn out form of Fortunatus's vision of Aura (MH: 267). But with the trope of praeterition (a figure by which summary mention of a thing is made by professing to omit it on such grounds as lack of time, etc.) all the tricks of the second scene (three typed pages) are condensed into a little more than a summary paragraph about how Taykin takes things out of empty saucepans, the Nurse walks out of a cupboard, and Taykin takes cats and cockatoos out of jars, makes mice and rabbits disappear and reappear and the lamp fly (MH: 274). All three forms of the cumbersome business with covered cabinets are reduced to Aura's transformation "before the astonished eyes of the nurse and the apprentice," the transposition of the rival princes "in the twinkling of an eye" (with a corresponding changing of the formula of Aura's promise), and Taykin's shrinking without being covered up in the gallows (MH: 269, 278, 280). The Magician's climactic transformation is significantly different between versions. In the play the metamorphosis of the Magician's into a child is in keeping with generic decorum but does not provide the pleasure of seeing the quickness of the hand deceiving the eye, as it is an obvious trick with a screen (so that a child substitutes for the adult actor via a trapdoor). In the prose version, all this is more economical, more suited to being read, but quite as "stage-magical" as the play and in no way wondrous or mysterious.

Further, a burlesque Kunstmärchen on the page can allude for comic effect to the conventions of dramatic burlesque, but not vice versa (at any rate I have never seen an instance of it). So, the prose recension of **"The Magician's Heart"** alludes to dramatic burlesque with the *addition of two elements which are spectacular to a degree that physical and financial restraints would perhaps obviate on the stage.* Thus, when Taykin curses the baby Fortunatus (which is only an allusion in the play), he "vanished in a puff of red smoke with a smell like the Fifth of November [fireworks] in a back garden" (MH: 261), in a reference to the traditional pantomime Demon King (cf. Nesbit's Malevola, the evil fairy of her semi-burlesque retelling of **"The Sleeping Beauty in the Wood,"** in *The Old Nursery Stories,* 1908, who appears with bats' wings and a bonnet rimmed with live snakes, to the accompaniment of thunder and lightning, like a pantomime Evil Fairy or Demon King. The play keeps the smoke or vapour for a less usual effect with the vision of Aura). Then in the tower, the stage-business with the Magician and the Apprentice vanishing in the cabinet is replaced by Taykin leaping into a cauldron and emerging as a red lion, and Fortunatus doing the same to emerge as a green dragon before vanishing, "a most uncomfortable sensation" (273). *Neither the added nor the substituted element further the plot,* and both provide as jocular but *more* spectacular and more pantomime-like magic than the actual play itself. This is like Noel's Langley's *Land of Green Ginger* (1937, rev. 1947

and 1966), another major burlesque Kunstmärchen (a long one, which draws upon some of the features of the fantasy novel) which is also very self-consciously "prosed pantomime" (most markedly in the third version) with lots of "stage effects" on the page, though Langley was drawing on an established stereotype of an "Aladdin" pantomime, rather than actually having scripted one himself, and his prosed pantomime was subsequently staged (Langley, letter: 1974).

The narrative voice of the prose version of **"The Magician's Heart"** also foregrounds the magician as conjurer, sometimes in sections which have no corresponding matter in the play. It introduces Taykin as "merely a wicked magician, who by economy and strict attention to customers had worked up a very good business of his own" (MH: 261). It refers to the imprisoned Taykin finding it dull to take rabbits out of a hat with no one to see him, glosses his tricks as being done "just like a conjurer does. Only of course he was a real magician," adds that Taykin delights in showing off because he was lonely for so many years and that he must have used magic to make his references from previous employers to get the job of palace cook, and, in the diction of conjurers' advertising, it calls Fortunatus's transposition of the rival princes "the purest and most high-class magic" (MH: 264, 266, 274, 273, 280).

Like the eighteenth-century harlequinade out of which it grew, pantomime/burlesque was originally silent, but it broadened out and became much more heterogeneous with the inclusion of dialogue, song, horseplay and jokes, and it was marked by many puns (see Booth: 38). The burlesque Kunstmärchen shares these features with the dramatic burlesque. Indeed, George MacDonald's "The Light Princess" in *Adela Cathcart* (1864) grows out of extended puns on lightness and gravity (which then go on to accrete theological reverberations), and one of the negative criticisms levelled against a burlesque Kunstmärchen by the fictive narratees in *Adela Cathcart* is that it is overfull of trivial puns, the lowest form of wit (see MacDonald: [1864] 1908: 62-68). The prose version of **"The Magician's Heart"** is light and playful and comic but it does away with the obvious aural jests of the play, which accord with the generic requirements of being seen and heard rather than read.

The comic basis of the plot of **"The Magician's Heart"** is a making literal of the phrase "offer you my hand and heart" (MH Mss 11, MH: 269), but the play version is full of crude punning heart/heartless jokes, treating the detachable heart as an object, and all but one of these disappear in the prose version. The play starts with the Magician taking his heart out and adducing the "Golden rule: Never carry objects of value about your person" (MH Mss: 3). He talks to his heart: "Be still, my heart! How odd now. I didn't know I'd got a heart" (MH Mss: 11, see also 16, 18, 18, 19). And the others make puns about it. Says the Princess to the Apprentice, who tells her to steal his heart, "I thought I *had* stolen [his heart]," and he replies, "Ah, girls often think things like that. No, his heart's on his cooking at present—in point of fact it's in that saucepan" (MH Mss: 19).

The play is also replete with other dreadful low puns for their own sake, all but two of which the prose recension omits. For example, when the Nurse's ham falls on the Magician's head, he says "I *am* touched by the ham" (MH Mss: 6, repeated 7), and when she slaps him he says "Your arguments touch me" (MH Mss: 19). The Princess orders a "sentimental bill of fare" which puns on the love-associations of "*Turtle* soup-*sole*-lamb-*duck*-sheep's *heart*-angel trifle-*love* pudding" (MH Mss: 19-20. see also 10, 16). The jester's long shaggy-dog stories turn on the puns "were/wear" and "ball" as pill/party (MH Mss: 25), and the King tells the rival suitor to keep his hand handy (MH Mss: 29). Only the punning on the different senses of "to take" a chair, some wine, and a veil off, and "to give" alms and medicine (MH Mss: 8, 9) are retained in the prose recension (MH: 268, 269).

The dialogue in the play is based on a series of word patterns for comic effect, built around various forms of repetition, parallelism and antithesis. The prose recension summarises and condenses much of the dialogue, so these mostly disappear as well. The Magician's initial exposition of his imprisonment uses a figure that is variously called gradatio, concatenatio or the tracer (a series of clauses with the last phrase of each clause repeated at the beginning of the next). "It's a great pity that people aren't more careful about sending out invitations. If the King hadn't forgotten to invite me to his daughter's christening I shouldn't have lost my temper, and I hadn't lost my temper, I shouldn't have changed the princess from pretty to ugly; and if I hadn't lost my temper . . . ." etc. (MH Mss: 3). The story condenses and gently mocks all the love talk of the lovers, which is based on chiasmus and antithesis and repetition: "I've more to lose than you have—and more to gain." / "We have each other to gain." / "But never to lose." / "Yours, yours." / "Yours!" (MH Mss: 13). The Nurse

and Apprentice comment on the flight to the palace: "His poor brain's gone." / "He's gone." / " . . . that rabbit—it'll be gone next." / "No—I shall be gone next . . . ." / "He can't do it. He has done it, though! Whatever *am* I to do!" (MH Mss: 14). The Magician first thinks the beggar girl is disguised as a Princess, then finds that she is one, with "I'll marry her all the same." / "I'll marry her all the more" (MH Mss: 17, retained in the prose version, MH: 275, with an additional instance of chiasmus, "Marry me—or drink [the uglifying potion]" / "Drink, or marry me"). The Magician threatens the Nurse, about to slap, "You might be struck so" / "You *are* struck so" (MH Mss: 21). The King kisses the Princess with "As the father of the future princess of the Fortunate Islands permit me to congratulate you!" and the Apprentice echoes, "As Prince of the Fortunate Islands, and as the Princess's bridegroom, permit me to congratulate myself" as he does the same (MH Mss: 31).

Sometimes repetition results in backchat, comic stichomythia (the retort in drama, with a form of words altered in a reply). So the Nurse suggests to the Magician, " . . . suppose some respectable person as wasn't a fool thought of [the idea of apprenticing a stupid person] for them?" / "Respectable persons who aren't fools have got other things to think about." / "I haven't." / "You don't mean to say you ever think?" / "Yes I do—quite often." (MH Mss: 6). The Magician says, "I'll think about it." / "Yes, do: I'll call him in; he's waiting outside.—You can go on thinking just the same." (MH Mss: 6). The Apprentice uses his stupidity, now removed, as a cover for insolence: "How dared you [let the Princess out]?" / "I don't know. I'm so stupid." "What disguise?" ponders the Magician. "Disguise yourself as a perfect gentleman," suggests the Apprentice. Replies the Magician "(*furious*) I'll disguise you as a hospital in patient" (MH Mss: 14). When the Magician as cook assures the Princess that he is her most obedient humble servant, she retorts that she doesn't want him to be her servant at all (MH Mss: 17). If he harms her, she says, the King will "have you locked up again." / "You, in the meantime, will have case to be worth locking up," comes the reply (MH Mss: 17). The enchained Magician, "(*hardened and resentful*)," accused of attempting to turn the Princess ugly, enquires, "Who made her a Pretty Princess I should like to know?" and the King retorts, "*I* did, in the first instance. You see she takes after her dear father" (MH Mss: 27). The King says that making the Princess love the Apprentice is high treason, all the world over, and the Nurse "(*indignantly*)" interjects that it's human nature the world over (MH Mss: 28). "[D/

Jon't be hard on my boy," pleads the Nurse; "Your boy has been hard on everyone else," retorts the King (MH Mss: 30). All this is omitted in the prose version.

The play of **"The Magician's Heart"** uses bathos for the pure facetiousness of dramatic burlesque in some of these retorts, which do not use stichomythia. So, the Nurse comments fondly on the Magician's Arabian Nightsy "Lady, you are the pearl of the Universe—the moon of perfect loveliness—the light of my eyes, the star of my destiny" with "There's nothing like a delicate compliment" (MH Mss: 11). The Princess's refusal of the Magician's offer of marriage goes "No thank you." / "Ah don't say that." / "No then" (MH Mss: 12). The Princess and the Apprentice discover each other in the kitchen with "You?" / "Yes, me—oh, never mind grammar" (MH Mss: 19). The Magician interrupts the King's judgement on him by offering information in exchange for clemency, and the information is that the King's "crown's all crooked," which the King knows already (MH Mss: 27).

All this and other bathos is omitted in the prose recension, as is much of the juxtaposition of parodic registers and shifting between them characteristic of the burlesque Kunstmärchen in general. In the play, the Magician is much more of a comic parody of a melodrama villain, who speaks at various points "(*with a dark expression*)," "(*dramatically*)," "(*impressively*)," "(*in his grandest manner*)" "(*Malignly*)" (MH Mss: 17, 18, 18, 19, 22), and uses such stock cliche phrases as "Then prepare to meet your doom" (MH Mss: 22). But he varies this manner with, for example, "(*mincingly*) How extremely vexatious. It's [the potion] all boiled away" (MH Mss: 22). The melodrama villain also takes on other roles and registers. The Magician's "If you won't marry me I'll—(*pauses with the air of one about to utter a terrible threat*) I'll—see you home! *No* trouble I assure you—a pleasure" (MH Mss: 12) combines the threat of a melodrama villain with the bathos of an ending with bourgeois politesse. The villain also speaks and is spoken to like a recalcitrant child: "Ha ha! I'll make every single person in the world hideous and miserable. Ha—I *am* going to enjoy myself. I'll—" / "Well, ducky, is it going to be a good boy now?" / (*violently*) "No, it's not. It's going to be a bad boy. As bad as ever it knows how" (MH Mss: 21). Dropping into the inflated language of melodrama is a very deliberate strategy of farce. In the manuscript, the King's ordinary phrase "They tell me that you love my daughter" is altered in (probably

Nesbit's) handwriting into "have the impertinence to love the princess" (MH Mss: 28). This inflated pomposity characterises the power-relation between the Magician and his "Aged retainer" (MH Mss: 19), as the play self-consciously emphasises his stagy villainy. "If I were not a thoroughly wicked magician I should be touched by the affection of this aged retainer," "Pardon me, Madam, you will not learn [= vulg. for "teach"] me. Overcome by the pleasures of memory I allowed you to take a liberty [of slapping me] just now" (MH Mss: 6, 21).

The Magician also drops into parodies of the register of a publisher, accepting the Apprentice's bond "not necessarily for publication, but as a guarantee of good faith," parodies the words of a house-agent, with "the kitchen's on the 52nd floor—replete with every modern inconvenience," then moves into the register of a tradesman (a plumber or housepainter) with the Princess, touting "All sorts of spells. Enchantments competently carried out. Magic performed with punctuality and despatch. Really reliable spells at popular prices. Love charms personally executed. What shall it be? We can do you a nice little spell at seven and six that'll make it always jam for tea"—perhaps a memory of *Through the Looking-Glass* (MH Mss: 7, 7, 9). This advertising magic as a commodity is in the tradition of Gilbert and Sullivan's magician's advertisement patter-song in Act I of *The Sorcerer* (1877): "We've a first rate assortment of magic / And for raising a posthumous shade / With effects that are comic or tragic / There's no cheaper a house in the trade. / Love Philtre, we've quantities of it / And for Knowledge if anyone burns / We're keeping a very small Prophet / A Prophet who brings us unbounded returns . . . ," etc. (Gilbert [1877]: 1959: 37). The Magician goes on to assume the "manner of a drawing-room entertainer" before his "little trick" with the Princess, describing it as

> a very difficult one, invented by myself, and might be performed with advantage on most of the crowned heads of Europe—I mean *before* the crowned heads of Europe. There is no deception, ladies and gentlemen. You see before you a beggar maid, just a plain beggar maid—a very plain beggar maid, I shall now proceed to change her into a beautiful beggar maid. There is no deception. I have no apparatus concealed about my person. You can see for yourselves that there is no beauty about me. (MH Mss: 10)

The Magician talks to the Princess with more mixing of registers: "have an acid drop and conceal your emotion" (MH Mss: 10), addresses his heart with the archness of a beau to a coquette, "Be still, little flutterer" (MH Mss: 18), speaks with the "accent and action of a French chef," "'Ighness, if her Ighness vill write ze menu, I am at ze orders of 'er Ighness" (MH Mss: 19). The King arraigns him in a parody of legalese, charging him with "feloniously attempting to turn a pretty Princess into an ugly one" (MH Mss: 25).

In keeping with the broad-comic emphasis on spectacle and aural comedy, where the play presents two purely comic low characters: the Nurse as agroikos (rustic), and the Jester as bomolochos (buffoon), the prose recension conflates the two, and omits the Jester entirely, for his function is purely to add spectacle and verbal play, with his comic asides in parallel sentences on the nature of girls, his flattery of the King (he claims that the attachment of the Apprentice for the Princess is the King's fault because it was he who made the Princess pretty in the first place), his comment about magic being as rule-bound as arithmetic and so on (MH Mss: 25, 27, 30).

In dramatic burlesque, the author shared responsibility with the cast (Booth: 51), so there was much ad libbing. The throne room scene begins with the Jester's feeble punning jokes, and the stage direction "(The Courtiers laugh, and if Messrs Maskelyne and Devant don't like these anecdotes others can be substituted, I am sure they know more good stories than I do)" (MH Mss: 25). There could have been other jokes added to the script, for dramatic burlesques often included topical jokes, such as the Magician's journey to the palace by magic underground railway (MH Mss: 14). There had been a rudimentary subway system since the 1860s and the first electric underground railway in London went into operation in 1890, but in 1900 Charles Tytson Yerkes, a U.S. railway magnate, had arrived in London, and much work had begun on subway extensions. Trains play the means of fantasy locomotion in Nesbit's **"The Aunt and Amabel,"** a fantasy short story in *The Magic World,* and also in, for example, G. E. Farrow's *The Cinematograph Train* (ser. earlier, pub. 1904) or E. F. Benson's *David Blaize and the Blue Door* (1918) in this period.

The characterisation is a little different between versions. In the play, we see a good deal more of the Apprentice's stupidity as he answers only "Yes" and "No" when the Magician interviews him about it, and when he dithers about whether the vision is inviting or repelling him (MH Mss: 7, 8). In the play he is meddlesome, for he mixes magic elements on purpose, and the vision arises, to be seen by the Ma-

gician and Nurse, whereas in the prose version, he mixes the elements only by accident, and alone. The King's character is much more developed in the play, and he is a good deal more reasonable, as he responds to the Jester's flattery, finds it quite pardonable that the young pair should love though quite out of the question that they should marry, cheers up quickly after being outwitted, and blesses the pair cheerfully rather than crossly (MH Mss: 28-30, cf MH: 278-279). There is also more of the Nurse's rambling and of her obsession with the Magician as a baby (eg. his reluctance to wash), and her other trademark word, "respectable" (MH Mss: 5-6), which the prose version completely omits. In the play, the Nurse comes with the intention of bringing the Magician an apprentice, though she does not know what his trade is (MH Mss: 6), but in the prose recension, she suggests that he apprentices the baker's boy, whom she has borrowed to hold her horse, after he says that he is lonely (MH: 266). In the revision, the element of chance in the lovers' coming together suggests the workings of fate much better.

The prose recension also omits not only the Magician's roleplaying, but his own constantly-repeated refrain, "And *that*'s all right." He is much more needlessly "sarcastic" in the play with the Nurse, with the Princess to whom he addresses a parody of the cliches of polite conversation, and about the (feigned) stupidity of the Apprentice (MH Mss: 5, 8, 9, 16). He is also more overtly childish, as he relishes his Nurse's cooking, offers the Princess a spell which will make everyone think you're good even if you aren't, reacts to the her rejection of his proposal with the childish diction of "you see if you aren't" sorry, and violently argues with his Nurse (MH Mss: 8, 9, 18, 21). Though the prose version omits all this, it heightens the one sign of his childishness which it retains, when the Magician, instead of asking the Nurse to brush his coat and sew on a button, asks her to tie his necktie (MH Mss: 12, MH: 270). In the play, he is trickier and less passive, as he tries to weasel his way out of any punishment at all after the revelation of the Apprentice's identity, by suggesting that he regain his heart and leave (MH Mss: 30). The cumulative effect of these changes is to render the prose Taykin less of a "stage villain" and, though he is still the main focus, to direct less attention on him relative to the hero and heroine. When the King is also reduced in humanity in the prose version, this has the same effect. Hence all the changes in characterisation work consistently, rather than undercutting and cancelling each other out, as Aura and Fortunatus still remain conventional type figures, but are given a little more of the attention that would automatically be directed to the princess and prince of a Märchen.

The play farcically observes the unity of time with an exposition and a sequence of action that covers the course of a day. Though the prose recension adds additional segments and does away with this unity of time, it is shorter and much tighter. In the first scene of the play, the Princess kisses the Apprentice into cleverness, tells him to come to the palace and escapes; then the Magician considers drugging the guards with pies for which he produces the animals to go into them, then the three left behind drink a potion to go to the palace by train. In the kitchen scene, the Magician plays with magic cooking, the Apprentice steals the Magician's notebook, the Magician threatens the Princess, the nurse interferes, he affects to spare the Princess, the Apprentice tells the Princess to steal the heart from a saucepan as she orders the menu, she establishes a rapport with the Nurse and goes out with her, the Magician repeats "That's all right," brews his uglifying potion twice, the ladies return, and he is then blackmailed. Then, the Nurse pleads with the Magician to be good and he refuses as he is arrested and again at the end (MH Mss: 24, 30), she twice pleads with the King (MH Mss: 26, 30), with whom she has much more byplay, and the babyfied Magician says he will be good twice.

The prose version moves much faster as it omits the putative drugging, gives the potion-drinking a reason (transmogrification), and conflates and condenses the rest. It has James steal the notebook and then the heart while Taykin threatens Aura, has Nurse plead with Taykin and the King simultaneously at the end, and the baby Taykin make his assertion once. Both versions foreground the improbability of the Magician getting the job as palace cook, but differently. In the play, the Magician says he forgets how he comes to be here, in the prose recension the narrator professes ignorance about how Taykin got the job so quickly and whether he made magic references from employers to get it (MH Mss: 17, MH: 273). Foregrounding and conjecturing about improbabilities and lacunae while taking actual fantasy events and characters for granted is one of the characteristics of Nesbit's rhetoric of fantasy, for example, drawing attention to the children being miraculously able to understand foreign languages in *The Story of the Amulet* (ser. earlier, pub. 1906).

The condensing of the prose recension also entirely omits the pathos of the Princess's situation just be-

fore the end in the play. The King orders her to give the Apprentice up, the Apprentice "impressively" says to her twice, "Do as your father says—always!," she cries out, "weeping," "Oh, I *did* think you'd *tell* him you'd rather die than give me up," there is a tableau of the Princess "dragging away from King" with the rival prince on her other hand, her pathetic resolve to obey the apprentice, and her plea to the King to let her say goodbye (MH Mss: 28-29). The prose version reduces this to two sentences about Aura following a signal from Fortunatus, before the transposition (MH: 278). It is not that the prose version therefore becomes less "human" and more heartless, more purely flippant, but a case of the play containing a wider range of elements and a broader spectrum of emotions in order to hold audience attention through a much longer time span than the prose recension.

Where the play has frolicsome spectacular fantasy, much broad aural and visual knockabout comedy, and stronger affinities with New Comedy, the prose recension is less facetious, tightens the plotting, emphasises the Märchen and the Kunstmärchen traditions, especially the conflict of good and evil, and heightens the socialist allusions and the theme of moral transformation which lightly reverberate through the text.

The stylisation of the burlesque Kunstmärchen and the pantomime genre imply an expectation that young lovers will be united at the end. But where this play introduces the separable heart and jokes on it right from the beginning, the prose recension introduces the figure of speech made concrete only at the point of Taykin's proposal. This works better, for it comes as a pleasant surprise, prepared for by all the other magic. Contrariwise, the prose version does away with the surprises in the play, which are connected with Taykin's christening curses. The prose recension elaborates the Magician's exposition about uglifying Aura, being imprisoned by the King, and obdurately refusing to undo his curse. And it consolidates it with Aura's kiss ("My fairy godmother gave me that kiss at my christening. It was a magic kiss, that had the power to turn a stupid person into a clever one. I've been saving up that kiss, for you, for twenty years"), the Apprentice's accusation of the Magician ("You made me stupid, because you were not invited to my christening"), and the revelation of his identity ("Now I'm clever again I know who I am") which are filtered through the play (MH Mss: 13, 23, 30), and which as we *read* it (though not during an enactment), feel somewhat like plot-gaps being hastily filled. In the prose recension, these become two long initial sections, and as a result of this rearranging and elaboration of material, the prose recension not only removes the surprises of the play, but from the start *emphasises its affinities with the Märchen*: the Sleeping Beauty, her christening curse, its modification, its implication of the power of fate and time.

The play starts in the Magician's Tower with the imprisoned Magician's exposition of *one* christening, so we only *hear* about the curses, though we see a good deal of his conjuring-magic. But the prose recension follows chronology, so it "shows" rather than merely tells of both christening curses. It has more about fairy godmothers, so that the White Witch (a new name) appears and speaks at Aura's christening rather than remaining a stray reference. As in "The Sleeping Beauty," the prose recension emphasises her power to mitigate but not to cancel out the power of evil, since she gives Aura the kiss, does not spell out its nature but tells her she will know what to do with it *when the time comes*. It is she, rather than the King, who prevents Taykin from vanishing, and warns that Taykin himself will undo the curse in time but not if he is asked (MH: 263). The prose recension repositions and alters the Magician's assertion that white magic (beautifying the Princess) is quite easy but black magic is "the very dickens" and his promise to do no more of it except at children's parties (MH Mss: 21, 23) into the narratorial assertion about the *White Witch*'s "White Magic [being] much stronger than Black Magic, as well as more suited for drawing-room performances" (MH: 263).

"The traditional fairy queen, gracefully waving her wand and uttering noble sentiments in a silvery voice, is a pale, meaningless cipher to those who have known" Nesbit's Psammead, Phoenix, Mouldiwarp (Moore: 193). Moore rightly points to Nesbit's achievement within the fantasy novel, but ignores the difference between generic paradigms. Nesbit works differently within the fantasy novel and the Kunstmärchen, and does deploy this figure of the traditional good fairy (sometimes called Benevola, and more redolent of pantomime than Märchen) when she writes burlesque Kunstmärchen, as she does in **"The Magician's Heart."** Oddly, the "dear White Witch" (MH: 263) does not appear in the very pantomime-like tableau at the end of the prose recension, where both a pantomime and burlesque Kunstmärchen would traditionally include her (cf. *The Rose and the Ring*)—perhaps Nesbit was tiring as she rewrote.

The play sets off the Magician only against the King. He is kept imprisoned only by the King, who "won't let [him] do Magic anywhere but here" (MH Mss: 1, 5). But the prose recension sets Taykin off against the White Witch, and indicates more clearly that Taykin is to be taken more seriously. In the prose recension, though Taykin says to his Nurse that he cannot get out because *King*'s orders must be respected, it is the *White Witch*'s charm that makes him unable to vanish after cursing Aura. Her charm will work till there is no further use for it, and allows him only to play with magic in the tower till he will willingly undo his curse (MH: 263, 266). Thus Taykin is much more supernatural than the Magician, much less subject to human power, and the prose recension puts a greater emphasis upon his role as the Kunstmärchen equivalent of the wicked fairy of "The Sleeping Beauty" who is not a comic figure, and even a frivolous burlesque version of whom carries a trace of her power to affect the fates of princes and nations.

For all the conjuring tricks in both versions, Taykin *is* a conjurer in the play, and *is* a "real magician" in the prose recension, as the play focusses almost exclusively on the spectacle of the Magician as conjurer, and the prose recension focuses more equally on Taykin as *both* as the Kunstmärchen equivalent of "The Sleeping Beauty" Märchen wicked fairy *and* as conjurer. When Taykin produces things out of the air "like a conjurer does" the immediate caveat "Only, of course he was a real magician" (MH: 266) means exactly what it says at one level (Taykin as evil fairy), though it means the opposite on another (Taykin merely as conjurer). The tension between the two aspects is absent in the play, and in the prose recension when Taykin is *like* a conjurer, the deflation works to indicate the moral that the power of evil is basically no more than trivial legerdemain.

Because the prose recension pits Taykin against the White Witch, it also irons out the inconsistencies of his magical escape to the palace in the play. There, the Magician just uses his magic to get out of the tower, which makes nonsense of him being imprisoned in the first place (a glaring inconsistency which would probably pass unnoticed on stage), but in the prose recension, when Taykin undoes Aura's curse, logically, the White Witch's spell that holds him is dissolved, he wishes that his old magic would work outside the tower; feels "in strange, confused, yet quite sure way" that it will, and is able to leave (MH: 273).

As the prose recension enhances the presence of the Märchen in the narrative, it also reduces the presence of New Comedy elements. It removes the conventional surprise of the revelation of the Apprentice's real identity, as the narrator constantly harps on the string that James is Prince Fortunatus, so there is no actual comic anagnorisis for the reader. It does indicate Taykin's association with the father when it adds to the bathos of the Magician's comic threat to see the Princess home the statement that Taykin will appeal to Aura's father who will not let her refuse a match so desirable for a beggar maid (MH Mss: 12, MH: 270). However, it plays down Taykin as father-figure in other ways. The Nurse offends the Magician in the play by talking of his old age, for he does not think he is old, but the prose recension clearly indicates that Taykin is only in his forties, which still allows him to have attended the babies' christenings twenty years before, yet does not give him the weight of patriarchal old age (MH Mss: 5, MH: 265). It omits the Magician's "and *that*'s all right" *and* the Apprentice using the same phrase when he overcomes him, which emphasises the sexual rivalry of the son obtaining what the father-figure wanted (MH Mss: 24, 31).

Finally, the prose recension changes the ending. It omits the babyfied Magician's echoing the King's blessing of the young pair, which underlines the doubling effect, it leaves out his last words, "and that's all right," and it elaborates the last stage direction, "(*Shower of roses*)" (MH Mss: 31). The prose version ends with Taykin's resolve to be good, and the sentence, "And so the story ends with love and a wedding, and showers of white roses" (MH: 280). This difference in tone nicely epitomises both the change between versions and the different generic decorum of the dramatic burlesque and the burlesque Kunstmärchen. It consists in playing down the New Comedy elements, the romantic softening of the *white* roses, and the self-consciousness of the allusion to "story" which emphasises the generic location of this burlesque Kunstmärchen in a tradition of Märchen and of Kunstmärchen before it.

For as the prose recension emphasises its Märchen affinities and decreases the New Comedy inflexions, it also emphasises its affinities with the burlesque Kunstmärchen tradition and an authorial oeuvre within it, a feature completely absent in the play. "The Sleeping Beauty" is the primary Märchen drawn upon by the Kunstmärchen tradition, by its burlesque variety in particular, and by Nesbit. The play touches on the affinities of the burlesque Kunstmärchen with the absurdity of the nursery rhyme, as the Magician says that five-and-twenty blackbirds will fly out of

his pie (MH Mss: 16). The prose recension omits this intergeneric touch, but instead brings in Aura's cousin, Princess Belinda. She is absent in the play, and here advises Aura to disguise herself and go to Taykin and pay him not more than £50 (exaggerating the £5 in the play) or he may suspect she is not a beggar maid. This Belinda is the heroine of "Belinda and Bellamant" (first published in a magazine), collected in the same volume, a tale of two other christening-curses of ugliness within the *same authorial Kunstmärchen world* built over various tales. This authorial world is the juvenile fantasy fiction equivalent of Piers Anthony's Xanth or Terry Pratchett's Discworld today. In Nesbit's Kunstmärchen world Malevola tends to be the bad fairy, and the inhabitants "know" Märchen plots as their "history," Kings and queens are aware of previous similar christenings and their dangers. There are similar devices in Thackeray, Lang and Hood, including the device of ancestry (a character being descended from a Märchen character), and here, the device of blood-relation to a previous Kunstmärchen character is a variation of it. Likewise, James as foundling / baker's boy / prince calls attention to the relation of **"The Magician's Heart"** to **"The Princess and the Hedge-Pig,"** also in the same volume.

The play has the Princess actively stealing the heart, which the prose recension omits, but the prose recension emphasises Aura's determination to change her own fate on Belinda's advice, and lessens her passive pathos before the transposition, so the feminist inflexions are similar in both versions. But the social satire and the class theme is much more focussed and foregrounded in the prose recension. In the play, the invitation to the Magician for the Princess's christening is *forgotten,* and later the Apprentice tells him in relation to his own, "You never were invited to any one's christening, and I don't wonder at it" (MH Mss: 3, 23). The Magician is offended when the Nurse asks him what his trade is, she explains she means what he gets his living by, he self satisfiedly tells her that he has *got* his living, that he is a magician by trade and "sarcastically" thanks her for her naive exclamation, "My! And what a nice respectable business—almost as respectable as being a water-rate collector or a watchmaker or an artist" (MH Mss: 4-5). When he proposes to the beautiful beggar maid, he talks of his willingness to stoop from his high estate to marry her, and the Nurse calls it most handsome, considering what a come down it is for him (MH Mss: 11). The Apprentice then insults him by suggesting he disguise himself as a perfect gentleman to escape (MH Mss: 14).

But the prose recension works up and emphasises the theme of Taykin's social origins right at the beginning. His invitations are not *forgotten* (as the wicked fairy was), nor is he not invited because he is a *nasty person*. The Nurse's exclamation is transformed into the clear narratorial statement in the first paragraph that he was not invited to royal christenings "because he was not a lord, or a duke, or a seller of bacon and tea, or anything really high class," but merely a successful wicked magician of whom no court would *know* (MH: 260), and the prose recension also *adds* his motivation for the curses—when he went to Fortunatus's christening unasked, the court's rudeness made him curse Fortunatus and go on to curse Aura. And his transformation, without the separable heart and with the addition of strange words in a foreign language much more strongly suggests baptism and the fantasy transformation as a theologically inflected metaphor for inward psychological change.

It is scarcely necessary in this forum to note the interest and the value of neglected works of fantasy fiction. But it should be remarked that academia today tends to pay more attention to prose fiction than to poetry and drama, and that we should not forget fairy plays and indeed songs and verse, for both children and adults, in our consideration of marvels and tales. Our comparison of the two versions of **"The Magician's Heart"** demonstrates not just that mimesis requires more space than diegesis or that Nesbit was getting tired and summarising old material as she rewrote it, but that Nesbit was a writer alert to different generic requirements, who knew that the stage can allow for more visual and aural comedy and looser plotting than the page, and who ironed out inconsistencies and heightened and played down elements as she transposed material from one medium to another. The comparison makes it abundantly clear that the stereotyped image of Nesbit as hasty, careless and throwaway in her attitude to writing is in need of revision, and simply does not fit the facts of these two texts.

The comparison shows that the prose recension of **"The Magician's Heart"** does not hide its affinities with dramatic burlesque but also condenses all the comic dialogue and the repeated elements, provides less conjuring, tightens the plotting, emphasises its Märchen origins and morals, plays down the New Comedy elements, allies the tale with other work in the tradition and authorial oeuvre, and heightens the class inflexions. While the prose version is still comic, the play is more farcical. Close reading of the two texts in juxtaposition enables us to see the minute but influential ways in which genre conventions and genre expectations actually shift and displace one another as Nesbit moves from pantomime script to prose narrative. In the process, the sum total of her alterations does, paradoxically, serve to underpin precisely that privileging of prose narrative at the expense of drama and verse, and that valuing of "seriousness" (the Märchen emphasis on good vs evil) which Tolkien, and many later critics, embody. For in the act of translating her farcical script into a burlesque Kunstmärchen, Nesbit in fact shifts from the broadest of broad comedy to a subtler form of it, which suggests that she, too, somehow conceived prose narrative as "higher" or more "serious" than drama.

Notes

1. The processes of gaining access to the playscript of *The Magician's Heart* (of which I informed Julia Briggs, author of the latest biography of Nesbit) illustrate the bibliographical/logistical problems (and the expenses) of a scholar in neglected fantasy fiction. Doris Langley Moore mentions that in January 1907, Nesbit "had a one-act play produced at Maskelyne and Devant's Theatre. It was called *The Magician's Heart,* and was devised to give the celebrated conjurers scope for the performance of 'magic'" (Moore: 237). In a bibliographical note, Roger Lancelyn Green also refers to "*The Magician's Heart,* which [E. Nesbit] wrote as a one-act play, given at St. George's Hall, London, in 1907, and later made into the last story of *The Magic World,* 1912" (Green: 1955: vi). Finally, in Clarence's standard bibliography of plays I found the entry "Magician's Heart, The. Fairy P. 3 a. E. Nesbit. St.Geo.H. Jan. 14, 1907" (Clarence [1909] 1970: 272).

I now had the exact date of the first performance, but was faced with the apparent contradiction of a play that was both three-act and one-act, performed at both Maskelyne and Devant's Theatre and in St. George's Hall. It seemed that Moore did not appear to have seen the script (Moore: letter, 1978; she also did not think such an examination as this of such a "minor" piece was worth doing), and Green informed me that his source too was Clarence (Green: letter, 1978). But it became clear that Maskelyne and Devant (formerly Maskelyne and Cooke, and named as such in the serialised but not the book version of *The Enchanted Castle*) were proprietors of St. George's Hall in Regent Street. Then followed a correspondence that lasted over a year. The Worshipful Company of Stationers directed me to the Public Record Offices, but neither had records of the play; the Office of the Lord Chamberlain first informed me that they had no record in their files, but then later found that the play had indeed been licensed, and directed me to the British Library, on whose indexes the play did not seem to appear. Finally, the Department of Manuscripts in the British Library informed me that they did indeed hold a copy of the play in their collection of plays submitted for licensing to the Lord Chamberlain (letters, 1978-1979), gave me a number, and a copy was obtained on Interlibrary Loan through the Australian National University, Canberra.

This copy appears to have been owned by the actor who played the King, since all pencil marks and emendations are made to the speeches made by this character. There are blank spaces in the dramatis personae and the first two scenes for the names of the Magician (Professor) and the Princess. The Magician is given a name only in Scene iii; and the Princess is called Candida, not Aura, so clearly Nesbit thought of *The Magician's Heart* at about the time of "The Charmed Life; or The Princess and the Lift Man" (coll. 1905) with its own Shavian-named heroine Princess Candida, and changed it in the printed version.

2. Primarily in the Edwardian period and after, this sort of drama was still called "pantomime" (a word which has well-nigh replaced "burlesque") as it also went beyond the Märchen and the Kunstmärchen to more original fantasy plots allied to those of the fantasy novel—eg. *Peter Pan, Pinkie and the Fairies, Where the Rainbow Ends, Katawampus, Bluebell and the Sleepy King, Toad of Toad Hall, The Wallypug of Why*—some of which started on the stage and moved into diegetic form, others the reverse.

3. It seems that the famous music hall artiste Dan Leno who moved to pantomime appears in the list of actors (not in the typescript of the play, but this information was given to me in correspondence either by the British Museum Library *or* the Office of the Lord Chamberlain, 1978-1979 (I cannot check the correspondence, which now reposes in a trunk in India). Dan Leno sometimes did dame parts (Booth: 382-383), and it is likely that he played the Nurse (if not, then he would have been the Jester in red and white motley).

Mavis Reimer

SOURCE: "Treasure Seekers and Invaders: E. Nesbit's Cross-Writing of the Bastables," in *Children's Literature,* Vol. 25, 1997, pp. 50-9.

A startling moment in Edwardian children's literature occurs in a book not written for children at all, when a remarkably spelled letter from the Junior Blackheath Society of Antiquaries and Field Club arrives at the breakfast table of Len and Chloe, protagonists of a domestic comedy, *The Red House,* published in 1902 by E. Nesbit. The Antiquaries turn out to be none other than the Bastable children and their friends, who have decided to recast the visit of the Maidstone antiquarian society to the Moat House, a visit that forms the basis of one of the stories in *The Wouldbegoods* (1901). The report of the genesis of the children's plan and Oswald's account of the Red House experience appear in yet another context, one of the stories in the *New Treasure Seekers* collection (1904).

Julia Briggs observes that the Bastables "put in a guest appearance" in Nesbit's adult novel (*WP* 215), a comment implying that the Bastables' presence is somehow incidental to the trajectory of the text. My experience of reading *The Red House,* however, was that the Bastables' eruption into Nesbit's novel radically disrupted the text. Not only does the "free" talk of the children (*RH* 226) generally undercut the conventionally sentimental and coy tone of Nesbit's narrator, Len, but also the children's discovery of the antique cradle "treasure" in the basement of the house allows the text to introduce, by decorous indirection, the fact of Chloe's pregnancy. Moreover, the Bastables' return by invitation to the Red House at the conclusion of the novel allows readers their first glimpse of the occupant of the cradle—Len's and Chloe's daughter, who is known only as "the pussy kitten" in the text. Nesbit, it seems, uses the Bastables to focus the representation of "the child" for her adult audience. How, I wondered, is that representation the same as and different from the representation of "the child" Nesbit constructs for her audience of children in the three collections of Treasure Seekers stories?[1]

Recent theories of children's literature suggest that such differences and similarities in the cross-writing of the child may point to significant ideological constructions. Jacqueline Rose (1984), James Kincaid (1992), and Perry Nodelman (1992) have demonstrated that Anglo-American culture sets childhood apart as a site of lost innocence and that children are constructed as Other for the benefit of adults. Those benefits include the exercise of power in various guises: the power to know and conceal desire, to preserve values on the verge of collapse, to reproduce children as commodities, and to define adulthood itself. But although the idea of the child as a site of lost innocence may have been produced for the benefit of adults, the relative stability and the persistence of that idea imply that it is not simply a coercive domination, but rather a domination that also manufactures consent.[2] Children's literature would seem to be a primary site for the production and reproduction of this complex subjectivity.

Nesbit's work for children fits into the late nineteenth-century "cult of the child" and what Roger Lancelyn Green (1962) named the Golden Age of children's books. Children's books of the period are distinguished in Green's view precisely by their attitude to childhood, an attitude Green—like Rose, Kincaid, and Nodelman after him—describes by borrowing the metaphor of colonization: childhood suddenly was presented as "a thing in itself . . . a new world to be explored, a new species to be observed and described" (44-45). The difference from earlier texts of children's literature, according to Green, is that there was no longer a sense of the child as an "undeveloped adult" being pushed toward a more fully realized humanity; rather, "you were enjoying the Spring for itself" (44-45). Rose develops her theory that children's literature is "one of the central means through which we regulate our relationship to language and images" (139) in her work with another text of the period, J. M. Barrie's *Peter Pan*. She remarks a similar change in the texts of children's literature over time: from the eighteenth century through the works of such nineteenth-century writers as Mary Molesworth, children's fiction delineates the division between the adult's and the child's "types of language and modes of address" (59), but that division progressively was removed after the late-nineteenth century, "as the adult intention has more and more been absorbed into the story and, apparently, rendered invisible" (60). The congruence between the relative ideas of "the child" and "the adult" that Green finds in Edwardian literature for children and the ideas that recent theorists describe as persisting in contemporary Anglo-American culture points to the possibility that texts from the turn of the century, such as Nesbit's, might demonstrate how this structural relation comes to be instituted. What cultural function does this formation serve? What contradictions does it resolve? How do Nesbit's texts represent to the child his or her position as subject in such a way that the child is likely to consent to this position?

The primary scene in which the Bastable children establish an important relation with an adult occurs in the first collection of stories. After spending fourteen chapters trying various ways to "restore the fallen fortunes of [their] House" (16), the Bastables finally find the "treasure, and no mistake" (200) they have been seeking in the person of their "Mother's Indian Uncle" (*STS,* 182). Not only does the Uncle arrive in a fairy-godmother coach laden with boxes and knobby parcels containing "heaps and heaps of presents" (200), but he also rescues Father's faltering business with a substantial capital investment and takes the whole family to live with him in the "jolly, big, ugly red" house "with a lot of windows" on the top of the hill (202). It is, as Oswald remarks, just like the ending of a fairy tale.

The abundance of treasure and happy surprises unpacked in this ending almost obscures the sequence of events by which the treasure seekers transform an irascible old man into a fairy godmother. The sequence is set in motion because the children make a series of mistakes in interpreting adult language. When their father announces that their "dear Mother's Indian Uncle" is coming to dinner (*STS,* 182), the children assume that the uncle is "the Red kind" (199), an imperial subject rather than an imperial functionary. They find evidence for their interpretation in the uncle's description of himself as "a poor, broken-down man" (186), a description that the Bastables hear as a literal statement about the uncle's material circumstances rather than as a metaphorical description of his health. Corroboration for this train of thought comes from their reading of English literature, specifically the line from Pope's *Essay on Man*—"Lo, the poor Indian!"—which Nesbit uses as the title for the chapter. Again, their misprision is a result of their confusion of Pope's metaphorical judgement of the Native American's "untutor'd mind" with literal pauperism, which exceeds even their own straitened circumstances. By reading literally the adults' figurative language, the children position the uncle with themselves as subjected Other rather than as subject.

In their assumption of equality—indeed, of superiority—to the uncle, the children offer him the pleasures of play. Their "play-dinner" includes teaching him "how to be a dauntless hunter," by slaying the rabbit/deer with "trusty yew bows" and the pudding/wild boar with forks (191); how to be an adventurer in an exotic land, by plucking almonds and raisins "from the boughs of the great trees" at the top of the chest of drawers; and how to be a cosmopolitan consumer, by choosing figs "from the cargo that the rich merchants brought" in their drawer/ship (193). Their play, in other words, reproduces three roles in the colonial project—that of the trophy hunter, that of the European traveler/adventurer, and that of the consumer back home. The uncle's subsequent appearances in the novel make it clear that he literally has enacted each of these "playful" roles before his momentous meeting with the Bastables: his red house is decorated with "swords and guns" and with "horns of stags and other animals" (202); the Christmas dinner he serves them is replete with such exotic comestibles as ginger wine (207); and the cargo disgorged from the coach includes "Japanese china tea-sets" (199) and "yards and yards of soft silk from India" for the girls, "a real Indian sword for Oswald and a book of Japanese pictures for Noël and some ivory chessmen for Dicky," as well as assorted carved fans, silver bangles, strings of amber beads, necklaces of uncut gems, shawls and scarves of silk, cabinets of brown and gold, ivory boxes, silver trays, and "brass things" (200). The children's reading of the metaphorical as the literal has allowed the uncle to release his literal experiences as colonizer into the play of metaphor.

The congruence the theorists find between the construction of the Other in colonial discourse and our discourse about "the child," it seems, not only offers an explanatory analogy, but also is historically apt. Jacqueline Rose, in fact, notes that the oppositional terms in which childhood currently is understood can be traced back from "Thomas Day and Peter Parley to Rousseau" (59) in the colonialist concepts of exploration, discovery, and adventure. A similar structural definition of the "primitive" in relation to the "civilized" was put in place by evolutionary theory in the middle of the nineteenth century. According to Daniel Bivona (1990), the "notions of the 'barbaric,' the 'uncivilized,' the 'primitive,' the 'childlike,' the alien in time and the alien in space overlap constantly in the Victorian imagination of the late nineteenth century" and eventually "the purely analogical relationships . . . begin to be broken down into more literal ones" (76-77).

Seen as "alien in time," the child retains the promise of growing up and crossing into adulthood. Seen as "alien in space," however, the child is fixed as irremediably Other. Peter Coveney insists that this fixity

distinguishes the cult of the child as an attitude "wholly different" from the Romantic view of childhood: "their interest in childhood serves not to integrate childhood and adult experience, but to create a barrier of nostalgia and regret between childhood and the potential responses of adult life" (240). What Nesbit does by staging the mechanisms through which her culture produces its version of "the child" is even more consequential than Bivona suggests, for her discourse is not about childhood—about the metaphor of the child—but is directed to actual children. This is a text of children's literature. To some extent, then, Nesbit's writing of the Bastables must be seen as an imperative to children to occupy a place in discourse that allows adults to effect the transaction of the literal and the metaphorical.

The immediate rewards of consent are abundantly obvious in *The Story of the Treasure Seekers:* the Bastables achieve safety, material comfort, the restitution of their class position (Oswald is headed for Rugby and Oxford at the conclusion of the story), and the ability to see themselves as coherent characters. "I can't help it if it is like Dickens," remarks Oswald, "because it happens this way. Real life is often something like books" (*STS,* 205).

The children also gain the illusion of power. They assume that they show the "poor Indian" "how to be a dauntless hunter" (191); it seems to be Oswald's saying so that brings "the coach of the Fairy Godmother" to a stop outside their house (197). That their power is illusory—in the sense both that their power lies in creating illusion and that they are deluded in assuming they have real power—becomes evident in the next book about the Bastables, *The Wouldbegoods.* The collection opens with a story about the children playing *The Jungle Book,* an escalated version of the same game that had captivated their uncle and had brought about the fairy-tale ending to their story of treasure-seeking. In this case, however, the children's playing comes too close to being real. They borrow several of the uncle's hunting trophies as props, even stuffing and animating the tiger skins he has brought from India. When the uncle walks in on this game, far from responding with expansive enjoyment, he madly begins to beat the children with the Malacca cane he is carrying. As a consequence of their misbehavior, the children are sent into the country to "stay till we had grown into better children" (*W,* 25), a resonant phrase for any argument about the constructedness of "the child." It is while they are staying at the Moat House that they meet the Maidstone Society of Antiquaries and Field Club, which inspires their trip to the Red House in the adult novel.

If in the children's novel the children's reading of the metaphorical as literal allows the adult to disperse the literal in play, in the adult novel the reverse transaction takes place: the children's restaging of a "real" event as play allows the adults to reconstitute their own play as reality.

Len and Chloe, writer and illustrator, respectively, are left the grand old Red House by the will of a deceased uncle identified, like the Indian uncle, as a "fairy godmother" (*RH,* 32). Their modest incomes as members of "the noble army of workers" (7) will not stretch to allow them to maintain the rambling house and the country property on which it sits. Yet when they cycle out to see the house, they immediately succumb to its charms and decide to move in. Housed in a manor, but inept at proper household management on such a scale, Len and Chloe repeatedly refer to themselves as "Babes in the Wood" (82) playing at housekeeping. Like "naughty children" (120), they picnic on newspapers in the kitchen, scandalize the vicar's wife by greeting her in bare feet because they are washing their own floors, and succeed in mounting a housewarming party only by borrowing dishes and draping packing cases for a table. At the same time, however, Len as narrator is careful to distinguish their play in the Red House from their play in the "doll's house" they first occupied after their marriage, allowing only the Red House experiences to be thought of as "real" (111). In order to hold together his contradictory definitions of play, he adopts the metaphors of exploration and colonization. The Red House, he muses, is "a new life—a primitive existence where law was not" (66); he and Chloe are "in the position of folk cast upon a desert island" (67). "Like Columbus," he tells Chloe, they must establish their own rules (111).

The visit of the Bastable children legitimizes the proprietary status they have assumed in play and ratifies their rule. The letter the Bastables copy and send to Len and Chloe names the Red House as having "great ihstoric [sic] interest" (*RH,* 212) and has the effect of making the adults feel like "lords of the manor" (215). When the children arrive, they assume the continuity of the house's past owner (a "celebrated amn [sic]" [213]) and its present owner ("a clever writer" (222)) and, despite their "discerning" observations (232) and "free" talk (226), they do not register any incogruities between the house and its occupants—they simply pronounce both to be splendid. That is, they do not register any such incongruities in this text directed to an adult audience. In the retelling of the incident in the children's book, Oswald does

remark that "the girls thought [the house] was bare" (*New Treasure Seekers,* 88). In *The Red House,* however, the Bastables are only focalized through the first-person narrator, Len, so that their private judgements are never introduced into the text. Even what Len calls their "very full flow of conversation" (*RH,* 225) is reported in the text in a summary marked by the narrator's insistence that the children's relationship to language is "close and unproblematic" (Rose 44)—a representation of the relation of children and language that Jacqueline Rose suggests underwrites children's literature from its beginnings in the mid-eighteenth century. Len comments: "They now threw away all shyness, and talked to us with simple directness of adventures, of contemporary literature, of the ways of Providence, and their own vital ambitions" (*RH,* 225). "Simple directness" is, I suspect, the last phrase most readers would use to describe Oswald Bastable's language as narrator of the Treasure Seekers stories. What purpose does it serve for Len to describe the children's language in this way in the adult novel?

As in *The Story of the Treasure Seekers,* it is the children's confusion of categories—in this case, their conflation of historical periods—that makes them available as agents of transaction. By suggesting that the children's uncertainty represents a higher truth, a simple and direct account of, among other things, "the ways of Providence," Len and Chloe can insert themselves into a line of historical "lords of the manor." Indeed the children's playful "invasion" of the house uncovers the props Len and Chloe need to give substance to their play: behind the door of an inner cellar, the Bastables locate a store of massive and solid, if somewhat dilapidated, furniture from various eras of the house's ownership. The dynastic cradle is among the treasures. Len's reverential conclusion to his story is an extended metaphor of lineage and inheritance: his daughter is a "usurper," a "princess," the occasion of Chloe's mounting from a "high estate" to "a higher" (*RH,* 274). It is a metaphor made literal by the person of his heir in the cradle.

Why did it become so important for adults to be able to manipulate the linguistic fields of the literal and the metaphorical in turn-of-the-century England? By the late nineteenth century, the Empire was producing unprecedented economic benefits for England, but, at the same time, the imperial project had become fraught with what Bivona calls "epistemological" difficulties, which shook British confidence in the Empire's right to exploit Indian and African territories for British benefit. Jenny Sharpe in *Allegories of Empire* dates this crisis from the Indian "Mutiny" of 1857. She argues that it was in the aftermath of the savage British restoration of order in India that a new discourse about imperialism emerged. Imperialism had long been regarded as a civilizing mission, but that mission unproblematically included "the profit-making enterprise of creating new markets for English manufactures" (7). It was only after the "violent upheavals that encouraged the colonizers to see themselves as the innocent victims of native hostility" that Britain began to figure its mission in terms of the "domestic virtues of self-sacrifice, moral duty, and devotion to others" (8). In Nesbit, the Indian Uncle's restaging of his part in colonial exploitation as play allows him to reproduce himself as a benevolent rescuer of the Bastables, as a fairy godmother.

But play, because it allows for such a reinvention of subjectivity by blurring the boundaries between the literal and the metaphorical, also allows for the opposite transaction, the conversion of game into history. It is this transaction that the Bastables facilitate in *The Red House.* Because adults not only create children in language, but also produce children through procreation, their play can be reified as fact. In *The Red House,* this reification allows Len and Chloe, who not incidentally are makers of texts, to use the pleasures of children's play—and the pleasures of playing with children—to institute a historical entitlement for their child. That the theorists of children's literature should find that we continue to recognize and reproduce this historical entitlement as a structural relation raises many troubling questions about the institution of children's literature and the criticism of it.

Nesbit's representation of "the child" alternatively to audiences of children and adults is literally a crosswriting, a staging and restaging of the chiasmic discursive mechanism by which her culture produced the structural relation of child and adult. Do her texts for children merely manufacture consent? Green himself suggests that Nesbit substitutes "tone for teaching" (46). Although I am not convinced that the two can be separated so neatly, it seems clear that the sceptical, self-deprecating, yet arrogant voice of Oswald Bastable exceeds the category of "this emptiness called a child" (Kincaid 71). The several levels and situations of narration—readers' consciousness of Oswald as Nesbit's creation, Oswald's self-conscious withholding of full information about himself as narrator, and Oswald's alternate reportage of other characters' words and feelings in direct quota-

tion and in the amalgamated narrative voice of free indirect discourse—point to the mediation of language between "the child" and the world and complicate any attempt to read the children's texts as straight instruction or as simple appropriation. Nesbit, after all, gives Oswald the last word on the Red House adventure, a last word he uses to insist on the intractability of actual children to adults' self-serving conceptualizations: "I suppose they thought it was wilful waste to have a cradle and no baby to use it. But it could so easily have been used for something else. It would have made a ripping rabbit-hutch, and babies are far more trouble than rabbits to keep, and not nearly so profitable, I believe" (*NTS,* 104).

Notes

1. [Reimer's point is underlined by Nesbit's chapter title in *The Red House:* the children's visit in ch. 10 is called "The Invaders." Interestingly, Nesbit also separates juvenile and adult texts not only by language and narrative perspective, but also by naming the invasive society in the *Red House* differently. The children style themselves the Maidstone Society of Antiquaries and Field Club in *The Wouldbegoods* and in "The Young Antiquaries" chapter of *New Treasure Seekers.* Eds.]

2. Stephen Slemon and Jo-Ann Wallace (11) suggest that locating the places where imperial power "manufacture[s] a domination by consent" is an important project for theorists of children's literature to investigate.

Erika Rothwell

SOURCE: "'You Catch It if You Try to Do Otherwise': The Limitations of E. Nesbit's Cross-Written Vision of the Child," in *Children's Literature,* Vol. 25, 1997, pp. 60-70.

Edith Nesbit did not begin writing for children consistently or particularly successfully until she produced *The Treasure Seekers* in 1899. After this success, the majority of her books were children's, but she also continued to write for adults. Nesbit, however, not only alternates between addressing child and adult audiences, but also crosswrites for adult and child *within* and *across* works. The children's books that make up the Bastable trilogy—*The Treasure Seekers* (1899), *The Wouldbegoods* (1901), and *The New Treasure Seekers* (1904)—though told from a child's point of view, address both child and adult readers and focus attention upon the common, but conflicting, experiences of adult and child. Meanwhile, the domestic novel *The Red House* (1902), which is intended for an adult audience, calls attention to the same phenomena of shared, yet conflicting, experience by introducing the child Bastable characters as "guest stars" and telling, from Len's adult point of view, an episode that is later renarrated by Oswald in *The Treasure Seekers.*

Virtually all critical consideration of Nesbit and her view of the child is based solely upon her children's books and does not incorporate the intersection of child and adult books that I have just described. Humphrey Carpenter finds Nesbit's Bastable trilogy "as condescending towards children as are any of the Beautiful Child books of the Molesworth era" (132), but more often Nesbit's children's books are thought of as iconoclastic.[1] Mary Croxson, for example, believes that Nesbit's purpose is to emancipate the child. Nesbit's children "are no longer enslaved by the repressive or over-indulgent adult domination of an earlier age. They converse freely with their elders, are at liberty to develop as they will and have the freedom of personal awareness given by a rich imaginative life" (Croxson 63). In short, Nesbit is typically defined as a juvenile author who writes for children as equals and as an uncompromising advocate of the child's viewpoint, rights, and freedoms.

I believe, however, that the cross-written vision of the child that emerges from the sum of the Bastable books and the *Red House* reveals that Nesbit's view of the child is more complex and contradictory than is usually acknowledged and that this perspective is neither liberating nor emancipating. It is true that the Bastables are remarkably free of regulations and inhibitions, and that Nesbit clearly does reject some Victorian manifestations of the child when she dismisses evangelical classics like Maria Charlesworth's *Ministering Children* (1854) as the "wrong sort of books" (328).[2] Nevertheless, I do not think that Nesbit's works truly can be said to address the child as an equal or to grant him or her any significant liberation. The Bastable books contain much that is inaccessible to the child reader, and the final picture that emerges from Nesbit's texts reveals the young as separate and powerless beings who are repeatedly subject to failure and confusion. Unable to understand fully or to affect knowingly the adult world, Nesbit's children can hope for no more than amused condescension from the kindest of adults.

Nesbit may well owe her reputation as a child-centered author to the creation of Oswald Bastable, who sees and speaks to the adult world from a child's

perspective. Alison Lurie writes that "the decision to tell her story through the persona of Oswald Bastable, a child much after her own pattern: bold, quick-tempered, egotistic, and literary," was a decision which "released Nesbit's genius" (424).[3] Oswald voices the collective opinions, observations, and conclusions of the Bastable children as they attempt to understand adults and the adult world. Thus, Oswald has been considered an "Everychild" who can speak directly to child readers in a way adult narrators cannot.

Oswald's jaunty narration, however, which combines detail, incident, observation, and reflection, balances the Bastable tales between child and adult readers through a style designed to suggest realism to the child reader while simultaneously communicating both realism and humor to the adult reader. Both child and adult readers can relate to the Bastable children's bewildering experiences with adults and respond to Oswald's realistic descriptions of games, meals, and the dynamics of sibling relationships. But many child readers, like the child narrator, will probably fail to appreciate at least some of the humor of circumstance that informs the Bastables' comic disasters or to perceive the motivation for adult characters' actions. In addition, the "mystery" of the narrator's identity, Denny's misquoted poetry, Oswald's misuse of various words and expressions, and the general misunderstanding of the adult world that pervades the trilogy are all jokes seemingly designed to be understood by and appeal to adult readers before child readers—and at the expense of children—because the joke is often between the adult reader and the author at Oswald's expense.

There is an air of quixotism about the Bastables in their first volume of adventures as they attempt to "restore the fallen fortunes of the house of Bastable" through various methods suggested by the children's reading (16). Ultimately, all of these ventures fail, although their amusing misapprehensions often induce kind adults to supply them with pocket money. These adventures also reveal circumstances and create comic situations that Oswald (and child readers like myself) never recognize: the money found in digging for treasure was planted by Albert's uncle; the criminals they capture in expectation of a generous reward are their own neighbors hiding out at home, who are ashamed of not being able to afford their usual seaside holiday; the "generous benefactor" is a money lender who cannot part with a sovereign; and the "Noble Editor" who admires and buys Noël's poetry is a tabloid journalist using the boys for his own ends. Oswald *is* critical of this journalist's article, which he says "describes [them] all wrong," and "seemed to make game of [Noël's poems]" (71), but he never understands the entire experience, further stressing the disjunction between adult and child worlds: children do not understand adults to adults' satisfaction, and adults do not see children as they see themselves. Thus, adults and children seem to occupy separate spheres that are firmly segregated from each other.

In *The Case of Peter Pan,* Jacqueline Rose suggests that the segregation of child and adult is a defining characteristic of fiction such as Nesbit's, which she identifies as "new realism"—essentially, the portrayal of real children. Rose theorizes that new realism is governed by a subtle rule which "demands that the narrator be adult *or* child" and use that "knowledge to hold the two instances safely apart on the page." This distance enforces the separateness of the child and, by extension, his permeable nature, which Rose believes is attractive to adults (69). Overall, Nesbit's construction of Oswald does provide a child narrator who is unable to interpret the codes of the adult world and who holds the realities of child and adult apart. I cannot completely endorse Rose's rule of total separation in relation to the Bastable chronicles, however, because there are times when Oswald brings the solitudes of child and adult reality together. Oswald has flashes of insight that allow him to perceive the truth of situations like the "Noble Editor's" mockery of him and Noël. Noël, however, is simply "quite pleased" (71). Thus, Nesbit breaks down the categories of "child" and "adult" by distinguishing between the perception of two unique child characters of different ages. This distinction suggests that Nesbit views children as individuals, recognizes graduations in the category of childhood, and under some circumstances, allows the adult and child realities to meet.

Furthermore, the very realism that arises from the inclusion of Oswald's inability to understand what may be easily elucidated by an adult reader brings the worlds of child and adult into collision, and thereby further undermines Rose's theory that the child and adult are purposely separated to provide the adult reader with a safe (that is, completely knowable) incarnation of childhood. When the children visit the moneylender Mr. Rosenbaum, they gain entrance with one of their father's cards and unknowingly touch Rosenbaum's heart. Afterward, Mr. Bastable receives a "kind" letter from Mr. Rosenbaum and declares "that letter took a weight off my mind" (130-31). Os-

wald "can't think what he meant" (130). He remains the innocent child narrator with no inkling of his father's financial struggles, and thus holds the reality of child and adult worlds apart. Simultaneously, however, Oswald's innocence or ignorance has brought the worlds of child misapprehension and adult reality together on the page. The Bastables cause Mr. Rosenbaum to play some aspect of the role of "Generous Benefactor" and relieve their astonished father of some pressing adult cares. Many child readers are likely to share Oswald's bewilderment over this adventure, but Nesbit's message for the adult reader is that real children like Bastables are separate and unaccountable beings whose decisions, actions, and conclusions are not easily elucidated and who may unexpectedly bring the worlds of child and adult into collision.

Despite such crossovers of influence, however, the Bastables are often forced to remain outside the adult world and are frequently bewildered to find that acting on good intentions results in accusations of naughtiness from adults. The children's naughtiness may be seen as simply an aspect of their realistic nature, and by extension of their lack of understanding, but, as James Kincaid notes in *Child-Loving* (1992), the naughty child is as much a construction as the angelic one—a "resisting child" that "keeps its distance from the professed standard, remains Other, does not so much rebel as respond more acutely to what is wanted" (246). In other words, although I do not believe that Nesbit presents the child as completely knowable or separate as Rose suggests, I do think that she flatters and appeals to adult readers by constructing child characters who take on the identity of an Other defined by the persistent inability to understand what is easily apparent to adults. Nesbit's Other is not a child who is willfully naughty and allows adults to rebel vicariously against prescriptive social norms, but rather an Other who cannot cope in the adult world and who is helplessly and unintentionally naughty.

This helpless, unintentional naughtiness is best illustrated in *The Wouldbegoods.* In this second volume of the Bastable trilogy, the children form a "New Society for Being Good In" (285), after they are sent to the country following a disastrous game of *Jungle Book* in which Uncle's possessions are the losers. But the gaps in their knowledge and ability make the desired goodness unattainable. Early in the novel, Oswald observes that "grown-up people" like "to keep things far different from what we would, and you catch it if you try to do otherwise" (292-93).

Throughout the novel, something always goes wrong in the Bastables' efforts to be good. When Dicky fixes a window in the dairy, the maids fail to notice his handiwork and prop the window with a milk pan as usual. The pan pushes the window all the way open and falls into the moat. The Bastables attempt to drag the moat, and Dora cuts her foot badly on a jagged piece of tin. Oswald observes that they looked for the pan not "to please ourselves, but because it was our duty. But that made no difference to our punishment when father came down. I have known this mistake to occur before" (305).[4]

Children not only "catch it" when they attempt to interact with the adult world; they also must endure the frustration that arises from being caught in a child world that is inherently separate. Alice expresses a child's frustration at this separation from the adult world when she cries, "It's no use! We *have* tried to be good. . . . You don't know how we've tried! And it's all no use. I believe we are the wickedest children in the whole world, and I wish we were all dead!" Albert's uncle assures Alice that although they can be "naughty and tiresome," they are not wicked; observes that they do not tell lies or do mean things; and explains that they "will learn to be good in other ways some day"—or, in other words, when they are adults (378-79). Children, it seems, are not capable of acts of significant goodness in Nesbit's adult world, but are confined to the separate role of the unintentionally naughty Other.

Anita Moss (226) writes that Nesbit "breathed new and vital life into the Romantic child" with the Bastable stories. Even when the Bastables manage to escape charges of naughtiness, however, their attempts to exercise influence through the traditional Romantic and Victorian child roles of rescuer or redeemer are generally ineffectual or unnecessary—and ultimately undermine, rather than reanimate, the Romantic vision of the child. Often an adult has anticipated their actions. The efforts made to find Albert-next-door's Uncle's sweetheart turn out to be for naught because Albert's uncle has already found her, arranged a Christmas wedding, and deliberately kept these events secret. Nor do Nesbit's children successfully play any of the other roles so often linked to the Romantic portrayal of the child; they do not function as agents of healing, rejuvenation, or salvation. Instead, they require adults to rescue them from the consequences of their actions and provide comfort and guidance. In other words, the Bastables do not exercise any real or lasting influence over the outcome of events in the adult world, nor do they pos-

sess any of the innate moral superiority often associated with the Romantic and Victorian visions of the child. The Bastables actually engage in some rather questionable moral activities like arranging to "rescue" Lord Tottenham from the "savagery" of their own dog, orchestrating the "Avenging Take-In" on the porter, or begging for money to enhance the contents of the Christmas pudding. After such incidents, they are inevitably ashamed, often half-realizing that they have done wrong even before an adult makes this clear. According to the definition advanced by Albert's uncle, the Bastables are generally good. They are not mean, selfish, or untruthful. In no way, however, does Nesbit allow them moral superiority, and her limited definition of a "good" child is certainly different from earlier definitions of "goodness," which generally incorporate piety, respectfulness, obedience, neatness, and productive industry.

Furthermore, Romantic and Victorian literature implicitly flatters the child and pays court to his or her superior innocence and sensitivity by granting the child power over adults. Nesbit does not. If she flatters anyone, it is adults, who are shown to be so necessary to children. Like many Victorian and Romantic predecessors, Nesbit's children are basically honorable, truthful, and well intentioned, in addition to being realistically quarrelsome, mischievous, and egoistic; moreover, they are granted new, Edwardian-inspired freedoms in terms of play and individuality. But ultimately Nesbit undercuts Romantic elevation and Victorian idealization by showing children as dependent upon the adult world, which defines and controls them, however benignly.

This deflation of the Romantic and Victorian visions of the child is confirmed by *The Red House* (1902). The novel's title page refers to Nesbit as "the author of *The Treasure Seekers.*" No additional cross-reference is provided, but Nesbit must expect her adult readers to be familiar with her children's books or her child readers to graduate to reading her adult books. Otherwise the joke, the sense of being "in" on something, would be lost. The joke begins when Len and Chloe receive a letter they can scarcely read and barely understand.[5] Sent from the Bastables and inexpertly typed by Noël, it requests permission to view their old country house. As usual, the Bastables are attempting to interact with the adult world as equals, but they lack the requisite skills and knowledge. Although they are initially stunned when the children appear, Len and Chloe quickly ascertain and evaluate their names, class, appearance, and manners and, approving of the children's imagination and initiative, enter into their visit with amused and kindly, though condescending, enthusiasm: Len, for instance, notes that the children are "much funnier than they meant to be" (*RH,* 228). Like an adult reader of the Bastable trilogy, Len sees that the Bastables are both ignorant and innocent of the adult world: "They are very trusting. The world must have been kind to them" (229). The Bastables' visit inspires Len and Chloe to muse briefly on the nature of children. Chloe, having expressed her emphatic dislike of Albert—whose velvet suits, frilly collar, and priggish manners seem reminiscent of Little Lord Fauntleroy in particular and the Victorian conception of the delicate seen-and-not-heard child—asks, "Why aren't all children nice?" Len replies, "They are—if they have nice grown-ups belonging to them" (224). In this conversation, Nesbit expresses a concept that is implicit to the Bastable trilogy's comparison and portrayal of the Bastables, the Ffoulkeses, and Albert—that the influence of the adult upon the child is an important and determining one. The children occupy similar places and evoke the same attitudes, themes, and responses in this adult novel as they do in the Bastable trilogy, but they are further reduced in terms of autonomy and importance through the sentimental attitudes of Len and Chloe. Len dwells on the children's picturesqueness—their rosy cheeks, their scarlet Tam-o'-Shanters, and their "young laughter" in the "old garden" (219). Len finds Alice more attractive than Dora because Alice is so pretty, and Chloe gushes over H. O. because he is the smallest, declaring him "simply a duck" (224). Len and Chloe reduce the children to the status of amusing, ornamental playthings that furnish the garden and are pretty to look at. In some ways, Oswald is less childish than these adults. He never mentions his siblings' appearances, and he judges them based upon what they do, not what they look like. To Oswald, each Bastable is an individual, not a trope of childhood that calls forth culturally conditioned, sentimental responses.

By itself in *The Treasure Seekers,* the visit to the Red House is merely another example of the Bastables' insouciant misunderstanding of the adult world, but read in concert with Len's, Oswald's account reveals differences in child and adult perceptions. The children think Len and Chloe are nice, but they see nothing untoward in their own behavior and do not realize that Len and Chloe are really extremely lenient adults stooping to a child's level. Len and Chloe are simply called "Mr. and Mrs. Redhouse." This nomenclature humorously reduces their importance in the child-centered text and sug-

gests that Nesbit may occasionally poke fun at adults' own self-importance, but it is also another example of Oswald's failure to grasp the significance of name and position in the adult world. Furthermore, Oswald's method of naming is a practice that is likely to be deemed amusing and naive by adults who would not indulge in it; thus it enforces once more the child's separation from the adult world. Nor does Oswald reflect on what makes some adults nicer than others or consider what effect the nature of children has on adults. The dual stories of the Red House make it doubly clear that adults have a power of definition and influence over children that is not reciprocated, and that adults can stoop to interact equally with children, but children cannot rise to the level of adults.

The Bastables' third volume of adventures, *The New Treasure Seekers,* is organized around the children's attempts to raise money for their (supposedly) poor landlady. Once again, the Bastables frequently find themselves in trouble in spite of their good intentions, and adults are needed to restore order, give explanations, administer punishments and rewards, and offer comfort and understanding. In *The New Treasure Seekers,* however, Oswald grows into a new consciousness of the adult world. After the "General" lets the children take part in the "war" and Benenden lets them participate in a "smuggling run," Oswald suspects that the adult world is benevolently deceiving him. Thinking over the military adventures, Oswald uneasily concludes that "we had made jolly fools of ourselves throughout" and that "the whole thing was a beastly sell" (586-87). He is perfectly right, but like a good adult-in-embryo, he does not undeceive his younger siblings.

Contemporary depictions of the child and childhood such as Kenneth Grahame's *The Golden Age* (1895) and *Dream Days* (1898) or James Barrie's *Peter Pan* (1911) portray growing up as a thoroughly negative process. Grahame's children refer to the adults as "The Olympians" and condemn them as "hopeless and incapable creatures" (4) whose "movements were confined and slow" and whose habits were "stereotyped and senseless" (5). Children are the "illuminati," the only ones capable of understanding "real life" (7). The opening page of *Peter Pan* laments the fact that children grow up and declares that "two is the beginning of the end" (1). Both books feature adult narrators looking back through time and both have been judged to be *about* rather than *for* children. Nesbit's view of childhood is more immediate due to her use of Oswald as narrator, but her view of childhood is, of course, also an adult's interpretation. For Nesbit, childhood is a time and a space set apart, and children are not to be looked up to with reverential awe as in Wordsworth's romantic vision, but thrown sidelong glances of condescending sympathy, amusement, and understanding. Growing up is not a tragedy. Oswald loses some of his innocence, but he gains in perception. Oswald does say that he sometimes feels "grownupness creeping inordiously upon him" and rather wishes that "you didn't grow up so quickly," but these rather trite, literary-sounding observations seem most likely to have been (imperfectly) culled from Oswald's reading and are probably intended to mock such sentiments (610).[6] At other times, Oswald is eager to grow up, to leave school, to travel, to become a soldier. In addition, I think that the Bastables' many misadventures teach that in growing up children gain in terms of power and knowledge, even if they do lose some of their innocence and sense of wonder.

In creating intersections between books for children and adults, Nesbit crosses the borders and challenges the boundaries separating children's books from adult books while she explores children's and adults' continuing and shifting attempts to understand and define one another. The picture of the child that emerges from Nesbit's attempts to appeal to both adult and child readers is curious and contradictory. In the Bastable trilogy, children are granted new freedoms and indulgences but are simultaneously marginalized and disenfranchised from the Romantic child's traditional roles of superiority and influence over the adult. *The Red House,* however, not only reinforces the child's difference, but further undermines the child's autonomy and status through sentimental and condescending attitudes. Therefore, the vision of the child that finally emerges from Nesbit's writing is not liberating, as most commentators suggest, but dominated by limitation and condescension.

Notes

1. All Nesbit references, except to *RH,* are to the 1928 *CHBF.* By late nineteenth-century standards, Edith Nesbit was a cross-dresser as well as a cross-writer. She wore pantaloons, cropped her hair short, and was rarely seen without cigarettes at a time when few respectable women smoked.

2. Daisy and Denny Ffoulkes, who have read such books under the tutelage of a Victorian aunt reminiscent of Miss Murdstone in *David Copperfield* (265), are considered repressed "little pinky, frightened things, like white mice" who must be re-formed

through their association with the hardy, independent Bastables (263).

3. Julia Briggs believes that Nesbit splits herself between the characters of the twins: Alice is "morally courageous and determined," and Noël is "vulnerable" and "subject to fits of poetry, fainting, and tears" (*WP* xvii). This is a very perceptive observation; nevertheless, I still concur with Lurie that a great deal of Nesbit's reported personality can be seen in Oswald. It probably isn't necessary to choose between the two interpretations; given that Oswald, Alice, and Noël are the most prominent of the six Bastable children, it is reasonable to suppose that Nesbit identified closely with all three characters.

4. Attempts to fill the empty lock with water after it has been emptied, to bury a fox the hunt was pursuing, to rescue an "abandoned high born babe," to entertain the Antiquarian society by planting relics in their excavation site, and to offer nonalcoholic "free drinks" to thirsty travelers also end in punishments and disasters of varying degrees, outcomes that further illustrate the truth of Oswald's observations.

5. Chloe believes that the writer of the letter must be mad or idiotic, but Len, seeing the children's address, says "I'm almost certain it's a workman's club" (*RH* 214). These two ideas represent traditional classifications of the child, who has historically been linked with the lower classes and the mentally deficient.

6. Oswald speaks grammatically correct English (a tribute to his middle-class education), which is sprinkled with slang and catchwords culled from his wide reading of children's classics, novels of all descriptions, and newspapers. Oswald is a self-reflexive author who cheerfully admits that his style is influenced by what he reads. In comparing the live farm animals to the mounted ones in his uncle's house, he says: "The stuffed denizens of our late-lamented Jungle pale into insignificance before the number of live things on the farm," and then he comments in an aside: "I hope you do not think that the words I use are getting too long. I know they are the right words. And Albert's uncle says your style is always altered a bit by what you read. And I have been reading the Vicomte de Bragelonne. Nearly all my new words came out of those" (387). Later Oswald tries out a different descriptive style: "In a very short space of time we would be wending our way back to Blackheath, and all the variegated delightfulness of the country would soon be only preserved in memory's

faded flowers." He observes, however, that "I don't care for that way of writing very much. It would be an awful swat to keep it up" (588).

Julia Briggs

SOURCE: "E. Nesbit, the Bastables, and *The Red House*: A Response," in *Children's Literature,* Vol. 25, 1997, pp. 71-85.

It is at once a pleasure and a responsibility to respond to two papers that address E. Nesbit's cross-writing, as demonstrated in Nesbit's description of the Bastables' visit to the Red House in the novel of that name. It is a pleasure to find Nesbit's work being treated with the seriousness it deserves, and a responsibility because any response risks narrowing, rather than opening up, the field. Mavis Reimer and Erika Rothwell contribute valuably to ongoing theoretical discussions concerning the construction of the child at the end of the last century; they set the figure of the child in the perspectives of empire and of earlier writing for children, and they explore the question of persuasion or even coercion implicit in the adult writer's address to the child reader. These are key issues, and their very centrality permits a response more closely focused upon the initial circumstances of publication of *The Story of the Treasure Seekers* as a text generated by and within a context of cross-writing. I am conscious of pursuing a rather different line of argument, but my approach through intertextuality and publishing history, which is intended to complement rather than to counter the arguments Reimer and Rothwell establish, is made possible by their more fundamental concern to define the relationship between adult and child as figured in Nesbit's *The Story of the Treasure Seekers, The Red House,* and *The New Treasure Seekers.*

> Yes, these stories are good. They are written on a rather original idea, on a line off the common run. Here we have the life of a family of children told by themselves in a candid, ingenuous and very amusing style. Of course, no child would write as E. Nesbit writes, but the result is that we have drawn for us a very charming picture of English family life . . . the stories are individual— they will please every grown up who reads them.
>
> Edward Garnett, Reader's Report to Fisher Unwin on Seven Stories from the *Pall Mall Magazine,* 1898

Garnett, a famous talent-spotter, seizes at once on the point made by Erika Rothwell at the outset of her essay: the stories that became *The Story of the Trea-*

sure Seekers were addressed to children and adults simultaneously, with the expectation that they would be read in different ways, like a pantomime that includes different types of jokes for different age groups. Unfortunately Nesbit left no record of the process by which she transformed her writing for children from the flat, simplistic narratives of her early work for Raphael Tuck and Ernest Nister to the complex and self-conscious rhetoric of Oswald Bastable, whose literary sense apparently directs him to relate his own story as a third-person narrative. She was, however, an ardent admirer of Henry James, whose work in the 1890s, particularly *What Maisie Knew* (1897) and *The Turn of the Screw* (1898) exploits the possibilities of literary misreadings created by unreliable narrators and the conflicting interpretations of events by children and adults.

Put to comic purpose, these devices dominate the narrative practice of *The Story of the Treasure Seekers* (1899), creating a cross-writing that simultaneously addresses adult and child readers by conferring on Oswald (and through him on his siblings) the full subjecthood implicit in a first-person narrative, a narrative that invites the childreader to identify with Oswald or his siblings. (When he is referred to in the third person or as a child among children confronting the adult world, however, Oswald is seen from an adult perspective as comically smaller and less significant than he supposes, as an amusing little boy, as "Other"; as Rothwell puts it, "the joke is often between the adult reader and the author at Oswald's expense.") Nesbit's introduction of the Bastables into her sentimental novel *The Red House* (1902) could thus be considered the logical outcome of a narrative strategy that had originated with their invention. Chloe's exclamation, "Aren't they perfect dears? . . . I don't like the Morrison boy—but the others are lovely" (175) is thus in danger of overstating what adult readers have already observed for themselves, and for a moment the speaker within the fiction and the author outside it betray an uneasy complicity.

If Henry James offers one literary paradigm, Kenneth Grahame affords another. *The Golden Age* (1895) and its successor *Dream Days* (1898) were outstandingly successful books written about children for adults, though they were soon passed on to children as well: Oswald considers *The Golden Age* "A1 except where it gets mixed up with grown-up nonsense" (*Wouldbegoods,* 94). Grahame's celebration of the child's world of imaginative play owes something to Stevenson's essay "Child's Play" (*Virginibus Puerisque,* 1881) and more to Richard Jefferies's evocation of childhood in *Bevis: The Story of a Boy* (1882), both texts written about rather than for children by writers who also wrote for children directly. *The Golden Age* established childhood as a pastoral or nostalgic world for adults and later lent its name to a particular way of writing for children that marks a distinctive development within the history of children's books as well as in the construction of the child—the point at which the adult, searching for a lost childhood, vicariously recovers it through a particular child's experience.

Such a pattern is always potentially present in the relation of child to adult—for example, when Wordsworth interrogated Basil Montagu in "Anecdote for Fathers," or when Dickens sought his own healing through exposing society's victimization of children—but it takes an intensified, even exaggerated form in Carroll's use of Alice, and later in Barrie's use of Peter Pan and "the Lost Boys." Positioning the nostalgic adult reader over the child's shoulder decisively alters the narrative voice and the angle of address. Whereas romantic poets and essayists recalled the *Arabian Nights* or chapbook heroes such as Jack the Giant-Killer with affection, a later generation of adult readers sought books they had enjoyed in childhood, while adult writers for children deliberately rework themes from earlier children's books. C. S. Lewis, who did both these things, even enunciated the principle that "a children's story which is enjoyed only by children is a bad children's story" (59). Adults gladly surrendered the "Olympian" status conferred on them by Grahame and joined in children's games in many "Golden Age" texts including Nesbit's, Kipling's *Just So Stories* (1902), and the opening sequence of *Winnie the Pooh* (1926).

The 1880s and 1890s saw an increasing overlap between writing addressed to children and that meant for adults: "boys' stories," adventures at the outposts of empire, historical tales, and detective stories, as well as ghost stories and sentimental or romantic narratives, were widely read and published in the illustrated magazines aimed at middle-class "family" reading. Here popular romance of all kinds was published alongside the serialized work of Thomas Hardy or even Henry James. E. Nesbit wrote up memories of her schooldays for *The Girl's Own Paper*, but the adventures of the Bastables appeared in the *Illustrated London News* (initially in the "Father Christmas" supplement, but later in the regular pages) as well as in the *Pall Mall Magazine*, the *Windsor Magazine*, *Crampton's*, and the *London Magazine* (where **The New Treasure Seekers** was immediately

followed by the serialization of **The Railway Children**). Her closest association, however, was with George Newnes's best-selling and high-paying magazine *The Strand*, where her children's stories appeared more or less continuously from 1902 to 1912.

Nearly all of the Bastable stories were published in magazines of this kind before they reached book form, as the appended list indicates. Unlike *Aunt Judy's Magazine*, recalled by Edward Garnett in the course of his reader's report, none of these magazines was addressed to children, though nothing they included would have "brought a blush to a young person's cheek." Nesbit herself also published short stories for adults in them, and these were often illustrated by the same artists as her stories for children: for example, Frances Ewan illustrated **"The Nobleness of Oswald"** when it appeared in the *Windsor Magazine*, as well as Nesbit's story **"A Perfect Stranger,"** later reprinted in a collection of short stories for adults, **Thirteen Ways Home** (1901). Another story from that collection, "G. H. and I," was illustrated by Lewis Baumer for the *Pall Mall Magazine*, for which he also illustrated the episode **"Being Detectives,"** later to become chapter 3 of **The Story of the Treasure Seekers.** Arthur Buckland, the main artist for **The Wouldbegoods** as it appeared serially in the *Illustrated London News*, also illustrated her romantic short story **"The Letter in Brown Ink"** for the *Windsor Magazine*.

All these magazines situated the children's stories they published within a context of adult reading and thus could be said to constitute a locus of crosswriting. Surprisingly, there seems to have been little anxiety to identify the readership being addressed in any individual piece of writing, presumably because it was evident from the outset and none of the material published was obviously "unsuitable for children." When the individual episodes that later made up **The Story of the Treasure Seekers** first appeared in the *Pall Mall* or the *Windsor Magazine*, they were not explicitly identified as stories for children. **"Noël's Princess,"** the third episode of the Bastables to appear in the *Pall Mall Magazine*, was subtitled (inaccurately, as it happened) "Passages from the life of Oswald Bastable, Esq., of Lewisham, in the County of Kent. No 2." This title was probably intended to indicate the humorous tone of the child aspiring to adult status; possibly it was intended to distinguish it from the comparable episode in *The Golden Age*. In any case, the experiment was not repeated.

One way in which the illustrated magazines conveyed the nature of their articles was through the subject matter of their illustrations. Another was the use of illustrative blocks appearing at the head and foot of a particular story or poem. These blocks were not specifically drawn for that piece, but served rather as indicators of mood or subject. The Bastable stories as they appeared in the *Pall Mall Magazine* were introduced by rather stiff little scenes in period costume of the type appropriate for a history book or for a series of historical episodes. These headers bore no relationship to the stories they introduced; they usually changed from month to month, though episodes published in July and August 1898 were introduced by the same picture. Dated four years earlier and signed "Gilbert James, '95," they had presumably been drawn for an earlier set of articles. *The Windsor Magazine* did not make use of introductory headings.

Many, but by no means all, of the illustrations made for the Bastable stories when they first appeared were reproduced when they were published in book form (*STS* 1899). Lewis Baumer and Gordon Browne, who illustrated episodes for the *Pall Mall Magazine,* were included, whereas the *Windsor Magazine* illustrators, Frances Ewan and Raymond Potter, who worked with wash rather than in line, were not. *The Wouldbegoods* (1901) reprinted the work of Arthur Buckland and John Hassall, first published in the *Illustrated London News*. Later, Wells, Gardner, and Darton, who published **Oswald Bastable and Others** (1905), appear to have commissioned Charles Brock to provide some extra pictures for stories such as **"An Object of Value and Virtue,"** which had originally appeared without illustrations. Nesbit's early illustrators, Lewis Baumer and Gordon Browne, have subsequently been overshadowed by H. R. Millar, who worked mainly for *The Strand* and illustrated the fantasies she published there. Browne, in particular, was an excellent artist in his own right: the son of Dickens's illustrator "Phiz" (Hablot K. Browne), he was particularly good at conveying movement: in his pictures the nursemaid sweeps out of the frame carrying the screaming German princess, or the Indian uncle attacks the pudding in high style. He did not illustrate **The Wouldbegoods** (which was mainly serialized in the *Illustrated London News*) but the drawings for **The New Treasure Seekers** (1904) were his, having originally appeared in the *London Magazine*. It was Gordon Browne who depicted the encounters between Len and Chloe of **The Red House** and the Bastables.

Children's books of this period tended to be illustrated more fully and often in a more decorative or stylized manner than those intended for adults, but the kind of periodicals referred to above were heavily illustrated, and adult books often included some illustrations, usually at least a frontispiece. **The Treasure Seekers** is cross-written insofar as it addresses adult readers in a magazine published for adults at the same time as it addresses child readers (or perhaps it speaks to the parent reading to the child; Kipling enjoyed reading Nesbit's stories to his children). It also reproduces features of its original publication context as part of its structural form and content. Journals and newspapers figure repeatedly in the text and are used in a variety of ways. Dicky's proposals for moneymaking, adopted in chapters 9 and 11, are inspired by "small ads" of various kinds, especially those that promise instant cash, offer lucrative partnerships in return for an investment of £100, promise loans without security, or give assurances that you can make £2 a week in your spare time (the sums involved should be multiplied by at least one hundred). Invitations of this kind, telltale signs of a degenerate capitalism, were (and still are) addressed to the gullible, and thus naturally appeal to the Bastables. In the following chapter (12), they study the commercial techniques displayed in patent medicine advertisements, inventing and bottling "Bastable's Certain Cure for Colds," a mixture of peppermint and nontoxic paint which they hope will bring in clear profit, if marketed effectively.

One of their earliest projects for making money is a visit to Fleet Street to sell Noël's poems. It is on this occasion that Oswald and Noël meet Mrs. Leslie, who, like Albert-Next-Door's Uncle, is a professional "author" (what other job would allow him to make himself available whenever he was needed?). The Bastables also write and edit their own journal, *The Lewisham Recorder:* its wide range of forms and genres closely parallels that of magazines such as the *Windsor* and the *Pall Mall* where the stories originally appeared (although this episode, ch. 7, had a significant forebear in Nesbit**'s "The Play Times,"** published as a series in *Nister's Holiday Annual* from 1894 to 1896.) Also composed by a family of children, **"The Play Times"** includes a number of pieces later attributed to the Bastables and written in imitation of the conventions of adult journalism; both newspapers deliberately rework the equivalent scenes in Dickens's *Holiday Romance* (1868). *The Lewisham Recorder* reveals the children's sensitivity to literary languages: in their different contributions, they recreate a variety of styles and genres as a mode of imitative play. All writing is stylized, and although particular languages are appropriate for particular games, they also shape the children's expectations and suggest to them a particular interpretation (or misinterpretation) of the events they encounter. This process is vividly displayed in chapter 3, **"Being Detectives,"** where literary fictions are used to expose social fictions. There the highly distinctive conventions of the detective story lead Oswald and Dicky to uncover their neighbors' guilty secret: that they are too poor for all of them to go on holiday. The girls' cheap meal is comically underlined by an engraving of the Prodigal Son that hangs on the wall above (*STS,* 44).

Nesbit could count on her readers' familiarity with a range of literary styles, a reliance that can be an obstacle for many of today's child readers. The Bastables are portrayed as avid readers who are delighted when they can communicate with adults through the shortcut of shared allusions: Albert's Uncle regularly scores by "talking like a book" and Mrs. Leslie knows her Kipling; the Jewish moneylender, on the other hand, is baffled by being addressed as "G. B.," short for "Generous Benefactor, like in Miss Edgeworth" (137, 142). The world of children's reading provided familiar reference points not only for child readers, but also for middle-class adults, a generation who had grown up with children's books. Nesbit's allusions are often substantial: she sets up either an announced or a concealed playing-out of an episode from an earlier text—*Sintram and His Companions,* Charlotte M. Yonge, Grahame, or Kipling—by drawing on its plot outline or perhaps its opening sequence of events. Such borrowings allow her to economize on original plot invention while she sets up a series of intertexts that create further moments of comedy or recognition.

Cross-writing implies a double perspective, lending complexity and richness while increasing uncertainty. There is an effect in Nesbit's works of being simultaneously inside and outside a story-shaped world, because books are "acted out" even though they are explicitly recognized as fictions. Oswald undercuts the implausible happy ending of *The Story of the Treasure Seekers* by observing "I can't help it if it is like Dickens, because it happens this way. Real life is often something like books" (294). Elsewhere the adult world seems as arbitrary as any game (a point of view that underpins the *Alice* books), so that the clichés of fiction provide at least one stable system of referents in an incomprehensible world, even though the expectations fiction creates also lead to difficulties: in *The New Treasure Seekers,* Noël and H. O. cut the wires Father has just installed for electricity

on the assumption that "It is dynamite . . . to blow up Father because he took part in the Lewisham election, and his side won" (156). The Bastables see themselves as empowered and independent, with an obligation to restore the family fortunes or to help those less privileged than themselves; yet, as Erika Rothwell observes, their assumptions are always undercut by adult interventions that reduce them to the status of children once more, leaving them intimidated or outmaneuvered, even ritually punished: "His face wore the look that means bed, and very likely no supper" (*Wouldbegoods,* 167). Their uncertain status defines the Bastables as closer to Carroll's Alice than to those children of the evangelical tradition whose spiritual resources give them unexpected power over the fallen adults around them.

Both Rothwell and Reimer read *The Red House* episode and its reworking in *The New Treasure Seekers* in terms of a redefinition of the power relations between adult and child, although they each approach the topic from rather different angles. **"Treasure Seekers and Invaders"** asserts the centrality of the Bastables' disruptive intervention to the structure of *The Red House* and defines the relationship between *The Red House* and the Bastables' earliest appearance in *The Story of the Treasure Seekers* in terms of a close reading of the latter's final chapter. Reimer comments on their differences: "If, in the children's novel, the reading of the metaphorical as literal allows the adult to disperse the literal in play, in the adult novel the reverse transaction takes place; the children's restaging of a 'real' event as play allows the adults to reconstitute their own play as reality." The relationship of play to reality here described is central not only to the ending but also to *The Treasure Seekers* as a whole: it occurs partly because Albert's Uncle enjoys playing up to the children's sense of wonder, for example, by popping a half crown into the hole they have dug for treasure; but also because on more than one occasion the children's intervention unexpectedly solves an adult problem in ways that could not have been expected or foreseen—as when the Generous Benefactor lives up to his title and extends Father's loan, when Noël finds a real princess (though she is not in the least their idea of one), or when, in the final chapters, the children's mistaken assumption about their Uncle's poverty enables him to recognize theirs.

The interplay between imagination and reality is inevitably a favorite theme in writing for children, but one crucial model for *The Story of the Treasure Seekers* was Frances Hodgson Burnett's *Sara Crewe, or What Happened at Miss Minchin*'s (1887), the earlier version of *A Little Princess* (1905). Nesbit's attitude to Burnett mingles admiration with an edge of resentment. Albert-next-door in his frilly collars and velvet knickerbockers registers her irritation with Fauntleroy as spoiled only child and "muff" (as Rothwell notices), whereas chapter 13, **"The Robber and the Burglar,"** blatantly reworks Burnett's *Editha's Burglar* (1888). The whole framework of *The Story of the Treasure Seekers,* that of a family come down in the world, bearing up bravely in reduced circumstances and later recovering its lost status and fortunes, has many parallels with the story of Sara Crewe, demoted from parlor boarder to slavey. Sara sustains herself during her trials through acts of the imagination, through her "supposings," much as the Bastables sustain themselves through their imaginative games, and her dreams finally come true through the intervention of another "poor, brokendown" Indian benefactor—in this case her father's lost business partner, who showers her with the accumulated wealth of the East. As Reimer observes, imperial wealth had a special significance at this period, and parallels between the oppression of colonial peoples, of children, and of the working class are sharply underscored in Burnett's text, which also introduces a colonial servant, the Lascar, and a sad little monkey to emphasize the point.

Nesbit reworks Burnett's ending, creating a series of misunderstandings around the word "poor," as Reimer shows: the Indian Uncle describes himself as "a poor, broken-down man" to excuse himself from drinking any more of Father's cheap wine, which the Bastables understand as a reference to his financial state. Their mistake establishes links between the final chapter and a discourse of "genteel" (that is, shameful and concealed) poverty that runs through the whole book but is set out in detail in the opening chapter. Although the precise significance of dunning letters and the long blue paper brought by a policeman is hidden from the children, they are not altogether deceived by the polite fictions offered to them: the silver "all went away to the shop to have the dents and scratches taken out of it and never came back. We think Father hadn't enough money to pay the silver man for taking out the dents and scratches" (5-6). The realism with which middle-class poverty is presented inhibits sentimentality, though by invoking Dickens in the final chapter Oswald seems to acknowledge that his narrative belongs ultimately to the mode of fairy tale rather than to a world of strict moral consequence, in which one person's gain is another's loss. Although "Lord Tottenham" in chapter 10 makes fun of Oswald's assumption "that the best way to restore fallen fortunes was to rescue an old gentleman in distress" (153), this turns out, in effect, to be what happens: the Bastables' sympathy for their Uncle's supposed poverty and their determination to give him a really good dinner function on one level as the good deed in the fairy tale, while on another, the children's involvement gives the Uncle the chance to recognize the hardship Father has so carefully concealed and thus to become the ultimate Generous Benefactor. Play becomes reality for the last time as Oswald announces his arrival: "Here comes the coach of the Fairy Godmother. It'll stop here, you see if it doesn't" (283). Such a transformation confers the illusion of power, but no more than that.

Both Reimer and Rothwell take up the crucial question of how much power or independence the Bastables actually achieve, only to be struck by its absence. For Reimer, the construction of the child is bound up with that of the colonial subject, and *The Story of the Treasure Seekers* aims to create "a domination that also manufactures consent," in a process that will allow the adult to make literal what has been metaphorical—that is, in terms of the book's final chapter, to convert fantasy and play into reality. Rothwell also finds the Bastables' lack of power, their constant subjection to adult wishes and to adult interpretation, to be debilitating, in contrast to earlier accounts that tend to represent the Bestables as free and emancipated, and thus as the fore-runners of Ransom's Swallows and Amazons or Blyton's Famous Five.

Nesbit's continual mockery of earlier children's books, including those written in the evangelical tradition, exposes the means to spiritual or moral power that they appear to offer. Instead, her own texts generally focus upon the possibilities of imaginative power, usually figured as magic, in a tradition that had flourished since the midcentury. Oswald himself accepts economic dependence and the arbitrary rules imposed by parents, servants, and other authorities, although at the same time he resists their implications by adopting condescending attitudes toward them whenever possible. The Bastables' sense of disempowerment is sharply focused in the opening events of *The Story of the Treasure Seekers:* a parent dies, and a loss of financial security and status follows. One of the worst consequences is that "we left off going to school, and Father said we should go to a good school as soon as he could manage it. He said a holiday would do us all good. We thought he was right, but we wished he had told us he couldn't afford it. For of course we knew" (6). The Bastables must find their own amusements because they do not have lessons or go to school, and they cannot attend the free Board Schools because that would have involved an open acknowledgement that they had lost their middle-class status. The search for a solution or a means of recovery or restoration from such a comedown is probably the commonest element in Nesbit's plots. The plight of Sara Crewe thus becomes a paradigm of what loss of social status involves, one that reveals the depths to which a once pampered and protected child might fall through no fault of her own.

If the Bastables' power is no more than an illusion, it may in part be a necessary illusion, acting as compensation for the increasingly infantilized and protected middle-class child. Nesbit's work was thought of as emancipating because within it the urban middle-class child was released from the oppressive safety of the nursery, school-room, or garden to have "adventures." The Bastables' games and excursions brought them into situations of danger, conflict, and risk largely because they *were* children and thus lacked sufficient experience or authority to anticipate or deal with the problems they might encounter. For them, the world of adventure, so often located in an "elsewhere," is imaginatively entered from any park or street, but it is always liable to disruption by "reality" as an irate adult breaks in. As Rothwell explains, they enjoy freedom (within limits), but not power, and it is precisely their lack of power which turns their urban environment into an adventure playground, a place of excitement not unmixed with anxiety.

Part of the process of disempowerment paradoxically involved a changing conception of what constituted subversive behavior in children. One reaction against the romantic and evangelical ideas of the child took the form of a revaluation of childish high spirits, notoriously celebrated in Catherine Sinclair's *Holiday House* (1839), but also strongly present in the May family in Charlotte M. Yonge's *The Daisy Chain* (1856), and later degenerating into sentimental pictures of scamps, scallywags, and lovable pickles. High spirits in the form of elaborate practical jokes or booby traps (such as those which Dicky Bastable favored) became fashionable among schoolboys and young men, and childish bad temper became an occasion for humor rather than punishment as Kipling's "the camelious hump" or Edward Abbott Parry's *Katawampus* (1895) indicate. Naughtiness might acquire a sinister aspect from the adult desire to pun-

ish, but it was increasingly accepted as part of childhood and might even be regarded as a virtue in the right circumstances: at the end of *The Wouldbegoods* we learn that Daisy and Denny, nicknamed "the white mice," "have thought of several quite new naughty things entirely on their own—and done them too— since they came back from the Moat House" (330). Once naughtiness came to be regarded as a manifestation of the energies natural to childhood, the Bastables could display it with impunity. A new and rather different code of behavior began to influence the upbringing and conduct of middle-class children in the second half of the nineteenth century, a code influenced by Thomas Arnold and the new public schools. It is this that the Bastables subscribe to, according to Albert's Uncle: "I have known you all for four years—and you know as well as I do how many scrapes I've seen you in and out of—but I've never known one of you tell a lie, and I've never known one of you do a mean or dishonourable action. And when you have done wrong you are always sorry. Now this is something to stand firm on. You'll learn to be good in other ways some day" (*Wouldbegoods,* 116). This is the code that Oswald himself upholds and that Nesbit's books seek to instill in her readers.

The active high spirits that welcome adventure and all too often lead to "naughtiness" were not unrelated to the qualities of courage and daring promoted in fiction for boys and were more often encouraged in boys than in girls. Both *The Story of the Treasure Seekers* and *The Red House* employ male narrators, but Oswald's narrative consistently celebrates masculine values at the expense of girls' interests and games, whereas the main claim to originality of *The Red House* lies in its use of a male narrator to valorize domestic life, love, and motherhood. As the girls stereotypically crowd around the cradle on the final page, Dicky asks if "they might not go and see the pig." Oswald's impatience with baby worship is voiced in his own later relation of events in *The New Treasure Seekers* (160), where his view that "babies are far more trouble than rabbits" strikes a welcome, if predictably "masculine," note. As he explains in *The Wouldbegoods,* he prefers love stories "where the hero parts with the girl at the garden-gate in the gloaming and goes off and has adventures, and you don't see her any more until he comes home to marry her at the end of the book" (329). The Bastables introduce a necessary astringency into *The Red House,* though they do so by means of a construction of masculinity that is now rightly suspect. Nesbit's cross-writing here negotiates not only the adult-child divide, but also the polarities of male and female values.

Amelia A. Rutledge

SOURCE: "E. Nesbit and the Woman Question," in *Victorian Women Writers and the Woman Question,* edited by Nicola Diane Thompson, Cambridge University Press, 1999, pp. 223-40.

In E. Nesbit's fantasy, *The Magic City* (1910), two children, Philip and Lucy, travel to a realm governed by an edict decreeing that "Girls are expected to be brave and the boys, kind."[1] The children are followed by Philip's nursemaid, who becomes the "Pretenderette" to the city-kingdom's throne. In this character (her title is derisively similar to "suffragette"), Nesbit satirizes both working-class resentment and the New Woman's political ambition.[2] After the children defeat the Pretenderette, her crimes are symbolically chastised by enforced "proper" female activity—learning to feel affection for others (nurturing) and reforming the allegorical dragon Sloth (the maintaining of moral standards). Although Lucy has successfully insisted that Philip obey the ruling precept and accept her agency on several occasions, her self-enforced emancipation is countered by the Pretenderette's fate, a strategy typical of Nesbit's ambivalence toward, if not compromise with, her contrary impulses toward sustaining and undermining the hegemony of conventional female roles.

Nesbit, born in 1858, did not begin her career as a novelist until she was nearly forty; thus her first novel, *The Secret of Kyriels* (1899), was written at the end of the period normally assigned to the New Woman novels; Nesbit is clearly a late entry into the field, but perhaps the currently stylish term "retro" best describes her adult fiction. An innovator in defining the children's time fantasy—although F. Anstey's *The Brass Bottle* (1900) preceded her stories, her work has influenced writers from C. S. Lewis to Edward Eager—her fiction for adults resembles what had been available to her in her twenties and thirties and is recognizably a holdover from the heyday of the New Woman novels. Children's fantasies inspired her most creative efforts; there was little that was original in her adult fiction. In form and content, *The Secret of Kyriels* most closely resembles the sensation novel, and shares with it an unusually aggressive heroine of the type that was to become characteristic for Nesbit—the girl just out of school. It focuses

more on enigmas surrounding maternity and marriage, complete with an imprisoned madwoman than on broader women's issues.[3] By the time she produced her later novels, the use of the emancipated female protagonist had lost much of its polemical edge. I wish to argue that Nesbit thus represents the appropriation by the dominant fictional discourse of material whose subversive force could now be contained by aligning it with nonthreatening "entertainment" in which the shocking is denatured to the mildly naughty—a "normalized" version of the "new" or "emancipated" woman. The novels, not reprinted in her lifetime, perhaps because of her being "type cast" as a children's writer and a producer of light verse, merit reexamination not only as documents of her expressive constructions of issues but in themselves, as complex, albeit not wholly successful, literary artifacts.

Nesbit's work resembles what Ann Ardis calls "boomerang" novels, i.e., those that present New Woman elements but then subvert them by a reversion to the marriage-plot at the end.[4] That there was a market for such stories in Nesbit's day argues for the persistent appeal of these more conservative works long after the initial flurry of New Woman novels. Nesbit's heroines submit gladly to matrimony; there is only minimal struggle to assert independence, and the unmarried state is merely a brief transitional period. These women can be free temporarily from some social constraints, yet completely acceptable to any but the most censorious conservatives. Thus, Nesbit's novels transmute the polemic of New Woman fiction into popular romance by means of a brief fling (a job and independence) that is resolved if not by marriage, then at least by the strong suggestion that that, too, will come.

If the first reviewers' alarm or vituperation catch the eyes of twentieth-century critics as they recuperate New Woman fiction, and most studies suggest this, then the superficial attention to Nesbit's fiction in its own day easily accounts for today's neglect. A perusal of newspaper reviews for her later novels shows that with the exception of *The Red House* (1902) and *Salome and the Head* (hereafter *Salome,* 1909), her later novels received only brief notice in the reviews of a month's crop of light fiction. To reviewers, some of her heroines—notably Daphne Carmichael of *Daphne in Fitzroy Street* (1909)— resemble the flightly schoolgirl more than the pioneers or martyrs of woman question fiction, but even when the content of her work might be viewed as controversial or scandalous, as was the case with

Salome, the reviewers criticized surface features—gruesome details or a reference to a contemporary figure that the reviewer considered ill advised—while paying little attention to the gender issues in the novel except as they were related to the "love interest." These reviewers certainly did not address any potentially subversive content of the novels. Although Nesbit's reviewers will be discussed at the end of this study, it suffices to note here that they tended to be perplexed by her forays into serious adult fiction and tended to suggest that light comedy and children's literature were her true fields of endeavor.[5] Before examining her children's fiction, it will be helpful to consider both the social and literary contexts that fostered Nesbit's ambivalences toward feminist issues and dictated her choices in the writing of fiction.

As one of the founding members of the Fabian Society, Nesbit was a member of the "Old Gang," the part of the membership that consistently evaded consideration of women's issues despite their advocacy of the rights of the (male) working class. In *The Magic City,* for example, Nesbit the Fabian socialist and "liberated" woman becomes an advocate of acquiescence to hierarchical social relationships who severely narrows the scope of the bravery she has mandated by edict. Bravery, it seems, is acceptable for little girls in resolving fantastic dilemmas; otherwise, along with self-assertion, it is a destabilizing impulse that must be ridiculed out of existence—especially when exhibited by a member of an underclass.

Nesbit was aware of all of the controversies subsumed under the woman question, but she refrained from active participation beyond her membership in the Fabian Society and her limited association with its Women's Group. On the other hand, she admired militant advocates such as Olive Schreiner, who offered a sincere tribute to Nesbit's personal warmth and kindness.[6] Her allegiances were consistently personal instead of ideological; on the other hand, she could use one ideology, socialism, as a defense against another, woman suffrage, as I will discuss below. In all of her writing, Nesbit employed strategies of displacement and distancing with regard to feminist issues, whether by adoption of the fantastic mode, as in her children's fiction and occasionally in her adult work, or by substituting for polemic the compensatory fantasy characteristic of popular romance.

While Nesbit's narrative strategies rendered her works non-controversial—she constructed an implied author and addressed an implied audience both of which were acceptable to the less radical, non-militant readership—these same strategies have left the adult fiction outside the serious critical attention that her children's fiction has received. In fact, the novels that most directly address women's social issues show Nesbit negotiating her conflicting and conflicted views of the place of women in society and the novels demonstrate the ways in which the pressure of a writing public inflected those views.

In her personal life, Nesbit was enmeshed in multiple quandaries; whatever her sentiments with regard to women's roles, she lived with the realities of patriarchal practice and sentiments, and she never resolved these many conflicts with any explicit act or statement. Nesbit had demonstrated her own essentially willful character by marrying Hubert Bland despite her mother's suspicious disapproval; she had already flouted convention, being seven months pregnant when she married. Bland, as all accounts indicate, was keeping a mistress at the time, and later had several affairs during his married life, fathering the two children born to his wife's housekeeper-companion, Alice Hoatson. Nesbit adopted both children as her own, and they long remained ignorant of their true parentage. Nesbit, bound in and to this marriage by social custom as well as by her expressed deep love for Bland, compensated by having several affairs of her own; these were of varying degrees of involvment, and included an extended, unconsummated affair with George Bernard Shaw. Further, it is quite likely that her reticence on suffrage issues is, in part, grounded in her deference to Bland's anti-suffrage views.[7]

Bland, for all of his socialist leanings, expressed in numerous articles and reviews after he established himself as a writer, was a touchstone of patriarchal ideology and male sexual privilege, considering women as ideally ornaments. His essay "If I Were a Woman" would seem a caricature of male chauvinism if its content were not repeated in various guises throughout his writings: "Woman's realm is the realm of the heart and the afternoon tea-table, not of the brain and the intelligence. It is hers to bewitch man, not to convince him."[8] He also declared, on the subject of women's franchise, "Votes for women? Votes for children! Votes for dogs!"[9] The most scathing criticism of Bland's hypocrisies is to be found in the autobiography of H. G. Wells, although the latter's commentary requires measured consideration since his unsuccessful attempt to elope with Bland's daughter, Rosamund, effectively ended what had been friendship between Wells, Bland, and Nesbit.[10]

More often than not the primary breadwinner of her household, Nesbit in no way conformed to the image of the "Angel in the House." Her Fabian allegiances do not necessarily contradict her conservatism, since the group was itself characterized by a limited, narrow set of radical impulses. Although she had written and published poetry prior to her marriage, Nesbit had not defined herself in any way as a professional writer. Nor had she, until becoming involved along with her husband in the newly formed Fabian Society, expressed any particular political opinions. In the Fabian ambience, she adopted the visible attributes of the "advanced" woman—bobbed hair, cigarette smoking, loose-fitting "aesthetic" clothing, knickers for cycling—but consistently demurred at any opportunity to become a public advocate for suffrage, at one point stating that she considered it a potential distraction from the advance of socialism.[11] In the May 29, 1908 meeting of the newly formed Fabian Women's Group, she astonished the audience when she announced that the subject of her invited address would be the "natural disabilities of woman." She had received the invitation to speak on "women and work" because of her success both as a wife and mother and as a published writer of some renown. She spoke instead in her persona as the wife of Hubert Bland. Dismayed, the Women's Group responded with a series of lectures, the first by a woman physician, that were clearly mounted to counter this reversal of expectations.[12] The Women's Group episode epitomizes Nesbit's fundamental ambivalence toward gender issues. The division between public acclaim and painful private compromises was never bridged in real life.

Nesbit did not participate when the Fabian Women's Group supported the women's suffrage movement, nor was there explicit engagement with feminist issues in her adult fiction. She did, however, allow herself some narrative liberties in the depiction of female characters, especially in her fairy tales; the use of the fantastic mode in the children's fiction allowed a "space" for non-traditional configurations.[13] Alison Lurie suggests that Nesbit's children's fiction presents elements of covert and explicit protest against the reinforcement of intellectual and social subjection of women in patriarchal culture by literature intended for the socialization of children.[14] When her children's stories were set in contemporary England, she used ironic depictions of male characters' investments in patriarchal practice as strategic displacements of feminist impulses; even a fictionalized contemporary setting exerted powerful constraints on her subversive impulses. In her fairy tales she could more explicitly counter gender stereotypes.

The fairy tale offered Nesbit a socially acceptable (and profitable) venue for publication and a flexible structure that would admit of variations in plot and even departures from convention, but the development of fairy tales from evening adult entertainment to vehicles for the socialization of children, especially girls, had long carried with it a diminution of female agency. The shift in the characterization of Red Riding Hood, signaled by Jack Zipes, from a successful trickster to a dead victim is an extreme case, but a similar sequence can be traced for other tales as well.[15] Many of Nesbit's earliest efforts do not depart from conventional depictions of male and female gender roles, but she profited from the "new tradition" in fairy tale writing that followed the publication of work by Lewis Carroll, George MacDonald, Juliana Horatia Ewing, and others. Lurie and U. C. Knoepflmacher have both pointed out that something of the original vigor of the female characters began to be recaptured in the nineteenth century, as women writers, Nesbit among them, published the increasingly popular fantastic tale.[16] Knoepflmacher has also suggested that although Nesbit is one of the writers who recaptures the children's story for women after an extended period of appropriation by male editors and authors such as Perrault and the brothers Grimm, thereby regaining "space" for active female characters, she does not depart in any marked fashion from the "patriarchal patterns," and "pronounced moralism" of nineteenth-century children's fiction; in this she is similar to George Eliot, whose work also manifests internalized gender ideology.[17]

Most discussions of Nesbit's fiction focus on her series books (the adventures of the Bastables or of the "Five Children"), although Lurie's text and the collection edited by Auerbach and Knoepflmacher discuss the short tales as well. When Nesbit does rework the fairy tale, the depictions of female characters are vital and intense, and suggest a response to what the public expected of a woman writing fairy tales operating concurrently with a desire for a break with convention. Since many folk tales and fairy tales focus on a single heroine, and present, in their earliest versions, examples of strong female agents, they offer a structure conceivably suited to weakening the force of convention.[18] The stories set in Nesbit's "present day" (even the fantasies of the "Five Children" begin in this world) were too firmly linked to mimesis to allow much freedom. The "carnivalesque" space she opens for her creative activity in the formal structures of the fairy tale demonstrates that Nesbit was able to "write out," but not necessarily to resolve in her own life, some of those tensions inherent in her ambivalence; her writing is thus a series of complex negotiations, complicated by her own vexed relationship to female roles, between transcending convention and marketing her work.

The term "carnivalesque" is used advisedly, since the experience of fantasy creates "nested" carnivalesque structures: first, the act of reading fantasy creates an interval of "freedom" in daily life that might be likened to the sanctioned break with customary activities and conventions that, according to Mikhail Bakhtin, characterizes the carnival.[19] Secondly, the fantastic narrative encloses another carnivalesque structure, since within it a brief period of reversal occurs that acts out its own precepts and then yields to its dissolution. It is within that carnivalesque story-space that Nesbit finds a controlled yet liberating freedom. On the other hand, this ludic "freedom" is carefully circumscribed, existing only within the limits of the narrative just as carnival exists within the dominant social structure, so that Nesbit cannot be said here, any more than in her own life, directly to confront or to challenge convention.[20]

The primary public manifestation of carnival is the temporary unsettling of hierarchical distinctions and "natural" oppositions. One such binary, and one that Nesbit addressed most frequently in her children's stories, was male active agency and aggression in opposition to female passivity and altruism. Nesbit's conservative tendencies are most evident in those stories—the greater percentage of her major fiction—in which the protagonists operate as a group.[21] In her stories of the "Five Children," the female characters, especially Anthea, the elder of the two girls, are the nurturing exemplars of empathy.[22] She also tended to select male characters as her narrators and protagonists—most notably Oswald Bastable, but also Dickie Harding of *The House of Arden* (1908) and *Harding's Luck* (1909), a practice that carried over into her adult fiction; even when the protagonist is a female, the action tends to be focalized through the principal male. These male narrators are transparently unreliable and their egotistical self-presentation ironically undermines their pretentiousness. For example, Gerald, in *The Enchanted Castle,* constantly narrativizes his own actions—he seems incapable of referring to himself except as a pseudo-literary adventure hero:

> "The young explorers . . . could see nothing. But their dauntless leader, whose eyes had grown used

to the dark while the clumsy forms of the others were bungling up the entrance, had made a discovery."

> "Oh, what!" both the others were used to Gerald's way of telling a story while he acted it, but they did sometimes wish that he didn't talk quite so long and so like a book in moments of excitement.[23]

Although Nesbit sustains this ironic depiction of spurious male superiority throughout the story, her treatment of male arrogance loses force because the children's effective power succumbs to the generally disastrous results attendant on all their escapades; her ironies cannot even begin to undercut the powerful presence of gender conventions when the adventures themselves are self-canceling.

John Stephens suggests that Nesbit employs the *conventions,* but not the spirit or the subversive potential, of the carnivalesque, in ways that reinforce the subjected status of her child protagonists and reaffirm the social codes governing adult-child relationships.[24] Thus adults' authority is never seriously (if at all) undermined. Stephens' strictures are valid, but when one examines Nesbit's *fairy tales,* I think it necessary to qualify these observations since Nesbit's use of a series of strategies ranging from arbitrary whimsy to complex and self-reflexive intertextuality enable her to reclaim not only the appropriated genre of the fairy tale, but also a subversive "voice." Nesbit self-reflexively reveals her manipulations of plots as well-known to the reader as to herself, explicitly calling attention to the "rules" of the fairy tale while simultaneously bending many of them, thus drawing her implied audience into her intertextual web and insuring that the shared humor retains its subversive force. A similar, although more constrained exploitation of carnivalesque freedom characterizes her adult novels, this time sanctioned by the relatively permissive "entertainment" environment of popular romance for women.

At this point, it is useful to examine the apparent sources of Nesbit's sense of freedom within the limits of the fairy tale by considering the dynamics of one of her lesser-known short stories, **"The Twopenny Spell,"** from *Oswald Bastable and Others* (1905). In this story, paired protagonists make the simplest gender subversion, role-reversal, both workable and acceptable, judging from the frequency with which she employed the device here and elsewhere.

In **"The Twopenny Spell,"** the prankish Harry is subjected to the vengeance of his sister, Lucy (not the heroine of *The Magic City*); she purchases a "twopenny" spell that preserves outward appearances but reverses the siblings' personality traits. The boy, one of the leaders among his schoolfellows, becomes pathetically timid and is repeatedly trounced, the girl plays malicious tricks on *her* schoolfellows and foments several quarrels. Even here, however, Nesbit cannot resolve the plot without a conventional gesture. Lucy regrets her act upon learning of Harry's humiliation: Lucy "[s]uddenly . . . was really sorry. She had done this, she had degraded her happy brother to a mere milksop . . . Remorse suddenly gripped her with tooth and claw."[25] On the other hand, she then proposes that Harry disguise himself as a girl and attend *her* school under her protection. His affectionate response and her apology cancel the spell (which, it must be admitted, had already done its punitive and reforming work), providing a moral fillip that reads almost apologetically after the obvious relish with which the girl's mischief has been narrated.

The passage is a study in shifting constructions; just at the moment that an affirmation of Lucy's independent agency seems to occur, we see instead that the spell has had no effect on Lucy's true, "innate" impulses. Despite the tendency to cancel any moves she makes toward alternative depiction, Nesbit does show that gender rivalry has been shifted toward androgyny and teamwork.[26] The siblings, especially Harry, have both gained more balanced personalities, integrating both altruism and self-assertion. Lucy apologizes, and Harry "thrashed Simpkins Minor thoroughly and scientifically on the first opportunity; but he did not thrash him extravagantly: he tempered pluck with mercy."[27]

This story illustrates Nesbit's tactics in negotiating the boundary between outright advocacy of female agency and an ultimate rejection of it in favor of domesticity. The same carnivalesque interval of the children's fantasy was also Nesbit's choice when she turned to her adult fiction; but the results are less impressive with her grown-up "princesses." In his study *Secret Gardens,* Humphrey Carpenter criticizes the absence of real risk in Nesbit's children's stories, and that same "safety net" is present in the protectors with whom she surrounds her heroines.[28] Carpenter's criticisms are valid, although harsh, when applied to Nesbit's children's stories; his reading is, however, an accurate assessment of Nesbit's practices in her *adult* fiction. Once the romantic dilemma of these novels has been resolved, the courtship structure is restored and the brief non-traditional episode of female power is ensconced in a "safe" narrative

framework. The surviving remnant of her fantasy—the unlikely rescues of her heroines from amorous scrapes—deprives her mimetic heroines, in most cases, of the opportunities to demonstrate the real bravery available to the least significant of her fairy tale heroines.

Katherine, the heroine of *The Incredible Honeymoon* (1916) most fully embodies Nesbit's game of adult wish-fulfillment. Unwilling to marry Edward Basingstoke, with whom she flees a confining family life, Katherine consents to a "mock marriage" (at a London registry!). Here the seriousness of free choice in love as presented by novelists such as Olive Schreiner and Mona Caird approaches bedroom farce. Likewise, Nesbit evades full affirmation of a woman's self-worth when Daphne Carmichael, the heroine of *Daphne of Fitzroy Street,* rejects suitors who value her for the artist who has exploited her as a model, brutally expressed his valuation of his work over any woman, and reneged after proposing marriage. Although the outcome of their relationship is less clear than Nesbit's reviewers and her biographers Doris Langley Moore and Julia Briggs suggest—there is no explicit acceptance of his final proposal—Daphne is the ethical opposite of the New Woman despite her bohemian career as an art student. Nesbit exploits the escapist potential of the now-old New Woman novel, but the underlying model of the fairy tale undercuts, without completely eliminating, elements of feminist polemic.

Nesbit's tendency to update by romanticizing the dilemmas of the New Woman continues in the novels that most resemble her children's fiction: *Daphne in Fitzroy Street, The Red House, The Incomplete Amorist* (1906) and *The Incredible Honeymoon.* In these works, Nesbit's most effective New Women are the independent spinsters who double as fairy godmothers; only *The Incredible Honeymoon* lacks such a character. These figures present female agency firmly domesticated as brusque nurturant behavior. The marginalized female rescuer was Nesbit's best effort at the New Woman, and this depiction is problematized only in Cecily, Lady Blair, of *Dormant* (1911).

Katherine, Daphne, and Betty are all variations on the "New Girl" story, directed to adolescents and young working women, which began to flourish between the years 1880 and 1915;[29] Nesbit was a contributor to *The Girl's Own Paper,* one of the most influential periodicals. These heroines, safely and unremittingly modest but not homebound, often act out a public version of angelic domesticity. Nesbit's adult fiction seems to represent an astute, but not necessarily cynical, market-awareness and an ability to translate the adventurous children for whom she is justly famous into callow but mildly pleasing young women who threaten no conservative mores. Such is not the case in her adult fantasy novels, sometimes called "sensational" by her reviewers—a dubious designation, since Nesbit's heroines are quite tame when contrasted with the Lady Audleys or even the Herminia Bartons of traditional sensational fiction. At the same time, however, Nesbit involves Sandra Mundy of *Salome and the Head* and Rose Royal of *Dormant* in serious confrontations with issues of female resistance to and subversion of gender stereotypes.

Salome is the story of Sandra, a young woman in flight from an impulsive and imprudent marriage; in fact, the marriage is a hoax to gain her money, but she is unaware of this for at least half of the novel. She establishes herself in London as an interpretive dancer, successfully maintaining her privacy and reputation; the "house" of the American title refers to the faceless house, lacking an address and any visible means of entry, in which she resides. When her "husband" is murdered and Sandra finds that the stage-prop head of her "Salome" dance is that of his corpse, her new lover, accepted in the belief that her husband had already died, deserts her, and she is rescued by an admirer who falsely claims the murder as his own.

Sandra finds the resolve at the end to reject, resoundingly, her vacillating lover in favor of the man who truly sacrifices for her; she does not yield to the importunities of an unworthy potential mate. Sandra embodies Nesbit's own contrary impulses—she is both "risky" and "safe"—and she is Nesbit's most sustained portait of self-determination in an adult female protagonist.

On the other hand, there is little focus on the risks—especially that of becoming *déclassée*—that Sandra takes in establishing her career; every element of notoriety is carefully removed from her life. Her career, clearly modeled on that of Maude Allan and her dance to music from Richard Strauss's *Salome*, also stands as a model of the careful cultivation of respectability by professional performers outlined by Mary Jane Corbett in *Representing Femininity*.[30] Without writing a fantastic narrative, Nesbit nevertheless idealizes Sandra's charmed life. Potentially serious consequences remain *in potentia,* and self-sacrificing male rescuers abound.

Dormant, a "Theosophical" romance of reincarnation, is Nesbit's most ambitious and most complex narrative, with the exception of the interconnected children's novels *Harding's Luck* and *The House of Arden.* Further, it is her darkest view of the "emancipated" heroine, one who is not only displaced from the center of her own narrative, but who is also rendered ineffectual by supernatural forces that ultimately destroy her lover, a "Frankenstein" in nature and activity. The "exploded" science of Paracelsus returns, becoming the Theosophy of Helena Blavatsky and Annie Besant—the latter a close friend of Nesbit and Bland. Nesbit had used the Frankenstein motif in some of her gothic tales; in *Dormant,* it is interwoven with the Sleeping Beauty motif in a confrontation of male with female power that can have no positive resolution.

Nesbit at first seems to place women's issues in the foreground, when Rose Royal, transparently the young Nesbit in appearance and outlook, resolves to live alone in a slum property that is the source of her income. Rose's agency is diminished as the novel increasingly focuses on her lover, Anthony Drelincourt, ostensibly a chemist and anatomist, but also a secret adept in "ancient wisdom" and the Paracelsian quest for the elixir of life. Anthony, if anything even more self-absorbed and narcissistic than Victor Frankenstein, falls in love with Eugenia, the woman whom he discovers and "resurrects," unaware that she is the lover of his namesake uncle who attempted to render her immortal; he perishes with Eugenia as a result of his attempts to render himself as immortal as she.

If Rose and Eugenia share between them the Sleeping Beauty role, then Cecily, Lady Blair, Eugenia's past rival and Anthony's mentor, is cast, and indeed named on many occasions, as the fairy godmother. In this role, she is pathetically lacking, especially in the ruses by which she tries to recall her long-vanished youth. Yet it is Lady Blair who supports Eugenia—with mixed motives, one is sure—in her resistance to Anthony's schemes, and she is consistently Rose's advocate as well.

Eugenia resembles the Sleeping Beauty who awakens in power even if her male counterpart seems to hold patriarchal mastery over her fate.[31] Her passage through "death" has given her both the will and the intellect to resist Anthony's plan; there is, even in her consent to his desire to undergo the ritual, a suggestion that she knows and welcomes the inevitable failure. The resistance to Anthony mounted by all three women, who are dispersed aspects of Nesbit herself both as young and as aging lover, represents Nesbit's critique of his blindness and arrogance. Her persistent focalization via Anthony renders the female characters a passive "Greek chorus," however; it seems that patriarchy can be punished, but not dethroned. It is a significant index of Nesbit's characteristic ambivalence that Rose, the contemporary and more mimetic character, is locked into a set of conventional behaviors—her rueful meditations accepting second place to Anthony's work affirm female acquiescence in the *status quo*—while the "magical" Eugenia, like the girl-heroines of her fairy tales, is able to act effectively, even though it means her destruction.

Nesbit was dismayed that she was marginalized as a writer of children's fiction.[32] Her first desire was to become a poet, and even after she won critical and public acclaim with her "Bastable" books and the "Five Children" series, she longed to be recognized as a "serious" writer, even to the point of attempting short stories, clearly imitative of Henry James, in *The Literary Sense* (1903). Nesbit seems to have been caught in a double bind that was partly of her own making and partly that of society's. In evading any real confrontation with New Woman issues in her fiction, she was unlikely to receive much critical notice, and the critics' general tendency to dismiss women's fiction insured that little notice was taken of her work.[33] When *Dormant,* for example, was mentioned at all by the critics, the novel's serious issues were passed over in silence, and the whole was treated as a comic episode—one critic emphasized the difficulties of transporting a catatonic body by rail to London.[34] Her critics met each of her adult novels with the same response, either praising her "light" or "humorous" touch, or expressing dismay that she had, in the words of one critic of her first novel, *The Secret of Kyriels:*

> done violence to her delicate imagination by challenging comparisons with Miss Florence Warden and Mrs. Williamson. *The Secret of Kyriels* is a clever *tour de force,* but it affords the author little scope for indulging in her sense of humor. Romantic comedy rather than melodrama is the domain in which she ought to achieve genuine success.[35]

This assessment, almost the first review of her fiction, was to be repeated throughout her career, either as praise or as blame. Even where possibilities for irony existed, such as the male-narrated *The Red House,* the critic for *The Academy* was uneasy at her "gender-bending":

> most people will agree that for a woman-writer to tell a story in the guise of a man is a distinct risk, and a risk not worth taking. And E. Nesbit is a particularly feminine woman-writer; that is the secret of her charm. So we feel resentful when she cheats us of what she has taught us to expect from her, for the sake of masquerading in doublet and hose . . . We wish very heartily that [the narrator] had been the person called Chloe, for by letting her husband tell the tale she has left us to form the impression of a most effeminate and rather tiresome young man.[36]

For a woman to satirize male unreliability and foibles as she had done when speaking in the voice of the boy Oswald Bastable will not do, it seems, when she speaks through the grown-up, Len.

In her life, Nesbit avoided public involvement with feminist issues; privately she raged and acquiesced to the impositions of her married life. By reducing the New Woman to an iconic "new" romantic heroine, Nesbit sidestepped engagement with the serious potential of such characters and lost desirable critical attention. It is necessary to read Nesbit selectively if one's agenda is to recuperate her for feminism, but in the interests of a "thick description" of the *feminisms* of the late nineteenth and early twentieth centuries, she remains a figure who provides a valuable middle term between equally adamant feminists and antifeminists. Imaginative release from socially constituted repressions is the true license of fantasy. It has been attested, for Nesbit and others, many times, and it is the hallmark of nineteenth-century fantasy. The demands of writing purely mimetic fiction effectively repressed much protest in Nesbit's work. It is perhaps inevitable that the most forthright and independent females Nesbit ever depicted are a dancer, one who is outside the pale or nearly so, and a woman magically recalled from the dead.

Notes

1. *The Magic City* (London: Ernest Benn, 1910; New York: MacMillan, 1910), p. 164.

2. Julia Briggs discusses the topicality of *The Magic City* in her biography of Nesbit, *A Woman of Passion: The Life of E. Nesbit, 1858-1924* (London: Hutchinson; New York: New Amsterdam Books, 1987), pp. 333-35. Nesbit is generally sympathetic to the hardships of working people, but, on occasion, the assumptions of her class are inscribed quite harshly.

3. *Ibid.,* pp. 193-95.

4. Ann Ardis, *New Women, New Novels* (New Brunswick, NJ: Rutgers University Press, 1990), p. 140.

5. Nesbit also produced a small number of competent gothic short stories, collected as *E. Nesbit's Tales of Terror* (London: Methuen, 1983), although only a few, most notably "Man-Sized in Marble," effectively exploit gender issues.

6. Doris Langley Moore, *E. Nesbit: A Biography,* revised edition (New York: Chilton Books, 1966). Langley Moore quotes from a letter of October 22, 1888 Olive Schreiner wrote to Havelock Ellis: "Mrs. Bland . . . was so kind to me before I left London. I don't think I should have got away without her. She came the last morning to finish packing my things and see me off. Do you know, she's one of the noblest women? I can't tell you about her life, because I mustn't, but it's grand . . . " (p. 110). Schreiner is obviously referring to the open secret of Hubert Bland's infidelities.

7. Briggs, *A Woman of Passion,* p. 333.

8. Hubert Bland, *Essays By Hubert,* ed. E. Nesbit (London: M. Goschen, 1914), p. 209. Ironically, Nesbit edited this and similar essays after Bland's death, dedicating them to "The readers who loved Hubert."

9. Quoted in Briggs, *A Woman of Passion,* p. 333.

10. Wells described Bland as one who lived an imagined persona of "a great Man of the World, a Business Man (he had no gleam of business ability)" (quoted in Ruth Braddon, *The New Women and the Old Men* [New York: Norton, 1990], p. 174).

11. Briggs, *A Woman of Passion,* p. 335.

12. This episode is attested to in the Fabian treatise *Three Years' Work* in Sally Alexander (ed.), *Women's Fabian Tracts* (New York, London: Routledge, 1988), p. 154. Nesbit is generally supposed to have been anti-suffrage, but the relevant documents suggest that her opposition may have developed over time.

13. Edith Lazaros Honig, *Breaking the Angelic Image: Woman Power in Victorian Children's Fiction* (New York: Greenwood Press: 1988). Honig states that "In humorous fantasy . . . an independent heroine could be readily dismissed as part of the delightful reversal of reality, all the while insidiously presenting a subversive feminist message that was there for the reader to note or to disregard" (p. 71).

14. Alison Lurie, *Don't Tell the Grownups* (New York: Avon, 1990), p. 105.

15. Jack Zipes, *Fairy Tales and the Art of Subversion* (New York: Routledge, 1983), pp. 28-30.

16. Lurie, *Don't Tell the Grownups,* p. 117, and U. C. Knoepflmacher, "Of Babylands and Babylons: E. Nesbit and the Reclamation of the Fairy Tale," *Tulsa Studies in Women's Literature* 6.2 (Fall 1987), 299-325. See also Nina Auerbach and Knoepflmacher (eds.), *Forbidden Journeys: Fairy Tales and Fantasies by Victorian Women Writers* (Chicago and London: University of Chicago Press, 1992). The introductions to the divisions of this anthology also emphasize the increasing prominence of women writers of fairy tales.

17. Knoepflmacher, "Of Babylands and Babylons," 302.

18. Lurie, *Don't Tell the Grownups,* p. 21.

19. Mikhail Bakhtin, *Rabelais and His World,* trans. Hélène Iswolsky (Bloomington: University of Indiana Press, 1984). Bahktin's theories have been exhaustively analyzed. William Touponce has indicated their applicability to some aspects of young readers' literature in his study "Laughter and Freedom in Ray Bradbury's *Something Wicked This Way Comes,*" *Children's Literature Association Quarterly* 13.1 (Spring 1988), 17-21.

20. Karen A. Hohne and Helen Wussow, *A Dialogue of Voices: Feminist Theory and Bakhtin* (Minneapolis: University of Minnesota Press, 1994). As the editors to this volume indicate, "It must be stressed that in Bakhtin's definition, carnival continues to exist within authority's framework . . . Instead of smashing social frameworks, carnival reinscribes them by being contained within them" (p. xii).

21. In addition to Elmar Schenkel's article "Utopie und Phantasktik in den Kinderbüchern von E. Nesbit," *Inklings: Jahrbuch für Literatur und Aesthetik* 8 (1990), 107, in *Long Ago When I Was Young,* Noel Streatfeild, ed., (London: Ronald Whiting and Wheaton, 1966), the editor has also pointed out that Nesbit's most positive experiences are grounded in the escapades with her brothers, in which, as the indulged youngest sibling, she was allowed to participate (pp. 14, 19).

22. One exception, however, is Elfrida in Nesbit's *The House of Arden* (London: Ernest Benn, 1908; New York: Coward, McCann, 1908), who is consistently depicted as being more courageous than Edred, her brother.

23. Nesbit, *The Enchanted Castle* (London: T. Fisher Unwin, 1907; New York: Harper, 1908), p. 15.

24. John Stephens, *Language and Ideology in Children's Fiction* (New York and London: Longman, 1992), pp. 125-32.

25. Nesbit, "The Twopenny Spell," in *Oswald Bastable and Others* (London: Wells, Gardner, Darton, and Co., 1905; New York: Coward, McCann, 1960), p. 177.

26. Claudia Nelson discusses the question of the tensions between the angelic and the virile ideals in representing masculinity in her book *Boys Will Be Girls: The Feminine Ethic and British Children's Fiction, 1857-1917* (New Brunswick, NJ: Rutgers University Press, 1991). Alan Richardson also discusses the representation of masculinity in "Reluctant Lords and Lame Princes: Engendering the Male Child in Nineteenth-Century Juvenile Fiction," *Children's Literature* 21 (1993), 3-19.

27. Nesbit, "The Twopenny Spell," p. 178.

28. Humphrey Carpenter, *Secret Gardens* (Boston: Houghton Mifflin), 1985, pp. 133-37.

29. Sally Mitchell, *The New Girl: Girls' Culture in England, 1880-1915* (New York: Columbia University Press, 1995), p. 3.

30. Mary Jane Corbett, *Representing Femininity: Middle-Class Subjectivity in Victorian and Edwardian Women's Autobiographies* (New York: Oxford University Press, 1992), pp. 107-29.

31. Nina Auerbach, *Woman and the Demon* (Cambridge, MA: Harvard University Press, 1982). Citing H. Rider Haggard's Ayesha in *She* as only one of several examples (p. 42), Auerbach suggests that the passivity of Sleeping Beauty is a matter more of societal wish-fulfillment, a way of containing female potential, rather than an emblem of female subjection.

32. Briggs, *A Woman of Passion,* pp. 399-401.

33. See Nicola Diane Thompson, *Reviewing Sex: Gender and the Reception of Victorian Novels* (London: Macmillan: New York: New York University Press, 1996) for a fuller discussion of these issues.

34. *The Saturday Review* (December 23, 1911), 805.

35. *The Spectator,* 81 (December 10, 1898), 873. One reviewer, in *The Literary World,* 31 (March 31, 1900), did praise Nesbit's control over her involved, suspense-filled plot, noting, however, that it was "not a study of character, but a tale of incident" (71).

36. Review of *The Red House, The Academy* (March 7, 1903), 225-26.

Additonal coverage of Nesbit's life and career is contained in the following sources published by the Gale Group: *Contemporary Authors,* **Vols. 118, 137;** *Dictionary of Literary Biography,* **Vols. 141,153, 178;** *Junior DISCovering Authors; Major Authors and Illustrators for Children and Young Adults; Major Twentieth-Century Writers,* **Second Edition;** *St. James Guide to Children's Writers; St. James Guide to Fantasy Writers; St. James Guide to Horror, Ghost, and Gothic Writers; Something about the Author,* **Vols. 100;** *Yesterday's Authors of Books for Children,* **Vol. 1.**

Helen Oxenbury
1938-

English illustrator and author of picture books for toddlers, pre-schoolers, and early readers.

Major works include *Beach Day* (1982), *Mother's Helper* (1982), *The Checkup* (1983), *The Dancing Class* (1983), *Helen Oxenbury's Nursery Story Book* (1985), and the "Tom and Pippo" series (1988-).

For further information on Oxenbury's life and works, see *CLR,* Volume 22.

INTRODUCTION

Children under the age of five, among them her own daughter, were blessed when Helen Oxenbury developed the Little Baby Board Books, and doubly blessed when she created the characters of Tom and his stuffed monkey, Pippo. A gifted artist, Oxenbury's illustrations and early reader books have drawn critical attention to her deep understanding and affection for young children and to her accurate, humorous, and insightful depictions of the everyday experiences of the young. A pioneer in the development of board books, her works directed to babies and small children, Oxenbury is considered one of the most influential contributors to the form. Her round faced babies and sturdy unassuming toddlers exhibit the ups and downs of baby and toddler life, and the books' small size fit easily into little hands. In an interview with *The Junior Bookshelf* Oxenbury said, "I believe children to be very canny people who immediately sense if adults talk, write, or illustrate down to them . . . I think most children appreciate, and more frighteningly recognize, honesty." She also said, "I look for warmth and humour—and characters that aren't absolutely wonderful and lovely!"

Critics have praised the wonderfully expressive faces of her children and animals, especially interesting since she uses little ink, and the masterly quality of her watercolor landscapes. Her gentle humor and warmth have been noted as the hallmarks of her down-to-earth stories that provide young children with both amusement and comfort. Amelia Edwards of Walker Books said, "She is so good, so endlessly creative . . . changing style, format, medium, and of course she created the Walker [Books logo] bear."

Besides her self-illustrated work, Oxenbury has illustrated the works of many other authors, including Edward Lear, Lewis Carroll, Alexei Tolstoy, Ivor Cutler, and Ruth Krauss.

BIOGRAPHICAL INFORMATION

Born and raised in East Suffolk on the coast of England, Oxenbury claims to love the bleak landscape with its "clear light, huge sky, mudflats, and wheeling birds." She attended a private girls' school in Ipswich which she disliked very much. She has suggested that she would have been much happier attending A. S. Neill's nearby Summerhill, a creative and free-form alternative school at which her husband-to-be, fellow illustrator John Burningham, was a student. After graduation, she attended Ipswich Art School, where she studied life drawing, and worked at the Ipswich Repertory Theatre as a designer. She enjoyed her time in the theater so much that she decided to study costume and scene design at the Central School in London. It was there that she met her husband, but one of her instructors told her that she should be an illustrator rather than a costume designer because she was so much more interested in the people than the clothes she was drawing.

She worked for a while as assistant designer for the Colchester Repertory Theater, then went to Israel to join Burningham. She worked there as an au pair and English teacher, then got a job as the design assistant for the Habimah Theatre in Tel Aviv. During the three years she was in Israel, she was given opportunities and responsibilities to design and construct whole sets and enormous backdrops. On her return to England, she worked for a time in film and television, but marriage and the demands of a growing family ended her theatrical career.

When she was pregnant with her first child, illustrator Jan Pieńkowski suggested she try illustrating Christmas cards. He further suggested she try an ABC or counting book. The result was Oxenbury's first book, *Numbers of Things* (1969), and this in turn led to more illustrations for her own and others' books. With two children to carry and care for, Oxenbury used pen and crayon for her work because they took up little space and were easy to carry.

When she was in the hospital with her third child, Oxenbury received a visit from the innovative publisher Sebastian Walker. Walker believed that children's literature was undervalued and that children deserved the best writers and illustrators. He revolutionized the publishing climate, and pay level, for artists and writers of children's books. Walker was to become the adored advocate for Oxenbury, among others, establishing a successful and highly respected publishing house for children's books.

One of Oxenbury's greatest successes, the Little Baby Board Books, were inspired by the youngest of her three children, Emily. She saw that there were no books available for toddlers and suggested to Walker that they create a book for children under five. Walker was very enthusiastic, and published an entire series of wordless picture books, sturdy and small enough for baby hands. Emily was Oxenbury's best audience. She recalled, "Emily would go stiff with excitement when I showed them to her." Emily's needs became a source of ideas for the books, and the baby in the books grew and learned as Emily did.

As her illustrating career flourished, Oxenbury was asked by the French children's magazine *Popi* to create two characters for them, one a child and one a toy. The five pages she produced for *Popi* were easily turned into a book, and the book soon became a series. Toddler Tom and his long suffering stuffed monkey, Pippo, have had over a dozen adventures since then.

MAJOR WORKS

Oxenbury is in great part responsible for the advent of board books for babies and first picture books designed especially for small hands. Inspired by and based on the experiences of her youngest daughter, Little Baby Board Books, Oxenbury's series of small, sturdy, wordless books, with titles such as *Beach Day* and *Mother's Helper* (both 1982), traces the growth of a round faced baby who plays, gets dressed, visits the zoo, and helps with dishes, becoming more mobile with age and advancing to more complicated activities. Slightly more advanced books move out into the world, with titles such as *The Checkup* and *The Dancing Class* (both 1983), depicting experiences such as these, a car trip, and the first day of school.

Beginning with *Tom and Pippo Go for a Walk* (1988), Oxenbury has written over a dozen books about little Tom and his stuffed monkey Pippo. Each book describes a different experience in the life of a small child; Tom and Pippo go for a walk, make a mess, read a story, take a bath, go to the beach, and engage in many other activities common to young children. Oxenbury needs only a few lines to give the long suffering but well-loved Pippo an extraordinarily expressive face.

Among the books she has illustrated for others are the award winning *We're Going on a Bear Hunt* retold by Michael Rosen, *Farmer Duck* by Martin Waddell, and *So Much* by Trish Cooke. Oxenbury's illustrations for the nursery song *We're Going on a Bear Hunt* feature a father and his four children. They hunt the bear through many terrains, then have to go back through them to escape the bear they find. Oxenbury's family is jubilant and energetic and full of fun. Her illustrations were called masterly characterizations full of delightful comedy and high drama. *Farmer Duck* is about a duck who lives on a farm and does all the work for the lazy farmer. When the other animals see how tired the duck is, they chase the farmer away and take over the farm themselves. Oxenbury's poor exhausted duck, with bags under its eyes, as it digs and washes and irons and slogs through the muddy yard in the rain, would garner anyone's sympathy. In *So Much*, all the baby's relatives come into the house one by one and show their complete adoration for the baby. Finally Daddy arrives home from work, and there is a surprise birthday party for him. Critics said of *So Much* that Oxenbury lent her characteristic richness and humor to an exuberant family party.

AWARDS

Oxenbury won the British Library Association's Kate Greenaway Medal in 1969 for her illustrations of Edward Lear's *The Quangle Wangle's Hat* and Margaret Mahy's *The Dragon of an Ordinary Family*. She received it again in 1989 and 1991. *The Helen Oxenbury Nursery Story Book* was runner-up for the Kurt Maschler Award in 1985. The Smarties Book Prize was awarded to her for *We're Going on a Bear Hunt* in 1989, and again in 1991 for *Farmer Duck*. *We're Going on a Bear Hunt* also won the *Boston Globe-Horn Book* Honor Book Award. In 1991 Oxenbury was also honored with the British Book Award for illustration. *So Much* received the Kurt Maschler Award and the Smarties Book Prize in the under-5 category in 1994, and was also awarded the Kate Greenaway Medal in 1995.

AUTHOR COMMENTARY

Helen Oxenbury

SOURCE: "Drawing for Children," in *The Junior Bookshelf,* Vol. 34, No. 4, August, 1970, pp. 199-201.

It is difficult to say what makes me want to illustrate certain children's stories. I only know the attraction is instant and lasts till the endpapers.

I felt this very strongly with Edward Lear's **The Quangle-Wangle's Hat,** and I know here what the attraction was. I loved the strangeness and quiet sad humour. Fortunately I believe children like it too, and it has the added pleasure of rhythmic verse and dotty names that children delight in repeating over and over.

The Hunting of the Snark by Lewis Carroll was my next choice and I think for the same reasons as I chose the Edward Lear—the marvellous mixture of weird people in dreamlike situations surprising one by doing and saying quite ordinary and down-to-earth things one minute, and absurd, outrageous things the next.

I am now working on a book called **Meal One** by Ivor Cutler, whom I consider to be the nearest thing to a present-day Lear or Carroll.

Mediocrity and boredom come quickly with books for which I have not felt this instant sympathy, and yet have talked myself into for reasons such as children will love it. The only answer then is to abandon the whole idea, as I can be sure if the characters left me cold at the beginning of the story, by the end I would be feeling murderous towards them.

I believe children to be very canny people who immediately sense if adults talk, write or illustrate down to them, hence the unpopularity of self-conscious, child-like drawings that appear in some children's books. The illustrator is misguidedly thinking the child will be able to identify more easily with drawings similar to his own, while probably he is disgusted that adults cannot do better.

Similarly, I think most children appreciate, and more frighteningly recognise, honesty. I know this is true of my two. They are for instance unmoved by pictures of neat Mums in neat kitchens, cooking neat meals. They know very well it isn't like that, nor do farmers' wives any longer scatter corn for chickens and farmers use unromantic modern machinery. This doesn't mean that the old books that have started these clichés aren't still loved dearly. It just seems a little pointless to be continually rehashing them.

I find with my two children that they will look with the same eagerness at good and bad illustrations, and listen rapt to both good and bad stories. This is why I think it is important to expose them as much as possible to the best, for I'm sure that how they see things when their young minds are like sponges lives with them all their lives.

Within reason I don't think there are any rules about what frightens children, and it depends entirely on the individual child. I can remember sitting through some of Walt Disney's films absolutely paralysed with fear, whereas my three-year-old son for some reason is horrified by the moon in both pictures and reality but can stand, and even enjoys, as many pictures of gnarled old witches and goblins as you can put in front of him. I just don't know how young children stomach some of Hans Christian Andersen's terrifying fairy stories, but obviously they do very well, as they've been around for over a hundred years.

When I have prepared the book dummy, I consider three-quarters of the work to be done. This is a set of pages cut to the same size and length as the book. It is the bone structure of the book and arranging it is far the hardest and most time-consuming part. All the thinking, measuring, reshuffling, planning, positioning of type and size of illustrations and a hundred other considerations go into this rough. For my last two books, which have had more text, my publisher has made up several galley proofs with correct size type. These I have cut around and positioned on the dummy pages. In this way one is sure of avoiding that irritating fault of type disappearing into the illustration and it is possible to visualise the finished book more clearly.

The next step is plain sailing and for me extremely enjoyable, the only problem being finding time between looking after the children and general housework. This is why I've arranged to be extremely mobile, using the minimum amount of materials, which can be gathered up quickly, and rushed out of reach of invading children. With this training there are not many situations that stop me working, and I am able to move with my equipment from the cooker, to the garden, to the television, to my own desk, and finally end up in bed with it.

Helen Oxenbury with Stephanie Nettell

SOURCE: An interview in *Books for Keeps,* No. 62, May, 1990, pp. 16-17.

'I can't tell if being a mother has influenced me. I know I love the shape of little children. I can stare at them for hours—I love their little limbs, little arms, little bums.'

But it was in fact the birth of Helen Oxenbury's own children that directed this much loved best-seller of the nursery towards book illustration of any kind. She was expecting her first child (now 24 and herself at Manchester School of Art), watching husband John Burningham doing *Borka* and its successor, needing money and wondering what on earth to do, when a friend of theirs—who happened to be Jan Pieńkowski of Gallery Five—suggested she did some Christmas cards.

He followed up with the notion that she might tackle a book—'an ABC or a counting book, where you don't have to worry about the text, something you can do at home.' *Numbers of Things* was at once accepted by Heinemann, and she's never stopped since. (John won the Kate Greenaway with *Borka;* five years later so did Helen, with illustrations for Lear and Margaret Mahy.)

Such small-scale, table-top work was a far cry from her earlier life. Her architect father became town planner for East Suffolk, and she was brought up in Felixstowe, on the Suffolk coast. 'We still have a boathouse right on the estuary: a lot of people think it's bleak, but I *love* that scenery—the clear light, the strip of land, the huge sky, the wheeling birds and the mudflats—oh, it's wonderful! The *freedom* that I and my brother, three years older, had was idyllic compared with today's children—we'd leave home in the mornings and not be seen or worried about till the evening meal.'

Only weekends and holidays like this allowed her to survive her Ipswich school—prim, all girls and very Victorian. 'I was absolutely miserable: they didn't like me and I didn't like them.' Her parents had struggled to send her there; a few miles away, her future husband (all unaware) was at A S Neill's Summerhill at Sizewell, which she's sure she'd have loved. (Could there be something about this coast to have produced, simultaneously though unknown to each other, Oxenbury, Burningham and Michael Foreman?)

'That school never caught my interest academically—perhaps art was the only thing I was good at. But Ipswich Art School was a whole new ballgame. It was like square-bashing—my goodness, you had to work—but I enjoyed it enormously: you were treated like an adult. And every holiday I used to do the menial tasks, like mixing paints and putting on base colours, in the Ipswich Repertory Theatre workshop. I *loved* it, and after two years thought I'd specialise in theatre design.

'I applied to the Central School in London, but didn't enjoy it like Ipswich. I had to do costume design—needlework, and how things are cut to get the look of the period—but I always got involved in how the people would look, and used to concentrate on their *faces!* One tutor said, "This is hopeless, you know. You ought to go and do illustration—you're more interested in the character and we don't *know* who's going to play the part!"

'It didn't click even then. I struggled on, sold on all the jolly times I'd had in the theatre at Ipswich.' After two years she became an assistant designer at Colchester Rep. at £7 a week. 'Now that was hard work—a play a week, a new set for each—but very interesting. We did the actual painting in a huge great warehouse: used to get *frozen!*'

But at the Central she'd met John. He'd gone out to Israel, where she now joined him as an au pair and teaching English conversation. 'I got work as assistant to the designer at the Habimah Theatre in Tel Aviv, unbelievably new and splendid. There wasn't that much competition then in Israel for set designers (I bet there is now), and I was given whole sets to do, with huge backdrops—it was I who had the assistant then!'

She was in Israel three years, off and on, and returned to a brief nine months with ABC TV at Teddington. Shepperton film studios followed—great fun. 'It was Judy Garland's last film—Carry On Singing? No, hardly . . . (actually, I Could Go On Singing)—and though I was totally insignificant, one of a huge team, I loved looking into the studios.'

She married John, and that was the end of the theatrical design. Exit huge backdrops; enter books for babies' hands.

'I began with pen and crayon because they're so easy to carry around (what a terrible reason!); when my first two were little we had a tiny flat, and a box of crayons, a pen and a bottle of ink take up little space.

I did **Pig Tale** in gouache, then moved on to watercolour; I want to try something else now, and am experimenting to see what I'm comfortable with.

'The difficulty with watercolour is that by its very nature you can't work on top of it—if you go wrong you have to scrap it and start again.' We spoke of the new problem confronting illustrators who like to work on card—watercolourists particularly, because of its effect on paper—when modern printing processes demand that the paper layer is peeled off. 'For Brian Alderson's **Cakes and Custard** I used crayon and pen on "fashion-plate" board (very shiny so won't take water), and when the shiny paper was peeled off it wrecked the whole thing. Might as well write it off. I shan't do that again!'

Analyse an Oxenbury face and it seems just eye-dots and a line, but this results from a thousand trial-runs. 'I enjoy trying to get expression with the minimum of line, though my early stuff was much more detailed—lips, eyelids, shading and hatching. Neither style is necessarily better—I may even change and go back. I love black and white line, but you come up against the sales force, who always want colour. You should have heard the "Oh-what-a-shame-it's-black-and- white" for **Bear Hunt:** if you do a cover that's limited in colour or black and white, they say it must be colour to stand out—but of course everyone else is in colour. Because the design team at Walker are brilliant, and they were all for having it as a drawing on the cover, we succeeded between us—but there was quite a resistance.'

Like so many who feel Sebastian Walker changed the whole climate for artists (and not only by his rates of pay), she slips easily into a paean of praise.

'They *listen* to you at Walker—I can't tell you what a breath of fresh air it was to be able to thrash things out with a designer! Nothing is too much trouble for Amelia Edwards, the design director. I can go in with an idea, or two, or three, and she'll say, "Helen, we'll try each way and see how they look." So often publishers say, "That's it," and off it goes to the design department; and you don't see it till it comes back, and then it's "Well, it's done now—sorry . . . "

'Sebastian has always said it's his artists and writers who make the books—without them there is nothing. I believe he's even started a crèche for his young mums. Simply, he's a genius: he's got it right!'

The Burninghams live on the edge of Hampstead Heath, having 'circulated around the area' since John's student days, in a splendidly idiosyncratic house that feels part baronial, part sunny farmhouse, overlooking a vast un-London garden. Like his older sister, their son is also at art school (Winchester), though they have great hopes that 11-year-old Emily will do something else . . . She'll have to be very determined, sandwiched between John's studio at garden level and Helen's up at the top of the house.

'It's John's flair that has made the house amazing. You see it now and you think, cor blimey!, but when we bought it, about 12 years ago, no one would have given tuppence for it. He loves architecture, goes to demolition sites, etc. and totally transforms everything.'

They were about to fly to France that afternoon, where a soft toy of Pippo, after years of problems and discussion (horrible velvet or washable, cuddly towelling? how to get the eyes sewn on straight? should the head be moulded?), is drawing near to actual production. Tom and his little monkey Pippo originated when the French, great magazine readers, for the first time started one for tinies, and asked her to create two characters, one of which would become a toy. Her five pages for the magazine turned easily into a book, and the series has become phenomenally successful. The same French company is talking of involving her in an animated film: very exciting.

She's open to any future idea, child or adult, and wistful that Emily's age group is now out of illustrated books. She enjoys working on texts by other writers, but couldn't work *with* them. 'The last one, **Bear Hunt,** was marvellous because it gave the illustrator so much—the characters were never defined in the text—but I had never met Michael Rosen until the actual Smarties Prize party. We know a few people from our world, but we're not "clubby".' Indeed, she's well-known as a quiet soul who shrinks from self-exposure, a reputation at odds with the sense of exuberance, of the joyful muddle of everyday life, in her work. She recognises at once a text she'll be comfortable with, rejecting hundreds on the way. The recipe also applies to her own books.

'It must have humour and be true to life—it can deal with a child's fantasy and still be rooted in things that are true. Above all, I look for warmth and humour—and characters that aren't absolutely wonderful and lovely!' And that's a recipe for not only a good book, but a good mum, too.

Helen Oxenbury

SOURCE: "The Artist at Work: Books for the Very Young," in *The Horn Book Magazine*, Vol. LXVIII, No. 5, October-November, 1992, pp. 555-59.

When I read a manuscript, either it instantly appeals to me or it doesn't. I can't convince myself to like a story. It's very difficult to put my finger on just what in a book attracts me. First, the story has to have a certain amount of humor. And I don't like very sentimental stories. I like books that are down to earth, that portray things and people as they are. I have to be able to see the characters. I read a lot of manuscripts and have a chance to make a choice in terms of what I illustrate. But very few texts appeal to me. A book constitutes over nine months of work, a good chunk of my life, so I have to really love what I'm working on.

My most recent book is Martin Waddell's **Farmer Duck,** about a duck on a farm who is left doing all the work while the lazy farmer stays in bed; eventually, the duck and all her friends give the farmer his comeuppance and end up running the farm. The plot appealed to me and gave me an extra edge to use in the illustrations.

We're Going on a Bear Hunt was a gift. I had free rein. The editor at Walker Books said that he had heard Michael Rosen act the song out and had told Michael that he must write his version down. I knew the song from when my children were little, and I knew instantly that I wanted to illustrate Michael's version. Up until then I hadn't done much landscape illustration because there had been no need—very young children like simple drawings and situations they can relate to. So here was an opportunity to add another dimension by creating atmosphere in different landscapes, and I found myself being drawn to the landscape of my childhood.

I was brought up in Suffolk by a river estuary, and the surrounding landscape was characterized by mud flats, huge East Anglian skies, and crisp air. The quality of light is very particular, clearer and brighter than the south and west of England. But Suffolk can be freezing cold and very bleak—which doesn't put off the huge variety of wading birds, though a lot of people find it too austere in the winter months.

I've always drawn. My father used to send my drawings off to competitions, and they seemed to do well. Drawing was one of the few things I was good at in school. My father was an architect, so there was no opposition to my going to art school. I thoroughly enjoyed art school; imagine every day being allowed to do something you really enjoy.

The first art school I went to was quite general; we did everything from sculpture to painting. I had some excellent teachers—one man in particular, who really made me think about color. He was a fabric designer. There was another, extremely good teacher of whom I was absolutely terrified. Thirty years later, I can still, in my head, hear his sarcastic—but hilarious—criticisms.

My husband, John Burningham, has been a very strong influence as well. I learned the rather specialized process of creating picture books—as opposed to fine art—mostly from him. John works in the most extraordinary way. He'll draw on a piece of tissue paper or some other little scrap of paper, and if the drawing has the right feel, he'll keep it. Then his publishers have to reprint it somehow. He uses everything, sticks his illustrations anywhere on a page, and creates these terribly messy drawings—but he knows what they are going to look like printed. A picture that is not "finished" can be enhanced by the printing process, whereas a beautifully perfected drawing can be a disappointment when printed.

John and I don't work in the same place. We've never worked together. I can think of a lot of people who do actually create books together, but I'm not sure that would work for us. We certainly ask each other, "What do you think about this drawing?"; we consult each other about our work. I hope we help each other. In a way it's quite nice to know, when very specific difficulties arise with drawings, that he has been through these problems as well. There are bad days when nothing goes right and you think you'll never produce anything again.

I met John at art school in London. I used to work in the theater during school holidays, painting scenery, and I thought it would be very nice to learn more about it, become more proficient. So I took a course in theater design at art school, and John was studying illustration. We eventually left; I went to work in the theater, and he started illustrating books. The more I saw him working on books, the more I thought that I would love to try it myself. When I had my first child, working in the theater became impossible. So I illustrated a children's book, a counting book without text. I took it to Heinemann Books, and they, amazingly, accepted it.

Then Walker Books started publishing. I was in the hospital having my third child, and Sebastian Walker came to see me there. I suspected it wasn't just the baby he had come to see, and books very soon came into the conversation. There was something about him that made me want to work with him. And, twenty-five books later, I'm still working with Walker Books, now an extremely successful children's book publisher.

Sebastian was the one who first interested me in the idea of creating books for very young children. My daughter was a baby at the time, and I found there was almost nothing for her age—except, of course, the excellent board books by Dick Bruna. So, when I was looking for board books for Emily, I thought I could perhaps fill that gap in the English market. Sebastian was very enthusiastic about the idea. I found that the actual process of working on a board book was the same as the process for any picture book. It's just a question of paring down for the age group, trying to keep the concepts extremely simple—objects and situations that very small children will recognize.

If you were to see the art for the book I'm working on at the moment, you would also see a pile of rejects about twice the size of the actual book—especially since I work in watercolor, which is quite a difficult medium. If I make a mistake, I have to start all over again. First of all, I work the drawing out on layout paper, making corrections before I am finally practiced enough to abandon it and attempt the final drawing with watercolor on watercolor paper. One has to be careful not to become too bogged down with technique. The illustrations, after all, are complementary to the text and, at best, add to it.

Personally, I don't like over-designed books, because even though they might be extremely beautiful, some can have a slightly dead quality. I would like to get freer in my work, but I know that I mustn't lose sight of the fact that these illustrations are for children.

The publishing climate in Britain has changed since I began doing children's books. There certainly wasn't the competition that there is now—although Brian Wildsmith, Charles Keeping, John, and a few others were creating exciting books. And there was, of course, a very distinguished backlist of children's books. There are so many more illustrators now. I would not like to start out as a new illustrator today. In those days we got a kind of nurturing; we were able to make mistakes, to think about what we wanted to do. We were very lucky.

I get quite a few letters from parents, especially about the board books. Babies seem to recognize the situations in the books, and the letters tell me that that's what babies really like. There were a surprising number of letters about the Pippo books. These actually started off as a feature of a monthly magazine in France called *Popi*. The editors there wanted me to create two characters, one being a toy and the other a child, and the Pippo stories are what we came up with.

I used to work at home, but it was difficult. I would just have put the washing in and finally started work when somebody would arrive at the door. There's always something to stop one working. So, I got a studio last summer. It's absolutely wonderful. I take my daughter to school; I drop her off at eight o'clock and am at my studio by half past eight. When she gets out of school at four, she comes to my studio and does her homework. It's lovely, after all these years, to have a whole day of uninterrupted time in which to work.

As far as editing is concerned, I think I know now what works and what doesn't in illustration. But still, there's no particular illustration that I can point to and say, "That's it. That's exactly what I wanted." It would be lovely, but it hasn't happened yet—not quite. There are artists who I think have achieved what I am striving for. Edward Ardizzone, for instance. His work has all the qualities that I love: great humor and warmth.

Seeing the finished product is not the best part of doing books. Absolutely not. I can't bear to look at the finished book, because I can't change anything at that point. No, the best part is when I think I know what I'm doing and I've completed a few drawings. In fact, when I get about a third of the way through, and I feel I'm on my way, when I'm happy. It's like reading a good book—you don't want it to end.

Helen Oxenbury and Susan Thomas

SOURCE: An interview in *The Times Educational Supplement,* No. 4111, April 14, 1995, pp. 17-18.

Helen Oxenbury clasps a steaming mug of coffee, leans back in her chair, gazes into space and smiles—a small crescent moon of pleasure, seeing not the garden, the elaborate terraces and early spring flowers but babies. Babies in baths and puddles, highchairs and swings—and particularly Emily, her last child, going stiff with excitement, entranced by the pictures her mother had made.

"You never forget how they look," she says. "The tiny fingernails, the little straight necks that go all the way down their backs and make you sit up." She is slim and dark-eyed, a mass of brown hair piled above a perfect oval face—an illustrator's dream.

Helen Oxenbury is married to John Burningham, fellow children's writer and illustrator. They live in a tall, gaunt house on the edge of Hampstead Health in north London which has been recreated and filled with all sorts of architectural delights tracked down in builders' yards—fireplaces, fancy tiles, grand balustrades. John, she says, is fearfully good at these things. These days she works in a separate studio but for long enough they worked at opposite ends of the house—Helen in the attic, John in the basement.

Childhood and the countryside are recurring themes in her conversation. Living opposite Hampstead Heath, she goes there every day to walk the dogs and observe—but not to draw. She is aghast at the thought. "People would look and I'd feel compelled to say—I'm much better than this really." And this from a Kate Greenaway medallist for illustration and twice winner of the Smarties Prize for children's books!

But in any case she draws more on the pale open landscapes of East Anglia for inspiration. "I grew up on the Suffolk coast—a wonderful free and easy childhood," she says, as we talk of children's lack of freedom now. "My brother and I used to go off for the whole day only coming back for food. And nobody worried."

School was dreadful. "John, funnily enough, was quite nearby at [A S Neill's] Summerhill—I'm sure I would have been much happier there—but we didn't meet till I went to the Central School (in London) after art school in Suffolk."

Helen did her "square bashing"—hours of life drawing, and the basis of theatre design—at Ipswich Art School, but John missed out on this basic training. He says that as a result Helen often points out where his anatomy doesn't work. She is, he says, fussy about shoulders.

They met again in Israel where Helen worked as an assistant set designer at the Habimah theatre in Tel Aviv. Marriage, a tiny flat in Hampstead and a dramatic change of scale followed. It was Jan Pieńkowski, illustrator and creator of the "Meg and Mog" series, who suggested that she try a children's book, and the new career was under way.

"I cannot imagine now where I found the energy. But as soon as the children were in bed I would clear a space on the kitchen table and start work."

For some reason, the two older children were never involved in her work—something which did not stop them making their own careers in art—but with the advent of Emily, her third child, her career took a

new turn. Emily's arrival coincided with the advent of Walker Books, a new publishing company, co-founded by the late Sebastian Walker, which took the then-unfashionable approach that children deserved only the best writers and illustrators.

"Sebastian didn't feel the fact the baby was imminent was any reason not to start work—only to start more promptly." He wrote afterwards that he was so delighted by Helen's agreement, so touched by her refusal of a paltry £500 downpayment, which was all he could afford in the early days, that he promptly reversed his car into a lamp post. "I never had the dent removed. I called it the Oxenbury bump and felt that it brought me luck." And so it did.

Those first Walker books were little spiral-bound sectional affairs with a choice of 729 improbable, and sometimes risqué, combinations of heads, bodies and legs—a sure-fire hit with toddlers and grandparents and still selling. But it was when Emily was aged three months that Helen found a whole new market niche.

"I suddenly discovered that there weren't any books for that age group. Yet Emily loved to look at bright pictures in magazines. That's how the Little Baby Board Books were born. When I showed them to her, her whole little body would go stiff with excitement.

"It was extraordinary. I had never involved the older children in my work at all, but I suppose I was just so much more relaxed with her."

From then on Emily's needs became a source of ideas. The board books were followed by picture story books for the under-fives, introducing those early rites of passage—the visit to the doctor, the dance class, the car journey which invariably leave the adult exhausted, the child triumphant.

While she continued to work for Heinemann, more and more books came in from Walkers. "All exciting. It was a new team, doing things differently, full of enthusiasm and determined to make it work."

She has illustrated Michael Rosen, Martin Waddell and recently Trish Cooke, whose *So Much,* a tale of a much-loved black toddler and his whole laughing, dancing, adoring extended family took her down to Brixton. "I used to sit in a cafe by the market just watching . . . smart grannies in hats, little girls in wonderful party frocks. And the boys! Those huge trainers, caps on back to front, jeans with the crotch half-way down to the knees, and wonderfully un-English combinations of colour."

So Much went on to win the Kurt Maschler Award and the Smarties Prize in the 0-5 category in 1994. All the best picture books, says Helen Oxenbury, leave the visual element entirely to the artist. Authors like Trish Cooke or Michael Rosen just stick to narrative.

"Sometimes, as in *We're going on a Bear Hunt* you don't even know who the characters are or how many. . . . that is an illustrator's delight!"

She never discusses the story or characters with the author, and often does not meet them until the book is finished.

The relationship with Walker Books continued after Sebastian Walker's death in July 1991. "He was such a lovely man—nothing was too much trouble. Everybody knows about the wonderful free lunches and fresh flowers for the staff, but they don't know how much care they take over the production of your work getting it absolutely right. I work very closely with Amelia Edwards, the art director, and I can say 'I'm not sure whether it would look better this way or that' and she will say 'We'll try it all ways.' And she does. No one else would do that."

Amelia Edwards is one of the intrepid band of three who set up the company including Wendy Boase, Walker's editorial director. Amelia is ecstatic about Helen's work. "It is not just that she was in at the beginning but that she is so good, so endlessly creative . . . changing style, format, medium, and of course she created the Walker bear."

David Lloyd, chairman of Walker Books, remembers that birth 10 years ago. "Sebastian and I were looking for a logo. We'd seen a rather nice Patrick Benson illustration for a book by William Mayne—a little old spirit called Hob walking along holding a candle and casting long shadows. It seemed a fearfully good image but we weren't sure we could have someone from the hidden world. So we decided on a bear and Helen came up with it. It did the trick."

Walker Books were the first publishers to make it through the supermarket checkouts, and Helen Oxenbury was in at the start. "There was rather a hoo-ha at first," she says, "because all the bookshops thought it was going to ruin their sales, but I was rather for it. In fact I think it has had the reverse effect and the supermarkets have reached a whole new set of people."

The only drawback is having to produce a format. "And now," she says darkly, "they are doing dreadful things to my covers—pink for this age, orange for that. And yes . . . I do think they know that I'm not keen."

Attitudes to books and, above all to the quality of illustration have changed over the past two decades. "As a nation we are becoming more and more visually literate," says Ameila Edwards. "And the quality of illustrators has just gone skyhigh. So many talented young people are coming out of art school with the most wonderful creative ideas."

It was Sebastian Walker, says Helen Oxenbury, who was largely responsible for this blossoming of children's books. "He took children seriously. Only the best was good enough for them. And he took writers and illustrators seriously while other publishers wanted people to be machines. The result was that more and more good people appeared on the doorstep, and more and more good books came out."

As for what makes a good book: "Good books are true," says David Lloyd. "It might seem strange that a book about a lazy farmer who makes his duck do all the work, or a little bear that is frightened of the dark, is true but children recognise the truth at once."

That's it then. Helen Oxenbury's books are true. They are about ordinary families where things go right or wrong, where people are happy and sad and funny and cross and in the end it is all right because they are, above all, loving families. The trick is to show it all in the angle of the head, the set of a chin, the line of the shoulder.

TITLE COMMENTARY

📖 *THE "TOM AND PIPPO" SERIES*

Kirkus Reviews

SOURCE: A review of *Tom and Pippo and the Washing Machine* and others, in *Kirkus Reviews,* Vol. 56, No. 20, October 15, 1988, p. 1532.

From one of the finest practitioners of the art of the picture book for the youngest children, four disarming vignettes about a toddler and his toy monkey: Pippo, who has played in the mud, goes into the washing machine after a poignant kiss goodbye in case he never gets out; after a walk on a cold day when both Tom and Pippo fall into a puddle, Mommy gives them separate baths and a warm drink together by the fire; Tom likes to do what Daddy does—including scolding poor Pippo as instigator when Tom makes a mess by "helping" with the painting; and when Daddy is tired of reading to Tom, Tom "reads" to Pippo. In each book, busy little Tom is happy to learn by doing, imagining Pippo as his surrogate.

Oxenbury uses simple language, though [***Tom and Pippo and the Washing Machine***] is lengthy enough to extend listeners' verbal ability and to contain some subtle nuances in these healthy relationships. Her clear, admirably drawn illustrations are full of amusing detail, including expressions on faces—Pippo's comically show emotion despite his limp, long-suffering form. Pages are very sturdy but flexible—fine alternative to board books for tiny fingers learning to turn pages. Wonderful.

Beth Herbert

SOURCE: A review of *Tom and Pippo Go Shopping* and others, in *Booklist,* Vol. 85, No. 14, March 15, 1989, pp. 1302-03.

Oxenbury serves up four more stories about the toddler, Tom, and his toy monkey, Pippo, to captivate the very young. As the duo participate in commonplace activities that to them seem like adventures, Pippo suffers the indignities of beloved stuffed animals everywhere. Not only is he fed dirt and blamed for his owner's mistake, but he also loses his snacks to Tom and is callously tossed aside in favor of Daddy. Yet Tom cannot fall asleep without his beloved monkey, an attachment that many children will readily understand. Oxenbury's graphics are, as always, charming; amply executed in soft colors, they take up the entire right hand page. The left side is devoted to an enticing mix of text and pen-and-ink drawings, integral to the stories. Printed on extra-sturdy paper, these winning books will help ease the transition from board books to longer stories.

Sharron McElmeel

SOURCE: A review of *Tom and Pippo and the Washing Machine* and others, in *School Library Journal,* Vol. 35, No. 8, April, 1989, pp. 88-9.

Four delightful books with single concepts developed through the simple texts. Tom and his stuffed monkey, Pippo, get into the types of mischief that children are bound to find. In the first book, Tom and Pippo play in the mud and get dirty; Tom is put in the bathtub and Pippo goes into the washing machine and is hung on the line to dry. In the second, they go for a walk and get dirty. In the next, the two of them watch Tom's dad paint a room, and they make a mess when they help. In the fourth book, the father reads to Tom and Pippo, and in turn Tom reads to Pippo and falls to sleep musing that he "hope[s] one day Pippo can read on his own." Brightly washed illustrations show the two friends realistically drawn. These are comfortable books for lap reading to young audiences, and the large, clear typeface is well chosen for children who are just beginning to read. They will surely want to hear the stories again and again (and to tell the stories themselves). These are well designed and appealing books.

Ellen Fader

SOURCE: A review of *Tom and Pippo Go Shopping* and others, in *The Horn Book Magazine,* Vol. LXV, No. 3, May-June, 1989, pp. 361-62.

Very young children are lucky, indeed, as Helen Oxenbury continues, in a second quartet of books, the adventures of Tom and his stuffed toy monkey Pippo. Identical in format to the previous four titles, the books offer brief but insightful glimpses into events of a small boy's life. In the limited experience of a toddler these incidents are the equivalent of full-blown adventures. In the first book Mommy takes everyone shopping for food, but Pippo gets nothing when all the snacks Tom requests for his monkey end up in his own stomach. Tom escorts Pippo on a bumpy walk around the garden in the second title and feeds him his lunch, dirt from a bucket. "Pippo makes a mess when he eats. He gets food all over his face. So I have to wipe him with a washcloth." In the third book Tom decides that one day he and Pippo will go on trip to the moon. The final book details the major events of Tom's day, from waking to sleeping, always accompanied by his monkey friend. "When it's bedtime, sometimes I don't know where Pippo is and I have to look everywhere until I find him. Because when it's time to go to sleep, I need to be with Pippo." The books have an open feeling, with a smaller line drawing on one side facing a full-page, brightly-colored picture on the opposite. Amusing visual details abound: in ***Tom and Pippo See the Moon*** Tom flies Pippo through the air like a rocket; Tom, Pippo, and Daddy wear space suits for their trip; and a painting of a cow jumping over the moon hangs over Tom's bed. On paper heavier than usual but not quite as sturdy as that used in the author's board books for younger children, these volumes have been designed with children in mind. Oxenbury understands her audience; young people as well as adults will find pleasure in repeated readings of these unassuming gems, and no one will be able to resist the facial expressions and postures of the long-suffering Pippo.

Books for Keeps

SOURCE: A review of *Tom and Pippo and the Dog* and others, in *Books for Keeps,* No. 60, January, 1990, p. 6.

Tom and his toy monkey Pippo go out for a walk with Mummy and meet a dog in the park. The dog runs away with Pippo. Happily Pippo is quickly restored to his owner and the bad dog suitably chastised.

Just right for small children battling with the problems of their world and it is beautifully drawn . . . as are the others in the series of ten. I particularly like *Tom and Pippo Make a Friend* which deals with the issue of sharing, and again in this simple story the sharing is happily resolved. *Tom and Pippo in the Snow* is fun too. It's about going sledging with Daddy and tells about that frightening feeling of being all by yourself on the sledge for the first time. *Pippo Gets Lost* deals with the homey everyday happening when a special toy is lost and the whole family is involved in looking for it everywhere. Eventually when it is found there is great relief all round.

These books are entirely suitable for small children (2-4s) I think and should be a most welcome addition to the Nursery shelves.

Carolyn Phelan

SOURCE: A review of *Tom and Pippo on the Beach,* in *Booklist,* Vol. 89, Nos. 19 & 20, June 1 & 15, 1993, pp. 1859-60.

When Daddy insists that little Tom needs a hat to protect him from the sun at the beach [in *Tom and Pippo on the Beach*], Tom reasons that if he needs a hat, his stuffed monkey, Pippo, does too. Generously, he puts the unwanted headgear on his monkey's head. Daddy makes Pippo a newspaper hat, which Pippo dislikes, so Tom wears it instead. That's the story,

and it wouldn't make much of a book, were it not for Oxenbury's beguiling illustrations. Enhanced by her sensitive line drawings, some washed with delicate, seaside colors, this little picture book is one that many toddlers and their parents will enjoy. The interplay of the three characters and the familiar activities and emotions acted out on the pages make this slight story into another charmer for Tom and Pippo fans.

Martha V. Parravano

SOURCE: A review of *Tom and Pippo on the Beach,* in *The Horn Book Magazine,* Vol. XXXIX, No. 8, July-August, 1993, p. 449.

When Daddy and Tom go to the beach for the day—"and of course Pippo came too"—Tom refuses to wear his blue-and-white checked sunhat, despite his father's urging, and puts it on Pippo instead. Daddy wisely counters by making a hat out of newspaper for Pippo to wear; Tom, deciding that his friend Pippo doesn't look happy in the tricornered paper hat, has another idea—not exactly what Daddy had in mind, but a solution that makes everyone happy nonetheless. Tom switches hats with Pippo. "I'm glad Pippo's got the best hat, so he won't feel sick in the sun." Once again, as in the other books about Tom and his stuffed monkey, Oxenbury humorously and gently illuminates toddler behavior as she portrays a warm, solicitous friendship. The illustrator's unpretentious pencil sketches and full-page watercolors have a child's-eye vantage point perfect for the child-centered story. At the end [of *Tom and Pippo on the Beach*], Tom and Pippo—each in their chosen hats—gaze out of the small, sturdy book, Tom with a protective arm around Pippo, as Daddy looks benevolently on. A lovely vignette.

Jeanne Marie Clancy

SOURCE: A review of *Tom and Pippo on the Beach,* in *School Library Journal,* Vol. 39, No. 8, August, 1993, p. 149.

Anyone who reads to toddlers will be thrilled with the return of Oxenbury's Tom and his stuffed monkey, Pippo. In this title, Daddy takes the guys to the beach for the day and wants Tom to wear a sun hat. When the toddler insists that Pippo needs it, the unflappable father has the answer—a handmade, newsprint hat. Tom happily dons the three-cornered creation because Pippo must, of course, wear the best one. While in a different format from the previous books about the pair (Aladdin), this title still features

Oxenbury's signature illustrations. The pages alternate pen-and-ink sketches with watercolor paintings in which Tom splashes in the waves, totes buckets of water, and builds castles while Pippo looks on. As ever, the author's simple plot is right on target for young listeners. Here's hoping there will be many more Tom and Pippo adventures to follow.

IT'S MY BIRTHDAY (1994)

Publishers Weekly

SOURCE: A review of *It's My Birthday,* in *Publishers Weekly* Vol. 241, No. 25, June 20, 1994, p. 104.

Oxenbury brings her considerable talents to bear on this slender but winsome picture book. "It's my birthday and I'm going to make a cake," announces a child, and one by one a host of animal friends offer their contributions—an egg from the chicken, flour from the bear, salt from the pig and so on. Perfectly paced, the story celebrates friendship and ends, naturally, with a party. Like the casts of Else Holmelund Minarik's classic tales, the animals are gently anthropomorphized, and the affection they display toward one another underscores the story's theme. Oxenbury deliberately leaves the child's gender ambiguous, making it all that much easier for every reader to identify with her character. As always, her understated watercolors are filled with whimsy—from a picnicking otter family that lends salt to the pig to a bespectacled sheep at the market cash register—and they shine with the quiet resplendence of happy family life.

Hazel Rochman

SOURCE: A review of *It's My Birthday,* in *Booklist,* Vol. 90, No. 21, July, 1994, p. 1956.

A toddler gathers the ingredients one by one and makes a cake for his birthday with the help of his animal friends. Without being cute or condescending, Oxenbury tells a cumulative story for the very young child with clear watercolors and a simple, cheerful text. The telling has a satisfying rhythm and repetition. "It's my birthday and I'm going to make a cake," says the boy each time he names the ingredients he has and asks for the one he needs. The pictures are funny and surprising: the cat grabs the butter and milk from the refrigerator when no one's looking: the pig gets a pinch of salt from a friendly beaver family on a picnic; the monkey picks some cherries for the top of the cake. In the end the friends help the boy mix the cake, and he invites them all to the party to eat it.

Additonal coverage of Oxenbury's life and career is contained in the following sources published by the Gale Group: *Contemporary Authors,* **Vols. 25-28R;** *Contemporary Authors,* **Vols. 35, 79;** *Dictionary of Literary Biography,* **Vols. 141,153, 178;** *Junior DISCovering Authors;* *Major Authors and Illustrators for Children and Young Adults;* *Major 20th-Century Writers;* *St. James Guide to Children's Writers;* *Something about the Author,* **Vols. 3, 68.**

How to Use This Index

The main reference

> **Baum, L(yman) Frank**
> 1856-1919 .... **15**

lists all author entries in this and previous volumes of *Children's Literature Review*.

The cross-references

> See also CA 103; 108; DLB 22; JRDA;
> MAICYA; MTCW; SATA 18; TCLC 7

list all author entries in the following Gale biographical and literary sources:

AAYA = *Authors & Artists for Young Adults*
AITN = *Authors in the News*
BLC = *Black Literature Criticism*
BLCS = *Black Literature Criticism Supplement*
BW = *Black Writers*
CA = *Contemporary Authors*
CAAS = *Contemporary Authors Autobiography Series*
CABS = *Contemporary Authors Bibliographical Series*
CANR = *Contemporary Authors New Revision Series*
CAP = *Contemporary Authors Permanent Series*
CDALB = *Concise Dictionary of American Literary Biography*
CDBLB = *Concise Dictionary of British Literary Biography*
CLC = *Contemporary Literary Criticism*
CMLC = *Classical and Medieval Literature Criticism*
DA = *DISCovering Authors*
DAB = *DISCovering Authors: British*
DAC = *DISCovering Authors: Canadian*
DAM = *DISCovering Authors: Modules*
    DRAM: *Dramatists Module;* **MST:** *Most-Studied Authors Module;*
    MULT: *Multicultural Authors Module;* **NOV:** *Novelists Module;*
    POET: *Poets Module;* **POP:** *Popular Fiction and Genre Authors Module*
DC = *Drama Criticism*
DLB = *Dictionary of Literary Biography*
DLBD = *Dictionary of Literary Biography Documentary Series*
DLBY = *Dictionary of Literary Biography Yearbook*
HLC = *Hispanic Literature Criticism*
HLCS = *Hispanic Literature Criticism Supplement*
HW = *Hispanic Writers*
JRDA = *Junior DISCovering Authors*
LC = *Literature Criticism from 1400 to 1800*
MAICYA = *Major Authors and Illustrators for Children and Young Adults*
MTCW = *Major 20th-Century Writers*
NCLC = *Nineteenth-Century Literature Criticism*
NNAL = *Native North American Literature*
PC = *Poetry Criticism*
SAAS = *Something about the Author Autobiography Series*
SATA = *Something about the Author*
SSC = *Short Story Criticism*
TCLC = *Twentieth-Century Literary Criticism*
WLC = *World Literature Criticism, 1500 to the Present*
WLCS = *World Literature Criticism Supplement*
YABC = *Yesterday's Authors of Books for Children*

CLR Cumulative Author Index

Sanchez, Sonia 1934- **18**
See also BLC 3; BW 2, 3; CA 33-36R;
CANR 24, 49, 74; CLC 5, 116; DAM
MULT; DA3; DLB 41; DLBD 8; MAI-
CYA; MTCW 1, 2; PC 9; SATA 22
Sanchez-Silva, Jose Maria 1911- **12**
See also CA 73-76; MAICYA; SATA 16
Sandburg, Carl (August) 1878-1967 ...... **67**
See also AAYA 24; CA 5-8R; 25-28R;
CANR 35; CDALB 1865-1917; CLC 1,
4, 10, 15, 35; DA; DAB; DAC; DAM
MST, POET; DA3; DLB 17, 54; MAI-
CYA; MTCW 1, 2; PC 2; SATA 8
Sandburg, Charles
See Sandburg, Carl (August)
Sandburg, Charles A.
See Sandburg, Carl (August)
Sanders, Winston P.
See Anderson, Poul (William)
San Souci, Robert D. 1946- **43**
See also CA 108; CANR 46, 79; SATA 40,
81, 117
Sasek, Miroslav 1916-1980 .... **4**
See also CA 73-76; 101; SATA 16; SATA-
Obit 23
Sattler, Helen Roney 1921-1992 .... **24**
See also CA 33-36R; CANR 14, 31; SATA
4, 74
Sawyer, Ruth 1880-1970 .... **36**
See also CA 73-76; CANR 37, 83; DLB 22;
MAICYA; SATA 17
Say, Allen 1937- **22**
See also CA 29-32R; CANR 30; JRDA;
MAICYA; SATA 28, 69, 110
Scarlett, Susan
See Streatfeild, (Mary) Noel
Scarry, Richard (McClure) 1919-1994 . **3, 41**
See also CA 17-20R; 145; CANR 18, 39,
83; DLB 61; MAICYA; SATA 2, 35, 75;
SATA-Obit 90
Schlein, Miriam 1926- **41**
See also CA 1-4R; CANR 2, 52, 87; SATA
2, 87
Schmidt, Annie M. G. 1911-1995 .... **22**
See also CA 135; 152; SATA 67; SATA-
Obit 91
Schwartz, Alvin 1927-1992 .... **3**
See also CA 13-16R; 137; CANR 7, 24, 49,
86; MAICYA; SATA 4, 56; SATA-Obit 71
Schwartz, Amy 1954- **25**
See also CA 110; CANR 29, 57; INT
CANR-29; SAAS 18; SATA 47, 83;
SATA-Brief 41
Schweitzer, Byrd Baylor
See Baylor, Byrd
Scieszka, Jon 1954- **27**
See also AAYA 21; CA 135; CANR 84;
SATA 68, 105
Scott, Jack Denton 1915-1995 .... **20**
See also CA 108; CANR 48, 86; MAICYA;
SAAS 14; SATA 31, 83
Sebastian, Lee
See Silverberg, Robert
Sebestyen, Ouida 1924- **17**
See also AAYA 8; AW; CA 107; CANR 40;
CLC 30; JRDA; MAICYA; SAAS 10;
SATA 39
Sefton, Catherine
See Waddell, Martin
Selden, George **8**
See also Thompson, George Selden
See also DLB 52
Selsam, Millicent Ellis 1912-1996 .... **1**
See also CA 9-12R; 154; CANR 5, 38;
MAICYA; SATA 1, 29; SATA-Obit 92
Sendak, Maurice (Bernard) 1928- **1, 17**
See also CA 5-8R; CANR 11, 39; DLB 61;
INT CANR-11; MAICYA; MTCW 1, 2;
SATA 1, 27, 113

Seredy, Kate 1899-1975 .... **10**
See also CA 5-8R; 57-60; CANR 83; DLB
22; MAICYA; SATA 1; SATA-Obit 24
Serraillier, Ian (Lucien) 1912-1994 .... **2**
See also AW; CA 1-4R; 147; CANR 1, 83;
DLB 161; MAICYA; SAAS 3; SATA 1,
73; SATA-Obit 83
Seton, Ernest (Evan) Thompson 1860-1946
.... **59**
See also CA 109; DLB 92; DLBD 13;
JRDA; SATA 18; TCLC 31
Seton-Thompson, Ernest
See Seton, Ernest (Evan) Thompson
Seuss, Dr.
See Dr. Seuss; Geisel, Theodor Seuss
Sewell, Anna 1820-1878 .... **17**
See also DLB 163; JRDA; MAICYA; SATA
24, 100
Sharp, Margery 1905-1991 .... **27**
See also CA 21-24R; 134; CANR 18, 85;
DLB 161; MAICYA; SATA 1, 29; SATA-
Obit 67
Shearer, John 1947- **34**
See also CA 125; SATA 43; SATA-Brief 27
Shepard, Ernest Howard 1879-1976 .... **27**
See also CA 9-12R; 65-68; CANR 23, 86;
DLB 160; MAICYA; SATA 3, 33, 100;
SATA-Obit 24
Shippen, Katherine B(inney) 1892-1980 . **36**
See also CA 5-8R; 93-96; CANR 86; SATA
1; SATA-Obit 23
Showers, Paul C. 1910-1999 .... **6**
See also CA 1-4R; 183; CANR 4, 38, 59;
MAICYA; SAAS 7; SATA 21, 92; SATA-
Obit 114
Shulevitz, Uri 1935- **5, 61**
See also CA 9-12R; CANR 3; DLB 61;
MAICYA; SATA 3, 50, 106
Silverberg, Robert 1935- **59**
See also AAYA 24; CA 1-4R; 186; CAAE
186; CAAS 3; CANR 1, 20, 36, 85; CLC
7, 140; DAM POP; DLB 8; INT CANR-
20; MAICYA; MTCW 1, 2; SATA 13, 91;
SATA-Essay 104; SCFW 2
Silverstein, Alvin 1933- **25**
See also CA 49-52; CANR 2; CLC 17;
JRDA; MAICYA; SATA 8, 69
Silverstein, Shel(don Allan) 1932-1999 ..... **5**
See also BW 3; CA 107; 179; CANR 47,
74, 81; JRDA; MAICYA; MTCW 2;
SATA 33, 92; SATA-Brief 27; SATA-Obit
116
Silverstein, Virginia B(arbara Opshelor)
1937- **25**
See also CA 49-52; CANR 2; CLC 17;
JRDA; MAICYA; SATA 8, 69
Simmonds, Posy **23**
Simon, Hilda Rita 1921- **39**
See also CA 77-80; SATA 28
Simon, Seymour 1931- **9, 63**
See also CA 25-28R; CANR 11, 29; MAI-
CYA; SATA 4, 73
Singer, Isaac
See Singer, Isaac Bashevis
Singer, Isaac Bashevis 1904-1991 .... **1**
See also AAYA 32; AITN 1, 2; AW; CA
1-4R; 134; CANR 1, 39; CDALB 1941-
1968; CLC 1, 3, 6, 9, 11, 15, 23, 38, 69,
111; DA; DAB; DAC; DAM MST, NOV;
DA3; DLB 6, 28, 52; DLBY 91; JRDA;
MAICYA; MTCW 1, 2; SATA 3, 27;
SATA-Obit 68; SSC 3
Singer, Marilyn 1948- **48**
See also AW; CA 65-68; CANR 9, 39, 85;
JRDA; MAICYA; SAAS 13; SATA 48,
80; SATA-Brief 38
Sis, Peter 1949- **45**
See also CA 128; SATA 67, 106

Sleator, William (Warner III) 1945- **29**
See also AAYA 5, 39; CA 29-32R; CANR
46, 83; JRDA; MAICYA; SATA 3, 68, 118
Slote, Alfred 1926- **4**
See also JRDA; MAICYA; SAAS 21; SATA
8, 72
Small, David 1945- **53**
See also SATA 50, 95; SATA-Brief 46
Smith, Dick King
See King-Smith, Dick
Smith, Jessie Willcox 1863-1935 .... **59**
See also CA 190; DLB 188; MAICYA;
SATA 21
Smith, Lane 1959- **47**
See also AAYA 21; CA 143; SATA 76
Smucker, Barbara (Claassen) 1915- **10**
See also CA 106; CANR 23; JRDA; MAI-
CYA; SAAS 11; SATA 29, 76
Sneve, Virginia Driving Hawk 1933- **2**
See also CA 49-52; CANR 3, 68; SATA 8,
95
Snyder, Zilpha Keatley 1927- **31**
See also AAYA 15; AW; CA 9-12R; CANR
38; CLC 17; JRDA; MAICYA; SAAS 2;
SATA 1, 28, 75, 110; SATA-Essay 112
Sobol, Donald J. 1924- **4**
See also CA 1-4R; CANR 1, 18, 38; JRDA;
MAICYA; SATA 1, 31, 73
Soto, Gary 1952- **38**
See also AAYA 10, 37; AW; CA 119; 125;
CANR 50, 74; CLC 32, 80; DAM MULT;
DLB 82; HLC 2; HW 1, 2; INT 125;
JRDA; MTCW 2; PC 28; SATA 80, 120
Souci, Robert D. San
See San Souci, Robert D.
Southall, Ivan (Francis) 1921- **2**
See also AAYA 22; AW; CA 9-12R; CANR
7, 47; JRDA; MAICYA; SAAS 3; SATA
3, 68
Speare, Elizabeth George 1908-1994 .... **8**
See also AW; CA 1-4R; 147; JRDA; MAI-
CYA; SATA 5, 62; SATA-Obit 83
Spence, Eleanor (Rachel) 1928- **26**
See also AW; CA 49-52; CANR 3; SATA
21
Spencer, Leonard G.
See Silverberg, Robert
Spier, Peter (Edward) 1927- **5**
See also CA 5-8R; CANR 41; DLB 61;
MAICYA; SATA 4, 54
Spinelli, Jerry 1941- **26**
See also AAYA 11; AW; CA 111; CANR
30, 45; JRDA; MAICYA; SATA 39, 71,
110
Spykman, E(lizabeth) C(hoate) 1896-1965
.... **35**
See also CA 101; SATA 10
Spyri, Johanna (Heusser) 1827-1901 ...... **13**
See also CA 137; MAICYA; SATA 19, 100
Stanley, Diane 1943- **46**
See also CA 112; CANR 32, 64; SAAS 15;
SATA 37, 80, 115; SATA-Brief 32
Stanton, Schuyler
See Baum, L(yman) Frank
Staples, Suzanne Fisher 1945- **60**
See also AAYA 26; AW; CA 132; CANR
82; SATA 70, 105
Starbird, Kaye 1916- **60**
See also CA 17-20R; CANR 38; MAICYA;
SATA 6
Staunton, Schuyler
See Baum, L(yman) Frank
Steig, William (H.) 1907- **2, 15**
See also AITN 1; CA 77-80; CANR 21, 44;
DLB 61; INT CANR-21; MAICYA; SATA
18, 70, 111
Steptoe, John (Lewis) 1950-1989 .... **2, 12**
See also BW 1; CA 49-52; 129; CANR 3,
26, 81; MAICYA; SATA 8, 63

CLR Cumulative Nationality Index

AMERICAN

Aardema, Verna **17**
Aaseng, Nathan **54**
Adkins, Jan **7**
Adler, Irving **27**
Adoff, Arnold **7**
Alcott, Louisa May **1, 38**
Aldrich, Bess Streeter **70**
Alexander, Lloyd (Chudley) **1, 5, 48**
Aliki **9**
Anderson, Poul (William) **58**
Angelou, Maya **53**
Anglund, Joan Walsh **1**
Armstrong, Jennifer **66**
Armstrong, William H(oward) **1**
Arnold, Caroline **61**
Arnosky, James Edward **15**
Aruego, Jose (Espiritu) **5**
Ashabranner, Brent (Kenneth) **28**
Asimov, Isaac **12**
Atwater, Florence (Hasseltine Carroll) **19**
Atwater, Richard (Tupper) **19**
Avi **24, 68**
Aylesworth, Thomas G(ibbons) **6**
Babbitt, Natalie (Zane Moore) **2, 53**
Bacon, Martha Sherman **3**
Ballard, Robert D(uane) **60**
Bang, Molly Garrett **8**
Baum, L(yman) Frank **15**
Baylor, Byrd **3**
Bellairs, John (A.) **37**
Bemelmans, Ludwig **6**
Benary-Isbert, Margot **12**
Bendick, Jeanne **5**
Berenstain, Jan(ice) **19**
Berenstain, Stan(ley) **19**
Berger, Melvin H. **32**
Bess, Clayton **39**
Bethancourt, T. Ernesto **3**
Block, Francesca Lia **33**
Blos, Joan W(insor) **18**
Blumberg, Rhoda **21**
Blume, Judy (Sussman) **2, 15, 69**
Bogart, Jo Ellen **59**
Bond, Nancy (Barbara) **11**
Bontemps, Arna(ud Wendell) **6**
Bova, Ben(jamin William) **3**
Boyd, Candy Dawson **50**
Brancato, Robin F(idler) **32**
Branley, Franklyn M(ansfield) **13**
Brett, Jan (Churchill) **27**
Bridgers, Sue Ellen **18**
Brink, Carol Ryrie **30**
Brooks, Bruce **25**
Brooks, Gwendolyn (Elizabeth) **27**
Brown, Marcia **12**
Brown, Marc (Tolon) **29**
Brown, Margaret Wise **10**
Bruchac, Joseph III **46**
Bryan, Ashley F. **18, 66**
Bunting, Eve **28, 56**
Burch, Robert J(oseph) **63**

Burnett, Frances (Eliza) Hodgson **24**
Burton, Virginia Lee **11**
Butler, Octavia E(stelle) **65**
Byars, Betsy (Cromer) **1, 16**
Caines, Jeannette (Franklin) **24**
Calhoun, Mary **42**
Cameron, Eleanor (Frances) **1**
Carle, Eric **10**
Carter, Alden R(ichardson) **22**
Cassedy, Sylvia **26**
Catalanotto, Peter **68**
Charlip, Remy **8**
Childress, Alice **14**
Choi, Sook Nyul **53**
Christopher, Matt(hew Frederick) **33**
Ciardi, John (Anthony) **19**
Clark, Ann Nolan **16**
Cleary, Beverly (Atlee Bunn) **2, 8**
Cleaver, Bill **6**
Cleaver, Vera (Allen) **6**
Clifton, (Thelma) Lucille **5**
Climo, Shirley **69**
Coatsworth, Elizabeth (Jane) **2**
Cobb, Vicki **2**
Cohen, Daniel (E.) **3, 43**
Cole, Brock **18**
Cole, Joanna **5, 40**
Collier, James L(incoln) **3**
Colum, Padraic **36**
Conford, Ellen **10**
Conrad, Pam **18**
Cooney, Barbara **23**
Cooper, Floyd **60**
Corbett, Scott **1**
Corcoran, Barbara **50**
Cormier, Robert (Edmund) **12, 55**
Cox, Palmer **24**
Creech, Sharon **42**
Crews, Donald **7**
Crutcher, Chris(topher C.) **28**
Cummings, Pat (Marie) **48**
Curry, Jane L(ouise) **31**
Curtis, Christopher Paul **68**
Cushman, Karen **55**
Dalgliesh, Alice **62**
Danziger, Paula **20**
d'Aulaire, Edgar Parin **21**
d'Aulaire, Ingri (Mortenson Parin) **21**
Davis, Ossie **56**
Day, Alexandra **22**
de Angeli, Marguerite (Lofft) **1**
DeClements, Barthe **23**
DeJong, Meindert **1**
Denslow, W(illiam) W(allace) **15**
dePaola, Tomie **4, 24**
Diaz, David **65**
Dillon, Diane (Claire) **44**
Dillon, Leo **44**
Disch, Thomas M(ichael) **18**
Dixon, Franklin W. **61**
Dodge, Mary (Elizabeth) Mapes **62**
Domanska, Janina **40**
Donovan, John **3**

Dorris, Michael (Anthony) **58**
Dorros, Arthur (M.) **42**
Draper, Sharon M(ills) **57**
Dr. Seuss **1, 9, 53**
Duke, Kate **51**
Duncan, Lois **29**
Duvoisin, Roger Antoine **23**
Eager, Edward McMaken **43**
Ehlert, Lois (Jane) **28**
Emberley, Barbara A(nne) **5**
Emberley, Ed(ward Randolph) **5**
Engdahl, Sylvia Louise **2**
L'Engle, Madeleine (Camp Franklin) **1, 14, 57**
Enright, Elizabeth **4**
Epstein, Beryl (M. Williams) **26**
Epstein, Samuel **26**
Estes, Eleanor (Ruth) **2, 70**
Ets, Marie Hall **33**
Feelings, Muriel (Grey) **5**
Feelings, Tom **5, 58**
Ferry, Charles **34**
Field, Rachel (Lyman) **21**
Fisher, Aileen (Lucia) **49**
Fisher, Leonard Everett **18**
Fitzgerald, John D(ennis) **1**
Fitzhugh, Louise **1**
Flack, Marjorie **28**
Fleischman, (Albert) Sid(ney) **1, 15**
Fleischman, Paul **20, 66**
Forbes, Esther **27**
Foster, Genevieve Stump **7**
Fox, Paula **1, 44**
Freedman, Russell (Bruce) **20**
Freeman, Don **30**
Fritz, Jean (Guttery) **2, 14**
Frost, Robert (Lee) **67**
Fujikawa, Gyo **25**
Gaberman, Judie Angell **33**
Gag, Wanda (Hazel) **4**
Gaines, Ernest J(ames) **62**
Galdone, Paul **16**
Gallant, Roy A(rthur) **30**
Gantos, Jack **18**
Garden, Nancy **51**
Gauch, Patricia Lee **56**
Geisel, Theodor Seuss **53**
George, Jean Craighead **1**
Gibbons, Gail **8**
Giblin, James Cross **29**
Giovanni, Nikki **6**
Glenn, Mel **51**
Glubok, Shirley (Astor) **1**
Goble, Paul **21**
Goffstein, (Marilyn) Brooke **3**
Gordon, Sheila **27**
Gorey, Edward (St. John) **36**
Graham, Lorenz (Bell) **10**
Gramatky, Hardie **22**
Greene, Bette **2**
Greene, Constance C(larke) **62**
Greenfield, Eloise **4, 38**
Grifalconi, Ann **35**

Nationality Index

CLR Cumulative Title Index

Title Index

Title Index

Title Index

Title Index